Sociology

Exploring the Architecture of Everyday Life

READINGS

A companion text entitled

Sociology: Exploring the Architecture of Everyday Life

accompanies this anthology and is available from
your instructor and college bookstore.

Sociology

Exploring the Architecture of Everyday Life

READINGS

FOURTH EDITION

David M. Newman

Department of Sociology and Anthropology
DePauw University

Jodi O'Brien

Department of Sociology
Seattle University

 PINE FORGE PRESS
An Imprint of Sage Publications, Inc.
Thousand Oaks, California • London • New Delhi

For information:

 Pine Forge Press
An imprint of Sage Publications, Inc.
2455 Teller Road
Thousand Oaks, California 91320
(805) 499-4224
E-mail: order@pfp.sagepub.com

Sage Publications Ltd.
6 Bonhill Street
London EC2A 4PU
United Kingdom

Sage Publications India Pvt. Ltd.
M-32 Market
Greater Kailash I
New Delhi 110 048 India

Printed in the United States of America

Library of Congress Cataloging-in-Publication Data
Sociology : exploring the architecture of everyday life : readings /
[edited by] David M. Newman, Jodi A. O'Brien. — 4th ed.
    p. cm.
  Includes bibliographical references.
   ISBN 0-7619-8748-7 (pbk.)
   1. Sociology.   I. Newman, David M., 1958–   II. O'Brien, Jodi.
   HM586 .S64 2002
   301—dc21

                                          2001007235

Production Management: *Scratchgravel Publishing Services*
Copy Editor: *Toni Ackley*
Typesetter: *Scratchgravel Publishing Services*
Cover Designers: *Ravi Balasuriya, Michelle Lee*

About the Editors

David M. Newman (Ph.D., University of Washington) is Associate Professor of Sociology at DePauw University. In addition to the introductory course, he teaches courses in research methods, family, social psychology, and deviance. He has won teaching awards at both the University of Washington and DePauw University. His other books include the companion textbook *Sociology: Exploring the Architecture of Everyday Life,* Fourth Edition, and (with co-author Liz Grauerholz) *Sociology of Families,* Second Edition (Pine Forge Press).

Jodi O'Brien is Associate Professor of Sociology at Seattle University. She teaches courses in social psychology, sexuality, inequality, and classical and contemporary theory. She writes and lectures on the cultural politics of transgressive identities and communities. Her other books include *Everyday Inequalities* (Basil Blackwell), *Social Prisms: Reflections on Everyday Myths and Paradoxes* (Pine Forge Press), and (with co-author Peter Kollock) *The Production of Reality: Essays and Readings on Social Interaction,* Third Edition (Pine Forge Press).

About the Publisher

Pine Forge Press is an educational publisher, dedicated to publishing innovative books and software throughout the social sciences. On this and any other of our publications, we welcome your comments.

Please write to:

Pine Forge Press
An imprint of Sage Publications, Inc.
2455 Teller Road
Thousand Oaks, CA 91320-2218
(805) 499-0871
E-mail: info.pineforge@sagepub.com

Visit our World Wide Web site, your direct link to a multitude of online resources:

www.pineforge.com

Contents

Preface

One of the greatest challenges we face as teachers of sociology is getting our students to see the relevance of the course material to their own lives and to appreciate fully its connection to the larger society. We teach our students to see that sociology is all around us. It's in our families, our careers, our media, our goals, our interests, our desires, even our minds. Sociology can be found at the neighborhood pub, the maintenance bay at the local gas station, and the highest offices of government. It's with us when we're alone and when we're in a mob of people. Sociology can answer questions of global as well as private significance—from how some countries create and maintain dominance over others to why we find some people attractive and not others; from why poverty, discrimination, crime, and homelessness exist to why many Americans eat scrambled eggs rather than rice for breakfast.

With these ideas in mind we set out to compile this collection of short articles, chapters, and excerpts designed to help introduce you to sociology. Instructors and students alike responded quite positively to the readings in the first three editions of this book. It would have been easy simply to include those same readings in this fourth edition. But we very much wanted the book to be fresh and contemporary. And we especially wanted to emphasize the importance of race, social class, and gender in people's everyday lives. Hence, twenty-one of the thirty-eight readings are new additions, most of which were written within the past five years.

As in the first three editions, these selections are intended to be vivid, provocative, and eye-opening examples of the practice of sociology. Many of the readings are drawn from carefully conducted social research. They provide important illustrations of how sociologists support their theories, insights, and ideas with empirical evidence. Others are personal narratives that put human faces on matters of sociological relevance. In addition to accurately representing the sociological perspective and providing rigorous coverage of the discipline, we hope the selections are thought-provoking and enjoyable to read.

The readings represent a variety of styles. Some use common, everyday experiences and phenomena (such as sadness, sports, college life, employment, marriage, childbirth, perceptions of time) to illustrate the relationship between the individual and society. Others focus on important social issues or problems (crime, race relations, poverty, educational inequalities, immigration, global economics, environmental degradation, political extremism) or on historical events (massacres during war, drug scares, early movements for women's rights). You need not be a trained sociologist to see the world sociologically. So this book includes articles written by psychologists, anthropologists, novelists, social commentators, and journalists as well as by sociologists.

To help you get the most out of these selections we've written brief introductions to each chapter that provide the sociological context for the readings. For those of you who are also reading the accompanying textbook, these introductions will furnish a quick intellectual link between the readings and information in the textbook. After each selection you will find a set of discussion questions to ponder. Many of these questions ask you to apply a specific author's conclusions to some contemporary issue in society or to your own life experiences. It is our hope that these questions will generate a lot of classroom debate and help you see the sociological merit of the readings.

A new World Wide Web site established for this fourth edition includes do-it-yourself reviews and tests for students, web-based activities designed to enhance learning, and a chat room where students and teachers can post messages and debate matters of sociological significance. The site can be accessed via the Pine Forge web site at www.pineforge.com.

Books like these are enormous projects. As with the first three editions, we would like to thank past president Steve Rutter along with Sherith Pankratz, Kirsten Stoller, Becky Smith, and the rest of the staff at Pine Forge Press for their useful advice and assistance in putting this reader together. We are grateful, as always, to Anne and Greg Draus at Scratchgravel Publishing for producing a high-quality book under extreme time pressure and to Sheri Gilbert for securing all the copyright permissions. We would also like to thank Bizz Steele for magically and promptly acquiring many of the books and articles we desperately needed.

Jodi O'Brien is also grateful to the following people for their helpful suggestions regarding the various readings that are new to this edition: Michele Berger, Wendy Chapkis, Judy Howard, Val Jenness, Townsand Price-Spratlen, Nicole Raeburn, Barbara Trepagnier, France Winddance Twine, and David Yamane. Finally, a heartfelt thanks to Samm Lindsey for continuously inspiring me to stretch.

Enjoy!

David M. Newman
Department of Sociology/Anthropology
DePauw University
Greencastle, IN 46135
E-Mail: DNEWMAN@DEPAUW.EDU

Jodi O'Brien
Department of Sociology
Seattle University
Seattle, WA 98122
E-mail: JOBRIEN@SEATTLEU.EDU

Acknowledgments

We appreciate the many helpful comments offered by the reviewers of the four editions of this book:

Sharon Abbott, Fairfield University
Deborah Abowitz, Bucknell University
Stephen Adair, Central Connecticut State University
Rebecca Adams, University of North Carolina, Greensboro
Ron Aminzade, University of Minnesota
Afroza Anwary, Carleton College
George Arquitt, Oklahoma State University
Carol Auster, Franklin and Marshall College
Ellen C. Baird, Arizona State University
David Bogen, Emerson College
Frances A. Boudreau, Connecticut College
Todd Campbell, Loyola University, Chicago
Wanda Clark, South Plains College
Thomas Conroy, St. Peter's College
Norman Conti, Cleveland State University
Doug Currivan, University of Massachusetts, Boston
Jeff Davidson, University of Delaware
Kimberly Davies, Augusta State University
Tricia Davis, North Carolina State University
James J. Dowd, University of Georgia
Charlotte Chorn Dunham, Texas Tech University
Charles Edgley, Oklahoma State University
Rachel Einwohner, Purdue University
Shalom Endleman, Quinnipiac College
Rebecca Erickson, University of Akron
Kimberly Faust, Fitchburg State University
Patrick Fontane, St. Louis College of Pharmacy
Michael J. Fraleigh, Bryant College
Barry Goetz, University of Dayton
Lorie Schabo Grabowski, University of Minnesota
Valerie Gunter, University of New Orleans
Roger Guy, Texas Lutheran University
Charles Harper, Creighton University
Doug Harper, Duquesne University
Peter Hennen, University of Minnesota
Max Herman, Oberlin College
Susan Hoerbelt, University of South Florida

Gary Hytreck, Georgia Southern University
Valerie Jenness, University of California, Irvine
Kathryn Johnson, Barat College
Richard Jones, Marquette University
Tom Kando, California State University, Sacramento
Steve Keto, Kent State University
Peter Kivisto, Augustana College
Marc LaFountain, State University of West Georgia
Melissa Latimer, West Virginia University
Joseph Lengermann, University of Maryland, College Park
Lynda A. Litteral, Clark State Community College
Fred Maher
Kristen Marcussen, University of Iowa
Benjamin Mariante, Stonehill College
Joseph Marolla, Virginia Commonwealth University
Michallene McDaniel, University of Georgia
James R. McIntosh, Lehigh University
Jerome McKibben, Fitchburg State University
Ted P. McNeilsmith, Adams State College
Melinda J. Milligan, Tulane Univeristy
Susannne Monahan, Montana State University
Kelly Murphy, University of Pittsburgh
Daniel Myers, University of Notre Dame
Elizabeth Ehrhardt Mustaine, University of Central Florida
Anne Nurse, College of Wooster
Marjukka Ollilainen, Weber State University
Toska Olson, University of Washington
Larry Perkins
Bernice Pescosolido, Indiana University, Bloomington
Mike Plummer, Boston College
Edward Ponczek, William Rainey Harper College
Tanya Poteet, Capitol University
Sharon E. Preves, Grand Valley State University

Judith Richlin-Klonsky, University of California, Los Angeles

Robert Robinson, Indiana University, Bloomington

Mary Rogers, University of West Florida

Sally S. Rogers, Montgomery College

Michael Ryan, Upper Iowa University

Mark Shibley, Southern Oregon University

Thomas Shriver, Oklahoma State University

Katherine Slevin, College of William and Mary

Lisa White Smith, Christopher Newport University

Eldon Snyder, Bowling Green State University

Nicholas Sofios, Providence College

Kandi Stinson, Xavier University

Richard Tardanico, Florida International University

Robert Tellander, Sonoma State University

Kathleen Tiemann, University of North Dakota

Steven Vallas, Georgia Institute of Technology

Tom Vander Ven, Hofstra University

John Walsh, University of Illinois, Chicago

Gregory Weiss, Roanoke College

Marty Wenglinsky, Quinnipiac College

Stephan Werba, Catonsville Community College

Cheryl E. Whitley, Marist College

Norma Williams, University of North Texas

Janelle Wilson, University of Minnesota, Duluth

Mark Winton, University of Central Florida

Cynthia A. Woolever, Lexington Theological Seminary

Ashraf Zahedi, Santa Clara University

Stephen Zehr, University of Southern Indiana

Sociology

Exploring the Architecture of Everyday Life

READINGS

PART I
The Individual and Society

Taking a New Look at a Familiar World

The primary theme of sociology is that our everyday thoughts and actions are the product of a complex interplay between massive social forces and personal characteristics. We can't understand the relationship between individuals and their societies without understanding both. The *sociological imagination* is the ability to see the impact of social forces on our private lives. It is an awareness that our lives lie at the intersection of personal biography and societal history. The sociological imagination encourages us to move beyond individualistic explanations of human experiences to an understanding of the mutual influence that individuals and society have on one another. So, rather than study what goes on *within* people, sociologists study what goes on *between* and *among* people, as individuals, groups, organizations, or entire societies. Sociology forces us to look outside the tight confines of our individual personalities to understand the social phenomena that shape us.

Consider athletic performance. I'm sure you've seen televised coverage of the Olympics. If you're like us, you probably sat in awe of those remarkable athletes—the elite of their respective sports—competing at a level far beyond the reach of most "normal" people. As we watch them perform, it's easy to conclude that such athletes are a different breed, that they have some inborn, personal quality—call it "talent"—that propels them to world-class achievements. But Daniel Chambliss, in "The Mundanity of Excellence," argues that, as much as we'd like to believe otherwise, these world-class athletes are not that different from the rest of us. Their excellence comes from fundamentally ordinary activities that take place within identifiable social worlds that have their own unique values, attitudes, and behavior patterns. By explaining athletic excellence in such a way, Chambliss helps introduce us to the sociological perspective on understanding social life: Behavior commonly attributed to innate qualities can be better understood by examining the broader social context within which it takes place.

The Mundanity of Excellence

An Ethnographic Report on Stratification and Olympic Swimmers

Daniel F. Chambliss

Olympic sports and competitive swimming in particular provide an unusually clear opportunity for studying the nature of excellence. In other fields, it may be less clear who are the outstanding performers: the best painter or pianist, the best businessperson, the finest waitress or the best father. But in sport (and this is one of its attractions) success is defined more exactly, by success in competition. There are medals and ribbons and plaques for first place, second, and third; competitions are arranged for the head-to-head meeting of the best competitors in the world; in swimming and track, times are electronically recorded to the hundredth of a second; there are statistics published and rankings announced, every month or every week. By the end of the Olympic Games every four years, it is completely clear who won and who lost, who made the finals, who participated in the Games, and who never participated in the sport at all.

Within competitive swimming in particular, clear stratification exists not only between individuals but also between defined levels of the sport as well. At the lowest level, we see the country club teams, operating in the summertime as a loosely run, mildly competitive league, with volunteer, part-time coaches. Above that there are teams that represent entire cities and compete with other teams from other cities around the state or region; then a "Junior Nationals" level of competition, featuring the best younger (under 18 years old) athletes; then the Senior Nationals level (any age, the best in the nation); and finally, we could speak of world- or Olympic-class competitors. At each such level, we find, predictably, certain people competing: one athlete swims in a summer league, never seeing swimmers from another town; one swimmer may consistently qualify for the Junior Nationals, but not for Seniors; a third may swim at the Olympics and never return to Junior Nationals. The levels of the sport are remarkably distinct from one another.

. . . Because success in swimming is so definable, . . . we can clearly see, by comparing levels and studying individuals as they move between and within levels, what exactly produces excellence. In addition, careers in swimming are relatively short; one can achieve tremendous success in a brief period of time. Rowdy Gaines, beginning in the sport when 17 years old, jumped from a country club league to a world record in the 100 meter freestyle event in only three years. This allows the researcher to conduct true longitudinal research in a few short years. . . .

. . . This report draws on extended experience with swimmers at every level of ability, over some half a dozen years. Observation has covered the span of careers, and I have had the chance to compare not just athletes within a certain level (the view that most coaches have), but between the most discrepant levels as well. Thus these findings avoid the usual . . . problem of an observer's being familiar mainly with athletes at one level. . . .

The Nature of Excellence

By "excellence" I mean "consistent superiority of performance." The excellent athlete regularly, even routinely, performs better than his or her competitors. Consistency of superior performances tells us that one athlete is indeed better than another, and that the difference between them is not merely the product of chance. This definition can apply at any level of the sport, differentiating athletes. The superiority discussed

3

here may be that of one swimmer over another, or of all athletes at one level (say, the Olympic class) over another. By this definition, we need not judge performance against an absolute criterion, but only against other performances. There are acknowledged leaders on every team, as well as teams widely recognized as dominant.

To introduce what are sources of excellence for Olympic athletes, I should first suggest—saving the demonstration for later—what *does not* produce excellence.

(1) Excellence is not, I find, the product of socially deviant personalities. These swimmers don't appear to be "oddballs," nor are they loners ("kids who have given up the normal teenage life").[1] If their achievements result from a personality characteristic, that characteristic is not obvious. Perhaps it is true, as the mythology of sports has it, that the best athletes are more self-confident (although that is debatable); but such confidence could be an effect of achievement, not the cause of it.[2]

(2) Excellence does *not* result from quantitative changes in behavior. Increased training time, *per se,* does not make one swim fast; nor does increased "psyching up," nor does moving the arms faster. Simply doing more of the same will not lead to moving up a level in the sport.

(3) Excellence does *not* result from some special inner quality of the athlete. "Talent" is one common name for this quality; sometimes we talk of a "gift," or of "natural ability." These terms are generally used to mystify the essentially mundane processes of achievement in sports, keeping us away from a realistic analysis of the actual factors creating superlative performances, and protecting us from a sense of responsibility for our own outcomes.

So where does excellence—consistent superiority of performance—come from?

I. Excellence Requires Qualitative Differentiation

Excellence in competitive swimming is achieved through qualitative differentiation from other swimmers, not through quantitative increases in activity. . . .

. . . I should clarify what is meant here by "quantitative" and "qualitative." By quantity, we mean the number or amount of something. Quantitative improvement entails an increase in the number of some one thing one does. An athlete who practices 2 hours a day and increases that activity to 4 hours a day has made a quantitative change in behavior. Or, one who swims 5 miles and changes to 7 miles has made a quantitative change. She does more of the same thing; there is an increase in quantity. Or again, a freestyle swimmer who, while maintaining the same stroke technique, moves his arms at an increased number of strokes per minute has made a quantitative change in behavior. Quantitative improvements, then, involve doing *more of the same thing.*

By quality, though, we mean the character or nature of the thing itself. A qualitative change involves modifying what is actually being done, not simply doing more of it. For a swimmer doing the breaststroke, a qualitative change might be a change from pulling straight back with the arms to sculling them outwards, to the sides; or from lifting oneself up out of the water at the turn to staying low near the water. Other qualitative changes might include competing in a regional meet instead of local meets; eating vegetables and complex carbohydrates rather than fats and sugars; entering one's weaker events instead of only one's stronger events; learning to do a flip turn with freestyle, instead of merely turning around and pushing off; or training at near-competition levels of intensity, rather than casually. Each of these involves doing things differently than before, not necessarily doing more. Qualitative improvements involve doing *different kinds of things.*

Now we can consider how qualitative differentiation is manifested:

Different levels of the sport are qualitatively distinct. Olympic champions don't just do much more of the same things that summer-league country club swimmers do. They don't just swim more hours, or move their arms faster, or attend more workouts. What makes them faster cannot be quantitatively compared with lower-level swimmers, because while there may be quantitative differences—and certainly there are, for instance in the number of hours spent in workouts—these are not, I think, the decisive factors at all.[3]

Instead, they do things differently. Their strokes are different, their attitudes are different, their groups of friends are different, their parents treat the sport differently, the swimmers prepare differently for their races, and they enter different kinds of meets and events. There are numerous discontinuities of this sort between, say, the swimmer who competes in a local City League meet and one who enters the Olympic Trials. Consider three dimensions of difference:

(1) Technique: The styles of strokes, dives and turns are dramatically different at different levels. A "C" (the lowest rank in United States Swimming's ranking system) breaststroke swimmer tends to pull her arms far back beneath her, kick the legs out very wide without bringing them together at the finish, lift herself high out of the water on the turn, fail to take a long pull underwater after the turn, and touch at the finish with one hand, on her side. By comparison, an "AAAA" (the highest rank) swimmer, sculls the arms out to the side and sweeps back in (never actually pulling backwards), kicks narrowly with the feet finishing together, stays low on the turns, takes a long underwater pull after the turn, and touches at the finish with both hands. Not only are the strokes different, they are so different that the "C" swimmer may be amazed to see how the "AAAA" swimmer looks when swimming. The appearance alone is dramatically different, as is the speed with which they swim. . . .

(2) Discipline: The best swimmers are more likely to be strict with their training, coming to workouts on time, carefully doing the competitive strokes legally (i.e., without violating the technical rules of the sport),[4] watch what they eat, sleep regular hours, do proper warmups before a meet, and the like. Their energy is carefully channeled. Diver Greg Louganis, who won two Olympic gold medals in 1984, practices only three hours each day—not a long time—divided into two or three sessions. But during each session, he tries to do every dive perfectly. Louganis

is never sloppy in practice, and so is never sloppy in meets.[5]

(3) Attitude: At the higher levels of competitive swimming, something like an inversion of attitude takes place. The very features of the sport that the "C" swimmer finds unpleasant, the top-level swimmer enjoys. What others see as boring—swimming back and forth over a black line for two hours, say—they find peaceful, even meditative,[6] often challenging, or therapeutic. They enjoy hard practices, look forward to difficult competitions, try to set difficult goals. Coming into the 5:30 A.M. practices at Mission Viejo, many of the swimmers were lively, laughing, talking, enjoying themselves, perhaps appreciating the fact that most people would positively hate doing it. It is incorrect to believe that top athletes suffer great sacrifices to achieve their goals. Often, they don't see what they do as sacrificial at all. They like it.

These qualitative differences are what distinguish levels of the sport. They are very noticeable, while the quantitative differences between levels, both in training and in competition, may be surprisingly small indeed. . . . Yet very small quantitative differences in performance may be coupled with huge qualitative differences: In the finals of the men's 100-meter freestyle swimming event at the 1984 Olympics, Rowdy Gaines, the gold medalist, finished ahead of second-place Mark Stockwell by .44 seconds, a gap of only 8/10 of 1%. Between Gaines and the 8th place finisher (a virtual unknown named Dirk Korthals, from West Germany), there was only a 2.2% difference in time. Indeed, between Rowdy Gaines, the fastest swimmer in the world that year, and a respectable 10-year-old, the quantitative difference in speed would only be about 30%.

Yet here, as in many cases, a rather small *quantitative* difference produces an enormous *qualitative difference:* Gaines was consistently a winner in major international meets, holder of the world record, and the Olympic Gold Medalist in three events.

Stratification in the sport is discrete, not continuous. There are significant, qualitative breaks—

discontinuities—between levels of the sport. These include differences in attitude, discipline, and technique which in turn lead to small but consistent quantitative differences in speed. Entire teams show such differences in attitude, discipline, and technique, and consequently certain teams are easily seen to be "stuck" at certain levels.[7] Some teams always do well at the National Championships, others do well at the Regionals, others at the County Meet. And certainly swimmers typically remain within a certain level for most of their careers, maintaining throughout their careers the habits with which they began. Within levels, competitive improvements for such swimmers are typically marginal, reflecting only differential growth rates (early onset of puberty, for instance) or the jockeying for position within the relatively limited sphere of their own level. . . .

. . . Athletes move up to the top ranks through *qualitative jumps:* noticeable changes in their techniques, discipline, and attitude, accomplished usually through a change in settings, e.g., joining a new team with a new coach, new friends, etc., who work at a higher level. Without such qualitative jumps, no major improvements (movements through levels) will take place. . . .

This is really several worlds, each with its own patterns of conduct. . . . If, as I have suggested, there really are qualitative breaks between levels of the sport, and if people really don't "work their way up" in any simple additive sense, perhaps our very conception of a single swimming world is inaccurate. I have spoken of the "top" of the sport, and of "levels" within the sport. But these words suggest that all swimmers are, so to speak, climbing a single ladder, aiming towards the same goals, sharing the same values, swimming the same strokes, all looking upwards towards an Olympic gold medal. But they aren't.[8] Some want gold medals, some want to make the team, some want to exercise, or have fun with friends, or be out in the sunshine and water. Some are trying to escape their parents. The images of the "top" and the "levels" of swimming which I have used until now may simply reflect the dominance of a cer-

tain faction of swimmers and coaches in the sport: top is what *they* regard as the top, and their definitions of success have the broadest political currency in United States Swimming. Fast swimmers take as given that faster is better—instead of, say, that more beautiful is better; or that parental involvement is better; or that "well-rounded" children (whatever that may mean) are better. . . .

So we should envision not a swimming world, but multiple worlds[9] (and changing worlds is a major step toward excellence), a horizontal rather than vertical differentiation of the sport. What I have called "levels" are better described as "worlds" or "spheres." In one such world, parents are loosely in charge, coaches are teenagers employed as lifeguards, practices are held a few times a week, competitions are scheduled perhaps a week in advance, the season lasts for a few weeks in the summertime, and athletes who are much faster than the others may be discouraged by social pressure even from competing, for they take the fun out of it.[10] The big event of the season is the City Championship, when children from the metropolitan area will spend two days racing each other in many events, and the rest of the time sitting under huge tents playing cards, reading, listening to music, and gossiping. In another world, coaches are very powerful, parents seen only occasionally (and never on the pool deck), swimmers travel thousands of miles to attend meets, they swim 6 days a week for years at a time, and the fastest among them are objects of respect and praise. The big event of the season may be the National Championships, where the athletes may spend much time—sitting under huge tents, playing cards, reading, listening to music and gossiping.[11]

Each such world has its own distinctive types of powerful people and dominant athletes, and being prominent in one world is no guarantee of being prominent in another.[12] At lower levels, the parents of swimmers are in charge; at the higher levels, the coaches; perhaps in the Masters teams which are made up only of swimmers over 25 years old, the swimmers themselves. Each world, too, has its distinctive goals: going to the Olympics, doing well at the National Junior Olympics, winning the City Meet, having a good time for a few weeks. In each world the techniques are at least somewhat distinct (as with the breaststroke, discussed above), and certain demands are made on family and friends. In all of these ways, and many more, each so-called "level" of competitive swimming is qualitatively different than others. The differences are not simply quantifiable steps along a one-dimensional path leading to the Olympic Games. Goals are varied, participants have competing commitments, and techniques are jumbled.

II. Why "Talent" Does Not Lead to Excellence

. . . "Talent" is perhaps the most pervasive lay explanation we have for athletic success. Great athletes, we seem to believe, are born with a special gift, almost a "thing" inside of them, denied to the rest of us—perhaps physical, genetic, psychological, or physiological. Some have "it," and some don't. Some are "natural athletes," and some aren't. While an athlete, we acknowledge, may require many years of training and dedication to develop and use that talent, it is always "in there," only waiting for an opportunity to come out. When children perform well, they are said to "have" talent; if performance declines, they may be said to have "wasted their talent." We believe it is that talent, conceived as a substance behind the surface reality of performance, which finally distinguishes the best among our athletes.

But talent fails as an explanation for athletic success, on conceptual grounds. It mystifies excellence, subsuming a complex set of discrete actions behind a single undifferentiated concept. To understand these actions and the excellence which they constitute, then, we should first debunk this concept of talent and see where it fails. On at least three points, I believe, "talent" is inadequate.

Factors other than talent explain athletic success more precisely. We can, with a little effort, see what these factors are in swimming: geographical location, particularly living in southern California where the sun shines year round and everybody swims; fairly high family income, which allows for the travel to meets and payments of the fees entailed in the sport, not to mention sheer access to swimming pools when one is young; one's height, weight, and proportions; the luck or choice of having a good coach, who can teach the skills required; inherited muscle structure—it certainly helps to be both strong and flexible; parents who are interested in sports. Some swimmers, too, enjoy more the physical pleasures of swimming; some have better coordination; some even have a higher percentage of fast-twitch muscle fiber. Such factors are clearly definable, and their effects can be clearly demonstrated. To subsume all of them, willynilly, under the rubric of "talent" obscures rather than illuminates the sources of athletic excellence.

It's easy to do this, especially if one's only exposure to top athletes comes once every four years while watching the Olympics on television, or if one only sees them in performances rather than in day-to-day training. Say, for instance, that one day I turn on the television set and there witness a magnificent figure skating performance by Scott Hamilton. What I see is grace and power and skill all flowing together, seemingly without effort; a single moving picture, rapid and sure, far beyond what I could myself do. . . . "His skating," I may say, referring to his actions as a single thing, "is spectacular." With that quick shorthand, I have captured (I believe) at a stroke the wealth of tiny details that Hamilton, over years and years, has fitted together into a performance so smoothly that they become invisible to the untrained eye.[13] Perhaps, with concentration, Hamilton himself can feel the details in his movements; certainly a great coach can see them, and pick out the single fault or mistake in an otherwise flawless routine. But to me, the performance is a thing entire.

Afterwards, my friends and I sit and talk about Hamilton's life as a "career of excellence," or as showing "incredible dedication," "tremendous motivation"—again, as if his excellence, his dedication, his motivation somehow exist all-at-once.

His excellence becomes a thing inside of him which he periodically reveals to us, which comes out now and then; his life and habits become reified. "Talent" is merely the word we use to label this reification.

But that is no explanation of success.

Talent is indistinguishable from its effects. One cannot see that talent exists until after its effects become obvious. Kalinowski's research on Olympic swimmers demonstrates this clearly.

> One of the more startling discoveries of our study has been that it takes a while to recognize swimming talent. Indeed, it usually takes being successful at a regional level, and more often, at a national level (in AAU swimming) before the child is identified as talented. (p. 173)

> "They didn't say I had talent until I started to get really good [and made Senior Nationals at sixteen]; then they started to say I had talent . . ." (p. 174)

> . . . despite the physical capabilities he was born with, it took Peter several years (six by our estimate) to appear gifted. This is the predominant, though not exclusive, pattern found in our data on swimmers. Most of them are said to be "natural" or "gifted" after they had already devoted a great deal of time and hard work to the field. (p. 194)

> . . . whatever superior qualities were attributed to him as he grew older and more successful, they were not apparent then [before he was thirteen]. (p. 200)

The above quotations suggest that talent is *discovered* later in one's career, the implication being that while the athlete's ability *existed* all along, we were unaware of it until late. Kalinowski, like many of us, holds to the belief that there must be this thing inside the athlete which precedes and determines success, only later to be discovered. But the recurring evidence he finds suggests a different interpretation: perhaps there is no such thing as "talent," there is only the outstanding performance itself. He sees success and immediately infers behind it a cause, a cause *for which he has no evidence other than the success itself.* Here, as elsewhere, talent (our name for this cause) cannot be measured, or seen, or felt in any form other than the success to which it supposedly gives rise. . . .

The "amount" of talent needed for athletic success seems to be strikingly low. It seems initially plausible that one must have a certain level of natural ability in order to succeed in sports (or music or academics). But upon empirical examination, it becomes very difficult to say exactly what that physical minimum is. Indeed, much of the mythology of sport is built around people who lack natural ability who went on to succeed fabulously. An entire genre of inspirational literature is built on the theme of the person whose even normal natural abilities have been destroyed: Wilma Rudolph had polio as a child, then came back to win the Olympic 100-Meter Dash. Glenn Cunningham had his legs badly burned in a fire, then broke the world record in the mile. Such stories are grist for the sportswriter's mill.

More than merely common, these stories are almost routine. Most Olympic champions, when their history is studied, seem to have overcome sharp adversity in their pursuit of success. Automobile accidents, shin splints, twisted ankles, shoulder surgery are common in such tales. In fact, they are common in life generally. While some necessary minimum of physical strength, heart/lung capacity, or nerve density may well be required for athletic achievement (again, I am *not* denying differential advantages), that minimum seems both difficult to define and markedly low, at least in many cases. Perhaps the crucial factor is not natural ability at all, but the willingness to overcome natural or unnatural disabilities of the sort that most of us face, ranging from minor inconveniences in getting up and going to work, to accidents and injuries, to gross physical impairments.

And if the basic level of talent needed, then, seems so low as to be nearly universally available, perhaps the very concept of talent itself—no longer differentiating among performers—is better discarded altogether. It simply doesn't explain the differences in outcomes. Rather than talk about talent and ability, we do better to look at what people actually do that creates outstanding performance.

The concept of talent hinders a clear understanding of excellence. By providing a quick . . . "explanation" of athletic success, it satisfies our casual curiosity while requiring neither an empirical analysis nor a critical questioning of our tacit assumptions about top athletes. At best, it is an easy way of admitting that we don't know the answer. . . . But the attempt at explanation fails. . . . Through the notion of talent, we transform particular actions that a human being does into an object possessed, held in trust for the day when it will be revealed for all to see.

This line of thought leads to one more step. Since talent can be viewed only indirectly in the effects that it supposedly produces, its very existence is a matter of faith. The basic dogma of "talent" says that what people do in this world has a cause lying behind them, that there is a kind of backstage reality where the real things happen, and what we—you and I—see here in our lives (say, the winning of a gold medal) is really a reflection of that true reality back there. Those of us who are not admitted to the company of the elect—the talented—can never see what that other world of fabulous success is really like, and can never share those experiences. And accepting this faith in talent, I suggest, we relinquish our chance of accurately understanding excellence. . . .

III. The Mundanity of Excellence

"People don't know how ordinary success is," said Mary T. Meagher, winner of 3 gold medals in the Los Angeles Olympics, when asked what the public least understands about her sport. She then spoke of starting her career in a summer league country club team, of working her way to AAU meets, to faster and faster competitions, of learning new techniques, practicing new habits, meeting new challenges.[14] What Meagher said—that success is ordinary—in some sense applies, I believe, to other fields of

endeavor as well: to business, to politics, to professions of all kinds, including academics. In what follows I will try to elaborate on this point, drawing some examples from the swimming research, and some from other fields, to indicate the scope of this conception.

Excellence is mundane. Superlative performance is really a confluence of dozens of small skills or activities, each one learned or stumbled upon, which have been carefully drilled into habit and then are fitted together in a synthesized whole. There is nothing extraordinary or superhuman in any one of those actions; only the fact that they are done consistently and correctly, and all together, produce excellence. When a swimmer learns a proper flip turn in the freestyle races, she will swim the race a bit faster; then a streamlined push off from the wall, with the arms squeezed together over the head, and a little faster; then how to place the hands in the water so no air is cupped in them; then how to lift them over the water; then how to lift weights to properly build strength, and how to eat the right foods, and to wear the best suits for racing, and on and on.[15] Each of those tasks seems small in itself, but each allows the athlete to swim a bit faster. And having learned and consistently practiced all of them together, and many more besides, the swimmer may compete in the Olympic Games. The winning of a gold medal is nothing more than the synthesis of a countless number of such little things—even if some of them are done unwittingly or by others, and thus called "luck."

So the "little things" really do count. We have already seen how a very small (in quantitative terms) difference can produce a noticeable success. Even apparent flukes can lead to gold medal performances:

> In the 100-Meter Freestyle event in Los Angeles, Rowdy Gaines, knowing that the starter for the race tended to fire the gun fast, anticipated the start; while not actually jumping the gun, it seems from video replays of the race that Gaines knew exactly when to go, and others were left on the blocks as he took off. But the starter turned his back, and the protests filed

afterwards by competitors were ignored. Gaines had spent years watching starters, and had talked with his coach (Richard Quick) before the race about this starter in particular. (Field notes; see Chambliss, 1988, for full description)

Gaines was not noticeably faster than several of the other swimmers in the race, but with this one extra tactic, he gained enough of an advantage to win the race. And he seemed in almost all of his races to find such an advantage; hence the gold medal. Looking at such subtleties, we can say that not only are the little things important; in some ways, the little things are the only things. . . .

In swimming, or elsewhere, these practices might at first glance seem very minimal indeed:

When Mary T. Meagher was 13 years old and had qualified for the National Championships, she decided to try to break the world record in the 200-Meter Butterfly race. She made two immediate qualitative changes in her routine: first, she began coming on time to all practices. She recalls now, years later, being picked up at school by her mother and driving (rather quickly) through the streets of Louisville, Kentucky, trying desperately to make it to the pool on time. That habit, that discipline, she now says, gave her the sense that every minute of practice time counted. And second, she began doing all of her turns, during those practices, correctly, in strict accordance with the competitive rules. Most swimmers don't do this; they turn rather casually, and tend to touch with one hand instead of two (in the butterfly, Meagher's stroke). This, she says, accustomed her to doing things one step better than those around her—always. Those are the two major changes she made in her training, as she remembers it.[16]

Meagher made two quite mundane changes in her habits, either one of which anyone could do, if he or she wanted. Within a year Meagher had broken the world record in the butterfly. . . .

Motivation is mundane, too. Swimmers go to practice to see their friends, to exercise, to feel strong afterwards, to impress the coach, to work towards bettering a time they swam in the last meet. Sometimes, the older ones, with a longer view of the future, will aim towards a meet that is still several months away. But even given the longer-term goals, the daily satisfactions need to be there. The mundane social rewards really are crucial (see Chambliss, 1988, Chapter 6). By comparison, the big, dramatic motivations—winning an Olympic gold medal, setting a world record—seem to be ineffective unless translated into shorter-term tasks. Viewing "Rocky" or "Chariots of Fire" may inspire one for several days, but the excitement stirred by a film wears off rather quickly when confronted with the day-to-day reality of climbing out of bed to go and jump in cold water. If, on the other hand, that day-to-day reality is itself fun, rewarding, challenging; if the water is nice and friends are supportive, the longer-term goals may well be achieved almost in spite of themselves. Again, Mary T. Meagher:

I never looked beyond the next year, and I never looked beyond the next level. I never thought about the Olympics when I was ten; at that time I was thinking about the State Championships. When I made cuts for Regionals [the next higher level of competition], I started thinking about Regionals; when I made cuts for National Junior Olympics, I started thinking about National Junior Olympics . . . I can't even think about the [1988] Olympics right now. . . .
Things can overwhelm you if you think too far ahead. (Interview notes)

This statement was echoed by many of the swimmers I interviewed. While many of them were working towards the Olympic Games, they divided the work along the way into achievable steps, no one of which was too big. They found their challenges in small things: working on a better start this week, polishing up their backstroke technique next week, focusing on better sleep habits, planning how to pace their swim. . . .

. . . Many top swimmers are accustomed to winning races in practice, day after day. Steve Lundquist, who won two gold medals in Los Angeles, sees his success as resulting from an early decision that he wanted to win every swim, every day, in every practice. That was the immediate goal he faced at workouts; just try to win every swim, every lap, in every stroke, no matter what. Lundquist gained a reputation in swimming for being a ferocious workout swimmer, one who competed all the time, even in the warmup. He became so accustomed to winning that he entered meets knowing that he could beat these people—he had developed the habit, every day, of never losing. The short-term goal of winning this swim, in this workout, translated into his ability to win bigger and bigger races. Competition, when the day arrived for a meet, was not a shock to him, nothing at all out of the ordinary.[17]

This leads to a third and final point.

In the pursuit of excellence, maintaining mundanity is the key psychological challenge. In common parlance, winners don't choke. Faced with what seems to be a tremendous challenge or a strikingly unusual event, such as the Olympic Games, the better athletes take it as a normal, manageable situation[18] ("It's just another swim meet," is a phrase sometimes used by top swimmers at a major event such as the Games) and do what is necessary to deal with it. Standard rituals (such as the warmup, the psych, the visualization of the race, the taking off of sweats, and the like) are ways of importing one's daily habits into the novel situation, to make it as normal an event as possible. Swimmers like Lundquist, who train at competition-level intensity, therefore have an advantage: arriving at a meet, they are already accustomed to doing turns correctly, taking legal starts, doing a proper warmup, and being aggressive from the outset of the competition. If each day of the season is approached with a seriousness of purpose, then the big meet will not come as a shock. The athlete will believe "I belong here, this is my world"—and not be paralyzed by fear or self-consciousness. The task then is to have training closely approximate competition conditions. . . .

The mundanity of excellence is typically unrecognized. I think the reason is fairly simple.

Usually we see great athletes only after they have become great—after the years of learning the new methods, gaining the habits of competitiveness and consistency, after becoming comfortable in their world. They have long since perfected the myriad of techniques that together constitute excellence. Ignorant of all of the specific steps that have led to the performance and to the confidence, we think that somehow excellence sprang full grown from this person, and we say he or she "has talent" or "is gifted." Even when seen close up, the mundanity of excellence is often not believed:

> Every week at the Mission Viejo training pool, where the National Champion Nadadores team practiced, coaches from around the world would be on the deck visiting, watching as the team did their workouts, swimming back and forth for hours. The visiting coaches would be excited at first, just to be here; then soon— within an hour or so usually—they grew bored, walking back and forth looking at the deck, glancing around at the hills around the town, reading the bulletin boards, glancing down at their watches, wondering, after the long flight out to California, when something dramatic was going to happen. "They all have to come to Mecca, and see what we do," coach Mark Schubert said. "They think we have some big secret." (Field notes)

But of course there is no secret; there is only the doing of all those little things, each one done correctly, time and again, until excellence in every detail becomes a firmly ingrained habit, an ordinary part of one's everyday life.

Conclusions

The foregoing analysis suggests that we have overlooked a fundamental fact about Olympic-class athletes; and the argument may apply far more widely than swimming, or sports. I suggest that it applies to success in business, politics, and academics, in dentistry, bookkeeping, food service, speechmaking, electrical engineering, selling insurance (when the clients are upset, you climb in the car and go out there to talk with them), and perhaps even in the arts.[19] Consider again the major points:

(1) *Excellence is a qualitative phenomenon.* Doing more does not equal doing better. High performers focus on qualitative, not quantitative, improvements; it is qualitative improvements which produce significant changes in level of achievement; different levels of achievement really are distinct, and in fact reflect vastly different habits, values, and goals.

(2) *Talent is a useless concept.* Varying conceptions of natural ability ("talent," e.g.) tend to mystify excellence, treating it as the inherent possession of a few; they mask the concrete actions that create outstanding performance; they avoid the work of empirical analysis and logical explanations (clear definitions, separable independent and dependent variables, and at least an attempt at establishing the temporal priority of the cause); and finally, such conceptions perpetuate the sense of innate psychological differences between high performers and other people.

(3) *Excellence is mundane.* Excellence is accomplished through the doing of actions, ordinary in themselves, performed consistently and carefully, habitualized, compounded together, added up over time. While these actions are "qualitatively different" from those of performers at other levels, these differences are neither unmanageable nor, taken one step at a time, terribly difficult. Mary T. Meagher came to practice on time; some writers always work for three hours each morning, before beginning anything else; a businessperson may go ahead and make that tough phone call; a job applicant writes one more letter; a runner decides, against the odds, to enter the race; a county commissioner submits a petition to run for Congress; a teenager asks for a date; an actor attends one more audition. Every time a decision comes up, the qualitatively "correct" choice will be made. The action, in itself, is nothing special; the care and consistency with which it is made is.

Howard Becker has presented a similar argument about the ordinariness of apparently unusual people in his book *Outsiders* (1961). But where he speaks of deviance, I would speak of excellence. Becker says, and I concur:

> We ought not to view it as something special, as depraved or in some magical way better than other kinds of behavior. We ought to see it simply as a kind of behavior some disapprove of and others value, studying the processes by which either or both perspectives are built up and maintained. Perhaps the best surety against either extreme is close contact with the people we study. (Becker, p. 176)

After three years of field work with world-class swimmers, having the kind of close contact that Becker recommends, I wrote a draft of some book chapters, full of stories about swimmers, and I showed it to a friend. "You need to jazz it up," he said. "You need to make these people more interesting. The analysis is nice, but except for the fact that these are good swimmers, there isn't much else exciting to say about them as individuals." He was right, of course. What these athletes do was rather interesting, but the people themselves were only fast swimmers, who did the particular things one does to swim fast. It is all very mundane. When my friend said that they weren't exciting, my best answer could only be, simply put: *That's the point.*

NOTES

The author wishes to thank Randall Collins and Gary Alan Fine for their comments on an earlier draft of this paper.

1. In fact, if anything they are more socially bonded and adept than their peers. The process by which this happens fits well with Durkheim's (1965) description of the sources of social cohesion.

2. These issues are addressed at length in "The Social World of Olympic Swimmers." Daniel F. Chambliss, in preparation.

3. True, the top teams work long hours, and swim very long distances, but (1) such workouts often begin after a swimmer achieves national status, not before, and (2) the positive impact of increased yardage seems to come with huge increases, e.g., the doubling of workout distances—in which case one could argue

that a *qualitative* jump has been made. The whole question of "how much yardage to swim" is widely discussed within the sport itself.

Compare the (specious, I think) notion that a longer school day/term/year will produce educational improvements.

4. One day at Mission Viejo, with some sixty swimmers going back and forth the length of a 50-meter pool, coach Mark Schubert took one boy out of the water and had him do twenty pushups before continuing the workout. The boy had touched the wall with one hand at the end of a breaststroke swim. The rules require a two-handed touch.

One hundred and twenty hands should have touched, one hundred and nineteen *did* touch, and this made Schubert angry. He pays attention to details.

5. From an interview with his coach, Ron O'Brien.

6. Distance swimmers frequently compare swimming to meditation.

7. For example: several well-known teams consistently do well at the National Junior Olympics ("Junior Nationals," as it is called informally), and yet never place high in the team standings at the National Championships ("Senior Nationals"), the next higher meet.

These teams actually prevent their swimmers from going to the better meet, holding them in store for the easier meet so that the team will do better at that lesser event. In this way, and in many others, teams choose their own level of success.

8. March and Olsen make a similar point with regard to educational institutions and organizations in general: organizations include a variety of constituents with differing goals, plans, motivations, and values. Unity of purpose, even with organizations, cannot simply be assumed. Coherence, not diversity, is what needs explaining. March and Olsen, 1976.

9. See Shibutani in Rose, 1962, on "social worlds." Blumer, 1969.

10. These fast swimmers who come to slow meets are called hot dogs, showoffs, or even jerks. (Personal observations.)

11. Again, personal observations from a large number of cases. While there are significant differences between swimmers of the Olympic class and a country club league, the basic sociability of their worlds is not one of them.

12. "Indeed, prestige ladders in the various worlds are so different that a man who reaches the pinnacle

of success in one may be completely unknown elsewhere." Shibutani in Rose, 1962.

Similarly in academia: one may be a successful professor at the national level and yet find it difficult to gain employment at a minor regional university. Professors at the regional school may suspect his/her motives, be jealous, feel that he/she "wouldn't fit in," "won't stay anyway," etc. Many top-school graduate students discover upon entering the markets that no-name colleges have no interest in them; indeed, by attending a Chicago or Harvard Ph.D. program one may limit oneself to the top ranks of employment opportunities.

13. "Now, no one can see in an artist's work how it evolved: that is its advantage, for wherever we can see the evolution, we grow somewhat cooler. The complete art of representation wards off all thought of its solution; it tyrannizes as present perfection" (Nietzsche, 1984, p. 111).

14. Meagher's entire career is described in detail in Chambliss, 1988.

15. Such techniques are thoroughly explained in Maglischo (1982) and Troup and Reese (1983).

16. Interview notes.

17. Interview notes.

18. An interesting parallel: some of the most successful generals have no trouble sleeping before and after major battles. For details on Ulysses Grant and the Duke of Wellington, see Keegan, p. 207.

19. Professor Margaret Bates, an opera enthusiast, tells me that this "mundanity of excellence" argument applies nicely to Enrico Caruso, the great singer, who carefully perfected each ordinary detail of his performance in an effort to overcome a recognized lack of "natural ability."

REFERENCES

Blumer, Herbert. 1969. *Symbolic Interactionism.* Englewood Cliffs: Prentice Hall.

Chambliss, Daniel F. 1988. *Champions: The Making of Olympic Swimmers.* New York: Morrow.

Durkheim, Emile. 1965. *The Elementary Forms of the Religious Life.* New York: Free Press.

Kalinowsky, Anthony G. "The Development of Olympic Swimmers," and "One Olympic Swimmer," in Bloom (1985), pp. 139–210.

Keegan, John. 1987. *The Mask of Command.* New York: Viking.

Maglischo, Ernest W. 1982. *Swimming Faster.* Palo Alto: Mayfield.

March, James G. and Olsen, Johan P. 1976. *Ambiguity and Choice in Organizations.* Bergen, Norway: Universitetsforlaget.

Nietzsche, Friedrich. 1984. *Human, All Too Human.* Lincoln.: University of Nebraska Press.

Shibutani, T. "Reference Groups and Social Control," in Rose, Arnold M. 1962. *Human Behavior and Social Process.* Boston: Houghton Mifflin, pp. 128–147.

Troup, John and Reese, Randy. 1983. *A Scientific Approach to the Sport of Swimming.* Gainesville, FL: Scientific Sports.

THINKING ABOUT THE READING

Why does Chambliss feel that "talent" is a useless concept in explaining success among world-class swimmers? Where, instead, does he think that athletic excellence comes from? Why do you suppose we have such a strong tendency to focus on "talent" or "natural ability" in explaining superior performances? If it's true, as Chambliss suggests, that factors such as geographical location, high family income and interest, and the luck of having a good coach can all play important roles in creating world-class swimmers, then there are probably many potentially successful athletes who don't have the opportunity to excel in certain sports because of their social circumstances. Relatively few inner-city kids grow up to succeed in "wealthy" sports such as swimming, tennis, and golf. However, the inner city produces many of the world's best basketball, football, and track stars. What kinds of social circumstances encourage success in these sports? Can you identify other areas of life (other than sports) where achievement might similarly be affected by the kinds of social circumstances described in this article?

2 Seeing and Thinking Sociologically

Although society exists as an objective entity, it is also a social construction that is created, reaffirmed, and altered through the day-to-day interactions of the very people it influences and controls. Humans are social beings. We constantly look to others to help define and interpret the situations in which we find ourselves. Other people can influence what we see, feel, think, and do. But it's not just other people who influence us. We also live in a *society*, which consists of socially recognizable combinations of individuals—relationships, groups, and organizations—as well as the products of human action—statuses, roles, culture, and institutions.

The influence of social structure on our personal actions is often felt most forcefully when we are compelled to obey the commands of someone who is in a position of authority. In "The My Lai Massacre: A Military Crime of Obedience," Herbert Kelman and Lee Hamilton describe a specific example of a crime in which the individuals involved attempted to deny responsibility for their actions by claiming that they were following the orders of a military officer who had the legitimate right to command them. This incident occurred in the midst of the Vietnam War. Arguably, people do things under such trying conditions that they wouldn't ordinarily do, even—as in this case—kill defenseless people. Kelman and Hamilton make a key sociological point by showing that these soldiers were not necessarily psychological misfits who were especially mean or violent. Instead, the researchers argue, they were ordinary people caught up in tense circumstances that made obeying the brutal commands of an authority seem like the normatively and morally acceptable thing to do.

The influence society has on our everyday lives is often obscured by our culture's tendency to see people's problems in individualistic terms. In his article, "Speaking of Sadness," David Karp shows us how the private experience of depression is shaped by social processes and cultural expectations. Karp, a sufferer of clinical depression himself, observes that our society's emphasis on individual achievement and self-fulfillment, not to mention Americans' ever-increasing sense of social isolation, conspires to create an environment in which more and more people suffer from debilitating depression. Karp's observations illustrate the profound power of the sociological imagination by showing that even such an apparently private "illness" as depression cannot be fully understood without seeing its relationship to the culture and the economy.

The My Lai Massacre

A Military Crime of Obedience

Herbert Kelman and V. Lee Hamilton

March 16, 1968, was a busy day in U.S. history. Stateside, Robert F. Kennedy announced his presidential candidacy, challenging a sitting president from his own party—in part out of opposition to an undeclared and disastrous war. In Vietnam, the war continued. In many ways, March 16 may have been a typical day in that war. We will probably never know. But we do know that on that day a typical company went on a mission—which may or may not have been typical—to a village called Son (or Song) My. Most of what is remembered from that mission occurred in the subhamlet known to Americans as My Lai 4.

The My Lai massacre was investigated and charges were brought in 1969 and 1970. Trials and disciplinary actions lasted into 1971. Entire books have been written about the army's year-long cover-up of the massacre (for example, Hersh, 1972), and the cover-up was a major focus of the army's own investigation of the incident. Our central concern here is the massacre itself—a crime of obedience—and public reactions to such crimes, rather than the lengths to which many went to deny the event. Therefore this account concentrates on one day: March 16, 1968.

Many verbal testimonials to the horrors that occurred at My Lai were available. More unusual was the fact that an army photographer, Ronald Haeberle, was assigned the task of documenting the anticipated military engagement at My Lai—and documented a massacre instead. Later, as the story of the massacre emerged, his photographs were widely distributed and seared the public conscience. What might have been dismissed as unreal or exaggerated was depicted in photographs of demonstrable authenticity. The dominant image appeared on the cover of *Life:* piles of bodies jumbled together in a ditch along a trail—the dead all apparently unarmed. All were Oriental, and all appeared to be children, women, or old men. Clearly there had been a mass execution, one whose image would not quickly fade.

So many bodies (over twenty in the cover photo alone) are hard to imagine as the handiwork of one killer. These were not. They were the product of what we call a crime of obedience. Crimes of obedience begin with orders. But orders are often vague and rarely survive with any clarity the transition from one authority down a chain of subordinates to the ultimate actors. The operation at Son My was no exception.

"Charlie" Company, Company C, under Lt. Col. Frank Barker's command, arrived in Vietnam in December 1967. As the army's investigative unit, directed by Lt. Gen. William R. Peers, characterized the personnel, they "contained no significant deviation from the average" for the time. Seymour S. Hersh (1970) described the "average" more explicitly: "Most of the men in Charlie Company had volunteered for the draft; only a few had gone to college for even one year. Nearly half were black, with a few Mexican-Americans. Most were eighteen to twenty-two years old. The favorite reading matter of Charlie Company, like that of other line infantry units in Vietnam, was comic books" (p. 18). The action at My Lai, like that throughout Vietnam, was fought by a cross-section of those Americans who either believed in the war or lacked the social resources to avoid participating in it. Charlie Company was indeed average for that time, that place, and that war.

Two key figures in Charlie Company were more unusual. The company's commander, Capt. Ernest Medina, was an upwardly mobile Mexican-American who wanted to make the army his career, although he feared that he might never advance beyond captain because of his lack of formal education. His eagerness had earned him a nickname among his men: "Mad Dog Medina." One of his admirers was the platoon leader Second Lt. William L. Calley, Jr., an undistinguished, five-foot-three-inch junior-college dropout who had failed four of the seven courses in which he had enrolled his first year. Many viewed him as one of those "instant officers" made possible only by the army's then-desperate need for manpower. Whatever the cause, he was an insecure leader whose frequent claim was "I'm the boss." His nickname among some of the troops was "Surfside 5½," a reference to the swashbuckling heroes of a popular television show, "Surfside 6."

The Son My operation was planned by Lieutenant Colonel Barker and his staff as a search-and-destroy mission with the objective of rooting out the Forty-eighth Viet Cong Battalion from their base area of Son My village. Apparently no written orders were ever issued. Barker's superior, Col. Oran Henderson, arrived at the staging point the day before. Among the issues he reviewed with the assembled officers were some of the weaknesses of prior operations by their units, including their failure to be appropriately aggressive in pursuit of the enemy. Later briefings by Lieutenant Colonel Barker and his staff asserted that no one except Viet Cong was expected to be in the village after 7 A.M. on the following day. The "innocent" would all be at the market. Those present at the briefings gave conflicting accounts of Barker's exact orders, but he conveyed at least a strong suggestion that the Son My area was to be obliterated. As the army's inquiry reported: "While there is some conflict in the testimony as to whether LTC Barker ordered the destruction of houses, dwellings, livestock, and other foodstuffs in the Song My area, the preponderance of the evidence indicates that such destruction was implied, if not specifically directed, by his orders of 15 March" (Peers Report, in Goldstein et al., 1976, p. 94).

Evidence that Barker ordered the killing of civilians is even more murky. What does seem clear, however, is that—having asserted that civilians would be away at the market—he did not specify what was to be done with any who might nevertheless be found on the scene. The Peers Report therefore considered it "reasonable to conclude that LTC Barker's minimal or nonexistent instructions concerning the handling of noncombatants created the potential for grave misunderstandings as to his intentions and for interpretation of his orders as authority to fire, without restriction, on all persons found in target area" (Goldstein et al., 1976, p. 95). Since Barker was killed in action in June 1968, his own formal version of the truth was never available.

Charlie Company's Captain Medina was briefed for the operation by Barker and his staff. He then transmitted the already vague orders to his own men. Charlie Company was spoiling for a fight, having been totally frustrated during its months in Vietnam—first by waiting for battles that never came, then by incompetent forays led by inexperienced commanders, and finally by mines and booby traps. In fact, the emotion-laden funeral of a sergeant killed by a booby trap was held on March 15, the day before My Lai. Captain Medina gave the orders for the next day's action at the close of that funeral. Many were in a mood for revenge.

It is again unclear what was ordered. Although all participants were alive by the time of the trials for the massacre, they were either on trial or probably felt under threat of trial. Memories are often flawed and self-serving at such times. It is apparent that Medina relayed to the men at least some of Barker's general message—to expect Viet Cong resistance, to burn, and to kill livestock. It is not clear that he ordered the slaughter of the inhabitants, but some of the men who heard him thought he had. One of those who claimed to have heard such orders was Lt. William Calley.

As March 16 dawned, much was expected of the operation by those who had set it into motion. Therefore a full complement of "brass" was present in helicopters overhead, including Barker, Colonel Henderson, and their superior, Major General Koster (who went on to become commandant of West Point before the story of My Lai broke). On the ground, the troops were to carry with them one reporter and one photographer to immortalize the anticipated battle.

The action for Company C began at 7:30 as their first wave of helicopters touched down near the subhamlet of My Lai 4. By 7:47 all of Company C was present and set to fight. But instead of the Viet Cong Forty-eighth Battalion, My Lai was filled with the old men, women, and children who were supposed to have gone to market. By this time, in their version of the war, and with whatever orders they thought they had heard, the men from Company C were nevertheless ready to find Viet Cong everywhere. By nightfall, the official tally was 128 VC killed and three weapons captured, although later, unofficial body counts ran as high as 500. The operation at Son My was over. And by nightfall, as Hersh reported: "the Viet Cong were back in My Lai 4, helping the survivors bury the dead. It took five days. Most of the funeral speeches were made by the Communist guerrillas. Nguyen Bat was not a Communist at the time of the massacre, but the incident changed his mind. 'After the shooting,' he said, 'all the villagers became Communists'" (1970, p. 74). To this day, the memory of the massacre is kept alive by markers and plaques designating the spots where groups of villagers were killed, by a large statue, and by the My Lai Museum, established in 1975 (Williams, 1985).

But what could have happened to leave American troops reporting a victory over Viet Cong when in fact they had killed hundreds of noncombatants? It is not hard to explain the report of victory; that is the essence of a cover-up. It is harder to understand how the killings came to be committed in the first place, making a cover-up necessary.

Mass Executions and the Defense of Superior Orders

Some of the atrocities on March 16, 1968, were evidently unofficial, spontaneous acts: rapes, tortures, killings. For example, Hersh (1970) describes Charlie Company's Second Platoon as entering "My Lai 4 with guns blazing" (p. 50); more graphically, Lieutenant "Brooks and his men in the second platoon to the north had begun to systematically ransack the hamlet and slaughter the people, kill the livestock, and destroy the crops. Men poured rifle and machine-gun fire into huts without knowing—or seemingly caring—who was inside" (pp. 49–50).

Some atrocities toward the end of the action were part of an almost casual "mopping-up," much of which was the responsibility of Lieutenant LaCross's Third Platoon of Charlie Company. The Peers Report states: "The entire 3rd Platoon then began moving into the western edge of My Lai (4), for the mop-up operation. . . . The squad . . . began to burn the houses in the southwestern portion of the hamlet" (Goldstein et al., 1976, p. 133). They became mingled with other platoons during a series of rapes and killings of survivors for which it was impossible to fix responsibility. Certainly to a Vietnamese all GIs would by this point look alike: "Nineteen-year-old Nguyen Thi Ngoc Tuyet watched a baby trying to open her slain mother's blouse to nurse. A soldier shot the infant while it was struggling with the blouse, and then slashed it with his bayonet." Tuyet also said she saw another baby hacked to death by GIs wielding their bayonets. "Le Tong, a twenty-eight-year-old rice farmer, reported seeing one woman raped after GIs killed her children. Nguyen Khoa, a thirty-seven-year-old peasant, told of a thirteen-year-old girl who was raped before being killed. GIs then attacked Khoa's wife, tearing off her clothes. Before they could rape her, however, Khoa said, their six-year-old son, riddled with bullets, fell and saturated her with blood. The GIs left her alone" (Hersh, 1970, p. 72). All of Company C was implicated in a pattern of death and destruction throughout the hamlet, much of which seemingly lacked rhyme or reason.

But a substantial amount of the killing was *organized* and traceable to one authority: the First Platoon's Lt. William Calley. Calley was originally charged with 109 killings, almost all of them mass executions at the trail and other locations.

He stood trial for 102 of these killings, was convicted of 22 in 1971, and at first received a life sentence. Though others—both superior and subordinate to Calley—were brought to trial, he was the only one convicted for the My Lai crimes. Thus, the only actions of My Lai for which *anyone* was ever convicted were mass executions, ordered and committed. We suspect that there are commonsense reasons why this one type of killing was singled out. In the midst of rapidly moving events with people running about, an execution of stationary targets is literally a still life that stands out and whose participants are clearly visible. It can be proven that specific people committed specific deeds. An execution, in contrast to the shooting of someone on the run, is also more likely to meet the legal definition of an act resulting from intent—with malice aforethought. Moreover, American military law specifically forbids the killing of unarmed civilians or military prisoners, as does the Geneva Convention between nations. Thus common sense, legal standards, and explicit doctrine all made such actions the likeliest target for prosecution.

When Lieutenant Calley was charged under military law it was for violation of the Uniform Code of Military Justice (UCMJ) Article 118 (murder). This article is similar to civilian codes in that it provides for conviction if an accused:

> without justification or excuse, unlawfully kills a human being, when he—
>
> 1. has a premeditated design to kill;
> 2. intends to kill or inflict great bodily harm;
> 3. is engaged in an act which is inherently dangerous to others and evinces a wanton disregard of human life; or
> 4. is engaged in the perpetration or attempted perpetration of burglary, sodomy, rape, robbery, or aggravated arson. (Goldstein et al., 1976, p. 507)

For a soldier, one legal justification for killing is warfare; but warfare is subject to many legal limits and restrictions, including, of course, the inadmissibility of killing unarmed noncombatants or prisoners whom one has disarmed. The pictures of the trail victims at My Lai certainly portrayed one or the other of these. Such an action would be illegal under military law; ordering another to commit such an action would be illegal; and following such an order would be illegal.

But following an order may provide a second and pivotal justification for an act that would be murder when committed by a civilian. American military law assumes that the subordinate is inclined to follow orders, as that is the normal obligation of the role. Hence, legally, obedient subordinates are protected from unreasonable expectations regarding their capacity to evaluate those orders:

> An order requiring the performance of a military duty may be inferred to be legal. An act performed manifestly beyond the scope of authority, or pursuant to an order that a man of ordinary sense and understanding would know to be illegal, or in a wanton manner in the discharge of a lawful duty, is not excusable. (Par. 216, Subpar. *d*, Manual for Courts Martial, United States, 1969 Rev.)

Thus what *may* be excusable is the good-faith carrying out of an order, as long as that order appears to the ordinary soldier to be a legal one. In military law, invoking superior orders moves the question from one of the action's consequences—the body count—to one of evaluating the actor's motives and good sense.

In sum, if anyone is to be brought to justice for a massacre, common sense and legal codes decree that the most appropriate targets are those who make themselves executioners. This is the kind of target the government selected in prosecuting Lieutenant Calley with the greatest fervor. And in a military context, the most promising way in which one can redefine one's undeniable deeds into acceptability is to invoke superior orders. This is what Calley did in attempting to avoid conviction. Since the core legal issues involved points of mass execution—the ditches and trail where America's image of My Lai was formed—we review these events in greater detail.

The day's quiet beginning has already been noted. Troops landed and swept unopposed into the village. The three weapons eventually reported as the haul from the operation were picked up from three apparent Viet Cong who fled the village when the troops arrived and were pursued and killed by helicopter gunships. Obviously the Viet Cong did frequent the area. But it appears that by about 8:00 A.M. no one who met the troops was aggressive, and no one was armed. By the laws of war Charlie Company had no argument with such people.

As they moved into the village, the soldiers began to gather its inhabitants together. Shortly after 8:00 a.m. Lieutenant Calley told Pfc. Paul Meadlo that "you know what to do with" a group of villagers Meadlo was guarding. Estimates of the numbers in the group ranged as high as eighty women, children, and old men, and Meadlo's own estimate under oath was thirty to fifty people. As Meadlo later testified, Calley returned after ten or fifteen minutes: "He [Calley] said, 'How come they're not dead?' I said, 'I didn't know we were supposed to kill them.' He said, 'I want them dead.' He backed off twenty or thirty feet and started shooting into the people—the Viet Cong—shooting automatic. He was beside me. He burned four or five magazines. I burned off a few, about three. I helped shoot 'em" (Hammer, 1971, p. 155). Meadlo himself and others testified that Meadlo cried as he fired; others reported him later to be sobbing and "all broke up." It would appear that to Lieutenant Calley's subordinates something was unusual, and stressful, in these orders.

At the trial, the first specification in the murder charge against Calley was for this incident; he was accused of premeditated murder of "an unknown number, not less than 30, Oriental human beings, males and females of various ages, whose names are unknown, occupants of the village of My Lai 4, by means of shooting them with a rifle" (Goldstein et al., 1976, p. 497).

Among the helicopters flying reconnaissance above Son My was that of CWO Hugh Thompson. By 9:00 or soon after, Thompson had noticed some horrifying events from his perch. As he spotted wounded civilians, he sent down smoke markers so that soldiers on the ground could treat them. They killed them instead. He reported to headquarters, trying to persuade someone to stop what was going on. Barker, hearing the message, called down to Captain Medina. Medina, in turn, later claimed to have told Calley that it was "enough for today." But it was not yet enough.

At Calley's orders, his men began gathering the remaining villagers—roughly seventy-five individuals, mostly women and children—and herding them toward a drainage ditch. Accompanied by three or four enlisted men, Lieutenant Calley executed several batches of civilians who had been gathered into ditches. Some of the details of the process were entered into testimony in such accounts as Pfc. Dennis Conti's: "A lot of them, the people, were trying to get up and mostly they was just screaming and pretty bad shot up. . . . I seen a woman tried to get up. I seen Lieutenant Calley fire. He hit the side of her head and blew it off" (Hammer, 1971, p. 125).

Testimony by other soldiers presented the shooting's aftermath. Specialist Four Charles Hall, asked by Prosecutor Aubrey Daniel how he knew the people in the ditch were dead, said: "There was blood coming from them. They were just scattered all over the ground in the ditch, some in piles and some scattered out 20, 25 meters perhaps up the ditch. . . . They were very old people, very young children, and mothers. . . . There was blood all over them" (Goldstein et al., 1976, pp. 501–502). And Pfc. Gregory Olsen corroborated the general picture of the victims: "They were—the majority were women and children, some babies. I distinctly remember one middle-aged Vietnamese male dressed in white right at my feet as I crossed. None of the bodies were mangled in any way. There was blood. Some appeared to be dead, others followed me with their eyes as I walked across the ditch" (Goldstein et al., 1976, p. 502).

The second specification in the murder charge stated that Calley did "with premeditation, murder an unknown number of Oriental human beings, not less than seventy, males and females of various ages, whose names are unknown, occupants of the village of My Lai 4, by means of shooting them with a rifle" (Goldstein et al., 1976, p. 497). Calley was also charged with and tried for shootings of individuals (an old man and a child); these charges were clearly supplemental to the main issue at trial—the mass killings and how they came about.

It is noteworthy that during these executions more than one enlisted man avoided carrying out Calley's orders, and more than one, by sworn oath, directly refused to obey them. For example, Pfc. James Joseph Dursi testified, when asked if he fired when Lieutenant Calley ordered him to: "No I just stood there. Meadlo turned to me after a couple of minutes and said 'Shoot! Why don't you shoot! Why don't you fire!' He was crying and yelling. I said, 'I can't! I won't!' And the people were screaming and crying and yelling. They kept firing for a couple of minutes, mostly automatic and semi-automatic" (Hammer, 1971, p. 143)....

Disobedience of Lieutenant Calley's own orders to kill represented a serious legal and moral threat to a defense *based* on superior orders, such as Calley was attempting. This defense had to assert that the orders seemed reasonable enough to carry out; that they appeared to be legal orders. Even if the orders in question were not legal, the defense had to assert that an ordinary individual could not and should not be expected to see the distinction. In short, if what happened was "business as usual," even though it might be bad business, then the defendant stood a chance of acquittal. But under direct command from "Surfside $5^1/2$," some ordinary enlisted men managed to refuse, to avoid, or at least to stop doing what they were ordered to do. As "reasonable men" of "ordinary sense and understanding," they had apparently found something awry that morning; and it would have been hard for an officer to plead successfully that he was more ordinary than his men in his capacity to evaluate the reasonableness of orders.

Even those who obeyed Calley's orders showed great stress. For example, Meadlo eventually began to argue and cry directly in front of Calley. Pfc. Herbert Carter shot himself in the foot, possibly because he could no longer take what he was doing. We were not destined to hear a sworn version of the incident, since neither side at the Calley trial called him to testify.

The most unusual instance of resistance to authority came from the skies. CWO Hugh Thompson, who had protested the apparent carnage of civilians, was Calley's inferior in rank but was not in his line of command. He was also watching the ditch from his helicopter and noticed some people moving after the first round of slaughter—chiefly children who had been shielded by their mothers' bodies. Landing to rescue the wounded, he also found some villagers hiding in a nearby bunker. Protecting the Vietnamese with his own body, Thompson ordered his men to train their guns on the Americans and to open fire if the Americans fired on the Vietnamese. He then radioed for additional rescue helicopters and stood between the Vietnamese and the Americans under Calley's command until the Vietnamese could be evacuated. He later returned to the ditch to unearth a child buried, unharmed, beneath layers of bodies. In October 1969, Thompson was awarded the Distinguished Flying Cross for heroism at My Lai, specifically (albeit inaccurately) for the rescue of children hiding in a bunker "between Viet Cong forces and advancing friendly forces" and for the rescue of a wounded child "caught in the intense crossfire" (Hersh, 1970, p. 119). Four months earlier, at the Pentagon, Thompson had identified Calley as having been at the ditch.

By about 10:00 A.M., the massacre was winding down. The remaining actions consisted largely of isolated rapes and killings, "clean-up" shootings of the wounded, and the destruction of the village by fire. We have already seen some examples of these more indiscriminate and possibly less premeditated acts. By the 11:00 A.M. lunch break, when the exhausted men of Company C were relaxing, two young girls wandered back from a hiding place only to be invited to share lunch. This surrealist touch illustrates the extent to which the soldiers' action had become dissociated from its meaning. An hour earlier, some of these men were making sure that not even a child would escape the executioner's bullet. But now the job was done and it was time for lunch—and in this new context it seemed only natural to ask the children who had managed to escape execution to join them. The massacre had ended. It remained only for the Viet Cong to reap the political rewards among the survivors in hiding.

The army command in the area knew that something had gone wrong. Direct commanders, including Lieutenant Colonel Barker, had firsthand reports, such as Thompson's complaints. Others had such odd bits of evidence as the claim of 128 Viet Cong dead with a booty of only three weapons. But the cover-up of My Lai began at once. The operation was reported as a victory over a stronghold of the Viet Cong Forty-eighth. . . .

William Calley was not the only man tried for the event at My Lai. The actions of over thirty soldiers and civilians were scrutinized by investigators; over half of these had to face charges or disciplinary action of some sort. Targets of investigation included Captain Medina, who was tried, and various higher-ups, including General Koster. But Lieutenant Calley was the only person convicted, the only person to serve time.

The core of Lieutenant Calley's defense was superior orders. What this meant to him—in contrast to what it meant to the judge and jury—can be gleaned from his responses to a series of questions from his defense attorney, George Latimer, in which Calley sketched out his understanding of the laws of war and the actions that constitute doing one's duty within those laws:

Latimer: Did you receive any training which had to do with the obedience to orders?

Calley: Yes, sir.

Latimer: . . . what were you informed [were] the principles involved in that field?

Calley: That all orders were to be assumed legal, that the soldier's job was to carry out any order given him to the best of his ability.

Latimer: . . . what might occur if you disobeyed an order by a senior officer?

Calley: You could be court-martialed for refusing an order and refusing an order in the face of the enemy, you could be sent to death, sir.

Latimer: [I am asking] whether you were required in any way, shape or form to make a determination of the legality or illegality of an order?

Calley: No, sir. I was never told that I had the choice, sir.

Latimer: If you had a doubt about the order, what were you supposed to do?

Calley: . . . I was supposed to carry the order out and then come back and make my complaint. (Hammer, 1971, pp. 240–241)

Lieutenant Calley steadfastly maintained that his actions within My Lai had constituted, in his mind, carrying out orders from Captain Medina. Both his own actions and the orders he gave to others (such as the instruction to Meadlo to "waste 'em") were entirely in response to superior orders. He denied any intent to kill individuals and any but the most passing awareness of distinctions among the individuals: "I was ordered to go in there and destroy the enemy. That was my job on that day. That was the mission I was given. I did not sit down and think in terms of men, women, and children. They were all classified the same, and that was the classification that we dealt with, just as enemy soldiers." When Latimer asked if in his own opinion Calley had acted "rightly and according to your understanding of your directions and orders," Calley replied, "I felt then and I still do that I acted as I was directed, and I carried out the orders that I was given, and I do not feel wrong in doing so, sir" (Hammer, 1971, p. 257).

His court-martial did not accept Calley's defense of superior orders and clearly did not share his interpretation of his duty. The jury evidently reasoned that, even if there had been orders to destroy everything in sight and to "waste the Vietnamese," any reasonable person would have realized that such orders were illegal and should have refused to carry them out. The defense of superior orders under such conditions is inadmissible under international and military law. The U.S. Army's *Law of Land Warfare* (Dept. of the Army, 1956), for example, states that "the fact that the law of war has been violated pursuant to an order of a superior authority, whether military or civil, does not deprive the act in question of its character of a war crime, nor does it constitute a defense in the trial of an accused individual, unless he did not know and could not reasonably have been expected to know that the act was unlawful" and that "members of the armed forces are bound to obey only lawful orders" (in Falk et al., 1971, pp. 71–72).

The disagreement between Calley and the court-martial seems to have revolved around the definition of the responsibilities of a subordinate to obey, on the one hand, and to evaluate, on the other. This tension . . . can best be captured via the charge to the jury in the Calley court-martial, made by the trial judge, Col. Reid Kennedy. The forty-one pages of the charge include the following:

> Both combatants captured by and noncombatants detained by the opposing force . . . have the right to be treated as prisoners. . . . Summary execution of detainees or prisoners is forbidden by law. . . . I therefore instruct you . . . that if unresisting human beings were killed at My Lai (4) while within the effective custody and control of our military forces, their deaths cannot be considered justified. . . . Thus if you find that Lieutenant Calley received an order directing him to kill unresisting Vietnamese within his control or within the control of his troops, *that order would be an illegal order.*
>
> A determination that an order is illegal does not, of itself, assign criminal responsibility to the person following the order for acts done in compliance with it. Soldiers are taught to follow orders, and special attention is given to obedience of orders on the battlefield. Military effectiveness depends on obedience to orders. On the other hand, the obedience of a soldier is not the obedience of an automaton. A soldier is a reasoning agent, obliged to respond, not as a machine, but as a person. The law takes these factors into account in assessing criminal responsibility for acts done in compliance with illegal orders.

> The acts of a subordinate done in compliance with an unlawful order given him by his superior are excused and impose no criminal liability upon him unless the superior's order is one which a man of *ordinary sense and understanding* would, under the circumstances, know to be unlawful, or if the order in question is actually known to the accused to be unlawful. (Goldstein et al., 1976, pp. 525–526; emphasis added)

By this definition, subordinates take part in a balancing act, one tipped toward obedience but tempered by "ordinary sense and understanding."

A jury of combat veterans proceeded to convict William Calley of the premeditated murder of no less than twenty-two human beings. (The army, realizing some unfortunate connotations in referring to the victims as "Oriental human beings," eventually referred to them as "human beings.") Regarding the first specification in the murder charge, the bodies on the trail, [Calley] was convicted of premeditated murder of not less than one person. (Medical testimony had been able to pinpoint only one person whose wounds as revealed in Haeberle's photos were sure to be immediately fatal.) Regarding the second specification, the bodies in the ditch, Calley was convicted of the premeditated murder of not less than twenty human beings. Regarding additional specifications that he had killed an old man and a child, Calley was convicted of premeditated murder in the first case and of assault with intent to commit murder in the second.

Lieutenant Calley was initially sentenced to life imprisonment. That sentence was reduced: first to twenty years, eventually to ten (the latter by Secretary of Defense Callaway in 1974). Calley served three years before being released on bond. The time was spent under house arrest in his apartment, where he was able to receive visits from his girlfriend. He was granted parole on September 10, 1975.

Sanctioned Massacres

The slaughter at My Lai is an instance of a class of violent acts that can be described as sanctioned massacres (Kelman, 1973): acts of indiscriminate, ruthless, and often systematic mass violence, carried out by military or paramilitary personnel while engaged in officially sanctioned campaigns, the victims of which are defenseless and unresisting civilians, including old men, women, and children. Sanctioned massacres have occurred throughout history. Within American history, My Lai had its precursors in the Philippine war around the turn of the century (Schirmer, 1971) and in the massacres of American Indians. Elsewhere in the world, one recalls the Nazis' "final solution" for European Jews, the massacres and deportations of Armenians by Turks, the liquidation of the kulaks and the great purges in the Soviet Union, and more recently the massacres in Indonesia and Bangladesh, in Biafra and Burundi, in South Africa and Mozambique, in Cambodia and Afghanistan, in Syria and Lebanon. . . .

The occurrence of sanctioned massacres cannot be adequately explained by the existence of psychological forces—whether these be characterological dispositions to engage in murderous violence or profound hostility against the target—so powerful that they must find expression in violent acts unhampered by moral restraints. Instead, the major instigators for this class of violence derive from the policy process. The question that really calls for psychological analysis is why so many people are willing to formulate, participate in, and condone policies that call for the mass killings of defenseless civilians. Thus it is more instructive to look not at the motives for violence but at the conditions under which the usual moral inhibitions against violence become weakened. Three social processes that tend to create such conditions can be identified: authorization, routinization, and dehumanization. Through authorization, the situation becomes so defined that the individual is absolved of the responsibility to make personal moral choices. Through routinization, the action becomes so organized that there is no opportunity for raising moral questions. Through dehumanization, the actors' attitudes toward the target and toward themselves be-

come so structured that it is neither necessary nor possible for them to view the relationship in moral terms.

Authorization

Sanctioned massacres by definition occur in the context of an authority situation, a situation in which, at least for many of the participants, the moral principles that generally govern human relationships do not apply. Thus, when acts of violence are explicitly ordered, implicitly encouraged, tacitly approved, or at least permitted by legitimate authorities, people's readiness to commit or condone them is enhanced. That such acts are authorized seems to carry automatic justification for them. Behaviorally, authorization obviates the necessity of making judgments or choices. Not only do normal moral principles become inoperative, but—particularly when the actions are explicitly ordered—a different kind of morality, linked to the duty to obey superior orders, tends to take over.

In an authority situation, individuals characteristically feel obligated to obey the orders of the authorities, whether or not these correspond with their personal preferences. They see themselves as having no choice as long as they accept the legitimacy of the orders and of the authorities who give them. Individuals differ considerably in the degree to which—and the conditions under which—they are prepared to challenge the legitimacy of an order on the grounds that the order itself is illegal, or that those giving it have overstepped their authority, or that it stems from a policy that violates fundamental societal values. Regardless of such individual differences, however, the basic structure of a situation of legitimate authority requires subordinates to respond in terms of their role obligations rather than their personal preferences; they can openly disobey only by challenging the legitimacy of the authority. Often people obey without question even though the behavior they engage in may entail great personal sacrifice or great harm to others.

An important corollary of the basic structure of the authority situation is that actors often do not see themselves as personally responsible for the consequences of their actions. Again, there are individual differences, depending on actors' capacity and readiness to evaluate the legitimacy of orders received. Insofar as they see themselves as having had no choice in their actions, however, they do not feel personally responsible for them. They were not personal agents, but merely extensions of the authority. Thus, when their actions cause harm to others, they can feel relatively free of guilt. A similar mechanism operates when a person engages in antisocial behavior that was not ordered by the authorities but was tacitly encouraged and approved by them—even if only by making it clear that such behavior will not be punished. In this situation, behavior that was formerly illegitimate is legitimized by the authorities' acquiescence.

In the My Lai massacre, it is likely that the structure of the authority situation contributed to the massive violence in both ways—that is, by conveying the message that acts of violence against Vietnamese villagers were *required,* as well as the message that such acts, even if not ordered, were *permitted* by the authorities in charge. The actions at My Lai represented, at least in some respects, responses to explicit or implicit orders. Lieutenant Calley indicated, by orders and by example, that he wanted large numbers of villagers killed. Whether Calley himself had been ordered by his superiors to "waste" the whole area, as he claimed, remains a matter of controversy. Even if we assume, however, that he was not explicitly ordered to wipe out the village, he had reason to believe that such actions were expected by his superior officers. Indeed, the very nature of the war conveyed this expectation. The principal measure of military success was the "body count"—the number of enemy soldiers killed—and any Vietnamese killed by the U.S. military was commonly defined as a "Viet Cong." Thus, it was not totally bizarre for Calley to believe that what he was doing at My Lai was to increase his body count, as any good officer was expected to do.

Even to the extent that the actions at My Lai occurred spontaneously, without reference to superior orders, those committing them had

reason to assume that such actions might be tacitly approved of by the military authorities. Not only had they failed to punish such acts in most cases, but the very strategies and tactics that the authorities consistently devised were based on the proposition that the civilian population of South Vietnam—whether "hostile" or "friendly"—was expendable. Such policies as search-and-destroy missions, the establishment of free-shooting zones, the use of antipersonnel weapons, the bombing of entire villages if they were suspected of harboring guerrillas, the forced migration of masses of the rural population, and the defoliation of vast forest areas helped legitimize acts of massive violence of the kind occurring at My Lai.

Some of the actions at My Lai suggest an orientation to authority based on unquestioning obedience to superior orders, no matter how destructive the actions these orders call for. Such obedience is specifically fostered in the course of military training and reinforced by the structure of the military authority situation. It also reflects, however, an ideological orientation that may be more widespread in the general population. . . .

Routinization

Authorization processes create a situation in which people become involved in an action without considering its implications and without really making a decision. Once they have taken the initial step, they are in a new psychological and social situation in which the pressures to continue are powerful. As Lewin (1947) has pointed out, many forces that might originally have kept people out of a situation reverse direction once they have made a commitment (once they have gone through the "gate region") and now serve to keep them in the situation. For example, concern about the criminal nature of an action, which might originally have inhibited a person from becoming involved, may now lead to deeper involvement in efforts to justify the action and to avoid negative consequences.

Despite these forces, however, given the nature of the actions involved in sanctioned massacres, one might still expect moral scruples to intervene; but the likelihood of moral resistance is greatly reduced by transforming the action into routine, mechanical, highly programmed operations. Routinization fulfills two functions. First, it reduces the necessity of making decisions, thus minimizing the occasions in which moral questions may arise. Second, it makes it easier to avoid the implications of the action, since the actor focuses on the details of the job rather than on its meaning. The latter effect is more readily achieved among those who participate in sanctioned massacres from a distance—from their desks or even from the cockpits of their bombers.

Routinization operates both at the level of the individual actor and at the organizational level. Individual job performance is broken down into a series of discrete steps, most of them carried out in automatic, regularized fashion. It becomes easy to forget the nature of the product that emerges from this process. When Lieutenant Calley said of My Lai that it was "no great deal," he probably implied that it was all in a day's work. Organizationally, the task is divided among different offices, each of which has responsibility for a small portion of it. This arrangement diffuses responsibility and limits the amount and scope of decision making that is necessary. There is no expectation that the moral implications will be considered at any of these points, nor is there any opportunity to do so. The organizational processes also help further legitimize the actions of each participant. By proceeding in routine fashion—processing papers, exchanging memos, diligently carrying out their assigned tasks—the different units mutually reinforce each other in the view that what is going on must be perfectly normal, correct, and legitimate. The shared illusion that they are engaged in a legitimate enterprise helps the participants assimilate their activities to other purposes, such as the efficiency of their performance, the productivity of their unit, or the cohesiveness of their group (see Janis, 1972).

Normalization of atrocities is more difficult to the extent that there are constant reminders of the true meaning of the enterprise. Bureaucratic inventiveness in the use of language helps to cover up such meaning. For example, the SS had a set of *Sprachregelungen,* or "language rules," to govern descriptions of their extermination program. As Arendt (1964) points out, the term *language rule* in itself was "a code name; it meant what in ordinary language would be called a lie" (p. 85). The code names for killing and liquidation were "final solution," "evacuation," and "special treatment." The war in Indochina produced its own set of euphemisms, such as "protective reaction," "pacification," and "forced-draft urbanization and modernization." The use of euphemisms allows participants in sanctioned massacres to differentiate their actions from ordinary killing and destruction and thus to avoid confronting their true meaning.

Dehumanization

Authorization processes override standard moral considerations; routinization processes reduce the likelihood that such considerations will arise. Still, the inhibitions against murdering one's fellow human beings are generally so strong that the victims must also be stripped of their human status if they are to be subjected to systematic killing. Insofar as they are dehumanized, the usual principles of morality no longer apply to them.

Sanctioned massacres become possible to the extent that the victims are deprived in the perpetrators' eyes of the two qualities essential to being perceived as fully human and included in the moral compact that governs human relationships: *identity*—standing as independent, distinctive individuals, capable of making choices and entitled to live their own lives—and *community*—fellow membership in an interconnected network of individuals who care for each other and respect each other's individuality and rights (Kelman, 1973; see also Bakan, 1966, for a related distinction between "agency" and "communion"). Thus, when a group of people is defined entirely in terms of a category to which they belong, and when this category is excluded from the human family, moral restraints against killing them are more readily overcome.

Dehumanization of the enemy is a common phenomenon in any war situation. Sanctioned massacres, however, presuppose a more extreme degree of dehumanization, insofar as the killing is not in direct response to the target's threats or provocations. It is not what they have done that marks such victims for death but who they are—the category to which they happen to belong. They are the victims of policies that regard their systematic destruction as a desirable end or an acceptable means. Such extreme dehumanization becomes possible when the target group can readily be identified as a separate category of people who have historically been stigmatized and excluded by the victimizers; often the victims belong to a distinct racial, religious, ethnic, or political group regarded as inferior or sinister. The traditions, the habits, the images, and the vocabularies for dehumanizing such groups are already well established and can be drawn upon when the groups are selected for massacre. Labels help deprive the victims of identity and community, as in the epithet "gooks" that was commonly used to refer to Vietnamese and other Indochinese peoples.

The dynamics of the massacre process itself further increase the participants' tendency to dehumanize their victims. Those who participate as part of the bureaucratic apparatus increasingly come to see their victims as bodies to be counted and entered into their reports, as faceless figures that will determine their productivity rates and promotions. Those who participate in the massacre directly—in the field, as it were—are reinforced in their perception of the victims as less than human by observing their very victimization. The only way they can justify what is being done to these people—both by others and by themselves—and the only way they can extract some degree of meaning out of the absurd events in which they find themselves participating (see Lifton, 1971, 1973) is by coming to believe that the victims are subhuman and deserve to be rooted out. And thus the process of dehumanization feeds on itself.

REFERENCES

Arendt, H. (1964). *Eichmann in Jerusalem: A report on the banality of evil.* New York: Viking Press.

Bakan, D. (1966). *The duality of human existence.* Chicago: Rand McNally.

Department of the Army. (1956). *The law of land warfare* (Field Manual, No. 27-10). Washington, DC: U.S. Government Printing Office.

Falk, R. A.; Kolko, G.; & Lifton, R. J. (Eds.). (1971). *Crimes of war.* New York: Vintage Books.

French, P. (Ed.). (1972). *Individual and collective responsibility: The massacre at My Lai.* Cambridge, MA: Schenkman.

Goldstein, J.; Marshall, B.; & Schwartz, J. (Eds.). (1976). *The My Lai massacre and its cover-up: Beyond the reach of law?* (The Peers report with a supplement and introductory essay on the limits of law). New York: Free Press.

Hammer, R. (1971). *The court-martial of Lt. Calley.* New York: Coward, McCann, & Geoghegan.

Hersh, S. (1970). *My Lai 4: A report on the massacre and its aftermath.* New York: Vintage Books.

_____. (1972). *Cover-up.* New York: Random House.

Janis, I. L. (1972). *Victims of groupthink: A psychological study of foreign-policy decisions and fiascoes.* Boston: Houghton Mifflin.

Kelman, H. C. (1973). Violence without moral restraint: Reflections on the dehumanization of victims and victimizers. *Journal of Social Issues,* 29(4), 25–61.

Lewin, K. (1947). Group decision and social change. In T. M. Newcomb & E. L. Hartley (Eds.), *Readings in social psychology.* New York: Holt.

Lifton, R. J. (1971). Existential evil. In N. Sanford, C. Comstock, & Associates, *Sanctions for evil: Sources of social destructiveness.* San Francisco: Jossey-Bass.

_____. (1973). *Home from the war—Vietnam veterans: Neither victims nor executioners.* New York: Simon & Schuster.

Manual for courts martial, United States (rev. ed.). (1969). Washington, DC: U.S. Government Printing Office.

Schirmer, D. B. (1971, April 24). My Lai was not the first time. *New Republic,* pp. 18–21.

Williams, B. (1985, April 14–15). "I will never forgive," says My Lai survivor. *Jordan Times* (Amman), p. 4.

THINKING ABOUT THE READING

According to Kelman and Hamilton, social processes can create conditions under which usual restraints against violence are weakened. What social processes were in evidence during the My Lai massacre? The incident they describe provides us with an uncomfortable picture of human nature. Do you think most people would have reacted the way the soldiers at My Lai did? Are we all potential massacrers? Does the phenomenon of obedience to authority go beyond the tightly structured environment of the military? Can you think of incidents in your own life when you've done something—perhaps harmed or humiliated another person—because of the powerful influence of others? How might Kelman and Hamilton explain the actions of the individuals who carried out the hijackings and attacks of September 11, 2001?

Speaking of Sadness

Depression, Disconnection, and the Meanings of Illness

David A. Karp

Living with Depression

In greater or lesser degree I have grappled with depression for almost 20 years. I suppose that even as a child my experience of life was as much characterized by anxiety as by joy and pleasure. And as I look back, there were lots of tip-offs that things weren't right. I find it difficult to remember much of my early years, but throughout high school and college I felt uncertain of myself, feared that I could not accomplish what was expected of me, and had plenty of sleepless nights. At college one of my roommates nicknamed me "weak heart," after a character-type in Dostoyevsky novels, because I often seemed a bit of a lost soul. During all those years, though, I had no real baseline for evaluating the "normalcy" of my feelings. At most, I had defined myself as more anxious than other people and as a "worrier." None of this seemed to warrant treatment of any sort. Even though I was muddling along emotionally, probably like having a constant low-grade fever, I was achieving well enough in school to presume that underneath it all I was okay. It wasn't until my early thirties that I was forced to conclude that something was "really wrong" with me.

People who have lived with depression can often vividly remember the situations that forced them to have a new consciousness as a troubled person. One such occasion for me was a 1974 professional meeting of sociologists in Montreal. By any objective standards I should have been feeling pretty good. I had a solid academic job at Boston College, had just signed my first book contract, and I had a great wife, beautiful son, and a new baby daughter at home. From the outside my life looked pretty good.

During the week I was in Montreal I got virtually no sleep. It's true, I was staying in a strange city and in a borrowed apartment—maybe this was the problem. But I had done a fair amount of traveling and never had sleeping difficulties quite as bad. Then, I thought, "Maybe I'm physically ill. It must be the flu." But again, it was unlike any flu I'd ever had. I wasn't just tired and achy. Each sleepless night my head was filled with disturbing ruminations and during the day I felt a sense of intolerable grief as though somebody close to me had died. I was agitated and sensed a melancholy qualitatively different from anything in the past. I couldn't concentrate because the top of my head felt as if it would blow off, and the excitement of having received the book contract was replaced by the dread and certainty that I wasn't up to the task of writing it. It truly was a miserable week and the start of what I now know was an extended episode of depression. It was also the beginning of a long pilgrimage to figure out what was wrong with me, what to name it, what to do about it, and how to live with it. It has been a bewildering, frustrating, often deeply painful journey.

Despite a progressive worsening of the feelings I first experienced in Montreal, it took me quite a while before I fully connected the word depression to my situation. Being depressed was not yet part of my self-description or identity. It was another prolonged and even more debilitating period of insomnia, compounded with anxiety and sadness, that pushed me to a doctor's office (an internist, not a psychiatrist). For the first time, I heard someone tell me that I was clinically depressed and that I needed "antidepressant medications." This too was a decisive moment in my growing self-definition as a troubled person. . . .

Like everyone who suffers with depression, I [have] spent a lot of time . . . considering its causes. Throughout the early 1970s I thought I had a pretty good explanation. I was a young assistant professor struggling to do enough publishing so that I would not lose my job. As they say in the academic business, 1977 was to be my "up or out year"; I would either be promoted or "terminated." In short, I was under enormous pressure for six years, juggling the tasks of teaching, counseling students, serving on departmental and university committees, presenting papers at professional meetings, and writing two books that had to be done before I was evaluated for tenure.

I thought for sure that my depression was rooted in these situational demands and that once I got tenure it would go away. I was promoted in 1977 and found that the depression actually deepened. Of course, this meant that my "tenure theory" was wrong and I needed to construct a new one. However, discarding it was no easy thing. The theory's failure suggested a wholly new and more frightening interpretation of depression's locus. Now I had to confront the possibility that my sickness might not arise from social situations, but somehow from my self.

By 1980 my sleeping, which has always been the key barometer of my psychic state, had become just awful. . . . Sometimes I might get to sleep, but even on my best nights I was up every hour or so. On my worst nights I got no sleep. I remember those nights especially well because they were so distinctly horrible. . . .

The two central feelings typifying my depression were frantic anxiety and a sense of grief. These feelings coupled to generate a sort of catastrophic thinking about events in my life as concrete as the next day's lecture and as amorphous as the quality of my relationships. None of these thoughts were productive. They were just insistently there, looping endlessly in my brain. Sometimes, as though God were serving up a particularly ironic punishment, I would drift off to sleep only shortly before I had to begin my day. The day did follow, filled with obligations that seemed burdensome and often impossible. Each day was spent struggling to appear competent, constantly feeling amazed that I had gotten through the last test and that I would certainly "shut down" in the face of the next. . . .

During all of this I felt deeply alone. Everyone else seemed to be moving through their days peacefully, laughing and having fun. I resented them because they were experiencing such an easy time of it; I felt utterly cut off from them emotionally. I was angry because there was no way they could understand what I was going through. Their very presence seemed to magnify my sense of isolation. I never felt seriously suicidal, but the combination of those days and nights often led me to feel that my life was not worth living. Although some days were far better than others, raising the elusive hope that I might be emerging from my difficulty, I basically dragged along, feeling barely alive. . . .

Given the pervasiveness of depression, it is not surprising that both medical and social scientists have tried to understand its causes and suggest ways of dealing with it. When I first considered writing about depression I did a computer search that turned up nearly 500 social science studies done in just the last few years. Researchers have tried to link the incidence of depression to every imaginable social factor. For example, since the rate of depression is twice as great for women than for men, studies have been conducted seeking to relate depression with gender roles, family structure, powerlessness, child rearing, and the like. Studies can also be found trying to link depression with, among other things, age (especially during adolescence and old age), unemployment, physical illness, disability, child abuse, ethnicity, race, and social class. . . .

Sickness, Self, and Society

. . . All human beings . . . think about the world in causal terms. All of us use cause and effect inferences in trying to understand important features of our lives. . . . Efforts to come to grips with depression turn on its presumed causes. . . . In this way, everyone suffering from depression inevitably becomes a theorist as they try to give order and coherence to their situation. With rare exceptions, the theories they generate locate the cause(s) of depression somewhere either in their biographies or their biologies. Occasionally, [people] spin out more complex theories that see depression as resulting from the subtle interplay of personal history, recent life events, and chemical imbalances. However, even those who name situational causes for their emotional problems typically restrict their conceptual vision to the immediate and local circumstances of their lives. Only rarely do sufferers of depression relate their condition to the kinds of broad cultural trends that, I believe, influence our consciousness about everything.

The reach of sociological thinking extends well beyond the immediate milieus of daily life. In fact, exercise of the sociological imagination *requires* analysis of the connections between daily life and larger cultural arrangements. . . . The abiding theoretical questions of sociology flow from consideration of the individual-society connection. Sociologists presume an ongoing intersection of personal biographies and the larger arenas of history and social structure. A sociological angle of vision sees an inseparability between the character of culture and even our innermost thoughts and feelings, including, of course, the deeply troubling thoughts and feelings we label as depression. As George Herbert Mead expressed it with the title of his famous book, an adequate *social* psychology of human experience must consider the ways in which *Mind, Self and Society*[1] mutually transform each other. [Next I will focus] on how the structure of contemporary American society may be implicated in the production of increasingly larger numbers of people who complain of and are diagnosed as having diseased minds and selves.

Like many sociologists, one of my favorite examples to illustrate the cultural roots of what initially appears to be an exclusively personal disorder is Émile Durkheim's classic study of suicide[2] that is generally seen as a sociological *tour de force*. Aside from the intrinsic importance of the topic, Durkheim presumably chose to study

suicide because, at first glance, it appears explicable *only* in individualistic, psychological terms. However, by testing a series of logically produced, deductive hypotheses linking suicide to such variables as religion, marital status, and membership in the military, Durkheim convincingly demonstrated the connection between suicide *rates* and degrees of *social integration*. Specifically, he argued that modernizing societies, like his own nineteenth century France, were less successful than earlier agrarian societies in providing sources of integration for their members. Such societies were characterized by what Durkheim termed *anomie*—a state of relative normlessness. His brilliant work verified that anomic societies that fail to integrate their members adequately also fail to insulate them from suicide. Suicide, in short, is as much a social as it is a psychological phenomenon.

Another first-rate sociologist, Kai Erikson, provides a valuable example for illustrating how a sociological perspective is necessary to see social patterns that would be missed if we only look at things "up close and personal," as they say on *Wide World of Sports*.[3] He has us imagine that we are walking along 42nd Street near Times Square. At the street level we can clearly see the faces of the thousands of people who pass us. We can see their individual expressions, their particular body idioms, their apparent ages, and so on. At this range, they normally seem to take no notice of anyone around them. Each stranger appears as a solitary atom, buzzing along in a wholly independent way.

Were we, however, to climb to the roof of a nearby 12-story building and look down on the flow of sidewalk traffic, we would see an extraordinary thing. It is true that from this vantage point we miss the particularities of each individual. However, we would instead witness a miraculous pattern—thousands of people moving along the street in an incredibly well-organized, efficient, and cooperative fashion. Moreover, each person on the street would likely be wholly unaware of their contribution to the web of behavior necessary to sustain such an enormously complex social order. It is as if each pedestrian is guided by an invisible social force, a kind of social gravity, about which they have only the vaguest awareness. I am proposing that most people suffering from depression, like street pedestrians, are only dimly aware of how the constitution of culture might be contributing to their depressed condition.

Although estimates of the number of Americans suffering from depression vary, there is general consensus that the number is in the vicinity of 11 million people and that economic losses from poor productivity, lost work days, hospitalization, outpatient care, and so on, is a staggering $43.7 billion dollars a year.[4] More important to my concerns are the data from a range of studies showing tremendous increases in the rates of depression. For example: (1) The incidence of depression among those born after World War II is much higher and the age of onset much earlier than in earlier population cohorts.[5] (2) In recent decades, there has been a continuing rise in depression among young women, but a disproportionate increase of depression among men has been closing the depression gender gap.[6] (3) There has been an absolute explosion of depression among "baby boomers."[7] These and similar findings warrant the conclusion that America is in the grip of a depression epidemic; that we have entered an "age of melancholy."[8]

. . . While any search for patterns necessarily suggests cause, I prefer to think about the link between cultural dimensions and depression in probabilistic terms. Epidemiologists, for example, describe poverty as a "risk factor" for a range of health problems. Poverty provides a context that makes individuals more vulnerable to disease. The notion of risk factors implies likelihoods rather than direct causal relationships. In Durkheimian fashion, [I will detail] the cultural dimensions of contemporary American society that provide the context for our collective vulnerability to emotional distress.[9] In particular, my thesis can be expressed as a theoretical equation. It is:

MEDICALIZATION + DISCONNECTION + POSTMODERNIZATION
= PERSONAL DISLOCATION

. . . I will define what I have in mind as each is discussed. Immediately, though, my argument is best advanced by showing how fundamentally the idea of depression is connected to culture. If the features of a particular culture truly influence what is even recognized as an illness, we should expect wide cultural variation in the labeling of particular physical and emotional experiences as health or illness.

Culture, Health, and Emotion

In a classic article written [over] 50 years ago, the medical historian Erwin H. Ackerknecht argued against the view that disease is a strictly physical phenomenon. Citing the important role played by social factors in the definition and treatment of illness, Ackerknecht maintained that "medicine's practical goal is not primarily a biological one, but that of social adjustment in a given society. . . . Even the notion of disease depends rather on the decisions of society than on objective facts."[10] As the following examples illustrate, societies differ dramatically in their response to the same physical symptoms:

> Pinto (dyschromic spirochetosis), a skin disease, is so common among many South American tribes that the few *healthy* men that *are not* suffering from pinto are regarded as *pathological* to the point of being excluded from marriage. The crippled feet of the traditional Chinese woman, diseased to us, were, of course, normal to the Chinese. Intestinal worms among the African Thongas are not at all regarded as pathological. They are thought to be necessary for digestion.[11]

Not only is the definition of what constitutes an illness or pathological condition subject to cultural variations, but, in an even more far-reaching sense, one's *experience* of bodily symptoms is shaped by social processes and expectations as well. In a now famous study, Mark Zborowski illustrated how responses to pain varied by the respondent's ethnicity.[12] Jewish-American patients, for example, evidenced substantial philosophical concern and anxiety about their condition and were pessimistic about the future course of their illness. Protestant patients felt optimistic about their prospects for recovery while viewing doctors as experts to whom one went for "mending," much like bringing a car to an auto mechanic for repairs. Italian-Americans, by contrast, wanted immediate pain relief, and, unlike Jewish respondents, had little concern about the larger "meanings" of the pain.

We should expect that the same principles apply to emotional pain and there is, indeed, substantial evidence that depression carries quite different meanings in different cultures. In a series of books and articles,[13] Arthur Kleinman, who is both an anthropologist and a physician, has written with eloquence and power on the value of looking at a range of emotional disorders cross culturally. Although he does not posit a particular theory as underlying his inquiries, Kleinman's analysis bears a striking resemblance to "symbolic interaction." . . . I say this because the underlying motif of his work is the *socially generated meanings of illness,* the importance of appreciating the dialectics of body and culture, symptom and society. In fact, Kleinman's mission seems nothing short of reforming the teaching and practice of medicine. By dismissing how illness carries very different symbolic meanings in different cultural settings, Western medicine, based nearly exclusively on a biomedical model, falls short in both its modes of diagnosis and treatment.

Like other medical anthropologists, Kleinman's thinking rests on the fundamental distinction between *illness* and *disease.* . . . Distinguishing the two words helps to make plain the difference between the subjective experience of bodily or emotional distress (illness) and the presumed biological cause of the distress (disease).

When first becoming sick we begin an interpretive process about the meaning of symptoms. We make assessments about the severity of our discomfort, and, usually in consultation with family and friends, assess the significance of our trouble, deciding what to name it and how to respond to it. The point here is that these interpretations can be rooted in widely varying normative orders and cultural symbol systems. Such culturally induced interpretations, moreover,

"orient us to how to act when ill, how to communicate distress, how to diagnose and treat, how to regard and manage the life problems illness creates, how to negotiate this social reality and interpret its meaning for ourselves and for others."[14] Disease, in contrast to illness, is "what the practitioner creates in the recasting of illness in terms of theories of disorder."[15] In Western medicine this typically means identifying the biological dysfunction presumably giving rise to the symptoms described by the patient.

Once we recognize the critical importance of cultural meanings in how symptoms are experienced and dealt with, we can also pinpoint a fundamental difficulty with the practice of Western medicine. American medicine is primarily concerned with disease and pays little attention to the patient's illness. The nearly single-minded efforts of physicians to quickly locate the presumed biological dysfunctions associated with symptoms leads to a problematic disjunction between what patients want from doctors and what they get. Evidence from a recent poll on dissatisfaction with conventional medicine[16] suggests that patients want to be heard by physicians and feel alienated when the full context of their illness experience is defined as irrelevant to their treatment. As a result, patients are seeking treatment from "alternative" healers in ever increasing numbers. Not incidentally, anxiety and depression rank one and two among the problems for which alternative help is sought.

Because of bureaucratic time imperatives[17] and physicians' felt need to quickly diagnose the patient's disease, most doctor/patient encounters in the United States are very short. While initial visits to a doctor might range up to 30 minutes, the average length of doctor/patient encounters is typically between 5 and 10 minutes. In a recent *Newsweek* story,[18] it was reported that patients' average time spent with psychiatrists in some clinics is an astonishing 3 minutes! Whether the figure is as low as 3 or as high as the 17 minutes reported in another study,[19] one thing is plain: Doctors are normally uninterested in hearing patients' illness experience—they listen only insofar as the information provided helps them to make a diagnosis. In fact, to let the patient "go on" about their symptoms and feelings is often seen as an obstacle to "good" medicine.[20] . . .

An anthropologically informed view sees diagnosis and treatment in very different terms. Illness narratives are deemed critical for appreciating precisely what physicians typically leave out of the picture—namely, how culturally prescribed meanings shape illness realities and, therefore, patients' likely responses to different modes of treatment. just as patients' experiences of symptoms arise out of particular symbol systems, so also must the likely efficacy of treatments be understood in cultural context. Nowhere is this line of thinking more apparently true than in psychiatry where emotional feelings define the problem and where the discovery of a clear disease entity is most elusive. Kleinman and his colleague Byron Good state with wonderful clarity what a cross-cultural perspective on depression teaches us. Based on a range of investigations, they say

> It is simply not tenable . . . to argue that dysphoric emotion and depressive illness are invariant across cultures. When culture is treated as a constant . . . it is relatively easy to view depression as [exclusively] a biological disorder. . . . From this perspective, culture appears epiphenomenal; cultural differences may exist, but they are not considered essential to the phenomenon itself. However, when culture is treated as a significant variable . . . many of our assumptions about the nature of emotions and illness are cast into sharp relief. Dramatic differences are found across cultures in the social organization, personal experience, and consequences of such emotions as sadness, grief, and anger, of behaviors such as withdrawal or aggression, and of psychological characteristics such as passivity and helplessness. . . . Dysphoria, even the pervasive loss of pleasure . . . is associated with quite different symptoms of distress and has widely varied consequences for the sufferer. . . . Depressive illness and dysphoria are thus not only interpreted differently in non-Western societies and across cultures; they are constituted as

fundamentally different forms of social reality.[21]

The essential finding of Kleinman's work and a number of other anthropologically oriented investigations on depression is that biological, psychological, and social processes are intricately woven together in creating the depression phenomenon. While there does appear to be a core syndrome of depression that can be observed universally across cultures, the equally clear findings of comparative research show wide variation in the experience of depression. Depressive disorders, in other words, display both universal and culture-specific properties.

Psychiatric medicine in the United States, with its heavily scientific bias, largely presumes biochemical pathology as the ultimate source of depressive disorders everywhere. Such a view is sustained despite the existence of "impressive data that there is no such thing as depression that occurs solely from biological causes."[22] To be sure, it would be equally plausible to say that real-world experiences produce depression by altering biochemistry and thus stand first in the hierarchy of depression's causes. Right now, though, it would be as presumptuous to make this claim as it is of American medicine to claim biology as the absolute foundation of depressive disorders. The truth is that there is no way to untangle the intersection of cultural and biological factors and, consequently, no sure way to claim the greater significance of either nature or nurture in causing depression. Despite this epistemological problem, the role of culture and the contributions of social science in understanding the course of illness remain very much at the margins of American medical training and practice.

This discussion asserts wide cultural variation in the incidence, meaning, and experience of psychiatric disorders, but is not grounded with concrete examples. To get specific, I can report that historically the best predictor of rates of admission to mental hospitals and suicides in North America is the health of the economy (the worse the economy the greater the rates); that the incidence and course of schizophrenia is tied to a society's level of technology (the more modernized a society the greater is the incidence of intractable schizophrenia); that a diagnostic category such as "narcissistic personality disorder," increasingly common in the United States, is virtually unheard of elsewhere; that in certain Asian societies "semen loss" resulting from nocturnal discharge is viewed with great alarm and anguish because sperm contains "qi" (vital energy), seen as absolutely necessary for health; that eating disorders such as anorexia and bulimia are most thoroughly characteristic of capitalist economies; that lack of joy, a central criterion for defining someone as depressed in the United States, would never be mentioned as a problem in Buddhist cultures such as Sri Lanka; that it is considered perfectly normal for American Indians grieving the loss of a spouse literally to hear the voices of the dead, and that the linguistic equivalents of anxiety and depression simply do not exist in many languages.[23]

In several of his books, Kleinman singles out China to illustrate how cultural sentiments influence the way doctors and their patients respond to the complex of feelings American doctors would unmistakably call depression. In contrast to the United States, depression is an infrequent diagnosis in China. Instead, patients suffering from a combination of such symptoms as anxiety, general debility, headaches, backaches, sadness, irritability, insomnia, poor appetite, and sexual dysfunction are diagnosed as suffering from "neurasthenia." Ironically, neurasthenia as a diagnostic category originated in the United States and was once thought of as "the American disease." Now, it is virtually never used in this country, just as the depression diagnosis is very rarely used in China. The choice of the neurasthenia diagnosis turns on cultural preferences. In China, where mental illness is deeply stigmatizing for both sick individuals and their families, doctors and patients find congenial a diagnosis—neurasthenia—that traces the disease to a neurological weakness rather than a mental disorder. In other words, the same symptoms are labeled, interpreted, responded to, and experienced quite differently in the two cultures. It

would be proper to say that, although suffering from nominally the same symptoms, the illness realities of Chinese and Americans are truly worlds apart.

Medicalization

The foregoing discussion implies that a necessary condition for widespread depressive illness is a culturally induced readiness to view emotional pain as a disease requiring medical intervention. The grounds for interpreting pain as an abnormal medical condition have been largely established through the increasing incursion of medical and other therapeutic experts into literally every aspect of our lives. Doctors in particular have become explorers, discovering every conceivable aspect of the human condition as potentially problematic and warranting their intervention. Such a "medicalization" process[24] has dramatically increased the number of uncomfortable or disliked feelings and behaviors that we now see as illnesses.

The so-called medical model is based on two apparently unassailable premises: (1) Normalcy is preferable to abnormalcy, and (2) normalcy is a synonym for health and abnormalcy a synonym for pathology. Definitions of health and pathology, in turn, are derived from laboratory research that is presumed to be thoroughly objective. In this way, medical definitions of health gain the status of scientific facts instead of merely collectively agreed on cultural designations.

Because it is better to be healthy than to be sick, the medical model legitimizes physicians' intervention, whether requested or not, to determine one's health status. No other profession provides for the extensive access to a person's body, mind, and self as do physical and psychiatric medicine. By defining certain features of the human condition as illnesses to be cured, physicians give themselves the right to explore every part of the human anatomy, to prescribe a myriad of curative agents, and even to compel treatment.

The term *healthy*, as used in the medical model, can be equated with *conformity*. In societies where it predominates, the medical model often supersedes legal or religious command-ments in regulating behavior. "Peculiar" indi-viduals who were once viewed as possessed or as agents of the devil are now classified as emotion-ally ill. In the name of science, the advice of medical experts is used in the courts to de-termine whether certain actions should be de-fined as crimes. Medicine, especially psychiatric medicine, is often used to "treat" individuals whose behaviors do not conform to the expecta-tions of the powerful or impinge on their moral sensitivities.

There can be little dispute that behavior in today's "postindustrial" society is dominated by "experts." Experts follow us through the life course, advising us on virtually every aspect of existence. They are there when we are born and accompany us each step along the way until we die. Among other things, we rely on experts to tell us how to maintain health, how to become edu-cated, how to make love, how to raise children, and how to age correctly. Most relevant here is that experts now tell us when our "selves" need repair and the proper procedures for doing it....

You might also understand that this depen-dence on therapeutic experts arises out of the distinctive problems posed by modern life. Every generation, because of its unique historical situa-tion, experiences the world differently than its predecessors. Whatever the historical conditions into which people are born, however, one prob-lem remains constant: Human beings need a co-herent framework for comprehending life and death. In some historical periods the traditional meanings transmitted from one generation to the next adequately perform this function. In other epochs, meaning coherence is not so easily established. As Peter Berger and Thomas Luck-mann note, the current moment in the Western world appears to be one in which many indi-viduals experience particular difficulty in under-standing themselves. They say that "In societies with a very simple division of labor . . . there is . . . no problem of identity. The question 'Who am I?' is unlikely to arise in consciousness, since the socially defined answer is massively real sub-jectively and consistently confirmed in all signifi-cant social interaction."[25]

When people come together and collectively act on their definitions of injustice, a social movement is born. In Ralph Turner's words, "The phenomenon of a man crying out with in-dignation because his society has not supplied him with a sense of personal worth and identity is the distinctive new feature of our era. The idea that a man who does not feel worthy and cannot find his proper place in life is to be pitied is an old one. The notion that he is indeed a victim of injustice is the new idea."[26] Today, alienation, previously seen as only a work-related phenom-enon, has a much broader connotation. In the present era, alienation refers to a psychological condition in which people are unable to locate a clear conception of self and feel a sense of whole-ness. In the context of such alienation, the "therapeutic state" has triumphed.[27]

As a more personalized conception of alien-ation has been taking root in American society, popular writings by psychiatrists, psychologists, and advice columnists have become increasingly influential. Television appearances have made "mind-tinkerers" such as Leo Buscaglia, "Dr. Ruth," Marianne Williamson, and John Bradshaw national celebrities. Their appeal attests to a per-vasive anxiety about questions of identity and psychological well-being in the society. Such ex-perts are constantly dispensing prescriptions for happiness, sexual fulfillment, and mental health.

The movement toward an all-embracing con-cern with psychological health and personal identity has been accompanied by a correspond-ing transformation in our explanations of human behavior. When people act in a way we consider deviant, our first impulse is to question their mental health and to probe their psychological makeup. Are they normal? Why are they doing that? What is wrong with them? Because of the medicalization process, such behaviors as alco-holism that years ago were viewed as evidence of sinfulness or moral degeneracy are now ex-plained as illness. A "sickness vocabulary" has re-placed a "sin vocabulary." For instance, the so-called "abuse excuse" as used in the celebrated trials of Erik and Lyle Menendez for murdering their parents has resulted in two hung juries. I would guess the same result would be virtually impossible had the Menendez brothers committed their crime 20 years ago.

Preoccupied with their dis-ease, huge numbers of Americans purchase the time and expertise of professionals in order to discover more about themselves. . . . We are in an era that has been characterized as the *age of narcissism*[28] and Americans are said to have constructed a "me, myself, and I" society. The availability of thousands of self-help books alone suggests that ours is a culture intensively absorbed with questions of self-fulfillment and self-realization.

The transformation in our self-conceptions has not been accomplished by mental health experts alone. Their orientation toward life is complemented by other self-oriented, self-discovery groups and movements. For example, large numbers of Americans continue to be involved in various fundamentalist and Eastern religious groups, as well as quasi-religious "personal growth" movements like Scientology and Transcendental Meditation.[29] Groups of this sort provide guidance for self-searching pilgrims, often by supplying absolutely definitive answers to the questions "Who am I and where do I fit in?" "New" religions thrive by providing world views alternative to the kind of scientific and bureaucratic rationality that insinuates even the innermost preserves of our everyday lives. The widespread interest in astrology, dianetics, and the paranormal is explicable as a reaction to a world in which science and technology have portrayed the universe as barren and bereft of meaning.

Yet another "revolution" directed toward the search for and repair of broken selves has been occurring in the last decade or so. In many ways, the springing up of self-help and support groups for dealing with almost every imaginable human trouble represents a combination of many of the elements I have been describing. The self-help revolution reflects the full flowering of a therapeutic culture in America. In self-help groups people turn to others afflicted with the same personal troubles and try, through conversation, to "heal" themselves of what they perceive to be their shared illness. An illness rhetoric (often implying biological causation) is sometimes joined with a spiritual vocabulary (as in programs like Alcoholics Anonymous) positing that "recovery" requires surrendering to a higher power. The self-help phenomenon thus derives its allure by combining elements of therapy with elements of religion and science. It is a powerful brew that has drawn the faith of millions.[30]

. . . As might be expected, the response of mental health professionals to the self-help phenomenon has been lukewarm.[31] While many mental health professionals are legitimately concerned about the wisdom of laypersons treating themselves, we should not miss the point that the self-help idea threatens their own claim to exclusive expertise about a number of mental health problems.

Recently a self-help backlash has developed. While people may individually feel better through participation in them, critics say that their collective effect may be the production of a national mentality in which virtually everyone perceives themselves as suffering from some sort of illness and as the "victim" of circumstances beyond their control. Dissidents wonder whether claims such as the one made by John Bradshaw, a leader of the "recovery movement," that 96 percent of American families are "dysfunctional," trivializes such real abuses as incest by grouping them with an enormous range of experiences that are somehow deemed as damaging people. Critics worry that the underlying illness ideology of support groups furthers the view—distinctly a product of the modern world—that individuals do not bear ultimate responsibility for their life problems and personal behaviors. Along these lines, the sociologist Edwin Shur pointed out several years ago that increased personal consciousness is too often achieved at the expense of a diminished social consciousness.[32]

As a final observation about the emergence of a therapeutic culture, I would add that self-absorption is consistent with the emphasis on self-satisfaction fostered by capitalism in general and advertising in particular. In the industrial age, society was primarily organized around the world of work. A person who did not work, for any reason other than physical disability, was defined as immoral, lazy, and worthless. This perspective on work was beautifully captured in Max Weber's notion of the Protestant Ethic which defines work as intrinsically valuable.[33] It appears, however, that the moral restraints of the work ethic have fundamentally been undermined by a consumption ethic. If workers imbued with the Protestant Ethic lived to work, now most of us work to consume.

The shift toward the social production of consumer-oriented selves has had far-reaching consequences. Since material possessions alone cannot ensure feelings of meaningfulness and satisfaction, many today find themselves caught up in an endless quest for personal significance; a quest made even more illusive by the built-in obsolescence of the products produced. There is always a "better" product in the works, and so the flames of advertising are always nearby heating the cauldron of contemporary anxiety.[34] In advanced capitalist societies virtually anything can be made into a commodity for sale, including our selves. . . .

. . . The experience of depression occurs within a cultural context that has enormously expanded the range of emotions defined as abnormal. Authors like Martin Gross have been skeptical about the legitimacy of such redefinitions. He comments, for example, that "what the psychological society has done is to redefine normality. It has taken the painful reactions to the normal vicissitudes of life . . . despair, anger, frustration—and labeled them as maladjustments. The semantic trick is in equating happiness with normality. By permitting this, we have given up our simple right to be normal and suffering at the same time."[35] While my sense is that such brush stroke observations about the "diseasing of America"[36] are unfair to millions of people whose suffering far exceeds what human beings ought to endure, they do properly sensitize us to an enormously increased readiness to interpret emotional discomfort as disease. Such a cultural mind-set has made it possible for medicine to "discover" depression and for millions of Americans to realize that they suffer from it.

The underlying metaphor . . . is of a cultural chemistry that catalyzes depression. Thus far I have outlined one piece of the mix that foments depression, a culturally induced readiness to interpret emotional pain as illness. Like any chemical mix, the elements involved cannot create a particular reaction until they are brought together. A second factor that really gets the depression reaction going is the increasing disconnection that appears to characterize Americans' relations with each other and with society. An elaboration of the social forces diminishing human connection extends my argument . . . that depression, at its root, is a disease of disconnection.

Disconnection

Sigmund Freud was once asked what people needed to be happy. The questioner no doubt expected a long, complicated answer reflecting Freud's years of deep reflection on the matter. His simple response, however, was "arbeiten und lieben,"—work and love. Happy people feel connected to others at work and through their intimate relationships. When those connections are threatened, diminished, or broken, people suffer. Today, millions of Americans are suffering from what my colleague Charles Derber calls "double trouble."[37] Those in double trouble have neither meaningful work nor sustaining intimate ties. The withering of community life in both domains fosters a rootlessness and social disintegration that unquestionably contributes to the growth of emotional disorders.[38]

. . . These ideas have a rich history. Classical sociological theorists (such as Émile Durkheim, Max Weber, and Ferdinand Toennies) fundamentally agreed that the bond between individuals and society had been dangerously weakened in "modern" society.[39] They were unanimous in their view that people were less morally constrained in urban societies because their relationships and commitments to communities of all sorts had become far more tenuous. These nineteenth century writers feared that the eclipse of community would foreshadow the demise of the family and would, in turn, precipitate an increase in all sorts of human pathologies—from crime to suicide.

Although these sociologists could not have had America in mind when they wrote, their analysis appears prophetic. Even the most optimistic among us must acknowledge that America has extraordinary problems. Each day the newspaper assails us with more bad news about rates of homelessness, poverty, suicide, drug addiction, AIDS, teenage pregnancy, illiteracy, and unemployment. In the midst of great wealth we are increasingly becoming two nations, the haves and the have nots, one nation black and the other white, one comfortable and the other destitute.[40] Racism, sexism, and ageism characterize ever-increasing antagonisms between groups that perceive each other only as adversaries. The focus here is more limited, however. My analysis turns on the question: "How do the increasingly loose human connections at work and at home contribute to the staggering and growing number of Americans who have fallen sick with depression?" Although any analytical separation of work and home is artificial since these life areas extensively affect each other,[41] I choose for simplicity's sake to discuss them one at a time.

The Work Disconnection. A well-established tradition of sociological literature illustrates the centrality of work to personal identity.[42] Occupational status may be the central yardstick by which we assess our own and others' "social value." In a very fundamental way, we *are* what we *do*. Our feelings of self-esteem and personal well-being are wrapped up in our work. Therefore, it is perfectly predictable that a legion of studies demonstrate how unemployment deprives individuals of much more than a regular paycheck. Loss of work bears a consistent relationship with serious family and psychiatric problems.[43] Our mental health unquestionably depends on being able to provide a satisfactory answer to the ubiquitous question "What kind of work do you do?" Without work, people feel lifeless, rootless, and marginal.

The disastrous consequences of joblessness for those at the bottom of the American class structure is an old story. If there is any news here it is, unfortunately, that things have gotten worse for the poorest and most marginalized popula-

tions in America's dying inner cities. Perhaps the outstanding fact bearing on this issue is the increasing concentration of nonwhites in central city areas. While there has been some modest movement of blacks to the suburbs since 1970, it has largely been the middle-class segment of the black population that has moved, leaving behind an increasing concentration of poor blacks within urban ghettoes. Blacks have been greatly overrepresented in inner-city areas since their initial migration from the rural South to the urban North beginning in the 1950s. However, according to William Julius Wilson,[44] poor blacks are experiencing ever increasing *social isolation* within central cities.

Such profoundly important demographic transformations in American society cannot be understood apart from the imperatives of corporate capitalism. We have entered into a new round of capitalist accumulation in which older, industrial cities are no longer favorable sites for the accumulation of profit. Corporations, free to move wherever there is cheaper labor and fewer legal restrictions, have largely fled the rustbelt cities of the midwest and the frostbelt cities of the northeast in favor of cities in the south and southwest. In yet another round of moves, corporations are now leaving the country altogether to "exploit" the cheap labor in Third World countries. These processes are part of the general "deindustrialization of America"[45] that has removed almost all meaningful job opportunities for the hyperghettoized minorities trapped in America's once great cities.

Without work, black men become less desirable marriage partners and are unable to support the families they do have. Poor black families are then increasingly headed by young women dependent on welfare or the few available jobs that provide less than bare subsistence wages. As a result, "children are being raised in an institutionless community, where everyone is poor, instability is the norm, and the social and psychological role of fatherhood is nonexistent.[46] Such a situation breeds depression that spreads easily from one generation to the next. The mechanism of transmission acts like this: (1) Unemployed women caring for children at home suffer from rates of depression as high as 40 percent.[47] (2) Depressed mothers simply cannot provide the care, nurturance, and empathy that is necessary for children to grow up with good emotional health. Understandably, (3) children whose primary caretaker is depressed are themselves at enormously high risk for becoming depressed.[48] (4) Depressed children become depressed adults who pass on their disease to their own children. And so on and on. So, we have another of the vicious cycles associated with depression. This one, however, is pushed along by an obviously dysfunctional *social* rather than biological system.[49]

The poor in America have always lived with occupational instability and its fallout. In contrast, middle-class workers have historically been immune from occupational insecurity. Indeed, achieving the American Dream of middle-class life has until recently been synonymous with tremendous occupational stability. In decades past, middle- to upper-middle-class workers in large organizations could count on being taken care of from "Womb to tomb." No more. Today, the catch-words "downsizing" and "reengineering" keep the fear of job loss at the forefront of middle-class workers' collective consciousness. Once again the logic of capitalist accumulation is creating a revolution. This one is qualitatively different than earlier economic restructurings because it directly touches the middle classes in hurtful ways. Instead of the strong bond of commitment and loyalty that organizations and middle-class workers previously felt toward each other, the new economic rules of corporate life emphasize efficiency, whatever the human cost. Knowing that they could be here today, but gone tomorrow, middle-class workers are constantly in "fear of falling."[50]

Along with those middle-class workers who continue to hold full-time jobs, however tenuously, is a growing army of well-educated "contingent workers" who are occupational nomads often working for "temp agencies." By 1988 one quarter of the American workforce worked on a contingent basis and the numbers are growing so rapidly that they will likely outnumber full-time workers by the turn of the century.[51] . . . Middle-class contingent workers *feel* contingent for good reason. They are disconnected from work in a way never before witnessed in the United States.

All social life involves a tension between freedom and constraint. Living in a society inevitably involves a trade-off between personal liberty and commitment to others. We judge some societies as immoral because they allow virtually no personal freedoms and others because they seem unable to constrain their members. For much of its history, the glory of American democracy seemed to be that it provided a healthy balance between commitment and freedom. For a long time, the pursuit of personal happiness and individual goals seemed compatible with a set of cultural values that Americans willingly embraced and held them together as a nation.

In the world of work, at least for "white collar" workers, there has been, until recently, a kind of *quid pro quo.* Organizations provided long-term security and received, in turn, worker loyalty, commitment, and responsibility. Loyalty, responsibility, security, commitment. These are the binding features of social systems, the glue that sustains the bond between individuals and social institutions. Unhappily, America's emerging "post-industrial" economy seems to have fundamentally altered the meaning of work for many by eroding loyalty, commitment, and mutual responsibility between organizations and workers.[52] Because emotional well-being is so unquestionably related to social attachment, the millions of Americans who are becoming occupationally marginal are at increasingly greater risk for being victimized by diseases of disconnection.

This section has sustained attention on how work is being reshaped in America's post-industrial, advanced capitalist society. Critics of capitalism, however, would maintain that the negative effects of capitalism on human relationships are far more inclusive than those in the workplace. In a more general way, the values underpinning capitalism are evident in a large variety of face-to-face encounters.

Competition, for example, is one of the cornerstones of capitalism. Advocates of capitalism maintain that competition is a necessary ingredient in both maintaining organizational efficiency and motivating individuals. On the negative side, however, competition pits individuals against each other, diminishes trust, and generally dehumanizes relationships. As the earlier discussion of advertising also intimates, capitalism contributes to a culture of inauthenticity. In a society where everything and everyone is evaluated by their profit potential, individuals are aware that they are constantly being manipulated, seduced, and conned by those who want to sell them or "take them." In a world held together by appearances and a tissue of illusions and deceptions, everyone becomes an enemy of sorts whose motives cannot be accepted at face value. In short, the abstract values of capitalism "trickle down" to everyday consciousness in a way that induces human beings to distrust and withdraw from each other. Withdrawal and increased isolation . . . are important features of the social dialectics of depression.

The Love Disconnection. Another underlying theme of nineteenth-century theory was the parallel development of capitalism and unbridled individualism. Although each of the classical theorists focused on somewhat different features of the social order, they agreed that while the central unit of earlier societies had been the larger collectivities of family and community, the central unit in their contemporary society had become the individual. Further, as the pursuit of financial gain and personal mobility became ascendant social values, relationships became more rational, impersonal, and contractual. Whereas people in earlier agrarian societies related to each other emotionally, with their hearts, those in the new social order related rationally, with their heads.

While the sociological analysis of individualism extends to the origins of the discipline, the conversation about its significance in understanding American character and social structure has recently been reinvigorated through the writings of Robert Bellah and his colleagues.[53] In 1985 they published a book entitled *Habits of the Heart* that details how individualism fosters self-absorption and guarantees a collective sense of strangeness, isolation, and loneliness. This book

has been widely praised as providing lucid, penetrating insights into our current cultural condition and has stimulated multiple responses to its ideas.

Bellah and his co-authors distinguish two forms of individualism, *instrumental individualism* and *expressive individualism.* Instrumental individualism refers to the freedom to pursue financial and career success. This is the kind of individualism celebrated in the maxims of Ben Franklin's "Poor Richard" and in the Horatio Alger "rags to riches" stories. Expressive individualism, in contrast, refers to the deep and abiding concerns that Americans have with personal self-fulfillment, with the idea that one of life's missions is to maximize personal happiness by discovering who you "really" are. This second form of individualism is thoroughly consistent with the "therapeutic culture" described earlier.

The essential problem posed by "excessive" individualism is that it privatizes the goals and pursuits of persons and thereby erodes the social attachments that provide society's moral anchor. Individualism undermines commitment to community since membership in any community (from the family to local community to nation) implies behavioral constraints that people perceive as inconsistent with personal fulfillment. The dilemma posed by the need both for attachment and freedom is beautifully captured in Bellah's analysis of romantic love in America. Americans believe deeply in romantic love as a necessary requirement for self satisfaction. At the same time, love and marriage, which are based on the free giving of self to another, pose the problem that in sharing too completely with another one might lose oneself. The difficulties that Americans have in maintaining intimate relationships stems in part from the uneasy balance between sharing and being separate. . . .

Among the many groups that have emerged as part of the self-help phenomenon, one deserves special mention in the context of this discussion. Across the country these days thousands flock to a group called "Co-Dependents Anonymous," a relatively new "12-stepper." Co-dependency is "a popular new disease, blamed for such diverse disorders as drug abuse, alcoholism, anorexia, child abuse, compulsive gambling, chronic late-ness, fear of intimacy, and low self esteem."[54] I find the idea of co-dependence interesting be-cause this newly discovered disorder arises out of widespread confusion about the permissible lim-its of human closeness. Members come to these groups because they see themselves as unable to sustain reasonable intimacy boundaries and feel overwhelmed by certain relationships. As previously, it would be unfair to minimize the real pain that pushes individuals to cure themselves of overinvolvement. It nevertheless seems clear that codependency can arise as a pathological condition only in a society that fosters deep am-bivalence about the value of extensive ties.

That Americans have problems with intimacy and commitment is surely reflected in the failure of half the marriages made in the country. Of course, marital problems and failures cannot be linked exclusively to patterns of self-absorption intrinsic to a cultural ethic of individualism. Failed relationships, as I indicated earlier, are also a result of the long-term, institutionalized pov-erty of some groups and the declining economic fortunes of others. Such difficult circumstances are hardly conducive to maintaining strong fam-ily and communal ties. Still, the passionate belief in individualism itself takes its toll. Americans feel incredibly ambivalent about all forms of so-cial attachments. Like moths to the proverbial flame, they are drawn to sources of connection for the comfort they provide, but equally fear what they perceive as the stifling features of all sorts of intimacies. Many are afraid that support-ive social bonds will evolve into bondage. They continuously flirt with intimacy and commit-ment, but in the end often choose a life style that maximizes both freedom and loneliness.

For a time the prevailing wisdom in America was that, on balance, children were better off when poor marriages split up. Yes, certainly there is substantial trauma when a marriage first ends, but children, the thinking went, are enormously resilient and eventually adapt in an emotionally healthy way. Whatever lingering problems they might have would surely have been worse if they too had to endure the bad marriage. Since the di-vorce revolution did not really begin until the 1970s, only now are we able to learn about the long-term emotional effects of broken marriages on children.

Immediately, let's recognize that children most usually live with their mothers after a di-vorce. This fact, coupled with compelling data on the "feminization of poverty"[55] post divorce, suggest the possible initiation of the same type of depression cycle earlier described as existing among poor inner-city, female-headed house-holds. In addition, recent data on the long-term effects of divorce debunk the notion that the negative emotional effects of divorce on children are short-lived. The 50 percent divorce rate seems instead to have produced an adult popula-tion with persistent and severe emotional prob-lems, depression among them.[56] Among the few issues that political conservatives and liberals agree on these days is that the disintegration of the traditional family across all social classes may be producing just the kinds of problems nine-teenth-century theorists presciently imagined.

It is said that when people on their death beds review their lives they rarely say they should have worked harder in order to own even more things than they do. Presumably, most regrets center on relationships that could have been better nur-tured and more fulfilling. However, as Bellah's analysis maintains, to live a life that truly centers on the quality of relations with others is exceed-ingly difficult for many, maybe most, Americans. The cultural pull away from others is often too powerful to resist. A culture that prizes individual self-realization above all else becomes a world held together by only the barest and most tenu-ous social connections. More and more Ameri-cans, identifying individual achievement as the primary medium for personal fulfillment, join the "lonely crowd" identified years ago by David Riesman.[57] To be part of the lonely crowd means being connected to many in general and few in particular. Having opted for loose intimate con-nections, increasing numbers of people then wonder why they feel the stirrings of emotional discontent that often evolves into the more dramatic malaise of depression.

NOTES

1. George Herbert Mead, *Mind, Self and Society* (Chicago: University of Chicago, 1934).

2. E. Durkheim, *Suicide* (New York: The Free Press, 1951).

3. K. Erikson, "On sociological prose," *The Yale Review* 78 (1989): 525–538.

4. M. Miller, "Dark days, the staggering cost of depression," *The Wall Street Journal,* Thursday, December 2, 1993, pp. B1, 6.

5. G. Klerman, "Evidence for increases in rates of depression in North America and Western Europe in recent decades." In H. Hippius, G. Klerman, and N. Matusssek (eds.), *New Results in Depression Research* (Berlin, Germany: Springer Verlag, 1986).

6. J. Brody, "Recognizing demons of depression, in either sex," *New York Times,* Wednesday, December 18,1991, p. C21.

7. See, G. Klerman, et. al., *Interpersonal Psychotherapy of Depression* (New York: Basic Books, 1984); B. Felton, "Cohort variation in happiness," *International Journal of Aging and Human Development* 25 (1987): 27–42; D. Regier, et al., "One month prevalence of mental disorders in the United States," *Archives of General Psychiatry* 45 (1988): 977–986.

8. T. Maher, "The withering of community life and the growth of emotional disorders." *Journal of Sociology and Social Welfare* 19 (1992), p. 138.

9. Although the context of the discussion here, as throughout the book, is on the ways social context shapes the depression experience, the broad social and cultural arrangements described in this chapter do not relate exclusively to depression. As indicated in the text, to pin generic features of American culture to depression alone would be like relating poverty in America to one social problem only. Just as poverty bears a strong relationship to a whole host of human difficulties, the features of American society that foster loneliness, depersonalization, distrust, inauthenticity, mutual indifference, and social disconnection are associated with multiple emotional illnesses. A whole range of disorders from anxiety to depression to paranoia to schizophrenia flourish in societies and situations that maximize the kinds of personal dislocations arising out of social disattachment.

10. E. Ackernecht, 'The role of medical history in medical education," *Bulletin of the History of Medicine* 21 (1947): 142–143.

11. Ibid., p. 143.

12. M. Zborowski, "Cultural components in responses to pain." In C. Clark and H. Robboy (eds.), *Social Interaction* (New York: St. Martin's, 1992).

13. Among his work demonstrating cross-cultural variation in the meanings of affective disorders, see A. Kleinman and B. Good (eds.), *Culture and Depression* (Berkeley: University of California Press, 1986), *Social Origins of Distress and Disease* (New Haven, CT: Yale University Press, 1986), *Rethinking Psychiatry* (New York: Free Press, 1988), and *The Illness Narratives* (New York: Basic Books, 1988).

14. A. Kleinman, *Social Origins of Distress and Disease,* op. cit., p. 145.

15. A. Kleinman, *The Illness Narratives,* op. cit., p. 5.

16. The results of this survey were reported in the *Boston Globe* on Thursday, January 28, 1993, p. 11.

17. See W. Yoels and J. Clair, 1994. "Never enough time: How medical residents manage a scarce resource," *The Journal of Contemporary Ethnography* 23 (1994): 185–213.

18. *Newsweek* (February 1, 1994).

19. H. Waitzkin, *The Politics of Medical Encounters: How Patients and Doctors Deal with Social Problem* (New Haven, CT: Yale University Press, 1991).

20. W. Yoels and W. Clair, op. cit.

21. A. Kleinman, *The Illness Narratives* (New York, Basic Books, 1988, p. 5).

22. A. Kleinman, *Rethinking Psychiatry,* op. cit., p. 73.

23. These and similar examples are found throughout the works of Arthur Kleinman noted above.

24. For a complete discussion of the medicalization process and particularly the medicalization of deviance, see P. Conrad and J. Schneider, *Deviance and Medicalization* (St. Louis: C. V. Mosby, 1980).

25. P. Berger and T. Luckmann, *The Social Construction of Reality* (New York: Doubleday Anchor, 1967), p. 164.

26. R. Turner, "The theme of contemporary social movements," *British Journal of Sociology* 20 (1969), p. 395.

27. See P. Rieff, *Triumph of the Therapeutic State* (New York: Harper & Row, 1966).

28. C. Lasch, *The Culture of Narcissism* (New York: W. W. Norton, 1978).

29. For a broadly based discussion of such groups, see R. Wuthnow, "Religious movements and counter-movements in North America." In J. Beckford (ed.), *New Religious Movements and Rapid Social Change* (London: Sage, 1986).

30. In his recent book entitled *Sharing the Journey Together: Support Groups and America's New Quest for Community* (New York: The Free Press, 1994), Robert Wuthnow argues that the ever-proliferating range of support groups now constitute the primary mechanism through which Americans achieve a sense of community and connection.

31. See T. Powell, *Self Help Organizations and Professional Practice* (Silver Spring, MD: National Association of Social Workers, 1987) and T. Powell (ed.), *Working with Self Help* (Silver Spring, MD: National Association of Social Workers, 1990).

32. E. Schur, *The Awareness Trap* (New York: McGraw-Hill, 1976).

33. M. Weber, *The Protestant Ethic and the Spirit of Capitalism,* translated by T. Parsons (New York: Scribner's, 1930).

34. Among those who have written about the relationship between capitalism and advertising, the work of Stewart Ewen is particularly cogent. See Ewen's two books entitled *Captains of Consciousness* (New York: McGraw-Hill, 1976) and *All Consuming Images* (New York: Basic Books, 1988).

35. M. Gross, *The Psychological Society* (New York: Random House, 1978), p. 6.

36. S. Peele, *Diseasing of America: Addiction Treatment Out of Control* (Lexington, MA: Lexington Books, 1989).

37. Personal conversation.

38. See T. Maher, "The withering of community life and the growth of emotional disorders," *Journal of Sociology and Social Welfare* 19 (1992): 125–143.

39. For a discussion of how nineteenth-century theorists considered the changing nature of the social bond with the advent of urban industrialization, see D. Karp, G. Stone, and W. Yoels, *Being Urban: A Sociology of City Life* (New York: Praeger, 1991).

40. A. Hacker, *Two Nations: Black and White, Separate, Hostile, Unequal* (New York: Scribner's, 1992).

41. R. Sennett and J. Cobb demonstrate, as an example, how the powerlessness of working-class men on their jobs helps to explain the widely observed pattern of male authoritarianism in working-class homes. This analysis is found in their book *The Hidden Injuries of Class* (New York: Random House, 1973).

42. See, for example, H. Becker and A. Strauss, "Careers, personality, and adult socialization," *American Journal of Sociology* 62 (1956): 253–263, and E. Hughes, *Men and Their Work* (New York: The Free Press, 1958).

43. See, R. Cohn, "The effects of employment status change on self attitudes," *Social Psychology* 41 (1978): 81–93; R. Coles, 'Work and self respect." In E. Erikson (ed.), *Adulthood* (New York: W. W. Norton, 1978); R. Rothman, *Working: Sociological Perspectives* (Englewood Cliffs, NJ: Prentice Hall, 1987).

44. W. Wilson, *The Truly Disadvantaged* (Chicago: University of Chicago Press, 1987).

45. B. Bluestone and B. Harrison, *The Deindustrialization of America* (New York: Basic Books, 1982).

46. T. Maher, op. cit., p. 134

47. Reported in T. Maher, op. cit.

48. Reported in T. Maher, op. cit.

49. If anything, the rate of severe depression among America's underclass is probably underestimated since this population segment is the most invisible, has the least access to information about depression, and has effectively been abandoned by the health care system.

50. B. Ehrenreich, *Fear of Falling: The Inner Life of the Middle Class* (New York: HarperCollins, 1989).

51. *Time,* "The temping of America," March 29, 1993.

52. See, for example, C. Davies, 'The throwaway culture: Job detachment and depression," *The Gerontologist* 25 (1985): 228–231.

53. R. Bellah, R. Madson, W. M. Sullivan, A. Swidler, and S. M. Tipton, *Habits of the Heart: Individualism and Commitment in American Life* (Berkeley: University of California Press, 1985).

54. W. Kaminer, "Chances are you're co-dependent too," *New York Times Book Review* (February, 11, 1990): 1, 26ff.

55. L. Weitzman, *The Divorce Revolution: The Unexpected Social and Economic Consequences in America* (New York: Free Press, 1985).

56. J. Wallerstein and S. Blakeulee, *Second Chances: Men, Women and Children: A Decade After Divorce* (New York: Ticknor and Fields, 1989).

57. D. Riesman, *The Lonely Crowd* (New Haven, CT: Yale University Press, 1950).

THINKING ABOUT THE READING

What does Karp mean when he says that depression is not an exclusively personal, biochemical disorder? What evidence does he provide to support his argument that this ailment is shaped by cultural and social processes? Why is depression so pervasive in technologically complex, postindustrial societies? Pay particular attention to the impact of individualism, occupational instability, and economic competition on people's emotions. If we take this argument one step further, it would imply that simple, preindustrial societies are somewhat inoculated against depression. Do you agree? Using Karp's argument as a starting point, discuss the effectiveness of drug therapy as the dominant treatment for depression. If it's true that people in different cultures experience depression differently, can the same antidepressant drug have similar effects across cultures?

PART II
The Construction of Self and Society

3 Building Reality: The Social Construction of Knowledge

Sociologists often talk about reality as a *social construction*. What they mean is that truth, knowledge, and so on, are discovered, made known, reinforced, and changed by members of society. As social beings, we respond to our interpretations and definitions of situations, not to the situations themselves, thereby shaping reality. How we distinguish fact from fantasy, truth from fiction, myth from reality are not merely abstract philosophical questions but are very much tied to interpersonal interaction, group membership, culture, history, power, economics, and politics. But not all of us possess the same ability to define reality. Individuals and groups in positions of power have the ability to control information, define values, create myths, manipulate events, and ultimately influence what others take for granted. The mass media are especially influential in shaping perceptions of reality.

In "The Crack Attack," Craig Reinarman and Harry Levine show us how the news media function to *create* a reality that the public comes to take for granted. They focus, in particular, on the emergence of "the crack problem" in American society. In the late 1980s, crack, a cocaine derivative, came to be seen as one of the most evil scourges on the social landscape. Even today we hear it described with terms like *plague* and *epidemic*. We hear horror stories about crack babies— children born addicted to the drug—whose lives are marked by emotional, intellectual, and behavioral suffering. But Reinarman and Levine point out that the terrified public concern over crack—the reality of the crack problem—is as much a function of media publicity, political opportunism, and the class, race, and ethnicity of crack users as it is a consequence of the actual chemical power and physical danger of the substance itself. In this sense, media representations don't merely *reflect* some "objective" reality, they actually help create it.

Discovering truth and amassing useful knowledge lay at the heart of any academic discipline. The purpose of a field such as sociology is to provide the public with useful and accurate information about how society works. This is typically accomplished through systematic social research—experiments, field research, unobtrusive research, and surveys. But gathering trustworthy data from people is a difficult task. People sometimes lie or have difficulty recalling past events in their lives. Sometimes the simple fact of observing people's behavior changes that behavior. And sometimes the information needed to answer questions about important, controversial issues is hard to obtain without raising ethical issues.

In "The Practice of Social Research," Julia O'Connell Davidson examines some of these dilemmas in conducting social research on sexuality and prostitution. O'Connell

Davidson employs a variety of face-to-face research techniques to study the life of a single prostitute (interviews, informal conversations, observations, participation as a receptionist). Only from this intimate vantage point does she feel she is fully capable of understanding the social forces at play in the lives of these women. In the interests of objectivity, most social researchers try to suppress or ignore their own emotions. O'Connell Davidson does the opposite, acknowledging and examining her own strong feelings about prostitutes and about the clients they serve.

The Crack Attack
Politics and Media in the Crack Scare

Craig Reinarman and Harry G. Levine

America discovered crack and overdosed on oratory. —New York Times (Editorial, October 4, 1988)

This *New York Times* editorial had a certain unintended irony, for "America's paper of record" itself had long been one of the leading orators, supplying a steady stream of the stuff on which the nation had, as they put it, "overdosed." Irony aside, the editorial hit the mark. The use of powder cocaine by affluent people in music, film, sports, and business had been common since the 1970s. According to surveys by the National Institute on Drug Abuse (NIDA), by 1985, more than twenty-two million Americans in all social classes and occupations had reported at least trying cocaine. Cocaine smoking originated with "freebasing," which began increasing by the late 1970s (see Inciardi, 1987; Siegel, 1982). Then (as now) most cocaine users bought cocaine hydrochloride (powder) for intranasal use (snorting). But by the end of the 1970s, some users had begun to "cook" powder cocaine down to crystalline or "base" form for smoking. All phases of freebasing, from selling to smoking, took place most often in the privacy of homes and offices of middle-class or well-to-do users. They typically purchased cocaine in units of a gram or more costing $80 to $100 a gram. These relatively affluent "basers" had been discovering the intense rush of smoking cocaine, as well as the risks, for a number of years before the term "crack" was coined. But most such users had a stake in conventional life. Therefore, when they felt their cocaine use was too heavy or out of control, they had the incentives and resources to cut down, quit, or get private treatment.

There was no orgy of media and political attention in the late 1970s when the prevalence of cocaine use jumped sharply, or even after middle-class and upper-class users began to use heavily, especially when freebasing. Like the crack users who followed them, basers had found that this mode of ingesting cocaine produced a much more intense and far shorter "high" because it delivered more pure cocaine into the brain far more directly and rapidly than by snorting. Many basers had found that crack's intense, brutally brief rush, combined with the painful "low" or "down" that immediately followed, produced a powerful desire immediately to repeat use—to binge (Waldorf et al., 1991).

Crack's pharmacological power alone does not explain the attention it received. In 1986, politicians and the media focused on crack— and the drug scare began—when cocaine smoking became visible among a "dangerous" group. Crack attracted the attention of politicians and the media because of its downward mobility to and increased visibility in ghettos and barrios. The new users were a different social class, race, and status (Duster, 1970; Washton and Gold, 1987). Crack was sold in smaller, cheaper, precooked units, on ghetto streets, to poorer, younger buyers who were already seen as a threat (*e.g., New York Times,* August 30, 1987; *Newsweek,* November 23, 1987; *Boston Globe,* May 18, 1988). Crack spread cocaine smoking into poor populations already beset with a cornucopia of troubles (Wilson, 1987). These people tended to have fewer bonds to conventional society, less to lose, and far fewer resources to cope with or shield themselves from drug-related problems.

The earliest mass media reference to the new form of cocaine may have been a *Los Angeles Times* article in late 1984 (November 25, p. cc1) on the use of cocaine "rocks" in ghettos and barrios in Los Angeles. By late 1985, the *New York Times* made the national media's first specific reference to "crack" in a story about three teenagers seeking treatment for cocaine abuse (November 17, p. B12). At the start of 1986, crack was known only in a few impoverished neighborhoods in Los Angeles, New York, Miami, and perhaps a few other large cities. . . .

The Frenzy: Cocaine and Crack in the Public Eye

When two celebrity athletes died in what news stories called "crack-related deaths" in the spring of 1986, the media seemed to sense a potential bonanza. Coverage skyrocketed and crack became widely known. "Dramatic footage" of black and Latino men being carted off in chains, or of police breaking down crack house doors, became a near nightly news event. In July 1986 alone, the three major TV networks offered seventy-four evening news segments on drugs, half of these about crack (Diamond et al., 1987; Reeves and Campbell, 1994). In the months leading up to the November elections, a handful of national newspapers and magazines produced roughly a thousand stories discussing crack (Inciardi, 1987, p. 481; Trebach, 1987, pp. 6–16). Like the TV networks, leading news magazines such as *Time* and *Newsweek* seemed determined not to be outdone; each devoted five cover stories to crack and the "drug crisis" in 1986 alone.

In the fall of 1986, the CBS news show *48 Hours* aired a heavily promoted documentary called "48 Hours on Crack Street," which Dan Rather previewed on his evening news show: "Tonight, CBS News takes you to the streets, to the war zone, for an unusual two hours of hands-on horror." Among many shots from hidden cameras was one of New York Senator Alphonse D'Amato and then-U.S. Attorney Rudolf Guiliani, *in cognito,* purchasing crack to dramatize the bra-

zenness of street corner sales in the ghetto. All this was good business for CBS: the program earned the highest Nielsen rating of any similar news show in the previous five years—fifteen million viewers (Diamond et al., 1987, p. 10). Three years later, after poor ratings nearly killed *48 Hours,* the show kicked off its season with a three-hour special, "Return to Crack Street."

The intense media competition for audience shares and advertising dollars spawned many similar shows. Three days after "48 Hours on Crack Street," NBC ran its own prime-time special, "Cocaine Country," which suggested that cocaine and crack use had become pandemic. This was one of dozens of separate stories on crack and cocaine produced by NBC alone—an unprecedented fifteen hours of air time—in the seven months leading up to the 1986 elections (Diamond et al., 1987; Hoffman, 1987). By mid-1986, *Newsweek* claimed that crack was the biggest story since Vietnam and Watergate (June 15, p. 15), and *Time* soon followed by calling crack "the Issue of the Year" (September 22, 1986, p. 25). The words "plague," "epidemic," and "crisis" had become routine. The *New York Times,* for example, did a three-part, front-page series called "The Crack Plague" (June 24, 1988, p. A1).

The crack scare began in 1986, but it waned somewhat in 1987 (a nonelection year). In 1988, drugs returned to the national stage as stories about the "crack epidemic" again appeared regularly on front pages and TV screens (Reeves and Campbell, 1994). One politician after another re-enlisted in the War on Drugs. In that election year, as in 1986, overwhelming majorities of both houses of Congress voted for new antidrug laws with long mandatory prison terms, death sentences, and large increases in funding for police and prisons. The annual federal budget for antidrug efforts surged from less than $2 billion in 1981 to more than $12 billion in 1993. The budget for the Drug Enforcement Administration (DEA) quadrupled between 1981 and 1992 (Massing, 1993). The Bush administration alone spent $45 billion—more than all other presidents since Nixon combined—mostly for law enforcement (Horgan, 1993; Office of National Drug Control Policy, 1992)....

An April 1988 ABC News special report termed crack "a plague" that was "eating away at the fabric of America." According to this documentary, Americans spend "$20 billion a year on cocaine," American businesses lose "$60 billion" a year in productivity because their workers use drugs, "the educational system is being undermined" by student drug use, and "the family" is "disintegrating" in the face of this "epidemic." This program did not give its millions of viewers any evidence to support such dramatic claims, but it did give them a powerful *vocabulary of attribution*: "drugs," especially crack, threatened all the central institutions in American life—families, communities, schools, businesses, law enforcement, even national sovereignty.

This media frenzy continued into 1989. Between October 1988 and October 1989, for example, the *Washington Post* alone ran 1565 stories—28,476 column inches—about the drug crisis. Even Richard Harwood (1989), the *Post's* own ombudsman, editorialized against what he called the loss of "a proper sense of perspective" due to such a "hyperbole epidemic." He said that "politicians are doing a number on people's heads." In the fall of 1989, another major new federal antidrug bill to further increase drug war funding (S-1233) began winding its way through Congress. In September, President Bush's "drug czar," William Bennett, unveiled his comprehensive battle plan, the *National Drug Control Strategy*. His introduction asks, "What . . . accounts for the intensifying drug-related chaos that we see every day in our newspapers and on television? One word explains much of it. That word is *crack*. . . . Crack is responsible for the fact that vast patches of the American urban landscape are rapidly deteriorating" (The White House, 1989, p. 3, original emphasis)....

On September 5, 1989, President Bush, speaking from the presidential desk in the Oval Office, announced his plan for achieving "victory over drugs" in his first major prime-time address to the nation, broadcast on all three national television networks. We want to focus on this incident as an example of the way politicians and the media systematically misinformed and deceived the public in order to promote the War on Drugs. During the address, Bush held up to the cameras a clear plastic bag of crack labeled "EVIDENCE." He announced that it was "seized a few days ago in a park across the street from the White House" (*Washington Post*, September 22, 1989, p. A1). Its contents, Bush said, were "turning our cities into battle zones and murdering our children." The president proclaimed that, because of crack and other drugs, he would "more than double" federal assistance to state and local law enforcement (*New York Times*, September 6, 1989, p. A11). The next morning the picture of the president holding a bag of crack was on the front pages of newspapers across America.

About two weeks later, the *Washington Post*, and then National Public Radio and other newspapers, discovered how the president of the United States had obtained his bag of crack. According to White House and DEA officials, "the idea of the President holding up crack was [first] included in some drafts" of his speech. Bush enthusiastically approved. A White House aide told the *Post* that the president "liked the prop. . . . It drove the point home." Bush and his advisors also decided that the crack should be seized in Lafayette Park across from the White House so the president could say that crack had become so pervasive that it was being sold "in front of the White House" (Isikoff, 1989).

This decision set up a complex chain of events. White House Communications Director David Demarst asked Cabinet Affairs Secretary David Bates to instruct the Justice Department "to find some crack that fit the description in the speech." Bates called Richard Weatherbee, special assistant to Attorney General Dick Thornburgh, who then called James Milford, executive assistant to the DEA chief. Finally, Milford phoned William McMullen, special agent in charge of the DEA's Washington office, and told him to arrange an undercover crack buy near the White House because "evidently, the President wants to show it could be bought anywhere" (Isikoff, 1989).

Despite their best efforts, the top federal drug agents were not able to find anyone selling crack (or any other drug) in Lafayette Park, or anywhere else in the vicinity of the White House. Therefore, in order to carry out their assignment, DEA agents had to entice someone to come to the park to make the sale. Apparently, the only person the DEA could convince was Keith Jackson, an eighteen-year-old African-American high school senior. McMullan reported that it was difficult because Jackson "did not even know where the White House was." The DEA's secret tape recording of the conversation revealed that the teenager seemed baffled by the request: "Where the [expletive deleted] is the White House?" he asked. Therefore, McMullan told the *Post,* "we had to manipulate him to get him down there. It wasn't easy" (Isikoff, 1989).

The undesirability of selling crack in Lafayette Park was confirmed by men from Washington, D.C., imprisoned for drug selling, and interviewed by National Public Radio. All agreed that nobody would sell crack there because, among other reasons, there would be no customers. The crack-using population was in Washington's poor African-American neighborhoods some distance from the White House. The *Washington Post* and other papers also reported that the undercover DEA agents had not, after all, actually seized the crack, as Bush had claimed in his speech. Rather, the DEA agents purchased it from Jackson for $2400 and then let him go.

This incident illustrates how a drug scare distorts and perverts public knowledge and policy. The claim that crack was threatening every neighborhood in America was not based on evidence; after three years of the scare, crack remained predominantly in the inner cities where it began. Instead, this claim appears to have been based on the symbolic political value seen by Bush's speech writers. When they sought, after the fact, to purchase their own crack to prove this point, they found that reality did not match their script. Instead of changing the script to reflect reality, a series of high-level officials instructed federal drug agents to *create* a reality that would fit the script. Finally, the president of the United States displayed the procured prop on national television. Yet, when all this was revealed, neither politicians nor the media were led to question the president's policies or his claims about crack's pervasiveness.

As a result of Bush's performance and all the other antidrug publicity and propaganda, in 1988 and 1989, the drug war commanded more public attention than any other issue. The media and politicians' antidrug crusade succeeded in making many Americans even more fearful of crack and other illicit drugs. A *New York Times/CBS News* poll has periodically asked Americans to identify "the most important problem facing this country today." In January 1985, 23% answered war or nuclear war; less than 1% believed the most important problem was drugs. In September 1989, shortly after the president's speech and the blizzard of drug stories that followed, 64% of those polled believed that drugs were now the most important problem, and only 1% thought that war or nuclear war was most important. Even the *New York Times* declared in a lead editorial that this reversal was "incredible" and then gently suggested that problems like war, "homelessness and the need to give poor children a chance in life" should perhaps be given more attention (September 28, 1989, p. A26).

A year later, during a lull in antidrug speeches and coverage, the percentage citing "drugs" as the nation's top problem had dropped to 10%. Noting this "precipitous fall from a remarkable height," the *Times* observed that an "alliance of Presidents and news directors" shaped public opinion about drugs. Indeed, once the White House let it be known that the president would be giving a prime-time address on the subject, all three networks tripled their coverage of drugs in the two weeks prior to his speech and quadrupled it for a week afterward (*New York Times,* September 6, 1990, p. A11; see also Reeves and Campbell, 1994). All this occurred while nearly every index of drug use was dropping.

The crack scare continued in 1990 and 1991, although with somewhat less media and political attention. By the beginning of 1992—the last year of the Bush administration—the War on Drugs in general, and the crack scare in particular, had begun to decline significantly in prominence and importance. However, even as the drug war was receiving less notice from politicians and the media, it remained institutionalized, bureaucratically powerful, and extremely well funded (especially police, military, and education/propaganda activities).

From the opening shots in 1986 to President Bush's national address in 1989, and through all the stories about "crack babies" in 1990 and 1991, politicians and the media depicted crack as supremely evil—*the* most important cause of America's problems. As recently as February of 1994, a prominent *New York Times* journalist repeated the claim that "An entire generation is being sacrificed to [crack]" (Staples, 1994). As in all drug scares since the nineteenth-century crusade against alcohol, a core feature of drug war discourse is the *routinization of caricature*—worst cases framed as typical cases, the episodic rhetorically recrafted into the epidemic.

Official Government Evidence

On those rare occasions when politicians and journalists cited statistical evidence to support their claims about the prevalence of crack and other drug use, they usually relied on two basic sources, both funded by the National Institute on Drug Abuse. One was the Drug Abuse Warning Network (DAWN), a monitoring project set up to survey a sample of hospitals, crisis and treatment centers, and coroners across the country about drug-related emergencies and deaths. The other was the National Household Survey on Drug Abuse among general population households and among young people. Other data sources existed, but these usually were either anecdotal, specific to a particular location, or based on a skewed sample. Therefore, we review what these two NIDA data sources had to say about crack because they were the only national data and because they are still considered by experts and claims makers to be the most reliable form of evidence available.

The Drug Abuse Warning Network

DAWN collects data on a whole series of drugs—from amphetamine to aspirin—that might be present in emergencies or fatalities. These data take the form of "mentions." A drug mention is produced when a patient, or someone with a patient, tells attending medical personnel that the patient recently used the drug, or occasionally, if a blood test shows the presence of the drug. These data provided perhaps the only piece of statistical support for the crack scare. They indicated that cocaine was "mentioned" in an increasing number of emergency room episodes in the 1980s. During 1986, as the scare moved into full swing, there were an estimated 51,600 emergency room episodes in which cocaine was mentioned (NIDA, 1993a). In subsequent years, the estimated number of such mentions continued to rise, providing clear cause for concern. By 1989, for example, the estimated number of emergency room episodes in which cocaine was mentioned had more than doubled to 110,000. Although the estimate dropped sharply in 1990 to 80,400, by 1992, it had risen again to 119,800 (NIDA, 1993a).

Unfortunately, the meaning of a mention is ambiguous. In many of these cases, cocaine was probably incidental to the emergency room visit. Such episodes included routine cases in which people went to emergency rooms, for example, after being injured as passengers in auto accidents and in home accidents. Moreover, in most cases, cocaine was only one of the drugs in the person's system; most people had also been drinking alcohol. Finally, the DAWN data do not include information about preexisting medical or mental health conditions that make any drug use, legal or illegal, more risky. For all these reasons, one cannot properly infer direct cause from the estimates of emergency room mentions. Cocaine did play a causal role in many of these emergency cases, but no one knows how many or what proportion of the total they were.

The DAWN data on deaths in which cocaine was mentioned by medical examiners also must be closely examined. When the crack scare got under way in 1986, coroners coded 1092 deaths as "cocaine related" (NIDA, 1986a), and as crack spread, this number, too, increased substantially. In 1989, the secretary of health and human services reported a 20% decline in both deaths and emergency room episodes in which cocaine was mentioned, but both indices rose again in 1991 and 1992. The 1992 DAWN figures showed 3020 deaths in which cocaine was mentioned (NIDA, 1992).

But cocaine *alone* was mentioned in only a fraction of these deaths; in 1986, for example, in less than one in five (NIDA, 1986a). In most of these cases, cocaine had been used with other drugs, again, most often alcohol. Although any death is tragic, cocaine's role in such fatalities remains ambiguous. "Cocaine related" is not the same as "cocaine caused," and "cocaine-related deaths" does not mean "deaths *due to* cocaine." There is little doubt that cocaine contributes to some significant (but unknown) percentage of such deaths. But journalists, politicians, and most of the experts on whom they relied never acknowledged the ambiguities in the data. Nor did they commonly provide any comparative perspective. For example, for every *one* cocaine-related death in the U.S., there have been approximately two hundred tobacco-related deaths and at least fifty alcohol-related deaths. Seen in this light, cocaine's role in mortality and morbidity was substantially less than media accounts and political rhetoric implied.

More serious interpretive and empirical difficulties appeared when the DAWN data were used to support claims about crack. Despite all the attention paid to the crack "plague" in 1986, when crack was allegedly "killing a whole generation," the DAWN data contained *no specific information on crack* as distinct from cocaine. In fact, the DAWN data show that in the vast majority of both emergencies and deaths in which cocaine received a mention, the mode of ingestion of cocaine was *not* "smoking" and therefore could not have been caused by crack. Thus, although it is likely that crack played a role in some of the emergencies and deaths in which cocaine was "mentioned," the data necessary to attribute them accurately to crack did not exist.

NIDA Surveys

The NIDA-sponsored surveys of drug use produce the data that are the statistical basis of all estimates of the prevalence of cocaine and other drug use. One of the core claims in the crack scare was that drug use among teenagers and young adults was already high and that it was growing at an alarming rate. Although politicians and the media often referred to teen drug use as an "epidemic" or "plague," the best official evidence available at the time did not support such claims. The National Household Survey on Drug Abuse surveys over eight thousand randomly selected households each year. These surveys show that the number of Americans who had used any illegal drug in the previous month began to decline in 1979, and in the early years of the crack scare, use of drugs, including cocaine, continued to decline (*New York Times*, September 24, 1989, p. A1; *Newsweek*, February 19, 1990, p. 74). Lifetime prevalence of cocaine use among young people (the percentage of those twelve through twenty-five years old who had "ever" tried it) peaked in 1982, *four years before the scare began*, and continued to decline after that (NIDA, 1991, p. 14). The sharpest rise in lifetime prevalence among young adults had taken place between 1972 and 1979; it produced no claims of an epidemic or plague by politicians and journalists (Johnston et al., 1988; NIDA, 1986b).

In February 1987, NIDA released the results of its 1986 annual survey of high school seniors. The *New York Times* handling of the story shows how even the most respectable media institutions sometimes skew facts about drug use to fit a story line. In the article's "lead," the *Times* announced a rise in the percentage of high school seniors reporting "daily" use of cocaine. Only later did one learn that this had risen very slightly and, more important for evaluating claims of a "plague," that daily use among seniors had now reached 0.4%. Daily crack use, even by this fraction of 1% of high school seniors, is surely troubling, but it hardly constituted a new drug epidemic or plague. Still later in the story, the *Times* presented a table showing other declines in cocaine use by young adults and high school seniors. Indeed, as the *Times* noted toward the end of its piece, virtually all forms of teenage drug use (including marijuana, LSD, and heroin) had declined—as they had in previous years (*New York Times*, February 24, 1987, p. A21; cf. Johnston et al., 1988; NIDA, 1991).

Two leading NIDA scholars, reporting in 1986 on the results of the household survey in *Science* magazine, wrote that "both annual prevalence and current prevalence [of all drug use] among college students and the total sample up to four years after high school has been relatively stable between 1980 and 1985" (Kozel and Adams, 1986, p. 973). The director of NIDA's high school surveys, Dr. Lloyd Johnston, made a similar point in 1987: "To some degree the fad quality of drugs has worn off" (*New York Times*, February 24, 1987, p. A21). When the findings of the high school senior survey for 1987 were released, the survey's director reported that "the most important" finding was that cocaine had again "showed a significant drop in use." He even reported a decline in the use of crack (Johnston et al., 1988).

These reported declines were in keeping with the general downward trend in drug use. In the early 1980s, according to the NIDA surveys, about one in six young Americans had tried cocaine powder. But between 1986 and 1987, the proportion of both high school seniors and young adults who had used cocaine in any form in the previous year dropped by 20% (Johnston et al., 1988). Further, two-thirds of those who had ever tried cocaine had not used it in the previous month. Although a significant minority of young people had tried cocaine powder at some point, the great majority of them did not continue to use it.

There had been a few signs of increasing cocaine use. The proportion of youngsters who reported using cocaine at least once in the previous month had increased slightly over the years, although it never exceeded 2% of all teens in the seven national household surveys between 1972 and 1985. The 1988 NIDA household survey found an increase in the number of adult daily users of cocaine, presumably the group that included crack addicts. But this group constituted only about 1.3% of those adults who had ever used cocaine. NIDA also estimated that about 0.5% of the total U.S. adult population had used cocaine in the week prior to the survey (NIDA, 1988).

But aside from these few slight increases, almost all other measures showed that the trends in official drug use statistics had been down even before the scare began. . . . The figures for cocaine use in particular were dropping just as crisis claims were reaching a crescendo, and had dropped still further precisely when the Bush/Bennett battle plan was being announced with such fanfare in 1989. Indeed, as White House officials anonymously admitted a few weeks after the president's "bag of crack" speech, the new plan's "true goals" were far more modest than its rhetoric: the Bush plan was "simply to move the nation 'a little bit' beyond where current trends would put it anyway" (*New York Times*, September 24, 1989, p. A1).

National Survey Data on Crack

Tom Brokaw reported on *NBC Nightly News* in 1986 (May 23) that crack was "flooding America" and that it had become "America's drug of choice." His colleagues at the other networks and in the print media had made similar claims. An ordinarily competent news consumer might well have gathered the impression that crack could be found in the lockers of most high school students. Yet, at the time of these press reports, *there were no prevalence statistics at all on crack* and no evidence of any sort showing that smoking crack had become the preferred mode even of cocaine use, much less of drug use.

When NIDA released the first official data on crack a few months later, they still did not support claims about widespread crack use. On the contrary, the NIDA survey found that most cocaine use could not have been crack because the preferred mode of use for 90% of cocaine users was "sniffing" rather than smoking (NIDA, 1986a; see also Inciardi, 1987). An all-but-ignored Drug Enforcement Administration press release issued in August 1986, during the first hysterical summer of the crack scare, sought to correct the misperception that crack use was now the major drug problem in America. The DEA said, "Crack is currently the subject of considerable media attention. . . . The result has been a distortion of the public perception of the extent of crack use as compared to the use of other drugs. . . . [Crack] presently appears to be a secondary rather than primary problem in most areas" (Drug Enforcement Administration, cited in Diamond et al., 1987, p. 10; Inciardi, 1987, p. 482).

The first official measures of the prevalence of teenage crack use began with NIDA's 1986 high school survey. It found that 4.1% of high school seniors reported having *tried* crack (at least once) in the previous year. This figure dropped to 3.9% in 1987 and to 3.1% in 1988, a 25% decline (Johnston et al., 1988; *National Report on Substance Abuse,* 1994, p. 3). This means that at the peak of crack use, 96% of America's high school seniors had never tried crack, much less gone on to more regular use, abuse, or addiction. Any drug use among the young is certainly worrisome, particularly when in such an intense form as crack. However, at the start of the crusade to save "a whole generation" of children from death by crack in the spring of 1986, the latest official data showed a national total of eight "cocaine-related" deaths of young people age eighteen and under for the preceding year (Trebach, 1987, p. 11). There was no way to determine whether any of these deaths involved crack use or even if cocaine was in fact the direct cause.

In general, the government's national surveys indicate that a substantial minority of teenagers and young adults experiment with illicit drugs. But as with other forms of youthful deviance, most tend to abandon such behavior as they assume adult roles. Politicians, the media, and antidrug advertisements often claimed that cocaine is inevitably addicting but that crack is still worse because it is "instantaneously addicting." However, according to the official national surveys, two-thirds of Americans of all ages who had ever tried cocaine had not used it in the month prior to the surveys. It is clear that the vast majority of the more than twenty-two million Americans who have tried cocaine do not use it in crack form, do not escalate to regular use, and do not end up addicted. . . .

In sum, the official evidence on cocaine and crack available during the crack scare gave a rather different picture than Americans received from the media and politicians. The sharp rise in mentions of cocaine in emergency room episodes and coroners' reports did offer cause for concern. But the best official evidence of drug use never supported the claims about an "epidemic" or "plague" throughout America or about "instantaneous addiction." Moreover, as media attention to crack was burgeoning, the actual extent of crack use was virtually unknown, and most other official measures of cocaine use were actually decreasing. Once crack use was actually measured, its prevalence turned out to be low to start with and to have declined throughout the scare (*National Report on Substance Abuse,* 1994, p. 3).

Crack as an Epidemic and Plague

The empirical evidence on crack use suggests that politicians and journalists have routinely used the words "epidemic" and "plague" imprecisely and rhetorically as words of warning, alarm, and danger. Therefore, on the basis of press reports, it is difficult to determine if there was any legitimacy at all in the description of crack use as an epidemic or plague. Like most other drug researchers and epidemiologists, we have concluded that crack addiction has never been anything but relatively rare across the great middle strata of the U.S. population. If the word "epidemic" is used to mean a disease or disease-like condition that is "widespread" or "prevalent," then there has never been an epidemic of crack addiction (or even crack use) among the vast majority of Americans. Among the urban poor, however, especially African-American and Latino youth, heavy crack use has been more common. An "epidemic of crack *use*" might be a description of what happened among a distinct minority of teenagers and young adults from impoverished urban neighborhoods in the mid to late 1980s. However, many more people use tobacco and alcohol heavily than use cocaine in any form. Alcohol drinking and tobacco smoking each kills far more people than all forms of cocaine and heroin use combined. Therefore, "epidemic" would be more appropriate to describe tobacco and alcohol use. But politicians and the media have not talked about tobacco and alcohol use as epidemics or plagues. The word "epidemic" also can mean a rapidly spreading disease. In this precise sense as well, in inner-city neighborhoods, crack use may have been epidemic (spreading rapidly) for a few years among impoverished young African-Americans and Latinos. However, crack use was never spreading fast or far enough among the general population to be termed an epidemic there.

"Plague" is even a stronger word than epidemic. Plague can mean a "deadly contagious disease," an epidemic "with great mortality," or it can refer to a "pestilence," an "infestation of a pest, [e.g.,] a plague of caterpillars." Crack is a central nervous system stimulant. Continuous and frequent use of crack often burns people out and does them substantial psychological and physical harm. But even very heavy use does not usually directly kill users. In this sense, crack use is not a plague. One could say that drug dealers were "infesting" some blocks of some poor neighborhoods in some cities, that there were pockets of plague in some specific areas; but that was not how "crack plague" was used.

When evaluating whether the extent and dangers of crack use match the claims of politicians and the media, it is instructive to compare how other drug use patterns are discussed. For example, an unusually balanced *New York Times* story (October 7, 1989, p. 26) compared crack and alcohol use among suburban teenagers and focused on the middle class. The *Times* reported that, except for a few "urban pockets" in suburban counties, "crack and other narcotics are rarely seen in the suburbs, whether modest or wealthy." . . .

The *Times* also reported that high school seniors were outdrinking the general adult population. Compared to the 64% of teenagers, only 55% of adults had consumed alcohol in the last month. Furthermore, teenagers have been drinking more than adults since at least 1972, when the surveys began. Even more significant is the *kind* of drinking teenagers do—what the *Times* called "excessive 'binge' drinking": "More than a third of the high school seniors had said that in the last two weeks they had had five or more drinks in a row." Drinking is, of course, the most widespread form of illicit drug use among high school students. As the *Times* explained, on the weekend, "practically every town has at least one underage party, indoors or out" and that "fake identification cards, older siblings, friends, and even parents all help teenagers obtain" alcohol.

The point we wish to emphasize is that even though illicit alcohol use was far more prevalent than cocaine or crack use, and even though it held substantial risk for alcohol dependence, addiction, drinking-driving deaths, and other alcohol-related problems, the media and politicians have not campaigned against teen drunkenness. Used as a descriptive term meaning "prevalent," the word "epidemic" fits teenage drinking far better than it does teenage crack use. Although many organizations have campaigned against drinking and driving by teenagers, the politicians and media have not used terms like "epidemic" or "plague" to call attention to illicit teenage drinking and drunkenness. Unlike the *Times* articles on crack, often on the front page, this article on teen drunkenness was placed in the second section on a Saturday.

It is also worth noting the unintentionally ironic mixing of metaphors, or of diagnoses and remedies, when advocates for the War on Drugs described crack use as an epidemic or plague. Although such disease terminology was used to call attention to the consequences of crack use, most of the federal government's domestic responses have centered on using police to arrest users. Treatment and prevention have always received a far smaller proportion of total federal antidrug funding than police and prisons do as a means of handling the "epidemic." If crack use is primarily a crime problem, then terms like "wave" (as in crime wave) would be more fitting. But if this truly is an "epidemic"—a widespread disease—

then police and prisons are the wrong remedy, and the victims of the epidemic should be offered treatment, public health programs, and social services. . . .

The Political Context of the "Crack Crisis"

If the many claims about an "epidemic" or "plague" endangering "a whole generation" of youth were at odds with the best official data, then what else was animating the new War on Drugs? In fact, even if all the exaggerated claims about crack had been true, it would not explain all the attention crack received. Poverty, homelessness, auto accidents, handgun deaths, and environmental hazards are also widespread, costly, even deadly, but most politicians and journalists never speak of them in terms of crisis or plague. Indeed, far more people were (and still are) injured and killed every year by domestic violence than by illicit drugs, but one would never know this from media reports or political speeches. The existence of government studies suggesting that crack contributed to the deaths of a small proportion of its users, that an unknown but somewhat larger minority of users became addicted to it, that its use was related to some forms of crime, and so on were neither necessary nor sufficient conditions for all the attention crack received (Spector and Kitsuse, 1977).

Like other sociologists, historians, and students of drug law and public policy, we suggest that understanding antidrug campaigns requires more than evidence of drug abuse and drug-related problems, which can be found in almost any period. It requires analyzing these crusades and scares as phenomena in their own right and understanding the broader social, political, and economic circumstances under which they occur (see, *e.g.,* Bakalar and Grinspoon, 1984; Brecher, 1972; Duster, 1970; Gusfield, 1963, 1981; Lindesmith, 1965; Morgan, 1978; Musto, 1973; Rumbarger, 1989). The crack scare also must be understood in terms of its political context and its appeal to important groups within American society. The mass media and politicians, however,

did not talk about drugs this way. Rather, they decontextualized the drama, making it appear as if the story had no authors aside from dealers and addicts. Their writing of the crack drama kept abusers, dealers, crimes, and casualties under spotlights while hiding other important factors in the shadows. We suggest that over and above the very real problems some users suffered with crack, the rise of the New Right and the competition between political parties in a conservative context contributed significantly to the making of the crack scare.

The New Right and Its Moral Ideology

During the post-Watergate rebuilding of the Republican Party, far right wing political organizations and fundamentalist Christian groups set about to impose what they called "traditional family values" on public policy. This self-proclaimed "New Right" felt increasingly threatened by the diffusion of modernist values, behaviors, and cultural practices—particularly by what they saw as the interconnected forms of 1960s hedonism involved in sex outside (heterosexual) marriage and consciousness alteration with (illicit) drugs. The New Right formed a core constituency for Ronald Reagan, an extreme conservative who had come to prominence as governor of California in part by taking a hard line against the new political movements and cultural practices of the 1960s.

Once he became president in 1981, Reagan and his appointees attempted to restructure public policy according to a radically conservative ideology. Through the lens of this ideology, most social problems appeared to be simply the consequences of *individual moral choices* (Ryan, 1976). Programs and research that had for many years been directed at the social and structural sources of social problems were systematically defunded in budgets and delegitimated in discourse. Unemployment, poverty, urban decay, school crises, crime, and all their attendant forms of human troubles were spoken of and acted upon as if they were the result of *individual* deviance, immorality, or weakness. The most basic premise of social science—that individual choices are influenced by social circumstances—was rejected as left-wing ideology. Reagan and the New Right constricted the aperture of attribution for America's ills so that only the lone deviant came into focus. They conceptualized people *in* trouble as people who *make* trouble (Gusfield, 1985); they made social control rather than social welfare the organizing axis of public policy (Reinarman, 1988).

With regard to drug problems, this conservative ideology is a form of *sociological denial.* For the New Right, people did not so much abuse drugs because they were jobless, homeless, poor, depressed, or alienated; they were jobless, homeless, poor, depressed, or alienated because they were weak, immoral, or foolish enough to use illicit drugs. For the right wing, American business productivity was not lagging because investors spent their capital on mergers and stock speculation instead of on new plants and equipment, or for any number of other economic reasons routinely mentioned in the *Wall Street Journal* or *Business Week.* Rather, conservatives claimed that businesses had difficulty competing partly because many workers were using drugs. In this view, U.S. education was in trouble not because it had suffered demoralizing budget cuts, but because a "generation" of students was "on drugs" and their teachers did not "get tough" with them. The new drug warriors did not see crime plaguing the ghettos and barrios for all the reasons it always has, but because of the influence of a new chemical bogeyman. Crack was a godsend to the Right. They used it and the drug issue as an ideological fig leaf to place over the unsightly urban ills that had increased markedly under Reagan administration social and economic policies. "The drug problem" served conservative politicians as an all-purpose scapegoat. They could blame an array of problems on the deviant individuals and then expand the nets of social control to imprison those people for causing the problems.

The crack crisis had other, more specific political uses. Nancy Reagan was a highly visible antidrug crusader, crisscrossing the nation to urge schoolchildren to "Just Say No" to drugs. Mrs. Reagan's crusade began in 1983 (before crack came into existence) when her "p.r.-conscious operatives," as *Time* magazine called them, convinced her that "serious-minded displays" of "social consciousness" would "make her appear more caring and less frivolous." Such a public relations strategy was important to Mrs. Reagan. The press had often criticized her for spending hundreds of thousands of dollars on new china for the White House, lavish galas for wealthy friends, and high-fashion evening gowns at a time when her husband's economic policies had induced a sharp recession, raised joblessness to near Depression-era levels, and cut funding for virtually all programs for the poor. *Time* explained that "the timing and destinations of her antidrug excursions last year were coordinated with the Reagan-Bush campaign officials to satisfy their particular political needs" (*Time,* January 14, 1985, p. 30). . . .

Political Party Competition

The primary political task facing liberals in the 1980s was to recapture some of the electorate that had gone over to the Right. Reagan's shrewdness in symbolically colonizing "middle American" fears put Democrats on the defensive. Most Democrats responded by moving to the right and pouncing upon the drug issue. Part of the early energy for the drug scare in the spring and summer of 1986 came from Democratic candidates trading charges with their Republican opponents about being "soft on drugs." Many candidates challenged each other to take urine tests as a symbol of their commitment to a "drug-free America." One Southern politician even proposed that candidates' spouses be tested. A California senatorial candidate charged his opponent with being "a noncombatant in the war on drugs" (*San Francisco Chronicle,* August 12, 1986, p. 9). By the fall of 1986, increasingly strident calls for a drug war became so much a part of candidates' standard stump speeches that even conservative columnist William Safire complained of antidrug "hysteria" and "narcomania"

(*New York Times,* September 11, 1986, p. A27). Politicians demanded everything from death penalties in North America to bombing raids in South America.

Crack could not have appeared at a more opportune political moment. After years of dull debates on budget balancing, a "hot" issue had arrived just in time for a crucial election. In an age of fiscal constraint, when most problems were seen as intractable and most solutions costly, the crack crisis was the one "safe" issue on which all politicians could take "tough stands" without losing a single vote or campaign contribution. The legislative results of the competition to "get tough" included a $2 billion law in 1986, the so-called "Drug-Free America Act," which whizzed through the House (392 to 16) just in time for members of Congress to go home and tell their constituents about it. In the heat of the preelection, antidrug hysteria, the symbolic value of such spending seemed to dwarf the deficit worries that had hamstrung other legislation. According to *Newsweek,* what occurred was "a can-you-top-this competition" among "election-bound members of both parties" seeking tough antidrug amendments. The 1986 drug bill, as Representative David McCurdy (D-Okla) put it, was "out of control," adding through a wry smile, "but of course I'm for it" (September 22, 1986, p. 39).

The prominence of the drug issue dropped sharply in both political speeches and media coverage after the 1986 election, but returned during the 1988 primaries. Once again the crack issue had political utility. One common observation about the 1988 presidential election campaigns was that there were no domestic or foreign policy crises looming on which the two parties could differentiate themselves. As a *New York Times* headline put it: "Drugs as 1988 Issue: Filling a Vacuum" (May 24, 1988, p. A14). In the 1988 primary season, candidates of both parties moved to fill this vacuum in part by drug-baiting their opponents and attacking them as "soft on drugs." In the fall, both Democrats Dukakis and Bentsen and Republicans Bush and Quayle claimed that their opponents were soft on drugs while asserting that their side would wage a "*real*

War on Drugs." And, just as they did before the 1986 election, members of Congress from both parties overwhelmingly passed a new, even more strict and costly antidrug bill.

The antidrug speeches favoring such expenditures became increasingly transparent as posturing, even to many of the speakers. For example, Senator Christopher Dodd (D-Conn) called the flurry of antidrug amendments a "feeding frenzy" (*New York Times,* May 22, 1988, p. E4). An aide to another senator admitted that "everybody was scrambling to get a piece of the action" (*New York Times,* May 24, 1988, p. A14). Even President Reagan's spokesperson, Marlin Fitzwater, told the White House press corps that "everybody wants to out-drug each other in terms of political rhetoric" (*Boston Globe,* May 18, 1988, p. 4). But however transparent, such election-year posturing—magnified by a media hungry for the readers and ratings that dramatic drug stories bring—enhanced the viability of claims about the menace of crack far more than any available empirical evidence could. In the fall of 1989, Congress finalized yet another major antidrug bill costing more than the other two combined. According to research by the Government Accounting Office, the federal government spent more than $23 billion on the drug war during the Reagan era, three-fourths of it for law enforcement (*Alcoholism and Drug Abuse Week,* 1989, p. 3). . . .

Politicians and the media were *forging,* not following, public opinion. The speeches and stories *led* the oft-cited poll results, not the other way around. In 1987, between elections—when drug problems persisted in the ghettos and barrios but when the drug scare was not so enflamed by election rhetoric and media coverage—only 3 to 5% of those surveyed picked drugs as our most important problem (*New York Times,* May 24, 1988, p. A14). But then again in 1989, immediately following President Bush's speech escalating the drug war, nearly two-thirds of the people polled identified drugs as America's most important problem. When the media and politicians invoked "public opinion" as the driving force behind their actions against crack, they inverted the actual causal sequence (Edelman, 1964, p. 172).

We argued in the previous section that the New Right and other conservatives found ideological utility in the crack scare. In this section, we have suggested that conservatives were not the only political group in America to help foment the scare and to benefit from it. Liberals and Democrats, too, found in crack and drugs a means of recapturing Democratic defectors by appearing more conservative. And they too found drugs to be a convenient scapegoat for the worsening conditions in the inner cities. All this happened at a historical moment when the Right successfully stigmatized the liberals' traditional solutions to the problems of the poor as ineffective and costly. Thus, in addition to the political capital to be gained by waging the war, the new chemical bogeyman afforded politicians across the ideological spectrum both an explanation for pressing public problems and an excuse for not proposing the unpopular taxing, spending, or redistributing needed to do something about them.

The End of the Crack Scare

In the 1980s, the conservative drive to reduce social spending exacerbated the enduring problems of impoverished African-American and Latino city residents. Partly in response, a minority of the young urban poor turned either to crack sales as their best shot at the American Dream and/or to the crack high as their best shot at a fleeting moment of pleasure. Inner-city churches, community organizations, and parent groups then tried to defend their children and neighborhoods from drug dealing and use on the one hand and to lobby for services and jobs on the other hand. But the crack scare did not inspire politicians of either party to address the worsening conditions and growing needs of the inner-city poor and working class or to launch a "Marshall Plan for cities." In the meantime, the white middle-class majority viewed with alarm the growing numbers, visibility, and desperation of the urban poor. And for years many Americans believed the central fiction of the crack scare: that drug use was not a symptom of urban decay but one of its most important causes.

All this gave federal and local authorities justification for widening the nets of social control. Of course, the new drug squads did not reduce the dangerousness of impoverished urban neighborhoods. But the crack scare did increase criminal justice system supervision of the underclass. By 1992, one in four young African-American males was in jail or prison or on probation or parole—more than were in higher education. . . . During the crack scare, the prison population more than doubled, largely because of the arrests of drug users and small dealers. This gave the U.S. the highest incarceration rate in the world (Currie, 1985; Irwin and Austin, 1994).

By the end of 1992, however, the crack scare seemed spent. There are a number of overlapping reasons for this. Most important was the failure of the War on Drugs itself. Democrats as well as Republicans supported the War on Drugs, but the Reagan and Bush administrations initiated and led it, and the drug war required support from the White House. George Bush appointed William Bennett to be a "tough" and extremely high profile "drug czar" to lead the campaign against drugs. But Bennett, criticized for his bombastic style, quit after only eighteen months (some press accounts referred to it as the "czar's abdication"). After that, the Bush administration downplayed the drug war, and it hardly figured at all in the presidential primaries or campaign in 1992. Bill Clinton said during the campaign that there were no easy solutions to drug problems and that programs that work only on reducing supply were doomed to fail. The Clinton administration eschewed the phrase "War on Drugs," and Lee Brown, Clinton's first top drug official, explicitly rejected the title of drug czar (Reinarman, 1994). After billions of tax dollars had been spent and millions of young Americans had been imprisoned, hard-core drug problems remained. With so little to show for years of drug war, politicians seemed to discover the limits of the drug issue as a political weapon. Moreover, with both parties firmly in favor of the "get tough" approach, there was no longer any partisan political advantage to be had.

The news media probably would have written dramatic stories about the appearance of smokeable cocaine in poor neighborhoods at any time. Television producers have found that drug stories, especially timely, well-advertised, dramatic ones, often receive high ratings. But the context of the Reagan-led drug war encouraged the media to write such pieces. Conservatives had long complained that the media had a liberal bias; in the mid-1980s, drug coverage allowed the media to rebut such criticism and to establish conservative credentials (Reeves and Campbell, 1994). As we have suggested, news coverage of drugs rose and fell with political initiatives, especially those coming from the president. Therefore, as the White House withdrew from the drug issue, so did the press.

After about 1989, it became increasingly difficult to sustain the exaggerated claims of the beginning of the crack scare. The mainstream media began to publish stories critical of earlier news coverage (though usually not their own). . . . *Newsweek* finally admitted in 1990 what it called the "dirty little secret" about crack that it had concealed in all of its earlier scare stories: "A lot of people use it without getting addicted," and that the anonymous "media" had "hyped instant and total addiction" (February 19, 1990, pp. 74–75). As early as 1988, it was clear that crack was not "destroying a whole generation"; it was not even spreading beyond the same poverty context that had long given rise to hard-core heroin addiction. Moreover, because of the obvious destructive effects of heavy use, people in ghettos and barrios had come to view "crack heads" as even lower in status than winos or junkies. Even crack dealers preferred powder cocaine and routinely disparaged crack heads (Williams, 1989). All of this meant that drugs in general, and crack in particular, declined in newsworthiness. Media competition had fueled the crack scare in its early years, and the same scramble for dramatic stories guaranteed that the media would move on to other stories. By 1992, the crack scare had faded beyond the media's horizon of hot new issues.

Finally, the crack scare could recede into the background partly because it had been *institu-*

tionalized. Between 1986 and 1992, Congress passed and two presidents signed a series of increasingly harsh antidrug laws. Federal antidrug funding increased for seven successive years, and an array of prison and police programs was established or expanded. All levels of government, from schools to cities, counties, and states, established agencies to warn about crack and other drug problems. And multimillion-dollar, corporate-sponsored, private organizations such as the Partnership for a Drug-Free America had been established to continue the crusade.

Conclusion

Smoking crack *is* a risky way to use an already potent drug. Despite all the exaggerations, heavy use of it *has* made life more difficult for many people—most of them from impoverished urban neighborhoods. If we agree that too many families have been touched by drug-related tragedies, why have we bothered criticizing the crack scare and the War on Drugs? If even a few people are saved from crack addiction, why should anyone care if this latest drug scare was in some measure concocted by the press, politicians, and moral entrepreneurs to serve their other agendas? Given the damage that drug abuse can do, what's the harm in a little hysteria? . . .

First, we suspect that drug scares do not work very well to reduce drug problems and that they may well promote the behavior they claim to be preventing. For all the repression successive drug wars have wrought (primarily upon the poor and the powerless), they have yet to make a measurable dent in our drug *problems.* For example, prompted by the crack crisis and inspired by the success of patriotic propaganda in World War II, the Partnership for a Drug-Free America ran a massive advertising campaign to "unsell drugs." From 1987 to 1993, the Partnership placed over $1 billion worth of advertising donated by corporations and the advertising industry. The Partnership claims to have had a "measurable impact" by "accelerating intolerance" to drugs and drug users. The Partnership claims it "can legitimately take some of the credit for the 25%

decline in illicit drug usage since our program was launched" (Hedrick, 1990). However, the association between the Partnership's antidrug advertising and the declines in drug use appears to be spurious. Drug use was declining well before the Partnership's founding; taking credit for what was already happening is a bit like jumping in front of a parade and then claiming to have been leading it all along. More important, drug *use* increased in the mid 1990s among precisely those age groups that had been targeted by Partnership ads, while drug *problems* continued throughout their campaign. Furthermore, Partnership ads scrupulously avoided any mention of the two forms of drug use most prevalent among youth: smoking and drinking. This may have something to do with the fact that the Partnership for a Drug-Free America is a partnership between the media and advertising industries, which make millions from alcohol and tobacco advertising each year, and with the fact that alcohol and tobacco companies contribute financially to the Partnership's campaign against illicit drugs. Surely public health education is important, but there is no evidence that selective antidrug propaganda and scare tactics have significantly reduced drug problems.

Indeed, hysterical and exaggerated antidrug campaigns may have increased drug-related harm in the U.S. There is the risk that all of the exaggerated claims made to mobilize the population for war actually arouse interest in drug use. In 1986, the *New England Journal of Medicine* reported that the frequency of teenage suicides increases after lurid news reports and TV shows about them (Gould and Shaffer, 1986; Phillips and Carstensen, 1986). Reports about drugs, especially of new and exotic drugs like crack, may work the same way. In his classic chapter, "How To Launch a Nation Wide Drug Menace," Brecher (1972) shows how exaggerated newspaper reports of dramatic police raids in 1960 functioned as advertising for glue sniffing. The arrests of a handful of sniffers led to anti–glue sniffing hysteria that actually spread this hitherto unknown practice across the U.S. In 1986, the media's desire for dramatic drug stories interacted with politicians' desire for partisan advantage and safe election-year issues, so news about crack spread to every nook and cranny of the nation far faster than dealers could have spread word on the street. When the media and politicians claimed that crack is "the most addictive substance known to man," there was some commonsense obligation to explain why. Therefore, alongside all the statements about "instant addiction," the media also reported some very intriguing things about crack: "whole body orgasm," "better than sex," and "cheaper than cocaine." For TV-raised young people in the inner city, faced with a dismal social environment and little economic opportunity, news about such a substance in their neighborhoods may have functioned as a massive advertising campaign for crack.

Further, advocates of the crack scare and the War on Drugs explicitly rejected public health approaches to drug problems that conflicted with their ideology. The most striking and devastating example of this was the total rejection of syringe distribution programs by the Reagan and Bush administrations and by drug warriors such as Congressman Charles Rangel. People can and do recover from drug addiction, but no one recovers from AIDS. By the end of the 1980s, the fastest growing AIDS population was intravenous drug users. Because syringes were hard to get, or their possession criminalized, injectors shared their syringes and infected each other and their sexual partners with AIDS. In the early 1980s, activists in a number of other Western countries had developed syringe distribution and exchange programs to prevent AIDS, and there is by now an enormous body of evidence that such programs are effective. But the U.S. government has consistently rejected such "harm reduction" programs on the grounds that they conflict with the policy of "zero tolerance" for drug use or "send the wrong message." As a result, cities such as Amsterdam, Liverpool, and Sydney, which have needle exchange programs, have very low or almost no transmission of AIDS by intravenous drug users. In New York City, however, roughly half the hundreds of thousands of injection drug users are HIV positive or already have AIDS. In short, the crack scare and the drug war policies it fueled will ultimately contribute to the deaths of tens of thousands of Americans, including the families, children, and sexual partners of the infected drug users.

Another important harm resulting from American drug scares is they have routinely blamed individual immorality and personal behavior for endemic social and structural problems. In so doing, they diverted attention and resources away from the underlying sources of drug abuse and the array of other social ills of which they are part. One necessary condition for the emergence of the crack scare (as in previous drug scares) was the linking of drug use with the problems faced by racial minorities, the poor, and youth. In the logic of the scare, whatever economic and social troubles these people have suffered were due largely to their drug use. Obscured or forgotten during the crack scare were all the social and economic problems that underlie crack abuse—and that are much more widespread—especially poverty, unemployment, racism, and the prospects of life in the permanent underclass.

Democrats denounced the Reagan and Bush administrations' hypocrisy in proclaiming "War on Drugs" while cutting the budgets for drug treatment, prevention, and research. However, the Democrats often neglected to mention an equally important but more politically popular development: the "Just Say No To Drugs" administrations had, with the help of many Democrats in Congress, also "just said no" to virtually every social program aimed at creating alternatives for and improving the lawful life chances of inner-city youth. These black and Latino young people were and are the group with the highest rate of crack abuse. Although, most inner-city youth have always steered clear of drug abuse, they could not "just say no" to poverty and unemployment. Dealing drugs, after all, was (and still is) accurately perceived by many poor city kids as the highest-paying job—straight or criminal—that they are likely to get.

The crack scare, like previous drug scares and antidrug campaigns, promoted misunderstandings of drug use and abuse, blinded people to the social sources of many social problems (including drug problems), and constrained the social policies that might reduce those problems. It routinely used inflated, misleading rhetoric and falsehoods such as Bush's televised account of how he came into possession of a bag of crack. At best, the crack scare was not good for public health. At worst, by manipulating and misinforming citizens about drug use and effects, it perverted social policy and political democracy.

REFERENCES

Alcoholism and Drug Abuse Week, "$23 Billion Spent on Federal Drug Effort Since 1981." July 5, 1989, pp. 3–4.

Anderson, Jack, and Michael Binstein, "Drug Informants Beating the System." *Washington Post,* September 10, 1992, p. D23.

Bakalar, James B., and Lester Grinspoon, *Drug Control in a Free Society.* Cambridge: Cambridge University Press, 1984.

Belenko, Steven, and Jeffrey Fagan, "Crack and the Criminal Justice System." New York: New York City Criminal Justice Agency, 1987.

Brecher, Edward M., *Licit and Illicit Drugs.* Boston: Little, Brown, 1972.

Chin K.-L, "Special Event Codes for Crack Arrests." Internal memorandum, New York City Criminal Justice Agency, 1988.

Currie, Elliott, *Confronting Crime.* New York: Pantheon, 1985.

Diamond, Edwin, Frank Accosta, and Leslie-Jean Thornton, "Is TV News Hyping America's Cocaine Problem?" *TV Guide,* February 7, 1987, pp. 4–10.

Drug Enforcement Administration, "Special Report: The Crack Situation in the U.S." Unpublished, Strategic Intelligence Section. Washington, DC: DEA, August 22, 1986.

Duster, Troy, *The Legislation of Morality.* New York: Free Press, 1970.

Edelman, Murray, *The Symbolic Uses of Politics.* Urbana: University of Illinois Press, 1964.

Gould, Madelyn S., and David Shaffer, "The Impact of Suicide in Television Movies: Evidence of Imitation." *New England Journal of Medicine* 315:690–694 (1986).

Grinspoon, Lester, and James B. Bakalar, *Cocaine: A Drug and Its Social Evolution.* New York: Basic Books, 1976.

Gusfield, Joseph R., *Symbolic Crusade.* Urbana: University of Illinois Press, 1963.

———, *The Culture of Public Problems.* Chicago: University of Chicago Press, 1981.

———, "Alcohol Problems—An Interactionist View," in J. P. von Wartburg et al., eds., *Currents in Alcohol Research and the Prevention of Alcohol Problems.* Berne, Switzerland: Hans Huber, 1985.

Harwood, Richard, "Hyperbole Epidemic." *Washington Post,* October 1, 1989, p. D6.

Hedrick, Thomas A., Jr., "Pro Bono Anti-Drug Ad Campaign Is Working." *Advertising Age,* June 25, 1990, p. 22.

Himmelstein, Jerome, *The Strange Career of Marijuana.* Westport, CT: Greenwood Press, 1983.

Hoffman, Abbie, *Steal This Urine Test: Fighting Drug Hysteria in America.* New York: Penguin Books, 1987.

Horgan, John, "A Kinder War." *Scientific American,* July 25, 1993, p. 6.

Inciardi, James, "Beyond Cocaine: Basuco, Crack, and Other Coca Products." *Contemporary Drug Problems* 14:461–492 (1987).

Irwin, John, and James Austin, *It's About Time: America's Imprisonment Binge.* Belmont, CA: Wadsworth, 1994.

Isikoff, Michael, "Drug Buy Set Up for Bush Speech: DEA Lured Seller to Lafayette Park." *Washington Post,* September 22, 1989, p. A1.

Johnson, Bruce D., et al., *Taking Care of Business: The Economics of Crime by Heroin Abusers.* Lexington, MA: Lexington Books, 1985.

Johnston, Lloyd D., Patrick M. O'Malley, and Jerald G. Bachman, *Illicit Drug Use, Smoking, and Drinking by America's High School Students, College Students, and Young Adults, 1975–1987.* Washington, DC: National Institute on Drug Abuse, 1988.

Kitsuse, John I., and Aaron V. Cicourel, "A Note on the Use of Official Statistics." *Social Problems* 11:131–139 (1963).

Kozel, Nicholas, and Edgar Adams, "Epidemiology of Drug Abuse: An Overview." *Science* 234:970–974 (1986).

Lindesmith, Alfred R., *The Addict and the Law.* Bloomington: Indiana University Press, 1965.

Massing, Michael, Review essay on "Swordfish," *New York Review of Books,* July 15, 1993, pp. 30–32.

Morgan, Patricia, "The Legislation of Drug Law: Economic Crisis and Social Control," *Journal of Drug Issues* 8:53–62 (1978).

Musto, David, *The American Disease: Origins of Narcotic Control.* New Haven, CT: Yale University Press, 1973.

National Institute on Drug Abuse, *Data from the Drug Abuse Warning Network: Annual Data 1985.* Statistical Series 1, #5. Washington, DC: National Institute on Drug Abuse, 1986a.

———, *National Household Survey on Drug Abuse, 1985.* Washington, DC: Division of Epidemiology and Statistical Analysis, National Institute on Drug Abuse, 1986b.

———, *National Household Survey on Drug Abuse: 1988 Population Estimates.* Washington, DC: Division of Epidemiology and Prevention Research, National Institute on Drug Abuse, 1988.

———, *National Household Survey on Drug Abuse: Main Findings 1990.* Washington, DC: Epidemiology and Prevention Research, National Institute on Drug Abuse, 1990.

———, *Annual Medical Examiner Data, 1991: Data from the Drug Abuse Warning Network.* Washington, DC: Division of Epidemiology and Prevention Research, National Institute on Drug Abuse, 1992.

———, *Estimates from the Drug Abuse Warning Network: 1992 Estimates of Drug-Related Emergency Room Episodes.* Washington, DC: Substance Abuse and Mental Health Services Administration, U.S. Dept. of Health and Human Services, 1993a.

———, *National Household Survey on Drug Abuse: Population Estimates 1992.* Washington, DC: Substance Abuse and Mental Health Services Administration, U.S. Dept. of Health and Human Services, 1993b.

National Report on Substance Abuse, "Federal Officials Express Alarm at Youth's Rising Illicit Drug Use." February 11, 1994, p. 2.

New York Times, "No Change in Basics: Bush Rejects Any Fundamental Shift, Instead Vowing Unprecedented Vigor." September 6, 1989, p. A11.

Office of National Drug Control Policy, *National Drug Control Strategy: Budget Summary.* Washington, DC: U.S. Government Printing Office, 1992.

Phillips, David P., and Lundie L. Carstensen, "Clustering of Teenage Suicides After Television News

Stories About Suicide." *New England Journal of Medicine* 315:685–689 (1986).

Reeves, Jimmie L., and Richard Campbell, *Cracked Coverage: Television News, the Anti-Cocaine Crusade, and the Reagan Legacy.* Durham, NC: Duke University Press, 1994.

Reinarman, Craig, "The Social Construction of an Alcohol Problem: The Case of Mothers Against Drunk Drivers and Social Control in the 1980s." *Theory and Society* 17:91–119 (1988).

———, "Glasnost in U.S. Drug Policy?: Clinton Constrained." *International Journal of Drug Policy* 5:42–49 (1994).

Rogin, Michael Paul, *Ronald Reagan, the Movie: and Other Episodes in Political Demonology.* Berkeley: University of California Press, 1987.

Rumbarger, John, *Profits, Power, and Prohibition,* Albany: State University of New York Press, 1989.

Ryan, William, *Blaming the Victim.* New York: Vintage, 1976.

Schneider, Joseph, and John I. Kitsuse, eds., *Studies in the Sociology of Social Problems.* Norwood, NJ: Ablex, 1984.

Siegel, Ronald, "Cocaine Smoking." *Journal of Psychoactive Drugs* 14:271–359 (1982).

Spector, Malcolm, and John Kitsuse, *Constructing Social Problems.* Menlo Park, CA: Cummings, 1977.

Staples, Brent, "Coke Wars." *New York Times Book Review,* February 6, 1994, p. 11.

Trebach, Arnold, *The Great Drug War.* New York: Macmillan, 1987.

University of Michigan, "Drug Use Rises Among American Teen-Agers." News and Information Services, January 27, 1994.

Waldorf, Dan, Craig Reinarman, and Sheigla Murphy, *Cocaine Changes.* Philadelphia: Temple University Press, 1991.

Washton, Arnold, and Mark Gold, "Recent Trends in Cocaine Abuse," *Advances in Alcohol and Substance Abuse* 6:31–47 (1987).

The White House, *National Drug Control Strategy.* Washington, DC: U.S. Government Printing Office, 1989.

Williams, Terry, *The Cocaine Kids.* Reading, MA: Addison-Wesley, 1989.

Wilson, William Julius, *The Truly Disadvantaged.* Chicago: University of Chicago Press, 1987.

Zinberg, Norman E., *Drug, Set, and Setting: The Basis for Controlled Drug Use.* New Haven, CT: Yale University Press, 1984.

THINKING ABOUT THE READING

How does Reinarman and Levine's article support the contention that reality is a social construction? Consider the broader implications of their argument: The use of certain substances becomes a serious social problem *not* because it is an objectively dangerous activity but because it receives sufficient media and political attention. What does this contention suggest about the way social problems and public fears are created and maintained in society? What does it tell us about our collective need to identify a scapegoat for our social problems? Why are there such vastly different public attitudes and legal responses to crack cocaine versus powder cocaine? Can you think of other situations in which heightened media coverage and political attention have created widespread public concern and moral outrage where none was warranted? How has this article affected your views about the "War on Drugs" and the decriminalization of illegal drugs?

The Practice of Social Research

Julia O'Connell Davidson

[In this article I am] concerned not simply with the technical problems and issues associated with a range of research methods, but also with the relationship between social research and social power, with the ethical dilemmas raised by social investigation, the need for reflexivity and the relevance of social research to our daily lives. This [article] aims to reiterate these themes and spell out their implications for the practice of research. It does so primarily through reference to a piece of research which [I am currently conducting].

Researching Prostitution

At the time of writing, I am involved in a small-scale ethnographic study of a prostitute, her receptionists, her clients and a number of her "hangers on." The prostitute (to whom I shall refer as "Desiree") is, her receptionists tell prospective clients, "a beautiful brown-eyed brunette, with a stunning figure measuring 44–26–40." She is neither a street prostitute nor a Madam. She works from home and runs what is effectively a fairly lucrative small business, although like other small businesses, Desiree's is adversely affected by the somewhat unsteady . . . British economy. . . . She provides clients with a range of services "from a basic massage through to a full personal service, which includes everything" and "offers a selection of toys and uniforms." Because she alone provides sexual services to clients, and because she does not solicit men to visit her, this business is quite legal. My research with Desiree has evolved in a fairly *ad hoc* way. One of her part-time receptionists, "Angie," was a student of mine, and knowing my interest in sex research, she arranged an interview with Desiree for me. I did not have a clear research agenda but spent about three hours talking to her. What she told me was not only fascinating in its own right but also tied in with a number of my theoretical preoccupations. Desiree gave me an open invitation to return, and after several weeks I did, this time with a rather sharper focus for the research.

First and foremost, I was interested in the issue of power and control. For some radical feminists, prostitution is one of the purest expressions of patriarchal domination, reducing women to nothing more than bought objects. Prostitution not only allows men to secure temporary (but direct) control over the prostitute, but also increases their existing social control over all women by developing and enhancing their powers of "sexual aggression." The prostitute's consent is explained primarily through reference to male hegemony. Other feminists contest this vision. They emphasize the skills and control of the prostitute in the commercial exchange itself and further hold that prostitutes effectively resist and defy male power by refusing to allow any one man ownership of their sexuality. According to Roberts, the "whore is dangerously free" (1992, 354), enjoying both the financial and the sexual autonomy that is denied to the majority of women in patriarchal societies. My initial interview with Desiree had led me to believe that issues of power, control and consent may be rather more complex than either of these positions suggest, and I therefore wanted to use ethnographic techniques to explore some of the contradictions of control within the prostitute–client relationship. I did not intend to limit the research to simply testing out this hypothesis, however. Since very little empirical research has been conducted in this field, I believe it will produce useful descriptive data. Such research also has potential for theory-constructing. All in all, I am adopting a flexible approach rather than restricting the research to theory-testing, empirical description or theory-constructing *per se.*

These ambitions have implications for the actual techniques employed in the research. There would be little point in administering a formal questionnaire to Desiree and her receptionists not just because they would be minuscule and unrepresentative sample, but also because I could hardly hope to tease out the subtle and complex contradictions which interest me with such a blunt and unresponsive instrument. . . . Unless a researcher already has a fairly clear idea of the questions that need answering, the survey method is inappropriate. I have therefore employed a range of techniques, including formal, topic based interviews, informal conversations, observation and participation (as a receptionist—answering phone calls, making appointments, taking coffee to waiting clients). I am now collecting data on clients of a more systematic kind. Because there are large numbers of clients—Desiree sees between 30 and 40 men per week—it would be too time consuming to conduct taped interviews about each one. Yet I want to know something about the range, nature and pattern of demand. Though Desiree could give me an impressionistic account, she finds it difficult to recall the exact details of every punter* she saw in a week. I therefore used interviews and conversations with Desiree to develop a questionnaire that monitors the sexual services each client receives . . . , and she now fills some of these in after clients leave.

There is an obvious problem with this technique, namely it relies upon Desiree, who is often very busy, remembering to fill forms out and remembering details accurately. Any data on client's marital status and employment will also have to be treated with extreme caution. Although some clients display a rather extraordi-

* "Punter" is British slang for a prostitute's client.

nary wish to "share" their lives with Desiree (showing her photographs of their wives or children after having received a sexual service, describing the details of their work life as she chains them up, even supplying her with a written curriculum vitae in one case "because we don't get a chance to talk much"), commonsense suggests that many will lie or conceal the truth about such matters. Furthermore, the questionnaire—like all questionnaires—has proved to have certain limitation. It is incapable of encompassing unanticipated sexual requirements. . . . Desiree kindly makes a note of such things, but these limitations will nonetheless have to be borne in mind when the data is analyzed and presented.

At present, I spend a day or an afternoon each week at the house, observing, participating and interviewing. I write up fieldnotes and transcribe taped interviews, code up the questionnaires and will soon begin to analyze them using SPSS (Statistical Package for the Social Sciences). But even though the research is in its infancy, it has already raised many . . . key methodological, ethical and political issues. . . .

Sampling

Desiree, her receptionists and her "hangers on" are an opportunistic sample, and it would be impossible for me to make generalized claims about all such prostitutes and their receptionists on the basis of interviews with these people. It would be better to broaden out the research by interviewing other women operating the same kind of setup. But this is extremely difficult to arrange. There are magazines and newspapers which advertise their phone numbers, but so far I have found it impossible to get past their receptionists, who are highly skilled at putting an end to "nuisance" and "time-wasting" calls. Receptionists treat a phone call from a woman with particular suspicion, since, Angie tells me, such calls are generally from other prostitutes doing a little market research on prices. In any event, a receptionist is hardly likely to agree to an interview on her employer's account. I could ask a male colleague or friend to phone and make a bogus appointment, thereby obtaining the addresses of other prostitutes, but wonder whether this would be ethical or even an effective way of securing access. I will probably have to rely on snowballing or volunteer methods to expand my sample, and there is thus little prospect of my ever being able to advance *generalized* claims about home-working prostitutes on the basis of the research.

The lack of a large or randomly selected or completely representative sample does not make the research worthless, however. To discover the ways in which Desiree exercises control within the prostitute–client relationship is informative and useful whether or not she is typical of *all* self-employed prostitutes, for example. Likewise, though the sample of clients is not a random selection of all men who visit prostitutes (Desiree's advertisement will attract a sample with particular sexual interests and from particular geographical locations), information about the nature and pattern of these particular men's demand for sexual services can make a valuable contribution to an area about which very little empirical data have been collected.

Ethical Issues

Although I have full and informed consent from Desiree, her receptionists and her "hangers on," my research involves covert observation of her clients and this raises some . . . ethical issues. . . . When I answer the phone and offer to provide details of services offered and prices charged, the men making inquiries (often masturbating as they do so) take me to be either a prostitute or a receptionist. Clients do not know that a sociologist is listening to their conversations . . . with Desiree in the hallway, or observing their fleeting forms as they run from the house having, as Desiree puts it, "shot their load." They have not consented to Desiree imparting information about their sexual preferences, commenting extensively and wittily on their physical and psychological defects. When I take coffee to a waiting punter, he is not aware that I am making

mental notes on his presentation of self, or that I will later be told whether he is a cross-dresser or a masochist or suffers from erection problems— or indeed all three.

It could be argued that I am invading these men's privacy and that, since I am firmly convinced few would give their informed consent, this is unethical. Yet I find myself untroubled by my uninvited intrusion into these men's world. This is mainly because the clients remain completely anonymous to me, and I am not therefore in a position to secure, store or disclose any information which could harm them. Moreover, Desiree has willingly offered to provide me with the details of their interaction, and since this knowledge belongs to her (in the sense that it is part of her lived experience, not a private experience of the client's and that she has not entered into any formal agreement with the client not to talk about their interaction), it seems to me that she is entitled to do what she likes with it. I recognize that purists could still make a case against my research practice. Some of the criticisms leveled against Humphreys' observational research in public toilets could also be leveled against me (although I hasten to add that I have no intention of noting the license plates of punters' cars in order to track them down for interviews). But such purism is a luxury that most researchers cannot afford. Virtually all social research is intrusive and exploitative to some degree, because though researchers may truly believe that their work is in the *interests* of their human subjects, it is seldom undertaken at the *behest* of these subjects and rarely, if ever, is it undertaken without a view to the professional advancement of the researcher. It therefore inevitably poses moral dilemmas, which, at the end of the day, can only be resolved through reference to the researcher's own moral and political values.

I feel a certain commitment towards Desiree and her receptionists, for example. I do not imagine for a moment that my research will help them as individuals, but I absolutely do not want it to damage them in any way. I would not want to deceive them about the research aims and feel obliged to allow them to make an informed choice about whether, and how much, to participate in the research. This is partly because I actually like and respect these women, and partly because I have no moral or political objection to the way they live their lives—rather the reverse. Desiree is an able, intelligent, independent and ambitious woman who lives in a society that does not value such qualities in women very highly. I am sympathetic towards her desire for financial and emotional autonomy, even though I personally would not wish to achieve it in the way she has chosen and have my doubts about whether she will ultimately attain it by engaging in commercial sex. But this sense of commitment does not extend towards her clients. I have no wish to advance their interests through the research, no personal liking and no real sympathy for them. I have a professional obligation to preserve and protect their anonymity and to ensure that they are not harmed by my research, but I feel no qualms about being less than frank with them, and no obligation to allow them to choose whether or not their actions are recorded.

In fact, my lack of sympathy for punters as a collective group actually raises another, rather different, set of ethical problems. Desiree introduced me to, then arranged an interview with, a man who I shall call "Dick." Dick's status at Desiree's house is ambiguous. He is useful to her in the sense of doing bits of DIY, walking the dogs, shopping and so on, but he is also a rather sad and lonely man, who might variously be described as an odd-ball, a misfit, perhaps a bit "simple." He does not buy sexual services from Desiree, but hangs around her, apparently dependent upon her in a number of ways. Though he does not buy sex in Britain, he takes an annual holiday in Thailand, where he spends three or four weeks "going through" as many prostitutes as he can. Desiree suggested that I might find it interesting to talk to him. I chatted to him once informally, and then conducted a two-hour, topic-based interview with him. It was certainly interesting, but I also found talking to him the most difficult and unpleasant experience I have ever had as a researcher. What he told me sickened and disturbed me. He spoke of the Thai prostitutes (many probably only 16 years of age or less) as nothing more than objects. He described, in profoundly racist terms, how the Otherness of "Orientals" made these "girls" especially appealing to him. He told me that the fact these women are from a "Third World" country makes him feel rich and powerful and how "fantastic" it is for the single man to get the choice of thousands of young and beautiful girls. He told me that he effectively haggles with human life, using safer sex as bargaining counter by offering them less money for sex with a condom. He described his experiences with what he terms "brand new" girls (those who have only just started to work as prostitutes) how they emerge from the shower clutching a towel to shield their naked bodies and try to get under the bedclothes without him seeing them—"I soon put a stop to that. I rip the towel off them and chuck it across the room." He described visits to brothels where women who are effectively owned by the pimp sit behind a glass screen with numbers round their necks waiting to be bought by men like Dick, and taken to be used and abused in anonymous hotel rooms.

Obviously, Dick would hardly have continued to disclose such information if I had openly expressed my horror and disgust. To maintain the rapport which makes an interview possible, I felt constrained to appear neutral and non-judgmental. This meant I was confronted by the dilemma which Scully faced in her research with rapists—neutrality could be interpreted as a signal approval, but disagreement or negative comments could destroy rapport (Scully 1990, 19). to Dick, I am an educated woman of relatively high social standing—a university lecturer. If I appear to accept his appallingly callous attitudes towards and exploitations of these women, will he see it as somehow more legitimate? Am I endorsing his activities by failing to outrightly and vigorously condemn them? For me, this is a far more serious ethical dilemma than any issue about invading Desiree's clients' privacy. I cannot claim to have resolved this problem, even to my own satisfaction. In defense of having thus far failed to roundly condemn him, I would argue as follows. My initial work with Desiree makes me think that the whole question of what exactly it is that men buy from prostitutes, and what exactly it is that prostitutes sell, is highly problematic. Though ostensibly a commercial exchange, because sex is so powerfully attached to ideologies about gender, biology and the proper relations between the sexes, the transaction between prostitute and client is not a simple market exchange. The interview with Dick made me begin to think about broadening my research to explore such ideas in more depth. The fact that he (and thousands of other men) apparently find it necessary or desirable to travel to Thailand to buy something from women, many of whom are kept as virtual slaves (thereby helping to sustain and reproduce the conditions of their oppression) seems to me to be worth investigating further. For the time being, therefore, I need Dick. He has information and contacts that may be invaluable to such research and I do not wish to alienate him by fully expressing my views.

I am not entirely happy with this formulation, but I do not believe that my failure to condemn him is actively encouraging him to persist with his activities. Moreover, if we insist that researchers are morally obliged to directly challenge the sexism and racism of their subjects during the research *process* (rather than in the work they publish), we will make it virtually impossible to undertake empirical research with such people. As a researcher, then, I can justify presenting a neutral façade to Dick and men like him. As a private individual, listening to such offensive views without attacking them leaves me with a sense of discomfort.

. . . [Many contemporary researchers have called] for research which is empathetic, non-hierarchical and non-exploitative. But this emphasis is especially difficult when coupled with an insistence that research should be emancipatory. To fully understand women's subordination it is necessary to study not just women, but also the men who oppress them. Of course, no [one] would recommend a non-hierarchical and non-exploitative approach to such research, insisting that I should enter into a genuinely caring and empathetic relationship with Dick, for ex-

ample. (It is worth noting that the fact he actually sat back, spread his legs and started masturbating through his trousers towards the end of the interview made it difficult for me to go through even the most orthodox, polite, end-of-interview formalities.) Most would presumably agree that my approach is justifiable under the circumstances, and merely insist that my emotional responses to Dick (and to everyone else) should be discussed and included in written accounts of the research. I should be aware that "being alive involves us in having emotions and involvements; and in doing research we cannot leave behind what is to be a person alive in the world" (Stanley and Wise 1993: 161). In other words, I should be *reflexive*. . . .

[Documenting Experience]

Equally important, so far as my research with Desiree goes, is the fact that she herself has several different versions of reality. She has an emotional life which she shifts and changes, and her accounts of the reality of her work shift and change with it. Moreover, Desiree cannot tell me or accurately describe *everything* about her lived experience. I say this not because I see myself as a scientist, expert or superior being, but simply because people's knowledge of their work life or daily routine rarely takes a very precise or exact form. If a researcher asked me to say how many students knocked on my office door each week, or to sit and describe a typical working day, the information I would give would be fairly vague and impressionistic, because I do not keep a systematic record of such things, not even a mental one. As a researcher, I therefore need to do more than simply ask and accept Desiree's account of her experience. I must try to check it against other versions of reality—that obtained by observation and by systematic monitoring of her clients, that provided by her receptionists and "hangers on," that achieved through my own observations. In other words, I need to adopt a form of triangulation to check the validity of any one account of her "lived experience."

Finally, I would argue that as a researcher who wishes to try to explain events, experiences and processes as well as to describe them, I need to employ theory and to apply theoretical concepts to the material I gather. The two different feminist positions on prostitution which I outline above, for example, are useful in focusing attention on issues of power, consent and control. They provide a conceptual framework within which I can try to understand some of the stories which Desiree tells me about clients and my observations of events in her house. If I did not apply such concepts to, say, the occasion on which Desiree exacted her revenge on a difficult client by beating him far longer and far harder than he actually wanted, then the accounts I produced would be nothing more than journalistic descriptions along the lines of "A Day in the Brothel" or perhaps similar to extracts from Desiree's own diary, if she happened to keep one.

Reflexivity

. . . Reflexivity is an awareness of the ways in which the researcher, as an individual with a given social identity, impacts upon that process. Even at this early stage of the research, I am conscious of the fact that my identity as a woman affects the data I collect. To begin with, it is only because I am woman that I am able to participate as a receptionist. A male researcher would not be able to answer the phone without putting Desiree's business at risk, and even if he did, men would be unlikely to say the kind of things that they say to women receptionists. . . . A male researcher could hardly show punters in or give them cups of coffee and chat to them. In other words, there are parts of the social world which are invisible to men simply because they are men, just as there are certain experiences which no woman is ever likely to have firsthand.

There are, no doubt, male researchers who could establish a rapport and obtain worthwhile information in the same setting, but I do also believe that it is easier for me, as a woman, to establish a rapport with Desiree and her receptionists, and that they would probably tone down the extremely crushing remarks they make about male sexuality and men in general if I were a male researcher. I have already observed, however, that

making contact with other prostitutes in order to widen the sample might be easier to achieve were I a man. The fact that I am a woman also makes me wary of taking up certain offers and "leads." I am more reluctant than a male researcher would be to interview one of Dick's friends in any setting other than the safety of Desiree's house or my own office, even though this increases the risk of him refusing to be interviewed. It is likewise important to note that both Desiree and I are white women. This . . . identity also has an effect on the data that is gathered. On the one hand, white people often feel able to express views in front of other whites that they would not give voice to in front of a Black person, on the other, white people sometimes reveal sides of themselves to Black people that remain largely invisible to white audiences. I am also aware that if I obtain access to interview Black women working as prostitutes, my "racialized" identity will impact upon the data I gather.

Furthermore, my class and gender identity probably combine to inhibit Desiree's male hangers on. Take Dick. He may have agreed to talk to me because I am female and because I am "from the University." But I am sure that my class identity led him to modify the account of his activities he gave, and to conceal certain things from me. He had previously told Angie, for example, that he did not bother to use condoms with "girls" he had "been with before" or "girls who look clean." When I asked him about safer sex, he told me very firmly that he *always* used condoms—"In fact, I introduce myself to the girls as Mr. Condom" he said (and of course, this itself was later contradicted by his statement to the effect that he bargained with condoms). His estimates of how many prostitutes he had sex with on his last visit to Thailand also fluctuated according to who asked him. Desiree was told 50, Angie (who makes her disapproval and disgust for his activities more than evident) was told 40. Dick told me that he had "gone through" 35. I assume that he would present himself differently again to a male researcher, and very differently to "the guys" who accompany him on his trips to Thailand.

My class and gender identity as well as my personality also affect the research in another way. One recurrent problem which Desiree faces stems from the fact that many men obtain enormous sexual excitement by simply entering a brothel and seeing a real, live prostitute. In the past such men would arrive for an appointment, then either sneak into the toilet and wank off, or simply meet her then leave to a much enhanced wank in their car without paying anything at all. To stop this happening, Desiree instituted a system whereby the receptionists only give her address when clients book a definite appointment, and she charges a set fee for the appointment whether or not they actually receive a massage or sexual service. In other words, once a man turns up on the doorstep, he will not be allowed to leave until he has paid the appointment fee. This, of course, can lead to conflict. The would-be wanker will assert that he did not make an appointment, but called on the off-chance, or that he has no money with him. Now Desiree and her receptionists strike me as tough women. They do not appear to feel intimidated by such men, in fact they often find such encounters hugely entertaining. But I am not renowned for having a fearless disposition, and my version of the reality of such conflicts, my estimation of the degree of aggression being expressed by each party, and even my assessment of Desiree and receptionists as "tough," are probably colored by my own past experiences of verbal and physical conflict. This again underlines the importance of triangulation. I make a point of checking my perceptions of these situations by asking Desiree and her receptionists how they perceived such events.

There are aspects of my social identity and personality which also affect the length and style of interviewing. I curtailed my interview with Dick when he began to masturbate, for example. Another interviewer might have been willing to persist (or to ask him to desist). Other people might also have adopted a more confrontational style of interviewing, directly challenging him on some of his views, and have managed to do so without completely destroying the rapport. My personal interviewing style has always been characterized more by sweet hypocrisy, plenty of nodding and meaningless affirmative noises than by pushy, challenging or incisive questioning. Nuances in interviewing style can have as much to do with personality and self-presentation as they have to do with adherence to a particular methodological school of thought.

The Role of Luck and Chance

Handbooks on research methods seldom mention what seems to me to be something that is absolutely critical to the research process, namely good fortune. I was more than lucky to know Angie, for without her I would not be doing this research and I was fortunate that the prostitute she happened to know happened to be Desiree. These two women's perspicacity, combined with their enthusiasm for the project, makes it possible for me, as a researcher, to find out more than I could possibly hope to discover without them. Desiree's willingness to fill out questionnaires (she requisitions more as they run out) and to have me hanging around her house seems to me unbelievably fortuitous. She is even "sounding out" various regulars to see whether they would agree to an interview with me. She is, in fact, little short of a dream research subject and I am enormously grateful to her. There is no doubt in my mind that no matter how polished my research skills or how carefully devised my research strategy, without this good fortune, my findings would be more limited.

For me, this is not the first time that luck and chance have exerted an influence over the progress of a research project. My research on employment relations in the privatized water industry (see O'Connell Davidson 1993) was facilitated by the fact that the senior manager who first granted me access to the organization left the company soon afterwards. The overall effect of this chance event was that I was left with almost unlimited access and freedom to move around the company, interviewing those people I wished to interview, without any accountability to management. I somehow got "lost." My presence was accepted, but no one asked to see what I was producing or prevented me from exploring "sensitive" areas. The fact that luck (or bad luck) and chance can sometimes play a pivotal role in the research process is another reason for emphasizing the importance of adopting a flexible approach to research. If researchers are too rigid about implementing a preconceived plan, they may miss opportunities to broaden, deepen or otherwise enhance their data.

Politics, Power and Social Research

[I have] stressed the centrality of politics and power to the process and practice of social research. At the most basic level, these issues affect what is researched, by whom and how, through the medium of funding. I intend to put together an application for funding to extend and broaden my research on prostitution. Whether it is successful depends in part upon the importance that is attached to such research by various funding agencies, as well as upon government policy in relation to funding academic research more generally. At present, I am able to do the research because I am fortunate enough to have a job which both requires and allows me to undertake research. In the current climate, however, most British academics are finding that the government's policy of expanding student intake without simultaneously expanding the universities' resources makes it increasingly difficult to pursue their research interests.

. . . Power and politics also intrude on the research process in other ways. My moral and political values mean that I approach the issue of prostitution from a particular angle and view it through a particular lens, for example. Researchers with different values would not necessarily ask the same questions or analyze the data produced in the same way. Moreover, the researcher's social identity (in terms of gender, "racialization" and class) affects the research process. Orthodox methodologists tend to overlook the fact that the researcher's relative power in relation to funding bodies, other academics, gatekeepers and the subjects of the research, impacts upon the kind of social identity, social power and social research which lead us to emphasize the need for reflexivity. For as Okely puts it:

In its fullest sense, reflexivity forces us to think through the consequences of our relations with others, whether it be conditions of reciprocity, asymmetry or potential exploitation. There are choices to be made in the field, within relationships and in the final text. (1992, 24)

Having said this, it is important to reiterate the fact that although social research is necessarily infused by the moral and political values of the researcher, it is not necessarily, and should not be, the simple rehearsal of prejudice. There are better and worse ways of doing research, and if it is undertaken critically, reflexively and competently, a more accurate picture of social reality will be produced. Of course, how this picture is then interpreted, what its implications are taken to be and so on, are moral and political issues.

Finally, [I want to emphasize the] interplay between social research and common-sense thinking (social researchers are members of society and therefore draw on a stock of common-sense knowledge and normative and moral values, their research feeds back into this stock of knowledge and value systems), and the fact that social research makes a significant impact not only upon policy but also upon ideological constructs. It follows from this that social research can contribute to social transformation as well as to the maintenance of the existing status quo. A concern with producing critical and reflexive social research may also allow us to begin to transcend to the sterile dualisms between objectivism and relativism, structural determinism and methodological individualism, quantitative and qualitative approaches. Marx observed that philosophers had merely interpreted the world, the point, however, was to change it. . . . My hope is that this [article] will be of some practical use to those readers whose desire is for change.

REFERENCES

O'Connell Davidson, J. 1993. *Privatization and Employment Relations: The Case of the Water Industry.* London: Mansell.

Okely, J. 1992. "Anthropology and Autobiography: Participatory Experience and Embodied Knowledge." In J. Okely and H. Callaway (eds.), *Anthropology and Autobiography,* London: Routledge.

Roberts, N. 1992. *Whores in History.* London: Grafton.

Scully, D. 1990. *Understanding Sexual Violence.* London: HarperCollins.

Stanley, L., and Wise, S. 1993. *Breaking Out Again: Feminist Ontology and Epistemology.* London: Routledge.

THINKING ABOUT THE READING

O'Connell Davidson did not divulge her identity as a sociologist to the male clients she came in contact with during her research. Do you think this deception was ethically justifiable? Why does O'Connell Davidson warn the reader against drawing conclusions about prostitutes in general from her single case study? Can you think of other ways to acquire accurate information about prostitutes? She admits to being more sympathetic to "Desiree," the prostitute, than to "Dick," her handyman. How might these feelings influence her observations? Is it desirable, or even possible, for researchers to completely suppress their feelings about the individuals they are studying? The author thinks that being female was a big advantage for her in researching prostitution. Do you agree? Can you think of other research settings where the gender of the researcher would be significant?

4 Building Order: Culture and History

Culture provides members of a society with a common bond, a sense that they see certain facets of society in similar ways. That members of a society can live together at all depends on the fact that they share a certain amount of cultural knowledge. Social norms—the rules and standards that govern all social encounters—provide order in our day-to-day lives. Norms reflect commonly held assumptions about conventional behavior. They tell us what to expect from others and what others can expect from us. Violations of norms mark the boundaries of acceptable behavior and symbolically reaffirm what a particular society defines as right and wrong.

Sociology tells us that virtually every aspect of our lives is influenced by culture. When we examine these influences, things that were once familiar and taken-for-granted suddenly become unfamiliar and curious. During the course of our lives we are rarely forced to examine *why* we do the common things we do, we just do them. But if we take a step back and examine our common customs and behaviors they begin to look as strange as the "mystical" rituals of some far off, exotic land. It is for this reason that Horace Miner's article, "Body Ritual Among the Nacirema" has become a classic in sociology and anthropology.

Norms, of course, vary greatly across cultures. Indeed, the more ethnically and culturally diverse a society is, the greater the likelihood of normative clashes between groups. We can see clear evidence of the power of cultural norms when we examine how members of a different society handle some taken-for-granted aspect of everyday life. Take, for instance, the experience of time. If you've ever traveled abroad you know that people perceive the importance of time differently. In some places everyday life is incredibly fast-paced; in others it seems frustratingly slow and lethargic. In the industrialized world, events are often meticulously timed and scheduled. But in less developed parts of the world, time is much less restrictive and events occur more spontaneously. In "A Geography of Time," Robert Levine uses his own travel experiences and anthropological observations to examine the impact of culture on the perception and use of time. He shows us how conflicts can result from clashes between people operating on different conceptions of time (what he calls *clock time* and *event time*). His comparison of the way time is experienced in other cultures versus our own reminds us that the time norms we consider to be normal and superior are in the end arbitrary and not shared worldwide. This is a humbling but important lesson for people who assume that their cultural way of life is natural and normal.

We don't have to travel to a foreign country, though, to see the clash of different cultural beliefs and expectations. Such clashes can be quite confusing and painful for newly arrived immigrants from countries with vastly different cultural traditions. In the article "The Melting Pot," Anne Fadiman examines the experiences of Hmong refugees in the United States. Hundreds of thousands of Hmong people have fled Laos since that country fell to communist forces in 1975. Most have settled in the United States. Virtually every element of Hmong culture and tradition lies in stark contrast to the standard assumptions of American life. They have been described in the American media as simplistic, primitive, and throwbacks to the Stone Age. The Hmong have had a particularly difficult time adapting to American society because they are a proud, independent people who are quick to reject the customs of other cultures. This article vividly portrays the everyday conflicts immigrants face as they straddle two vastly different cultures.

Body Ritual Among the Nacirema

Horace Miner

The anthropologist has become so familiar with the diversity of ways in which different peoples behave in similar situations that he is not apt to be surprised by even the most exotic customs. In fact, if all of the logically possible combinations of behavior have not been found somewhere in the world, he is apt to suspect that they must be present in some yet undescribed tribe. This point has, in fact, been expressed with respect to clan organization by Murdock (1949, p. 71). In this light, the magical beliefs and practices of the Nacirema present such unusual aspects that it seems desirable to describe them as an example of the extremes to which human behavior can go.

Professor Linton first brought the ritual of the Nacirema to the attention of anthropologists twenty years ago (1936, p. 326), but the culture of this people is still very poorly understood. They are a North American group living in the territory between the Canadian Cree, the Yaqui and Tarahumara of Mexico, and the Carib and Arawak of the Antilles. Little is known of their origin, although tradition states that they came from the east. According to Nacirema mythology, their nation was originated by a culture hero, Notgnihsaw, who is otherwise known for two great feats of strength—the throwing of a piece of wampum across the river Pa-To-Mac and the chopping down of a cherry tree in which the Spirit of Truth resided.

Nacirema culture is characterized by a highly developed market economy which has evolved in a rich natural habitat. While much of the people's time is devoted to economic pursuits, a large part of the fruits of these labors and a considerable portion of the day are spent in ritual activity. The focus of this activity is the human body, the appearance and health of which loom as a dominant concern in the ethos of the people. While such a concern is certainly not unusual, its ceremonial aspects and associated philosophy are unique.

The fundamental belief underlying the whole system appears to be that the human body is ugly and that its natural tendency is to debility and disease. Incarcerated in such a body, man's only hope is to avert these characteristics through the use of the powerful influences of ritual and ceremony. Every household has one or more shrines devoted to this purpose. The more powerful individuals in this society have several shrines in their houses and, in fact, the opulence of a house is often referred to in terms of the number of such ritual centers it possesses. Most houses are of wattle and daub construction, but the shrine rooms of the more wealthy are walled with stone. Poorer families imitate the rich by applying pottery plaques to their shrine walls.

While each family has at least one such shrine, the rituals associated with it are not family ceremonies but are private and secret. The rites are normally only discussed with children, and then only during the period when they are being initiated into these mysteries. I was able, however, to establish sufficient rapport with the natives to examine these shrines and to have the rituals described to me.

The focal point of the shrine is a box or chest which is built into the wall. In this chest are kept the many charms and magical potions without which no native believes he could live. These preparations are secured from a variety of specialized practitioners. The most powerful of these are the medicine men, whose assistance must be rewarded with substantial gifts. However, the medicine men do not provide the curative potions for their clients, but decide what the ingredients should be and then write them down in an ancient and secret language. This writing is understood only by the medicine men and by the herbalists who, for another gift, provide the required charm.

The charm is not disposed of after it has served its purpose, but is placed in the charm-box of the household shrine. As these magical materials are specific for certain ills, and the real or imagined maladies of the people are many, the charm-box is usually full to overflowing. The magical packets are so numerous that people forget what their purposes were and fear to use them again. While the natives are very vague on this point, we can only assume that the idea in retaining all the old magical materials is that their presence in the charm-box, before which the body rituals are conducted, will in some way protect the worshipper.

Beneath the charm-box is a small font. Each day every member of the family, in succession, enters the shrine room, bows his head before the charm-box, mingles different sorts of holy water in the font, and proceeds with a brief rite of ablution. The holy waters are secured from the Water Temple of the community, where the priests conduct elaborate ceremonies to make the liquid ritually pure.

In the hierarchy of magical practitioners, and below the medicine men in prestige, are specialists whose designation is best translated "holy-mouth-men." The Nacirema have an almost pathological horror of and fascination with the mouth, the condition of which is believed to have a supernatural influence on all social relationships. Were it not for the rituals of the mouth, they believe that their teeth would fall out, their gums bleed, their jaws shrink, their friends desert them, and their lovers reject them. They also believe that a strong relationship exists between oral and moral characteristics. For example, there is a ritual ablution of the mouth for children which is supposed to improve their moral fiber.

The daily body ritual performed by everyone includes a mouth-rite. Despite the fact that these people are so punctilious about care of the mouth, this rite involves a practice which strikes the uninitiated stranger as revolting. It was reported to me that the ritual consists of inserting a small bundle of hog hairs into the mouth, along with certain magical powders, and then moving the bundle in a highly formalized series of gestures.

In addition to the private mouth-rite, the people seek out a holy-mouth-man once or twice a year. These practitioners have an impressive set of paraphernalia, consisting of a variety of augers, awls, probes, and prods. The use of these objects in the exorcism of the evils of the mouth involves almost unbelievable ritual torture of the client. The holy-mouth-man opens the client's mouth and, using the above-mentioned tools, enlarges any holes which decay may have created in the teeth. Magical materials are put into these holes. If there are no naturally occurring holes in the teeth, large sections of one or more teeth are gouged out so that the supernatural substance can be applied. In the client's view, the purpose of these ministrations is to arrest decay and to draw friends. The extremely sacred and traditional character of the rite is evident in the fact that the natives return to the holy-mouth-man year after year, despite the fact that their teeth continue to decay.

It is to be hoped that, when a thorough study of the Nacirema is made, there will be careful inquiry into the personality structure of these people. One has but to watch the gleam in the eye of a holy-mouth-man, as he jabs an awl into an exposed nerve, to suspect that a certain amount of sadism is involved. If this can be established, a very interesting pattern emerges, for most of the population shows definite masochistic tendencies. It was to these that Professor Linton referred in discussing a distinctive part of the daily body ritual which is performed only by men. This part of the rite involves scraping and lacerating the surface of the face with a sharp instrument. Special women's rites are performed only four times during each lunar month, but what they lack in frequency is made up in barbarity. As part of this ceremony, women bake their heads in small ovens for about an hour. The theoretically interesting point is that what seems to be a preponderantly masochistic people have developed sadistic specialists.

The medicine men have an imposing temple, or *latipso,* in every community of any size. The more elaborate ceremonies required to treat very sick patients can only be performed at this temple. These ceremonies involve not only the thaumaturge but a permanent group of vestal maidens who move sedately about the temple chambers in distinctive costume and headdress.

The *latipso* ceremonies are so harsh that it is phenomenal that a fair proportion of the really sick natives who enter the temple ever recover. Small children whose indoctrination is still incomplete have been known to resist attempts to take them to the temple because "that is where you go to die." Despite this fact, sick adults are not only willing but eager to undergo the protracted ritual purification, if they can afford to do so. No matter how ill the supplicant or how grave the emergency, the guardians of many temples will not admit a client if he cannot give a rich gift to the custodian. Even after one has gained admission and survived the ceremonies, the guardians will not permit the neophyte to leave until he makes still another gift.

The supplicant entering the temple is first stripped of all his or her clothes. In everyday life the Nacirema avoids exposure of his body and its natural functions. Bathing and excretory acts are performed only in the secrecy of the household shrine, where they are ritualized as part of the body-rites. Psychological shock results from the fact that body secrecy is suddenly lost upon entry into the *latipso.* A man, whose own wife has never seen him in an excretory act, suddenly finds himself naked and assisted by a vestal maiden while he performs his natural functions into a sacred vessel. This sort of ceremonial treatment is necessitated by the fact that the excreta are used by a diviner to ascertain the course and nature of the client's sickness. Female clients, on the other hand, find their naked bodies are

subjected to the scrutiny, manipulation, and prodding of the medicine men.

Few supplicants in the temple are well enough to do anything but lie on their hard beds. The daily ceremonies, like the rites of the holy-mouth-men, involve discomfort and torture. With ritual precision, the vestals awaken their miserable charges each dawn and roll them about on their beds of pain while performing ablutions, in the formal movements of which the maidens are highly trained. At other times they insert magic wands in the supplicant's mouth or force him to eat substances which are supposed to be healing. From time to time the medicine men come to their clients and jab magically treated needles into their flesh. The fact that these temple ceremonies may not cure, and may even kill the neophyte, in no way decreases the people's faith in the medicine men.

There remains one other kind of practitioner, known as a "listener." This witch-doctor has the power to exorcise the devils that lodge in the heads of people who have been bewitched. The Nacirema believe that parents bewitch their own children. Mothers are particularly suspected of putting a curse on children while teaching them the secret body rituals. The counter-magic of the witch-doctor is unusual in its lack of ritual. The patient simply tells the "listener" all his troubles and fears, beginning with the earliest difficulties he can remember. The memory displayed by the Nacirema in these exorcism sessions is truly remarkable. It is not uncommon for the patient to bemoan the rejection he felt upon being weaned as a babe, and a few individuals even see their troubles going back to the traumatic effects of their own birth.

In conclusion, mention must be made of certain practices which have their base in native esthetics but which depend upon the pervasive aversion to the natural body and its functions. There are ritual fasts to make fat people thin and ceremonial feasts to make thin people fat. Still other rites are used to make women's breasts larger if they are small, and smaller if they are large. General dissatisfaction with breast shape is symbolized in the fact that the ideal form is virtually outside the range of human variation. A few women afflicted with almost inhuman hypermammary development are so idolized that they make a handsome living by simply going from village to village and permitting the natives to stare at them for a fee.

Reference has already been made to the fact that excretory functions are ritualized, routinized, and relegated to secrecy. Natural reproductive functions are similarly distorted. Intercourse is taboo as a topic and scheduled as an act. Efforts are made to avoid pregnancy by the use of magical materials or by limiting intercourse to certain phases of the moon. Conception is actually very infrequent. When pregnant, women dress so as to hide their condition. Parturition takes place in secret, without friends or relatives to assist, and the majority of women do not nurse their infants.

Our review of the ritual life of the Nacirema has certainly shown them to be a magic-ridden people. It is hard to understand how they have managed to exist so long under the burdens which they have imposed upon themselves. But even such exotic customs as these take on real meaning when they are viewed with the insight provided by Malinowski when he wrote (1948, p. 70):

> Looking from far and above, from our high places of safety in the developed civilization, it is easy to see all the crudity and irrelevance of magic. But without its power and guidance early man could not have mastered his practical difficulties as he has done, nor could man have advanced to the higher stages of civilization.

REFERENCES

Linton, R. (1936). *The study of man*. New York: Appleton-Century.

Malinowski, B. (1948). *Magic, science, and religion*. Glencoe, IL: Free Press.

Murdock, G. P. (1949). *Social structure*. New York: Macmillan.

THINKING ABOUT THE READING

How long did it take you to realize that Miner was describing *American* culture? This article was written over 40 years ago and, of course, much has changed since then. How might you update this description of the "Nacirema" to account for current values and rituals? Imagine you are an anthropologist from a culture completely unfamiliar with Western traditions. Using your own life as a starting point, think of common patterns of work, leisure, learning, intimacy, eating, sleeping, and so forth. Are there some customs that distinguish your group (religious, racial, ethnic, friendship, and so on) from others? See if you can find the reasons why these customs exist. Which customs serve an obvious purpose (for example, health)? Which might seem arbitrary and silly to an outside observer?

A Geography of Time

Robert Levine

Living on Event Time

Anyone who has traveled abroad—or waited in a doctor's office, for that matter—knows that the clock, or even the calendar, is sometimes no more than an ornament. The event at hand, on these occasions, often begins and ends with complete disregard for the technicalities of a timepiece. We in the industrialized world expect punctuality. But life on clock time is clearly out of line with virtually all of recorded history. And it is not only from a historical perspective that these temporal customs are so deviant. Still today, the idea of living by the clock remains absolutely foreign to much of the world.

One of the most significant differences in the pace of life is whether people use the hour on the clock to schedule the beginning and ending of activities, or whether the activities are allowed to transpire according to their own spontaneous schedule. These two approaches are known, respectively, as living by clock time and living by event time. The difference between clock and event time is more than a difference in speed, although life certainly does tend to be faster for people on clock time. Let me again turn to a personal example.

A few years after my stay in Brazil I became eligible for a sabbatical leave from my university. I decided to invest my term of "rest and renewal" in a study of international differences in the pace of life. I also chose to use the opportunity to live out a childhood dream—to travel around the world.

Precisely where I would go wasn't altogether clear. The phrase "travel around the world" had a lovely ring to it, but I must admit that I wasn't certain just what it entailed. Never having done very well in geography, I had very little grasp of how the nations of the world are arranged and even less notion of their innards. Not knowing what I'd encounter, it was impossible to plan exactly where to visit or how long I would stay in each country. I decided, instead, to let the trip evolve its own form. Fortunately, the research I had designed allowed me the flexibility to decide where and when to collect data along the way.

I bought a map of the world and marked the locations of the four most exotic sights I could invoke: The Great Wall of China, Mount Everest, the Taj Mahal and the Great Pyramids of Egypt. I drew a line connecting the marks. Although I was uncertain how many of these wonders I'd actually see, they gave my trip a rough outline. I decided to fly to the edge of Western Asia and then make my way by land, moving in a rough westerly direction, around the globe. Searching the map for Asia's outside edge, my finger landed on Indonesia.

I purchased a one-way plane ticket to Jakarta, with stops along the way in Japan, Taiwan, and Hong Kong. Beyond that, I had no tickets. From Indonesia I would travel up the Malaysian peninsula toward Thailand, and then west across Asia toward home. My only rules would be to travel no better than second class and to stay on the ground as much as possible. I gave up my house lease, loaned out my car, put my possessions in storage, and told everyone who needed to know I'd be gone for the semester. (Professors don't think in terms of months. Our unit of time is the semester.) The semester stretched into two semesters (one year, tossing in a summer vacation).

The trip began with a flight from San Francisco to Tokyo. Settling in for the long ride, I tried to focus on what I was beginning. My first thought was that I had no keys in my pocket. Next, that in place of an appointment calendar, I was carrying, for the first time in my life, a journal. Then came the realization that I had no commitments. There was nothing, other than carrying out my very flexible research plans, that needed to be done. I didn't have to be any place at any specific time for six whole months. There were no plans or schedules to interfere with whatever might come along. I could let my opportunities come forth on their own and I would choose those I wished to follow. I was free, free, free!

My joy lasted nearly half a minute. Then the terror: What in the world would I do for a whole semester without a schedule or plans? I looked ahead and saw layers and layers of nothing. How would I fill my time? I have never in my life so yearned for an appointment—with anyone for anything. It really was pitiful. Here I was freer and more mobile than most people in the world could ever dream of being. I was Marlon Brando on his motorcycle—with a passport, a Ph.D., and a steady paycheck. And I responded with an anxiety attack.

When I dozed off a little later on the flight, I dreamed about a passage from William Faulkner's *Light in August*. It is when the character named Christmas, hungry and fleeing from the sheriff, becomes obsessed with time. I later looked up the actual quotation:

> . . . *I have not eaten since I have not eaten since* trying to remember how many days it had been since Friday in Jefferson, in the restaurant where he had eaten his supper, until after a while, in the lying still with waiting until the men should have eaten and gone to the field, the name of the day of the week seemed more important than the food. Because when the men were gone at last and he descended, emerged, into the level, jonquil-colored sun and went to the kitchen door, he didn't ask for food at all . . . he heard his mouth saying "Can you tell me what day this is? I just want to know what day this is."
>
> "What day it is?" Her face was gaunt as his, her body as gaunt and as tireless and as driven.

She said: "You get away from here! It's Tuesday! You get away from here! I'll call my man!"

He said, "Thank you," as the door banged.

After finally arriving in Tokyo, I checked into a hotel room an ex-student had reserved for me. This was the only room reservation I had for the next six months (twelve months, actually—but, mercifully, I didn't know that then). After unpacking, I put on the robe and slippers provided by the hotel. The bottom of the robe showed considerably more thigh than its maker had intended and the slippers only fit over three of my toes. But I liked the image and, coupled with a dip in the hot tub and a very large bottle of Sapporo beer, I went to sleep with some iota of hope for my immediate future.

The next morning I awoke to a view of green tiled roofs, banyan trees, and an enormous reclining Buddha. At the sight of my little robe and slippers my anticipation returned. I was ready to let events take their own course. What to do first? I loved my hot tub the night before, so decided to start my day with another long dip. Then I found a tea shop next door. The waiter spoke a little English, the food was good, and there was even a *Herald Tribune* to keep me company. After breakfast I explored my neighborhood reclining Buddha, who turned out to be resting in a large temple surrounded by a lovely park. I took out a book to read, stretched my legs and watched life in Tokyo parade by.

Next? A friend had given me a list of gardens he thought I'd enjoy seeing. Why not? I randomly chose one, and thoroughly enjoyed the visit. That evening I had a nice dinner at a restaurant near my hotel. I ended my day with a hot tub, my robe and slippers, and a Sapporo.

The following morning I shot out of bed with an adrenalin charge. What might this new day have in store? How to begin? A hot bath first, of course. Then, recalling the pleasant morning before, I returned to my tea shop for breakfast. After that I could think of no place on earth I would rather be than sitting beside my local Buddha. That afternoon I tried another garden. In the evening I returned to the same restaurant. And, of course, I took a hot bath and nursed my Sapporo before turning in. Another lovely day.

Day three went something like: hot tub/breakfast at the tea shop/Buddha/gardens/dinner/hot tub/Sapporo. The next day was the same. As was the next. And the next.

Looking back at that first week, I see you could have set a clock by my activities. What time is it, you ask? "He's reading his book in the park, so it must be 10 o'clock." "Now he's leaving the hot tub, so that must mean a little after eight." Without intending it, I'd created the structure I so craved on my plane trip. Ironically, one of the very reasons I chose a career in academia in the first place was because it, more than other professions, allowed me to arrange my own time. But when confronted with no limits, I had bounced to the other extreme. To my surprise as well as humbling disappointment, I had built a tighter schedule than the one I lived at work.

Drowning in Event Time

My behavior, I now recognize, was a textbook struggle between the forces of clock time, on the one hand, and event time on the other. Under clock time, the hour on the timepiece governs the beginning and ending of activities. When event time predominates, scheduling is determined by activities. Events begin and end when, by mutual consensus, participants "feel" the time is right. The distinction between clock and event time is profound. The sociologist Robert Lauer conducted in his book *Temporal Man* an intensive review of the literature concerning the meaning of time throughout history. The most fundamental difference, he found, has been between people operating by the clock versus those who measure time by social events.[1]

Many countries extoll event time as a philosophy of life. In Mexico, for example, there is a popular adage to "Give time to time" (*Darle tiempo al tiempo)*. Across the globe in Africa, it is said that "Even the time takes its time." Psychologist Kris Eysell, while a Peace Corps volunteer in Liberia, was confronted by a variation on this African expression. She describes how every day, as she made her eight-mile walk from home to work, complete strangers would call out to her along the way: "Take time, Missy."

My experiences in Japan were those of a clock time addict floundering in situations where programming by the clock had lost its effectiveness. I was, I have since come to learn, drowning in good company. The social psychologist James Jones had even more complicated temporal challenges during his stay in Trinidad. Jones, an African-American, is quite familiar with the casualness of what used to be called "colored people's time" (CPT). But he was unprepared for the quagmire of life on event time. Jones first confronted the popular motto "Anytime is Trinidad time" soon after arriving, and said he spent the rest of his stay trying to understand just what it meant:

> CPT simply implied that coming late to things was the norm and contrasted with the Anglo-European penchant for punctuality and timeliness. Over the course of my year in Trinidad, though, I came to understand that Trinidadians had personal control over time. They more or less came and went as they wanted or felt. "I didn't feel to go to work today," was a standard way of expressing that choice. Time was reckoned more by behavior than the clock. Things started when people arrived and ended when they left, not when the clock struck 8:00 or 1:00.[2]

To visitors from the world of clocks, life conducted on event time often appears, in James Jones's words, to be "chronometric anarchy."

Where are the Cows?: Measuring Time in Burundi

When event time people do listen to the clock, it is often nature's clock they hear. Salvatore Niyonzima, one of my former graduate students, describes his home country of Burundi as a classic example of this.

As in most of Central Africa, Niyonzima says, life in Burundi is guided by the seasons. More than 80 percent of the population of Burundi are farmers. As a result, "people still rely on the phases of nature," he explains. "When the dry season begins it is time for harvesting. And when the rainy season comes back—then, of course, it's time to return to the fields and plant and grow things, because this is the cycle."

Appointment times in Burundi are also often regulated by natural cycles. "Appointments are not necessarily in terms of a precise hour of the day. People who grew up in rural areas, and who haven't had very much education, might make an early appointment by saying, 'Okay, I'll see you tomorrow morning when the cows are going out for grazing.'" If they want to meet in the middle of the day, "they set their appointment for the time 'when the cows are going to drink in the stream,' which is where they are led at midday." In order to prevent the youngest cows from drinking too much, Niyonzima explains, farmers typically spend two or three hours with them back in a sheltered place, while their elders are still drinking from the stream. "Then in the afternoon, let's say somewhere around three o'clock, it's time again to get the young cows outside for the evening graze. So if we want to make a late appointment we might say 'I'll see you when the young cows go out.'"

Being any more precise—to say, for example, "I'll meet you in the latter part of the time when the cows are out drinking"—would be, Niyonzima says, "just too much. If you arrange to come to my place when the cows are going to drink water, then it means it's around the middle of the day. If it's an hour earlier or an hour later, it doesn't matter. He knows that he made an appointment and that he'll be there." Precision is difficult and mostly irrelevant because it is hard to know exactly at what time people will be leading the cows out in the first place. "I might decide to lead them to the river one hour later because I either got them out of the home later or it didn't look like they really had that much to eat because the place where they were grazing didn't have very much pasture."

People in Burundi use similarly tangible images to mark the nighttime. "We refer to a very dark night as a 'Who are you?' night," Niyonzima explains. "This means that it was so dark that you couldn't recognize anybody without hearing their voice. You know that somebody is there but can't see them because it is so dark, so you say 'Who are you?' as a greeting. They speak and I hear their voice and now I recognize who they are. 'Who are you?'—time is one way to describe when it gets dark. We might refer back to an occasion as having occurred on a 'Who are you?' night."

Specifying precise nighttime appointments, Niyonzima says, "gets difficult. 'Who are you?' simply refers to the physical condition of darkness. I certainly wouldn't give a time like 8 P.M. or 9 P.M. When people want to name a particular time of the night, they might use references to aspects of sleep. They may, for example, say something occurred at a time 'When nobody was awake' or, if they wanted to be a little more specific, at the time 'When people were beginning the first period of their sleep.' Later in the night might be called 'Almost the morning light' or the time 'When the rooster sings'; or, to get really specific, 'When the rooster sings for the first time' or the second time, and so on. And then we're ready for the cows again."

Contrast the natural clocks of Burundi to the clock time scheduling that prevails in the dominant Anglo culture of the United States. Our watches dictate when it is time to work and when to play; when each encounter must begin and end.

Even biological events are typically scheduled by the clock. It is normal to talk about it being "too early to go to sleep" or "not yet dinner time," or too late to take a nap or eat a snack. The hour on the clock, rather than the signal from our bodies, usually dictates when it is time to begin and stop. We learn these habits at a very early age. A newborn is fully capable of recognizing when he or she is hungry or sleepy. But it is not long before parents either adjust their baby's routine to fit their own or, in response to whatever may be the prevailing cultural standards (often defined by popular Dr. Spock–type advice manuals), train the child to eat and sleep to more "healthy" rhythms. The baby then learns when to be hungry and when to be sleepy.

As adults, some people are particularly susceptible to the control of the clock. Several years ago, in a series of classic studies, social psychologist Stanley Schachter and his colleagues observed the eating behaviors of obese and normal-weight people. Schachter theorized that a major factor in obesity is a tendency for eating to be governed by external cues from the surrounding environment. People of normal weight, he believed, are more responsive to their internal hunger pangs. One powerful external cue, Schachter hypothesized, is the clock.

To test his theory, Columbia University dormitory students were brought into a room in which the experimenters had doctored the clocks so that some subjects thought it was earlier than their usual dinner time and others thought it was later than their usual dinner time. Participants were told to help themselves to a bowl of crackers in front of them. As Schachter predicted, the obese people ate more crackers when they thought it was after their dinner time than when they were made to believe that it was not yet time for dinner. The time on the clock had no bearing on how many crackers the normal-weight subjects ate. They ate when they were hungry. The overweight people ate when the time on the clock said it was appropriate.[3] As my over-three-hundred-pound uncle replied when I once asked him if he was hungry, "I haven't been hungry in 45 years."

Is Time Money?

When the clock predominates, time becomes a valuable commodity. Clock time cultures take for granted the reality of time as fixed, linear, and measurable. As Ben Franklin once advised, "Remember that time is money." But to event time cultures, for whom time is considerably more flexible and ambiguous, time and money are very separate entities.

The clash between these attitudes can be jarring. When, on my sabbatical trip, I moved out of my hot tub/breakfast/Buddha routine and made a trip to the Taj Mahal, for example, the most frequent comments I heard spoken by first-world visitors referred to the amount of work that went into the building—variations on the question, "How long must that have taken?" Perhaps the second most frequent comment I heard from tourists in India went something like: "That embroidery must have taken forever. Can you imagine how much that would cost back home?" Finding bargains on foreigners' time is, in fact, a favorite vacation activity of many Westerners. But these comments wouldn't mean much to the Indian artist who spent months embroidering a fabric or to their ancestors who'd built the Taj Mahal. When event time predominates, the economic model of clock time makes little sense. Time and money are independent entities. You need to give time to time, as they say in Mexico.

In my travels in South America and Asia I have repeatedly been confused, and sometimes even harassed, by comments such as: "Unlike you Americans, time is not money for us." My usual response is something like: "But our time is all we have. It's our most valuable, our only really valuable, possession. How can you waste it like that?" Their typical retort—usually in a less frantic tone than my own—begins with unqualified agreement that time is, indeed, our most valuable commodity. But it is for exactly this reason, event timers argue, that time shouldn't be wasted by carving it into inorganic monetary units.

Burundi again provides a case in point. "Central Africans," Salvatore Niyonzima says, "generally disregard the fact that time is always money. When I want the time to wait for me, it does. And when I don't want to do something today—for any reason, whatever reason—I can just decide to do it tomorrow and it will be as good as today. If I lose some time I'm not losing something very important because, after all, I have so much of it."

Jean Traore, an exchange student from Burkina Faso in Eastern Africa, finds the concept of "wasting time" confusing. "There's no such thing as wasting time where I live," he observes. "How can you waste time? If you're not doing one thing, you're doing something else. Even if you're just talking to a friend, or sitting around, that's what you're doing." A responsible Burkina Faso citizen is expected to understand and accept this view of time, and to recognize that what is truly wasteful—sinful, to some—is to not make sufficient time available for the people in your life.

Mexico is another example. Frustrated U.S. business people often complain that Mexicans are *plagued* by a lack of attachment to time. But as writer Jorge Castaneda points out, "they are simply different . . . Letting and watching time go by, being late (an hour, a day, a week), are not grievous offenses. They simply indicate a lower rung on the ladder of priorities. It is more important to see a friend of the family than to keep an appointment or to make it to work, especially when work consists of hawking wares on street corners." There is also an economic explanation: "There is a severe lack of incentives for being on time, delivering on time, or working overtime. Since most people are paid little for what they do, the prize for punctuality and formality can be meaningless: time is often not money in Mexico."

Event time and clock time are not totally unrelated. But event time encompasses considerably more than the clock. It is a product of the larger gestalt; a result of social, economic, and environmental cues, and, of course, of cultural values. Consequently, clock time and event time often constitute worlds of their own. As Jorge Castaneda observes about Mexico and the United States, "time divides our two countries as much as any other single factor."[4]

Other Event Time Cultures

Life in industrialized society is so enmeshed with the clock that its inhabitants are often oblivious to how eccentric their temporal beliefs can appear to others. But many people in the world aren't as "civilized" as us. (Psychologist Julian Jaynes defines civilization as "the art of living in towns of such size that everyone does not know everyone else.") Even today, organic clocks like Burundi's time of the cows are often the only standard that insiders are willing to accept. For many, if not most, people in the world, living by mechanical clocks would feel as abnormal and confusing as living without a concrete schedule would to a Type A Westerner.

Anthropologists have chronicled many examples of contemporary event time cultures. Philip Bock, for example, analyzed the temporal sequence of a wake conducted by the Micmac Indians of Eastern Canada. He found that the wake can be clearly divided into gathering time, prayer time, singing time, intermission, and mealtime. But it turns out that none of these times are directly related to clock time. The mourners simply move from one time to another by mutual consensus. When do they begin and end each episode? When the time is ripe and no sooner.[5]

Robert Lauer tells of the Nuers from the Sudan, whose calendars are based on the seasonal changes in their environment. They construct their fishing dams and cattle camps, for example, in the month of *kur*. How do they know when it is *kur*? It's *kur* when they're building their dams and camps. They break camp and return to their villages in the months of *dwat*. When is it *dwat*? When people are on the move.[6] There's an old joke about an American on a whirlwind tour of Europe who is asked where he is. "If it's Tuesday," he responds, "this must be Belgium." If Nuers were asked the same question they might answer: "If it's Belgium, this must be Tuesday."

Many people use their social activities to mark time rather than the other way around. In parts of Madagascar, for example, questions about how long something takes might receive an answer like "the time of a rice-cooking" (about half an hour) or "the frying of a locust" (a quick moment). Similarly, natives of the Cross River in Nigeria have been quoted as saying "the man died in less than the time in which maize is not yet completely roasted" (less than fifteen minutes). Closer to home, not too many years ago the *New English Dictionary* included a listing for the term "pissing while"—not a particularly exact measurement, perhaps, but one with a certain cross-cultural translatability.

Most societies have some type of week, but it turns out it's not always seven days long. The Incas had a ten-day week. Their neighbors, the

Muysca of Bogota, had a three-day week. Some weeks are as long as sixteen days. Often the length of the week reflects cycles of activities, rather than the other way around. For many people, their markets are the main activity requiring group co-ordination. The Khasis of Assam, Pitirim Sorokin reports, hold their market every eighth day. Being practical people, they've made their week eight days long and named the days of the week after the places where the main markets occur.[7]

Natives of the Andaman jungle in India are another people with little need to buy calendars. The Andamanese have constructed a complex annual calendar built around the sequence of dominant smells of trees and flowers in their environment. When they want to check the time of year, the Andamanese simply smell the odors outside their door.[8]

The monks in Burma have developed a fool-proof alarm clock. They know it is time to rise at daybreak "when there is light enough to see the veins in their hand."[9]

There are groups who, even though they have wristwatches, prefer to measure time imprecisely. The anthropologist Douglas Raybeck, for example, has studied the Kelantese peasants of the Malay Peninsula, a group he refers to as the "coconut-clock" people. The Kelantese approach to time is typified by their coconut clocks—an invention they use as a timer for sporting competitions. This clock consists of a half coconut shell with a small hole in its center that sits in a pail of water. Intervals are measured by the time it takes the shell to fill with water and then sink—usually about three to five minutes. The Kelantese recognize that the clock is inexact, but they choose it over the wristwatches they own.[10]

Some people don't even have a single-word equivalent of "time." E. R. Leach has studied the Kachin people of North Burma. The Kachin use the word *ahkying* to refer to the time of the clock. The word *na* refers to a long time, and *tawng* to a short time. The word *ta* refers to springtime and *asak* to the time of a person's life. A Kachin wouldn't regard any of these words as synonymous with another. Whereas time for most West-

erners is treated as an objective entity—it is a noun in the English language—the Kachin words for time are treated more like adverbs. Time has no tangible reality for the Kachin.[11]

Many North American Indian cultures also treat time only indirectly in their language. The Sioux, for example, have no single word in their language for "time," "late," or "waiting." The Hopi, observes Edward Hall, have no verb tenses for past, present, and future. Like the Kachin people, the Hopi treat temporal concepts more like adverbs than nouns. When discussing the seasons, for example, "the Hopi cannot talk about summer being hot, because summer is the quality hot, just as an apple has the quality red," Hall reports. "Summer and hot are the same! Summer is a *condition:* hot." It is difficult for the Kachin and the Hopi to conceive of time as a quantity. Certainly, it is not equated with money and the clock. Time only exists in the eternal present.

Many Mediterranean Arab cultures define only three sets of time: no time at all, now (which is of varying duration), and forever (too long). As a result, American businessmen have often encountered frustrating communication break-downs when trying to get Arabs to distinguish between different waiting periods—between, say, a long time and a very long time.[12]

I ran into similar dictionary problems once when trying to translate a time survey into Spanish for a Mexican sample. Three of my original English questions asked people when they would "expect" a person to arrive for a certain appointment, what time they "hoped" that person would arrive, and how long they would "wait" for them to arrive. It turns out that the three English verbs "to expect," "to hope," and "to wait" all translate into the single Spanish verb "*esperar*." (The same verb is used in Portuguese.) I eventually had to use roundabout terms to get the distinctions across.

There is an old Yiddish proverb that says, "It's good to hope, it's the waiting that spoils it." Compare this to a culture whose language does not routinely distinguish between expecting, hoping, and waiting, and you have a pretty clear picture of how the latter feels about the clock. At first, I was frustrated by the inability to translate my questionnaires. Later, though, I came to see that my translation failures were telling me as much about Latin American concepts of time as were their responses to my formal questions. The silent and verbal languages of time feed upon each other.

Keeping Everything from Happening at Once

The primary function of clock time, it may be argued, is to prevent simultaneously occurring events from running into one another. "Time is nature's way of keeping everything from happening at once," observes a contemporary item of graffiti. The more complex our network of activities, the greater the need to formalize scheduling. A shared commitment to abide by clock time serves to coordinate traffic. The Khasis and Nuers are able to avoid governance by the clock because the demands on their time are relatively distinct and uncomplicated.

But we don't have to cross continents to see groups still operating on event time. Even in clock-time-dominated cultures, there are people whose temporal demands more closely resemble the sparsity of Asian villagers than that of the surrounding clock-coordinated society. In these subcultures, life takes on the cadence of event time.

Alex Gonzalez, a fellow social psychologist raised in a Mexican-American barrio in Los Angeles, has described the attitude toward time among his childhood friends who remain in his old neighborhood. Many of these people are unemployed, have little prospect of employment, and, he observes, almost no future time perspective. His old neighborhood, Gonzalez says, is filled with people who congregate loosely each day and wait for something to capture their interest. Their problem is not so much finding time for their activities as it is to find activities to fill their time. They stay with the event until, by mutual consent, it feels like time to move on. Time is flat. Watches are mostly ornaments and symbols of status. They're rarely for telling time.[13]

How would these people react if you gave them a Day Runner? Probably like Jonathan Swifts's Lilliputians did to Gulliver, who looked at his watch before doing anything. He called it his oracle. The Lilliputians he met in his travels decided that Gulliver's watch must be his God. In other words, they thought he was crazy.

The Advantage of Temporal Flexibility

Clock time cultures tend to be less flexible in how they schedule activities. They are more likely to be what anthropologist Edward Hall calls monochronic or M-time schedulers: people who like to focus on one activity at a time. Event time people, on the other hand, tend to prefer polychronic or P-time scheduling: doing several things at once.[14] M-time people like to work from start to finish in linear sequence: the first task is begun and completed before turning to another, which is then begun and completed. In polychronic time, however, one project goes on until there is an inclination or inspiration to turn to another, which may lead to an idea for another, then back to the first, with intermittent and unpredictable pauses and resumptions of one task or another. Progress on P-time occurs a little at a time on each task.

P-time cultures are characterized by a strong involvement with people. They emphasize the completion of human transactions rather than keeping to schedules. Two Burundians deep in conversation, for example, will typically choose to arrive late for their next appointment rather than cut into the flow of their discussion. Both would be insulted, in fact, if their partner were to abruptly terminate the conversation before it came to a spontaneous conclusion. "If you value people," Hall explains about the sensibility of P-time cultures, "you must hear them out and cannot cut them off simply because of a schedule."

P-time and M-time don't mix well. Allen Bluedorn, a professor of management at the University of Missouri, and his colleagues have found that M-time individuals are happier and more productive in M-time organizations while polychronic people do better in polychronic ones. These findings are applicable not only to foreign cultures, but also to different organizational cultures in the United States.[15]

Both M-time and clock time thinking tend to be concentrated in achievement-oriented, industrialized societies like the United States. P-time and event time are more common in third-world economies. In general, people who live on P-time are less productive—by Western economic standards, at least—than are M-time people. But there are occasions when polychronicity is not only more people-oriented, but also more productive. Rigid adherence to schedules can cut things short just when they are beginning to move forward. And as the invention of the word processor has taught even the most rigid of M-time people, working in nonlinear progression, spontaneously shifting attention from one section of a project to another, making connections from back to front as well as vice versa, can be both liberating and productive.

The most fruitful approach of all, however, is one that moves flexibly between the worlds of P-time and M-time, event time and clock time, as suits the situation. Some of the newer entrants into the economics of industrialization have managed monetary success without wholesale sacrifice of their traditional commitment to social obligations. Once again, the Japanese, with their blend of traditional Eastern and modern Western cultures, provide a noteworthy example.

A few years ago, I received a letter from Kiyoshi Yoneda, a businessman from Tokyo who has spent more than five years living in the West. My research on cross-national differences in the pace of life, which found that the Japanese had the fastest pace of life in the world, had just been reported in the international press. Mr. Yoneda wrote because he was concerned (with good reason, I might add) about the superficiality of my understanding of Japanese attitudes toward time. He wanted me to understand that the Japanese may be fast, but that doesn't mean that they treat the clock with the same reverence as people in the West.

Meetings in Japan, he pointed out, start less punctually and end much more "sluggishly" than they do in the United States. "In the Japanese company I work for," he wrote, "meetings go all the way until some agreement is made, or until everybody is tired; and the end is not sharply predefined by a scheduled time. The agreement is often not clearly stated. Perhaps in order to compensate [for] the unpredictability of the closing time of a meeting, you are not blamed if you [go] away before the meeting is over. Also, it's quite all right to sleep during the meeting. For instance, if you are an engineer and not interested in the money-counting aspects of a project, nobody expects you to stay wide awake paying attention to discussions concerning details of accounting. You may fall asleep, do your reading or writing, or stand up to get some coffee or tea."

Monochronic and polychronic organizations each have their weaknesses. Monochronic systems are prone to undervaluing the humanity of their members. Polychronic ones tend toward unproductive chaos. It would seem that the most healthy approach to P-time and M-time is to hone skills for both, and to execute mixtures of each to suit the situation. The Japanese blend offers one provocative example of how people take control of their time, rather than the other way around.

More Time Wars

Because cultural norms are so widely shared by the surrounding society, people often forget that their own rules are arbitrary. It is easy to confuse cultural normalcy with ethnocentric superiority. When people of different cultures interact, the potential for misunderstanding exists on many levels. For example, members of Arab and Latin cultures usually stand much closer when they're speaking to people than we do in the United States, a fact we frequently misinterpret as aggression or disrespect. Similarly, we often misconstrue the intentions of people with temporal customs different from our own. Such are the difficulties of communicating the silent languages of culture.

Nearly every traveler has experienced these blunders, in the forms of their own misunderstanding of the motives of the surrounding culture as well as others' misinterpretations of theirs. A particularly frequent source of mishaps involves clashes between clock time and event time. Fortunately, most of our stumblings are limited to unpleasant miscommunications. When misunderstandings occur at a higher level, however, they can be serious business.

An example of this occurred in 1985, when a group of Shiite Muslim terrorists hijacked a TWA jetliner and held 40 Americans hostage, demanding that Israel release 764 Lebanese Shiite prisoners being held in prison. Shortly after, the terrorists handed the American hostages over to Shiite Muslim leaders, who assured everybody that nothing would happen if the Israelis met their demands.

At one point during the delicate negotiations Ghassan Sablini, the number-three man in the Shiite militia Amal (who had assumed the role of militant authorities), announced that the hostages would be handed back to the hijackers in two days if no action was taken on their demand that Israel release its Shiite prisoners. This created a very dangerous situation. The U.S. negotiators knew that neither they nor the Israelis could submit to these terrorist demands without working out a face-saving compromise. But by setting a limit of "two days" the Shiite leaders made a compromise unlikely and had elevated the crisis to a very dangerous level. People held their breath. At the last minute, however, Sablini was made to understand how his statement was being interpreted. To everyone's relief, he explained: "We said a couple of days but we were not necessarily specifying 48 hours."[16]

Forty deaths and a possible war were nearly caused by a miscommunication over the meaning of the word "day." To the U.S. negotiators, the word referred to a technical aspect of time: 24 hours. For the Muslim leader, a day was merely a figure of speech meaning "a while." The U.S. negotiators were thinking on clock time. Sablini was on event time.

NOTES

1. Lauer, R. (1981). *Temporal Man: The Meaning and Uses of Social Time.* New York: Praeger.

2. Jones, J. (1993). An exploration of temporality in human behavior. In Schank, R., and Langer, E. (eds.), *Beliefs, Reasoning, and Decision-Making: Psycho-Logic in Honor of Bob Abelson.* Hillsdale, NJ: Lawrence Erlbaum.

3. Schachter, S., and Gross, L. (1968). Manipulated time and eating behavior. *Journal of Personality and Social Psychology* 10, 93–106.

4. Castaneda, J. (1995, July). Ferocious differences. *The Atlantic Monthly,* 68–76, 73, 74.

5. Bock, P. (1964). Social structure and language structure. *Southwestern Journal of Anthropology* 20, 393–403.

6. Lauer, R. H. (1981). *Temporal Man: The Meaning and Uses of Social Time.* New York: Praeger.

7. Sorokin, P. (1964). *Sociocultural Causality, Space, Time.* New York: Russel and Russel.

8. Rifkin, J. (1987, September/October). Time wars: A new dimension shaping our future. *Utne Reader,* 46–57.

9. Thompson, E. P. (1967). Time, work-discipline, and industrial capitalism. *Past and Present* 38, 56–97.

10. Raybeck, D. (1992). The coconut-shell clock: Time and cultural identity. *Time and Society* 1 (3), 323–40.

11. Leach, E. R. (1961). *Rethinking Anthropology.* London: Athlone Press.

12. Hall, E. (1983). *The Dance of Life.* Garden City, NY: Doubleday.

13. Gonzalez has also done important research on the subject of time. See Gonzalez, A., and Zimbardo, P. (1985, March). Time in perspective. *Psychology Today,* 20–26.

14. Hall, E. (1983). *The Dance of Life.* Garden City, NY: Doubleday.

15. Bluedorn, A., Kaufman, C., and Lane, P. (1992). How many things do you like to do at once? An introduction to monochronic and polychronic time. *Academy of Management Executive* 6, 17–26.

16. UPI (1985, June 23). Ships with 1,800 Marines off Lebanon. Reprinted in *The Fresno Bee,* A1.

THINKING ABOUT THE READING

What is the difference between *clock time* and *event time?* How are these different types of time related to the level of development of a particular culture? Levine seems to be arguing that event time is a less stressful, more healthy way for people to live their lives than clock time, even though clock time is a characteristic of more advanced societies. Do you think an achievement-oriented, technologically complex society like the United States could ever exist on event time? If not, are there ways that society could reduce the stressful effects of clock time? As you ponder this question, make sure you address how other institutions (economy, family, politics, education, and so on) would be affected. What lessons can you draw from this article about Americans' strong tendency to view societies that aren't as "sophisticated" as theirs as somehow inferior?

The Melting Pot

Anne Fadiman

The Lee family—Nao Kao, Foua, Chong, Zoua, Cheng, May, Yer, and True—arrived in the United States on December 18, 1980. Their luggage consisted of a few clothes, a blue blanket, and a wooden mortar and pestle that Foua had chiseled from a block of wood in Houaysouy. They flew from Bangkok to Honolulu, and then to Portland, Oregon, where they were to spend two years before moving to Merced. Other refugees told me that their airplane flights—a mode of travel that strained the limits of the familiar Hmong concept of migration—had been fraught with anxiety and shame: they got airsick, they didn't know how to use the bathroom but were afraid to soil themselves, they thought they had to pay for their food but had no money, they tried to eat the Wash'n Dris. The Lees, though perplexed, took the novelties of the trip in stride. Nao Kao remembers the airplane as being "just like a big house."

Their first week in Portland, however, was miserably disorienting. Before being placed by a local refugee agency in a small rented house, they spent a week with relatives, sleeping on the floor. "We didn't know anything so our relatives had to show us everything," Foua said. "They knew because they had lived in America for three or four months already. Our relatives told us about electricity and said the children shouldn't touch those plugs in the wall because they could get hurt. They told us that the refrigerator is a cold box where you put meat. They showed us how to open the TV so we could see it. We had never seen a toilet before and we thought maybe the water in it was to drink or cook with. Then our relatives told us what it was, but we didn't know whether we should sit or whether we should stand on it. Our relatives took us to the store but we didn't know that the cans and packages had food in them. We could tell what the meat was, but the chickens and cows and pigs were all cut up in little pieces and had plastic on them. Our relatives told us the stove is for cooking the food, but I was afraid to use it because it might explode. Our relatives said in America the food you don't eat you just throw away. In Laos we always fed it to the animals and it was strange to waste it like that. In this country there were a lot of strange things and even now I don't know a lot of things and my children have to help me, and it still seems like a strange country."

Seventeen years later, Foua and Nao Kao use American appliances, but they still speak only Hmong, celebrate only Hmong holidays, practice only the Hmong religion, cook only Hmong dishes, sing only Hmong songs, play only Hmong musical instruments, tell only Hmong stories, and know far more about current political events in Laos and Thailand than about those in the United States. When I first met them, during their eighth year in this country, only one American adult, Jeanine Hilt, had ever been invited to their home as a guest. It would be hard to imagine anything further from the vaunted American ideal of assimilation, in which immigrants are expected to submerge their cultural differences in order to embrace a shared national identity. *E pluribus unum:* from many, one.

During the late 1910s and early 1920s, immigrant workers at the Ford automotive plant in Dearborn, Michigan, were given free, compulsory "Americanization" classes. In addition to English lessons, there were lectures on work habits, personal hygiene, and table manners. The first sentence they memorized was "I am a good American." During their graduation ceremony they gathered next to a gigantic wooden pot, which their teachers stirred with ten-foot ladles. The students walked through a door into the pot, wearing traditional costumes from their countries of origin and singing songs in their native languages. A few minutes later, the door in the pot opened, and the students walked out again, wearing suits and ties, waving American flags, and singing "The Star-Spangled Banner."

The European immigrants who emerged from the Ford Motor Company melting pot came to the United States because they hoped to assimilate into mainstream American society. The Hmong came to the United States for the same reason they had left China in the nineteenth century: because they were trying to *resist* assimilation. As the anthropologist Jacques Lemoine has observed, "they did not come to our countries only to save their lives, they rather came to save their selves, that is, their Hmong ethnicity." If their Hmong ethnicity had been safe in Laos, they would have preferred to remain there, just as their ancestors—for whom migration had always been a problem-solving strategy, not a footloose impulse—would have preferred to remain in China. Unlike the Ford workers who enthusiastically, or at least uncomplainingly, belted out the "The Star-Spangled Banner" (of which Foua and Nao Kao know not a single word), the Hmong are what sociologists call "involuntary migrants." It is well known that involuntary migrants, no matter what pot they are thrown into, tend not to melt.

What the Hmong wanted here was to be left alone to be Hmong: clustered in all-Hmong enclaves, protected from government interference, self-sufficient, and agrarian. Some brought hoes in their luggage. General Vang Pao has said, "For many years, right from the start, I tell the American government that we need a little bit of land where we can grow vegetables and build homes like in Laos. . . . I tell them it does not have to be the best land, just a little land where we can live." This proposal was never seriously considered. "It

was just out of the question," said a spokesman for the State Department's refugee program. "It would cost too much, it would be impractical, but most of all it would set off wild protests from [other Americans] and from other refugees who weren't getting land for themselves." . . .

Just as newly arrived immigrants in earlier eras had been called "FOBs"—Fresh Off the Boat—some social workers nicknamed the incoming Hmong, along with the other Southeast Asian refugees who entered the United States after the Vietnamese War, "JOJs": Just Off the Jet. Unlike the first waves of Vietnamese and Cambodian refugees, most of whom received several months of vocational and language training at regional "reception centers," the Hmong JOJs, who arrived after the centers had closed, were all sent directly to their new homes. (Later on, some were given "cultural orientation" training in Thailand before flying to the United States. Their classes covered such topics as how to distinguish a one-dollar bill from a ten-dollar bill and how to use a peephole.) The logistical details of their resettlement were contracted by the federal government to private nonprofit groups known as VOLAGs, or national voluntary resettlement agencies, which found local sponsors. Within their first few weeks in this country, newly arrived families were likely to deal with VOLAG officials, immigration officials, public health officials, social service officials, employment officials, and public assistance officials. The Hmong are not known for holding bureaucrats in high esteem. As one proverb puts it, "To see a tiger is to die; to see an official is to become destitute." In a study of adaptation problems among Indochinese refugees, Hmong respondents rated "Difficulty with American Agencies" as a more serious problem than either "War Memories" or "Separation from Family." Because many of the VOLAGs had religious affiliations, the JOJs also often found themselves dealing with Christian ministers, who, not surprisingly, took a dim view of shamanistic animism. A sponsoring pastor in Minnesota told a local newspaper, "It would be wicked to just bring them over and feed and clothe them and let them go to hell. The God who made us wants them to be converted. If anyone thinks that a gospel-preaching church would bring them over and not tell them about the Lord, they're out of their mind." The proselytizing backfired. According to a study of Hmong mental health problems, refugees sponsored by this pastor's religious organization were significantly more likely, when compared to other refugees, to require psychiatric treatment.

The Hmong were accustomed to living in the mountains, and most of them had never seen snow. Almost all their resettlement sites had flat topography and freezing winters. The majority were sent to cities, including Minneapolis, Chicago, Milwaukee, Detroit, Hartford, and Providence, because that was where refugee services—health care, language classes, job training, public housing—were concentrated. To encourage assimilation, and to avoid burdening any one community with more than its "fair share" of refugees, the Immigration and Naturalization Service adopted a policy of dispersal rather than clustering. Newly arrived Hmong were assigned to fifty-three cities in twenty-five different states: stirred into the melting pot in tiny, manageable portions, or, as John Finck, who worked with Hmong at the Rhode Island Office of Refugee Resettlement, put it, "spread like a thin layer of butter throughout the country so they'd disappear." In some places, clans were broken up. In others, members of only one clan were resettled, making it impossible for young people, who were forbidden by cultural taboo from marrying within their own clan, to find local marriage partners. Group solidarity, the cornerstone of Hmong social organization for more than two thousand years, was completely ignored.

Although most Hmong were resettled in cities, some nuclear families, unaccompanied by any of their extended relations, were placed in isolated rural areas. Disconnected from traditional supports, these families exhibited unusually high levels of anxiety, depression, and paranoia. In one such case, the distraught and delusional father of the Yang family—the only Hmong family sponsored by the First Baptist Church of Fairfield,

Iowa—attempted to hang himself in the basement of his wooden bungalow along with his wife and four children. His wife changed her mind at the last minute and cut the family down, but she acted too late to save their only son. An Iowa grand jury declined to indict either parent, on the grounds that the father was suffering from Post-Traumatic Stress Disorder, and the mother, cut off from all sources of information except her husband, had no way to develop an independent version of reality.

Reviewing the initial resettlement of the Hmong with a decade's hindsight, Lionel Rosenblatt, the former United States Refugee Coordinator in Thailand, conceded that it had been catastrophically mishandled. "We knew at the start their situation was different, but we just couldn't make any special provisions for them," he said. "I still feel it was no mistake to bring the Hmong here, but you look back now and say, 'How could we have done it so shoddily?'" Eugene Douglas, President Reagan's ambassador-at-large for refugee affairs, stated flatly, "It was a kind of hell they landed into. Really, it couldn't have been done much worse."

The Hmong who sought asylum in the United States were, of course, not a homogeneous lump. A small percentage, mostly the high-ranking military officers who were admitted first, were multilingual and cosmopolitan, and a larger percentage had been exposed in a desultory fashion to some aspects of American culture and technology during the war or while living in Thai refugee camps. But the experience of tens of thousands of Hmong was much like the Lees'. It is possible to get some idea of how monumental the task of adjustment was likely to be by glancing at some of the pamphlets, audiotapes, and videos that refugee agencies produced for Southeast Asian JOJs. For example, "Your New Life in the United States," a handbook published by the Language and Orientation Resource Center in Washington, D.C., included the following tips:

Learn the meaning of "WALK"–"DON'T WALK" signs when crossing the street.

To send mail, you must use stamps.

To use the phone:
1) Pick up the receiver
2) Listen for dial tone
3) Dial each number separately
4) Wait for person to answer after it rings
5) Speak.

The door of the refrigerator must be shut.

Never put your hand in the garbage disposal.

Do not stand or squat on the toilet since it may break.

Never put rocks or other hard objects in the tub or sink since this will damage them.

Always ask before picking your neighbor's flowers, fruit, or vegetables.

In colder areas you must wear shoes, socks, and appropriate outerwear. Otherwise, you may become ill.

Always use a handkerchief or a kleenex to blow your nose in public places or inside a public building.

Never urinate in the street. This creates a smell that is offensive to Americans. They also believe that it causes disease.

Spitting in public is considered impolite and unhealthy. Use a kleenex or handkerchief.

Picking your nose or your ears in public is frowned upon in the United States.

The customs they were expected to follow seemed so peculiar, the rules and regulations so numerous, the language so hard to learn, and the emphasis on literacy and the decoding of other unfamiliar symbols so strong, that many Hmong were overwhelmed. Jonas Vangay told me, "In America, we are blind because even though we have eyes, we cannot see. We are deaf because even though we have ears, we cannot hear." Some newcomers wore pajamas as street clothes; poured water on electric stoves to extinguish them; lit charcoal fires in their living rooms;

stored blankets in their refrigerators; washed rice in their toilets; washed their clothes in swimming pools; washed their hair with Lestoil; cooked with motor oil and furniture polish; drank Clorox; ate cat food; planted crops in public parks; shot and ate skunks, porcupines, woodpeckers, robins, egrets, sparrows, and a bald eagle; and hunted pigeons with crossbows in the streets of Philadelphia.

If the United States seemed incomprehensible to the Hmong, the Hmong seemed equally incomprehensible to the United States. Journalists seized excitedly on a label that is still trotted out at regular intervals: "the most primitive refugee group in America." (In an angry letter to the *New York Times,* in which that phrase had appeared in a 1990 news article, a Hmong computer specialist observed, "Evidently, we were not too primitive to fight as proxies for United States troops in the war in Laos.") Typical phrases from newspaper and magazine stories in the late seventies and eighties included "low-caste hill tribe," "Stone Age," "emerging from the mists of time," "like Alice falling down a rabbit hole." Inaccuracies were in no short supply. A 1981 article in the *Christian Science Monitor* called the Hmong language "extremely simplistic"; declared that the Hmong, who have been sewing *paj ntaub* [embroidered cloth] with organic motifs for centuries, make "no connection between a picture of a tree and a real tree"; and noted that "the Hmong have no oral tradition of literature.... Apparently no folk tales exist." Some journalists seemed to shed all inhibition, and much of their good sense as well, when they were loosed on the Hmong. My favorite passage is a 1981 *New York Times* editorial about the large number of Hmong men who had died unexpectedly in their sleep, killed—or so it was widely believed at the time— by their own nightmares.[1] After explaining that the Hmong "attributed conscious life to natural objects," the writer asked,

> What were these nightmares? Did a palm tree's fronds turn into threatening fingers? Did a forest move and march with the implacability

of the tide? Did a rose stretch on its stalk and throttle the sleeper?

Or did a gasoline hose curl and crush like a python? Was one of the dreamers pinned by a perambulating postbox? Or stabbed by scissors run amok?

("Or did the editorial writer drop acid?" I wrote in the newspaper margin when I first read this.)

Timothy Dunnigan, a linguistic anthropologist who has taught a seminar at the University of Minnesota on the media presentation of Hmong and Native Americans, once remarked to me, "The kinds of metaphorical language that we use to describe the Hmong say far more about us, and our attachment to our own frame of reference, than they do about the Hmong." So much for the Perambulating Postbox Theory. Dunnigan's comment resonates with Dwight Conquergood's observation about the uneasiness Westerners feel when confronted with the Other—for who could be more Other than the Hmong? Not only did they squat on toilets and eat skunks, not only did they bang gongs and sacrifice cows, but they also displayed what struck many people as an offensively selective interest in adopting the customs of the majority culture. For example, many Hmong quickly learned how to use telephones and drive cars, because those skills fit their own agenda of communicating with other Hmong, but failed to learn English. In 1987, when Senator Alan Simpson, then the ranking minority member of the Senate Subcommittee on Immigration and Refugee Affairs, called the Hmong "the most indigestible group in society," he sounded much like the authorities in China long ago, who were grievously insulted when the Hmong refused to speak Chinese or eat with chopsticks.

It could not be denied that the Hmong were genuinely mysterious—far more so, for instance, than the Vietnamese and Cambodians who were streaming into the United States at the same time. Hardly anyone knew how to pronounce the word "Hmong." Hardly anyone—except the anthropology graduate students who suddenly realized they could write dissertations on patrilineal exogamous clan structures without leaving their hometowns—knew what role the Hmong had played during the war, or even what war it had been, since our government had succeeded all too well in keeping the Quiet War quiet. Hardly anyone knew they had a rich history, a complex culture, an efficient social system, and enviable family values. They were therefore an ideal blank surface on which to project xenophobic fantasies.

The most expedient mode of projection has always been the rumor, and the Hmong attracted more than their share. This was to be expected. After all, the Hmong of China had had wings under their armpits and small tails. In prevalence and nastiness, American rumors about the Hmong are at least an even match for the Hmong rumors about America that circulated in the refugee camps of Thailand. Some samples: The Hmong run a white slave trade. The Hmong are given cars by the government. The Hmong force their children to run in front of cars in order to get big insurance settlements. The Hmong sell their daughters and buy their wives. Hmong women think speed bumps are washboards for scrubbing clothes, and they get run over by eighteen-wheelers. The Hmong eat dogs.[2] (That one comes complete with its own set of racist jokes. "What's the name of the Hmong cookbook? *101 Ways to Wok Your Dog.*") The dog-eating rumor has joined the national pantheon of deathless urban legends, right up there with alligators in the sewers and worms in the Big Macs. . . .

Not everyone who wanted to make the Hmong feel unwelcome stopped at slander. In the words of the president of a youth center in Minneapolis, his Hmong neighbors in the mid-eighties were "prime meat for predators." In Laos, Hmong houses had no locks. Sometimes they had no doors. Cultural taboos against theft and intra-community violence were poor preparation for life in the high-crime, inner-city neighborhoods in which most Hmong were placed. Some of the violence directed against them had nothing to do with their ethnicity; they were simply easy marks. But a good deal of it was motivated by resentment, particularly in urban areas, for what was perceived as preferential welfare treatment.[3]

In Minneapolis, tires were slashed and windows smashed. A high school student getting off a bus was hit in the face and told to "go back to China." A woman was kicked in the thighs, face, and kidneys, and her purse, which contained the family's entire savings of $400, was stolen; afterwards, she forbade her children to play outdoors, and her husband, who had once commanded a fifty-man unit in the Armée Clandestine, stayed home to guard the family's belongings. In Providence, children were beaten walking home from school. In Missoula, teenagers were stoned. In Milwaukee, garden plots were vandalized and a car was set on fire. In Eureka, California, two burning crosses were placed on a family's front lawn. In a random act of violence near Springfield, Illinois, a twelve-year-old boy was shot and killed by three men who forced his family's car off Interstate 55 and demanded money. His father told a reporter, "In a war, you know who your enemies are. Here, you don't know if the person walking up to you will hurt you."

In Philadelphia, anti-Hmong muggings, robberies, beatings, stonings, and vandalism were so commonplace during the early eighties that the city's Commission on Human Relations held public hearings to investigate the violence. One source of discord seemed to be a $100,000 federal grant for Hmong employment assistance that had incensed local residents, who were mostly unemployed themselves and believed the money should have been allocated to American citizens, not resident aliens. In one of the most grievous incidents, Seng Vang, a Hmong resident of Quebec who was visiting his mother, brothers, and sisters in west Philadelphia, was beaten with steel rods and a large rock, and left on the street with two broken legs and a brain injury. Later that day, a rifle shot was fired into his mother's apartment, breaking a window near the spot where she stood washing dishes. When Vang was treated at the University of Pennsylvania hospital, he was given a blood transfusion that was probably tainted. He was gravely ill for months with a rare form of hepatitis, and, seized by justifiable paranoia, became convinced that his doctors, too, had tried to kill him.

One thing stands out in all these accounts: the Hmong didn't fight back. I pondered that fact one day as I was thumbing through the index of Charles Johnson's *Dab Neeg Hmoob: Myths, Legends and Folk Tales from the Hmong of Laos,* which contained the following entries:

Fighting
    Enemies fighting . . . 29–46, 52–58, 198, 227,
        470–471
Revenge
    Murdered man reincarnated to revenge his
        death . . . 308–309
    Cruel 9-tongued eagle has tongues cut
        out . . . 330
    Ngao Njua boils king who sent away her
        husband . . . 362
    Family kills tiger murderer of daughter,
        husband & children . . . 403
    . . .
Vengeance
    Punishment of evil-doers by lightning . . . 11,
        20
    Wildcat tortured & killed to avenge murder
        of woman . . . 436–437

To quote from the last folktale cited: "Quickly, the rooster came down, seized the cat, threw him into the mortar of the rice mill, and started in immediately pounding him with the heavy pestle: DA DUH NDUH! DA DUH NDUH! He kept pounding until all the wildcat's bones were completely broken. And that's how the wildcat died, and that's how the story ends." It was clear that the Hmong were hardly the docile, passive, mild-mannered Asians of popular stereotype. Why hadn't the Americans who tormented the Hmong ended up like that wildcat?

Charles Johnson's background notes to another tale in *Dab Neeg Hmoob* provide a partial explanation:

Our interviews indicate that the Hmong do not fight very much. When they do, it is with fists and feet. (In contrast with some neighboring peoples [in Laos] who tend to fight a lot, seem to take it lightly, and can be friends later, if two Hmong fight once, they are likely to take it very seriously, as a big issue which they do not forget, and may remain enemies forever.)

. . . The Hmong do have an ideal of patience and stoical self-control, alluded to in the idiomatic expression often used by the Hmong to admonish someone who is acting impatiently or impulsively, or by parents in teaching good behavior to their children: "Ua siab ntev" (literally, Make, do, or act with a long liver, that is, a spirit or attitude of long-suffering, patient endurance of wrongs or difficulties).

Although on the battlefield the Hmong were known more for their fierceness than for their long livers, in the United States many were too proud to lower themselves to the level of the petty criminals they encountered, or even to admit they had been victims. An anthropologist named George M. Scott, Jr., once asked a group of Hmong in San Diego, all victims of property damage or assault, why they had not defended themselves or taken revenge. Scott wrote, "several Hmong victims of such abuse, both young and old, answered that to have done so, besides inviting further, retaliatory, abuse, would have made them feel 'embarrassed' or ashamed. . . . In addition, the current president of Lao Family [a Hmong mutual assistance organization], when asked why his people did not 'fight back' when attacked here as they did in Laos, replied simply, 'because nothing here is worth defending to us.'"

There were exceptions, of course. If he was threatened with what he perceived as unbearable *poob ntsej muag* (loss of face), a Hmong sometimes decided that his shame and embarrassment would be even greater if he didn't fight back than if he did. Several Hmong in Fresno, hearing rumors that their welfare grants might be terminated because they owned cars, sent death threats ("You take away my grant and I'm going to blow your head off") to the county Social Services Department. As visual aids, they enclosed bullets and pictures of swords in their envelopes. (The grants were not terminated, and the bullets and swords were never used.) In Chicago, an elderly Hmong man and his son, in-

sulted because an American driver had honked at them loudly and persistently, hit the American over the head with a steering-wheel locking device. The injury required thirteen stitches. When the men, Ching and Bravo Xiong, were brought to trial for aggravated battery, they asked the judge to allow each party to tell his side of the story and then drink a mixture of water and the blood of a sacrificed rooster. According to Hmong tradition, anyone who drinks rooster blood after telling a lie is destined to die within a year, so if a man partakes willingly, he is recognized as a truthteller. The judge denied this request. Instead, he sentenced the younger Xiong to two weekends in jail and six hundred hours of community service. He also ordered both men to learn English and study American culture.

Such incidents were rare. Most Hmong kept an apprehensive distance from the American penal system, which was radically different from their own. There were no prisons in their villages in Laos. The Hmong sense of justice was pragmatic and personal: how would incarceration benefit the victim? Corporal punishment was also unknown. Instead, various forms of public humiliation—a powerful deterrent in a society where loss of face was considered a worse fate than death—were employed. For example, a thief who had stolen four bars of silver might be forced to repay five bars to the victim and then be hauled off to the village chief with his hands tied, while the entire community jeered. The victim ended up enriched, the criminal suffered the shame he deserved, the criminal's innocent family kept its primary provider in the household, and any would-be thieves in the village were discouraged from potential crimes by witnessing the disgraceful spectacle. The Hmong who came to this country had heard that if they hurt someone, for whatever the reason, they would be sent to an American prison, and most of them were willing to do almost anything to avoid such an unimaginable calamity. Chao Wang Vang, a Fresno resident who had been charged with misdemeanor manslaughter after a fatal traffic accident, hanged himself in the county jail before his case came to court, not knowing he had the right to a trial and believing he would be imprisoned for the rest of his life.

In any case, Hmong who were persecuted by their neighbors could exercise a time-honored alternative to violence: flight. . . . Between 1982 and 1984, three quarters of the Hmong population of Philadelphia simply left town and joined relatives in other cities. During approximately the same period, one third of all the Hmong in the United States moved from one city to another. When they decided to relocate, Hmong families often lit off without notifying their sponsors, who were invariably offended. If they couldn't fit one of their possessions, such as a television set, in a car or bus or U-Haul, they left it behind, seemingly without so much as a backward glance. Some families traveled alone, but more often they moved in groups. When there was an exodus from Portland, Oregon, a long caravan of overloaded cars motored together down Interstate 5, bound for the Central Valley of California. With this "secondary migration," as sociologists termed it, the government's attempt to stir the Hmong evenly into the melting pot was definitively sabotaged.

Although local violence was often the triggering factor, there were also other reasons for migrating. In 1982, when all refugees who had lived in the United States for more than eighteen months stopped receiving Refugee Cash Assistance—the period of eligibility had previously been three years—many Hmong who had no jobs and no prospects moved to states that provided welfare benefits to two-parent families. Their original host states were often glad to get rid of them. For a time, the Oregon Human Resources Department, strapped by a tight state budget, sent refugees letters that pointedly detailed the levels of welfare benefits available in several other states. California's were among the highest. Thousands of Hmong also moved to California because they had heard it was an agricultural state where they might be able to farm. But by far the most important reason for relocating was reunification with other members of

one's clan. Hmong clans are sometimes at odds with each other, but within a clan, whose thousands of members are regarded as siblings, one can always count on support and sympathy. A Hmong who tries to gain acceptance to a kin group other than his own is called a *puav,* or bat. He is rejected by the birds because he has fur and by the mice because he has wings. Only when a Hmong lives among his own subspecies can he stop flitting restlessly from group to group, haunted by the shame of not belonging.

The Hmong may have been following their venerable proverb, "There's always another mountain," but in the past, each new mountain had yielded a living. Unfortunately, the most popular areas of secondary resettlement all had high unemployment rates, and they got higher. For example, in the Central Valley—which had no Hmong in 1980 and more than 20,000 three years later—the economic recession of 1982 shut down dozens of factories and other businesses, driving up local unemployment and forcing the Hmong to compete with out-of-work Americans for even the most unskilled jobs. The dream of farming quickly fizzled for all but a few hundred. Hmong farmers knew a great deal about torching fields for slash-and-burn agriculture, planting mountain rice with dibble sticks, and tapping opium pods, but they had much to learn (to quote from the course plan for a not-very-successful Hmong training program) about

> crop varieties, soil preparation, machinery and equipment, timing and succession of planting, seeds and transplants, fertilizer, pest and weed management, disease control, irrigation, erosion control, record-keeping, harvesting, washing and handling, grading and size selection, packing, conditioning, market selection, product planning, pricing strategies, shipping and receiving, advertising, merchandising, verbal and non-verbal communication skills for dealing with consumers, etc.

By 1985, at least eighty percent of the Hmong in Merced, Fresno, and San Joaquin counties were on welfare.

That didn't halt the migration. Family reunification tends to have a snowball effect. The more Thaos or Xiongs there were in one place, the more mutual assistance they could provide, the more cultural traditions they could practice together, and the more stable their community would be. Americans, however, tended to view secondary migration as an indication of instability and dependence. . . .

Seeing that the Hmong were redistributing themselves as they saw fit, and that they were becoming an economic burden on the places to which they chose to move, the federal Office of Refugee Resettlement tried to slow the migratory tide. The 1983 Highland Lao Initiative, a three-million-dollar "emergency effort" to bolster employment and community stability in Hmong communities outside California, offered vocational training, English classes, and other enticements for the Hmong to stay put. Though the initiative claimed a handful of modest local successes, the California migration was essentially unstoppable. By this time, most Hmong JOJs were being sponsored by relatives in America rather than by voluntary organizations, so the government no longer had geographic control over their placements. The influx therefore came—and, in smaller increments, is still coming—from Thailand as well as from other parts of America. Therefore, in addition to trying to prevent the Hmong from moving to high-welfare states, the Office of Refugee Resettlement started trying to encourage the ones who were already there to leave. Spending an average of $7,000 per family on moving expenses, job placement, and a month or two of rent and food subsidies, the Planned Secondary Resettlement Program, which was phased out in 1994, relocated about 800 unemployed Hmong families from what it called "congested areas" to communities with "favorable employment opportunities"—i.e., unskilled jobs with wages too low to attract a full complement of local American workers.

Within the economic limitations of blue-collar labor, those 800 families have fared well. Ninety-five percent have become self-sufficient.

They work in manufacturing plants in Dallas, on electronics assembly lines in Atlanta, in furniture and textile factories in Morganton, North Carolina. More than a quarter of them have saved enough money to buy their own houses, as have three quarters of the Hmong families who live in Lancaster County, Pennsylvania, where the men farm or work in food-processing plants, and the women work for the Amish, sewing quilts that are truthfully advertised as "locally made." Elsewhere, Hmong are employed as grocers, carpenters, poultry processors, machinists, welders, auto mechanics, tool and die makers, teachers, nurses, interpreters, and community liaisons. In a survey of Minnesota employers, the respondents were asked "What do you think of the Hmong as workers?" Eighty-six percent rated them "very good." . . .

Some younger Hmong have become lawyers, doctors, dentists, engineers, computer programmers, accountants, and public administrators. Hmong National Development, an association that promotes Hmong self-sufficiency, encourages this small corps of professionals to serve as mentors and sponsors for other Hmong who might thereby be induced to follow suit. The cultural legacy of mutual assistance has been remarkably adaptive. Hundreds of Hmong students converse electronically, trading gossip and information—opinions on the relevance of traditional customs, advice on college admissions, personal ads—via the Hmong Channel on the Internet Relay Chat system. . . . There is also a Hmong Homepage on the World Wide Web (http://www.stolaf.edu/people/cdr/hmong/) and several burgeoning Hmong electronic mailing lists, including Hmongnet, Hmongforum, and Hmong Language Users Group.[4]

The M.D.s and J.D.s and digital sophisticates constitute a small, though growing, minority. Although younger, English-speaking Hmong who have been educated in the United States have better employment records than their elders, they still lag behind most other Asian-Americans. As for Hmong workers over thirty-five, the majority are immovably wedged at or near entry level. They can't get jobs that require better English, and they can't learn English on their current jobs. The federal *Hmong Resettlement Study* cited, as an example, a Hmong worker in Dallas who after three years on the job was unable to name the machine he operated. He stated that he never expected a promotion or a pay raise other than cost-of-living increases. Other Hmong have been thwarted by placing a higher value on group solidarity than on individual initiative. In San Diego, the manager of an electronics plant was so enthusiastic about one Hmong assembly worker that he tried to promote him to supervisor. The man quit, ashamed to accept a job that would place him above his Hmong coworkers.

For the many Hmong who live in high-unemployment areas, questions of advancement are often moot. They have no jobs at all. This is the reason the Hmong are routinely called this country's "least successful refugees." It is worth noting that the standard American tests of success that they have flunked are almost exclusively economic. If one applied social indices instead—such as rates of crime, child abuse, illegitimacy, and divorce—the Hmong would probably score better than most refugee groups (and also better than most Americans), but those are not the forms of success to which our culture assigns its highest priority. Instead, we have trained the spotlight on our best-loved index of failure, the welfare rolls. In California, Minnesota, and Wisconsin, where, not coincidentally, benefits tend to be relatively generous and eligibility requirements relatively loose, the percentages of Hmong on welfare are approximately forty-five, forty, and thirty-five (an improvement over five years ago, when they were approximately sixty-five, seventy, and sixty). The cycle of dependence that began with rice drops in Laos and reinforced with daily handouts at Thai refugee camps has been completed here in the United States. The conflicting structures of the Hmong culture and the American welfare system make it almost impossible for the average family to become independent. In California, for example, a man with seven children—a typical Hmong family size—would have to make $10.60 an hour, working forty hours a week, to equal his welfare stipend and food stamp allowance. But with few marketable skills and little English, he would probably be ineligible for most jobs that paid more than minimum wage, at which, even at the newly elevated rate of $5.15 an hour, he would have to work an improbable eighty-two hours a week in order to equal his welfare allotment. In addition, until the mid-nineties in most states, if he worked more than one hundred hours a month—as a part-time worker trying to acquire job skills, for example, or a farmer in the start-up phase—his family would lose their entire welfare grant, all their food stamps, and their health insurance.[5]

The 1996 welfare reform bill, which in its present form promises to deny benefits to legal immigrants, has stirred up monumental waves of anxiety among the Hmong. Faced with the possibility of having their assistance cut off, some have applied for citizenship, although many middle-aged Hmong find the English language requirement an insuperable obstacle. (The hurdles are lower for older Hmong who came to the United States shortly after the end of the war in Laos. The language rule is waived for "lawful permanent residents" age fifty or older who have been in this country for at least twenty years, and for those age fifty-five or older who have been here at least fifteen years. The Lees, who are considering applying for citizenship, would qualify for this waiver.) Some Hmong have moved, or are planning to move, to states with better job markets. Some will become dependent on their relatives. Because a few states will probably elect to use their own funds to assist legal immigrants, some will simply continue to depend on welfare in altered, reduced, and more precarious forms.

Few things gall the Hmong more than to be criticized for accepting public assistance. For one thing, they feel they deserve the money. Every Hmong has a different version of what is commonly called "The Promise": a written or verbal contract, made by CIA personnel in Laos, that if they fought for the Americans, the Americans would aid them if the Pathet Lao won the war. After risking their lives to rescue downed American pilots, seeing their villages flattened by incidental American bombs, and being forced to flee their country because they had supported the "American War," the Hmong expected a hero's welcome here. According to many of them, the first betrayal came when the American airlifts rescued only the officers from Long Tieng, leaving nearly everyone else behind. The second betrayal came in the Thai camps, when the Hmong who wanted to come to the United States were not all automatically admitted. The third betrayal came when they arrived here and found they were ineligible for veterans' benefits. The fourth betrayal came when Americans condemned them for what the Hmong call "eating welfare." The fifth betrayal came when the Americans announced that the welfare would stop.

Aside from some older people who consider welfare a retirement benefit, most Hmong would prefer almost any other option—if other options existed. What right-thinking Hmong would choose to be yoked to one of the most bureaucratic institutions in America? (A tip from "Your New Life in the United States," on applying for cash assistance: "You should have as many of the following documents available as possible: I-94—take the original, if you can; rent bill or lease; Social Security card; any pay stubs; bank account statement or savings passbook; utility bills; medical bills or proof of medical disability; employment registration card.") What Hmong would choose to become addicted to a way of life that some clan leaders have likened to opium? And what Hmong would choose the disgrace of being *dev mus nuam yaj*, a dog waiting for scraps? Dang Moua, the Merced businessman who had kept his family alive en route to Thailand by shooting birds with a homemade crossbow, once told me, "One time when I am first in America, a Korean man tell me that if someone is lazy and doesn't work, the government still pay them. I say, you crazy! That doesn't ring my bell at all! I am not afraid of working! My parents raised me as a man! I work till the last day I leave this earth!" And indeed, Dang held three concurrent nearly full-time jobs, as a grocer, an interpreter, and a pig farmer. He was once a clerk-typist in the

American Embassy in Vientiane and speaks five languages, so his success is not one most Hmong could reasonably be expected to emulate. More typical are two middle-aged men who were interviewed in San Diego for a survey on refugee adaptation. The first said:

> I used to be a real man like any other man, but not now any longer. . . . We only live day by day, just like the baby birds who are only staying in the nest opening their mouths and waiting for the mother bird to bring the worms.

The second said:

> We are not born to earth to have somebody give us feed; we are so ashamed to depend on somebody like this. When we were in our country, we never ask anybody for help like this. . . . I've been trying very hard to learn English and at the same time looking for a job. No matter what kind of job, even the job to clean people's toilets; but still people don't even trust you or offer you such work. I'm looking at me that I'm not even worth as much as a dog's stool. Talking about this, I want to die right here so I won't see my future.

These men were both suffering from a global despair to which their economic dependence was only one of many contributing factors. In the survey for which they were interviewed, part of a longitudinal study of Hmong, Cambodians, Vietnamese, and Chinese-Vietnamese refugees, the Hmong respondents scored lowest in "happiness" and "life satisfaction." In a study of Indochinese refugees in Illinois, the Hmong exhibited the highest degree of "alienation from their environment." According to a Minnesota study, Hmong refugees who had lived in the United States for a year and a half had "very high levels of depression, anxiety, hostility, phobia, paranoid ideation, obsessive compulsiveness and feelings of inadequacy." (Over the next decade, some of these symptoms moderated, but the refugees' levels of anxiety, hostility, and paranoia showed little or no improvement.) The study that I found most disheartening was the 1987 California Southeast

Asian Mental Health Needs Assessment, a state-wide epidemiological survey funded by the Office of Refugee Resettlement and the National Institute of Mental Health. It was shocking to look at the bar graphs comparing the Hmong with the Vietnamese, the Chinese-Vietnamese, the Cambodians, and the Lao—all of whom, particularly the Cambodians, fared poorly compared to the general population—and see how the Hmong stacked up: Most depressed. Most psychosocially dysfunctional. Most likely to be severely in need of mental health treatment. Least educated. Least literate. Smallest percentage in labor force. Most likely to cite "fear" as a reason for immigration and least likely to cite "a better life."

The same bleak ground was covered from the Hmong point of view by Bruce Thowpaou Bliatout, a public health administrator in Portland, Oregon. Dr. Bliatout, who is Hmong, explained in an article on mental health concepts that such issues as job adjustment and family happiness are regarded by the Hmong as problems of the liver. If patience, as Charles Johnson noted in *Dab Neeg Hmoob*, is attributed to a long—that is, a robust and healthy—liver, what Americans would call mental illness is attributed to a liver that has become diseased or damaged through soul loss. According to Bliatout, who provided case histories for each one, some illnesses common among Hmong in the United States are:

Nyuab Siab
Translation: Difficult liver.
Causes: Loss of family, status, home, country, or any important item that has a high emotional value.
Symptoms: Excessive worry; crying; confusion; disjointed speech; loss of sleep and appetite; delusions.

Tu Siab
Translation: Broken liver.
Causes: Loss of family member; quarrel between family members; break of family unity.
Symptoms: Grief; worry; loneliness; guilt; feeling of loss; insecurity.

Lwj Siab
Translation: Rotten liver.
Causes: Stressful family relations; constant unfulfillment of goals.
Symptoms: Loss of memory; short temper; delusions.

Before I came to Merced, Bill Selvidge described to me the first Hmong patient he had ever seen. Bruce Thowpaou Bliatout would have diagnosed this patient as having a difficult liver; Bill thought of it, not so differently, as a broken heart. "Mr. Thao was a man in his fifties," said Bill. "He told me through an interpreter that he had a bad back, but after I listened for a while I realized that he'd really come in because of depression. It turned out he was an agoraphobe. He was afraid to leave his house because he thought if he walked more than a couple of blocks he'd get lost and never find his way home again. What a metaphor! He'd seen his entire immediate family die in Laos, he'd seen his country collapse, and he never *was* going to find his way home again. All I could do was prescribe antidepressants."

Mr. Thao turned out to be the first of a long procession of depressed Hmong patients whom Bill was to treat over the next three years. Bill cut to the nub of the matter when he described the man's profound loss of "home." For the Hmong in America—where not only the social mores but also the sound of every birdsong, the shape of every tree and flower, the smell of the air, and the very texture of the earth are unfamiliar—the ache of homesickness can be incapacitating. . . .

The home to which the older Hmong dream of returning—which they call *peb lub tebchaws*, "our fields and our lands"—is prewar Laos. Their memories of wartime Laos are almost unrelievedly traumatic: a "bereavement overload" that critically magnifies all their other stresses. Richard Mollica, a psychiatrist who helped found the IndoChinese Psychiatry Clinic in Boston, found that during the war and its aftermath, Hmong refugees had experienced an average of fifteen "major trauma events," such as witnessing killings and torture. Mollica has observed of his patients, "Their psychological reality is both full and empty. They are 'full' of the past; they are 'empty' of new ideas and life experiences."

"Full" of both past trauma and past longing, the Hmong have found it especially hard to deal with present threats to their old identities. I once went to a conference on Southeast Asian mental health at which a psychologist named Evelyn Lee, who was born in Macao, invited six members of the audience to come to the front of the auditorium for a role-playing exercise. She cast them as a grandfather, a father, a mother, an eighteen-year-old son, a sixteen-year-old daughter, and a twelve-year-old daughter. "Okay," she told them, "line up according to your status in your old country." Ranking themselves by traditional notions of age and gender, they queued up in the order I've just mentioned, with the grandfather standing proudly at the head of the line. "Now they come to America," said Dr. Lee. "Grandfather has no job. Father can only chop vegetables. Mother didn't work in the old country, but here she gets a job in a garment factory. Oldest daughter works there too. Son drops out of high school because he can't learn English. Youngest daughter learns the best English in the family and ends up at U.C. Berkeley. Now you line up again." As the family reshuffled, I realized that its power structure had turned completely upside down, with the twelve-year-old girl now occupying the head of the line and the grandfather standing forlornly at the tail.

Dr. Lee's exercise was an eloquent demonstration of what sociologists call "role loss." Of all the stresses in the Hmong community, role loss . . . may be the most corrosive to the ego. Every Hmong can tell stories about colonels who became janitors, military communications specialists who became chicken processors, flight crewmen who found no work at all. Dang Moua's cousin Moua Kee, a former judge, worked first in a box factory and then on the night shift in a machine shop. "When you have no country, no land, no house, no power, everyone is the same," he said with a shrug. Major Wang Seng Khang, a former battalion commander who served as leader for 10,000 Hmong in his refugee camp,

took five years to find a job as a part-time church liaison. Even then, he depended on his wife's wages from a jewelry factory to pay the rent and on his children to translate for him. Of himself and his fellow leaders, he said, "We have become children in this country."

And in this country the real children have assumed some of the power that used to belong to their elders. The status conferred by speaking English and understanding American conventions is a phenomenon familiar to most immigrant groups, but the Hmong, whose identity has always hinged on tradition, have taken it particularly hard. "Animals are responsible to their masters, and children to their parents," advised a Hmong proverb that survived unquestioned for countless generations. In prewar Laos, where families worked in the fields all day and shared a single room at night, it was not uncommon for children and their parents to be together around the clock. Remoteness and altitude insulated their villages from the majority culture. Hmong children here spend six hours in school and often several more at large in their communities, soaking up America. "My sisters don't feel they're Hmong at all," my interpreter, May Ying Xiong, once told me. "One of them has spiked hair. The youngest one speaks mostly English. I don't see the respect I gave elders at that age." Lia's sister May said, "I know how to do *paj ntaub*, but I hate sewing. My mom says, why aren't you doing *paj ntaub*? I say, Mom, this is America."

Although Americanization may bring certain benefits—more job opportunities, more money, less cultural dislocation—Hmong parents are likely to view any earmarks of assimilation as an insult and a threat. "In our families, the kids eat hamburger and bread," said Dang Moua sadly, "whereas the parents prefer hot soup with vegetables, rice, and meat like tripes or liver or kidney that the young ones don't want. The old ones may have no driver's licenses and they ask the young ones to take them some place. Sometimes the kid say I'm too busy. That is a serious situation when the kid will not obey us. The old ones are really upset." Rebellious young Hmong sometimes go beyond refusing to chauffeur their parents, and tangle with drugs or violence. In 1994, Xou Yang, a nineteen-year-old high-school dropout from Banning, California, robbed and murdered a German tourist. His father, a veteran of the war in Laos, told a reporter, "We have lost all control. Our children do not respect us. One of the hardest things for me is when I tell my children things and they say, 'I already know that.' When my wife and I try to tell my son about Hmong culture, he tells me people here are different, and he will not listen to me."

Sukey Waller, Merced's maverick psychologist, once recalled a Hmong community meeting she had attended. "An old man of seventy or eighty stood up in the front row," she said, "and he asked one of the most poignant questions I have ever heard: 'Why, when what we did worked so well for two hundred years, is everything breaking down?'" When Sukey told me this, I understood why the man had asked the question, but I thought he was wrong. Much has broken down, but not everything. Jacques Lemoine's analysis of the postwar hegira—that the Hmong came to the West to save not only their lives but their ethnicity—has been at least partially confirmed in the United States. I can think of no other group of immigrants whose culture, in its most essential aspects, has been so little eroded by assimilation. Virtually all Hmong still marry other Hmong, marry young, obey the taboo against marrying within their own clans, pay bride-prices, and have large families. Clan and lineage structures are intact, as is the ethic of group solidarity and mutual assistance. On most weekends in Merced, it is possible to hear a death drum beating at a Hmong funeral or a *txiv neeb's* gong and rattle sounding at a healing ceremony. Babies wear strings on their wrists to protect their souls from abduction by *dabs*. People divine their fortunes by interpreting their dreams. (If you dream of opium, you will have bad luck; if you dream you are covered with excrement, you will have good luck; if you dream you have a snake on your lap, you will become pregnant.) Animal sacrifices are common, even among Christian converts, a fact I first learned when May Ying Xiong told me that she would be un-

available to interpret one weekend because her family was sacrificing a cow to safeguard her niece during an upcoming open-heart operation. When I said, "I didn't know your family was so religious," she replied, "Oh yes, we're Mormon."

Even more crucially, the essential Hmong temperament—independent, insular, antiauthoritarian, suspicious, stubborn, proud, choleric, energetic, vehement, loquacious, humorous, hospitable, generous—has so far been ineradicable. Indeed, as George M. Scott, Jr., has observed, the Hmong have responded to the hardships of life in the United States "by becoming *more* Hmong, rather than less so." Summing up his impressions of the Hmong in 1924, François Marie Savina, the French missionary, attributed their ethnic durability to six factors: religion; love of liberty; traditional customs; refusal to marry outside their race; life in cold, dry, mountainous areas; and the toughening effects of war. Even though their experience here has been suffused with despair and loss, the 180,000 Hmong who live in the United States are doing passably or better on the first four counts.[6]

I was able to see the whole cycle of adjustment to American life start all over again during one of my visits to Merced. When I arrived at the Lees' apartment, I was surprised to find it crammed with people I'd never met before. These turned out to be a cousin of Nao Kao's named Joua Chai Lee, his wife, Yeng Lor, and their nine children, who ranged in age from eight months to twenty-five years. They had arrived from Thailand two weeks earlier, carrying one piece of luggage for all eleven of them. In it were packed some clothes, a bag of rice, and, because Joua is a *txiv neeb's* assistant, a set of rattles, a drum, and a pair of divinatory water-buffalo horns. The cousins were staying with Foua and Nao Kao until they found a place of their own. The two families had not seen each other in more than a decade, and there was a festive atmosphere in the little apartment, with small children dashing around in their new American sneakers and the four barefooted adults frequently throwing back their heads and laughing. Joua said to me, via May Ying's translation, "Even though there are a lot of us, you can spend the night here too." May Ying explained to me later that Joua didn't really expect me to lie down on the floor with twenty of his relatives. It was simply his way, even though he was in a strange country where he owned almost nothing, of extending a face-saving bit of Hmong hospitality.

I asked Joua what he thought of America. "It is really nice but it is different," he said, "It is very flat. You cannot tell one place from another. There are many things I have not seen before, like that"—a light switch—"and that"—a telephone—"and that"—an air conditioner. "Yesterday our relatives took us somewhere in a car and I saw a lady and I thought she was real but she was fake." This turned out to have been a mannequin at the Merced Mall. "I couldn't stop laughing all the way home," he said. And remembering how funny his mistake had been, he started to laugh again.

Then I asked Joua what he hoped for his family's future here. "I will work if I can," he said, "but I think I probably cannot. As old as I am, I think I will not be able to learn one word of English. If my children put a heart to it, they will be able to learn English and get really smart. But as for myself, I have no hope."

NOTES

1. Sudden Unexpected Death Syndrome, which until the early 1980s was the leading cause of death among young Hmong males in the United States, is triggered by cardiac failure, often during or after a bad dream. No one has been able to explain what produces the cardiac irregularity, although theories over the years have included potassium deficiency, thiamine deficiency, sleep apnea, depression, culture shock, and survivor guilt. Many Hmong have attributed the deaths to attacks by an incubuslike *dab* [spirit] who sits on the victim's chest and presses the breath out of him.

2. Like most false rumors, these all grew from germs of truth. The white-slavery rumor originated in press accounts of Vietnamese crimes in California, most of which were themselves probably unfounded. The car rumor originated in the Hmong custom of pooling the savings of several families to buy cars and other items too expensive for one family to afford. The insurance rumor originated in the $78,000 that a Hmong family in Wisconsin was awarded after their fourteen-year-old son was killed after being hit by a car. The daughter-selling rumor originated in the Hmong custom of brideprice, or "nurturing charge," as it is now sometimes called in the United States in order to avoid just such misinterpretations. The speed-bump rumor originated in the many nonlethal domestic faux pas the Hmong have actually committed. The dog-eating rumor, which, as I've mentioned elsewhere, is current in Merced, originated in Hmong ritual sacrifices.

3. Like all low-income refugees, newly arrived Hmong were automatically eligible for Refugee Cash Assistance. The RCA program enabled Hmong who would otherwise have been ineligible for welfare in some states—for instance, because an able-bodied male was present in the home—to receive benefits. But it did not enable Hmong families to receive more money than American families. In a given state, Refugee Cash Assistance payments were always identical to benefits from AFDC (Aid to Families with Dependent Children, the form of public assistance most people mean by the word "welfare").

4. The Hmong Channel is accessed almost exclusively by Hmong users. The Hmong Homepage and the electronic mailing lists also have an audience of Americans with an academic or professional interest in Hmong culture, as well as a number of Mormon elders who have been assigned missionary work in Hmong communities.

5. At the request of local public assistance agencies, the infamous "100-Hour Rule," which prevented so many Hmong from becoming economically self-sufficient, was waived in the majority of states, starting with California, between 1994 and 1996. "Basically, it required people not to work," explained John Cullen, who directed Merced's Human Services Agency during the last years of the rule's sway. The 100-Hour Rule was replaced by a formula of gradually decreasing benefits based on earnings.

6. About 150,000 Hmong—some of whom resettled in countries other than the United States, and some of whom are still in Thailand—fled Laos. The Hmong now living in the United States exceed that number because of their high birthrate.

THINKING ABOUT THE READING

Why has it been so difficult for Hmong refugees to adjust to the American way of life? Why are the Hmong such as popular target of anti-immigrant violence and persecution? Why is American society so unwilling to grant the Hmong their wish to be "left alone"? In other words, why is there such a strong desire to assimilate them into American culture? On a more general level, why is there such distaste in this society when certain ethnic groups desire to retain their traditional way of life? How do the experiences of younger Hmong compare to those of their elders?

5 Building Identity: Socialization

ociology teaches us that humans don't develop in a social vacuum. Other people, cultural practices, historical events, and social institutions can determine not only what we do and say but what we value and who we become. Our self-concept, identity, and sense of self-worth are derived from the reactions, real or imagined, of other people.

The fundamental task of any society is to reproduce itself—to create members whose behaviors, desires, and goals correspond to those defined as appropriate by that particular society. *Socialization* is the process by which individuals learn their culture and learn to live according to the norms of their society. It is how we learn to perceive our world, gain a sense of our own identity, and interact appropriately with others. This learning process occurs within the context of several social institutions—schools, religious institutions, the mass media, and the family—and it extends beyond childhood. Adults must be resocialized into a new galaxy of norms, values, and expectations each time they leave or abandon old roles and enter new ones.

The socialization process is also strongly influenced by race and social class. In "Life as the Maid's Daughter," sociologist Mary Romero describes a research interview with a young Chicana regarding her recollections of growing up as the daughter of a live-in maid for white, upper-class families living in Los Angeles. Romero describes the many ways in which this girl learns to move between different social settings, adapting to different expectations and occupying different roles. This girl must constantly negotiate the boundaries of inclusion and exclusion, as she struggles between the socializing influence of her ethnic group and that of the white, middle-class employers she and her mother live with. In so doing, she illustrates the sociological contention that we take on different identities in different situations.

Negotiating the boundaries between inclusion and exclusion is also the theme of "Boyhood, Organized Sports, and the Construction of Masculinities." Here author Michael Messner uses the world of organized sports to describe the many ways boys learn to be boys. He shows that many of the behaviors and traits commonly associated with masculinity are not inborn but are learned, especially through organized competitive sports. Participation (and success) in sports is one very significant place where boys learn the meaning and expression of masculinity and what it takes to be accepted by their peers.

The construction of identity is particularly difficult for people whose behavior is stigmatized by others. In "Coming Out: Lesbian Identities and the Categorization

Problem," Valerie Jenness notes that there is a gap between sexual behavior and sexual identity. Individuals may engage in homosexual behavior but do not necessarily identify themselves as gay or lesbian. She describes a process of "typification" whereby a woman must first be aware of the category of "lesbian" and then have multiple reasons to type herself as such before actually taking on the identity of "lesbian." Jenness shows us that the socialization process is not a solitary one. It requires input from others and always takes place in a social context that can either be supportive or, in this case, antagonistic.

Life as the Maid's Daughter

An Exploration of the Everyday Boundaries of Race, Class, and Gender

Mary Romero

Introduction

. . . My current research attempts to expand the sociological understanding of the dynamics of race, class, and gender in the everyday routines of family life and reproductive labor. . . . I am lured to the unique setting presented by domestic service . . . and I turn to the realities experienced by the children of private household workers. This focus is not entirely voluntary. While presenting my research on Chicana private household workers, I was approached repeatedly by Latina/os and African Americans who wanted to share their knowledge about domestic service—knowledge they obtained as the daughters and sons of household workers. Listening to their accounts about their mothers' employment presents another reality to understanding paid and unpaid reproductive labor and the way in which persons of color are socialized into a class-based, gendered, racist social structure. The following discussion explores issues of stratification in everyday life by analyzing the life story of a maid's daughter. This life story illustrates the potential of the standpoint of the maid's daughter for generating knowledge about race, class, and gender. . . .

Social Boundaries Presented in the Life Story

The first interview with Teresa,[1] the daughter of a live-in maid, eventually led to a life history project. I am intrigued by Teresa's experiences with her mother's white, upper-middle-class employers while maintaining close ties to her relatives in Juarez, Mexico, and Mexican friends in Los Angeles. While some may view Teresa's life as a freak accident, living a life of "rags to riches," and certainly not a common Chicana/o experience, her story represents a microcosm of power relationships in the larger society. Life as the maid's daughter in an upper-middle-class neighborhood exemplifies many aspects of the Chicano/Mexicano experience as "racial ethnics" in the United States, whereby the boundaries of inclusion and exclusion are constantly changing as we move from one social setting and one social role to another.

Teresa's narrative contains descriptive accounts of negotiating boundaries in the employers' homes and in their community. As the maid's daughter, the old adage "Just like one of the family" is a reality, and Teresa has to learn when she must act like the employer's child and when she must assume the appropriate behavior as the maid's daughter. She has to recognize all the social cues and interpret social settings correctly—when to expect the same rights and privileges as the employer's children and when to fulfill the expectations and obligations as the maid's daughter. Unlike the employers' families, Teresa and her mother rely on different ways of obtaining knowledge. The taken-for-granted reality of the employers' families do not contain conscious experiences of negotiating race and class status, particularly not in the intimate setting of the home. Teresa's status is constantly changing in response to the wide range of social settings she encounters—from employers' dinner parties with movie stars and corporate executives to Sunday dinners with Mexican garment workers in Los Angeles and factory workers in El Paso. Since Teresa remains bilingual and bicultural throughout her life, her story reflects the constant struggle and resistance to maintain her Mexican identity, claiming a reality that is neither rewarded nor acknowledged as valid.

Teresa's account of her life as the maid's daughter is symbolic of the way that racial ethnics participate in the United States; sometimes we are included and other times excluded or ignored. Teresa's story captures the reality of social stratification in the United States, that is, a racist, sexist, and class-structured society upheld by an ideology of equality. I will analyze the experiences of the maid's daughter in an upper-middle-class neighborhood in Los Angeles to investigate the ways that boundaries of race, class, and gender are maintained or diffused in everyday life. I have selected various excerpts from the transcripts that illustrate how knowledge about a class-based and gendered, racist social order is learned, the type of information that is conveyed, and how the boundaries between systems of domination impact everyday life. I begin with a brief history of Teresa and her mother, Carmen.

Learning Social Boundaries: Background

Teresa's mother was born in Piedras Negras, a small town in Aguas Calientes in Mexico. After her father was seriously injured in a railroad accident, the family moved to a small town outside Ciudad Juarez. Teresa's mother soon became involved in a variety of activities to earn money. She sold food and trinkets at the railroad station and during train stops boarded the trains seeking customers. By the time she was fifteen she moved to Juarez and took a job as a domestic, making about eight dollars a week. She soon crossed the border and began working for Anglo families in the country club area in El Paso. Like other domestics in El Paso, Teresa's mother returned to Mexico on weekends and helped support her mother and sisters. In her late twenties she joined several of her friends in their search for better-paying jobs in Los Angels. The women immediately found jobs in the garment industry. Yet, after six months in the sweatshops, Teresa's mother went to an agency in search of domestic

work. She was placed in a very exclusive Los Angeles neighborhood. Several years later Teresa was born. Her friends took care of the baby while Carmen continued working; childcare became a burden, however, and she eventually returned to Mexico. At the age of thirty-six Teresa's mother returned to Mexico with her newborn baby. Leaving Teresa with her grandmother and aunts, her mother sought work in the country club area. Three years later Teresa and her mother returned to Los Angels.

Over the next fifteen years Teresa lived with her mother in the employer's (Smith) home, usually the two sharing the maid's room located off the kitchen. From the age of three until Teresa started school, she accompanied her mother to work. She continued to live in the Smiths' home until she left for college. All of Teresa's live-in years were spent in one employer's household. The Smiths were unable to afford a full-time maid, however, so Teresa's mother began doing day work throughout the neighborhood. After school Teresa went to whatever house her mother was cleaning and waited until her mother finished working, around 4 or 6 P.M., and then returned to the Smiths' home with her mother. Many prominent families in the neighborhood knew Teresa as the maid's daughter and treated her accordingly. While Teresa wanted the relationship with the employers to cease when she went to college and left the neighborhood, her mother continued to work as a live-in maid with no residence other than the room in the employer's home; consequently, Teresa's social status as the maid's daughter continued.

Entrance into the Employers' World

Having spent her first three years in a female-dominated and monolingual, Spanish-speaking household in Juarez and in a Mexican immigrant community in Los Angeles, Teresa had a great deal to learn about the foreign environment presented by her mother's working conditions as a live-in maid. As a pre-schooler, Teresa began to learn that her social status reflected her mother's social position. In Mexico her mother was the primary wage earner for her grandmother and aunts. In this Mexican household dominated by women, Teresa received special attention and privileges as Carmen's daughter. Teresa recalled very vivid memories about entering the employers' world and being forced to learn an entirely new set of rules and beliefs of a Euro-American social order that consisted of a white, monolingual, male-dominated, and upper-middle-class family life. Teresa's account of her early years in the employers' homes is clearly from the perspective of the maid's daughter. She was an outsider and had to learn the appropriate behavior for each setting.

Rules were a major theme in Teresa's recollections of growing up in the employers' homes. She was very much aware of different rules operating in each home and of the need to act accordingly. In one of her mother's work sites, she was expected to play with the employer's children, in another she was allowed to play with their toys in specific areas of the house, and in other workplaces she sat quietly and was not allowed to touch the things around her. From the beginning she was socialized by the employers and their children, who emphasized conformity and change to their culture. The employers did not make any attempt to create a bicultural or multicultural environment in their homes or community. Teresa was expected to conform to their linguistic norms and acquiesce to becoming "the other"—the little Spanish-speaking Mexican girl among the English-speaking white children.

In the following excerpt Teresa describes her first encounter with the boundaries she confronted in the employers' homes. The excerpt is typical of her observances and recollections about her daily life, in which she is constantly assessing the practices and routines and reading signs in order to determine her position in each social setting and, thus, select the appropriate behavior. While the demands to conform and change were repeated throughout her experiences, Teresa did not embrace the opportunity to assimilate. Her resistance and struggle against assimilation is evident throughout her account, as indicated by her attempt to leave the employer's home and her refusal to speak English:

I started to realize that every day I went to somebody else's house. Everybody's house had different rules. . . . My mother says that she constantly had to watch me, because she tried to get me to sit still and I'd be really depressed and I cried or I wanted to go see things, and my mother was afraid I was going to break something and she told me not to touch anything. The kids wanted to play with me. To them, I was a novelty and they wanted to play with the little Mexican girl. . . .

I think I just had an attitude problem as I describe it now. I didn't want to play with them, they were different. My mother would tell me to go play with them, and in a little while later I'd come back and say: "Mama no me quieren aguntar"—obviously it was the communication problem. We couldn't communicate. I got really mad one day at these girls, because "no me quieran aguntar," and they did not understand what I was trying to say. They couldn't, we couldn't play, so I decided that I was going to go home, and that I didn't like this anymore. So I just opened the door and I walked out. I went around the block and I was going to walk home, to the apartment where we lived. I went out of the house, and walked around and went the opposite direction around the block. The little girls came to my mom and said: "Carmen your little daughter she left!" So my mom dropped everything and was hysterical and one of the older daughters drove my mom around and she found me on the corner. My mom was crying and crying, upset, and she asked me where I was going and I said: "Well, I was going to go home, porque no me quieran aguntar," and I didn't want to be there anymore, and I was gonna walk home. So my mother had to really keep an eye on me.

I would go to the Jones' [employers], and they had kids, and I would just mostly sit and play with their toys, but I wouldn't try to interact with them. Then they tried to teach me

English. I really resented that. They had an aquarium and fishes and they would say: "Teresa, can you say Fiishh?" and I would just glare at them, just really upset. Then I would say "Fish, no, es pescado." You know, like trying to change me, and I did not want to speak their language, or play with their kids, or do anything with them. At the Smiths they tried to teach me English. There were different rules there. I couldn't touch anything. The first things I learned were "No touch, no touch," and "Don't do this, don't do that."

At different houses, I started picking up different things. I remember that my mother used to also work for a Jewish family, when I was about five, the Altman's. We had to walk to their house. Things were different at the Altman's. At the Altman's they were really nice to me. They had this little metal stove that they let me play with. I would play with that. That was like the one thing I could play with, in the house. I immediately—I'd get there and sit down in my designated area that I could be in, and I'd play there. Sometimes, Ms. Altman would take me to the park and I'd play there. She would try to talk to me. Sometimes I would talk and sometimes I would just sit there.

Teresa's account of going to work with her mother as a toddler was not a story of a child running freely and exploring the world around her; instead, her story was shaped by the need to learn the rules set by white, monolingual, English-speaking adults and children. The emphasis in her socialization within employers' homes was quite different than that given to the employers' male children; rather than advocating independence, individuality, and adventure, Teresa was socialized to conform to female sex roles, restricting her movement and playing with gendered toys. Learning the restrictions that limit her behavior—"No touch. Don't do this"—served to educate Teresa about her social status in the employers' homes. She was clearly different from the other children, "a novelty," and was bound by rules regulating her use of social space and linguistic behavior. Teresa's resistance

against changing her language points to the strong self-esteem and pride in her culture and Mexican identity that she obtained from her experience in a Mexican household. Teresa's early memories were dominated by pressure to assimilate and to restrain her movement and activity to fit into a white, male-dominated, upper-middle-class household.

The context in which Teresa learned English was very significant in acquiring knowledge about the social order. English was introduced into her life as a means of control and to restrict her movement within employers' homes. The employers' children were involved in teaching Teresa English, and they exerted pressure that she conform to the linguistic norms governing their households. Teresa was not praised or rewarded for ability to speak Spanish, and her racial and cultural differences were only perceived positively when they served a function for the employer's family, such as a curiosity, entertainment, or a cross-cultural experience. While her mother continued to talk to Teresa in Spanish when they were alone, Carmen was not able to defend her daughter's right to decide which language to speak in the presence of the employers' families. Furthermore, Teresa observed her mother serving and waiting on the employers' families, taking orders, and being treated in a familiar manner. While Teresa referred to the employers formally, by their last names, the employers' children called Teresa's mother by her first name. The circumstances created an environment whereby all monolingual, Spanish-speaking women, including her mother, were in powerless positions. The experiences provided Teresa with knowledge about social stratification—that is, the negative value placed on the Spanish language and Mexican culture—as well as about the social status of Spanish-speaking Mexican immigrant women.

One of the Family

As Teresa got older, the boundaries between insider and outsider became more complicated, as employers referred to her and Carmen as "one of the family." Entering into an employer's world as the maid's daughter, Teresa was not only subjected to the rules of an outsider but also had to recognize when the rules changed, making her momentarily an insider. While the boundaries dictating Carmen's work became blurred between the obligations of an employee and that of a friend or family member, Teresa was forced into situations in which she was expected to be just like one of the employer's children, and yet she remained the maid's daughter. . . .

Living under conditions established by the employers made Teresa and her mother's efforts to maintain a distinction between their family life and an employer's family very difficult. Analyzing incidents in which the boundaries between the worker's family and employer's family were blurred highlights the issues that complicate the mother-daughter relationship. Teresa's account of her mother's hospitalization was the first of numerous conflicts between the two that stemmed from the live-in situation and their relationships with the employer's family. The following excerpt demonstrates the difficulty in interacting as a family unit and the degree of influence and power employers exerted over their daily lives:

When I was about ten my mother got real sick. That summer, instead of sleeping downstairs in my mother's room when my mother wasn't there, one of the kids was gone away to college, so it was just Rosalyn, David and myself that were home. The other two were gone, so I was gonna sleep upstairs in one of the rooms. I was around eight or nine, ten I guess. I lived in the back room. It was a really neat room because Rosalyn was allowed to paint it. She got her friend who was real good, painted a big tree and clouds and all this stuff on the walls. So I really loved it and I had my own room. I was with the Smiths all the time, as my parents, for about two months. My mother was in the hospital for about a month. Then when she came home, she really couldn't do anything. We would all have dinner, the Smiths were really, really supportive. I went to summer school and I took math and English and stuff like that. I was in this drama

class and I did drama and I got to do the leading role. Everybody really liked me and Ms. Smith would come and see my play. So things started to change when I got a lot closer to them and I was with them alone. I would go see my mother everyday, and my cousin was there. I think that my cousin kind of resented all the time that the Smiths spent with me. I think my mother was really afraid that now that she wasn't there that they were going to steal me from her. I went to see her, but I could only stay a couple of hours and it was really weird. I didn't like seeing my mother in pain and she was in a lot of pain. I remember before she came home the Smiths said that they thought it would be a really good idea if I stayed upstairs and I had my own room now that my mother was going to be sick and I couldn't sleep in the same bed 'cause I might hurt her. It was important for my mother to be alone. And how did I feel about that? I was really excited about that [having her own room]—you know. They said, "Your mom she is probably not going to like it and she might get upset about it, but I think that we can convince her that it is ok." When my mom came home, she understood that she couldn't be touched and that she had to be really careful, but she wanted it [having her own room] to be temporary. Then my mother was really upset. She got into it with them and said, "No, I don't want it that way." She would tell me, "No, I want you to be down here. ¿Qué crees que eres hija de ellos? You're gonna be with me all the time, you can't do that." So I would tell Ms. Smith. She would ask me when we would go to the market together, "How does your mom seem, what does she feel, what does she say?" She would get me to relay that. I would say, " I think my mom is really upset about me moving upstairs. She doesn't like it and she just says no." I wouldn't tell her everything. They would talk to her and finally they convinced her, but my mom really, really resented it and was really angry about it. She was just generally afraid. All these times that my mother wasn't there, things happened and they would take me places with them, go out to dinner with them and their friends. So that was a real big change, in that I slept upstairs and had different rules. Everything changed. I was more independent. I did my own homework; they would open the back door and yell that dinner was ready—you know. Things were just real different.

The account illustrates how assuming the role of insider was an illusion because neither the worker's daughter nor the worker ever became a member of the white, middle-class family. Teresa was only allowed to move out of the maid's quarter, where she shared a bed with her mother, when two of the employer's children were leaving home, vacating two bedrooms. This was not the first time that "space" determined whether Teresa was included in the employer's family activities. Her description of Thanksgiving dinner illustrates that she did not decide when to be included but, rather, the decision was based on the available space at the table:

> I never wanted to eat with them, I wanted to eat with my mom. Like Thanksgiving, it was always an awkward situation, because I never knew, up until dinnertime, where I was going to sit, every single time. It depended on how many guests they had, and how much room there was at the table. Sometimes, when they invited all their friends, the Carters and the Richmans, who had kids, the adults would all eat dinner in one room and then the kids would have dinner in another room. Then I could go eat dinner with the kids or sometimes I'd eat with my mom in the kitchen. It really depended.

Since Teresa preferred to eat with her mother, the inclusion was burdensome and unwanted. In the case of moving upstairs, however, Teresa wanted to have her "own" bedroom. The conflict arising from Teresa's move upstairs points to the way in which the employer's actions threatened the bonds between mother and daughter.

Teresa and Carmen did not experience the boundaries of insider and outsider in the same way. Teresa was in a position to assume a more active family role when employers made certain requests. Unlike her mother, she was not an employee and was not expected to clean and serve the employer. Carmen's responsibility for the housework never ceased, however, regardless of the emotional ties existing between employee and employers. She and her employers understood that, whatever family activity she might be participating in, if the situation called for someone to clean, pick up, or serve, that was Carmen's job. When the Smiths requested Teresa to sit at the dinner table with the family, they placed Teresa in a different class position than her mother, who was now expected to serve her daughter alongside her employer. Moving Teresa upstairs in a bedroom alongside the employer and their children was bound to drive a wedge between Teresa and Carmen. There is a long history of spatial deference in domestic service, including separate entrances, staircases, and eating and sleeping arrangements. Carmen's room reflected her position in the household. As the maid's quarter, the room was separated from the rest of the bedrooms and was located near the maid's central work area, the kitchen. The room was obviously not large enough for two beds because Carmen and Teresa shared a bed. Once Teresa was moved upstairs, she no longer shared the same social space in the employer's home as her mother. Weakening the bonds between the maid and her daughter permitted the employers to broaden their range of relationships and interaction with Teresa.

Carmen's feelings of betrayal and loss underline how threatening the employers' actions were. She understood that the employers were in a position to buy her child's love. They had already attempted to socialize Teresa into Euro-American ideals by planning Teresa's education and deciding what courses she would take. Guided by the importance they place on European culture, the employers defined the Mexican Spanish spoken by Teresa and her mother as inadequate and classified Castillan Spanish as "proper" Spanish. As a Mexican immigrant woman working as a live-in maid, Carmen was able to experience certain middle-class privileges, but her only access to these privileges was through her relationship with employers. Therefore, without the employers' assistance, she did not have the necessary connections to enroll Teresa in private schools or provide her with upper-middle-class experiences to help her develop the skills needed to survive in elite schools. Carmen only gained these privileges for her daughter at a price; she relinquished many of her parental rights to her employers. To a large degree the Smiths determined Carmen's role as a parent, and the other employers restricted the time she had to attend school functions and the amount of energy left at the end of the day to mother her own child.

Carmen pointed to the myth of "being like one of the family" in her comment, "¿Qué crees que eres hija de ellos? You're gonna be with me all the time, you can't do that." The statement underlines the fact that the bond between mother and daughter is for life, whereas the pseudofamily relationship with employers is temporary and conditional. Carmen wanted her daughter to understand that taking on the role of being one of the employer's family did not relinquish her from the responsibility of fulfilling her "real" family obligations. The resentment Teresa felt from her cousin who was keeping vigil at his aunt's hospital bed indicated that she had not been a dutiful daughter. The outside pressure from an employer did not remove her own family obligations and responsibilities. Teresa's relatives expected a daughter to be at her mother's side providing any assistance possible as a caretaker, even if it was limited to companionship. The employer determined Teresa's activity, however, and shaped her behavior into that of a middle-class child; consequently, she was kept away from the hospital and protected from the realities of her mother's illness. Furthermore, she was submerged into the employer's world, dining at the country club and interacting with their friends.

Her mother's accusation that Teresa wanted to be the Smiths' daughter signifies the feelings of betrayal or loss and the degree to which Carmen was threatened by the employer's power and authority. Yet Teresa also felt betrayal and loss and viewed herself in competition with the employers for her mother's time, attention, and love. In this excerpt Teresa accuses her mother of wanting to be part of employers' families and community:

> I couldn't understand it—you know—until I was about eighteen and then I said, "It is your fault. If I treat the Smiths differently, it is your fault. you chose to have me live in this situation. It was your decision to let me have two parents, and for me to balance things off, so you can't tell me that I said this. You are the one who wanted this." When I was about eighteen we got into a huge fight on Christmas. I hated the holidays because I hated spending them with the Smiths. My mother always worked. She worked on every holiday. She loved to work on the holidays! She would look forward to working. My mother just worked all the time! I think that part of it was that she wanted to have power and control over this community, and she wanted the network, and she wanted to go to different people's houses.

As employers, Mr. and Mrs. Smith were able to exert an enormous amount of power over the relationship between Teresa and her mother. Carmen was employed in an occupation in which the way to improve working conditions, pay, and benefits was through the manipulation of personal relationships with employers. Carmen obviously tried to take advantage of her relationship with the Smiths in order to provide the best for her daughter. The more intimate and interpersonal the relationship, the more likely employers were to give gifts, do favors, and provide financial assistance. Although speaking in anger and filled with hurt, Teresa accused her mother of choosing to be with employers and their families rather than with her own daughter. Underneath Teresa's accusation was the understanding that the only influence and status her mother had as a domestic was gained through her personal relationships with employers. Although her mother had limited power in rejecting the Smiths' demands, Teresa held her responsible for giving them too much control. Teresa argued that the positive relationship with the Smiths was done out of obedience to her mother and denied any familial feelings toward the employers. The web between employee and employers' families affected both mother and daughter, who were unable to separate the boundaries of work and family.

Maintaining Cultural Identity

A major theme in Teresa's narrative was her struggle to retain her Mexican culture and her political commitment to social justice. Rather than internalizing meaning attached to Euro-American practices and redefining Mexican culture and bilingualism as negative social traits, Teresa learned to be a competent social actor in both white, upper-middle-class environments and in working- and middle-class Chicano and Mexicano environments. To survive as a stranger in so many social settings, Teresa developed an acute skill for assessing the rules governing a particular social setting and acting accordingly. Her ability to be competent in diverse social settings was only possible, however, because of her life with the employers' children, Teresa and her mother maintained another life—one that was guarded and protected against any employer intrusion. Their other life was Mexican, not white, was Spanish speaking, not English speaking, was female dominated rather than male dominated, and was poor and working-class, not upper-middle-class. During the week Teresa and her mother visited the other Mexican maids in the neighborhoods, on weekends they occasionally took a bus into the Mexican barrio in Los Angeles to have dinner with friends, and every summer they spent a month in Ciudad Juarez with their family. . . .

Teresa's description of evening activity with the Mexican maids in the neighborhood provides insight into her daily socialization and explains how she learned to live in the employer's home without internalizing all their negative attitudes toward Mexican and working-class culture. Within the white, upper-class neighborhood in which they worked, the Mexican maids got together on a regular basis and cooked Mexican food, listened to Mexican music, and gos-

siped in Spanish about their employers. Treated as invisible or as confidants, the maids were frequently exposed to the intimate details of their employers' marriages and family life. The Mexican maids voiced their disapproval of the lenient child-rearing practices and parental decisions, particularly surrounding drug usage and the importance of material possessions:

> Raquel was the only one[maid] in the neighborhood who had her own room and own tv set. So everybody would go over to Raquel's. . . . This was my mother's support system. After hours, they would go to different people's [maid's] rooms depending on what their rooms had. Some of them had kitchens and they would go and cook all together, or do things like play cards and talk all the time. I remember that in those situations they would sit, and my mother would talk about the Smiths, what they were like. When they were going to negotiate for raises, when they didn't like certain things, I would listen and hear all the different discussions about what was going on in different houses. And they would talk, also, about the family relationships. The way they interacted, the kids did this and that. At the time some of the kids were smoking pot and they would talk about who was smoking marijuana. How weird it was that the parents didn't care. They would talk about what they saw as being wrong. The marriage relationship, or how weird it was they would go off to the beauty shop and spend all this money, go shopping and do all these weird things and the effect that it had on the kids.

The interaction among the maids points to the existence of another culture operating invisibly within a Euro-American and male-dominated community. The workers' support system did not include employers and addressed their concerns as mothers, immigrants, workers, and women. They created a Mexican-dominated domain for themselves. Here they ate Mexican food, spoke Spanish, listened to the Spanish radio station, and watched novellas on TV. Here Teresa was not a cultural artifact but, instead, a member of the Mexican community.

In exchanging gossip and voicing their opinions about the employers' lifestyles, the maids rejected many of the employers' priorities in life. Sharing stories about the employers' families allowed the Mexican immigrant women to be critical of white, upper-middle-class families and to affirm and enhance their own cultural practices and beliefs. The regular evening sessions with other working-class Mexican immigrant women were essential in preserving Teresa and her mother's cultural values and were an important agency of socialization for Teresa. For instance, the maids had a much higher regard for their duties and responsibilities as mothers than as wives or lovers. In comparison to their mistresses, they were not financially dependent on men, nor did they engage in the expensive and time-consuming activity of being an ideal wife, such as dieting, exercising, and maintaining a certain standard of beauty in their dress, makeup, and hairdos. Unlike the employers' daughters, who attended cotillions and were socialized to acquire success through marriage, Teresa was constantly pushed to succeed academically in order to pursue a career. The gender identity cultivated among the maids did not include dependence on men or the learned helplessness that was enforced in the employers' homes but, rather, promoted self-sufficiency. However, both white women employers and Mexican women employees were expected to be nurturing and caring. These traits were further reinforced when employers asked Teresa to babysit for their children or to provide them with companionship during their husbands' absences.

So, while Teresa observed her mother adapting to the employers' standards in her interaction with their children, she learned that her mother did not approve of their lifestyle and understood that she had another set of expectations to adhere to. Teresa attended the same schools as employers' children, wore similar clothes, and conducted most of her social life within the same socioeconomic class, but she remained the maid's daughter—and learned the limitations of that position. Teresa watched her mother uphold higher standards for her and apply a different set of standards to the employers' children; most of the time, however, it appeared to Teresa as if they had no rules at all.

Sharing stories about the Smiths and other employers in a female, Mexican, and worker-dominated social setting provided Teresa with a clear image of the people she lived with as employers rather than as family members. Seeing the employers through the eyes of the employees forced Teresa to question their kindness and benevolence and to recognize their use of manipulation to obtain additional physical and emotional labor from the employees. She became aware of the workers' struggles and the long list of grievances, including no annual raises, no paid vacations, no social security or health benefits, little if any privacy, and sexual harassment. Teresa was also exposed to the price that working-class immigrant women employed as live-in maids paid in maintaining white, middle-class, patriarchal communities. Employers' careers and lifestyles, particularly the everyday rituals affirming male privilege, were made possible through the labor women provided for men's physical, social, and emotional needs. Female employers depended on the maid's labor to assist in the reproduction of their gendered class status. Household labor was expanded in order to accommodate the male members of the employers' families and to preserve their privilege. Additional work was created by rearranging meals around men's work and recreation schedules and by waiting on them and serving them. Teresa's mother was frequently called upon to provide emotional labor for the wife, husband, mother, and father within an employer's family, thus freeing members to work or increase their leisure time.

Discussion

Teresa's account offers insight into the ways racial ethnic women gain knowledge about the social order and use the knowledge to develop survival strategies. As the college-educated daughter of an immigrant Mexican woman employed as a live-in maid, Teresa's experiences in the employers' homes, neighborhood, and school and her experiences in the homes of working-class Mexicano families and barrios provided her with the skills to cross the class and cultural boundaries separating the two worlds. The process of negotiating social boundaries involved an evaluation of Euro-American culture and its belief system in light of an intimate knowledge of white, middle-class families. Being in the position to compare and contrast behavior within different communities, Teresa debunked notions of "American family values" and resisted efforts toward assimilation. Learning to function in the employers' world was accomplished without internalizing its belief system, which defined ethnic culture as inferior. Unlike the employers' families, Teresa's was not able to assume the taken-for-granted reality of her mother's employers because her experiences provided a different kind of knowledge about the social order.

While the employers' children were surrounded by positive images of their race and class status, Teresa faced negative sanctions against her culture and powerless images of her race. Among employers' families she quickly learned that her "mother tongue" was not valued and that her culture was denied. All the Mexican adults in the neighborhood were in subordinate positions to the white adults and were responsible for caring for and nurturing white children. Most of the female employers were full-time homemakers who enjoyed the financial security provided by their husbands, whereas the Mexican immigrant women in the neighborhood all worked as maids and were financially independent; in many cases they were supporting children, husbands, and other family members. By directly observing her mother serve, pick up after, and nurture employers and their families, Teresa learned about white, middle-class privileges. Her experiences with other working-class Mexicans were dominated by women's responsibility for their children and extended families. Here the major responsibility of mothering was financial; caring and nurturing were secondary and were provided by the extended family or children did without. Confronted with a working

mother who was too tired to spend time with her, Teresa learned about the racial, class, and gender parameters of parenthood, including its privileges, rights, responsibilities, and obligations. She also learned that the role of a daughter included helping her mother with everyday household tasks and, eventually, with the financial needs of the extended family. Unlike her uncles and male cousins, Teresa was not exempt from cooking and housework, regardless of her financial contributions. Within the extended family Teresa was subjected to standards of beauty strongly weighted by male definitions of women as modest beings, many times restricted in her dress and physical movements. Her social worlds became clearly marked by race, ethnic, class, and gender differences.

Successfully negotiating movement from a white, male, and middle-class setting to one dominated by working-class, immigrant, Mexican women involved a socialization process that provided Teresa with the skills to be bicultural. Since neither setting was bicultural, Teresa had to become that in order to be a competent social actor in each. Being bicultural included having the ability to assess the rules governing each setting and to understand her ethnic, class, and gender position. Her early socialization in the employers' households was not guided by principles of creativity, independence, and leadership but, rather, was based on conformity and accommodation. Teresa's experiences in two different cultural groups allowed her to separate each and to fulfill the employers' expectations without necessarily internalizing the meaning attached to the act. Therefore, she was able to learn English without internalizing the idea that English is superior to Spanish or that monolingualism is normal. The existence of a Mexican community within the employers' neighborhood provided Teresa with a collective experience of class-based racism, and the maids' support system affirmed and enhanced their own belief system and culture. As Philomena Essed (1991, 294) points out, "The problem is not only how knowledge of racism is acquired but also what kind of knowledge is being transmitted."

Teresa's life story lends itself to a complex set of analyses because the pressures to assimilate were challenged by the positive interactions she experienced within her ethnic community. Like other bilingual persons in the United States, Teresa's linguistic abilities were shaped by the linguistic practices of the social settings she had access to. Teresa learned the appropriate behavior for each social setting, each marked by different class and cultural dynamics and in which women's economic roles and relationships to men were distinct. An overview of Teresa's socialization illustrates the process of biculturalism—a process that included different sets of standards and rules governing her actions as a woman, as a Chicana, and as the maid's daughter. . . .

NOTES

This essay was originally presented as a paper at the University of Michigan, "Feminist Scholarship: Thinking through the Disciplines," 30 January 1992. I want to thank Abigail J. Stewart and Donna Stanton for their insightful comments and suggestions.

1. The names are pseudonyms

REFERENCE

Essed, Philomena. 1991. *Understanding Everyday Racism.* Newbury Park, Calif.: Sage Publications.

THINKING ABOUT THE READING

Teresa's childhood is unique in that she and her mother lived in several employers' homes, requiring her to learn different sets of rules and to adjust her behavior to these new expectations each time they moved. Unlike most children who are free to explore the world around them, her childhood was shaped by the need to read signals from others to determine her position in each social setting. What were some of the different influences in Teresa's early socialization? Did she accept people's attempts to mold her, or did she resist? How did she react to her mother's employers referring to her as "one of the family"? Teresa came from a poor family, but she spent her childhood in affluent households. With respect to socialization, what advantages do you think these experiences provided her? What were the disadvantages? How do you think these experiences would have changed if she was a *son* of a live-in maid rather than a daughter? If she was a poor *white* girl rather than Latina?

Boyhood, Organized Sports, and the Construction of Masculinities

Michael A. Messner

The rapid expansion of feminist scholarship in the past two decades has led to fundamental reconceptualizations of the historical and contemporary meanings of organized sport. In the nineteenth and twentieth centuries, modernization and women's continued movement into public life created widespread "fears of social feminization," especially among middle-class men (Hantover, 1978; Kimmel, 1987). One result of these fears was the creation of organized sports as a homosocial sphere in which competition and (often violent) physicality were valued, while "the feminine" was devalued. As a result, organized sport has served to bolster a sagging ideology of male superiority, and has helped to reconstitute masculine hegemony (Bryson, 1987; Hall, 1988; Messner, 1988; Theberge, 1981).

The feminist critique has spawned a number of studies of the ways that women's sport has been marginalized and trivialized in the past (Greendorfer, 1977; Oglesby, 1978; Twin, 1978), in addition to illuminating the continued existence of structural and ideological barriers to gender equality within sport (Birrell, 1987). Only recently, however, have scholars begun to use feminist insights to examine men's experiences in sport (Kidd, 1987; Messner, 1987; Sabo, 1985). This article explores the relationship between the construction of masculine identity and boyhood participation in organized sports.

I view gender identity not as a "thing" that people "have," but rather as a *process of construction* that develops, comes into crisis, and changes as a person interacts with the social world. Through this perspective, it becomes possible to speak of "gendering" identities rather than "masculinity" or "femininity" as relatively fixed identities or statuses.

There is an agency in this construction; people are not passively shaped by their social environment. As recent feminist analyses of the construction of feminine gender identity have pointed out, girls and women are implicated in the construction of their own identities and personalities, both in terms of the ways that they participate in their own subordination and the ways that they resist subordination (Benjamin, 1988; Haug, 1987). Yet this self-construction is not a fully conscious process. There are also deeply woven, unconscious motivations, fears, and anxieties at work here. So, too, in the construction of masculinity. Levinson (1978) has argued that masculine identity is neither fully "formed" by the social context, nor is it "caused" by some internal dynamic put into place during infancy. Instead, it is shaped and constructed through the interaction between the internal and the social. The internal gendering identity may set developmental "tasks," may create thresholds of anxiety and ambivalence, yet it is only through a concrete examination of people's interactions with others within social institutions that we can begin to understand both the similarities and differences in the construction of gender identities.

In this study I explore and interpret the meanings that males themselves attribute to their boyhood participation in organized sports. In what ways do males construct masculine identities within the institution of organized sports? In what ways do class and racial differences mediate this relationship and perhaps lead to the construction of different meanings, and perhaps different masculinities? And what are some of the problems and contradictions within these constructions of masculinity?

Description of Research

Between 1983 and 1985, I conducted interviews with 30 male former athletes. Most of the men I interviewed had played the (U.S.) "major sports"—football, basketball, baseball, track. At the time of the interview, each had been retired from playing organized sports for at least five years. Their ages ranged from 21 to 48, with the median, 33; 14 were black, 14 were white, and two were Hispanic; 15 of the 16 black and Hispanic men had come from poor or working-class families, while the majority (9 of 14) of the white men had come from middle-class or professional families. All had at some time in their lives based their identities largely on their roles as athletes and could therefore be said to have had "athletic careers." Twelve had played organized sports through high school, 11 through college, and seven had been professional athletes. Though the sample was not randomly selected, an effort was made to see that the sample had a range of difference in terms of race and social class backgrounds, and that there was some variety in terms of age, types of sports played, and levels of success in athletic careers. Without exception, each man contacted agreed to be interviewed.

The tape-recorded interviews were semi-structured and took from one and one-half to six hours, with most taking about three hours. I asked each man to talk about four broad eras in his life: (1) his earliest experiences with sports in boyhood, (2) his athletic career, (3) retirement or disengagement from the athletic career, and (4) life after the athletic career. In each era, I focused the interview on the meanings of "success and failure," and on the boy's/man's relationships with family, with other males, with women, and with his own body.

In collecting what amounted to life histories of these men, my overarching purpose was to use feminist theories of masculine gender identity to explore how masculinity develops and changes as boys and men interact within the socially constructed world of organized sports. In addition to using the data to move toward some generalizations about the relationship between "masculinity and sport," I was also concerned with sorting out some of the variations among boys, based on class and racial inequalities that led them to relate differently to athletic careers. I divided my sample into two comparison groups. The first group was made up of 10 men from higher-status backgrounds, primarily white, middle-class, and professional families. The second group was made up of 20 men from lower-status backgrounds, primarily minority, poor, and working-class families.

Boyhood and the Promise of Sports

Zane Grey once said, "All boys love baseball. If they don't they're not real boys" (as cited in Kimmel, 1990). This is, of course, an ideological statement. In fact, some boys do *not* love baseball, or any other sports, for that matter. There are millions of males who at an early age are rejected by, become alienated from, or lose interest in organized sports. Yet all boys are, to a greater or lesser extent, judged according to their ability, or lack of ability, in competitive sports (Eitzen, 1975; Sabo, 1985). In this study I focus on those males who did become athletes—males who eventually poured thousands of hours into the development of specific physical skills. It is in boyhood that we can discover the roots of their commitment to athletic careers.

How did organized sports come to play such a central role in these boys' lives? When asked to recall how and why they initially got into playing sports, many of the men interviewed for this study seemed a bit puzzled: after all, playing sports was "just the thing to do." A 42-year-old black man who had played college basketball put it this way:

> It was just what you did. It's kind of like, you went to school, you played athletics, and if you didn't, there was something wrong with you. It was just like brushing your teeth: it's just what you did. It's part of your existence.

Spending one's time playing sports with other boys seemed as natural as the cycle of the seasons: baseball in the spring and summer, football in the fall, basketball in the winter—and then it was time get out the old baseball glove and begin again. As a black 35-year-old former professional football star said:

> I'd say when I wasn't in school, 95% of the time was spent in the park playing. It was the only thing to do. It just came as natural.

And a black, 34-year-old professional basketball player explained his early experiences in sports:

> My principal and teacher said, "Now if you work at this you might be pretty damned good." So it was more or less a community thing—everybody in the community said, "Boy, if you work hard and keep your nose clean, you gonna be good." Cause it was natural instinct.

"It was natural instinct." "I was a natural." Several athletes used words such as these to explain their early attraction to sports. But certainly there is nothing "natural" about throwing a ball through a hoop, hitting a ball with a bat, or jumping over hurdles. A boy, for instance, may have amazingly dexterous inborn hand-eye coordination, but this does not predispose him to a career of hitting baseballs any more than it predisposes him to a life as a brain surgeon. When one listens closely to what these men said about their early experiences in sports, it becomes clear that their adoption of the self-definition of "natural athlete" was the result of what Connell (1990) has called "a collective practice" that constructs masculinities. The boyhood development of masculine identity and status—truly problematic in a society that offers no official rite of passage into adulthood—results from a process of interaction with people and social institutions. Thus, in discussing early motivations in sports, men commonly talk of the importance of relationships with family members, peers, and the broader community.

Family Influences

Though most of the men in this study spoke of their mothers with love, respect, even reverence, their descriptions of their earliest experiences in sports are stories of an exclusively male world. The existence of older brothers or uncles who served as teachers and athletic role models—as well as sources of competition for attention and status within the family—was very common. An older brother, uncle, or even close friend of the family who was a successful athlete appears to have acted as a sort of standard of achievement against whom to measure oneself. A 34-year-old black man who had been a three-sport star in high school said:

> My uncles—my Uncle Harold went to the Detroit Tigers, played pro ball—all of 'em, everybody played sports, so I wanted to be better than anybody else. I knew that everybody in this town knew them—their names were something. I wanted my name to be just like theirs.

Similarly, a black 41-year-old former professional football player recalled:

> I was the younger of three brothers and everybody played sports, so consequently I was more or less forced into it. 'Cause one brother was always better than the next brother and then I came along and had to show them that I was just as good as them. My oldest brother was an all-city ballplayer, then my other brother comes along and he's all-city and all-state, and then I have to come along.

For some, attempting to emulate or surpass the athletic accomplishments of older male family members created pressures that were difficult to deal with. A 33-year-old white man explained that he was a good athlete during boyhood, but the constant awareness that his two older brothers had been better made it difficult for him to feel good about himself, or to have fun in sports:

> I had this sort of reputation that I followed from the playgrounds through grade school, and through high school. I followed these guys who were all-conference and all-state.

Most of these men, however, saw their relationships with their athletic older brothers and uncles in a positive light; it was within these relationships that they gained experience and developed motivations that gave them a competitive "edge" within their same-aged peer group. As a 33-year-old black man describes his earliest athletic experiences:

My brothers were role models. I wanted to prove—especially to my brothers—that I had heart, you know, that I was a man.

When asked, "What did it mean to you to be 'a man' at that age?" he replied:

Well, it meant that I didn't want to be a so-called scaredy-cat. You want to hit a guy even though he's bigger than you to show that, you know, you've got this macho image. I remember that at that young an age, that feeling was exciting to me. And that carried over, and as I got older, I got better and I began to look around me and see, well hey! I'm competitive with these guys, even though I'm younger, you know? And then of course all the compliments come—and I began to notice a change, even in my parents—especially in my father—he was proud of that, and that was very important to me. He was extremely important . . . he showed me more affection, now that I think of it.

As this man's words suggest, if men talk of their older brothers and uncles mostly as role models, teachers, and "names" to emulate, their talk of their relationships with their fathers is more deeply layered and complex. Athletic skills and competition for status may often be learned from older brothers, but it is in boys' relationships with fathers that we find many of the keys to the emotional salience of sports in the development of masculine identity.

Relationships with Fathers

The fact that boys' introductions to organized sports are often made by fathers who might otherwise be absent or emotionally distant adds a powerful emotional charge to these early experiences (Osherson, 1986). Although playing organized sports eventually came to feel "natural" for all of the men interviewed in this study, many

needed to be "exposed" to sports, or even gently "pushed" by their fathers to become involved in activities like Little League baseball. A white, 33-year-old man explained:

I still remember it like it was yesterday—Dad and I driving up in his truck, and I had my glove and my hat and all that—and I said, "Dad, I don't want to do it." He says, "What?" I says, "I don't want to do it." I was nervous. That I might fail. And he says, "Don't be silly. Lookit: There's Joey and Petey and all your friends out there." And so Dad says, "You're gonna do it, come on." And in my memory he's never said that about anything else; he just knew I needed a little kick in the pants and I'd do it. And once you're out there and you see all the other kids making errors and stuff, and you know you're better than those guys, you know: Maybe I *do* belong here. As it turned out, Little League was a good experience.

Some who were similarly "pushed" by their fathers were not so successful as the aforementioned man had been in Little League baseball, and thus the experience was not altogether a joyous affair. One 34-year-old white man, for instance, said he "inherited" his interest in sports from his father, who started playing catch with him at the age of four. Once he got into Little League, he felt pressured by his father, one of the coaches, who expected him to be the star of the team:

I'd go 0-for-four sometimes, strike out three times in a Little League game, and I'd dread the ride home. I'd come home and he'd say, "Go in the bathroom and swing the bat in the mirror for an hour," to get my swing level. . . . It didn't help much, though, I'd go out and strike out three or four times again the next game too [laughs ironically].

When asked if he had been concerned with having his father's approval, he responded:

Failure in his eyes? Yeah, I always thought that he wanted me to get some kind of [athletic] scholarship. I guess I was afraid of him when I was a kid. He didn't hit that much, but he had a rage about him—he'd rage, and that voice would just rattle you.

Similarly, a 24-year-old black man described his awe of his father's physical power and presence, and his sense of inadequacy in attempting to emulate him:

My father had a voice that sounded like rolling thunder. Whether it was intentional on his part or not, I don't know, but my father gave me a sense, an image of him being the most powerful being on earth, and that no matter what I ever did I would never come close to him. . . . There were definite feelings of physical inadequacy that I couldn't work around.

It is interesting to note how these feelings of physical inadequacy relative to the father lived on as part of this young man's permanent internalized image. He eventually became a "feared" high school football player and broke school records in weight-lifting, yet,

As I grew older, my mother and friends told me that I had actually grown to be a larger man than my father. Even though in time I required larger clothes than he, which should have been a very concrete indication, neither my brother nor I could ever bring ourselves to say that I was bigger. We simply couldn't conceive of it.

Using sports activities as a means of identifying with and "living up to" the power and status of one's father was not always such a painful and difficult task for the men I interviewed. Most did not describe fathers who "pushed" them to become sports star. The relationship between their athletic strivings and their identification with their fathers was more subtle. A 48-year-old black man, for instance, explained that he was not pushed into sports by his father, but was aware from an early age of the community status his father had gained through sports. He saw his own athletic accomplishments as a way to connect with and emulate his father:

I wanted to play baseball because my father had been quite a good baseball player in the Negro

leagues before baseball was integrated, and so he was kind of a model for me. I remember, quite young, going to a baseball game he was in—this was before the war and all—I remember being in the stands with my mother and seeing him on first base, and being aware of the crowd. . . . I was aware of people's confidence in him as a serious baseball player. I don't think my father ever said anything to me like "play sports." . . . [But] I knew he would like it if I did well. His admiration was important . . . he mattered.

Similarly, a 24-year-old white man described his father as a somewhat distant "role model" whose approval mattered:

My father was more of an example . . . he definitely was very much in touch with and still had very fond memories of being an athlete and talked about it, bragged about it. . . . But he really didn't do that much to teach me skills, and he didn't always go to every game I played like some parents. But he approved and that was important, you know. That was important to get his approval. I always knew that playing sports was important to him, so I knew implicitly that it was good and there was definitely a value on it.

First experiences in sports might often come through relationships with brothers or older male relatives, and the early emotional salience of sports was often directly related to a boy's relationship with his father. The sense of commitment that these young boys eventually made to the development of athletic careers is best explained as a process of development of masculine gender identity and status in relation to same-sex peers.

Masculine Identity and Early Commitment to Sports

When many of the men in this study said that during childhood they played sports because "it's just what everybody did," they of course meant that it was just what *boys* did. They were introduced to organized sports by older brothers and fathers, and once involved, found themselves playing within an exclusively male world. Though the separate (and unequal) gendered worlds of boys and girls came to appear as "natural," they were in fact socially constructed. Thorne's observations of children's activities in schools indicated that rather than "naturally" constituting "separate gendered cultures," there is considerable interaction between boys and girls in classrooms and on playgrounds. When adults set up legitimate contact between boys and girls, Thorne observed, this usually results in "relaxed interactions." But when activities in the classroom or on the playground are presented to children as sex-segregated activities and gender is marked by teachers and other adults ("boys line up here, girls over there"), "gender boundaries are heightened, and mixed-sex interaction becomes and explicit arena of risk" (Thorne, 1986; 70). Thus sex-segregated activities such as organized sports, as structured by adults, provide the context in which gendered identities and separate "gendered cultures" develop and come to appear natural. For the boys in this study, it became "natural" to equate masculinity with competition, physical strength, and skills. Girls simply did not (could not, it was believed) participate in these activities.

Yet it is not simply the separation of children, by adults, into separate activities that explains why many boys came to feel such strong connection with sports activities, while so few girls did. As I listened to men recall their earliest experiences in organized sports, I heard them talk of insecurity, loneliness, and especially a need to connect with other people as a primary motivation in their early sports strivings. As a 42-year-old white man stated, "The most important thing was just being out there with the rest of the guys—being friends." Another 32-year-old interviewee was born in Mexico and moved to the United States at a fairly young age. He never knew his father, and his mother died when he was only nine years old. Suddenly he felt rootless, and threw himself into sports. His initial motivations, however, do not appear to be based on a need to compete and win:

Actually, what I think sports did for me is it brought me into kind of an instant family. By being on a Little League team, or even just playing with all kinds of different kids in the neighborhood, it brought what I really wanted, which was some kind of closeness. It was just being there, and being friends.

Clearly, what these boys needed and craved was that which was most problematic for them: connection and unity with other people. But why do these young males find *organized sports* such an attractive context in which to establish "a kind of closeness" with others? Comparative observations of young boys' and girls' game-playing behaviors yield important insights into this question. Piaget (1965) and Lever (1976) both observed that girls tend to have more "pragmatic" and "flexible" orientations to the rules of games; they are more prone to make exceptions and innovations in the middle of a game in order to make the game more "fair." Boys, on the other hand, tend to have a more firm, even [in]flexible orientation to the rules of a game; to them, the rules are what protect any fairness. This difference, according to Gilligan (1982), is based on the fact that early developmental experiences have yielded deeply rooted differences between males' and females' developmental tasks, needs, and moral reasoning. Girls, who tend to define themselves primarily through connection with others, experience highly competitive situations (whether in organized sports or in other hierarchical institutions) as threats to relationships, and thus to their identities. For boys, the development of gender identity involves the construction of positional identities, where a sense of self is solidified through separation from others (Chodorow, 1978). Yet feminist psychoanalytic theory has tended to oversimplify the internal lives of men (Lichterman, 1986). Males do appear to develop positional identities, yet despite their fears of intimacy, they also retain a human need for closeness and unity with others. This ambivalence toward intimate relationships is a major thread running through masculine development throughout the life course. Here we can conceptualize what Craib (1987) calls the "elective affinity" between personality and social structure: For the boy who both seeks and fears attachment with others, the rule-bound structure of organized sports can promise to be a safe place in which to seek nonintimate attachment with others within a context that maintains clear boundaries, distance, and separation.

Competitive Structures and Conditional Self-Worth

Young boys may initially find that sports give them the opportunity to experience "some kind of closeness" with others, but the structure of sports and athletic careers often undermines the possibility of boys learning to transcend their fears of intimacy, thus becoming able to develop truly close intimate relationships with others (Kidd, 1990; Messner, 1987). The sports world is extremely hierarchical, and an incredible amount of importance is placed on winning, on "being number one." For instance, a few years ago I observed a basketball camp put on for boys by a professional basketball coach and his staff. The youngest boys, about eight years old (who could barely reach the basket with their shots) played a brief scrimmage. Afterwards, the coaches lined them up in a row in front of the older boys who were sitting in the grandstands. One by one, the coach would stand behind each boy, put his had on the boy's head (much in the manner of a priestly benediction), and the older boys in the stands would applaud and cheer, louder or softer, depending on how well or poorly the young boy was judged to have performed. The two or three boys who were clearly the exceptional players looked confident that they would receive the praise they were due. Most of the boys, though, had expressions ranging from puzzlement to thinly disguised terror on their faces as they awaited the judgments of the older boys.

This kind of experience teaches boys that it is not "just being out there with the guys—being friends" that ensures the kind of attention and connection that they crave; it is being *better* than the other guys—*beating* them—that is the key to acceptance. Most of the boys in this study did have some early successes in sports, and thus their ambivalent need for connection with others was met, at least for a time. But the institution of sport tends to encourage the development of what Schafer (1975) has called "conditional self-worth" in boys. As boys become aware that acceptance by others is contingent upon being good—a "winner"—narrow definitions of success, based upon performance and winning, become increasingly important to them. A 33-year-old black man said that by the time he was in his early teens:

> It was expected of me to do well in all my contests—I mean by my coaches, my peers, and my family. So I in turn expected to do well, and if I didn't do well, then I'd be very disappointed.

The man from Mexico, discussed above, who said that he had sought "some kind of closeness" in his early sports experiences began to notice in his early teens that if he played well, was a *winner*, he would get attention from others:

> It got to the point where I started realizing, noticing that people were always there for me, backing me all the time—sports got to be really fun because I always had some people there backing me. Finally my oldest brother started going to all my games, even though I had never really seen who he was [laughs]—after the game, you know, we never really saw each other, but he was at all my baseball games, and it seemed like we shared a kind of closeness there, but only in those situations. Off the field, when I wasn't in uniform, he was never around.

By high school, he said, he felt "up against the wall." Sports hadn't delivered what he had hoped it would, but he thought if he just tried harder, won one more championship trophy, he would get the attention he truly craved. Despite his efforts, this attention was not forthcoming. And, sadly, the pressures he had put on himself to excel in sports had taken most of the fun out of playing.

For many of the men in this study, throughout boyhood and into adolescence, this conscious striving for successful achievement became the primary means through which they sought connection with other people (Messner, 1987). But it is important to recognize that young males' internalized ambivalence about intimacy do not fully determine the contours and directions of their lives. Masculinity continues to develop through interaction with the social world—and because boys from different backgrounds are interacting with substantially different familial, educational, and other institutions, these differences will lead them to make different choices and define situations in different ways. Next, I examine the differences in the ways that boys from higher- and lower-status families and communities related to organized sports.

Status Differences and Commitments to Sports

In discussing early attractions to sports, the experiences of boys from higher- and lower-status backgrounds are quite similar. Both groups indicate the importance of fathers and older brothers in introducing them to sports. Both groups speak of the joys of receiving attention and acceptance among family and peers for early successes in sports. Note the similarities, for instance, in the following descriptions of boyhood athletic experiences of two men. First, a man born in a white, middle-class family:

> I loved playing sports so much from a very early age because of early exposure. A lot of the sports came easy at an early age, and because they did, and because you were successful at something, I think that you're inclined to strive for that gratification. It's like, if you're good, you like it, because it's instant gratification. I'm doing something that I'm good at and I'm gonna keep doing it.

Second, a black man from a poor family:

> Fortunately I had some athletic ability, and, quite naturally, once you start doing good in whatever it is—I don't care if it's jacks—you

show off what you do. That's you ability, that's your blessing, so you show it off as much as you can.

For boys from both groups, early exposure to sports, the discovery that they had some "ability," shortly followed by some sort of family, peer, and community recognition, all eventually led to the commitment of hundreds and thousands of hours of playing, practicing, and dreaming of future stardom. Despite these similarities, there are also some identifiable differences that begin to explain the tendency of males from lower-status backgrounds to develop higher levels of commitment to sports careers. The most clear-cut difference was that while men from higher-status backgrounds are likely to describe their earliest athletic experiences and motivations almost exclusively in terms of immediate family, men from lower-status backgrounds more commonly describe the importance of a broader community context. For instance, a 46-year-old man who grew up in a "poor working class" black family in a small town in Arkansas explained:

> In that community, at the age of third or fourth grade, if you're a male, they expect you to show some kind of inclination, some kind of skill in football or basketball. It was an expected thing, you know? My mom and my dad, they didn't push at all. It was the general environment.

A 48-year-old man describes sports activities as a survival strategy in his poor black community:

> Sports protected me from having to compete in gang stuff, or having to be good with my fists. If you were an athlete and got into the fist world, that was your business, and that was okay—but you didn't have to if you didn't want to. People would generally defer to you, give you your space away from trouble.

A 35-year-old man who grew up in "a poor black ghetto" described his boyhood relationship to sports similarly:

> Where I came from, either you were one of two things: you were in sports or you were out on

the streets being a drug addict, or breaking into places. The guys who were in sports, we had it a little easier, because we were accepted by both groups. . . . So it worked out to my advantage, cause I didn't get into a lot of trouble—some trouble, but not a lot.

The fact that boys in lower-status communities faced these kinds of realities gave salience to their developing athletic identities. In contrast, sports were important to boys from higher-status backgrounds, yet the middle-class environment seemed more secure, less threatening, and offered far more options. By the time most of these boys got into junior high or high school, many had made conscious decisions to shift their attentions away from athletic careers to educational and (nonathletic) career goals. A 32-year-old white college athletic director told me that he had seen his chance to pursue a pro baseball career as "pissing in the wind," and instead, focused on education. Similarly, a 33-year-old white dentist who was a three-sport star in high school, decided not to play sports in college, so he could focus on getting into dental school. As he put it,

I think I kind of downgraded the stardom thing. I thought it was small potatoes. And sure, that's nice in high school and all that, but on a broad scale, I didn't think it amounted to all that much.

This statement offers an important key to understanding the construction of masculine identity within a middle-class context. The status that this boy got through sports had been *very* important to him, yet he could see that "on a broad scale," this sort of status was "small potatoes." This sort of early recognition is more than a result of the oft-noted middle-class tendency to raise "future-oriented" children (Rubin, 1976; Sennett and Cobb, 1973). Perhaps more important, it is that the *kinds* of future orientations developed by boys from higher-status backgrounds are consistent with the middle-class context. These men's descriptions of their boyhoods reveal that they grew up immersed in a wide range of institutional frameworks, of which organized

sports was just one. And—importantly—they could see that the status of adult males around them was clearly linked to their positions within various professions, public institutions, and bureaucratic organizations. It was clear that access to this sort of institutional status came through educational achievement, not athletic prowess. A 32-year-old black man who grew up in a professional-class family recalled that he had idolized Wilt Chamberlain and dreamed of being a pro basketball player, yet his father discouraged his athletic strivings:

He knew I liked the game. I *loved* the game. But basketball was not recommended; my dad would say, "That's a stereotyped image for black youth. . . . When your basketball is gone and finished, what are you gonna do? One day, you might get injured. What are you gonna look forward to?" He stressed education.

Similarly, a 32-year-old man who was raised in a white, middle-class family, had found in sports a key means of gaining acceptance and connection in his peer group. Yet he was simultaneously developing an image of himself as a "smart student," and becoming aware of a wide range of non-sports life options:

My mother was constantly telling me how smart I was, how good I was, what a nice person I was, and giving me all sorts of positive strokes, and those positive strokes became a self-motivating kind of thing. I had this image of myself as smart, and I lived up to that image.

It is not that parents of boys in lower-status families did not also encourage their boys to work hard in school. Several reported that their parents "stressed books first, sports second." it's just that the broader social context—education, economy, and community—was more likely to *narrow* lower-status boys' perceptions of real-life options, while boys from higher-status backgrounds faced an expanding world of options. For instance, with a different socioeconomic background, one 35-year-old black man might have become a great musician instead of a star professional football running back. But he did not. When he was a child, he said, he was most interested in music:

> I wanted to be a drummer. But we couldn't afford drums. My dad couldn't go out and buy me a drum set or a guitar even—it was just one of those things; he was just trying to make ends meet.

But he *could* afford, as could so many in his socioeconomic condition, to spend countless hours at the local park, where he was told by the park supervisor

> that I was a natural—not only in gymnastics or baseball—whatever I did, I was a natural. He told me I shouldn't waste this talent, and so I immediately started watching the big guys then.

In retrospect, this man had potential to be a musician or any number of things, but his environment limited his options to sports, and he made the best of it. Even within sports, he, like most boys in the ghetto, was limited:

> We didn't have any tennis courts in the ghetto—we used to have a lot of tennis balls, but not racquets. I wonder today how good I might be in tennis if I had gotten a racquet in my hands at an early age.

It is within this limited structure of opportunity that many lower-status young boys found sports to be *the* place, rather than *a* place, within which to construct masculine identity, status, and relationships. A 36-year-old white man explained that his father left the family when he was very young and this mother faced a very difficult struggle to make ends meet. As his words suggest, the more limited a boy's options, and the more insecure his family situation, the more likely he is to make an early commitment to an athletic career:

> I used to ride my bicycle to Little League practice—if I'd waited for someone to pick me up and take me to the ball park I'd have never played. I'd get to the ball park and all the other kids would have their dad bring them to practice or games. But I'd park my bike to the side and when it was over I'd get on it and go home. Sports was the way for me to move everything to the side—family problems, just all the embarrassments—and think about one thing, and that was sports. . . . In the third grade, when the teacher went around the classroom and asked everybody, "What do you want to be when your grow up?" I said, "I want to be a major league baseball player," and everybody laughed their heads off.

This man eventually did enjoy a major league baseball career. Most boys from lower-status backgrounds who make similar early commitments to athletic careers are not so successful. As stated earlier, the career structure of organized sports is highly competitive and hierarchical. In fact, the chances of attaining professional status in sports are approximately 4:100,000 for a white man, 2:100,000 for a black man, and 3:1 million for a Hispanic man in the United States (Leonard and Reyman, 1988). Nevertheless, the immediate rewards (fun, status, attention), along with the constricted (nonsports) structure of opportunity, attract disproportionately large numbers of boys from lower-status backgrounds to athletic careers as their major means of constructing a masculine identity. These are the boys who later, as young men, had to struggle with "conditional self-worth," and, more often than not, occupational dead ends. Boys from higher-status backgrounds, on the other hand, bolstered their boyhood, adolescent, and early adult status through their athletic accomplishments. Their wide range of experiences and life changes led to an early shift away from sports careers as the major basis of identity (Messner, 1989).

Conclusion

The conception of the masculinity-sports relationship developed here begins to illustrate the idea of an "elective affinity" between social structure and personality. Organized sports is a "gendered institution"—an institution constructed by gender relations. As such, its structure and values (rules, formal organization, sex composition, etc.) reflect dominant conceptions of masculinity and femininity. Organized sports is also a "gendering institution"—an institution that helps to construct the current gender order. Part of this construction of gender is accomplished through the "masculinizing" of male bodies and minds.

Yet boys do not come to their first experiences in organized sports as "blank slates," but arrive with already "gendering" identities due to early developmental experiences and previous socialization. I have suggested here that an important thread running through the development of masculine identity is males' ambivalence toward intimate unity with others. Those boys who experience early athletic success find in the structure of organized sports an affinity with this masculine ambivalence toward intimacy: The rule-bound, competitive, hierarchical world of sport offers boys an attractive means of establishing an emotionally distant (and thus "safe") connection with others. Yet as boys begin to define themselves as "athletes," they learn that in order to be accepted (to have connection) through sports, they must be winners. And in order to be winners, they must construct relationships with others (and with themselves) that are consistent with the competitive and hierarchical values and structure of the sports world. As a result, they often develop a "conditional self-worth" that leads them to construct more instrumental relationships with themselves and others. This ultimately exacerbates their difficulties in constructing intimate relationships with others. In effect, the interaction between the young male's preexisting internalized ambivalence toward intimacy with the competitive hierarchical institution of sports has resulted in the construction of a masculine personality that is characterized by instrumental rationality, goal-orientation, and difficulties with intimate connection and expression (Messner, 1987).

This theoretical line of inquiry invites us not simply to examine how social institutions "socialize" boys, but also to explore the ways that boys' already-gendering identities interact with social institutions (which, like organized sports,

are themselves the product of gender relations). This study has also suggested that it is not some singular "masculinity" that is being constructed through athletic careers. It may be correct, from a psychoanalytic perspective, to suggest that all males bring ambivalences toward intimacy to their interaction with the world, but "the world" is a very different place for males from different racial and socioeconomic backgrounds. Because males have substantially different interactions with the world, based on class, race, and other differences and inequalities, we might expect the construction of masculinity to take on different meanings for boys and men from differing backgrounds (Messner, 1989). Indeed, this study has suggested that boys from higher-status backgrounds face a much broader range of options than do their lower-status counterparts. As a result, athletic careers take on different meanings for these boys. Lower-status boys are likely to see athletic careers as *the* institutional context for the construction of their masculine status and identities, while higher-status males make an early shift away from athletic careers toward other institutions (usually education and nonsports careers). A key line of inquiry for future studies might begin by exploring this irony of sports careers: Despite the fact that "the athlete" is currently an example of an exemplary form of masculinity in public ideology, the vast majority of boys who became most committed to athletic careers are never well-rewarded for their efforts. The fact that class and racial dynamics lead boys from higher-status backgrounds, unlike their lower-status counterparts, to move into nonsports careers illustrates how the construction of different kinds of masculinities is a key component of the overall construction of the gender order.

REFERENCES

Benjamin, J. (1988) *The Bounds of Love: Psychoanalysis, Feminism, and the Problem of Domination.* New York: Pantheon.

Birrell, S. (1987) "The woman athlete's college experience: knowns and unknowns." *J. of Sport and Social Issues* 11:82–96.

Bryson, L. (1987) "Sport and the maintenance of masculine hegemony." Women's Studies International *Forum* 10:349–360.

Chodorow, N. (1978) *The Reproduction of Mothering.* Berkeley: Univ. of California Press.

Connell, R. W. (1990) "An iron man: the body and some contradictions of hegemonic masculinity," in M. A. Messner and D. F. Sabo (eds.) *Sport, Men and the Gender Order: Critical Feminist Perspectives.* Champaign, IL: Human Kinetics.

Craib, I. (1987) "Masculinity and male dominance." *Soc. Rev.* 38:721–743.

Eitzen, D. S. (1975) "Athletics in the status system of male adolescents: a replication of Coleman's *The Adolescent Society.*" *Adolescence* 10:268–276.

Gilligan, C. (1982) *In a Different Voice: Psychological Theory and Women's Development.* Cambridge, MA: Harvard Univ. Press.

Greendorfer, S. L. (1977) "The role of socializing agents in female sport involvement." *Research Q.* 48:304–310.

Hall, M.A. (1988) "The discourse on gender and sport: from femininity to feminism." *Sociology of Sport J.* 5:330–340.

Hantover, J. (1978) "The boy scouts and the validation of masculinity." *J. of Social Issues* 34:184–195.

Haug, F. (1987) *Female Sexualization.* London: Verso.

Kidd, B. (1987) "Sports and masculinity," pp. 250–265 in M. Kaufman (ed.) *Beyond Patriarchy: Essays by Men on Pleasure, Power, and Change.* Toronto: Oxford Univ. Press.

Kidd, B. (1990) "The men's cultural centre: sports and the dynamic of women's oppression/ men's repression," in M. A. Messner and D. F. Sabo (eds.) *Sport, Men and the Gender Order: Critical Feminist Perspective.* Champaign, IL: Human Kinetics.

Kimmel, M. S. (1987) "Men's responses to feminism at the turn of the century." *Gender and Society* 1:261–283.

Kimmel, M. S. (1990) "Baseball and the reconstitution of American masculinity: 1880–1920," in M. A. Messner and D. F. Sabo (eds.) *Sport, Men and the Gender Order: Critical Feminist Perspectives.* Champaign, IL: Human Kinetics.

Leonard, W. M. II and J. M. Reyman (1988) "The odds of attaining professional athlete status: refining the computations." *Sociology of Sport J.* 5:162–169.

Lever, J. (1976) "Sex differences in the games children play." *Social Problems* 23:478–487.

Levinson, D. J. et al. (1978) *The Seasons of a Man's Life.* New York: Ballantine.

Lichterman, P. (1986) "Chodorow's psychoanalytic sociology: a project half-completed." *California Sociologist* 9:147–166.

Messner, M. (1987) "The meaning of success: the athletic experience and the development of male identity," pp. 193–210 in H. Brod (ed.) *The Making of Masculinities: The New Men's Studies.* Boston: Allen & Unwin.

Messner, M. (1988) "Sports and male domination: the female athlete as contested ideological terrain." *Sociology of Sport J.* 5:197–211.

Messner, M. (1989) "Masculinity and athletic careers." *Gender and Society* 3:71–88.

Oglesby, C. A. (ed.) (1978) *Women and Sport: From Myth to Reality.* Philadelphia: Lea & Farber.

Osherson, S. (1986) *Finding our Fathers: How a Man's Life Is Shaped by His Relationship with His Father.* New York: Fawcett Columbine.

Piaget, J. H. (1965) *The Moral Judgment of the Child.* New York: Free Press.

Rubin, L. B. (1976) *Worlds of Pain: Life in the Working Class Family.* New York: Basic Books.

Sabo, D. (1985) "Sport, patriarchy and male identity: new questions about men and sport." *Arena Rev.* 9:2.

Schafer, W. E. (1975) "Sport and male sex role socialization." *Sport Sociology Bull.* 4:47–54.

Sennett, R. and J. Cobb (1973) *The Hidden Injuries of Class.* New York: Random House.

Theberge, N. (1981) "A critique of critiques: radical and feminist writings on sport." *Social Forces* 60:2.

Thorne, B. (1986) "Girls and boys together . . . but mostly apart: gender arrangements in elementary schools," pp. 167–184 in W. W. Hartup and Z. Rubin (eds.) *Relationships and Development.* Hillsdale, NJ: Lawrence Erlbaum.

Twin, S. L. (ed.) (1978) *Out of the Bleachers: Writings on Women and Sport.* Old Westbury, NY: Feminist Press.

THINKING ABOUT THE READING

What does Messner mean when he calls organized sports a "gendered" as well as a "gendering" institution? In what ways do sports provide men with opportunities to establish their masculinity? How does the rule-bound structure of organized sports provide boys with a "safe place" to express feelings of closeness to other boys? Why do you suppose athletic success is such an important source of masculine identity for adolescent boys? Why do you suppose adolescent boys aren't able to achieve as much esteem from academic success as they are from athletic success? What role do you think the media plays in perpetuating this idea? How does social class influence the relationship between sports and masculine self-worth? As girls' athletics become more popular and a more visible feature in the culture, what is the likelihood that girls will begin to define their self-worth in terms of athletic success?

Coming Out

Lesbian Identities and the Categorization Problem

Valerie Jenness

For the last twenty years, gay and lesbian studies have focused on understanding lesbianism as a particular form of homoerotic and political experience. Central to this pursuit has been a preoccupation with rendering visible heretofore "invisible lesbians" of the past, documenting the bases upon which women have come to engage in behavior that may be identified as homosexual by themselves or by others, and describing the multitude of ways in which women come to identify themselves as lesbians. At this point in the early history of gay and lesbian studies, there is an abundance of literature which conceptualizes and comments upon these types of concerns. In general, this literature has been sensitive to the historical and cultural context in which these processes occur and produce different types of women, lesbians, and lesbian communities.

A clear message emanates from the *mélange* produced by this literature: there is a theoretical and an empirical difference between "doing" behaviors associated with lesbianism and "being" a lesbian. For example, in her now classic article "The female world of love and ritual: relations between women in nineteenth-century America," Carol Smith-Rosenberg (1975) documents the way in which romantic female friendships were comparatively common in the nineteenth century. Yet, imputations of lesbianism were absent from these relationships as they were understood to be socially acceptable and fully compatible with heterosexual marriage. Similarly, Lillian Faderman (1981) examined various psychological and social reasons why romantic friendships between women were accepted and flourished during the eighteenth century, although they did not become understood as lesbian relationships

by the participants. More recently, Martha Vicinus (1984) has examined the social origins and various phases of adolescent crushes between women in the late nineteenth and early twentieth centuries, including the ways in which participants in these relationships spoke of them as replications of heterosexual love rather than emergent lesbian relationships. In short, a "doing" is not a "being."

Taking this well-documented gap between women's behaviors, the cultural imputations of lesbianism, and the adoption of lesbian identities as a starting point, this [article] discusses the ways in which women who ultimately come to define themselves as lesbians understand the very concept of "lesbian" and relate themselves to this cultural construct at different points in their lives. The specific question pursued here is: *what is the nature of the process by which some women come to see themselves as* being *lesbian?* I grapple with the question of self-categorization by focusing on the interaction between culturally available categories, the interpretation of experiences, and the adoption of identities. To this end, this [article] relies upon existing autobiographical accounts of self-defined lesbians.[1]

. . . I argue that the adoption of a lesbian identity—the difference between "doing" and "being"—fundamentally hinges upon a process that I refer to as detypification. *Detypification is the process of redefining and subsequently reassessing the social category 'lesbian'' such that it acquires increasingly concrete and precise meanings, positive connotations, and personal applicability.* Transformations along these lines point to a patterned process of interpreting, evaluating, and adjusting to the social world that women proceed through in order to arrive at a lesbian identity, and thus claim membership in the social category of lesbian. Of course, the corresponding substantive changes in meaning associated with these shifts vary along a variety of dimensions, such as race and class, religion and ethnicity, region and nation, and education and political beliefs.

In what follows, I discuss the nature of this process. First, I note the relationship between social categories and personal identities, and argue that an awareness of the concept lesbian is a necessary prerequisite for the adoption of a lesbian identity. Then I detail the way in which "lesbian" is detypified in the process of women coming to understand themselves as an instance of that particular construct. Finally, I conclude this article with some thoughts on gay and lesbian studies' participation in the detypification process, as well as the construction of lesbianism, as we enter the twenty-first century.

Social Categories and Personal Identities

In the first instance, we interpret our world in terms of social categories. Social categories serve as a basis for self-evaluation in so far as we utilize our understanding of them as interpretative schemata to assess our experience of ourselves as an object existing in a larger social world. Put simply, identities emerge from the "kinds" of people it is possible to be in society. Accordingly, our identities emerge and are transformed as we place ourselves in various categories recognized in the community.

The construction of a lesbian identity is firmly located in a developmental process that begins with an awareness of the social category "lesbian." Regardless of how the category is understood, an awareness of the social category lesbian must be present for a woman eventually to categorize herself as a lesbian and adopt a lesbian identity. If the woman is not aware of the social category, she cannot assess her experiences in terms of that social construct and its affiliated identity. In essence, the commitment to a lesbian identity cannot occur in an environment where

the social construct "lesbian" does not exist (D'Emilio 1983; Ettore 1980; Weeks 1977). Although various behaviors, emotions, and thoughts may be experienced prior to an awareness of the social category lesbian, they cannot be (retrospectively) interpreted as such until the woman acquires an awareness of the social category lesbian.[2] Indeed, the term lesbian provides a necessary interpretative framework for women to utilize in assessing themselves.

Typifications of the Social Category Lesbian

There are many ways of becoming aware of and understanding any social category in a given socio-historical *milieu*. How one becomes aware of the social category lesbian is historically specific, yet diverse. For the purposes of this [article], how a woman becomes aware of the category lesbian is not at issue. Instead, the nature of the meanings associated with the category lesbian is of importance.

Not surprisingly, prior to the adoption of a lesbian identity, the meanings associated with the term lesbian derive from cultural typifications. Typifications are cognitive representations of a supposed . . . group; in this case, the woman's image of lesbians "in general." As a function of our stock of common knowledge, typifications are unexamined understandings that represent oversimplified opinions and images. Thus, by definition, typified understandings abstract from the concrete uniqueness of objects.[3]

For women who ultimately come to adopt a lesbian identity, the social category lesbian has three critical characteristics prior to self-categorization. First, understandings of the social category lesbian are relatively vague and derive from sources fairly removed from direct experience. Second, with rare exception, the connotations associated with the term lesbian are at best neutral and usually negative. Third and finally, the imagery associated with what it means to be a lesbian is perceived as incongruent with individual lived experience, and thus prohibits self-categorization.

During periods of their lives in which women reported understanding the social category lesbian along these lines, they did not identify themselves as lesbians. Regardless of content, typifications with these characteristics effectively allow women to disassociate themselves from the category lesbian. As Nancy clearly expressed:

> I compared this information with my own "case history." My childhood had been relatively happy. I possessed no glaring deformities that I had noticed and my biggest sexual thrill had been holding Joanie's hand. Half of me felt relieved. If that was lesbianism, clearly I had nothing to worry about. (Quoted in Cruikshank 1980: 141)

Similarly, Cynthia explained:

> It's funny, I had no idea at that point. First of all, I didn't even know what a lesbian was—well, no that's not true. There were always queer days in high school and things like that, but I never thought about it in terms of myself. I can't remember thinking about it ever—except to wear the right color on the right day so that you wouldn't be considered a queer. On the other hand, I was really programmed to be a heterosexual. But—I don't know—I don't think any more so than most kids. On the other hand, when I thought about it, my whole vision of it was just of the sleazy, gutter kind of depressing life, you know? I don't know where I got that! 'Cause I don't remember reading any books, or really hearing anything concrete. I don't remember anyone ever talking to me about it. So it had just seeped into my head is all I could figure . . . it sounded so creepy to me; I couldn't imagine doing it with someone of the same sex . . . I wasn't defining myself as a lesbian. (Quoted in Adair 1978: 141)

Finally, consider the words of Ruth who, after living with a woman for over five years, did not define herself as a lesbian:

> We considered ourselves married, although of course it was unofficial: we were both women.

> Never did I attach the label "lesbian" to either of us. I rarely thought of the term, and when I did I simply assumed that lesbians were women "out there" who were probably sick or deranged and at any rate were trying to be men. (Quoted in Baetz 1980: 17)

These comments suggest ways women implicitly and explicitly assess themselves through their general understandings of what it means to be a lesbian and then exclude themselves from membership of the category lesbian based on their typifications.

The practice of excluding oneself from the social category lesbian when it is typified in the above described manner contradicts the findings of others. For example, Grammick (1984:35) found that "physical/genital behavior and the establishment of a physical relationship directly and substantially influenced the woman to define herself as a lesbian." However, I argue that critical changes in the categorical meaning of lesbian are the decisive factor for self-categorization. The presence or absence of same-sex genital behavior or whether or not other women are found to be erotic or worthy of primary affiliation is crucial in the process of self-categorization only in so far as it facilitates a change in the typification of the social category lesbian.

Critical Revisions and Detypification

While the social categories we apply to ourselves are in a constant state of flux, they are not arbitrary. We are active in the establishment of our identities as we undergo changes in our knowledge base, including our understandings and interpretations of social categories and ourselves as an instance of them. As our understandings of the meanings associated with the kinds of people it is possible to be in society undergo substantive changes, we continually reassess the personal applicability of any given category.

Typified understandings are assumed to be an accurate assessment of reality until demonstrated otherwise. Our understandings of the world, including ourselves as an object, are generally held intact until a problematic situation al-lows—or forces—us to suspend belief in previ-ously unquestioned assumptions. As pragmatists have stressed, habitual behaviors, thoughts, and beliefs are often interrupted and suspended when the individual encounters a problematic situation, or what I refer to as a crisis.[4] Dewey succinctly explained:

> The individual has a stock of old opinions already, but she meets a new experience that puts them to a strain. Somebody contradicts them; or in a reflective moment she discovers that they contradict each other; or she hears of facts with which they are incompatible; or desires arise in her which they cease to satisfy. The result is inward trouble which she seeks to escape by modifying her previous mass of opinion. (Quoted in Thayer 1982: 216)

These modifications often result in "critical revi-sions" wherein typifications become detypified (Bittner, 1963).

Since typifications are inherently general and undetailed understandings of social objects, they inevitably fall short of complete understanding and are thus susceptible to change at any mo-ment. By definition, typifications are indetermi-nate, open-ended, and capable of revision. The question then becomes: in what ways is the social category lesbian shaded by the individuals who ultimately define themselves as a member of that category? Specifically, are the meanings and con-notations associated with the term lesbian modi-fied in specific ways which facilitate women be-ing able to categorize themselves as lesbians?

Detypification of the Social Category Lesbian

I argue that the detypification of the social category lesbian is a prerequisite for self-categorization. Detypification refers to a process through which the acquisition of a new (alterna-tive) interpretative schema allows women to rede-fine the social construct lesbian such that it is altered in three characteristic ways. First, under-standings of the social category lesbian are en-riched with detail as they are subjected to lived experiences and located in biographical contin-gencies. In the process, more concrete and precise understandings of what it means to be a lesbian are embraced. Second, the connotations associ-ated with the term lesbian become increasingly positive. And third, the imagery associated with what it means to be a lesbian is perceived as con-gruent with individual lived experience, and thus the possibility for self-categorization is enhanced.

The process of detypification is prompted by a crisis, either large or small, which results in the restructuring of the category lesbian. Quite of-ten, rethinking what it means to be a lesbian is sparked by new knowledge:

> Then, in a magazine shop in Greenwich Village, I found *The Ladder*. This small, rough periodi-cal was not full of unhappy endings. I sensed that its very existence proclaimed a kind of healthy survival I hadn't imagined possible. There were stories and poems and articles, advertisements and letters and editorials, just like in a real magazine. To a sadsack little kid who'd been badly beaten by the blows of persuasion to hide and mourn her very being, *The Ladder* allowed entry into a legitimate universe. (Lynch 1990: 45)

As another example, consider the words of Cynthia, who was introduced in the previous section:

> A girl I had known in high school who had gone out to California came to town . . . she started telling me about all these people in California who were bisexual! I'd never heard that term before. I don't know where I'd been all my life . . . I just started thinking "Weird." That sort of started me thinking about myself and about how I didn't seem to get along that well with men—in terms of romantic, I mean, it just didn't seem to happen. I started thinking. Like I had this one girlfriend who was a very physical person. Whenever she talked to people she touched them, so from then on, whenever she'd touch me I would think "Am I enjoying it?" (Quoted in Adair 1978: 141–143)

Cynthia failed to consider herself a member of the social category lesbian prior to this moment. At this point, however she "rethinks" the nature of the construct lesbian as well as her relationship to it. Specifically, as she (re)defines what it means to be lesbian, she re-evaluates herself with reference to those images.

Typifications get revised to become less general and more specific as they are employed to clarify ambiguous situations. That is, typifications undergo elaboration and/or qualification as they are shaped by experiences that arise in the course of women's lives. For example, Carol reported that she:

> Finally did make love [with another woman], but it happened just because we loved each other a lot, and I didn't connect it to lesbianism. It was a separate unit in my life. Then, I joined a consciousness-raising group in Mobile. A few months after I joined, the first two lesbian feminists ever to hit Mobile joined it. They said, "We are lesbians. We've been lovers for five years." Things started connecting in my mind. The more they would say, the more I would think, "Oh wow! This is what is going on with me." They just made everything fit together. (Quoted in Baetz 1980: 62)

As another example, Donna reflected:

> I might not have made this connection if I had only my vague attachments to women to go on. But there was a second development in my psyche when I was in my early twenties: the knowledge I got from reading a few lesbian novels and one or two studies on homosexuality. The sketchy reading did tell me a great deal about myself. In fact, by giving me a tentative sexual identity, it gave me a great deal. I was quietly satisfied to have figured it all out . . . thus was confirmed my suspicion of my emotional preferences for women which had come from reading. No longer could I interpret my unsatisfactory dating experience as a matter of mismatched minds. . . . All of the pieces of the puzzle had finally sorted themselves out and

their configuration stood the test of everyday life. (Quoted in Cruikshank 1980: 55)

Passages such as these reveal that women simultaneously reconstruct what it means to be a lesbian and reassess themselves as an instance of that particular category.

However, just because a woman retypifies what it means to be a lesbian does not ensure that she will come to understand herself as a lesbian. Retypification of what it means to be a lesbian is necessary, but not sufficient, for self-categorization. Women who categorize themselves as lesbians ultimately perceive similarities between themselves as objects and the cultural category lesbian. Congruence along these lines is *achieved* to the degree that personal experience converges with the retypified understandings. However, this in no way implies that the source or the content of the retypified construct is similar for all women. Obviously, the source and content of the retypification varies to the degree that individual lived experience varies.

Future Lesbianisms

Clearly, the process of detypification does not account for all that is included in the adoption of a lesbian identity. However, it does lie at the core of the difference between "doing" and "being," or what I call "the categorization problem." The process of detypification points to the way in which women are actively involved in ordering and interpreting their world, including themselves as an object in a larger social milieu. This is evidenced by the delicate interplay between the awareness of "lesbian" as a kind of person that it is possible to be in the world, the typification and detypification of what it means to be a lesbian, and the achievement of convergence between imagery and experience. Self-categorization as a lesbian arises out of a partial reconstruction of the social world, including ourselves, as type constructs. In essence, lesbian identities are simultaneously products of and resources for social categories.

The development of lesbian identity is, in the first instance, dependent upon the meanings that women attach to the social category lesbian. Such meanings are directly related to the meanings that are available in their immediate environment, as well as the meanings that are allowed to circulate in the wider society. Indeed, the historical invisibility of women's relationships with each other in general and lesbianism in particular, coupled with the insistence that sexual expression within women's relationships is deviant and unnatural, has constituted the greatest barrier to women's untroubled assumption of a lesbian identity.

Regardless of the now well-documented historical shifts and corresponding individual variation in the meaning of the term lesbian, since the concept "lesbian" emerged in common usage in the 1890s it has mostly been ideologically linked with invisibility and with deviance (Jay and Glasgow 1990; Katz 1976; Schur 1984). However, over twenty years of gay and lesbian studies have done much to challenge these links by making visible the range of women's experiences with each other, as well as the contexts within which they occur. In the process, lesbian research has implicitly or explicitly constructed new images of lesbians through the production and dissemination of "gay affirmative models" (Kitzinger 1987).

With the help of the gay and lesbian movement, as well as the women's movement, there has been and continues to be a proliferation of understandings of what it means to be lesbian (adjective) or *a* lesbian (noun). O'Brien (1984) has pointed out that same-sex genital sexual behavior experience has often been used as a least common denominator criterion. However, many have taken issue with this understanding by offering alternative conceptions which make genital experience and an erotic component only secondarily important. For example, Cook (1979) and Rich (1980) extend the term lesbian to refer to a range of woman-identified experiences, while radical feminists and lesbian separatists understand lesbianism as fundamentally a political statement representing the bonding of women against male supremacy. Others, such as Martin, argue that the word lesbian is "not an identity with predictable content constituting a total political and self-identification. It is a position from which to speak" (quoted in Jay and Glasgow 1990: 6). From this perspective, lesbian is not a type of person at all, it is a metaphor.

In short, throughout the 1970s and 1980s the term lesbian has become increasingly expansive—some would say problematic. For over two decades, gay and lesbian studies have contributed to this expansion by providing a now institutionalized forum for lesbians' voices to be heard in the articulation of what it means to be a lesbian. At this point in the history of lesbian studies, it may be useful to step back from our "cumulative discoveries" and examine them as our "collective constructions."

It is well past time to take inventory of the typifications of what it means to be a lesbian that emanate from lesbian studies and assess the degree to which they adequately capture and reflect distinctive new forms of women's same sex/gender relations in the so-called "post-modern era." As Stimpson surmised:

> A "lesbian identity" once entailed invisibility because no one wanted to see her. Now a "lesbian" identity might entail invisibility because the lesbian, like some supernatural creature of myth and tale, shows that no identity is stable enough to claim the reassurances of permanent visibility. (Stimpson 1990: 381)

Accordingly, are the conceptualizations of lesbianism emanating from gay and lesbian studies and remaining in common currency currently rendering invisible certain types of women, women's experiences, and women's relationships? Put another way, have the typifications emanating from lesbian studies been constructed in such a way that enable a diversity of women to locate themselves in that construct in light of their racial, class, ethnic, and religious identities, as well as the practical experiences and relevances of their lives in the course of engagement with their socio-symbolic world? At this point in our collective efforts, it is time to think seriously about the ways in which gay and lesbian studies have generated typifications which simultaneously facilitate and hinder the adoption of lesbian identities for particular women.

NOTES

1. Due to space limitations, a discussion of the materials used for this work has been reduced to a footnote. For a more lengthy discussion, see the larger work from which this article derives (Jenness 1987). What follows is a brief overview of the types of "voices" that were considered in this work. I relied upon a corpus of published material by surveying literally hundreds of autobiographical accounts of self-defined lesbians. While availability and usefulness ultimately directed the selection process, in each case the narrative was written in the first-person singular by a woman who defined herself as a lesbian. Ultimately, a diverse selection of lesbians was considered. That is, self-defined lesbians who account for a number of historical periods, a range of ages and socio-economic statuses, a variety of political camps and religious backgrounds, and a multitude of races and ethnicities were incorporated.

2. Zimmerman (1984: 558) has pointed out that "many of us would like to believe that we were born lesbian, free from the original sin of heterosexuality. Thus, as the Furies collective demonstrated, lesbians tend to reconstruct personal histories in accordance with norms established by either the dominant culture or the lesbian subculture." In her more recent work, Zimmerman (1990) has made evident the array of meanings attached to lesbianism through the proliferation of novels with lesbian themes, characters, etc.

3. The term typification should not be confused with the term stereotype. A stereotype is an image that conforms to a fixed pattern that constitutes a standardized mental picture that is held in common by others. While both stereotypes and typifications represent oversimplified opinions and understandings, the critical distinction is that a stereotype is assumed to be held in common by others, thus lacking variation in imagery. A typification, on the other hand, is not necessarily held in common by others, nor does it lack variation in imagery.

4. Crisis situations arise whenever new events are incomprehensible in terms of established assumptions. When existing expectations are violated, new sensitivities arise and new ideas emerge to be tested (Shibutani 1961, 1966).

REFERENCES

Adair, N. (1978) *Word Is Out,* San Francisco: New Glide Publications.

Baetz, J. (1980) *Lesbian Crossroads: Personal Stories of Lesbian Struggles & Triumphs,* New York: William and Morrow.

Bittner, E. (1963) "Radicalism and the organization of radical movements," *American Sociological Review* 28:928–940.

Cook, B.W. (1979) "Women alone stiff in my imagination: lesbianism and the cultural tradition," *Signs* 5:718–739.

Cruishank, M. (1980) *The Lesbian Path,* Tallahassee, FL: Naiad.

D'Emilio, J. (1983) *Sexual Politics, Sexual Communities: The Making of the Homosexual Minority in the United States,* Chicago: University of Chicago Press.

Ettore, E.M. (1980) *Lesbians, Women & Society,* London: Routledge & Kegan Paul.

Faderman, L. (1991) *Odd Girls and Twilight Lovers: A History of Lesbian Life in Twentieth-Century America,* New York: University of Columbia Press.

Grammick, J. (1984) "Developing a lesbian identity," in T. Darty and S. Potter (eds.) *Women-Identified Women,* Palo Alto, CA: Mayfield.

Jay, K., and Glasgow, J. (eds.) (1990) *Lesbian Texts and Contexts: Radical Revisions,* New York: New York University Press.

Jenness, V. (1987) *It's All a State of Mind: Social Categories, Constructed Conceptions, and Lesbian Identities,* (unpublished) Masters thesis, University of California, Santa Barbara.

Katz, J. (1990) "The invention of heterosexuality," *Socialist Review* 21:1.

Kitzinger, C. (1987) *The Social Construction of Lesbianism,* London: Sage.

Lynch, L. (1990) "Cruising the libraries," in K. Jay and J. Glasgow (eds.) *Lesbian Texts and Contexts: Radical Revisions,* New York: New York University Press.

O'Brien, S. (1984) " 'The thing not named': Willa Cather as a lesbian writer," *Signs* 9:576–599.

Rich, A. (1980) "Compulsory heterosexuality and lesbian existence" *Signs* 5:631–657.

Schur, E. (1984) *Labelling Women Deviant: Gender, Stigma, and Social Control*, Philadelphia: Temple University Press.

Shibutani, T. (1961) *Society and Personality*, Englewood Cliffs, NJ: Prentice-Hall.

Smith-Rosenberg, C. (1975) "The female world of love and ritual: relations between women in nineteenth century America," *Signs* 9:1–29.

Stimpson, C.R. (1990) "Afterward: lesbian studies," in K. Jay and J. Glasgow (eds.) *Lesbian Texts and Contexts: Radical Revisions*, New York: New York University Press, pp. 37–82.

Thayer, H. S. (1982) *Pragmatism: The Classic Writings*, Indianapolis: Harlett Publishing.

Vicinus, M. (1988) " 'They wonder to which sex I belong': the historical roots of modern lesbian identity," in *Homosexuality, Which Homosexuality?* Amsterdam: An Dekker/Schorrer, pp.171–188.

Weeks, J. (1977) *Coming Out: Homosexual Politics in Britain from the Nineteenth Century to the Present*, London: Quartet (2nd Edition 1990).

Zimmerman, B. (1984) "The politics of transliteration: lesbian personal narratives," *Signs* 9:663–682.

THINKING ABOUT THE READING

What does Jenness mean when she says that there's a difference between "doing" behaviors associated with lesbianism and "being" a lesbian? She points out that women typically begin the process of "becoming" a lesbian with vague—and sometimes negative—notions of what the category "lesbian" means. Ironically, at first they're quick to exclude themselves from this category. Eventually they modify their definition of "lesbian" (what Jenness calls "detypification"), enabling them to place themselves into the category. What prompts this redefinitional process? What roles do other people play in it? Do you think the culture assists or impedes this reconstruction of identity? How do you think this process differs for gay men who publicly acknowledge their sexuality? Can the stages of self-categorization Jenness identifies be applied to heterosexuals? In other words, is there a difference between "doing" heterosexual behaviors and "being" heterosexual?

6 Building Image: The Presentation of Self

A significant portion of social life is influenced by the images we form of others. We typically form impressions of people based on an initial assessment of their social group membership (race, age, gender, and so on), their personal attributes (for example, physical attractiveness), and the verbal and nonverbal messages they provide. Such assessments are usually accompanied by a set of expectations we've learned to associate with members of certain social groups or people with certain attributes. Such judgments allow us to place people in broad categories and provide a degree of predictability to forthcoming interactions.

But while we are gathering information about others to form impressions of them, we are fully aware that they are doing the same thing with us. Early in life, most of us learn that it is to our advantage to have people think highly of us. Hence, through a process called *impression management*, we attempt to control and manipulate information about ourselves to influence the impressions others form of us. Impression management provides the link between the way we perceive ourselves and the way we want others to perceive us. We've all been in situations—a first date, a job interview, meeting a girlfriend's or boyfriend's family for the first time—in which we've felt compelled to "make a good impression." What we often fail to realize, however, is that personal impression management can often be influenced by larger organizational and institutional forces.

In "Frederick the Great or Frederick's of Hollywood?" sociologist Melissa Herbert shows us how impression management in some institutional settings is made especially difficult by conflicting expectations. She draws from her research interviews to explore the different impression management strategies of women in the military. These women are under constant pressure to present themselves as tough women who are capable of doing work that has been traditionally considered a "man's job." They must be able to prove to their fellow soldiers that they are up to the task and can be counted on in life-or-death situations. At the same time, they must take care to maintain the impression that they are still feminine. Military women use a variety of strategies to manage this double-bind, although their choice of strategy can have important implications regarding the perpetuation of gender stereotypes.

Having to deal with the uncomfortable or inaccurate impressions others form of us is also the theme of Jill Nelson's article, "Volunteer Slavery: My Authentic Negro Experience." Here, Nelson, who is a journalist, describes a job interview she had for a position at the *Washington Post*. She paints a vivid picture of how she was consciously aware of having to manage the impression that she presented to her interviewer, an older, upper-class, white man. During the course of the interview, she notices how certain aspects of her class and cultural background enable the interviewer to think he has a connection to her despite her being a black woman.

Sometimes our very survival requires astute impression management. In their article, "Suspended Identity," Thomas Schmid and Richard Jones show that whereas people are sometimes motivated to present an image of themselves as likable and sophisticated, other times identity transformations require more drastic impression management techniques. Through participant observation in a maximum security prison—one of the researchers was an inmate serving a year-long felony sentence—the authors show how inmates must suspend their preprison identities and construct an inauthentic and often fearsome prison identity to survive the rigors of prison life. Most inmates discover that they can never fully recover their preprison identity upon release. They cannot return to being the same person they were before imprisonment. Here, too, we see how institutional demands can dictate the types of impressions we want others to form of us.

Frederick the Great or Frederick's of Hollywood?

The Accomplishment of Gender Among Women in the Military

Melissa S. Herbert

Introduction

In an article on military culture, Karen Dunivin writes, "the combat, masculine-warrior paradigm is the essence of military culture" (1994: 534). For military women, this may pose something of a contradiction. Women are often expected, by virtue of the perceived relationship between sex and gender, to display societal norms of femininity. What is expected when women fill an occupational role whose defining characteristics are inexorably linked with masculinity? While these women, by virtue of being in the military, fill a masculine work-role, it is quite possible that they are also penalized for being "too masculine," or, in essence, violating the societal expectations that they maintain some degree of femininity.

Masculinity in military men is not only rewarded, but is the primary construct around which resocialization as a soldier takes place. It is not surprising that femininity, or characteristics believed to be associated with femininity, would be discouraged. On the other hand, the military, reflecting the broader society, may find that women's femininity serves "to validate male identity and both individual and collective male power" (Lenskyj 1986: 56). This is, I believe, illustrated by the recently abandoned Marine Corps policy of requiring female Marines to undergo make-up and etiquette training and in current regulations that require women's hair not be cut "so short as to appear masculine." Additionally, the military is highly traditional, primarily conservative, institution in which we may expect the expression, "men are men and women are women" to be taken seriously. Exactly how are women in the military supposed to "be women?"...

Perceptions of women and their "fit" with what is believed to be gender appropriate may be critical to the ability of women to become accepted as members of the military. The integration of women into an institution *defined* by its association with masculinity may pose an interesting dilemma for military women. Can one truly be a soldier[1] and a woman and not be viewed as deviating either from what it means to be a soldier, or from what it means to be a woman? I can recall being asked by a fellow soldier why I, and other women, didn't "dress up" when we were off duty. It struck me then, as it does now, that we were expected to do our jobs "like the men," and transform "into women" once we removed our flak jackets and helmets and turned in our rifles and ammunition. One respondent spoke to these contradictions when, addressing men's perceptions, she wrote, "If you're too feminine, then you're not strong enough to command respect and lead men into battle, but if you're strong and aggressive you're not being a woman."

Those in the military, but particularly women, must "do gender." In their article, "Doing Gender," West and Zimmerman argue that gender is "a routine accomplishment embedded in everyday interaction" (1987: 125). . . . . Gender is "the local management of conduct in relation to normative conceptions of appropriate attitudes and activities for particular sex categories" (West and Fenstermaker 1993: 156). Although women in the military are clearly recognized as women, that is, as belonging to both the female sex (i.e., physiologically female) and female sex category (i.e., perceived as physiologically female; what others might call gender), given their role as members of the military, these women must constantly create and manage their gendered identities. While all women must do so, it should be noted that men also "do gender," on a daily basis. As Ronnie Steinberg notes, men "actively recreate their dominance every day" (1992: 576).

The military, I believe, is a particularly good site in which to examine the "everyday" ways in which women negotiate a world in which they must simultaneously be recognized and accepted as women, but must perform a job that has been perceived by many as appropriate only for men. Not only has the "soldier" been constructed, both ideologically and historically, as male, but soldiering has been the very means by which men have "become" men. Thus, the masculinity of soldiering is not "just" masculinity, but hyper-masculinity.... While women and men throughout society must "do gender," the increased salience of gender within the military makes it possible that it may be even more true within that setting, at least with regard to traditional conceptions of gender.

... [In this article I focus on the interactional processes related to the performance of gender in institutional settings.] "Interaction between individuals and groups is the medium for much institutional functioning, for decision making and image production" (Acker 1992: 568). It is through this process that gender is created and re-created. Goffman, addressing the "interactional field" and the interactions themselves, argues that "these scenes do not so much allow for the expression of natural differences between the sexes as for the production of that difference itself" (1977: 324). Gender is not accomplished solely on the basis of specific actions (e.g., wearing a skirt instead of pants), but it requires that interactions occur in which the action is recognized as placing the actor in a particular gendered context. West and Zimmerman write:

> While it is individuals who do gender, the enterprise is fundamentally interactional and institutional in character, for accountability is a feature of social relationships and its idiom is

drawn from the institutionalized arena in which those relationships are enacted (1987: 136–137).

... West and Zimmerman (1987) pose three central questions: "If, for example, individuals strive to achieve gender in encounters with others, how does a culture instill the need to achieve it? What is the relationship between the production of gender at the level of interaction and such institutional arrangements as the division of labor in society? And, perhaps most important, how does doing gender contribute to the subordination of women by men?" (140). In this [article] I respond to these questions by examining the place of gender in the lives of women in the United States military....

Methodology

The findings in this paper are based on 256 surveys collected from women who are veterans of, or currently serving in, the United States military. I used a variety of avenues to identify potential respondents including posting notices at women's bookstores, gay and lesbian community centers, on computer bulletin boards, in publications such as *Minerva's Bulletin Board, The Register* (the newsletter of the Women in Military Service for America Project), and at college and university veterans' program offices around the nation. The 15-page questionnaire contained seven sections with items in formats varying among yes/no questions, multiple choice questions, open-ended questions, check off items, and Likert-scale items. Each section has a different focus. The sections of the questionnaire assess the following: (1) personal information, (2) military service, (3) education, (4) personal assessment of military service, (5) personal resources, (6) gender, and (7) sexuality. The surveys were used to create a computerized data set as well as text files of the answers to open-ended questions. I should note that my own military service formed the basis for many of the questions. Though my experience is limited to the

Army, I was able to formulate questions about uniforms, on-post and off-post activities, chain of command, etc., on the basis of not only familiarity with scholarship on women in the military, but with the aid of 15 years experience in both the active and reserve components of the US Army as both enlisted and officer.

The women who answered the survey came from over 40 states, all branches, all ranks except flag officer (i.e., General/Admiral), and served as early as the 1950s. . . .

The survey asked respondents to indicate whether they believed that penalties exist for women who are perceived as "too feminine." In a separate question, it asked whether they believe that penalties exist for women who are perceived as "too masculine" and to provide examples of what the penalties might be. The results presented here are based on descriptive statistics and analyses of the open-ended responses about types of penalties.

The survey also included a list of 28 behaviors. Respondents were asked to "check any of the following that you believe applied to yourself" (while on active duty). These items consisted of behaviors such as polishing one's fingernails, wearing cologne on duty, keeping one's hair trimmed above the collar, socializing with the men in the unit, and so on. Respondents were then asked, "Do you believe that any of those behaviors checked . . . were part of a conscious attempt to insure that others perceived you as feminine?" The survey also asked, "Do you believe that any of those behaviors checked . . . were part of a conscious attempt to insure that others perceived you as masculine?"

Respondents were asked the question: "Are there other things that you did that you believe were a conscious attempt to insure that others perceived you as feminine/masculine?" This question was included in the survey because it was impossible to identify a list of all possible strategies. Answers to questions, both closed-ended and open-ended, illuminate how women strategize about gender.

By examining if and/or how military women believe that gender is policed and what they do in response, we can begin to understand how women engage in the accomplishment of gender as opposed to simply "being" feminine or masculine. By "policed," I mean that their behaviors are monitored or censured by other members of the military, female and male and at all levels, to insure that women are not seen as violating norms of gender appropriateness. The strategies that women employ are both interactional and internal. . . . The strategies are interactional in that their existence, and perpetuation, is dependent upon the response that the individual receives from others. And, they are internal in that, to some degree, they become incorporated into the persona of the person deploying them.

. . . In this research . . . I wanted to see if women would recognize and acknowledge their consciously engaging in strategies to manage gender.

Perceptions of Femininity

Do women believe that they are penalized for being perceived as "too feminine" or "too masculine?" Findings indicate that there is very little latitude for women when it comes to perceptions of gender. Sixty-four percent believe there are penalties for being perceived as "too feminine," while 60 percent of respondents indicate that they believe there are penalties for being perceived as "too masculine." . . .

Those women who believed there are penalties were asked to describe what they believed such penalties to be. One-hundred and sixty-five women described penalties for femininity. One hundred and fifty-seven described penalties for masculinity. Rather than starting with expected categories and coding the answers for whether or not they "fit" a particular category, I conducted a content analysis on the responses to see what categories emerged. Some answers could be coded into more than one category, as some respondents provided numerous examples, sometimes just listing words (e.g., "being perceived as an airhead, bimbo, or slut"). . . .

Though the penalties for femininity were quite varied, six common themes emerged: (1)

ostracism or disapproval from other women, (2) being viewed as a slut or sexually available, (3) being perceived as weak, (4) being perceived as incompetent or incapable, (5) not being taken seriously, and (6) career limitations. While some of these categories overlap and might even be perceived as one and the same (e.g., weak vs. incompetent), the specific words were used enough, and often within the same response, that it seemed as though they had different meanings for the respondents and should be coded accordingly.

The first five penalties are related to the sixth, and most frequently mentioned penalty: that of career limitations. This is true almost by definition, in that if there were no potentially negative impact on one's performance or career aspirations, one might question the way in which a given situation constituted a penalty. It is difficult to think of a situation in which a woman is penalized that does not carry with it the potential to damage one's work relationships and/or career.

"Career limitations" is actually a catch-all phrase for a number of career penalties. As illustrated by the respondents, they include, but are certainly not limited to, obvious limitations such as not being allowed to perform the job for which one was trained, not being promoted, not sent to a school needed for promotion, not getting choice assignments, etc. One woman wrote, "They are not assigned to 'career building' areas such as pilots, maintenance, security police—the generally thought of 'male jobs.'" Another woman wrote:

> I was a long haired blonde, outstanding figure, long beautiful nails (my own!) etc., etc. I was constantly told I couldn't do my job (working on aircraft) as I was a dumb blonde, I'd get my nails dirty, I was a danger to the guys working on aircraft because I distracted them, etc., etc. My first rating was not a favorable one even though I scored higher on the OJT [on-the-job-training] tests than anyone had ever scored in that shop!

Another indicated that "you don't get the tough jobs you need to be in good shape for promotion, and women who are too feminine usually get ignored or put in office jobs with no troops." Command positions, leading troops, are critical to the promotion of those in the officer ranks. Many women mentioned the penalty of being "removed from position[s] of authority and placed in somebody's office," or being "given more feminine jobs to do." Command positions are definitely not considered "feminine." One woman expressed her opinion on this issue:

> It is a great privilege as an officer to be in a command position. Part of being a commander is having a "command presence." I greatly doubt that women who wear lots of perfume, make-up, speak softly, and/or make strong efforts to appear feminine are considered frequently as serious contenders for command positions.

The categories of penalties clearly overlap. Especially in a military that "has no place for weakness," it is difficult to discuss attributions of weakness without discussing incompetence as well. It is difficult to discuss perceptions of incompetence without noting its relationship to not being taken seriously and suffering career limitations. In sum, while about one-quarter of the respondents mentioned career limitations explicitly ("Not selected for schools, promotion."), virtually all the penalties discussed are related, whether directly or indirectly, to the ability of women to be treated equally with men and, therefore, to achieve the same degree of success as their male counterparts. While the penalties for being perceived as too feminine are varied, they do share a common theme. Whether at the informal (e.g., perceived as a slut by other members of the unit) or formal level (e.g., not selected to attend leadership training), each of these penalties serves as a mechanism for insuring that women remain "outsiders" to the boys' club of the military.

Perceptions of Masculinity

If women who are perceived as too feminine experience penalties, what happens to those women who are perceived as too masculine? Are they polar opposites on some scale of acceptability? One might argue that the best mechanism for combating penalties for being too feminine is to insure that one is perceived as masculine. Examination of the data reveals that this is not the case.

Of the 157 women who described the penalties for being perceived as too masculine, over half indicated that such women would be labeled as lesbians. There were a number of responses that seemed as though that was what was being inferred, but because it wasn't stated explicitly I opted for a conservative approach and did not code them as such. Consider these examples: "Comments," "Many lewd remarks were made about 'masculine' type women," "I think they may have to prove themselves more especially if not married," and "'Too masculine' tends to be equated with 'man hating.'" If descriptions of this type were included, about two-thirds of the responses could be considered to address lesbianism.

Although the label "lesbian" emerges as a single category of penalty, it is illustrative to look at the different ways in which the issue is addressed. In many cases women stated very plainly, "Perceived as being a lesbian," "Perceived as lesbians," "Lesbo, dyke, etc.—Need I say more!" In other cases their descriptions were much more colorful or detailed. Consider the following description:

> Being teased by other service members . . .
> called "butch," "bitch," "dyke," a lesbian. If a
> female can't be told apart visually, at first
> glance, from a male she *will* be subjected to
> being called sir vs. ma'am and may be kicked
> out of a few female restrooms, at first glance.[2]

A number of respondents, as was the case when a woman is perceived as too feminine, indicated that penalties also came from other women. One woman wrote:

> If you go past gender neutral (the "ideal"
> woman officer), past masculine (conspicuous),
> to too masculine, you were courting being
> labeled a lesbian. Too masculine made men and
> women nervous. Me, too.

Another indicated that "they are often avoided by both male and female soldiers. They are the outcasts of the unit."

One of the most revealing findings regarding the penalty of being labeled a lesbian is the understanding that this label was often applied to women regardless of sexual orientation. This fact serves as a wonderful illustration of the way in which homophobia and perceptions of sexual orientation serve as mechanisms for the subjugation of all women. "I believe they are labeled as homosexuals, 'dykes,' whether they are or not." "Of course, they are tagged or stereotyped as lesbians, whether they are or not." The impact of such allegations can extend well beyond having to tolerate "talk." As one woman writes:

> One of the women in the unit who had a
> masculine appearance was accused of being a
> lesbian even though she wasn't. When her time
> was up she got out because of the accusations
> she was gay. She was a good soldier.

Being labeled a lesbian was the only category that clearly emerged from a content analysis of these items. Some answers occurred more frequently than others, but none so much as the penalty of being labeled a lesbian. Other penalties that respondents described included: (1) ostracism and ridicule and, (2) career limitations. Though they each constituted only about 10 percent of the descriptions, in these "nonsexualized" instances women are receiving social and career penalties for exhibiting behavior that is highly desirable in male soldiers. It is critical to understand that women are being penalized for exhibiting gendered behaviors that are consistent with the work-role of "soldier."

Bearing in mind that I am talking about the military, consider this description of how, and for what, women are penalized. "Women who were seen as too aggressive—too much focus on aggressive or violent activities were not seen as 'normal' or to be 'trusted.'" Exhibiting interests in activities that many would agree form the core of military ideology (i.e., aggression and violence) results in the penalty of not being considered "normal" or "trustworthy." Another respondent indicated the "women were discouraged from being aggressive, displaying leadership skills, being self-assured and independent."

The ostracism that women describe is often, but not always, linked to the subject of lesbianism. While some women offered comments such as, "They are shunned, called names (e.g. dyke)," others were less specific in their remarks. "Rejected by both male and female peers," or "A woman who appears too masculine may be ridiculed for it." One woman wrote, "Yeah, everybody hates them." Whether explicitly related to sexual orientation or not, it seems apparent that women who violate gender norms of femininity are "outsiders" to the same degree, albeit in a different fashion, as are women who violate the masculine work-role of the military by being too feminine.

By understanding that women receive career penalties for being perceived as too masculine, as well as too feminine, we begin to understand the degree to which women are required to walk a fine line. One woman's comments capture this contradiction beautifully:

[I] knew a female airman [*sic*] who could do her job on the flight line better than most of the guys in her unit. This convinced some people she was a "dyke"—just had to be a lesbian otherwise she wouldn't have been so good at a "man's job."

Although cast in the light of sexual orientation, such a description illustrates the difficulties women face when simply trying to do the job for which they were recruited. Another wrote:

A female commander who does the exact same discipline as a male commander is probably seen as a bitch on a power trip. You're derided and not respected for playing tough by the rules. . . .You play by their rules but then you lose because they didn't consider you part of their game.

In other instances, the examples described specific career penalties such as "not selected for 'high profile' jobs," "poor evaluations or less than

deserved marks," and "overlooked for awards/ promotions." As one woman described, "I believe it can affect performance reviews, assignments, and coaching or counseling which is provided for developmental growth." While the cynic might argue that women "just have to tough it out," it is clear that there are plenty of formal mechanisms by which women can be penalized if they are perceived as gender deviant, regardless of the direction of the alleged deviance. What, then, do women do?

Conscious Strategies—Femininity

. . . Forty-one percent, or close to half, of the sample indicated that they engaged in some form of gender management, or strategizing. . . .

Of those respondents who indicated employing strategies to be perceived as feminine, at least one-third chose each of the following strategies: wearing make-up on duty (40 percent), wearing long hair (38 percent), wearing earrings while in uniform when permitted (37 percent) (this figure may have been even higher if women had always been permitted to wear earrings; it was only in the 1980s that women were granted permission to wear earrings with certain dress uniforms), wearing cologne or perfume (35 percent), and wearing make-up off duty (34 percent). Slightly less than one-third indicated that they wore pumps instead of flat shoes (low quarters) with the dress uniform (32 percent) and that they wore skirt uniforms instead of pants uniforms (28 percent) as strategies to be perceived as feminine. The fact that these items focus on clothing is primarily a function of the choices that were provided in the survey.

One of the most interesting aspects of clothing as a strategy for being perceived as feminine was the *way* in which clothing was often worn. This is of interest not only because it goes beyond the issue of clothing *choice*, but because the way in which an item was worn was often in violation of the regulations. Consider the following examples of strategies that women described: "My uniform skirt was always too short," "[I} did not wear a t-shirt under fatigues," and "I wore my BDU cap and Class A cap way back on my head to look more like a female." Such violations could lead to formal punishment, such as receiving a counseling statement, or to informal punishment, such as being the subject of negative comments. In my military experience, women were frequently ridiculed for not wearing their uniforms properly. Such women were viewed as not being serious soldiers and as being more concerned about their appearance than doing their job. Thus, women may highlight femininity as a means of being viewed more favorably, but to do so they may choose a strategy that has negative repercussions as well.

Women not only strategize with props such as clothing, jewelry, and make-up, but they also used their bodies to highlight femininity. One example of this is seen in the closed-ended item regarding hair length. As indicated above, 38 percent of those who indicated strategizing said that they wore their hair long as a strategy for being perceived as feminine. In the open-ended question, others referred to hair styling in general: "I tried to keep my hair in a feminine style that suited me. This involved getting a perm every 3–4 months."

Another strategy was the intentional avoidance of swearing. One woman wrote that she "never used bad language like many other women in [the] military do," while another wrote that she simply, "did not swear much." Other strategies that appeared repeatedly included home and office décor ("Flowers on my desk, my Noritake coffee cup, and picture frames on my desk"), and watching one's weight ("I kept a close watch on my weight because I was under the false assumption that 'thinness' and feminine were related"). In sum, conscious manipulation of one's appearance and engaging in behaviors traditionally marked as "female" were common strategies for managing the perceptions others had about one's status as feminine.

All of the strategies discussed thus far focus on appearance, personal space, and personal habits. None of these strategies are particularly surprising, nor can most immediately be labeled as detrimental to one's physical or emotional well-being. The same cannot be said of the last group of strategies.

It is evident from the data that both men and women not only shape ideas of femininity, but also mete out the penalties for gender violations. While men were not surveyed or interviewed, the women gave many examples of how both women and men let women know when they were seen as deviating from accepted norms of gender. Most strategies, while influenced by others, were engaged in on an individual basis. That is, they did not involve the active participation of another individual, but could be accomplished alone (e.g., wearing make-up or a knife). In the last group of strategies addressing femininity, discussed below, men play a key role. These strategies are those in which women intentionally engaged in social or sexual relations with men.

The closed-ended question revealed that anywhere from 6 to 10 percent of those who strategized either socialized with the men in their units (seven percent), dated men in their units (11 percent), or married while on active duty (six percent) as a conscious attempt to be perceived as feminine. Four percent indicated that, as a strategy for being perceived as feminine, when they had a boyfriend they "made sure people knew it." These numbers may seem inconsequential until we realize that this means that people are intentionally engaging in personal relationships as strategies for altering or enhancing the perceptions that others have of them.

One woman wrote, "I believe I did a little 'indiscriminate' dating, more than I should have, maybe to feel more feminine." Another "Made up stories re: boyfriends, [heterosexual] sex, dates; even slept with man/men (when I was drunk) to cover for myself and the company." One woman said that she "tried to date civilian men," while another said, "I felt that I *had* to have a boyfriend." The relationship between femininity and heterosexuality is a key element to understanding why such social and sexual relations with men would serve as strategies. As one woman said, "I mostly made conscious attempts to appear heterosexual v. feminine." Another woman answered, "Hanging around with nothing but males and having sex with them to prove I wasn't a lesbian." Because of the obvious link to displays of heterosexuality, it is worth noting at this point that there was an entirely separate question, not analyzed here, about strategies to avoid being perceived as lesbian. The responses provided here are specifically in response to the question about being perceived as feminine. This is powerful evidence of the link between the ways gender and sexuality have been constructed.

Conscious Strategies—Masculinity

Although a majority of women who strategized did so toward femininity, this was not true for everyone. Twelve percent of those who employed strategies aimed some or all of their efforts at masculinity. Seventy-four percent of the respondents who indicated employing at least one masculine strategy said they wanted to be considered "one of the guys." Forty-one percent said that they "socialized with men" in their unit as a strategy. Thirty-one percent wore pants uniforms rather than skirt uniforms as a strategy and 30 percent indicated that their preference for work uniforms (e.g., camouflage uniforms) to dress uniforms was a strategy for being perceived as more masculine. Thus, clothing was also a strategy for being perceived as masculine, but not nearly as frequently as it was a strategy for being perceived as feminine. Clearly, being seen as "one of the guys" and/or socializing with men were key strategies for women wishing to be perceived as masculine.

Analysis of the open-ended items revealed strategies similar to those above. The four main strategies identified in the qualitative data are: swearing, drinking, working out, and doing other "guy things." In the findings concerning feminine strategies we saw that avoidance of swearing was considered by some to be a strategy for being perceived as feminine. In the results presented here we see the opposite approach. In answer to the open-ended question about strategies, one woman wrote, "My favorite cuss word is 'shit.' I cussed when I wanted to make a point."

Other examples include: "Started cursing," "Swearing," "Perhaps a bit cruder, earthier way of talking," "Talk nasty like guys, swear and stuff," "Use foul language to the extent men did," and "Used profanity when around men." Clearly, the expression "the mouth of a sailor" held some meaning for these women, as a number of them put the cliché to work.

A number of women indicated that drinking also served as a strategy. One woman said that she drank more than she should have. Another said, "Drinking with the guys—trying to keep up." One woman, however, did not acknowledge employing strategies, but then wrote, "Maybe—I tried beer because all of the guys were drinking it." Yet another mentioned "the amount of substance abuse" as a strategy for being perceived as masculine. As one woman wrote, "Foul language, smoking, drinking, joking—I am undeniably feminine—but I tried in many ways to 'compensate' (unfortunately)." While not all would agree, many would argue that swearing and drinking are more acceptable in men, relative to women, especially in the military.[3] Thus, it is not surprising that if women wished to emphasize masculinity, they would seize on these "available" behaviors as strategies for doing so.

A third strategy described by respondents was "working out" or concentrating on physical fitness. In the military, especially in recent years, we would expect this to be a "positive" strategy because of the military's emphasis on physical fitness. Additionally, if feminine women are perceived as weak, then it makes sense that some women might try to ensure that they are perceived as physically fit. As one woman described, "I made sure that I was physically fit to avoid being perceived as a weak female." Another wrote, "[I] Thought many other women were weak and pathetic. Made sure I was *very strong* physically." Several made specific mention of training in weight lifting, a stereotypically masculine mode of working out.

In a related vein, a number of women mentioned not allowing co-workers to help them with physical tasks. Typical responses included: "Not asking assistance of others when lifting heavy things" and [I] "lifted heavier things on the job than I should have." Another wrote:

> I did not let others (men) help me, unless a job normally required 2 people, and the guy was *assigned* to work with me. I only asked other women to help me, or went to great lengths to use leverage and improvise.

Demonstration of physical strength, whether through physical development or task accomplishment, is apparently one mechanism by which women try to be perceived as masculine and, as such, to fit in.

Though the last decade has led to significant change in this arena, the strategy of "working out," especially weight lifting, is viewed by some as "doing guy things." Some would say the same of swearing and drinking. If this weren't the case then it is unlikely that these would be identified as strategies for being perceived as masculine. Yet, the frequency with which these behaviors were mentioned warranted their being considered separate categories. The fourth strategy, "doing guy things," is distinct. Women mentioned a variety of behaviors, apart from those discussed above, that they exhibited as a means of being perceived as masculine. In some cases, these were specific behaviors (e.g., "learned to scuba and skydive"); in others they were general statements (e.g., "Go out with the guys and do the types of things they like to do"). The following comments illustrate these findings: "I drove a Pinto station wagon with a tool box in the back. I did my own oil changes." "Talked about stuff I did as a civilian—played in rock band, rode motorcycle, etc." "Auto hobby shop—fixed guys' cars—took flying lessons and mechanics with the guys." Again, certain behaviors, hobbies, etc., are culturally defined as masculine. If participation in these events is readily available then it is understandable that they would be part of the behavioral repertoire of those women who wish to be perceived as masculine.

"Demeanor" is another strategy of "doing guy things." One woman discussed "using the language and mannerisms of men," while another said she "became more assertive/aggressive." One woman said she "learned to be aggressive when necessary," while another said, "High assertiveness; low exhibited emotionality." As one woman described it, "Developed a tougher attitude and tried to hide my softer side at work."

Related to the strategy of "doing guy things" was the strategy of *not* doing "female things." One woman "attempted to downplay feminine 'traits' such as gossiping, flowers on desk, being emotional" while another wrote:

> Whenever I deployed, I reduced my attachment to "feminine" stuff; no contacts, no make-up, no complaints if I couldn't shower/wash hair, no perfume—made fun of women who continued these trappings while deployed.

In some instances, and as would be the case with some weight lifters, such behaviors involved physical change. One woman said, "I didn't wear make-up, I never swayed my hips, I strode along." Another said, "I kept my fingernails short and never polished them!" To some degree, the absence of the feminine may be seen, by default, as an approximation of the masculine. . . .

Results show that the types of strategies employed by women seeking to manage gender are numerous and diverse. Whether one is trying to be perceived as feminine or masculine there is an available repertoire of strategies from which one may choose. As I have shown, close to half of the women in this sample acknowledge the employment of strategies to manage gender. While most opt toward femininity, some do strategize toward masculinity. . . .

Doing Gender/Doing Sexuality

The first question posed by West and Zimmerman addressed the question of how a culture instills the need to achieve gender. . . . By establishing ideas about what is essentially female or male, what is "normal" or "natural" the culture instills within us a need to maintain these gendered identities. That is, we must continually create and recreate our identities as gendered beings.

I believe that this analysis is accurate, but fails to consider another important mechanism for insuring that we feel compelled to engage in the active accomplishment of gender. I argue that the link between gender and sexuality also serves to reinforce our need to "do gender." There are at least two ways in which sexuality functions to reinforce our need to do gender. First, notions of what types of sexual behavior are appropriate are used to insure that women work to be seen as "good women." For example, a woman who does not want to be viewed as a "whore," or a "tramp," must modify her appearance, and possibly demeanor, so that she fits "acceptable" ideas of how a "good woman" looks or acts. Similarly, men who have a certain "look" are assumed to possess, or not posses, a degree of sexual prowess. And, sexuality is viewed as being composed of the good vs. the bad. If all sexuality were viewed positively, there would be no negative connotations to labels such as whore or tramp. Homosexuality would not be viewed as bad; homophobia would not exist. If there were nothing "wrong" with being labeled a whore or a lesbian the labels would not be threatening.

Second, perceptions of gender are used to make assessments of one's sexual orientation. In women, femininity implies heterosexuality, masculinity implies homosexuality. And conversely, a woman known to be a lesbian may be assumed to possess more masculine traits than her heterosexual counterpart. Thus, perceptions about gender are used to make inferences about sexuality, and vice versa. This research provides ample evidence for the way that "masculinity" is used to "determine" that a woman is a lesbian.

Our culture instills the need to achieve gender not only by creating a sense of the "natural" or the "normal," but also by threatening social actors with penalties for violating prescribed notions of acceptable gendered behavior and acceptable sexual behavior. By linking the two together, we insure that violations in either arena result in penalties. Specifically, and because gendered behaviors are the more visible, the threat of being labeled sexually deviant may function to insure that we "do gender" in the appropriate fashion. That is, women enact femininity, and men enact masculinity. West and Fenstermaker make clear

that "doing gender does not always mean living up to normative conceptions of femininity or masculinity" (1993: 157). But, they also note that "To the extent that members of society know their actions are accountable, they will design their actions in relation to how they might be seen and described by others" (1993: 157). They write:

> First, and perhaps most important, conceiving of gender as an ongoing accomplishment, accountable to interaction, implies that we must locate its emergence in *social situations*, rather than within the individual or some ill-defined set of role expectations. . . . What it involves is crafting conduct that can be evaluated in relation to normative conceptions of manly and womanly natures (Fenstermaker and Berk 1985, p. 203), and assessing conduct in light of those conceptions—given the situation at hand (West and Zimmerman 1987, p. 139–140). (157)

Thus, it is not simply that women, for example, seek to enact femininity because it is expected of them, but also that situations call for such enactment. The social situation in which femininity serves as an indicator of heterosexuality can only compel one to enact femininity if there is some reason to want to insure that one is perceived to be heterosexual. Sociocultural attitudes toward homosexuality function to insure that this is the case. But, some situations are especially strongly marked, or call more strongly for gendered behavior. The military is one such situation.

The ban on lesbians, gay men, and bisexuals exacerbates this situation even further. As of this writing, military policy "allows" lesbians, gay men, and bisexuals to serve as long as they "don't tell." This, of course, requires that lesbians in the military do what they can to mask all potential "markers" of homosexuality. While the policymakers claim that they would not "ask" about sexual orientation and servicemembers could "be" homosexual as long as they didn't "tell" the military has not upheld their end of the bargain. People continue to be harassed, investigated, and discharged for being lesbian, gay, or bisexual. While there are many instances outside the military where this is so, there are few, if any, places where federal law supports such discrimination. Federal law may not *protect* civilians, but neither does it compel an employer to fire them if it is discovered that they are lesbian, gay, or bisexual.

As was addressed earlier, to be perceived as masculine may result in one being labeled a lesbian. Not only may women be "shunned," or lose the respect of their peers, but the institutional requirement that lesbians be discharged may result in investigation and, ultimately, discharge. One way of avoiding such charges is to insure that one is perceived as feminine, and thus, heterosexual. While I would not argue that this is the sole explanation for women enacting femininity, I do believe that it is a significant factor. As a number of women indicated, it was more important to be perceived as heterosexual than feminine, but the latter helps insure the former. Remember, one woman wrote, "I mostly made conscious attempts to appear heterosexual v. feminine." . . .

. . . For women in the military, women must "do femininity" to insure that they are perceived as heterosexual and, as such, are somewhat protected from potential stigma and/or expulsion.

Gender and the Institution

The second question posed by West and Zimmerman (1987) is : "What is the relationship between the production of gender at the level of interaction and such institutional arrangements as the division of labor in society?" In the case of the military, gender is produced at the level of interaction, but the result is the reinforcement of perceptions of women as unfit for military service. These perceptions are not merely micro-level assessments, but perceptions that permeate the broader institution. When the majority of women can be labeled "feminine," and anything feminine is viewed as inappropriate for military service, women, as a group, can become viewed as "inconsistent" with, or less than capable of performing, military service. Thus, by producing gender at the level of interaction (e.g., enacting

femininity), a broader ideology, as well as institutional arrangements (e.g., job restrictions) in which women are perceived to be second class soldiers is maintained.

If women were aggressive they were seen as lesbians; if women were not aggressive enough they were seen as incapable of leading troops and could receive poor evaluation reviews. In either case, the ultimate penalty could be discharge. At the least, women as a group are subject to the label of "unfit." Women have to prove themselves the exception to the rule. One interesting example of this is the experience of the male sergeant who, together with a female flight surgeon, was captured by the Iraqis during Desert Storm. After their experience as prisoners of war, he acknowledged that she could go into battle with him anytime, but that he wasn't prepared to say the same for all women. SGT Troy Dunlap stated, "I was really amazed . . . I was overwhelmed by the way she handled herself. . . . She can go to combat with me anytime" (Pauley 1992). He made it clear that she was the exception. One woman had proven herself; women as a group remained questionable. As MAJ Rhonda Cronum said in response, "I don't think I'll ever change his mind that says that women as a category of people shouldn't go to combat, but I think I did change his mind that this one individual person who happens to be female can go" (Pauley 1992).

When women "produce enactments of their 'essential' femininity" (West and Zimmerman 1987: 144), they are not being good soldiers. When they are "good soldiers," they often risk being labeled as lesbians. As Navy Vice Admiral Joseph S. Donnell wrote in 1990, lesbian sailors are "generally hard-working, career-oriented, willing to put in long hours on the job and among the command's top performers" (Gross, 1990: 24). It is not difficult to imagine how women who fit this description, regardless of sexual orientation, may be labeled as lesbian (Shilts 1993). Thus, the enactment of gender at the interactional level has the potential to reinforce perceptions of women as inappropriate for military service for a number of reasons. Such a perception of women then reinforces the belief that men are somehow uniquely suited to serving in the nation's military. Thus, the production of gender at the interactional level reinforces both ideological and institutional arrangements that place women at the margins of military participation.

It should be noted that stereotypical gay men do not fit the model of "soldier," in that they are not seen as masculine "enough." If gay male soldiers, or *any* male soldier for that matter, were not seen as appropriately masculine they would risk censure. The paradox is that the stereotypical lesbian *does* fit the model of "soldier," and, yet, risks censure for being "gender appropriate" to the work role of soldier. While a gay man can "pass" by "doing masculinity" in the appropriate fashion, women are faced with the contradiction that "doing masculinity" results in being perceived as a lesbian.

Gender as a Tool of Male Dominance

The third question posed by West and Zimmerman (1987) is "how does doing gender contribute to the subordination of women by men?" If, as described above, women in the military are perceived as second class soldiers, or as less than capable, it is not farfetched to argue that women are being subordinated by men. It is important to reiterate that clearly not all women, as individuals, are seen as second rate or unsuccessful. There are thousands of women who have served admirably and have earned the respect of their male co-workers, peers and superiors alike.[4] The case I am making here is that military women *as a group* are viewed as second class and are subordinated by the male institution of the military. Whether women are sexually harassed, denied assignments, or prohibited from performing particular jobs, we must realize that it is not simply the case of a poor performing individual that allows such incidents to occur. The social and institutional arrangements (e.g., the prohibition of women from most combat jobs) which permit women to be viewed as poor substitutes for male soldiers subordinate women to men and limit their participation as full members of the mili-

tary. In some cases, attributions of inadequacy have followed women to their deaths.

LT Kara Hultgreen was one of the first women to qualify to fly a Naval fighter jet, the F-14. LT Hultgreen died on October 25, 1994 when she crashed in the Pacific during a training exercise. The Navy rumor mill immediately spun into action with some going "so far as to send out false information in anonymous phone calls and faxes purporting that Hultgreen was unqualified and received special treatment by a politically correct Navy. In fact, Hultgreen was third out of seven flyers in her class" (*Minerva's Bulletin Board* Fall/ Winter, 1994: 3). Subsequent investigation revealed that the aircraft had lost an engine and that even skilled pilots would have had a difficult time landing successfully. CDR Trish Beckman, president of Women Military Aviators, writes:

> A combination of factors and limited time to recognize and correct them, put Kara in a "deep hole" which cost her life (an would have done the same to skilled Test Pilots in the same situation). What is different in this circumstance is that unnamed Navy men have attempted to slander and libel her reputation publicly (something that has never been done to a deceased male aviator, no matter how incompetent he was known to be or how many lives he took with him)." (*Minerva's Bulletin Board* Fall/Winter, 1994: 3–4)

In contrast, when two Navy pilots flew their helicopter past the demilitarized zone into North Korea in December 1994, resulting in the death of one and the capture of the other, no mention was made of blame or incompetence. No one suggested that perhaps permitting men to fly was a mistake.

Does the above question address the issue of the relationship between doing gender in the military and the subordination of women to men? I believe so. When military women enact femininity, they are subject to accusations that they are not capable of performing tasks, etc., that have been labeled as "masculine." When military women enact masculinity, they are subject to accusations of lesbianism. Doing gender results in women being subjected to an endless range of accusations which together result in the subordination of women as a class of citizens. The question, however, remains, is it possible to avoid doing gender?

West and Zimmerman (1987) write:

> If we do gender appropriately, we simultaneously sustain, reproduce, and render legitimate the institutional arrangements that are based on sex category. If we fail to do gender appropriately, we as individuals—not the institutional arrangements—may be called to account (for our character, motives, and predispositions). (146)

While it is unlikely, given the existing social order, that we can avoid doing gender, we can begin to tackle the resulting inequities in a number of ways. "Social change, then, must be pursued both at the institutional and cultural level of sex category and at the interactional level of gender" (West and Zimmerman 1987: 147). That is, we must challenge the institutional and cultural arrangements that perpetuate distinctions made on the basis of sex, or sex category. In the military, one way to accomplish this would be to eliminate prohibitions of women in combat. Another would be to eliminate the ban on lesbians, gay men, and bisexuals in the military. If we eliminate the importance of sex category in the "politics of sexual-object choice" (Connell 1985: 261) we eliminate the need for compulsory heterosexuality. That is, if whether a potential mate is female or male is irrelevant, heterosexuality loses it hegemonic stranglehold on society and its institutions. Thus, eliminating compulsory heterosexuality would do much to reduce the pressures women feel to be seen as feminine as well as the fear of being seen as too masculine, and not without significance, the fear men have of being seen as too feminine.

Conclusion

. . . There are some very real implications for women's day to day participation in the military. Women are likely to be subjected to a variety of unpleasantries ranging from sexual harassment

to being shunned, from being denied access to schooling to being denied promotions. While the penalties are varied, they share one potential outcome. All of the penalties discussed in this research may lead to women being discharged or feeling compelled to leave the service. Thus, the major implication of this research is that the perpetuation of an ideology in which soldiering and masculinity are closely bound results in the perpetuation of a military which is not only ideologically, but numerically, male as well.

There are several mechanisms which function to keep the military "male." In addition to women leaving the service, whether by force or choice, perceptions of the military as male also limit the numbers of women who will consider the military as a career option. As of late 1993, the proportion of enlistees who were women was, in fact, on the rise (*Minerva's Bulletin Board* Spring, 1994: 1–2). As of this writing, the Army had experienced a slight drop in women recruits after widespread sexual harassment was exposed in late 1996. Whether this will have any long term effect on Army recruiting is not yet known. It is impossible, at this point, to determine if women are finding the military more attractive than has been true in the past, or whether smaller numbers of male recruits are inflating the proportion of female recruits.

In addition, the ideology of the "male military" and restrictions on the participation of women function together to limit the number of positions open to women. Thus, fewer women, compared to men, can enter the service. That is, even if huge numbers of women wished to enlist, their numbers would be suppressed by the comparatively fewer numbers of available positions, especially in the Army where large numbers of jobs are classified as combat arms and, as such, are off limits to women.

As long as the military is viewed as the domain of men, women will be outsiders and their participation will be challenged. Thus, a cycle of male dominance is perpetuated. The military is defined as male, a small proportion of women are allowed to participate, the participation of these women is challenged and penalized, the military remains ideologically and numerically male dominated, the numbers of women remain small. How can this cycle be broken? First, we can challenge cultural constructions of sex/gender. Second, we can challenge institutional arrangements which allow the perpetuation of distinctions on the basis of sex/sex category. That is, reduce the importance of being feminine or masculine and female or male.

The first of these institutional arrangements is the classification of military job eligibility by sex. That is, one is eligible for a particular job only if one is male. In the military this is the case for jobs coded as having a high likelihood of engaging the enemy. Women, as a group, are thus excluded from some specific occupations and some specific assignments. Barriers are being broken, but many remain. As long as women are eligible only for some jobs they will be viewed as second class soldiers (or sailors, "airmen," etc.). If we eliminate such barriers and assign individuals on the basis of their performance, ability, etc., it is highly likely that we will see a corresponding increase in the acceptance of women as participants in the military.

The second arrangement which will improve the ability of women to participate on equal terms with men is the repeal of the laws prohibiting the participation of lesbians, gay men, and bisexuals in the United States military. It is painfully apparent that this ban hurts many lesbians, gay men, and bisexuals. Many wish to serve in the military, but know that to do so is not without risk. Many do join the military only to have their careers ended prematurely. But, as I have indicated, the ban on lesbians, gay men, and bisexuals also impacts negatively on all women and men, regardless of sexual orientation. If the confirmation of heterosexuality were not imperative, women would be free to engage in a much wider range of behaviors, particularly those labeled as masculine. If women did not feel compelled to ensure that they are seen as heterosexual, there would be less pressure to enact femininity, a marker of heterosexuality.

By having to confirm heterosexuality, women enact femininity, thereby ensuring that they will be perceived as less capable than their male counterparts. The link between gender and sexuality, situated in an organization which has an institutional mandate for heterosexuality, ensures the subordination of women. To eliminate compulsory heterosexuality would greatly enhance the more equal participation of women. To be sure, eliminating the degree to and manner in which women deploy gender at the interactional level would also enhance equal participation. But, without corresponding changes at the institutional level such changes are unlikely to occur. By understanding: (1) how gender is produced at the interactional level, (2) how the interactional level is related to existing institutional arrangements, and (3) how the link between gender and sexuality empowers this relationship, we can offer a new vision for the equal participation of women and men in the military and, more importantly, throughout society.

NOTES

1. Members of the military are also referred to as airmen [*sic*], sailors, Marines, etc., depending upon their branch. For ease of discussion I use the term soldiers, as the Army is the largest branch and in common parlance many often refer to all members of the military as soldiers, regardless of branch.

2. For an interesting, non-military, account of the experiences of androgynous women see Holly Devor's *Gender Blending: Confronting the Limits of Duality*, Bloomington, IN: Indiana University Press, 1989.

3. In the past swearing was not viewed as inappropriate or unprofessional and drinking was not only tolerated, but encouraged. New policies on sexual harassment and alcohol abuse have led to significant changes in recent years.

4. Of course, one could argue as well that while women have to *earn* the respect of the men with whom they work, men begin with that respect and must do something to lose it.

REFERENCES

Acker, Joan. 1992. "Gendered Institutions." *Contemporary Sociology* 21(5): 565–569.

Connell, Robert W. 1985. "Theorizing Gender." *Sociology* 19(2) 260–272.

Dunivin, Karen. 1994. "Military Culture: Change and Continuity." *Armed Forces & Society* 20(4): 531–547.

"Freedom of Press Seen on Trial Now." 1942. *New York Times,* 17 April, 8.

Goffman, Erving. 1977. "The Arrangement Between the Sexes." *Theory and Society* 4(3): 301–331.

Gross, Jane, 1990. "Navy Is Urged to Root Out Lesbians Despite Abilities." *New York Times,* 2 September, 24.

Lenskyj, Helen. 1986. *Out of Bounds: Women, Sport and Sexuality.* Toronto: The Women's Press.

The MINERVA Center. Spring, 1994. "Proportion of Women Growing Among New Recruits." *Minerva's Bulletin Board,* 1–2.

———. Fall/Winter, 1994. "Second Woman to Qualify as F-14 Pilot Dies in Crash." *Minerva's Bulletin Board,* 3–4.

Pauley, Jane. 1992. *Dateline NBC:* Interview with MAJ Rhonda L. Cornum. New York.

Shilts, Randy. 1993. *Conduct Unbecoming: Lesbians and Gays in the U. S. Military Vietnam to the Persian Gulf.* New York, NY: St. Martin's Press.

Steinberg, Ronni. 1992. "Gender on the Agenda: Male Advantage in Organizations." *Contemporary Sociology* 21(5): 576–581.

Veterans Administration. 1985. *Survey of Female Veterans: A Study of the Needs, Attitudes, and Experiences of Women Veterans.* Office of Information Management and Statistics, IM & SM 70–85–7.

West, Candace and Sarah Fenstermaker. 1993. "Power, Inequality and the Accomplishment of Gender: An Ethnomethodological View," in *Theory on Gender/Feminism on Theory,* P. England (ed.). Hawthorne, NY: Aldine de Gruyter, 151–174.

West, Candace and Don H. Zimmerman. 1987. "Doing Gender." *Gender & Society* 1(2): 125–151.

THINKING ABOUT THE READING

Which do you think is worse for female soldiers: being perceived as "too masculine" or being perceived as "too feminine"? How is female soldiers' need to "walk a fine line" between masculinity and femininity related to impression management? Can you think of a comparable situation for men—one in which an occupation requires a certain degree of femininity, while at the same time demanding that they present an image of themselves as "real men"? Given the extreme, potentially life-and-death demands of military combat, do you think that female soldiers will ever be accepted as equals to male soldiers?

Volunteer Slavery
My Authentic Negro Experience

Jill Nelson

"Well, this is the final stage of the *Washington Post* interview procedure," says the editor of the newspaper's new Sunday magazine. "Talking to Ben."

Jay Lovinger and I walk through the cavernous newsroom toward executive editor Ben Bradlee's glassed-in office on the north wall. Around me, hundreds of reporters sit at computer terminals, banging away. A few sneak surreptitious glances at me. No one makes eye contact except the two sisters at the switchboard. I feel like a side of beef hooked on a pulley in a meat refrigerator, circling for the buyer's inspection. It is April, 1986.

"Everyone hired at the *Post* talks to Ben. He is an incredible interviewer," Lovinger says.

"Oh really?" I say. I almost say "Ow really," as a needle of excruciating pain shoots up from the cramped space between my little toe and the one next to it. My feet, in three-inch heels, are killing me.

"So far, everyone really likes you."

"Great," I say. What I really want to say is, "Likes me? Who gives a damn if they like me? This is a writing job, not a personality contest, isn't it?"

"The Metro editors even want you for their staff," he says, as if conferring some much coveted status. "They were intrigued by your perspective."

I'm not surprised. Two white males running the Metropolitan desk in a 70-percent black city that is also the nation's capital are probably in a constant state of intrigue. Mostly involving how to parlay that job into a better, whiter one.

"If everything goes well with Ben, then we'll talk money," he says as we near the glass office, guarded by a fierce-looking redhead. "Just be yourself," he cautions.

I turn to look at him to see if he's trying to be funny, but of course he's dead serious. I decide not to ask him who else but myself he imagines I am, or could be. Instead, I smooth the folds of my turquoise ultrasuede dress, lick my lips, and wiggle my feet, trying to get the wad of Dr. Scholl's lambswool between my toes—the only thing standing between me and triple minority status: black, female, and handicapped—back into a more functional position.

But by now I am tired of being on. For me, the notion of coming to work at the *Washington Post* is mostly about money, but that's a black thing, which these people wouldn't understand. For twelve years, I have lived happily in New York as a successful yet poor freelance writer. I never thought about working for anyone but myself. Then one night the phone rang, and it was the man who's now escorting me to Bradlee's office.

"Hello," he said. "I'm the new editor of the new *Washington Post* magazine, and we'd like to talk to you about working with us."

After the obligatory yah-yah about purpose, art, and objectives, I cut to the chase: "What salary range are you offering?" The figure, twice what I earned the year before, gets me on a plane to this interview.

"What's Bradlee's interview technique like?" I ask.

"Fascinating. Absolutely fascinating. Don't be surprised if he does most of the talking, he usually does. He'll tell you about himself to find out about you. Even though you may not say much, Ben is incredibly insightful about people. He's an amazing judge of character."

"That's interesting," I say, and relax. This I can definitely deal with. White boy interview technique 101, in which he talks about himself in order to see if I can deal with him, which means he can deal with me. I didn't go to prep school and Columbia Journalism for nothing. My parents will be happy their money wasn't wasted.

"This is Jill Nelson. She's here to see Ben," Lovinger says to the secretary/sentinel.

"Go right in," she says, and smiles.

"Good luck," says Lovinger.

"Thank you," I say, smiling, wondering what I'm getting into. Then I remember that I'm just a piece of meat, dark meat at that. And after all, the blacker the berry, the sweeter the juice. It wasn't until years later that Daisy, one of the few friends I made in Washington, pointed out, "Yeah, but who wants sugar diabetes?" She ought to know. Short and olive-shaped, Daisy is Washington's smallest P.R. maven, a native of Boston who escaped via the East Village of the 1960s and ended up in D.C. Smart, acerbic, and outspoken, she pays homage to no one and has everyone's ear.

I am momentarily stunned when I enter Bradlee's office. I'm expecting Jason Robards from *All The Presidents Men,* tall, gray, and handsome. Instead I'm greeted by a short, gray, wrinkled gnome.

"Ben Bradlee. Nice to meet you. Sit down," he booms. Well, at least he has Jason Robards' voice. I sit.

"Tell me something about yourself."

Temporarily, my mind is null and void. All I can think to tell him is that my feet are killing me and that, in a static-cling war with my dress, my slip has risen up to encircle my waist. Then an ancient Temptations song pops into my head— "Papa was a Rollin' Stone." For years the words to this song, which I didn't particularly like when it was a hit in 1972, spring into mind when I'm queried about myself by white folks. I suspect many think the song defines the authentic Negro experience.

But truthfully, Papa wasn't a rolling stone, he was a dentist, Mommy was a businesswoman and librarian, we were solidly upper-middle-class. Besides, I remind myself, this is the 1980s. The day of the glorification of the stereotypical poor, pathological Negro is over. Just like the South, it is time for the black bourgeoisie to rise again. I am a foot soldier in that army. So I tell Bradlee, briefly, about my educational and journalistic background. Am I imagining it, or is he really impatient for me to shut up?

"Let me tell you about my magazine," Bradlee says, almost before my lips have closed over my last word.

"I want it to have an identity of its own, but at the same time be a mixture of *Esquire, New York* magazine, and *The New York Times Magazine.* I want it to be provocative, insightful, funny, and controversial . . ." He goes on.

I sit there looking at him, halfway listening as he talks and talks, struck by the notion of defining a new magazine by old ones, and old tired ones at that. I try to imagine myself, an African-American female, working and thriving at a publication that's an amalgam of white man at his best, a celebration of yuppie-dom, and all the news that fits, we print. I come up blank.

"I want the fashions to be exciting, new, to portray women who dress with style, like my wife," Bradlee is saying when I tune in again. I know he's married to Sally Quinn, but I'll be damned if I know what she wears. I don't remember reading her name in *W* or the fashion columns. What am I doing here?

"I want it to illuminate what really goes on in this city, to get under Washington's skin . . ."

It's when he says *skin* that I remember why I'm here. I'm black and female. The magazine, to debut in a few months, has no black or female writers. In 1986, I'm about to realize my destiny—or pay off some terrible karmic debt—and become a first. Hallelujah!

"So, have you always lived in New York?"

Again, I snap back. "Yes. Except for three years at prep school in Pennsylvania and a year I lived on Martha's Vineyard."

"Martha's Vineyard. How'd you wind up there?" It is the first time he has seemed sincerely interested in anything I've said. After all, only the best people wind up on the Vineyard.

"My parents have a home there. I've spent summers on the Vineyard since I was a child and just decided to spend a year there and write," I say.

He grins. It's as if he's suddenly recognized that the slightly threatening black guy asking for a hand-out on the street is actually a Harvard classmate fallen on hard times. The bond of the Vineyard makes me safe, a person like him.

"Ahhh," he says, "So you're part of that whole black bourgeoisie scene with the Bullocks and the Washingtons?"

"I guess you could say that," I say, and chuckle. So does he. I don't know what he's grinning about, but the notion of myself as part of the black socialite scene I've spent a lifetime avoiding on and off the Vineyard strikes me as laughable. So does his evocation of the Bullocks, old Washingtonians, and former Mayor Walter Washington, who is married to a Bullock. The Washingtons, after all, don't own, they visit—an important distinction in Vineyard society.

Our eyes meet, our chuckle ends, and I know I'm over. The job is mine. Simply by evoking residence on Martha's Vineyard, I have separated wheat from chaff, belongers from aspirers, rebellious chip-on-the-shoulder Negroes from middle-class, responsible ones.

Vanquished is the leftist ghost of my years writing for the *Village Voice.* Gone are the fears he might have had about my fitting in after a life as a freelance writer, an advocacy journalist, a free black. By dint of summers spent on Martha's Vineyard, I am, in his eyes, safe. I may be the darker sister, but I'm still a sister. I will fit into the *Washington Post* family.

Bradlee launches into a story about his house on the Vineyard, traded in for one in the more social media enclave of the Hamptons. I relax, stop listening, and start counting dollars. Unfortunately, there aren't enough of them to last the length of Bradlee's story. He keeps on talking and I just sit there, smiling. A feeling of foreboding expands geometrically around me. I shake it off and concentrate on willing my brain and feet into numbness.

THINKING ABOUT THE READING

This brief story is less about the stereotypical preconceptions of Ben Bradlee, the interviewer, as it is about Jill Nelson's interpretations of those preconceptions. How is what she says to herself different from what she expresses to Bradlee? Why does it seem to bother her so much that this upper-class white man sees a connection to her based on her parents' affluence? Toward the end of the essay, she says, "I am, in his eyes, safe." What do you suppose she means by this statement? Explain the significance of the title of this article, "Volunteer Slavery." Have you ever been in a situation, like Jill Nelson, where you had to deal with someone else's stereotypical impression of you? How did you handle the situation? Imagine that Jill was white and the interviewer was black. How would the dynamics of the interview change? In general, how do you think people feel when they are forced to present a certain image of themselves to others in order to get what they need?

Suspended Identity

Identity Transformation in a Maximum Security Prison

Thomas J. Schmid and Richard S. Jones

The extent to which people hide behind the masks of impression management in everyday life is a point of theoretical controversy (Goffman 1959; Gross and Stone 1964; Irwin 1977; Douglas et al. 1980; Douglas and Johnson 1977; Messinger et al. 1962; Blumer 1972, 1969). A variety of problematic circumstances can be identified, however, in which individuals find it necessary to accommodate a sudden but encompassing shift in social situations by establishing temporary identities. These circumstances, which can range from meteoric fame (Adler and Adler 1989) to confinement in total institutions, place new identity demands on the individual, while seriously challenging his or her prior identity bases.

A prison sentence constitutes a "massive assault" on the identity of those imprisoned (Berger 1963: 100–101). This assault is especially severe on first-time inmates, and we might expect radical identity changes to ensue from their imprisonment At the same time, a prisoner's awareness of the challenge to his identity affords some measure of protection against it. . . .

Data for the study are derived principally from ten months of participant observation at a maximum security prison for men in the upper midwest of the United States. One of the authors was an inmate serving a felony sentence for one year and one day, while the other participated in the study as an outside observer. Relying on traditional ethnographic data collection and analysis techniques, this approach offered us general observations of hundreds of prisoners, and extensive fieldnotes that were based on repeated, often daily, contacts with about fifty inmates, as well as on personal relationships established with a smaller number of inmates. We subsequently returned to the prison to conduct focused interviews with other prisoners; using information provided by prison officials, we were able to identify and interview twenty additional first-time inmates who were serving sentences of two years or less. . . .

Three interrelated research questions guided our analysis: How do first-time, short-term inmates define the prison world, and how do their definitions change during their prison careers? How do these inmates adapt to the prison world, and how do their adaptation strategies change during their prison careers? How do their self-definitions, change during their prison careers? . . .

Preprison Identity

Our data suggest that the inmates we studied have little in common before their arrival at prison, except their conventionality. Although convicted of felonies, most do not possess "criminal" identities (cf. Irwin 1970: 29–34). They begin their sentences with only a vague, incomplete image (Boulding 1961) of what prison is like, but an image that nonetheless stands in contrast to how they view their own social worlds. Their prison image is dominated by the theme of violence: they see prison inmates as violent, hostile, alien human beings, with whom they have nothing in common. They have several specific fears about what will happen to them in prison, including fears of assault, rape, and death. They are also concerned about their identities, fearing that—if they survive prison at all—they are in danger of changing in prison, either through the intentional efforts of rehabilitation personnel or through the unavoidable hardening effects of the prison environment Acting on this imagery (Blumer 1969)—or, more precisely, on the inconsonance of their self-images with this prison image—they develop an anticipatory survival strategy . . . that consists primarily of protective resolutions: a resolve to avoid all hostilities; a resolve to avoid all nonessential contacts with inmates and guards; a resolve to defend themselves in any way possible; and a resolve not to change, or to be changed, in prison.

A felon's image and strategy are formulated through a running self-dialogue, a heightened state of reflexive awareness (Lewis 1979) through which he ruminates about his past behavior and motives, and imaginatively projects himself into the prison world. This self-dialogue begins shortly after his arrest, continues intermittently during his trial or court hearings, and becomes especially intense at the time of his transfer to prison. . . .

> My first night in the joint was spent mainly on kicking myself in the butt for putting myself in the joint. It was a very emotional evening. I thought a lot about all my friends and family, the good-byes, the things we did the last couple of months, how good they had been to me, sticking by me. I also thought about my fears: Am I going to go crazy? Will I end up fighting for my life? How am I going to survive in here for a year? Will I change? Will things be the same when I get out?

His self-dialogue is also typically the most extensive self-assessment he has ever conducted; thus, at the same time that he is resolving not to change, he is also initiating the kind of introspective analysis that is essential to any identity transformation process.

Self-Insulation

A felon's self-dialogue continues during the initial weeks and months of his sentence, and it remains a solitary activity, each inmate struggling to come to grips with the inconsonance of his established (preprison) identity and his present predicament. Despite the differences in their preprison identities, however, inmates now share a common situation that affects their identities. With few exceptions, their self-dialogues involve feelings of vulnerability, discontinuity, and differentiation from other inmates, emotions that reflect both the degradations and deprivations of institutional life (cf. Goffman 1961; Sykes 1958; and Garfinkel 1956) and their continuing outsiders' perspective on the prison world. These feelings are obviously the result of everything that has happened to the inmates, but they are something else as well: they are the conditions in which every first-time, short-term inmate finds himself. They might even be called the common attributes of the inmates' selves-in-prison, for the irrelevance of their preprison identities within the prison world reduces their self-definitions, temporarily, to the level of pure emotion. These feelings, and a consequent emphasis on the "physical self" (Zurcher 1977: 176), also constitute the essential motivation for the inmates' self-insulation strategies.

An inmate cannot remain wholly insulated within the prison world, for a number of reasons. He simply spends too much of his time in the presence of others to avoid all interaction with them. He also recognizes that his prison image is based on incomplete and inadequate information, and that he must interact with others in order to acquire first-hand information about the prison world. His behavior in prison, moreover, is guided not only by his prison image but by a fundamental ambivalence he feels about his situation, resulting from his marginality between the prison and outside social worlds (Schmid and Jones 1987). His ambivalence has several manifestations throughout his prison career, but the most important is his conflicting desires for self-insulation and for human communication.

Managing a Dualistic Self

An inmate is able to express both directions of his ambivalence (and to address his need for more information about the prison) by drawing a distinction between his "true" identity (i.e., his outside, preprison identity) and a "false" identity he creates for the prison world. For most of a new inmate's prison career, his preprison identity remains a "subjective" or "personal" identity while his prison identity serves as his "objective" or "social" basis for interaction in prison (see Weigert 1986; Goffman 1963). This bifurcation of his self . . . is not a conscious decision made at a single point in time, but it does represent two conscious and interdependent identity-preservation tactics, formulated through self-dialogue and refined through tentative interaction with others.

First, after coming to believe that he cannot "be himself" in prison because he would be too vulnerable, he decides to "suspend" his preprison identity for the duration of his sentence. He retains his resolve not to let prison change him, protecting himself by choosing not to reveal himself (his "true" self) to others. . . . An inmate's decision to suspend his preprison identity emanates directly from his feelings of vulnerability, discontinuity and differentiation from other inmates. These emotions foster something like a "proto-sociological attitude" (Weigert 1986: 173; see also Zurcher 1977), in which new inmates find it necessary to step outside their taken-for-granted preprison identities. Rather than viewing these identities and the everyday life experience in which they are grounded as social constructions, however, inmates see the *prison* world as an artificial construction, and judge their "naturally occurring" preprison identities to be out of place within this construction. By attempting to suspend his preprison identity for the time that he spends in prison an inmate believes that he will again "be his old self" after his release.

While he is in confinement, an inmate's decision to suspend his identity leaves him with little or no basis for interaction. His second identity tactic, then, is the creation of an identity that allows him to interact, however cautiously, with others. This tactic consists of his increasingly sophisticated impression management skills (Goffman 1959; Schlenker 1980), which are ini-

tially designed simply to hide his vulnerability, but which gradually evolve into an alternative identity felt to be more suitable to the prison world. The character of the presented identity is remarkably similar from inmate to inmate:

> Well, I learned that you can't act like—you can't get the attitude where you are better than they are. Even where you might be better than them, you can't strut around like you are. Basically, you can't stick out. You don't stare at people and things like that. I knew a lot of these things from talking to people and I figured them out by myself. I sat down and figured out just what kind of attitude I'm going to have to take.

> Most people out here learn to be tough, whether they can back it up or not. If you don't learn to be tough, you will definitely pay for it. This toughness can be demonstrated through a mean look, tough language, or an extremely big build. . . . One important thing is never to let your guard down.

An inmate's prison identity, as an inauthentic presentation of self, is not in itself a form of identity transformation but is rather a form of identity construction. His prison identity is simply who he must pretend to be while he is in prison. It is a false identity created for survival in an artificial world. But this identity nonetheless emerges in the same manner as any other identity: it is learned from others, and it must be presented to, negotiated with, and validated by others. A new inmate arrives at prison with a general image of what prisoners are like, and he begins to flesh out this image from the day of his arrival, warily observing others just as they are observing him. Through watching others, through eavesdropping, through cautious conversation and selective interaction, a new inmate refines his understanding of what maximum security prisoners look like, how they talk, how they move, how they act. Despite his belief that he is different from these other prisoners, he knows that he cannot appear to be too different from them, if he is to hide his vulnerability. His initial image of other prisoners, his early observations, and his concern over how he appears to others thus provide a foundation for the identity he gradually creates through impression management.

Impression management skills, of course, are not exclusive to the prison world; a new inmate, like anyone else, has had experience in presenting a "front" to others, and he draws upon his experience in the creation of his prison identity. He has undoubtedly even had experience in projecting the very attributes—strength, stoicism, aplomb—required by his prison identity. Impression management in prison differs, however, in the totality with which it governs interactions and in the perceived costs of failure: humiliation, assault, or death. For these reasons the entire impression management process becomes a more highly conscious endeavor. When presenting himself before others, a new inmate pays close attention to such minute details of his front as eye contact, posture, and manner of walking:

...

> The way you look seems to be very important. The feeling is you shouldn't smile, that a frown is much more appropriate. The eyes are very important. You should never look away; it is considered a sign of weakness. Either stare straight ahead, look around, or look the person dead in the eyes. The way you walk is important. You shouldn't walk too fast; they might think you were scared and in a hurry to get away.

To create an appropriate embodiment (Weigert 1986; Stone 1962) of their prison identities, some new intimates devote long hours to weightlifting or other body-building exercises, and virtually all of them relinquish their civilian clothes—which might express their preprison identities—in favor of the standard issue clothing that most inmates wear. Whenever a new inmate is open to the view of other inmates, in fact, he is likely to relinquish most overt symbols of his individuality, in favor of a standard issue "prison inmate" appearance.

By acting self-consciously, of course, a new inmate runs the risk of exposing the fact that he *is*

acting. But he sees no alternative to playing his part better; he cannot "not act" because that too would expose the vulnerability of his "true" identity. He thus sees every new prison experience, every new territory that he is allowed to explore, as a test of his impression management skills. Every nonconfrontive encounter with another inmate symbolizes his success at these skills, but it is also a social validation of his prison identity. Eventually he comes to see that many, perhaps most, inmates are engaging in the same kind of inauthentic presentations of self (cf. Glaser and Strauss 1964). Their identities are as "false" as his, and their validations of his identity may be equally false. But he realizes that he is powerless to change this state of affairs, and that he must continue to present his prison identity for as long as he remains in prison....

By the middle of his sentence, a new inmate comes to adopt what is essentially an insider's perspective on the prison world. His prison image has evolved to the point where it is dominated by the theme of boredom rather than violence. (The possibility of violence is still acknowledged and feared, but those violent incidents that do occur have been redefined as the consequences of prison norm violations rather than as random predatory acts; see Schmid and Jones 1990.) His survival strategy, although still extant, has been supplemented by such general adaptation techniques as legal and illegal diversionary activities and conscious efforts to suppress his thoughts about the outside world.... His impression management tactics have become second nature rather than self-conscious, as he routinely interacts with others in terms of his prison identity.

An inmate's suspension of his preprison identity, of course, is never absolute, and the separation between his suspended identity and his prison identity is never complete. He continues to interact with his visitors at least partially in terms of his preprison identity, and he is likely to have acquired at least one inmate "partner" with whom he interacts in terms of his preprison as well as his prison identity. During times of introspection, however—which take place less frequently but do not disappear—he generally continues to think of himself as being the same person he was before he came to prison. But it is also during these periods of self-dialogue that he begins to have doubts about his ability to revive his suspended identity. . . . At this point, both the inmate's suspended preprison identity and his created prison identity are part of his "performance consciousness" (Schechner 1985), although they are not given equal value. His preprison identity is grounded primarily in the memory of his biography (Weigert 1986) rather than in self-performance. His concern, during the middle of his sentence, is that he has become so accustomed to dealing with others in terms of his prison identity—that he has been presenting and receiving affirmation of this identity for so long—that it is becoming his "true" identity.

An inmate's fear that he is becoming the character he has been presenting is not unfounded. All of his interactions within the prison world indicate the strong likelihood of a "role-person merger" (Turner 1978). An inmate views his presentation of his prison identity as a necessary expression of his inmate status. Unlike situational identities presented through impression management in the outside world, performance of the inmate role is transsituational and continuous. For a new inmate, prison consists almost exclusively of front regions, in which he must remain in character. As long as he is in the maximum security institution, he remains in at least partial view of the audience for which his prison identity is intended: other prison inmates. Moreover, because the stakes of his performance are so high, there is little room for self-mockery or other forms of role distance (Ungar 1984; Coser 1966) from his prison identity, and there is little possibility that an inmate's performance will be "punctured" (Adler and Adler 1989) by his partner or other prison acquaintances. And because his presentation of his prison identity is continuous, he also receives continuous affirmation of this identity from others—affirmation that becomes more significant in light of the fact that he also remains removed from day-to-day

reaffirmation of his preprison identity by his associates in the outside world. The inauthenticity of the process is beside the point. Stone's (1962: 93) observation that "one's identity is established when others *place* him as a social object by assigning him the same words of identity that he appropriates for himself or *announces*" remains sound even when both the announcements and the placements are recognized as false. . . .

Identity Dialectic

When an inmate's concerns about his identity first emerge, there is little that he can do about them. He recognizes that he has no choice but to present his prison identity so, following the insider's perspective he has now adopted, he consciously attempts to suppress his concerns. Eventually, however, he must begin to consider seriously his capacity to revive his suspended identity; his identity concerns, and his belief that he must deal with them, become particularly acute if he is transferred to the minimum security unit of the prison for the final months of his sentence. At the conclusion of his prison career, an inmate shifts back toward an outsider's perspective on the prison world . . . ; this shift involves the dissipation of his maximum security adaptation strategy, further revision of his prison image, reconstruction of an image of the outside world, and the initial development of an outside plan. The inmate's efforts to revive his suspended identity are part of this shift in perspectives.

It is primarily through a renewed self-dialogue that the inmate struggles to revive his suspended identity—a struggle that amounts to a dialectic between his suspended identity and his prison identity. Through self-dialogue he recognizes, and tries to confront, the extent to which these two identities really do differ. He again tries to differentiate himself from maximum security inmates.

> There seems to be a concern with the inmates here to be able to distinguish . . . themselves from the other inmates. That is—they feel they are above the others. . . . Although they may

associate with each other, it still seems important to degrade the majority here.

And he does have some success in freeing himself from his prison identity.

> Well, I think I am starting to soften up a little bit. I believe the identity I picked up in the prison is starting to leave me now that I have left the world of the [maximum security] joint. I find myself becoming more and more involved with the happenings of the outside world. I am even getting anxious to go out and see the sights, just to get away from this place.

But he recognizes that he *has* changed in prison, and that these changes run deeper than the mask he has been presenting to others. He has not returned to his "old self" simply because his impression management skills are used less frequently in minimum security. He raises the question—though he cannot answer it—of how permanent these changes are. He wonders how much his family and friends will see him as having changed. As stated by one of our interview respondents:

> I know I've changed a little bit. I just want to realize how the people I know are going to see it, because they [will] be able to see it more than I can see it. . . . Sometimes I just want to go somewhere and hide.

He speculates about how much the outside world—especially his own network of outside relationships—has changed in his absence. (It is his life, not those of his family and friends, that has been suspended during his prison sentence; he knows that changes have occurred in the outside world, and he suspects that some of these changes may have been withheld from him, intentionally or otherwise.) He has questions, if not serious doubts, about his ability to "make it" on the outside, especially concerning his relationships with others; he knows, in any case, that he cannot simply return to the outside world as if nothing has happened. Above all, he repeatedly confronts the question of who he is, and who he will be in the outside world.

An inmate's struggle with these questions, like his self-dialogue at the beginning of his prison career, is necessarily a solitary activity. The identity he claims at the time of his release, in contrast to his prison identity, cannot be learned from other inmates. Also like his earlier periods of self-dialogue, the questions he considers are not approached in a rational, systematic manner. The process is more one of rumination—of pondering one question until another replaces it, and then contemplating the new question until it is replaced by still another, or suppressed from his thoughts. There is, then, no final resolution to any of the inmate's identity questions. Each inmate confronts these questions in his own way, and each arrives at his own understanding of who he is, based on this unfinished, unresolved self-dialogue. In every case, however, an inmate's release identity is a synthesis of his suspended preprison identity and his prison identity.

Postprison Identity

Because each inmate's release identity is the outcome of his own identity dialectic, we cannot provide a profile of the "typical" release identity. But our data do allow us to specify some of the conditions that affect this outcome. Reaffirmations of his preprison identity by outsiders—visits and furloughs during which others interact with him as if he has not changed—provide powerful support for his efforts to revive his suspended identity. These efforts are also promoted by an inmate's recollection of his preprison identity (i.e., his attempts, through self-dialogue, to assess who he was before he came to prison), by his desire to abandon his prison identity, and by his general shift back toward an outsider's perspective. But there are also several factors that favor his prison identity, including his continued use of diversionary activities; his continued periodic efforts to suppress thoughts about the outside world; his continued ability to use prison impression management skills; and his continuing sense of injustice about the treatment he has received. Strained or cautious interactions with outsiders, or unfulfilled furlough expectations, inhibit the revival of his preprison identity. And he faces direct, experiential evidence that he has changed: when a minimum security resident recognizes that he is now completely unaffected by reports of violent incidents in maximum security, he acknowledges that he is no longer the same person that he was when he entered prison. . . .

Just as we cannot define a typical release identity, we cannot predict these inmates' future, postprison identities, not only because we have restricted our analysis to their prison experiences but because each inmate's future identity is inherently unpredictable. What effect an ex-inmate's prison experience has on his identity depends on how he, in interaction with others, defines this experience. Some of the men we have studied will be returned to prison in the future; others will not. But all will have been changed by their prison experiences. They entered the prison world fearing for their lives; they depart with the knowledge that they have survived. On the one hand, these men are undoubtedly stronger persons by virtue of this accomplishment. On the other hand, the same tactics that enabled them to survive the prison world can be called upon, appropriately or not, in difficult situations in the outside world. To the extent that these men draw upon their prison survival tactics to cope with the hardships of the outside world—to the extent that their prison behavior becomes a meaningful part of their "role repertoire" (Turner 1978) in their everyday lives—their prison identities will have become inseparable from their "true" identities.

The Suspended Identity Model

As identity preservation tactics, an inmate's suspension of his preprison identity and development of a false prison identity are not, and cannot be, entirely successful. At the conclusion of his sentence, no inmate can ever fully revive his suspended identity; he cannot remain the same person he was before he came to prison. But his tactics do not fail entirely either. An inmate's resolve not to change, his decision to suspend his

preprison identity, his belief that he will be able to revive this identity, and his subsequent struggle to revive this identity undoubtedly minimize the identity change that would otherwise have taken place. The inmate's tactics, leading up to his suspended identity dialectic, constitute an identity transformation process . . . that differs from both the gradual, sequential model of identity transformation and models of radical identity transformation (Strauss 1959). It also shares some characteristics with each of these models.

As in cases of brainwashing and conversion, there is an external change agency involved, the inmate does learn a new perspective (an insider's perspective) for evaluating himself and the world around him, and he does develop new group loyalties while his old loyalties are reduced. But unlike a radical identity transformation, the inmate does not interpret the changes that take place as changes in a *central* identity; the insider's perspective he learns and the new person he becomes in prison are viewed as a false front that he must present to others, but a front that does not affect who he really is. And while suspending his preprison identity necessarily entails a weakening of his outside loyalties, it does not, in most cases, destroy them. Because he never achieves more than a marginal status in the prison world, the inmate's ambivalence prevents him from accepting an insider's perspective too fully, and thus prevents him from fully severing his loyalties to the outside world (Schmid and Jones 1987). He retains a fundamental, if ambivalent, commitment to his outside world throughout his sentence, and he expects to reestablish his outside relationships (just as he expects to revive his suspended identity) when his sentence is over.

Like a religious convert who later loses his faith, an inmate cannot simply return to his old self. The liminal conditions (Turner 1977) of the prison world have removed him, for too long, from his accustomed identity bearings in everyday life. He does change in prison, but his attempts to suspend and subsequently revive his preprison identity maintain a general sense of identity continuity for most of his prison career.

As in the gradual identity transformation process delineated by Strauss (1959), he recognizes changes in his identity only at periodic "turning points," especially his mid-career doubts about his ability to revive his suspended identity and his self-dialogue at the end of his sentence. Also like a gradual identity transformation, the extent of his identity change depends on a balance between the situational adjustments he has made in prison and his continuing commitments to the outside world (Becker 1960, 1964). His identity depends, in other words, on the outcome of the dialectic between his prison identity and his suspended preprison identity.

The suspended identity model is one component of a holistic analysis of the experiences of first-time, short-term inmates at a specific maximum security prison. Like any holistic analysis, its usefulness lies primarily in its capacity to explain the particular case under study (Deising 1971). We nonetheless expect similar identity transformation processes to occur under similar circumstances: among individuals who desire to preserve their identities despite finding themselves involved in temporary but encompassing social worlds or social situations that subject them to new and disparate identity demands and render their prior identities inappropriate. The suspended identity model presented here provides a basis for further exploration of these circumstances.

REFERENCES

Adler, Patricia A. and Peter Adler. 1989. "The Gloried Self: The Aggrandizement and the Constriction of Self." *Social Psychology Quarterly* 52:299–310.

Becker, Howard S. 1960. "Notes on the Concept of Commitment." *American Journal of Sociology* 66:32–40.

———. "Personal Change in Adult Life." 1964. *Sociometry* 27:40–53.

Berger, Peter L. 1963. *Invitation to Sociology. A Humanistic Perspective.* Garden City, NY: Doubleday/Anchor Books.

Blumer, Herbert. 1972. "Action vs. Interaction: Review of *Relations in Public* by Erving Goffman." *Transaction* 9:50–53.

———. 1969. *Symbolic Interactionism: Perspective and Method.* Englewood Cliffs, NJ: Prentice Hall.

Boulding, Kenneth. 1961. *The Image.* Ann Arbor: University of Michigan Press.

Coser, R. 1966. "Role Distance, Sociological Ambivalence and Traditional Status Systems." *American Journal of Sociology* 72:173–187.

Deising, Paul. 1971. *Patterns of Discovery in the Social Sciences.* Chicago: Aldine-Atherton.

Douglas, Jack D., Patricia A. Adler, Peter Adler, Andrea Fontana, Robert C. Freeman, and Joseph A. Kotarba. 1980. *Introduction to the Sociologies of Everyday Life.* Boston: Allyn & Bacon.

Douglas, Jack D. and John M. Johnson. 1977. *Existential Sociology.* Cambridge: Cambridge University Press.

Garfinkel, Harold. 1956. "Conditions of Successful Degradation Ceremonies." *American Journal of Sociology* 61:420–424.

Glaser, Barney G. and Anselm L. Strauss. 1964. "Awareness Contexts and Social Interaction." *American Sociological Review* 29:269–279.

Goffman, Erving. 1961. *Asylums.* Garden City, NY: Doubleday/Anchor Books.

———. 1959. The *Presentation of Self in Everyday Life.* Garden City, NY: Doubleday/Anchor Books.

———. 1963. *Stigma: Notes on the Management of Spoiled Identity.* Englewood Cliffs, NJ: Prentice Hall.

Gross, Edward and Gregory P. Stone. 1964. "Embarrassment and the Analysis of Role Requirements." *American Journal of Sociology* 70:1–15.

Irwin, John. 1970. *The Felon.* Englewood Cliffs, NJ: Prentice Hall.

———. 1977. *Scenes.* Beverly Hills: Sage.

Lewis, David J. 1979. "A Social Behaviorist Interpretation of the Median I." *American Journal of Sociology* 84:261–287.

Messinger, Sheldon E., Harold Sampson, and Robert D. Towne. 1962. "Life as Theater: Some Notes on the Dramaturgic Approach to Social Reality." *Sociometry* 25: 98–111.

Schechner, Richard. 1985. *Between Theater and Anthropology.* Philadelphia. University of Pennsylvania Press.

Schlenker, B. 1980. *Impression Management. The Self Concept, Social Identity and Interpersonal Relations.* Belmont, CA: Wadsworth.

Schmid, Thomas and Richard Jones. 1987. "Ambivalent Actions: Prison Adaptation Strategies of New

Inmates." American Society of Criminology, annual meetings, Montreal, Quebec.

Schmid, Thomas and Richard Jones. 1990. "Experiential Orientations to the Prison Experience: The Case of First-Time, Short-Term Inmates." Pp. 189–210 in *Perspectives on Social Problems,* edited by Gale Miller and James A. Holstein. Greenwich, CT: JAI Press.

Stone, Gregory P. 1962. "Appearance and the Self." Pp. 86–118 in *Human Behavior and Social Processes,* edited by Arnold Rose. Boston: Houghton Mifflin.

Strauss, Anselm L. 1959. *Mirrors and Masks: The Search for Identity,* Glencoe: Free Press.

Sykes, Gresham. 1958. *The Society of Captives: A Study of a Maximum Security Prison.* Princeton: Princeton University Press.

Turner, Ralph H. 1978. "The Role and the Person." *American Journal of Sociology* 84:1–23.

Turner, Victor. 1977. *The Ritual Process: Structure and Anti-Structure.* Ithaca, NY: Cornell University Press.

Ungar, Sheldon. 1984. "Self-Mockery: An Alternative Form of Self-Presentation." *Symbolic Interaction* 7:121–133.

Weigert, Andrew J. 1986. "The Social Production of Identity: Metatheoretical Foundations." *Sociological Quarterly* 27:165–183.

Zurcher, Louis A. 1977. *The Mutable Self.* Beverly Hills: Sage.

THINKING ABOUT THE READING

What happens to inmates' self-concepts in prison? Given the stigmatizing effects of being identified as an "ex-con," do you think it is ever possible for people to reclaim their normal, law-abiding identities once they get out of prison? How would the identity transformations described by Schmid and Jones differ for female prisoners? Consider another environment (for instance, military boot camp, a violent street gang, a religious cult) where such a dramatic shift in public identity must take place. How would the experiences of people in these situations differ and/or resemble those of the inmates described by Schmid and Jones? What does the process of identity transformation imply about the strength and permanence of identity?

7 Constructing Difference: Social Deviance

According to most sociologists, deviance is not an inherent feature or personality trait. Instead, it is a consequence of a definitional process. Like beauty, it is in the eye of the beholder. Deviant labels can impede everyday social life by forming expectations in the minds of others. Some sociologists argue that the definition of deviance is a form of social control exerted by more powerful people and groups over less powerful ones.

William Chambliss, in "The Saints and the Roughnecks," shows that deviant labels can have serious negative consequences and can determine future opportunities, especially for young people. What makes this idea important, sociologically, is that the application of these labels is not just a function of lawbreaking behavior but is influenced by the social characteristics of the people engaging in such behavior. Most of us participate in some form of deviant activity when we are young: minor shoplifting, underage drinking, illegal drug use, driving over the speed limit, wearing bizarre clothes, skipping school, and so on. For most of us, these acts don't have any lasting impact on our identities, but for some they do.

Vivyan Adair expands on this idea that deviant labels are not simply applied to people who engage in undesirable behaviors. In "Branded with Infamy: Inscriptions of Poverty and Class in America," she describes the various ways in which poor women's bodies are marked as "unclean" or "unacceptable." These markings are the result of a life of poverty: lack of access to adequate health care, lack of proper nutrition and shelter, and a consequence of difficult and demanding physical labor. But more affluent people often come to view these women (and their children) not as victims of economic circumstances but as deviants who deserve to be disciplined, controlled, and punished.

The definitional process that results in the labeling of some people as deviant can occur at the institutional as well as the individual level. Powerful institutions are capable of creating a conception of deviance that the public comes to accept as truth. One such institution is the field of medicine. We usually think of medicine as a benevolent institution whose primary purpose is to help sick people get better. But in "Medicine as an Institution of Social Control," Peter Conrad and Joseph Schneider show how medical vocabularies and ideologies shape public perceptions of deviance. They show how various types of problematic behavior, previously considered crimes or sins, come to be seen as illnesses. We usually think of the individuals and organizations who make up the criminal justice system (police, courts, prisons) as the agents responsible for controlling deviance. But a medicalized view of deviance has given rise to a system of social control made up of physicians, psychiatrists, psychologists, counselors, and other specialists. The authors describe the important social implications of conceiving of deviance as a "disorder" that can and should be "treated" and "cured."

The Saints and the Roughnecks

William J. Chambliss

Eight promising young men—children of good, stable, white upper-middle-class families, active in school affairs, good pre-college students—were some of the most delinquent boys at Hanibal High School. While community residents and parents knew that these boys occasionally sowed a few wild oats, they were totally unaware that sowing wild oats completely occupied the daily routine of these young men. The Saints were constantly occupied with truancy, drinking, wild driving, petty theft and vandalism. Yet not one was officially arrested for any misdeed during the two years I observed them.

This record was particularly surprising in light of my observations during the same two years of another gang of Hanibal High School students, six lower-class white boys known as the Roughnecks. The Roughnecks were constantly in trouble with police and community even though their rate of delinquency was about equal with that of the Saints. What was the cause of this disparity? the result? The following consideration of the activities, social class and community perceptions of both gangs may provide some answers.

The Saints from Monday to Friday

The Saints' principal daily concern was with getting out of school as early as possible. The boys managed to get out of school with minimum danger that they would be accused of playing hookey through an elaborate procedure for obtaining "legitimate" release from class. The most common procedure was for one boy to obtain the release of another by fabricating a meeting of some committee, program or recognized club. Charles might raise his hand in his 9:00 chemis-try class and ask to be excused—a euphemism—for going to the bathroom. Charles would go to Ed's math class and inform the teacher that Ed was needed for a 9:30 rehearsal of the drama club play. The math teacher would recognize Ed and Charles as "good students" involved in numerous school activities and would permit Ed to leave at 9:30. Charles would return to his class, and Ed would go to Tom's English class to obtain his release. Tom would engineer Charles' escape. The strategy would continue until as many of the Saints as possible were freed. After a stealthy trip to the car (which had been parked in a strategic spot), the boys were off for a day of fun.

Over the two years I observed the Saints, this pattern was repeated nearly every day. There were variations on the theme, but in one form or another, the boys used this procedure for getting out of class and then off the school grounds. Rarely did all eight of the Saints manage to leave school at the same time. The average number avoiding school on the days I observed them was five.

Having escaped from the concrete corridors the boys usually went either to a pool hall on the other (lower-class) side of town or to a cafe in the suburbs. Both places were out of the way of people the boys were likely to know (family or school officials), and both provided a source of entertainment. The pool hall entertainment was the generally rough atmosphere, the occasional hustler, the sometimes drunk proprietor and, of course, the game of pool. The cafe's entertainment was provided by the owner. The boys would "accidentally" knock a glass on the floor or spill cola on the counter—not all the time, but enough to be sporting. They would also bend spoons, put salt in sugar bowls and generally tease whoever was working in the cafe. The owner had opened the cafe recently and was dependent on the boys' business which was, in fact, substantial since between the horsing around and the teasing they bought food and drinks.

The Saints on Weekends

On weekends the automobile was even more critical than during the week, for on weekends the Saints went to Big Town—a large city with a population of over a million 25 miles from Hanibal. Every Friday and Saturday night most of the Saints would meet between 8:00 and 8:30 and would go into Big Town. Big Town activities included drinking heavily in taverns or nightclubs, driving drunkenly through the streets, and committing acts of vandalism and playing pranks.

By midnight on Fridays and Saturdays the Saints were usually thoroughly high, and one or two of them were often so drunk they had to be carried to the cars. Then the boys drove around town, calling obscenities to women and girls; occasionally trying (unsuccessfully so far as I could tell) to pick girls up; and driving recklessly through red lights and at high speeds with their lights out. Occasionally they played "chicken." One boy would climb out the back window of the car and across the roof to the driver's side of the car while the car was moving at high speed (between 40 and 50 miles an hour); then the driver would move over and the boy who had just crawled across the car roof would take the driver's seat.

Searching for "fair game" for a prank was the boys' principal activity after they left the tavern. The boys would drive alongside a foot patrolman and ask directions to some street. If the policeman leaned on the car in the course of answering the question, the driver would speed away, causing him to lose his balance. The Saints were careful to play this prank only in an area where they were not going to spend much time and where they could quickly disappear around a corner to avoid having their license plate number taken.

Construction sites and road repair areas were the special province of the Saints' mischief. A soon-to-be-repaired hole in the road inevitably invited the Saints to remove lanterns and wooden barricades and put them in the car, leaving the hole unprotected. The boys would find a safe vantage point and wait for an unsuspecting motorist to drive into the hole. Often, though not always, the boys would go up to the motorist and commiserate with him about the dreadful way the city protected its citizenry.

Leaving the scene of the open hole and the motorist, the boys would then go searching for an appropriate place to erect the stolen barricade. An "appropriate place" was often a spot on a highway near a curve in the road where the barricade would not be seen by an oncoming motorist. The boys would wait to watch an unsuspecting motorist attempt to stop and (usually) crash into the wooden barricade. With saintly bearing, the boys might offer help and understanding.

A stolen lantern might well find its way onto the back of a police car or hang from a street lamp. Once a lantern served as a prop for a reenactment of the "midnight ride of Paul Revere" until the "play," which was taking place at 2:00 A.M. in the center of a main street of Big Town, was interrupted by a police car several blocks away. The boys ran, leaving the lanterns on the street, and managed to avoid being apprehended.

Abandoned houses, especially if they were located in out-of-the-way places, were fair game for destruction and spontaneous vandalism. The boys would break windows, remove furniture to the yard and tear it apart, urinate on the walls and scrawl obscenities inside.

Through all the pranks, drinking and reckless driving the boys managed miraculously to avoid being stopped by police. Only twice in two years was I aware that they had been stopped by a Big Town policeman. Once was for speeding (which they did every time they drove whether they were drunk or sober), and the driver managed to convince the policeman that it was simply an error. The second time they were stopped they had just left a nightclub and were walking through an alley. Aaron stopped to urinate and the boys began making obscene remarks. A foot patrolman came into the alley, lectured the boys and sent them home. Before the boys got to the car one began talking in a loud voice again. The policeman, who had followed them down the alley, arrested this boy for disturbing the peace and took him to the police station where the other Saints gathered. After paying a $5.00 fine and with the assurance that there would be no permanent record of the arrest, the boy was released.

The boys had a spirit of frivolity and fun about their escapades. They did not view what they were engaged in as "delinquency," though it surely was, by any reasonable definition of that word. They simply viewed themselves as having a little fun and who, they would ask, was really hurt by it? The answer had to be no one, although this fact remains one of the most difficult things to explain about the gang's behavior. Unlikely though it seems, in two years of drinking, driving, carousing and vandalism no one was seriously injured as a result of the Saints' activities.

The Saints in School

The Saints were highly successful in school. The average grade for the group was "B," with two of the boys having close to a straight "A" average. Almost all of the boys were popular and many of them held offices in the school. One of the boys was vice-president of the student body one year. Six of the boys played on athletic teams.

At the end of their senior year, the student body selected ten seniors for special recognition as the "school wheels"; four of the ten were Saints. Teachers and school officials saw no problem with any of these boys and anticipated that they would all "make something of themselves."

How the boys managed to maintain this impression is surprising in view of their actual behavior while in school. Their technique for covering truancy was so successful that teachers did not even realize that the boys were absent from school much of the time. Occasionally, of course, the system would backfire and then the boy was on his own. A boy who was caught would be most contrite, would plead guilty and ask for mercy. He inevitably got the mercy he sought.

Cheating on examinations was rampant, even to the point of orally communicating answers to exams as well as looking at one another's papers. Since none of the group studied, and since they were primarily dependent on one another for help, it is surprising that grades were so high. Teachers contributed to the deception in their admitted inclination to give these boys (and presumably others like them) the benefit of the doubt. When asked how the boys did in school, and when pressed on specific examinations, teachers might admit that they were disappointed in John's performance, but would quickly add that they "knew that he was capable of doing better," so John was given a higher grade than he had actually earned. How often this happened is impossible to know. During the time that I observed the group, I never saw any of the boys take homework home. Teachers may have been "understanding" very regularly.

One exception to the gang's generally good performance was Jerry, who had a "C" average in his junior year, experienced disaster the next year and failed to graduate. Jerry had always been a little more nonchalant than the others about the liberties he took in school. Rather than wait for someone to come get him from class, he would offer his own excuse and leave. Although he probably did not miss any more classes than most of the others in the group, he did not take the requisite pains to cover his absences. Jerry was the only Saint whom I ever heard talk back to a teacher. Although teachers often called him a "cut up" or a "smart kid," they never referred to him as a troublemaker or as a kid headed for trouble. It seems likely, then, that Jerry's failure his senior year and his mediocre performance his junior year were consequences of his not playing the game the proper way (possibly because he was disturbed by his parents' divorce). His teachers regarded him as "immature" and not quite ready to get out of high school.

The Police and the Saints

The local police saw the Saints as good boys who were among the leaders of the youth in the community. Rarely, the boys might be stopped in town for speeding or for running a stop sign. When this happened the boys were always polite, contrite and pled for mercy. As in school, they received the mercy they asked for. None ever received a ticket or was taken into the precinct by the local police.

The situation in Big Town, where the boys engaged in most of their delinquency, was only slightly different. The police there did not know the boys at all, although occasionally the boys were stopped by a patrolman. Once they were caught taking a lantern from a construction site. Another time they were stopped for running a stop sign, and on several occasions they were stopped for speeding. Their behavior was as before: contrite, polite and penitent. The urban police, like the local police, accepted their demeanor as sincere. More important, the urban police were convinced that these were good boys just out for a lark.

The Roughnecks

Hanibal townspeople never perceived the Saints' high level of delinquency. The Saints were good boys who just went in for an occasional prank. After all, they were well dressed, well mannered and had nice cars. The Roughnecks were a different story. Although the two gangs of boys were the same age, and both groups engaged in an equal amount of wild-oat sowing, everyone agreed that the not-so-well-dressed, not-so-well-mannered, not-so-rich boys were heading for trouble. Townspeople would say, "You can see the gang members at the drugstore, night after night, leaning against the storefront (sometimes drunk) or slouching around inside buying cokes, reading magazines, and probably stealing old Mr. Wall blind. When they are outside and girls walk by, even respectable girls, these boys make suggestive remarks. Sometimes their remarks are downright lewd."

From the community's viewpoint, the real indication that these kids were in for trouble was that they were constantly involved with the police. Some of them had been picked up for stealing, mostly small stuff, of course, "but still it's

stealing small stuff that leads to big time crimes." "Too bad," people said. "Too bad that these boys couldn't behave like the other kids in town; stay out of trouble, be polite to adults, and look to their future."

The community's impression of the degree to which this group of six boys (ranging in age from 16 to 19) engaged in delinquency was somewhat distorted. In some ways the gang was more delinquent than the community thought; in other ways they were less.

The fighting activities of the group were fairly readily and accurately perceived by almost everyone. At least once a month, the boys would get into some sort of fight, although most fights were scraps between members of the group or involved only one member of the group and some peripheral hanger-on. Only three times in the period of observation did the group fight together: once against a gang from across town, once against two blacks and once against a group of boys from another school. For the first two fights the group went out "looking for trouble"—and they found it both times. The third fight followed a football game and began spontaneously with an argument on the football field between one of the Roughnecks and a member of the opposition's football team.

Jack had a particular propensity for fighting and was involved in most of the brawls. He was a prime mover of the escalation of arguments into fights.

More serious than fighting, had the community been aware of it, was theft. Although almost everyone was aware that the boys occasionally stole things, they did not realize the extent of the activity. Petty stealing was a frequent event for the Roughnecks. Sometimes they stole as a group and coordinated their efforts; other times they stole in pairs. Rarely did they steal alone.

The thefts ranged from very small things like paperback books, comics and ballpoint pens to expensive items like watches. The nature of the thefts varied from time to time. The gang would go through a period of systematically shoplifting items from automobiles or school lockers. Types of thievery varied with the whim of the gang.

Some forms of thievery were more profitable than others, but all thefts were for profit, not just thrills.

Roughnecks siphoned gasoline from cars as often as they had access to an automobile, which was not very often. Unlike the Saints, who owned their own cars, the Roughnecks would have to borrow their parents' cars, an event which occurred only eight or nine times a year. The boys claimed to have stolen cars for joy rides from time to time.

Ron committed the most serious of the group's offenses. With an unidentified associate the boy attempted to burglarize a gasoline station. Although this station had been robbed twice previously in the same month, Ron denied any involvement in either of the other thefts. When Ron and his accomplice approached the station, the owner was hiding in the bushes beside the station. He fired both barrels of a double-barreled shotgun at the boys. Ron was severely injured; the other boy ran away and was never caught. Though he remained in critical condition for several months, Ron finally recovered and served six months of the following year in reform school. Upon release from reform school, Ron was put back a grade in school, and began running around with a different gang of boys. The Roughnecks considered the new gang less delinquent than themselves, and during the following year Ron had no more trouble with the police.

The Roughnecks, then, engaged mainly in three types of delinquency: theft, drinking and fighting. Although community members perceived that this gang of kids was delinquent, they mistakenly believed that their illegal activities were primarily drinking, fighting and being a nuisance to passersby. Drinking was limited among the gang members, although it did occur, and theft was much more prevalent than anyone realized.

Drinking would doubtless have been more prevalent had the boys had ready access to liquor. Since they rarely had automobiles at their disposal, they could not travel very far, and the bars in town would not serve them. Most of the boys had little money, and this, too, inhibited their purchase of alcohol. Their major source of liquor was a local drunk who would buy them a fifth if they would give him enough extra to buy himself a pint of whiskey or a bottle of wine.

The community's perception of drinking as prevalent stemmed from the fact that it was the most obvious delinquency the boys engaged in. When one of the boys had been drinking, even a casual observer seeing him on the corner would suspect that he was high.

There was a high level of mutual distrust and dislike between the Roughnecks and the police. The boys felt very strongly that the police were unfair and corrupt. Some evidence existed that the boys were correct in their perception.

The main source of the boys' dislike for the police undoubtedly stemmed from the fact that the police would sporadically harass the group. From the standpoint of the boys, these acts of occasional enforcement of the law were whimsical and uncalled for. It made no sense to them, for example, that the police would come to the corner occasionally and threaten them with arrest for loitering when the night before the boys had been out siphoning gasoline from cars and the police had been nowhere in sight. To the boys, the police were stupid on the one hand, for not being where they should have been and catching the boys in a serious offense, and unfair on the other hand, for trumping up "loitering" charges against them.

From the viewpoint of the police, the situation was quite different. They knew, with all the confidence necessary to be a policeman, that these boys were engaged in criminal activities. They knew this partly from occasionally catching them, mostly from circumstantial evidence ("the boys were around when those tires were slashed"), and partly because the police shared the view of the community in general that this was a bad bunch of boys. The best the police could hope to do was to be sensitive to the fact that these boys were engaged in illegal acts and arrest them whenever there was some evidence that they had been involved. Whether or not the boys had in fact committed a particular act in a particular way was not especially important. The police had a broader view: their job was to stamp out these kids' crimes; the tactics were not as important as the end result.

Over the period that the group was under observation, each member was arrested at least once. Several of the boys were arrested a number of times and spent at least one night in jail. While most were never taken to court, two of the boys were sentenced to six months' incarceration in boys' schools.

The Roughnecks in School

The Roughnecks' behavior in school was not particularly disruptive. During school hours they did not all hang around together, but tended instead to spend most of their time with one or two other members of the gang who were their special buddies. Although every member of the gang attempted to avoid school as much as possible, they were not particularly successful and most of them attended school with surprising regularity. They considered school a burden—something to be gotten through with a minimum of conflict. If they were "bugged" by a particular teacher, it could lead to trouble. One of the boys, Al, once threatened to beat up a teacher and, according to the other boys, the teacher hid under a desk to escape him.

Teachers saw the boys the way the general community did, as heading for trouble, as being uninterested in making something of themselves. Some were also seen as being incapable of meeting the academic standards of the school. Most of the teachers expressed concern for this group of boys and were willing to pass them despite poor performance, in the belief that failing them would only aggravate the problem.

The group of boys had a grade point average just slightly above "C." No one in the group failed either grade, and no one had better than a "C" average. They were very consistent in their achievement or, at least, the teachers were consistent in their perception of the boys' achievement.

Two of the boys were good football players. Herb was acknowledged to be the best player in the school and Jack was almost as good. Both boys were criticized for their failure to abide by training rules, for refusing to come to practice as often as they should, and for not playing their best during practice. What they lacked in sportsmanship they made up for in skill, apparently, and played every game no matter how poorly they had performed in practice or how many practice sessions they had missed.

Two Questions

Why did the community, the school and the police react to the Saints as though they were good, upstanding, nondelinquent youths with bright futures but to the Roughnecks as though they were tough, young criminals who were headed for trouble? Why did the Roughnecks and the Saints in fact have quite different careers after high school—careers which, by and large, lived up to the expectations of the community?

The most obvious explanation for the differences in the community's and law enforcement agencies' reactions to the two gangs is that one group of boys was "more delinquent" than the other. Which group was more delinquent? The answer to this question will determine in part how we explain the differential responses to these groups by the members of the community and, particularly, by law enforcement and school officials.

In sheer number of illegal acts, the Saints were the more delinquent. They were truant from school for at least part of the day almost every day of the week. In addition, their drinking and vandalism occurred with surprising regularity. The Roughnecks, in contrast, engaged sporadically in delinquent episodes. While these episodes were frequent, they certainly did not occur on a daily or even a weekly basis.

The difference in frequency of offenses was probably caused by the Roughnecks' inability to obtain liquor and to manipulate legitimate excuses from school. Since the Roughnecks had less money than the Saints, and teachers carefully supervised their school activities, the Roughnecks' hearts may have been as black as the Saints', but their misdeeds were not nearly as frequent.

There are really no clear-cut criteria by which to measure qualitative differences in antisocial behavior. The most important dimension of the difference is generally referred to as the "seriousness" of the offenses.

If seriousness encompasses the relative economic costs of delinquent acts, then some assessment can be made. The Roughnecks probably stole an average of about $5.00 worth of goods a week. Some weeks the figure was considerably higher, but these times must be balanced against long periods when almost nothing was stolen.

The Saints were more continuously engaged in delinquency but their acts were not for the most part costly to property. Only their vandalism and occasional theft of gasoline would so qualify. Perhaps once or twice a month they would siphon a tankful of gas. The other costly items were street signs, construction lanterns and the like. All of these acts combined probably did not quite average $5.00 a week, partly because much of the stolen equipment was abandoned and presumably could be recovered. The difference in cost of stolen property between the two groups was trivial, but the Roughnecks probably had a slightly more expensive set of activities than did the Saints.

Another meaning of seriousness is the potential threat of physical harm to members of the community and to the boys themselves. The Roughnecks were more prone to physical violence: they not only welcomed an opportunity to fight, they went seeking it. In addition, they fought among themselves frequently. Although the fighting never included deadly weapons, it was still a menace, however minor, to the physical safety of those involved.

The Saints never fought. They avoided physical conflict both inside and outside the group. At the same time, though, the Saints frequently endangered their own and other people's lives. They did so almost every time they drove a car, especially if they had been drinking. Sober, their driving was risky; under the influence of alcohol it was horrendous. In addition, the Saints endangered the lives of others with their pranks. Street excavations left unmarked were a very serious hazard.

Evaluating the relative seriousness of the two gangs' activities is difficult. The community reacted as though the behavior of the Roughnecks was a problem, and they reacted as though the behavior of the Saints was not. But the members of the community were ignorant of the array of delinquent acts that characterized the Saints' behavior. Although concerned citizens were unaware of much of the Roughnecks' behavior as well, they were much better informed about the Roughnecks' involvement in delinquency than they were about the Saints'.

Visibility

Differential treatment of the two gangs resulted in part because one gang was infinitely more visible than the other. This differential visibility was a direct function of the economic standing of the families. The Saints had access to automobiles and were able to remove themselves from the sight of the community. In as routine a decision as to where to go to have a milkshake after school, the Saints stayed away from the mainstream of community life. Lacking transportation, the Roughnecks could not make it to the edge of town. The center of town was the only practical place for them to meet, since their homes were scattered throughout the town and any noncentral meeting place put an undue hardship on some members. Through necessity the Roughnecks congregated in a crowded area where everyone in the community passed frequently, including teachers and law enforcement officers. They could easily see the Roughnecks hanging around the drugstore.

The Roughnecks, of course, made themselves even more visible by making remarks to passersby and by occasionally getting into fights on the corner. Meanwhile, just as regularly, the Saints were either at the cafe on one edge of town or in the pool hall at the other edge of town. Without any particular realization that they were making themselves inconspicuous, the Saints were able to hide their time-wasting. Not only were they removed from the mainstream of traffic, but they were almost always inside a building.

On their escapades the Saints were also relatively invisible, since they left Hanibal and travelled to Big Town. Here, too, they were mobile, roaming the city, rarely going to the same area twice.

Demeanor

To the notion of visibility must be added the difference in the responses of group members to outside intervention with their activities. If one of the Saints was confronted with an accusing policeman, even if he felt he was truly innocent of a wrongdoing, his demeanor was apologetic and penitent. A Roughneck's attitude was almost the polar opposite. When confronted with a threatening adult authority, even one who tried to be pleasant, the Roughneck's hostility and disdain were clearly observable. Sometimes he might attempt to put up a veneer of respect, but it was thin and was not accepted as sincere by the authority.

School was no different from the community at large. The Saints could manipulate the system by feigning compliance with the school norms. The availability of cars at school meant that once free from the immediate sight of the teacher, the boys could disappear rapidly. And this escape was well enough planned that no administrator or teacher was nearby when the boys left. A Roughneck who wished to escape for a few hours was in a bind. If it were possible to get free from class, downtown was still a mile away, and even if he arrived there, he was still very visible. Truancy for the Roughnecks meant almost certain detection, while the Saints enjoyed almost complete immunity from sanctions.

Bias

Community members were not aware of the transgressions of the Saints. Even if the Saints had been less discreet, their favorite delinquencies would have been perceived as less serious than those of the Roughnecks.

In the eyes of the police and school officials, a boy who drinks in an alley and stands intoxicated on the street corner is committing a more serious offense than is a boy who drinks to inebriation in a nightclub or a tavern and drives

around afterwards in a car. Similarly, a boy who steals a wallet from a store will be viewed as having committed a more serious offense than a boy who steals a lantern from a construction site.

Perceptual bias also operates with respect to the demeanor of the boys in the two groups when they are confronted by adults. It is not simply that adults dislike the posture affected by boys of the Roughneck ilk; more important is the conviction that the posture adopted by the Roughnecks is an indication of their devotion and commitment to deviance as a way of life. The posture becomes a cue, just as the type of the offense is a cue, to the degree to which the known transgressions are indicators of the youths' potential for other problems.

Visibility, demeanor and bias are surface variables which explain the day-to-day operations of the police. Why do these surface variables operate as they do? Why did the police choose to disregard the Saints' delinquencies while breathing down the backs of the Roughnecks?

The answer lies in the class structure of American society and the control of legal institutions by those at the top of the class structure. Obviously, no representative of the upper class drew up the operational chart for the police which led them to look in the ghettoes and on street corners—which led them to see the demeanor of lower-class youth as troublesome and that of upper-middle-class youth as tolerable. Rather, the procedures simply developed from experience—experience with irate and influential upper-middle-class parents insisting that their son's vandalism was simply a prank and his drunkenness only a momentary "sowing of wild oats"—experience with cooperative or indifferent, powerless, lower-class parents who acquiesced to the law's definition of their son's behavior.

Adult Careers of the Saints and the Roughnecks

The community's confidence in the potential of the Saints and the Roughnecks apparently was justified. If anything, the community members underestimated the degree to which these youngsters would turn out "good" or "bad."

Seven of the eight members of the Saints went on to college immediately after high school. Five of the boys graduated from college in four years. The sixth one finished college after two years in the army, and the seventh spent four years in the Air Force before returning to college and receiving a B.A. Of these seven college graduates, three went on for advanced degrees. One finished law school and is now active in state politics, one finished medical school and is practicing near Hanibal, and one boy is now working for a Ph.D. The other four college graduates entered submanagerial, managerial or executive training positions with larger firms.

The only Saint who did not complete college was Jerry. Jerry had failed to graduate from high school with the other Saints. During his second senior year, after the other Saints had gone on to college, Jerry began to hang around with what several teachers described as a "rough crowd"—the gang that was heir apparent to the Roughnecks. At the end of his second senior year, when he did graduate from high school, Jerry took a job as a used-car salesman, got married and quickly had a child. Although he made several abortive attempts to go to college by attending night school, when I last saw him (ten years after high school) Jerry was unemployed and had been living on unemployment for almost a year. His wife worked as a waitress.

Some of the Roughnecks have lived up to community expectations. A number of them were headed for trouble. A few were not.

Jack and Herb were the athletes among the Roughnecks, and their athletic prowess paid off handsomely. Both boys received unsolicited athletic scholarships to college. After Herb received his scholarship (near the end of his senior year), he apparently did an about-face. His demeanor became very similar to that of the Saints. Although he remained a member in good standing of the Roughnecks, he stopped participating in most activities and did not hang on the corner as often.

Jack did not change. If anything, he became more prone to fighting. He even made excuses for accepting the scholarship. He told the other gang members that the school had guaranteed him a "C" average if he would come to play football—an idea that seems far-fetched, even in this day of highly competitive recruiting.

During the summer after graduation from high school, Jack attempted suicide by jumping from a tall building. The jump would certainly have killed most people trying it, but Jack survived. He entered college in the fall and played four years of football. He and Herb graduated in four years, and both are teaching and coaching in high schools. They are married and have stable families. If anything, Jack appears to have a more prestigious position in the community than does Herb, though both are well respected and secure in their positions.

Two of the boys never finished high school. Tommy left at the end of his junior year and went to another state. That summer he was arrested and placed on probation on a manslaughter charge. Three years later he was arrested for murder; he pleaded guilty to second-degree murder and is serving a 30-year sentence in the state penitentiary.

Al, the other boy who did not finish high school, also left the state in his senior year. He is serving a life sentence in a state penitentiary for first-degree murder.

Wes is a small-time gambler. He finished high school and "bummed around." After several years he made contact with a bookmaker who employed him as a runner. Later he acquired his own area and has been working it ever since. His position among the bookmakers is almost identical to the position he had in the gang; he is always around but no one is really aware of him. He makes no trouble and he does not get into any. Steady, reliable, capable of keeping his mouth closed, he plays the game by the rules, even though the game is an illegal one.

That leaves only Ron. Some of his former friends reported that they had heard he was "driving a truck up north," but no one could provide any concrete information.

Reinforcement

The community responded to the Roughnecks as boys in trouble, and the boys agreed with that perception. Their pattern of deviancy was reinforced, and breaking away from it became increasingly unlikely. Once the boys acquired an image of themselves as deviants, they selected new friends who affirmed that self-image. As that self-conception became more firmly entrenched, they also became willing to try new and more extreme deviances. With their growing alienation came freer expression of disrespect and hostility for representatives of the legitimate society. This disrespect increased the community's negativism, perpetuating the entire process of commitment to deviance. Lack of a commitment to deviance works the same way. In either case, the process will perpetuate itself unless some event (like a scholarship to college or a sudden failure) external to the established relationship intervenes. For two of the Roughnecks (Herb and Jack), receiving college athletic scholarships created new relations and culminated in a break with the established pattern of deviance. In the case of one of the Saints (Jerry), his parents' divorce and his failing to graduate from high school changed some of his other relations. Being held back in school for a year and losing his place among the Saints had sufficient impact on Jerry to alter his self-image and to virtually assure that he would not go on to college as his peers did. Although the experiments of life can rarely be reversed, it seems likely in view of the behavior of the other boys who did not enjoy this special treatment by the school that Jerry, too, would have "become something" had he graduated as anticipated. For Herb and Jack outside intervention worked to their advantage; for Jerry it was his undoing.

Selective perception and labeling—finding, processing and punishing some kinds of criminality and not others—means that visible, poor, nonmobile, outspoken, undiplomatic "tough" kids will be noticed, whether their actions are seriously delinquent or not. Other kids, who have established a reputation for being bright (even though underachieving), disciplined and involved in respectable activities, who are mobile and monied, will be invisible when they deviate from sanctioned activities. They'll sow their wild oats—perhaps even wider and thicker than their lower-class cohorts—but they won't be noticed. When it's time to leave adolescence most will follow the expected path, settling into the ways of the middle class, remembering fondly the delinquent but unnoticed fling of their youth. The Roughnecks and others like them may turn around, too. It is more likely that their noticeable deviance will have been so reinforced by police and community that their lives will be effectively channelled into careers consistent with their adolescent background.

THINKING ABOUT THE READING

Have you ever known someone who had a "bad reputation"? How did this reputation affect the way people perceived that person? How did it affect the way people interpreted that person's actions? Compare your own "deviant" activities in high school with those of the "Saints" and the "Roughnecks." How were you able to overcome the potential negative effects of labeling? If you were labeled as a bad kid, how were you able to shed the label? Chambliss describes "deviant" activities that were relatively minor. How would the labeling processes he identifies differ if these groups were involved in serious, violent forms of deviance?

Branded with Infamy
Inscriptions of Poverty and Class in America

Vivyan Adair

"My kids and I been chopped up and spit out just like when I was a kid. My rotten teeth, my kids' twisted feet. My son's dull skin and blank stare. My oldest girl's stooped posture and the way she can't look no one in the eye no more. This all says we got nothing and we deserve what we got. On the street good families look at us and see right away what they'd be if they don't follow the rules. They're scared too, real scared."
—Welfare recipient and activist, Olympia, Washington, 1998

I begin with the words of a poor, White, single mother of three. Although officially she has only a tenth-grade education, she expertly reads and articulates a complex theory of power, bodily inscription, and socialization that arose directly from material conditions of her own life. She sees what many far more "educated" scholars and citizens fail to recognize: that the bodies of poor women and children are produced and positioned as texts that facilitate the mandates of a . . . profoundly brutal and mean-spirited political regime. . . .

Over the past decade or so, a host of inspired feminist welfare scholars and activists have addressed and examined the relationship between state power and the lives of poor women and children. As important and insightful as these exposés are, with few exceptions, they do not get at the closed circuit that fuses together systems of power, the material conditions of poverty, and the bodily experiences that allow for the perpetuation—and indeed the justification—of these systems. They fail to consider what the speaker of my opening passage recognized so as-

tutely: that systems of power produce and patrol poverty through the reproduction of both social and bodily markers. . . .

. . . [In this article I employ the theory of Michel Foucault to describe how the body is] the product of historically specific power relations. Feminists have used this notion of social inscription to explain a range of bodily operations from cosmetic surgery (Brush 1998, Morgan 1991), prostitution (Bell 1994), and Anorexia Nervosa (Hopwood 1995, Bordo 1993) to motherhood (Chandler 1999, Smart 1992), race (Stoler 1995, Ford-Smith 1996), and cultural imperialism (Desmond 1991). As these analyses illustrate, Foucault allows us to consider and critique the body as it is invested with meaning and inserted into regimes of truth via the operations of power and knowledge. . . .

Foucault clarifies and expands on this process of bodily/social inscription in his early work. In "Nietzsche, Genealogy, History," he positions the physical body as virtual text, accounting for the fact that "the body is the inscribed surface of events that are traced by language and dissolved by ideas" (1977, 83). . . . For Foucault, the body and [power] are inseparable. In his logic, power constructs and holds bodies. . . .

In *Discipline and Punish* Foucault sets out to depict the genealogy of torture and discipline as it reflects a public display of power on the body of subjects in the 17th and 18th centuries. In graphic detail Foucault begins his book with the description of a criminal being tortured and then drawn and quartered in a public square. The crowds of good parents and their growing children watch and learn. The public spectacle works as a patrolling image, socializing and controlling bodies within the body politic. Eighteenth century torture "must mark the victim: it is intended, either by the scar it leaves on the body or by the spectacle that accompanies it, to brand the victim with infamy . . . it traces around or rather on the very body of the condemned man signs that can not be effaced" (1984, 179). For Foucault, public exhibitions of punishment served as a socializing process, writing culture's codes and values on the minds and bodies of its subjects. In the process punishment . . . rearranged bodies.

. . . Foucault's point in *Discipline and Punish* is . . . that public exhibition and inscription have been replaced in contemporary society by a much more effective process of socialization and self-inscription. According to Foucault, today discipline has replaced torture as the privileged punishment, but the body continues to be written on. Discipline produces "subjected and practiced bodies, docile bodies" (1984, 182). We become subjects . . . of ideology, disciplining and inscribing our own bodies/minds in the process of becoming stable and singular subjects. . . . The body continues to be the site and operation of ideology. . . .

Indeed, while we are all marked discursively by ideology in Foucault's paradigm, in the United States today poor women and children of all races are multiply marked with signs of both discipline and punishment that cannot be erased or effaced. They are systematically produced through both 20th century forces of socialization and discipline and 18th century exhibitions of public mutilation. In addition to coming into being as disciplined and docile bodies, poor single welfare mothers and their children are physically inscribed, punished, and displayed as dangerous and pathological "other." It is important to note when considering the contemporary inscription of poverty as moral pathology etched onto the bodies of profoundly poor women and children, that these are more than metaphoric and self-patrolling marks of discipline. Rather on myriad levels—sexual, social, material and physical—poor women and their children, like the "deviants" publicly punished in Foucault's scenes of

torture, are marked, mutilated, and made to bear and transmit signs in a public spectacle that brands the victim with infamy.

. . . The (Not So) Hidden Injuries of Class

Recycled images of poor, welfare women permeate and shape our national consciousness.[1] Yet—as is so often the case—these images and narratives tell us more about the culture that spawned and embraced them than they do about the object of the culture's obsession. . . .

These productions orchestrate the story of poverty as one of moral and intellectual lack and of chaos, pathology, promiscuity, illogic, and sloth, juxtaposed always against the order, progress, and decency of "deserving" citizens. . . .

I am, and will probably always be, marked as a poor woman. I was raised by a poor, single, White mother who had to struggle to keep her four children fed, sheltered, and clothed by working at what seemed like an endless stream of minimum wage, exhausting, and demeaning jobs. As a child poverty was written onto and into my being at the level of private and public thought and body. At an early age my body bore witness to and emitted signs of the painful devaluation carved into my flesh; that same devaluation became integral to my being in the world. I came into being as disciplined body/mind while at the same time I was taught to read my abject body as the site of my own punishment and erasure. In this excess of meaning the space between private body and public sign was collapsed.

For many poor children this double exposure results in debilitating . . . shame and lack. As Carolyn Kay Steedman reminds us in *Landscape for a Good Woman,* the mental life of poor children flows from material deprivation. Steedman speaks of the "relentless laying down of guilt" she experienced as a poor child living in a world where identity was shaped through envy and unfulfilled desire and where her own body "told me stories of the terrible unfairness of things, of the subterranean culture of longing for that which one can never have" (1987, 8). For Steedman, public devaluation and punishment "demonstrated to us all the hierarchies of our illegality, the impropriety of our existence, our marginality within the social system" (1987, 9). Even as an adult she recalls that:

> . . . the baggage will never lighten for me or my sister. We were born, and had no choice in the matter; but we were social burdens, expensive, unworthy, never grateful enough. There was nothing we could do to pay back the debt of our existence. (1987, 19)

Indeed, poor children are often marked with bodily signs that cannot be forgotten or erased. Their bodies are physically inscribed as "other" and then read as pathological, dangerous, and undeserving. What I recall most vividly about being a child in a profoundly poor family was that we were constantly hurt and ill, and because we could not afford medical care, small illnesses and accidents spiraled into more dangerous illnesses and complications that became both a part of who we were and written proof that we were of no value in the world.

In spite of my mother's heroic efforts, at an early age my brothers and sister and I were stooped, bore scars that never healed properly, and limped with feet mangled by illfitting, used Salvation Army shoes. When my sister's forehead was split open by a door slammed in frustration, my mother "pasted" the angry wound together on her own, leaving a mark of our inability to afford medical attention, of our lack, on her very forehead. When I suffered from a concussion, my mother simply put borrowed ice on my head and tried to keep me awake for a night. And when throughout elementary school we were sent to the office for mandatory and very public yearly checks, the school nurse sucked air through her teeth as she donned surgical gloves to check only the hair of poor children for lice.

We were read as unworthy, laughable, and often dangerous. Our school mates laughed at our "ugly shoes," our crooked and ill-serviced teeth, and the way we "stank," as teachers excoriated us for inability to concentrate in school, our "re-

fusal" to come to class prepared with proper school supplies, and our unethical behavior when we tried to take more than our allocated share of "free lunch."[2] Whenever backpacks or library books came up missing, we were publicly interrogated and sent home to "think about" our offences, often accompanied by notes that reminded my mother that as a poor single parent she should be working twice as hard to make up for the discipline that allegedly walked out the door with my father. When we sat glued to our seats, afraid to stand in front of the class in ragged and ill-fitting handmedowns, we were held up as examples of unprepared and uncooperative children. And when our grades reflected our otherness, they were used to justify even more elaborate punishment. . . .

Friends who were poor as children, and respondents to a survey I conducted in 1998,[3] tell similar stories of the branding they received at the hands of teachers, administrators, and peers. An African-American woman raised in Yesler Terrace, a public housing complex in Seattle, Washington, writes:

> Poor was all over our faces. My glasses were taped and too weak. My big brother had missing teeth. My mom was dull and ashy. It was like a story of how poor we were that anyone could see. My sister Evie's lip was bit by a dog and we just had dime store stuff to put on it. Her lip was a big scar. Then she never smiled and no one smiled at her cause she never smiled. Kids called her "Scarface." Teachers never smiled at her. The principle put her in detention all the time because she was mean and bad (they said).

And, a White woman in the Utica, New York, area remembers:

> We lived in dilapidated and unsafe housing that had fleas no matter how clean my mom tried to be. We had bites all over us. Living in our car between evictions was even worse—then we didn't have a bathroom so I got kidney problems that I never had doctor's help for. When

my teachers wouldn't let me got to the bath-room every hour or so I would wet my pants in class. You can imagine what the kids did to me about that. And the teachers would refuse to let me go to the bathroom because they said I was willful.

Material deprivation is publicly written on the bodies of poor children in the world. In the United States poor families experience violent crime, hunger, lack of medical and dental care, utility shut-offs, the effects of living in unsafe housing and/or of being homeless, chronic ill-ness, and insufficient winter clothing (Lein and Edin 1996, 224–231). According to Jody Raphael of the Taylor Institute, poor women and their children are also at five times the risk of experi-encing domestic violence (Raphael, 2000).

As children, our disheveled and broken bodies were produced and read as signs of our inferior-ity and undeservedness. As adults our mutilated bodies are read as signs of inner chaos, immatu-rity, and indecency as we are punished and then read as proof of need for further discipline and punishment. When my already bad teeth started to rot and I was out of my head with pain, my choices as an adult welfare recipient were to ei-ther let my teeth fall out or have them pulled out. In either case the culture would then read me as a "toothless illiterate," as a fearful joke. In order to pay my rent and to put shoes on my daughter's feet I sold blood at two or three different clinics on a monthly basis until I became so anemic that they refused to buy it from me. A neighbor of mine went back to the man who continued to beat her and her children after being denied wel-fare benefits, when she realized that she could not adequately feed, clothe and house her family on her own minimum wage income. My good friend sold her ovum to a fertility clinic in a painful and potentially damaging process. Other friends ex-posed themselves to all manner of danger and disease by selling their bodies for sex in order to feed and clothe their babies.

Exhaustion also marks the bodies of poor women in indelible script. Rest becomes a privi-lege we simply cannot afford. After working full

shifts each day, poor mothers trying to support themselves at minimum wage jobs continue to work to a point of exhaustion that is inscribed on their faces, their bodies, their posture, and their diminishing sense of self and value in the world. My former neighbor recently recalled:

> I had to take connecting buses to bring and pick up my daughters at childcare after working on my feet all day. As soon as we arrived at home, we would head out again by bus to do laundry. Pick up groceries. Try to get to the food bank. Beg the electric company to not turn off our lights and heat again. Find free winter clothing. Sell my blood. I would be home at nine or ten o'clock at night. I was loaded down with one baby asleep and one crying. Carrying lots of heavy bags and ready to drop on my feet. I had bags under my eyes and no shampoo to wash my hair so I used soap. Anyway I had to stay up to wash diapers in the sink. Otherwise they wouldn't be dry when I left the house in the dark with my girls. In the morning I start all over again.

This bruised and lifeless body, hauling sniffling babies and bags of dirty laundry on the bus, was then read as a sign that she was a bad mother and a threat that needed to be disciplined and made to work even harder for her own good. Those who need the respite less go away for weekends, take drives in the woods, take their kids to the beach. Poor women without educa-tion are pushed into minimum wage jobs and have no money, no car, no time, no energy, and little support, as their bodies are made to display marks of their material deprivation as a socializ-ing and patrolling force.

Ultimately, we come to recognize that our bodies are not our own; that they are rather pub-lic property. State mandated blood tests, interro-gation of the most private aspects of our lives, the public humiliation of having to beg officials for food and medicine, and the loss of all right to privacy, teach us that our bodies are only useful as lessons, warnings, and signs of degradation that everyone loves to hate. In "From Welfare to Academe: Welfare Reform as College-Educated

Welfare Mothers Know It," Sandy Smith-Madsen describes the erosion of her privacy as a poor welfare mother:

> I was investigated. I was spied upon. A welfare investigator came into my home and after thoughtful deliberation, granted me permission to keep my belongings. . . . Like the witch hunts of old, if a neighbor reports you as a welfare queen, the guardians of the state's compelling interest come into your home and interrogate you. While they do not have the right to set your body ablaze on the public square, they can forever devastate heart and soul by snatching away children. Just like a police officer, they may use whatever they happen to see against you, including sexual orientation. Full-fledged citizens have the right to deny an officer entry into their home unless they possess a search warrant; welfare mothers fork over citizenship rights for the price of a welfare check. In Tennessee, constitutional rights go for a cash value of $185 per month for a family of three. (2000, 185)

Welfare reform policy is designed to publicly expose, humiliate, punish and display "deviant" welfare mothers. "Workfare" and "Learnfare"—two alleged successes of welfare reform—require that landlords, teachers, and employers be made explicitly aware of the second class status of these very public bodies. In Ohio, the Department of Human Services uses tax dollars to pay for advertisements on the side of Cleveland's RTA busses that show a "Welfare Queen" behind bars with a logo that proclaims "Crime does not pay. Welfare fraud is a crime" (Robinson 1999). In Michigan a pilot program mandating drug tests for all welfare recipients began on October 1, 1999. Recipients who refuse the test will lose their benefits immediately (Simon 1999). In Buffalo, New York, a County Executive proudly announced that his county will begin intensive investigation of all parents who refuse minimum wage jobs that are offered to them by the state. He warned: "We have many ways of investigating and exposing these errant parents who choose to exploit their children in this way" (Anderson 1999). And, welfare

reform legislation enacted in 1996 as the Personal Responsibility and Work Opportunities Reconciliation Act (PRWORA), requires that poor mothers work full-time, earning minimum wage salaries with which they cannot support their children. Often denied medical, dental, and childcare benefits, and unable to provide their families with adequate food, heat, or clothing, through this legislation the state mandates child neglect and abuse. The crowds of good parents and their growing children watch and learn. . . .

Reading and Rewriting the Body . . .

The bodies of poor women and children, scarred and mutilated by state mandated material deprivation and public exhibition, work as spectacles, as patrolling images socializing and controlling bodies within the body politic. . . .

Spectacular cover stories of the "Welfare Queen" play and re-play in the national mind's eye, becoming a prescriptive lens through which the American public as a whole reads the individual dramas of the bodies of poor women and their place and value in the world. These dramas produce "normative" citizens as singular, stable, rational, ordered, and free. In this dichotomous, hierarchical frame the poor welfare mother is juxtaposed against a logic of "normative" subjectivity as the embodiment of disorder, disarray, and other-ness. Her broken and scarred body becomes proof of her inner pathology and chaos, suggesting the need for further punishment and discipline.

In contemporary narrative welfare women are imagined to be dangerous because they refuse to sacrifice their desires and fail to participate in legally sanctioned heterosexual relationships; theirs is read, as a result, as a selfish, "unnatural," and immature sexuality. In this script, the bodies of poor women are viewed as being dangerously beyond the control of men and are as a result construed as the bearers of perverse desire. In this androcentric equation fathers become the sole bearers of order and of law, defending poor women and children against their own unchecked sexuality and lawlessness.

For Republican Senator [now Attorney General] John Ashcroft writing in *The St. Louis Dispatch,* the inner city is the site of "rampant illegitimacy" and a "space devoid of discipline" where all values are askew. For Ashcroft, what is insidious is not material poverty, but an entitlement system that has allowed "out-of-control" poor women to rupture traditional patriarchal authority, valuation, and boundaries (1995, A:23). Impoverished communities then become a site of chaos because without fathers they allegedly lack any organizing or patrolling principle. George Gilder agrees with Ashcroft when he writes in the conservative *American Spectator* that:

> The key problem of the welfare culture is not unemployed women and poor children. It is the women's skewed and traumatic relationships with men. In a reversal of the pattern of civilized societies, the women have the income and the ties to government authority and support.... This balance of power virtually prohibits marriage, which is everywhere based on the provider role of men, counterbalancing the sexual and domestic superiority of women. (1995, B:6)

For Gilder, the imprimatur of welfare women's sordid bodies unacceptably shifts the focus of the narrative from a male presence to a feminized absence.

In positioning welfare mothers as sexually chaotic, irrational, and unstable, their figures are temporarily immobilized and made to yield meaning as a space that must be brought under control and transformed through public displays of punishment. Poor single mothers and children who have been abandoned, have fled physical, sexual, and/or psychological abuse, or have in general refused to capitulate to male control within the home are mythologized as dangerous, pathological, out of control, and selfishly unable—or unwilling—to sacrifice their "naturally" unnatural desires. They are understood and punished as a danger to a culture resting on a foundation of inviolate male authority and absolute privilege in both public and private spheres.

William Raspberry disposes poor women as selfish and immature, when in "Ms. Smith Goes After Washington," he warrants that:

> ... unfortunately AFDC is paid to an unaccountable, accidental and unprepared parent who has chosen her head of household status as a personal form of satisfaction, while lacking the simple life skills and maturity to achieve love and job fulfillment from any other source. I submit that all of our other social ills—crime, drugs, violence, failing schools ... are a direct result of the degradation of parenthood by emotionally immature recipients. (1995, A:19)

Raspberry goes on to assert that like poor children, poor mothers must be made visible reminders to the rest of the culture of the "poor choices" they have made. He claims that rather than "coddling" her, we have a responsibility to "shame her" and to use her failure to teach other young women that it is "morally wrong for unmarried women to bear children," as we "cast single motherhood as a selfish and immature act" (1995, A:19).

Continuous, multiple, and often seamless public inscription, punishing policy, and lives of unbearable material lack leave poor women and their children scarred, exhausted, and confused. As a result their bodies are imagined as an embodiment of decay and cultural dis-ease that threatens the health and progress of our nation.... In a 1995 *USA Today* article entitled "America at Risk: Can We Survive Without Moral Values?" for example, the inner city is portrayed as a "*dark*" realm of "*decay* rooted in the *loss* of values, the *death* of work ethics, and the *deterioration* of families and communities." Allegedly here, "all morality has *rotted* due to a *breakdown* in gender discipline." This space of disorder and disease is marked with tropes of race and gender. It is also associated with the imagery of "communities of women *without* male leadership, cultural values and initiative [emphasis added]" (1995, C:3). In George Will's *Newsweek* editorial he proclaims that "*illogical* feminist and racial *anger* coupled with *misplaced* American emotion may be part or a cause of the *irresponsible* behavior *rampant* in poor neighborhoods." Will continues, proclaiming that here "mothers *lack* control over their children and have *selfishly* taught them to embrace a *pathological* ethos that values *self-need* and *self-expression* over self-control [emphasis added]" (1995, 23).

Poor women and children's bodies, publicly scarred and mutilated by material deprivation, are read as expressions of an essential lack of discipline and order. In response to this perception, journalist Ronald Brownstein of the *L.A. Times* proposed that the *Republican Contract with America* will "*restore* America to its path, *enforcing* social *order* and common *standards* of behavior, and replacing *stagnation* and *decay* with *movement* and *forward* thinking *energy* [emphasis added]" (1994, A:20). In these rhetorical fields poverty is . . . linked to lack of progress that would allegedly otherwise order, stabilize, and restore the culture. What emerges from these diatribes is the positioning of patriarchal, racist, capitalist, hierarchical, and heterosexist "order" and movement against the alleged stagnation and decay of the body of the "Welfare Queen."

Race is clearly written on the body of the poor single mother. The welfare mother, imagined as young, never married, and Black (contrary to statistical evidence[4]), is framed as dangerous and in need of punishment because she "naturally" emasculates her own men, refuses to service White men, and passes on—rather than appropriate codes of subservience and submission—a disruptive culture of resistance, survival, and "misplaced" pride to her children (Collins 1991). In stark contrast, widowed women with social security and divorced women with child support and alimony are imaged as White, legal, and propertied mothers whose value rests on their abilities to stay in their homes, care for their own children, and impart traditional cultural morals to their offspring, all for the betterment of the culture. In this narrative welfare mothers have only an "outlaw" culture to impart. Here the welfare mother is read as both the product and the producer of a culture of disease and disorder. These narratives imagine poor women as powerful contagion capable of, perhaps even lying in

wait to infect their own children as raced, gendered, and classed agents of their "diseased" nature. In contemporary discourses of poverty racial tropes position poor women's bodies as dangerous sites of "naturalized chaos" and as potentially valuable economic commodities who refuse their proper role.

Gary McDougal in "The Missing Half of the Welfare Debate" furthers this image by referring to the "crab effect of poverty" through which mothers and friends of individuals striving to break free of economic dependency allegedly "pull them back down." McDougal affirms—again despite statistical evidence to the contrary—that the mothers of welfare recipients are most often themselves "generational welfare freeloaders lacking traditional values and family ties who can not, and will not, teach their children right from wrong." "These women" he asserts "would be better off doing any kind of labor regardless of how little it pays, just to get them out of the house, to break their cycles of degeneracy" (1996, A:16).

In this plenitude of images of evil mothers, the poor welfare mother threatens not just her own children, but all children. The Welfare Queen is made to signify moral aberration and economic drain; her figure becomes even more impacted once responsibility for the destruction of the "American Way of Life" is attributed to her. Ronald Brownstein reads her "spider web of dependency" as a "crises of character development that leads to a morally bankrupt American ideology" (1994, A:6).

These representations position welfare mothers' bodies as sites of destruction and as catalysts for a culture of depravity and disobedience; in the process they produce a reading of the writing on the body of the poor woman that calls for further punishment and discipline. In New York City, "Workfare" programs force *lazy* poor women to take a job—"any job"—including working for the city wearing orange surplus prison uniforms picking up garbage on the highway and in parks for about $1.10 per hour (Dreier 1999). "Bridefare" programs in Wisconsin give added benefits to *licentious* welfare women who marry a man—"any man"—and publish a celebration of their "reform" in local newspapers (Dresand 1996). "Tidyfare" programs across the nation allow state workers to enter and inspect the homes of poor *slovenly* women so that they can monetarily sanction families whose homes are deemed to be appropriately tidied.[5] "Learnfare" programs in many states publicly expose and fine *undisciplined* mothers who for any reason have children who don't (or can't) attend school on a regular basis (Muir 1993). All of these welfare reform programs are designed to expose and publicly punish the *misfits* whose bodies are read as proof of their refusal or inability to capitulate to androcentric, capitalist, racist, and heterosexism values and mores.

The Power of Poor Women's Communal Resistance

Despite the rhetoric and policy that mark and mutilate our bodies, poor women survive. Hundreds of thousands of us are somehow good parents despite the systems that are designed to prohibit us from being so. We live on the unlivable and teach our children love, strength, and grace. We network, solve irresolvable dilemmas, and support each other and our families. If we somehow manage to find a decent pair of shoes, or save our foodstamps to buy our children a birthday cake, we are accused of being cheats or living too high. If our children suffer, it is read as proof of our inferiority and bad mothering; if they succeed we are suspect for being too pushy, for taking more than our share of free services, or for having too much free time to devote to them. Yet, as former welfare recipient Janet Diamond says in the introduction to *For Crying Out Loud:*

> In spite of public censure, welfare mothers graduate from school, get decent jobs, watch their children achieve, make good lives for themselves . . . welfare mothers continue to be my inspiration, not because they survive, but because they dare to dream. Because when you are a welfare recipient, laughter is an act of rebellion. (1986, 1)

. . . Because power is diffuse, heterogeneous, and contradictory, poor women struggle against the marks of their degradation. . . .

Poor women rebel by organizing for physical and emotional respite, and eventually for political power. My own resistance was born in the space between self-loathing and my love of and respect for poor women who were fighting together against oppression. In the throes of political activism (at first I was dragged blindly into such actions, ironically, in a protest that required, according to the organizer, just so many poor women's bodies) I became caught up in the contradiction between my body's meaning as despised public sign, and our shared sense of communal power, knowledge, authority, and beauty. Learning about labor movements, fighting for rent control, demanding fair treatment at the welfare office, sharing the costs, burdens, and joys of raising children, forming good cooperatives, working with other poor women to go to college, and organizing for political change, became addictive and life affirming acts of resistance.

Communal affiliation among poor women is discouraged, indeed in many cases prohibited, by those with power over our lives. Welfare offices, for example, are designed to prevent poor women from talking together; uncomfortable plastic chairs are secured to the ground in arrangements that make it difficult to communicate, silence is maintained in waiting rooms, case workers are rotated so that they do not become too "attached" to their clients, and, reinforced by "Welfare Fraud" signs covering industrially painted walls, we are daily reminded not to trust anyone with the details of our lives for fear of further exposure and punishment. And so, like most poor women, I had remained isolated, ashamed, and convinced that I was alone in, and responsible for, my suffering.

Through shared activism we became increasingly aware of our individual bodies as sites of contestation and of our collective body as a site of resistance and as a source power.

Noemy Vides in "Together We Are Getting Freedom," reminds us that "by talking and writing about learned shame together, [poor women] pursue their own liberation" (305). Vides adds that it is through this process that she learned to challenge the dominant explanations that decreed her value in the world,

> provoking an awareness that the labels— ignorant peasant, abandoned woman, broken-English speaker, welfare cheat—have nothing to do with who one really is, but serve to keep women subjugated and divided. [This communal process] gives women tools to understand the uses of power; it emboldens us to move beyond the imposed shame that silences, to speak out and join together in a common liberatory struggle. (305)

In struggling together we contest the marks of our bodily inscription, disrupt the use of our bodies as public sign, change the conditions of our lives, and survive. In the process we come to understand that the shaping of our bodies is not coterminous with our beings or abilities as a whole. Contestation and the deployment of new truths cannot erase the marks of our poverty, but the process does transform the ways in which we are able to interrogate and critique our bodies and the systems that have branded them with infamy. As a result these signs are rendered fragile, unstable, and ultimately malleable.

NOTES

1. Throughout this paper I use the terms "welfare recipients," and "poor working women" interchangeably because as the recent *Urban Institute* study made clear, today these populations are, in fact, one and the same. (Loprest 1999)

2. As recently as 1995, in my daughter's public elementary school cafeteria, "free lunchers" (poor children who could not otherwise afford to eat lunch, including my daughter) were reminded with a large and colorful sign to "line up last."

3. The goal of my survey was to measure the impact of the 1996 welfare reform legislation on the lives of profoundly poor women and children in the United States. Early in 1998 I sent fifty questionnaires and narrative surveys to four groups of poor women on the West and the East coasts; thirty-nine were returned to me. I followed these surveys with forty-five minute interviews with twenty of the surveyed women.

4. In the two years directly preceding the passage of the PRWORA, as a part of sweeping welfare reform, in the United States the largest percentage of people on welfare were white (39%) and fewer than 10% were teen mothers. (1994. U.S. Department of Health and Human Services, "An Overview of Entitlement Programs")

5. *Tidyfare* programs additionally required that caseworkers inventory the belongings of AFDC recipients so that they could require them to "sell-down" their assets. In my own case, in 1994 a HUD inspector came into my home, counted my daughter's books, checked them against his list to see that as a nine year old she was only entitled to have twelve books, calculated what he perceived to be the value of the excess books, and then had my AFDC check reduced by that amount in the following month.

REFERENCES

Abramovitz, Mimi. 1989. *Regulating the lives of women, social welfare policy from colonial times to the present.* Boston: South End Press.

———. 2000. *Under attack, fighting back.* New York: Monthly Review Press.

Albelda, Randy. 1997. *Glass ceilings and bottomless pits: women's work, women's poverty.* Boston: South End Press.

"America at risk; can we survive without moral values." 1995. *USA Today.* October, Sec. C: 3.

Amott, Teresa. 1993. *Caught in the crises: women and the U.S. economy today.* New York: Monthly Review Press.

Anderson, Dale. 1999. "County to investigate some welfare recipients." *The Buffalo News.* August 18, Sec. B: 5.

Ashcroft, John. 1995. "Illegitimacy rampant." *The St. Louis Dispatch.* July 2, Sec. A: 23.

Bell, Shannon. 1994. *Reading, writing and rewriting the prostitute body.* Bloomington and Indianapolis: Indiana University Press.

Bordo, Susan, 1993. *Unbearable Weight: feminism, western culture and the body.* Berkeley: University of California Press.

Brownstein, Ronald. 1994. "GOP welfare proposals more conservative." *Los Angeles Times,* May 20, Sec. A: 20.

————1994. "Latest welfare reform plan reflects liberals' priorities." *Los Angeles Times.* May 20, Sec. A: 6.

Chandler, Mielle. 1999. "Queering maternity." *Journal of the Association for Research on Mothering.* Vol. 1, no. 2, (21–32).

Collins, Patricia Hill. 2000. *Black feminist thought: knowledge, consciousness, and the politics of empowerment.* New York: Routledge.

Crompton, Rosemary. 1986. *Gender and stratification.* New York: Polity Press.

Desmond, Jane. 1991. "Dancing out the difference; cultural imperialism and Ruth St. Denis's Radna of 1906." *Signs.* Vol. 17, no. 1, Autumn, (28–49).

Diamond, Janet. 1986. *For crying out loud: women and poverty in the United States.* Boston: Pilgrim Press.

Dreier, Peter. 1999. "Treat welfare recipients like workers." *Los Angeles Times.* August 29, Sec. M: 6.

Dresang, Joel. 1996. "Bridefare designer, reform beneficiary have role in governor's address." *Milwaukee Journal Sentinel.* August 14, Sec. 9.

Dujon, Diane and Ann Withorn. 1996. *For crying out loud: women's poverty in the Unites States.* South End Press

Edin, Kathryn and Laura Lein. 1997. *Making ends meet: how single mothers survive welfare and low wage work.* Russell Sage Foundation.

Ford-Smith, Honor. 1995. "Making white ladies: race, gender and the production of identity in late colonial Jamaica." *Resources for Feminist Research,* Vol. 23, no. 4, Winter, (55–67).

Foucault, Michel. 1984. *Discipline and punish.* In P. Rabinow (ed.) *The Foucault reader.* New York: Pantheon Books.

————. 1978. *The history of sexuality: an introduction.* Trans. R. Hurley. Harmondsworth: Penguin.

————. 1984. "Nietzsche, genealogy, history." In P. Rabinow (ed.) *The Foucault reader.* New York Pantheon Books.

————. 1980. *Power/knowledge: selected interviews and other writings 1972–1977.* C. Gordon (ed.) Brighton: Harvester.

Funiciello, Theresa. 1998. "The brutality of bureaucracy." *Race, class and gender: an anthology,* 3rd ed. Eds. Margaret L. Andersen and Patricia Hill Collins. Belmont: Wadsworth Publishing Company, (377–381).

Gilder, George. 1995. "Welfare fraud today." *American Spectator.* September 5, Sec. B: 6.

Gordon, Linda. 1995. *Pitied, but not entitled: single mothers and the history of welfare.* New York: Belknap Press, 1995.

Hooks, Bell. "Thinking about race, class, gender and ethics" 1999. Presentation at Hamilton College, Clinton, New York.

Hopwood, Catherine. 1995. "My discourse/myself: therapy as possibility (for women who eat compulsively)." *Feminist Review.* No. 49, Spring, (66–82).

Langston, Donna. 1998. "Tired of playing monopoly?" In *Race, class and gender: an anthology,* 3rd ed. Eds. Margaret L. Andersen and Patricia Hill Collins. Belmont: Wadsworth Publishing Company, (126–136).

Lerman, Robert. 1995. "And for fathers?" *The Washington Post.* August 7, Sec. A: 19.

Loprest, Pamela. 1999. "Families who left welfare: who are they and how are they doing?" *The Urban Institute,* Washington, D.C. August, No. B-1.

McDougal, Gary. 1996. "The missing half of the welfare debate." *The Wall Street Journal.* September 6, Sec. A: 16 (W).

McNay, Lois. 1992. *Foucault and feminism: power, gender and the self.* Boston: Northeastern University Press.

Mink, Gwendoly. 1998. *Welfare's end.* Cornell University Press.

————. 1996. *The wages of motherhood: inequality in the welfare state 1917–1942,* Cornell University Press.

Morgan, Kathryn. 1991. "Women and the knife: cosmetic surgery and the colonization of women's bodies." *Hepatia.* V6, No 3. Fall, (25–53).

Muir, Kate. 1993. "Runaway fathers at welfare's final frontier. *The Times.* Times Newspapers Limited. July 19, Sec. A: 2.

"An overview of entitlement programs." 1994. U.S. Department of Health and Human Services. Washington, DC: U.S. Government Printing Office.

Piven, Frances Fox and Richard Cloward. 1993. *Regulating the poor: the functions of public welfare.* New York: Vintage Books.

Raspberry, William. 1995. "Ms. Smith goes after Washington." *The Washington Post.* February 1, Sec. A: 19.

————. 1996. "Uplifting the human spirit." *The Washington Post.* August 8, Sec. A: 31.

Robinson, Valerie. 1999. "State's ad attacks the poor." *The Plain Dealer,* November 2, Sec. B: 8.

Sennett, Richard and Jonathan Cobb. 1972. *The hidden injuries of class.* New York: Vintage Books.

Sidel, Ruth. 1998. *Keeping women and children last: America's war on the poor.* New York: Penguin Books.

Simon, Stephanie. 1999. "Drug tests for welfare applicants." *The Los Angeles Times.* December 18, Sec. A: 1. National Desk.

Smart, Carol. 1997. *Regulating womanhood: essays on marriage, motherhood and sexuality.* New York: Routledge.

———. *"Disruptive bodies and unruly sex: the regulation of reproduction and sexuality in the nineteenth century."* New York: Routledge, (7–32).

Smith-Madsen, Sandy. 2000. "From welfare to academe: welfare reform as college-educated welfare mothers know it." *And still we rise: women, poverty and the promise of education in America.* Forthcoming. Vivyan Adair and Sandra Dahlber, Eds. Philadelphia: Temple University Press, (160–186).

Steedman, Carolyn Kay. 1987. *Landscape for a good woman.* New Brunswick, N.J., Rutgers University Press.

Stoler, Ann Laura. 1995. *Race and the education of desire: Foucault's history of sexuality and the colonial order of things.* Durham: Duke University Press.

Sylvester, Kathleen. 1995. "Welfare debate." *The Washington Post.* September 3, Sec. E: 15.

Tanner, Michael. 1995. "Why welfare pays." *The Wall Street Journal.* September 28, Sec. A: 18 (W).

Vides, Noemy and Victoria Steinitz. 1996. "Together we are getting freedom." *For crying out loud.* Diane Dujon and Ann Withorn (eds.) Boston: South End Press, (295–306).

Will, George. 1995. "Welfare gate." *Newsweek.* February 5, Sec. 23.

THINKING ABOUT THE READING

When we think of people's bodies being labeled as deviant, we usually assume the bodies in question either deviate from cultural standards of shape and size or are marked by some noticeable physical handicap. However, Adair shows us that poor women's and children's bodies are tagged as deviant in ways that are just as profound and just as hard to erase. What does she mean when she says that the illnesses and accidents of youth became part of a visible reminder of who poor people are in the eyes of others? How do the public degradations suffered by poor people (for instance, having a school nurse wear surgical gloves to check only the hair of poor children for lice) reinforce their deviant status in society? Why do you think Adair continually evokes the images of "danger," "discipline," and "punishment" in describing the ways non-poor people perceive and respond to the physical appearance of poor people? Explain how focusing on the "deviance" of poor people deflects public attention away from the deviant acts committed by more affluent citizens. Do you see any connection between Adair's argument and the overrepresentation of poor people in prison?

Medicine as an Institution of Social Control

Peter Conrad and Joseph W. Schneider

In our society we want to believe in medicine, as we want to believe in religion and our country; it wards off collective fears and reduces public anxieties (see Edelman, 1977). In significant ways medicine, especially psychiatry, has replaced religion as the most powerful extralegal institution of social control. Physicians have been endowed with some of the charisma of shamans. In the 20th century the medical model of deviance . . . ascended with the glitter of a rising star, expanding medicine's social control functions. . . .

Types of Medical Social Control

Medicine was first conceptualized as an agent of social control by Talcott Parsons (1951) in his seminal essay on the "sick role." . . . Elliot Freidson (1970a) and Irving Zola (1972) have elucidated the jurisdictional mandate the medical profession has over anything that can be labeled an illness, regardless of its ability to deal with it effectively. The boundaries of medicine are elastic and increasingly expansive (Ehrenreich & Ehrenreich, 1975), and some analysts have expressed concern at the increasing medicalization of life (Illich, 1976). Although medical social control has been conceptualized in several ways, including professional control of colleagues (Freidson, 1975) and control of the micropolitics of physician-patient interaction (Waitzkin & Stoeckle, 1976), the focus here is narrower. Our concern . . . is with the medical control of deviant behavior, an aspect of the medicalization of deviance (Conrad, 1975; Pitts, 1968). Thus by medical social control we mean the ways in which medicine functions (wittingly or unwittingly) to secure adherence to social norms—specifically, by using medical means

to minimize, eliminate, or normalize deviant behavior. This section illustrates and catalogues the broad range of medical controls of deviance and in so doing conceptualizes three major "ideal types" of medical social control.

On the most abstract level medical social control is the acceptance of a medical perspective as the dominant definition of certain phenomena. When medical perspectives of problems and their solutions become dominant, they diminish competing definitions. This is particularly true of problems related to bodily functioning and in areas where medical technology can demonstrate effectiveness (e.g., immunization, contraception, antibacterial drugs) and is increasingly the case for behavioral and social problems (Mechanic, 1973). This underlies the construction of medical norms (e.g., the definition of what is healthy) and the "enforcement" of both medical and social norms. Medical social control also includes medical advice, counsel, and information that are part of the general stock of knowledge: for example, a well-balanced diet is important, cigarette smoking causes cancer, being overweight increases health risks, exercising regularly is healthy, teeth should be brushed regularly. Such directives, even when unheeded, serve as road signs for desirable behavior. At a more concrete level, medical social control is enacted through professional medical intervention [and] treatment (although it may include some types of self-treatment such as self-medication or medically oriented self-help groups). This intervention aims at returning sick individuals to compliance with health norms and to their conventional social roles, adjusting them to new (e.g., impaired) roles, or, short or these, making individuals more comfortable with their condition (see Freidson, 1970a; Parsons, 1951). Medical social control of deviant behavior is usually a variant of medical intervention that seeks to eliminate, modify, isolate, or regulate behavior socially defined as deviant, with medical means and in the name of health.

Traditionally, psychiatry and public health have served as the clearest examples of medical control. Psychiatry's social control functions with mental illness, especially in terms of institutionalization, have been described clearly (e.g., Miller, K. S., 1976; Szasz, 1970). Recently it has been argued that psychotherapy, because it reinforces dominant values and adjusts people to their life situations, is an agent of social control and a supporter of the status quo (Halleck, 1971; Hurvitz, 1973). Public health's mandate, the control and elimination of conditions and diseases that are deemed a threat to the health of community, is more diffuse. It operates as a control agent by setting and enforcing certain "health" standards in the home, workplace, and community (e.g., food, water, sanitation) and by identifying, preventing, treating and, if necessary, isolating persons with communicable diseases (Rosen, 1972). A clear example of the latter is the detection of venereal disease. Indeed, public health has exerted considerable coercive power in attempting to prevent the spread of infectious disease.

There are a number of types of medical control of deviance. The most common forms of medical social control include medicalizing deviant behavior—that is, defining the behavior as an illness or a symptom of an illness or underlying disease—and subsequent direct medical intervention. This medical social control takes three general forms: medical technology, medical collaboration, and medical ideology.

Medical Technology

The growth of specialized medicine and the concomitant development of medical technology has produced an armamentarium of medical controls. Psychotechnologies, which include various forms of medical and behavioral technologies (Chorover, 1973), are the most common means of medical control of deviance. Since the emergence of phenothiazine medications in the early 1950s for the treatment and control of mental disorder, there has been a virtual explosion in the development and use of psychoactive medications to control behavioral deviance: tranquilizers such as chlordiazepoxide (Librium) and diazepam (Valium) for anxiety, nervousness, and general malaise; stimulant medications for hyperactive children; amphetamines for overeating and obesity; disulfiram (Antabuse) for alcoholism; methadone for heroin, and many others. These pharmaceutical discoveries, aggressively promoted by a highly profitable and powerful drug industry (Goddard, 1973), often become the treatment of choice for deviant behavior. They are easily administered under professional medical control, quite potent in their effects (i.e., controlling, modifying, and even eliminating behavior), and are generally less expensive than other medical treatments and controls (e.g., hospitalization, altering environments, long-term psychotherapy).

Psychosurgery, surgical procedures meant to correct certain "brain dysfunctions" presumed to cause deviant behavior, was developed in the early 1930s as prefrontal lobotomy, and has been used as a treatment for mental illness. But psychosurgery fell into disrepute in the early 1950s because the "side effects" (general passivity, difficulty with abstract thinking) were deemed too undesirable, and many patients remained institutionalized in spite of such treatments. Furthermore, new psychoactive medications were becoming available to control the mentally ill. By the middle 1950s, however, approximately 40,000 to 50,000 such operations were performed in the United States (Freeman, 1959). In the late 1960s a new and technologically more sophisticated variant of psychosurgery (including laser technology and brain implants) emerged and was heralded by some as a treatment for uncontrollable violent outbursts (Delgado, 1969; Mark & Ervin, 1970).

Although psychosurgery for violence has been criticized from both within as well as outside the medical profession (Chorover, 1974b), and relatively few such operations have been performed, in 1976 a blue-ribbon national commission reporting to the Department of Health, Education and Welfare endorsed the use of psychosurgery as having "potential merit" and judged its risks "not excessive." This may encourage an increased use of this form of medical control.

Behavior modification, a psychotechnology based on B.F. Skinner's and other behaviorists' learning theories, has been adopted by some medical professionals as a treatment modality. A variety of types and variations of behavior modification exist (e.g., token economies, tier systems, positive reinforcement schedules, aversive conditioning). While they are not medical technologies per se, they have been used by physicians for the treatment of mental illness, mental retardation, homosexuality, violence, hyperactive children, autism, phobias, alcoholism, drug addiction, eating problems, and other disorders. An irony of the medical use of behavior modification is that behaviorism explicitly denies the medical model (that behavior is a symptom of illness) and adopts an environmental, albeit still individual, solution to the problem. This has not, however, hindered its adoption by medical professionals.

Human genetics is one of the most exciting and rapidly expanding areas of medical knowledge. Genetic screening and genetic counseling are becoming more commonplace. Genetic causes are proposed for such a variety of human problems as alcoholism, hyperactivity, learning disabilities, schizophrenia, manic depressive psychosis, homosexuality, and mental retardation. At this time, apart from specific genetic disorders such as pheylketonuria (PKU) and certain forms of retardation, genetic explanations tend to be general theories (i.e., at best positing "predispositions"), with only minimal empirical support, and are not at the level at which medical intervention occurs. The most well-publicized genetic theory of deviant behavior is that an XYY chromosome arrangement is a determinant factor in "criminal tendencies." Although this XYY research has been criticized severely (e.g., Fox, 1971), the controversy surrounding it may be a harbinger of things to come. Genetic anomalies may be discovered to have a correlation with deviant behavior and may become a causal explanation for this behavior. Medical control, in the form of genetic counseling (Sorenson, 1974), may discourage parents from having offspring with a high risk (e.g., 25%) of genetic impairment. Clearly the potentials for medical control go far beyond present use; one could imagine the possibility of licensing selected parents (with proper genes) to have children, and further manipulating gene arrangements to produce or eliminate certain traits.

Medical Collaboration

Medicine acts not only as an independent agent of social control (as above), but frequently medical collaboration with other authorities serves social control functions. Such collaboration includes roles as information provider, gatekeeper, institutional agent, and technician. These interdependent medical control functions highlight the extent to which medicine is interwoven in the fabric of society. Historically, medical personnel have reported information on gunshot wounds and venereal disease to state authorities. More recently this has included reporting "child abuse" to child welfare or law enforcement agencies (Pfohl, 1977).

The medical profession is the official designator of the "sick role." This imbues the physician with authority to define particular kinds of deviance as illness and exempt the patient from certain role obligations. These are general gatekeeping and social control tasks. In some instances the physician functions as a specific gatekeeper for special exemptions from conventional norms; here the exemptions are authorized because of illness, disease, or disability. A classic example is the so-called insanity defense in certain crime cases. Other more commonplace examples include competency to stand trial, medical deferment from the draft or a medical discharge from the military, requiring physicians' notes to legitimize missing an examination or excessive absences in school, and, before abortion was legalized, obtaining two psychiatrists' letters testifying to the therapeutic necessity of the abortion. Halleck (1971) has called this "the power of medical excuse." In a slightly different vein, but still forms of gatekeeping and medical excuse, are medical examinations for disability or workman's compensation benefits. Medical reports required for insurance coverage and employment or medical certification of an epileptic as seizure free to obtain a driver's license are also gatekeeping activities.

Physicians in total institutions have one of two roles. In some institutions, such as schools for the retarded or mental hospitals, they are usually the administrative authority; in others, such as in the military or prisons, they are employees of the administration. In total institutions, medicine's role as agent of social control (for the institution) is more apparent. In both the military and prisons, physicians have the power to confer the sick role and to offer medical excuse for deviance (see Daniels, 1969; Waitzkin & Waterman, 1974). For example, discharges and sick call are available medical designations for deviant behavior. Since physicians are both hired and paid by the institution, it is difficult for them to be fully an agent of the patient, engendering built-in role strains. An extreme example is in wartime when the physician's mandate is to return the soldier to combat duty as soon as possible. Under some circumstances physicians act as direct agents of control by prescribing medications to control unruly or disorderly inmates or to help a "neurotic" adjust to the conditions of a total institution. In such cases "captive professionals" (Daniels, 1969) are more likely to become the agent of the institution than the agent of the individual patient (Szasz, 1965; see also Menninger, 1967).

Under rather rare circumstances physicians may become "mere technicians," applying the sanctions of another authority who purchases their medical skills. An extreme example would be the behavior of the experimental and death physicians in Nazi Germany. a less heinous but nevertheless ominous example is provided by physicians who perform court-ordered sterilizations (Kittrie, 1971). . . . [Today, physicians administer] drugs as the "humanitarian" and painless executioners [in capital punishment cases.]

Medical Ideology

Medical ideology is a type of social control that involves defining a behavior or condition as an illness primarily because of the social and ideological benefits accrued by conceptualizing it in medical terms. These effects of medical ideology may benefit the individual, the dominant interests in the society, or both. They exist independently of any organic basis for illness or any available treatment. Howard Waitzkin and Barbara Waterman (1974) call one latent function of medicalization "secondary gain," arguing that assumption of the sick role can fulfill personality and individual needs (e.g., gaining nurturance or attention) or legitimize personal failure (Shuval & Antonovsky, 1973). One of the most important functions of the disease model of alcoholism and to a lesser extent drug addiction is the secondary gain of removing blame from, and constructing a shield against condemnation of, individuals for their deviant behavior, Alcoholics Anonymous, a nonmedical quasireligious self-help organization, adopted a variant of the medical model of alcoholism independent of the medical profession. One suspects the secondary gain serves their purposes well.

Disease designations can support dominant social interests and institutions. A poignant example is prominent 19th-century New Orleans physician S. W. Cartwright's antebellum conceptualization of the disease drapetomania, a condition that affected only slaves. Its major symptom was running away from their masters (Cartwright, S. W., 1851). Medical conceptions and controls often support dominant social values and morality: the 19th-century Victorian conceptualization of the illness of and addiction to masturbation and the medical treatments developed to control this disease make chilling reading in the [21st century] (Comfort, 1967: Englehardt,

1974). The [former] Soviet labeling of political dissidents as mentally ill is another example of the manipulation of illness designations to support dominant political and social institutions (Conrad, 1977). These examples highlight the sociopolitical nature of illness designations in general (Zola, 1975).

In sum, medicine as an institution of social control has a number of faces. The three types of medical social control discussed here do not necessarily exist as discrete entities but are found in combination with one another. For example, court-ordered sterilizations or medical prescribing of drugs to unruly nursing home patients combines both technological and collaborative aspects of medical control; legitimating disability status includes both ideological and collaborative aspects of medical control; and treating Soviet dissidents with drugs for their mental illness combines all three aspects of medical social control. It is clear that the enormous expansion of medicine in the past [70] years has increased the number of possible ways in which problems could be medicalized beyond those discussed in earlier chapters. In the next section we point out some of the consequences of this medicalization.

Social Consequences of Medicalizing Deviance

Jesse Pitts (1968), one of the first sociologists to give attention to the medicalization of deviance, suggests that "medicalization is one of the most effective means of social control and that it is destined to become the main mode of *formal* social control" (p. 391, emphasis in original). Although his bold prediction is far-reaching (and, in light of recent developments, perhaps a bit premature), his analysis . . . was curiously optimistic and uncritical of the effects and consequences of medicalization. Nonsociologists, especially psychiatric critic Thomas Szasz (1961, 1963, 1970, 1974) and legal scholar Nicholas Kittrie (1971), are much more critical in their evaluations of the ramifications of medicalization. Szasz's critiques are polemical and attack the medical, especially psychiatric, definitions

and treatments for deviant behavior. Szasz's analyses, although path breaking, insightful, and suggestive, have not been presented in a particularly systematic form. Both he and Kittrie tend to focus on the effects of medicalization on individual civil liberties and judicial processes rather than on social consequences. Their writings, however, reveal that both are aware of sociological consequences.

In this section we discuss some of the more significant consequences and ramifications of defining deviant behavior as a medical problem. We must remind the reader that we are examining the *social* consequences of medicalizing deviance, which can be analyzed separately from the validity of medical definitions or diagnoses, the effectiveness of medical regimens, or their individual consequences. These variously "latent" consequences inhere in medicalization itself and occur *regardless* of how efficacious the particular medical treatment or social control mechanism. As will be apparent, our sociological analysis has left us skeptical of the social benefits of medical social control. We separate the consequences into the "brighter" and "darker" sides of medicalization. The "brighter" side will be presented first.

Brighter Side

The brighter side of medicalization includes the positive or beneficial qualities that are attributed to medicalization. We review briefly the accepted socially progressive aspects of medicalizing deviance. They are separated more for clarity of presentation than for any intrinsic separation in consequence.

First, medicalization is related to a longtime *humanitarian* trend in the conception and control of deviance. For example, alcoholism is no longer considered a sin or even a moral weakness; it is now a disease. Alcoholics are no longer arrested in many places for "public drunkenness"; they are now somehow "treated," if only to be dried out for a time. Medical treatment for the alcoholic can be seen as a more humanitarian means of social control. It is not retributive or punitive, but at least ideally, therapeutic. Troy

Duster (1970, p. 10) suggests that medical definitions increase tolerance and compassion for human problems and they "have now been reinterpreted in an almost nonmoral fashion." (We doubt this, but leave the morality issue for a later discussion.) Medicine and humanitarianism historically developed concurrently and, as some have observed, the use of medical language and evidence increases the prestige of human proposals and enhances their acceptance (Wootton, 1959; Zola, 1975). Medical definitions are imbued with the prestige of the medical profession and are considered the "scientific" and humane way of viewing a problem. . . . This is especially true if an apparently "successful" treatment for controlling the behavior is available, as with hyperkinesis.

Second, medicalization allows for the extension of the *sick role* to those labeled as deviants. . . . Many of the perceived benefits of the medicalization of deviance stem from the assignment of the sick role. Some have suggested that this is the most significant element of adopting the medical model of deviant behavior (Sigler & Osmond, 1974). By defining deviant behavior as an illness or a result of illness, one is absolved of responsibility for one's behavior. It diminishes or *removes blame* from the individual for deviant actions. Alcoholics are no longer held responsible for their uncontrolled drinking, and perhaps hyperactive children are no longer the classroom's "bad boys" but children with a medical disorder. There is some clear secondary gain here for the individual. The label "sick" is free of the moral opprobrium and implied culpability of "criminal" or "sinner." The designation of sickness also may reduce guilt for drinkers and their families and for hyperactive children and their parents. Similarly, it may result in reduced stigma for the deviant. It allows for the development of more acceptable accounts of deviance: a recent film depicted a child witnessing her father's helpless drunken stupor; her mother remarked, "It's okay. Daddy's just sick."

The sick role allows for the "conditional legitimization" of a certain amount of deviance, so

long as the individual fulfills the obligation of the sick role. As Renée Fox (1977) notes:

> The fact that the exemptions of sickness have been extended to people with a widening arc of attitudes, experiences and behaviors in American society means primarily that what is regarded as "conditionally legitimated deviance" has increased. . . . So long as [the deviant] does not abandon himself to illness or eagerly embrace it, but works actively on his own or with medical professionals to improve his condition, he is considered to be responding appropriately, even admirably, to an unfortunate occurrence. Under these conditions, illness is accepted as legitimate deviance. (p. 15)

The deviant, in essence, is medically excused for the deviation. But, as Talcott Parsons (1972) has pointed out, "the conditional legitimization is bought at a 'price,' namely, the recognition that illness itself is an undesirable state, to be recovered from as expeditiously as possible" (p. 108). Thus the medical excuse for deviance is only valid when the patient-deviant accepts the medical perspective of the inherent undesirability of his or her sick behavior and submits to a subordinate relationship with an official agent of control (the physician) toward changing it. This, of course, negates any threat the deviant may pose to society's normative structure, for such deviants do not challenge the norm; by accepting deviance as sickness and social control as "treatment," the deviant underscores the validity of the violated norm.

Third, the medical model can be viewed as portraying an *optimistic* outcome for the deviant. Pitts (1968) notes, "the possibility that a patient may be exploited is somewhat minimized by therapeutic ideology, which creates an optimistic bias concerning the patient's fate" (p. 391). The therapeutic ideology, accepted in some form by all branches of medicine, suggests that a problem (e.g., deviant behavior) can be changed or alleviated if only the proper treatment is discovered and administered. Defining deviant behavior as an illness may also mobilize hope in the individual patient that with proper treatment a "cure" is possible (Frank, J. 1974). Clearly this could have beneficial results and even become a self-fulfilling prophecy. although the medical model is interpreted frequently as optimistic about individual change, under some circumstances it may lend itself to pessimistic interpretations. The attribution of physiological cause coupled with the lack of effective treatment engendered a somatic pessimism in the late 19th-century conception of madness. . . .

Fourth, medicalization lends the *prestige of the medical profession* to deviance designations and treatments. The medical profession is the most prestigious and dominant profession in American society (Freidson. 1970a). As just noted, medical definitions of deviance become imbued with the prestige of the medical profession and are construed to be the "scientific" way of viewing a problem. The medical mantle of science may serve to deflect definitional challenges. This is especially true if an apparently "successful" treatment for controlling the behavior is available. Medicalization places the problem in the hands of healing physicians. "The therapeutic value of professional dominance, from the patient's point of view, is that it becomes the *doctor's* problem" (Ehrenreich & Ehrenreich, 1975, p. 156, emphasis in original). Physicians are assumed to be beneficent and honorable. "The medical and paramedical professions," Pitts (1968) contends, "especially in the United States, are probably more immune to corruption than are the judicial and parajudicial professions and relatively immune to political pressure" (p. 391).

Fifth, medical social control is more *flexible* and often more *efficient* than judicial and legal controls. The impact of the flexibility of medicine is most profound on the "deviance of everyday life," since it allows "social pressures on deviance [to] increase without boxing the deviant into as rigid a category as 'criminal'" (Pitts, 1968, p. 391). Medical controls are adjustable to fit the needs of the individual patient, rather than being a response to the deviant act itself. It may be more efficient (and less expensive) to control opiate addiction with methadone maintenance than with long prison terms or mental hospital-

ization. The behavior of disruptive hyperactive children, who have been immune to all parental and teacher sanctions, may dramatically improve after treatment with medications. Medical controls circumvent complicated legal and judicial procedures and may be applied more informally. This can have a considerable effect on social control structures. For example, it has been noted that defining alcoholism as a disease would reduce arrest rates in some areas up to 50%.

In sum, the social benefits of medicalization include the creation of humanitarian and nonpunitive sanctions; the extension of the sick role to some deviants; a reduction of individual responsibility, blame, and possible stigma for deviance; an optimistic therapeutic ideology; care and treatment rendered by a prestigious medical profession; and the availability of a more flexible and often more efficient means of social control.

Darker Side

There is, however, another side to the medicalization of deviant behavior. Although it may often seem entirely humanitarian to conceptualize deviance as sickness as opposed to badness, it is not that simple. There is a "darker" side to the medicalization of deviance. In some senses these might be considered as the more clearly latent aspects of medicalization. In an earlier work Conrad (1975) elucidated four consequences of medicalizing deviance; building on that work, we expand our analysis to seven. Six are discussed here; the seventh is described separately in the next section.

Dislocation of responsibility. As we have seen, defining behavior as a medical problem removes or profoundly diminishes responsibility from the individual. Although affixing responsibility is always complex, medicalization produces confusion and ambiguity about who is responsible. Responsibility is separated from social action; it is located in the nether world of biophysiology or psyche. Although this takes the individual officially "off the hook," its excuse is only a partial one. The individual, the putative deviant, and the undesirable conduct are still associated. Aside from where such conduct is "seated," the sick deviant is the medium of its expression.

With the removal of responsibility also comes the lowering of status. A dual-class citizenship is created: those who are deemed responsible for their actions and those who are not. The not-completely-responsible sick are placed in a position of dependence on the fully responsible non-sick (Parsons, 1975, p. 108). Kittrie (1971, p. 347) notes in this regard that more than half the American population is no longer subject to the sanctions of criminal law. Such persons, among others, become true "second-class citizens."

Assumption of the moral neutrality of medicine. Cloaked in the mantle of science, medicine and medical practice are assumed to be objective and value free. But this profoundly misrepresents reality. The very nature of medical practice involves value judgement. To call something a disease is to deem it undesirable. Medicine is influenced by the moral order of society—witness the diagnosis and treatment of masturbation as a disease in Victorian times—yet medical language of disease and treatment is assumed to be morally neutral. It is not, and the very technological-scientific vocabulary of medicine that defines disease obfuscates this fact.

Defining deviance as disease allows behavior to keep its negative judgment, but medical language veils the political and moral nature of this decision in the guise of scientific fact. There was little public clamor for moral definitions of homosexuality as long as it remained defined an illness, but soon after the disease designation was removed, moral crusaders (e.g., Anita Bryant) launched public campaigns condemning the immorality of homosexuality. One only needs to scratch the surface of medical designations for deviant behavior to find overtly moral judgments.

Thus, as Zola (1975) points out, defining a problem as within medical jurisdiction

> is not morally neutral precisely because in establishing its relevance as a key dimension for

action, the moral issue is prevented from being squarely faced and occasionally from even being raised. By the acceptance of a specific behavior as an undesirable state the issue becomes not whether to treat an individual problem but how and when. (p. 86)

Defining deviance as a medical phenomenon involves moral enterprise.

Domination of expert control. The medical profession is made up of experts; it has a monopoly on anything that can be conceptualized as an illness. Because of the way the medical profession is organized and the mandate it has from society, decisions related to medical diagnoses and treatment are controlled almost completely by medical professionals.

Conditions that enter the medical domain are not ipso facto medical problems, whether we speak of alcoholism, hyperactivity, or drug addiction. When a problem is defined as medical, it is removed from the public realm, where there can be discussion by ordinary people, and put on a plane where only medical people can discuss it. As Janice Reynolds (1973) succinctly states,

> The increasing acceptance, especially among the more educated segments of our populace, of technical solutions—solutions administered by disinterested and morally neutral experts—results in the withdrawal of more and more areas of human experience from the realm of public discussion. For when drunkenness, juvenile delinquency, sub par performance and extreme political beliefs are seen as symptoms of an underlying illness or biological defect the merits and drawbacks of such behavior or beliefs need not be evaluated. (pp. 220–221)

The public may have their own conceptions of deviant behavior, but those of the experts are usually dominant. Medical definitions have a high likelihood for dominance and hegemony: they are often taken as the last scientific word. The language of medical experts increases mystification and decreases the accessibility of public debate.

Medical social control. Defining deviant behavior as a medical problem allows certain things to be done that could not otherwise be considered; for example, the body may be cut open or psychoactive medications given. As we elaborated above, this treatment can be a form of social control.

In regard to drug treatment, Henry Lennard (1971) observes: "Psychoactive drugs, especially those legally prescribed, tend to restrain individuals from behavior and experience that are not complementary with the requirements of the dominant value system" (p. 57). These forms of medical social control presume a prior definition of deviance as a medical problem. Psychosurgery on an individual prone to violent outbursts requires a diagnosis that something is wrong with his brain or nervous system. Similarly, prescribing drugs to restless, overactive, and disruptive schoolchildren requires a diagnosis of hyperkinesis. These forms of social control, what Stephan Chorover (1973) has called "psychotechnology," are powerful and often efficient means of controlling deviance. These relatively new and increasingly popular forms of medical control could not be used without the prior medicalization of deviant behavior. As is suggested from the discovery of hyperkineses and to a lesser extent the development of methadone treatment of opiate addiction, if a mechanism of medical social control seems useful, then the deviant behavior it modifies will be given a medical label or diagnosis. We imply no overt malevolence on the part of the medical profession; rather, it is part of a larger process, of which the medical profession is only a part. The larger process might be called the individualization of social problems.

Individualization of social problems. The medicalization of deviance is part of a larger phenomenon that is prevalent in our society: the individualization of social problems. We tend to look for causes and solutions to complex social problems in the individual rather than in the social system. William Ryan (1971a) has identified this process as "blaming the victim": seeing the causes of the problem in individuals (who are usually of low status) rather than as endemic to the society. We seek to change the "victim" rather than the society. The medical practice of diagnosing an illness in an individual lends itself to the individualization of social problems. Rather than seeing certain deviant behaviors as symptomatic of social conditions, the medical perspective focuses on the individual, diagnosing and treating the illness itself and generally ignoring the social situation.

Hyperkinesis serves as a good example of this. Both the school and parents are concerned with the child's behavior; the child is difficult at home and disruptive in school. No punishments or rewards seem consistently effective in modifying the behavior, and both parents and school are at their wits' end. A medical evaluation is suggested. The diagnosis of hyperkinetic behavior leads to prescribing stimulant medications. The child's behavior seems to become more socially acceptable, reducing problems in school and home. Treatment is considered a medical success.

But there is an alternative perspective. By focusing on the symptoms and defining them as hyperkinesis, we ignore the possibility that the behavior is not an illness but an adaptation to a social situation. It diverts our attention from the family or school and from seriously entertaining the idea that the "problem" could be in the structure of the social system. By giving medications, we are essentially supporting the existing social and political arrangements in that it becomes a "symptom" of an individual disease rather than a possible "comment" on the nature of the present situation. Although the individualization of social problems aligns well with the individualistic ethic of American culture, medical intervention against deviance makes medicine a de facto agent of dominant social and political interests.

Depoliticization of deviant behavior. Depoliticization of deviant behavior is a result of both the process of medicalization and the individualization of social problems. Probably one of the clearest . . . examples of such depoliticization occurred when political dissidents in the [former] Soviet Union were declared mentally ill and confined to mental hospitals (Conrad, 1977). This strategy served to neutralize the meaning of political protest and dissent, rendering it (officially, at least) symptomatic of mental illness.

The medicalization of deviant behavior depoliticizes deviance in the same manner. By defining the overactive, restless, and disruptive child as hyperkinetic, we ignore the meaning of the behavior in the context of the social system. If we focused our analysis on the school system, we might see the child's behavior as a protest against some aspect of the school or classroom situation, rather than symptomatic of an individual neurological disorder. Similar examples could be drawn of the opiate addict in the ghetto, the alcoholic in the workplace, and others. Medicalizing deviant behavior precludes us from recognizing it as a possible international repudiation of existing political arrangements.

There are other related consequences of the medicalization of deviance beyond the six discussed. The medical ideal of early intervention may lead to early labeling and secondary deviance (see Lemert, 1972). The "medical decision rule," which approximates "when in doubt, treat," is nearly the converse of the legal dictum "innocent until proven guilty" and may unnecessarily enlarge the population of deviants (Scheff, 1963). Certain constitutional safeguards of the judicial system that protect individuals' rights are neutralized or by-passed by medicatization (Kittrie, 1971). Social control in the name of benevolence is at once insidious and difficult to confront. Although these are all significant, we wish to expand on still another consequence of considerable social importance, the exclusion of evil.

Exclusion of Evil

Evil has been excluded from the imagery of modern human problems. We are uncomfortable with notions of evil; we regard them as primitive and nonhumanitarian, as residues from a theological era. Medicalization contributes to the exclusion of concepts of evil in our society. Clearly medicalization is not the sole cause of exclusion of evil, but it shrouds conditions, events, and people and prevents them from being confronted as evil.

The roots of the exclusion of evil are in the Enlightenment, the diminution of religious imagery of sin, the rise of determinist theories of human behavior, and the doctrine of cultural relativity. Social scientists as well have excluded the concept of evil from their analytic discourses (Wolff, 1969; for exceptions, see Becker, E., 1975, and Lyman, 1978).

Although we cannot here presume to identify the forms of evil in modern times, we would like to sensitize the reader to how medical definitions of deviance serve to further exclude evil from our view. It can be argued that regardless of what we construe as evil (e.g., destruction, pain, alienation, exploitation, oppression), there are at least two general types of evil: evil intent and evil consequence. Evil intent is similar to the legal concept mens rea, literally, "evil mind." Some evil is intended by a specific line of action. Evil consequence is, on the other hand, the result of action. No intent or motive to do evil is necessary for evil consequence to prevail; on the contrary, it often resembles the platitude "the road to hell is paved with good intentions." In either case medicalization dilutes or obstructs us from seeing evil. Sickness gives us a vocabulary of motive (Mills, 1940) that obliterates evil intent. And although it does not automatically render evil consequences good, the allegation that they were products of a "sick" mind or body relegates them to a status similar to that of "accidents."

For example, Hitler orchestrated the greatest mass genocide in modern history, yet some have reduced his motivation for the destruction of the Jews (and others) to a personal pathological condition. To them and to many of us, Hitler was sick. But this portrays the horror of the Holocaust as a product of individual pathology; as Thomas Szasz frequently points out, it prevents us from seeing and confronting man's inhumanity to man. Are Son of Sam, Charles Manson, the assassins of King and the Kennedys, the Richard Nixon of Watergate, Libya's Muammar Kaddafi, or the all-too-common child beater sick? Although many may well be troubled, we argue that there is little to be gained by deploying such a medical vocabulary of motives. It only hinders us from comprehending the human element in the decisions we make, the social structures we create, and the actions we take. Hannah Arendt (1963), in her exemplary study of the banality of evil, contends that Nazi war criminal Adolph Eichmann, rather than being sick, was "terribly, terrifyingly normal."

Susan Sontag (1978) has suggested that on a cultural level, we use the metaphor of illness to speak of various kinds of evil. Cancer, in particular, provides such a metaphor: we depict slums and pornography shops as "cancers" in our cities; J. Edgar Hoover's favorite metaphor for communism was "a cancer in our midst"; and Nixon's administration was deemed "cancerous," rotting from within. In our secular culture, where powerful religious connotations of sin and evil have been obscured, cancer (and for that matter, illness in general) is one of the few available images of unmitigated evil and wickedness. As Sontag (1978) observes:

> But how to be . . . [moral] in the late twentieth century? How, when . . . we have a sense of evil but no longer the religious or philosophical language to talk intelligently about evil. Trying to comprehend "radical" or "absolute" evil, we search for adequate metaphors. But the modern disease metaphors are all cheap shots. . . . Only in the most limited sense is any historical event or problem like an illness. It is invariably an encouragement to simplify what is complex. . . . (p. 85)

Thus we suggest that the medicalization of social problems detracts from our capability to see and confront the evils that face our world.

In sum, the "darker" side of the medicalization of deviance has profound consequences for the putative or alleged deviant and society. . . .

Medicalizing Deviance: A Final Note

The potential for medicalizing deviance has increased in the past few decades. The increasing dominance of the medical profession, the discovery of subtle physiological correlates of human behavior, and the creation of medical technolo-gies (promoted by powerful pharmaceutical and medical technology industry interests) have advanced this trend. Although we remain skeptical of the overall social benefits of medicalization and are concerned about its "darker" side, it is much too simplistic to suggest a wholesale condemnation of medicalization. Offering alcoholics medical treatment in lieu of the drunk tank is undoubtedly a more humane response to deviance; methadone maintenance allows a select group of opiate addicts to make successful adaptations to society; some schoolchildren seem to benefit from stimulant medications for hyperkinesis; and the medical discovery of child abuse may well increase therapeutic intervention. Medicalization in general has reduced societal condemnation of deviants. But these benefits do not mean these conditions are in fact diseases or that the same results could not be achieved in another manner. And even in those instances of medical "success," the social consequences indicated . . . are still evident.

The most difficult consequence of medicalization for us to discuss is the exclusion of evil. In part this is because we are members of a culture that has largely eliminated evil from intellectual and public discourse. But our discomfort also stems from our ambivalence about what can meaningfully be construed as evil in our society. If we are excluding evil, what exactly are we excluding? We have no difficulty depicting such conditions as pain, violence, oppression, exploitation, and abject cruelty as evil. Social scientists of various stripes have been pointing to these evils and their consequences since the dawn of social science. It is also possible for us to conceive of "organizational evils" such as corporate price fixing, false advertising (or even all advertising), promoting life-threatening automobiles, or the wholesale drugging of nursing home patients to facilitate institutional management. We also have little trouble in seeing ideologies such as imperialism, chauvinism, and racial supremacy as evils. Our difficulty comes with seeing individuals as evil. While we would not adopt a Father-Flanagan-of-Boys-Town attitude of "there's no such thing as a bad boy," our own socialization and "liberal" assumptions as well as sociological perspective make it difficult for us to conceive of any individual as "evil." As sociologists we are more likely to see people as products of their psychological and social circumstances: there may be evil social structures, ideologies, or deeds, but not evil people. Yet when we confront a Hitler, an Idi Amin, or a Stalin of the forced labor camps, it is sometimes difficult to reach any other conclusion. We note this dilemma more as clarification of our stance than as a solution. There are both evils in society and people who are "victims" to those evils. Worthwhile social scientific goals include uncovering the evils, understanding and aiding the victims, and ultimately contributing to a more humane existence for all.

REFERENCES

Arendt, H. *Eichmann in Jerusalem.* New York: Viking Press, 1963.

Becker, E. *Escape from evil.* New York: The Free Press, 1975.

Cartwright, S. W. Report on the diseases and physical peculiarities of the negro race. *N.O. Med. Surg. J.*, 1851, *7*, 691–715.

Chorover, S. Big Brother and psychotechnology. *Psychol. Today,* 1973, *7*, 43–54 (Oct.).

Chorover, S. Psychosurgery: a neuropsychological perspective. *Boston U. Law Rev.,* 1974, *74*, 231–248 (March). (b)

Comfort, A. *The anxiety makers.* London: Thomas Nelson & Sons, 1967.

Conrad, P. The discovery of hyperkinesis: notes on the medicalization of deviant behavior. *Social Prob.,* 1975, *23*, 12–21 (Oct.).

Conrad, P. Soviet dissidents, ideological deviance, and mental hospitalization. Presented at Midwest Sociological Society Meetings, Minneapolis, 1977.

Daniels, A. K. The captive professional: bureaucratic limitation in the practice of military psychiatry. *J. Health Soc. Behav.,* 1969, *10*, 255–265 (Dec.).

Delgado, J. M. R. *Physical control of the mind: toward a psychocivilized society.* New York: Harper & Row, Publishers, 1969.

Duster, T. *The legislation of morality.* New York: The Free Press, 1970.

Edelman, M. *Political language: words that succeed and policies that fail.* New York: Academic Press, Inc., 1977.

Ehrenreich, B., & Ehrenreich, J. Medicine and social control. In B. R. Mandell (Ed.), *Welfare in America: controlling the "dangerous" classes.* Englewood Cliffs, N.J.: Prentice-Hall, Inc., 1975.

Englehardt, H. T., Jr. The disease of masturbation: values and the concept of disease. *Bull. Hist. Med.,* 1974, *48*, 234–248 (Summer).

Fox, Renée. The medicalization and demedicalization of American society. *Daedalus,* 1977, *106*, 9–22.

Fox, Richard G. The XYY offender: a modern myth? *J. Crimin. Law, Criminol., and Police Sci.,* 1971, *62* (1), 59–73.

Frank, J. *Persuasion and healing.* (Rev. ed.). New York: Schocken Books. Inc., 1974.

Freeman, W. Psychosurgery. In S. Arieti (Ed.), *American handbook of psychiatery* (Vol. 2). New York: Basic Books, Inc., 1959.

Freidson, E. *Profession of medicine.* New York: Harper & Row, Publishers Inc., 1970. (a)

Freidson, E. *Doctoring together.* New York: Elsevier North-Holland, Inc., 1975.

Goddard, J. The medical business. *Sci. Am.,* 1973, *229,* 161–168 (Sept.).

Halleck, S. L. *The politics of therapy.* New York: Science House, 1971.

Hurvitz, N. Psychotherapy as a means of social control. *J. Consult. Clin. Psychol.,* 1973, *40*, 232–239.

Illich, I. *Medical nemesis.* New York: Pantheon Books, Inc., 1976.

Kittrie, N. *The right to be different: deviance and enforced therapy.* Baltimore: Johns Hopkins University Press, 1971. Copyright The Johns Hopkins Press, 1971.

Lemert, E. M. *Human deviance, social problems and social control* (2nd ed.). Englewood Cliffs, N.J.: Prentice-Hall, 1972.

Lennard, H. L., Esptein, L. J., Bernstein, A., & Ranson, D. C. *Mystification and drug misuse.* New York: Perennial Library, 1971.

Lyman, S. *The seven deadly sins: society and evil.* New York: St. Martin's Press, Inc., 1978.

Mark, V., & Ervin, F. *Violence and the brain.* New York: Harper & Row Publishers, Inc., 1970.

Mechanic, D. Health and illness in technological societies. *Hastings Center Stud.* 1973, *1*(3), 7–18.

Menninger, W. C. *A psychiatrist for a troubled world.* B. H. Hall (Ed.), New York: Viking Press, 1967.

Miller, K. S. *Managing madness.* New York: The Free Press, 1976.

Mills, C. W. Situated actions and vocabularies of motive. *Am. Sociol. Rev.,* 1940, 6, 904–913.

Parsons, T. *The social system.* New York: The Free Press, 1951.

Parsons, T. Definitions of illness and health in light of American values and social structure. In E. G. Jaco (Ed.), *Patients, physicians and illness.* (2nd ed.). New York: The Free Press, 1972.

Parsons, T. The sick role and the role of the physician reconsidered. *Health Society,* 1975 53, 257–278 (Summer).

Pfohl, S. J. The 'discovery' of child abuse. *Social Prob.,* 1977, 24, 310–323 (Feb.).

Pitts, J. Social control: the concepts. In D. Sills (Ed.), *International encyclopedia of social sciences.* (Vol. 14). New York: Macmillan Publishing Co., Inc., 1968.

Reynolds, J. M. The medical institution: the death and disease-producing appendage. In L.T. Reynolds & J. M. Henslin (Eds.), *American society: a critical analysis.* New York: David McKay Co., Inc., 1973.

Rosen, G. The evolution of social medicine. In H. E. Freeman, S. Levine, & L. Reeder (Eds.), *Handbook of medical sociology* (2nd ed.). Englewood Cliffs, N.J.: Prentice-Hall, Inc., 1972.

Ryan, W. *Blaming the victim.* New York: Vintage Books, 1971. (a)

Scheff, T. J. Decision rules, types of errors, and their consequences in medical diagnosis. *Behav. Sci.,* 1963, 8, 97–107.

Shuval, J. T., & Antonovsky, A. Illness: a mechanism for coping with failure. *Soc. Sci. Med.,* 1973, 7, 259–265.

Sigler, M., & Osmond, H. *Models of madness, models of medicine.* New York: Macmillan Publishing Co., Inc., 1974.

Sontag, S. *Illness as metaphor.* New York: Farrar, Straus & Giroux, 1978.

Sorenson, J. Biomedical innovation, uncertainty, and doctor-patient interaction. *J. Health Soc. Behav.,* 1974, 15, 366–374 (Dec.).

Szasz, T. *The myth of mental illness.* New York: Hoeber-Harper, 1961.

Szasz, T. *Law, liberty and psychiatry.* New York: Macmillan Publishing Co., Inc., 1963.

Szasz, T. Legal and moral aspects of homosexuality. In J. Marmor (Ed.), *Sexual inversion: the multiple roots of homosexuality.* New York: Basic Books, Inc., 1965.

Szasz, T. *The manufacture of madness,* New York: Harper & Row, Publishers, Inc., 1970.

Szasz, T. *Ceremonial chemistry.* New York: Anchor Books, 1974.

Waitzkin, H., & Stoeckle, J. Information control and the micropolitics of health care: summary of an ongoing project. *Soc. Sci. Med.,* 1976, 10, 263–276 (June).

Waitzkin, H. K., & Waterman, B. *The exploitation of illness in capitalist society.* Indianapolis: The Bobbs-Merrill Co., Inc., 1974.

Wolff, K. For a sociology of evil. *J. Soc. Issues,* 1969, 25, 111–125.

Wootton, B. *Social science and social pathology.* London: George Allen & Unwin, 1959.

Zola, I. K. Medicine as an institution of social control. *Sociological Rev.,* 1972, 20, 487–504.

Zola, I. K. In the name of health and illness: on some socio-political consequences of medical influence. *Soc. Sci. Med.,* 1975, 9, 83–87.

THINKING ABOUT THE READING

How does medicine function as a means of social control? What do the authors mean when they say, "Evil has been excluded from the imagery of modern human problems"? Do you agree that perceiving troublesome behavior as an "illness" prevents us from confronting such behavior as evil? Why do you suppose we have such a profound desire to use the vocabulary of medicine to describe deviant behavior? Clearly some people are helped when their problematic behaviors are conceived as illnesses or disorders and they are prescribed drugs or some sort of surgical treatment. Do you think that Conrad and Schneider overstate the negative consequences of the medicalization of deviance?

8 Building Social Relationships: Intimacy and Families

In this culture, close, personal relationships are the standard by which we judge the quality and happiness of our everyday lives. Yet in a complex, individualistic society like ours, these relationships are becoming more difficult to establish and sustain. Although we like to think that the things we do in our relationships are completely private experiences, they are continually influenced by large-scale political interests and economic pressures. Like every other aspect of our lives, close relationships can be understood only within the broader social context. Laws, customs, and social institutions often regulate the way we form these relationships, how we act inside them, and how we dispose of them when they are no longer working. At a more fundamental level, societies determine which relationships can be considered "legitimate" and therefore entitled to cultural and institutional recognition. Those relationships that lack such societal validation are often scorned and stigmatized.

Such social validation is particularly difficult to obtain for homosexual couples, who are often portrayed by others as a threat to the institution of family. In "No Place Like Home," sociologist Christopher Carrington describes how lesbians and gay men construct and sustain a sense of family in their own lives. From his research, Carrington argues that *family* isn't necessarily determined by blood or law but by a consistent pattern of loving and caring. *Family* resides in the unremarkable, everyday things that partners do with and for each other. In that sense, same-sex couples establish extensive life-long bonds, just like those found in long-term heterosexual couples.

Sherman Alexie also explores the theme of who gets to be called a family in his fictional short story, "Jesus Christ's Half-Brother Is Alive and Well on the Spokane Indian Reservation." It is the tale of a Spokane Indian man who is forced by circumstances to care for a young child. Like Carrington's research, this story highlights the ways in which the definition of *family* is a matter of heart and responsibility, not something defined by blood or law and not something that can always be easily and universally recognized.

No matter how we define families, one undeniable fact of family life in the early 21st century is that the adults in a household are likely to work outside the home. Hence, most families today must figure out ways to balance home life with the demands of work. Most of us assume that "home" is the more pleasant, soothing place to be. It's where we can relax and receive emotional sustenance. Work, on the other hand, has traditionally been characterized as a harried, dehumanizing, and insecure place. It's where we go, out of economic necessity, to earn money that serves as a means to an end. If given the choice, most people would rather be at home than at work, right?

Not necessarily. Arlie Hochschild finds in "The Time Bind" that the traditional images of work and home are changing. Many parents say they want to spend more time with their families and less time at work, but relatively few are taking advantage of opportunities to reduce their work time. The workers she interviewed seem to prefer being at work. Hochschild argues that new management techniques have made the workplace a more personal and appreciative place to be. At the same time, pressing time demands on working parents have made the home a frenzied, busy place where efficiency and scheduling are overriding concerns. Such a shift will have important consequences for people's family expectations and, according to Hochschild, children's lives in the future.

No Place Like Home

Christopher Carrington

This was a law developed for the purpose of ensuring that people can care for their families. It's inappropriate for a senator to cheapen the meaning of family by saying family is a "fill in the blank."
—Kristi Hamrick, spokesperson for the Family Research Council, commenting on New Jersey Sen. Robert Torricelli's decision to voluntarily extend some of the provisions of the 1993 Family and Medical Leave Act to lesbian and gay members of his staff (www. glinn.com March 13, 1997)

As I write these words, a cultural debate in the United States rages over the status of lesbian and gay families, most notably in the struggles over lesbian and gay marriage, as well as in the struggles to gain "domestic partnership" benefits. Much of the current debate about lesbian and gay families stems from the threat that such families are perceived to pose to the dominant organization of family practices in contemporary Western societies (Mohr 1994; Stacey 1996). However, a pervasive sense of crisis in the American family has existed throughout much of American history (Skolnick 1991; Coontz 1992), and the national debate concerning lesbian and gay families is but the latest grist for the mill. This sense of family crisis pervades the political efforts to block lesbian and gay people from attaining legal marriage and benefits of domestic partnership. The sense of crisis, and the rhetorical overkill that accompanies it, not only makes it difficult for political debate to focus on the everyday realities of lesbian and gay families but insures that many people will both understand such families in stereotypical ways and impede efforts to improve the quality of lesbian and gay

family life. The quotation at the beginning of this chapter from Ms. Hamrick denies the possibility that lesbian and gay families exist, much less acknowledges that they should enjoy any kind of cultural recognition.

. . . Actual lesbigay families, like most other American families, face the struggles of balancing work and family commitments, of managing the stresses and strains of waxing and waning sexual desires, of maintaining open and honest communication, of fighting over household responsibilities, and, most frequently, of simply trying to make ends meet. The latter point deserves much more attention, for if any phantom lurks in the lives of lesbian and gay families, it is their inability to achieve financial security, the foundation of a happy, communicative, and stable relationship (Voydanoff 1992).

This is a study of "family life" among a group of fifty-two lesbian and gay families (twenty-six female and twenty-six male). This study provides an ethnographic and empirical account of how lesbians and gay men actually construct, sustain, enhance, or undermine a sense of family in their lives. . . . I use the term *lesbigay*, which is coming into wider use, because it includes lesbians, bisexuals, and gay men, all of whom participate in the families I studied. Of the fifty-two adult women participants, two consider themselves bisexual, as does one of the fifty-three adult men.

In this study I reflect upon the *details* of everyday life in the households of the lesbigay families, and explore the relationship of such detail to the actual experience of and creation of family in the lives of lesbigay people. The participants in this research, similar to many other citizens, use the term *family* in diverse and often contradictory ways. At one moment a participant will conceive of family as a legal and biological category, a category that they reject, and might even define themselves as over and against. In a different place and time that same participant will conceive of family in favor of an understanding that emphasizes the labors involved and not the socially sanctioned roles. And at yet another place and time that same participant will embrace the legal and biological definitions of family with the hopes of achieving lesbigay inclusion into those categorizations (for example, advocating lesbigay legal marriage or attempting to secure custody of a child on the basis of biological linkage).

In my analysis the crucial element for defining what or who constitutes a family derives from whether the participants engage in a consistent and relatively reciprocal pattern of loving and caring activities and understand themselves to be bound to provide for, and entitled to partake of, the material and emotional needs and/or resources of other family members. I understand family as consisting of people who love and care for one another. This makes a couple a family. In other words, through their loving and caring activities, and their reflections upon them, people conceive of, construct, and maintain social relationships that they come to recognize and treat as family (Schneider 1984). In this sense a family, any family, is a social construction, or set of relationships recognized, edified, and sustained through human initiative. People "do" family.

This research ponders the deceptively simple activities that constitute love and care, activities that frequently go unnoticed in most families, including most lesbigay families. These may entail trips to the store to pick up something special for dinner, phoning an order to a catalog company for someone's birthday, tallying the money owed to friends, sorting the daily mail, remembering a couple's anniversary, finishing up the laundry before one's spouse returns home, maintaining a photo album, remembering the vegetables that family members dislike, or attending to myriad other small, often hidden, seemingly insignificant matters. Decidedly not insignificant, these small matters form the fabric of our daily lives as participants in families.

Moreover, the proliferation of these small matters produces a stronger and more pervasive sense of the relationship(s) as a family, both in the eyes of the participants and in the eyes of others. . . .

Kin Work Among Lesbigay Families

In recent years, scholars of family life have begun to document the forms of work that heterosexual women do in order to establish and sustain family relations. Some of this research reveals the forms of hidden and frequently unrecognized labor involved in maintaining kin relations (Rosenthal 1985; Di Leonardo 1987; Gerstel and Gallagher 1993 1994). Di Leonardo refers to these kinds of activities as "kin work":

> The conception, maintenance, and ritual celebration of cross-household kin ties, including visits, letters, telephone calls, presents and cards to kin; the organization of holiday gatherings; the creation and maintenance of quasi-kin relations; decisions to neglect or to intensify particular ties; the mental work of reflection about all of these activities; and the creation and communication of altering images of family and kin vis-à-vis the images of others, both folk and mass media. (1987, 442–43)

The forms of kin work Di Leonardo delineates appear in lesbigay families as well, although much of the aforementioned empirical research fails to include such families. In writing letters, making phone calls, organizing holiday and social occasions, selecting and purchasing gifts, as well as the forethought and decisions about how to do these things, how much to do, and for whom to do them, lesbigay families engage in a great deal of kin work. In fact, engaging in kin work is essential to creating lesbigay family life.

Kith as Family

In most respects, lesbigay families engage in forms of kin work quite similar to heterosexual families, though many do so among intimate friends rather than among biolegally defined relatives (Weston 1991; Nardi 1992; Nardi and Sherrod 1994). In contrast to the traditional Anglo-Saxon distinction made between kith (friends and acquaintances) and kin (relatives), many lesbigay families operate with a different set of distinctions where kith become kin and, sometimes, kin become kith. For example, Mary Ann Callihan, a thirty-eight-year-old artist now living in Oakland, reflects:

> I do consider my close friends as my family. They are my real family, I mean, my other family lives back East, and I don't have much to do with them and they don't have much to do with me. They really aren't a family, not at least in how I think a family should be. The people who care for me, listen to me, and love me are right here. They are my kin.

And while Mary Ann's comments diminishing the importance of biolegally defined kin reflect the views of roughly a third of the sample, her sentiments regarding the definition of family capture a common theme found in many lesbigay households: a normative sense of family as a voluntary association, as *chosen*. Sociologist Judith Stacey identifies this pattern of chosen kin and voluntary family ties as the "postmodern family" (Stacey 1990, 17, 270). Many lesbigay household operate with this postmodern conception of kin. Many respondents use the phrase "gay family" to designate their chosen family.

This conception of friends as family notwithstanding, lesbigay families make clear distinctions among friends. Anthropologist Kath Weston notes, "Although many gay families included friends, not just any friend would do" (1991, 109). Weston argues that "gay families differed from networks to the extent that they quite consciously incorporated symbolic demonstrations of love, shared history, material and emotional assistance and other signs of enduring solidarity" (109). Bringing the perspectives and findings of the literature on kin work to bear on Weston's findings raises a number of questions: What activities constitute symbolic demonstrations of love? What kind of work does material and emotional assistance involve and who per-

forms that work? What activities/behaviors serve as signs of enduring solidarity and what forms of work come to play in those activities? Peter Nardi, describing the role of friendships in lives of gay people, points out that

> in addition to providing opportunities for expressions of intimacy and identity, friendships for gay men and lesbians serve as sources for various kinds of social support (ranging from the monetary to health care) and provide them with a network of people with whom they can share celebrations, holidays, and other transitional rituals. (1992, 112)

Nardi's delineation of activities crucial to friendship suggests the presence of kin work: planning, provisioning, and coordinating visits, celebrations, holidays, and transitional rituals; making phone calls and sending e-mail on a consistent basis; sending notes, cards, and flowers at the appropriate times; selecting, purchasing, and wrapping gifts; providing or arranging for the provision of healthcare (not a minor matter given the HIV/AIDS epidemic); and reflecting upon and strategizing about relationships. All of these activities constitute kin work, and performing these activities *creates* and sustains family.

When laying claim to the term *family* to describe lesbigay relationships, most respondents point to particular phenomena as evidence of family: sharing meals, sharing leisure, sharing holidays, sharing religious community, sharing resources, relying on someone for emotional or medical care, turning to someone in an emergency, and/or sharing a common history. For example, many lesbians and gay men point to the sharing of holiday meals as indicative of the presence of family in their lives. Susan Posner, reflecting on those people with whom she and her partner, Camille, spend their holidays, comments:

> Well, we have them over to eat or they have us over. We have been together through thick and thin for so long from when we first came out of the closet, through our commitment ceremony, and through buying this house. That makes us family. I have known one of them for a very

long time, that's a lot of eating and sharing and crying and stuff.

Susan began to cry as she reflected on these events in her life. She then recounted several holiday gatherings where the joy that she experienced with her lesbigay family was so overwhelming that she began to cry during the events. Many lesbigay people can recount similar stories. In part, these are tears of exile from biolegal kin, but they are more than that. They are also tears of joy—joy in the discovery of a new home and a new family.

In addition to sharing holiday meals, other participants pointed to other kinds of kin work as evidence of family. Daniel Sen Yung, a twenty-eight-year-old accountant for a small nonprofit agency, offers another instance of kith becoming kin via various forms of kin work. Daniel, responding to my question about whether he considers his close friends as family, replies:

> Oh, yes, I know that I can depend on them for certain things that you would get from a family. If I were to get really ill, they would take care of me, house me, provide for me. We eat together, just like families should. I consider friends as family, especially as a gay person, I think that way. I definitely have a gay family. They look out for me and check in on me. They are the people who pay my bills when I go overseas for work, or who were with me when I had to take my cat to the veterinary hospital. They are the ones who came and visited me in the hospital, for God's sake.

Another participant, Raquel Rhodes, a thirty-one-year-old woman working as an assistant manger for a rental car agency, identified those who had loaned her money as central to her conception of family:

> I think you know who your real family is when you fall on hard times. My friends Rebecca and Sue, they came through for me when I lost my job. They lent me the money I needed to keep going. My own mother wouldn't because of all of her homophobic bullshit. That tells you who really counts and for me—Rebecca and Sue really count.

Loaning people money involves kin work. Managing and negotiating the feelings incumbent in such lending, particularly when a couple is doing the lending, as well as managing the money itself are both forms of kin work. Other forms of lesbigay kin work include all the efforts that people put into recognizing and celebrating their own and other people's relationships. The recent work by anthropologist Ellen Lewin (1998) exploring the commitment ceremonies of lesbian and gay couples reveals the extensive work entailed in creating these ceremonies. Lewin chronicles the efforts these couples put into selecting invitations, attire, and locations for the ceremony, as well as making arrangements for out-of-town guests. She also reveals the extensive emotional labor that goes into deciding who to invite—a sometimes gut-wrenching and potentially combative enterprise. When we do these things, we create family.

The Lesbigay Family Kin Keepers

Quite frequently, relationships function as a center for extended kinship structures. To use an astronomical metaphor, these relationships become planets around whom a series of moons (frequently, single individuals) revolve. The planning, organization, and facilitation of social occasions (picnics, holiday gatherings, vacations, commitment ceremonies/holy unions, birthday parties, gay-pride celebrations, hiking trips) bring these individuals into an orbit around lesbigay relationships. These occassions often take place in the homes of couples, as contrasted with individuals, and one member of the couple often performs the work involved. In answering questions about holiday gatherings, lesbigay families frequently recount stories of shared Thanksgiving meals, Jewish Sedarim, gay-pride celebrations, and Christmas Eve gatherings. Many speak of the importance of making sure that everyone "has a place to go" on such occasions.

For example, Matthew Corrigan and his partner, Greg Fuss, have been together for thirteen years and live in San Francisco's Castro district. Matthew works as an administrator in a nearby hospital and Greg works as a salesperson for a large pharmaceutical company. Matthew responds to my question about how he decides whom to invite for holiday occasions by saying:

> We have a lot of single friends. Many of them would like to be in couples, but they just haven't found Mr. or Mrs. Right yet. So, we are kind of their family. I mean, we will still be family after they find someone, but right now, they come here for holidays. I try to make sure that no one spends their Christmas alone. When we talk about who to invite, we always think about who doesn't have a place to go.

Matthew's comments capture a common dynamic where lesbigay families function as the center of kin relations for many single individuals. The lesbigay families can also function as a place where single individuals come into contact with one another and begin new relationships (Harry 1984, 143). These families become the center due to a number of socioeconomic factors. First, the formation of lesbigay families leads to pooling of resources. The shared resources of family groupings allow for larger residences, larger meal expenditures, and, interestingly, more time for kin work. Family status brings with it the possibility of at least one member in a family reducing the number of hours they work at paid labor and spending more time on family/household matters. Second, as lesbigay couples and threesomes come to perceive of their relationship in familial terms, they begin to act in familial ways: inviting others over for dinner, and creating holiday occasions, among other things. Third, it seems that unpartnered individuals view couples in familial ways and hold expectations that these individuals will act in familial terms. Angela DiVincenzo, a thirty-three-year-old elementary school teacher, felt this expectation from her lesbigay family:

> I think that our friends have a stake in our relationship. A lot of them are single and they kind of view us as the ideal family. I mean, partly, I think, it's about their hopes of having their own relationship, but also, it's about the fact that we are their family. They look to us to

act like a family. We all do things together, go on little trips or hiking or whatever. We are kind of a stabilizing influence in their lives. They know we are here and are interested in their lives, unlike many of their real families, that is, *supposedly* real families. We are the real family.

Moreover, in a number of the longer-term and more affluent lesbigay families, there emerges a person who becomes a family "kinkeeper" (Rosenthal 1985). This person functions as a sort of center for an extended lesbigay family. This individual actually coordinates some of the kin work across families. For example, Randy Ambert, a forty-two-year-old flight attendant, plans and coordinates many joint occasions for an extended kin group who he and his partner, Russ Pena, both consider their extended family. They include in this extended family a lesbian couple, another gay-male couple, a single lesbian, and two single gay men. In talking with Randy about these activities, he observes:

> I am sort of the family mom, if you get my drift. I tend to be the first person who thinks about what is coming up. I get everyone thinking about what we're going to do for summer travel, and I like to make sure that we don't forget anyone's birthday. With the other couples, that's not too much of an issue because they keep on top of each other's birthdays. But sometimes, the couples seem pretty busy and too worn out to make plans for things, you know, so I try to keep us all together. I plan a big celebration for Gay Pride each year that brings us all together.

In addition to planning these joint occasions, Randy reports making calls to gay family members who now live out of town and keeping them abreast of the news of the various people in the extended kin group. Randy's work sustains kinship; it makes real the claim of many lesbigay people, the claim to chosen family. Yet the work and the claim to family status occurs under a particular set of social conditions. Randy's relatively flexible work schedule and the relative affluence of his household allow Randy to invest more time in kin work, and to become a kinkeeper.

Arranging for such gatherings takes a great deal of kin work. In addition to the actual planning, provisioning and preparation of the food—all examples of feeding work—a number of other less observed labors make such family meals possible. Someone must envision such occasions and make decisions about whom to invite and when. Some people tend to think of the envisioning of such meals as a form of leisure, but in fact, this envisioning entails various hidden forms of labor. The envisioning of shared meals requires one to think and act in response to a number of different factors: individual, corporate, and societal calendars; whom to invite and how frequently; who gets along with whom and what mix of people would work; making phone calls or sending invitations; knowledge of social etiquette; and learning what foods guests like or dislike. Rich Niebuhr, a forty-one-year-old attorney working part-time, reveals the mental effort involved in deciding which people to invite to dinner:

> Well, it can be kind of awkward sometimes deciding whom to invite. Usually, I handle it because Joe doesn't like dealing with that kind of stuff. But, sometimes, I find myself torn because I know that we owe someone dinner, either we haven't seen them in a while and we run into them in Castro or at a movie, but I don't really feel like inviting them. Usually, I break down and invite them because I feel like a worm if I don't. I will think about whom to invite over at the same time—sort of to take the edge off, to make it a little less intense. It's okay. But, I kind of get mad that Joe just sort of expects me to negotiate all this stuff. Sometimes, I put my foot down, and make him call them. It can be real draining trying to stay on top of all this stuff.

Rich exemplifies the kinds of considerations that constitute kin work. Note how Rich bears responsibility for managing the interpersonal conflict and for strategizing the occasion because "Joe doesn't like dealing with that kind of stuff." Participant observation in Joe and Rich's home reveals that Rich performs much of the kin work,

both in its visible forms (making calls and planning events), as well as in its invisible forms (thinking about whom they should call and planning when to make the calls).

Variations in Kin Work Patterns

Not surprisingly the character and extent of kin work varies dramatically depending on a number of different social factors. Class identities, . . . the presence or absence of children, gender identities, . . . and ethnic and racial identities all influence the context in which kin work happens and the character of that kin work.

Social class and lesbigay kin work. While most lesbigay families in this study fall into the middle and upper middle class, clear distinctions emerge between these groups in terms of kin work. More affluent, upper-middle-class lesbigay households engage in significantly more kin work and much more frequently conceive of friends as family than their middle-class counterparts. Those families earning more than the median annual household income ($61,500) report twice as many close friends (twelve per household) as those households earning below the median (five). This pattern conforms to other empirical research revealing that patterns of informal association become more extensive as one moves up the socioeconomic hierarchy (Hodges 1964; Curtis and Jackson 1977). Among the ten most affluent households, all family members conceive of friends as family. In contrast, among the ten least affluent, only within four households does even one family member conceive of friends as family. In part this pattern may reflect the relatively younger age of the less affluent families. It also appears that among the more affluent, friendship/family networks become more strongly lesbigay. Less affluent respondents' friendship/family networks, while smaller, consist of a greater proportion of straight people. Overall, more affluent households maintain larger family structures and they do family with other lesbigay people.

This means that the work of creating and sustaining such relationships becomes more extensive and requires more labor for more affluent lesbigay families. For instance, they invite others over for shared meals more often, entertain larger numbers of people at dinner parties and other occasions, and go out to dinner with others more consistently. These activities require extensive kin work in the form of planning for such occasions, deciding whom to invite, extending invitations, deciding where to go out to eat, and maintaining a record (mental or written) of previous engagements.

Lawrence Sing and Henry Goode, together as a family for over two decades, live in a restored Edwardian flat in a rapidly gentrifying neighborhood in San Francisco. Lawrence works part-time as a real estate agent, and Henry works as a physician. They both possess postgraduate degrees. Lawerence, who performs much of the kin-related work in the family, makes the following comments about some of that work:

> I'm the keeper of the social calendar. I decide whom to invite over and when. I keep a mental record of who came last and whom we would like to see. I ask Henry if there is anyone he would like to see, but generally, I know how he feels about certain people. I keep up our obligations. Some people we see once a year, but there is a core of twenty-five to thirty people who I maintain contact with and whom we see with some frequency.

Lawerence, speaking with great enthusiasm and affection for his family of gay friends, denotes other forms of kin work in the effort to maintain those family relationships:

> I write letters to our closest friends who live farther away, and we always send them birthday presents and cards and, of course, presents at Christmastime. We try to plan holiday travel and our vacations with some of them. I often call them on Sundays; that's the day I make many of the long-distance calls to everybody. It's a lot of effort to keep it all together, but I think it's worth it. They're our family.

Lawrence's observations reflect common forms of kin work among more affluent lesbigay households. In contrast to less affluent lesbigay families, the affluent ones engage in some forms of kin work much more frequently: writing letters; buying and mailing gifts for birthdays and holidays; sending flowers; sending birthday, anniversary, and get-well cards; and sending a larger number of holiday greeting cards. When dividing up the sample into thirds, the most affluent one-third sent an average of seventy-five cards; and the lower one-third, fifteen cards per household. The more affluent families keep in contact with out-of-town friends and biolegal relatives much more frequently than less affluent families. The affluent make more long-distance calls and spend more time talking. All of these efforts constitute kin work: deciding upon and purchasing gifts and cards, writing and mailing the gifts and cards, remembering to call and write and deciding for whom to do these things.

In like manner, the more affluent households report more extensive holiday celebrations, and they often point to the sharing of holidays together as evidence of the family status of their intimate friends. Kathy Atwood and Joan Kelsey live in the Oakland hills in an Arts and Crafts style cottage in a neighborhood with many other lesbian families. Kathy works as an accountant for a prominent bank headquartered in downtown San Francisco. Joan works part-time as a finance manager for a local savings and loan. Together they earn slightly over $100,000 per year. Joan has a master's degree in accounting from a prestigious college in the East and Kathy has a bachelor's degree from the University of California. Kathy expresses her conception of friends as constituting family:

> I consider my friends as family. I see them as often as I see my biolegal family. I discuss our relationship with them. They come here for holidays or we go to their house. Our shared holidays are symbolic of our familiness. We share personal experiences. I would want them here for significant events, like Christmas or our Holy Union or whatever.

Joan, who does much of the kin work in the family, engages in a great deal of effort to make the holidays pleasant and meaningful to her chosen family:

> I put quite a bit of effort into getting the house together for Christmas. We had a lot of people over at different times, and our chosen family over on Christmas Eve, and we went to their house on Christmas day. I mean, I planned out the meals, a very special one for Christmas Eve. I bought and mailed invitations for a Sunday afternoon holiday party. I went to the Flower-mart in the city and bought greens and stuff like that. I bought a new tablecloth with a holiday theme. We chose presents for them together, but I had the time to wrap them and stuff like that.

Nearly a dozen individuals from more affluent families conceive of shared holidays as constitutive of family, while only two individuals from families earning below the median speak in these terms.

Conversely, in most cases, less affluent households more often conceive of family in biolegally defined terms, they engage in less kin work and to some extent they do different kinds of kin work. In terms of household income, most respondents perceiving of family as uniquely consisting of biolegal relatives fall below the median. I would characterize many of them as "minimal families" (Dizard and Gadlin 1990). They do not create and sustain large kin structures, either biolegally defined or lesbigay defined, and their conceptions of family emphasize biolegal links. Although these families afford less time and energy to maintaining kin relations, the efforts they do make often focus on biolegal relatives. These families often feel isolated and spend more time alone. Social researchers made the discovery long ago that the wealthy and the poor maintain stronger ties to kin for economic reasons than do middle-class Americans (Schneider and Smith 1973; Stack 1974). Most of those lesbigay families falling below the median income in this sample clearly fall into the middle or the lower middle class, as opposed to the working class or the poor. For instance, Amy Gilfoyle and Wendy Harper, a lesbian family living in a distant suburb north of San Francisco, a place where they could afford to buy a home, spend much of their time alone. They spend major holidays "alone together," without the presence of others. They both conceive of family as consisting of their own relationship and possibly Amy's biolegal parents. They report one close friend between the two of them, and both express disappointment about this. They would like more friends, but they seem conflicted. Wendy, a student and landscape gardener, feels somewhat threatened by new friends:

> I would worry about getting too close to a lot of other lesbians. There are always issues about falling in love with friends and that ruining your relationship. And, we live so far away from the places where we might meet friends. I suppose we could become friends with some gay men, but they don't live out here, or at least we don't have any way of finding those who do.

Wendy's comments point to issues partly beyond social class, to concerns about gender and sexuality. But the fact that Wendy and Amy live so far away from San Francisco speaks clearly of social class and the ability of more affluent families to buy and rent homes in the city. Interview questions focusing on the reasons for living in suburban communities almost always point to the cost of housing in the city as a factor in deciding where to live. Wendy and Amy bring in a household income of $35,000 per year. This places them somewhat below the Bay Area median household income of $41,459 (U.S. Census 1991). Like many other middle- and lower middle-class lesbigay families, they exert less effort in the maintenance of kinship structures than do more affluent families. They infrequently call friends or biolegal relatives. They rarely send cards of any sort. Together they sent eight holiday greeting cards in 1993. They rarely invite people over, though they actually have the space to entertain. Only once every few months do they go out to dinner, and then usually just the two of them go. They lead relatively isolated lives and feel ambiguous about changing this. . . .

In sum, social class appears to play a central role in the extent and the character of kin work among lesbigay families. As one ascends the so-cial-class hierarchy of lesbigay families in this sample from lower middle class to upper middle class, the intensity of kin work increases. The character of kin work shifts from concerns about establishing kin relationships to managing and sustaining kin relationships. The flow of material exchange intensifies with affluent lesbigay fami-lies buying more gifts, throwing more parties, hosting more dinners, making more phone calls, and sending more cards. Explaining why more affluent households do more kin work than less affluent ones involves several interrelated influ-ences. First, more affluent families live closer to the lesbigay enclaves due to the higher cost of liv-ing in the city. Proximity to other lesbigay people leads to larger kin networks. Yet, some lower middle-class lesbigay families live in the center of lesbigay enclaves and engage in significantly less kin work than their more affluent neighbors. Second, more affluent lesbigay families turn to the marketplace for other forms of domestic la-bor (for example, laundry and housekeeping) thus freeing these families to invest more energy in kin work. . . .

Lesbigay parenting and kin work. The presence of children diminishes the conception of friends as family in lesbian and gay households. In four of the five households with children present in this study, neither primary partner conceives of their close friends as family. Rather, these households limit family to the primary couple, the children, and to biolegal relatives. Emily Fortune and Alice Lauer, parents of two young infants, understand family in strongly biolegal terms. Emily states: "Some people use the term *family* very loosely. I don't call friends that. The kids and our relatives, they feel like family to me. To me, my family is my biolegal family. We have a natural bond to one another." Her partner, Alice:

> My concept of family has changed a great deal in the past few months. I think before the children were born I might have considered my friends as family. My relationship with my own sister has changed since the kids were born. I

have more of a sense of this family right here. I have a new appreciation for my family of origin. We can turn to them in a crisis, even though they may not be that comfortable with our sexuality.

Gay and lesbian parents appear more vested in biolegal conceptions of family, perhaps for very concrete reasons. To establish biolegal links in the American kinship structure often also establishes and legitimates economic links. Three of the les-bian families, all with infants, report relying on biolegal kin for resources, either in the form of providing housing, making loans, lending auto-mobiles, or providing daycare. Anthropologist Ellen Lewin suggests that the pattern of intensify-ing relations to blood kin among lesbian parents expresses an attempt to legitimate the claim to family and to provide a stable socioeconomic en-vironment for the children (1993, 91–94).

Moreover, the presence of children within some families distracts from the ability to main-tain friends. Clarice Perry, a college professor who is also deaf, expresses her feelings about family:

> My experience with family is strange. It's not easy to draw the line since I have Cheryl's children. I share responsibility for the kids, that's my idea of family. As an individual, my close friends, mostly deaf, we can't share that much because of the kids. The kids have changed my relationship with my friends. I have mixed feelings about it. I resent the kids sometimes. They took my friends away. It was not my plan to have kids, but they are now my family and I love them.

The addition of children changes one's social cir-cumstances, both for lesbigay people and for het-erosexuals. However, given that relatively few lesbigay families have children, and that parents often befriend parents in American culture, lesbi-gay parents may find it quite difficult to establish social links. This further encourages lesbigay families with kids to establish stronger relations with biolegal kin. The possibility exists that lesbian and gay friends may also intentionally diminish relationships with friends who have children. Some scholars find a fairly strong sentiment against children, especially among some gay men (Newton 1993).

Gender identities and lesbigay kin work. Gender appears central to explaining kin work in many settings. For instance, Di Leonardo posits that kin work reflects the influence of gender much more strongly than the influence of social class in heterosexual families (1987, 449). I can make no such unilateral claim about gender within lesbigay families. I detect gender-related concerns in terms of how lesbians and gay men both portray and do kin work, but this is complicated by the impact of socioeconomic factors. Interestingly, in this study, gay men do significantly more kin work than lesbian women. This parallels the finding of Blumstein and Schwartz (1983, 149–50) and my own research that gay men do more housework than lesbian women do. Blumstein and Schwartz argue this emerges from an effort among lesbians to avoid the low-status role assigned to housework in American society. I think additional factors play a role here.

While Blumstein and Schwartz find lesbian women shunning domestic work to avoid the low-status stigma attached to it, in the case of kin work I find both patterns of avoidance and a significantly diminished rationale for the generally less affluent lesbian families to engage in extensive kin work. When considering the economic affluence, educational level, and occupational prestige of all lesbigay households, the more affluent the household, the more educated and the more prestigious the career, the more extensive the kin work becomes regardless of gender. Dividing the lesbian families on the basis of household income into three groups (high, medium, and low) shows that those with high income report twice as many friends as those with low incomes. The same holds for males. Affluent families, regardless of gender, engage in much more extensive kin work. Due to the persistence of gender inequality, and the barriers women face in achieving higher-status, higher-paid employ-

ment, the resources necessary to sustain larger kin structures do not exist for many lesbian households as much as they do for gay men. Nor does maintaining such a network provide any economic advantage, as it does for those in occupational categories where extensive networks provide business and client contacts (lawyers, private-practice physicians, and psychologists).

Nonetheless, I am not suggesting that gender has no relevance here, but its relevance eludes easy classification. On the one hand, lesbian women may well avoid kin work activity in order to escape the devalued status associated with doing the work. After all, who wants to be "just a housewife" (Matthews 1987)? On the other hand, if one hopes to create and live within a family, then someone has to do this work. And in most lesbigay families these forms of work do occur. However, doing kin work, or failing to do it, carries different risks for gay men and lesbians. For the men, engaging in kin work produces threats to gender identity. Making calls to family, sending cards, buying presents, inviting dinner guests and worrying about soured relationships with family all carry the potential to become gender-producing phenomena (Berk 1985; West and Zimmerman 1987). A woman failing to engage in these nurturing/caring activities runs the risk of stigma. This "nurturing imperative" exists for women regardless of sexual orientation (Westkott 1986). I suspect that many lesbian women answering questions about kin work felt an obligation to do kin work. For instance, Melinda Rodriguez, a twenty-seven-year-old human resources administrator comments when I ask about making phone calls to biolegal relatives:

> Should I answer that the way I am supposed to or should I be more honest about it? *[Laughter]* I don't call too much. I feel guilty about it. But hey, my brothers don't call my parents. My mother complains to me about that, but not to my brothers. Why should I be judged differently? I guess it's not a very feminine attitude, but I don't care. Well, I do care, but I wish they would have more realistic expectations. You know, I work a lot, as much as my brothers do.

So I don't have that much time. Not like my mother, who doesn't work. She has time to call people.

Meanwhile, men engaging in extensive kin work frequently struggle with even more intense concerns about gender identity. Lance Meyter and Mike Tuzin, both in their late twenties, together for three years, and both working in the healthcare field (one in clerical, the other in higher administration), illustrate the dilemma some male couples face in negotiating kin work. Mike does most of the limited amount of kin work for their relationship. Lance feels that because Mike works at a less stressful job and has more time at home, he should do more of the "arranging of the social life." Mike, while accepting Lance's calculus, comments:

> I feel kind of weird about doing this stuff sometimes. I mean, I work, basically, as a secretary because I can't decide what to do with my life. That's already kind of embarrassing and hard on my self-esteem. I like to do a lot of social-type stuff, like talking to our friends, and arranging for things, but you know, it's hard. I was talking to my mother recently, and she wanted to know what we were doing that weekend and I told her everything I had planned and she said: "My, aren't you the little housewife." She was just joshing me, but I sort of, I wanted to puke. I mean, I think it's important to do this stuff, but it's kind of embarrassing, you know? *I do go to the gym quite a bit, so I guess that sort of makes up for it* (emphasis added).

Here we see the potential for the stigmatization of men who do these activities. Mike, in attempting to manage both a feminine-defined occupation and responsibility for kin work (among other forms of domestic work), turns to the realm of athletics "to make up for it." Many gay-male families must manage the threatening character of domestic work (including kin work) to male gender identity. Let it suffice to say that there are many ways to resolve this issue, including constructing myths, using rhetorical strate-

gies that hide the true division of domestic labor, and, for a few, simply violating conventional expectations. . . .

Ethnic and racial distinctions and lesbigay kin work. The influence of ethnic and racial identity upon kin work eludes easy analysis. The confluence of class and race in American culture often conceals distinctions between race and class (Steinberg 1989). This study captures the diversity of lesbigay families in terms of ethnic/racial identity, with over 40 percent of the respondents identifying themselves as Latino-, African-, or Asian-American. However, comparisons are limited by the fact that many of these same respondents are middle class. I know from my attempts to identify lower middle-class and working-class respondents within these groups and among Euro-Americans that lesbigays with fewer economic resources are far more hesitant to participate in this kind of research due to concerns about exposure of sexual identity. That said, let me turn to some discussion of the possible influence of ethnic/racial identity upon the extent and character of kin work.

On the one hand, because most of these families' household earnings, education and occupational identities place them in the middle class, they exhibit kin work patterns similar to their Euro-American middle-class counterparts. Most live in what Dizard and Gadlin would characterize as "minimal families" (1990). Similar to many middle-class families, and in contrast to more affluent families, these families report fewer close friends, they invite nonbiolegal kin over less often, they send fewer cards, write fewer letters, make fewer visits, make fewer long-distance calls, buy, send and give fewer presents, and organize fewer social occasions. On the other hand, Latino/Asian/African-identified lesbigay families recurrently report more extensive connections to biolegal relatives than do Euro-American families, and further, they more often than not conceive of family in strongly biolegal terms. For instance, they report greater exchange of money and material goods with biolegal relatives. A number of factors help to explain these dynamics.

First, the wide majority of African-, Asian- and Latino-American lesbigays grew up in California. This contrasts markedly with the Euro-Americans, 90 percent of whom grew up elsewhere and relocated to California. This means that, because Asian-, African- and Latino-American biolegal kin live in the area, kin relations become more extensive and more pressing. This dynamic appears more strongly related to geographical proximity than to ethnic/racial distinction. Euro-Americans who grew up in this region also exhibit stronger ties to biolegal kin. However, many lesbigay people of color strongly link conceptions of racial/ethnic identity with conceptions of kinship, something not heard among Euro-Americans. Deborah James, an African-American woman, and her partner, Elsa Harding, also African-American, both speak of their connections to biolegal family as a component of their racial identity. Deborah, who works as a daycare provider, states:

> I think that Anglo-Americans don't value family as much as Black people do. I mean, I know some lesbians who think of each other as their family, but I really don't get that. I mean, I think you gotta love your family, even if they aren't that accepting of you. For us, part of being African-American is keeping your connections to your family and your church and stuff like that.

Barbara Cho, a thirty-eight-year-old Chinese-American woman working as a hotel clerk, holds a similar view: "I think of my family as my relatives. I love Barbara [her partner], but she is not really a part of my relatives. I don't want to say she isn't like family to me, but she's not my family. My mother and father, and my sisters, they are my family."

Although most Asian-, African-, and Latino-American lesbigay families conceive of family in biolegal terms (many respondents use the phrase "blood is thicker than water"), not all share this conception. Ceasar Portes and Andy Yanez, together for seventeen years and living in San Francisco's Mission district, a predominantly Latino neighborhood, exhibit an alternative pattern. Ceasar comes from a large Mexican-American family, most of whom live within a half-day's drive. Andy comes from a somewhat smaller, though equally close, Filipino-American family. Ceasar, diminishing the distinction between biolegal and lesbigay kin, asserts:

> We try to include all of our family, I mean both our gay family and our blood family, who live in San Jose or in Pacifica, in our lives. We also have our religious family, you know, many brothers and sisters in the faith, who are a part of our community. We invite everyone to be here. At first, it was hard. I don't think my blood relatives really understood gay people. But they have really changed. My mother loves all of our gay family now, and so we are all family together.

Andy reports that his family, while less accepting of his sexual identity than Ceasar's family, remains strongly committed to "keeping the family together," and includes Ceasar in family activities. Ceasar says that one of his sisters thinks of Andy as a "padrino," or godfather, to her children and makes an effort to include him in family activities.

Derrick Harding and Andrew Joust, both African-American men, provide another counterexample to the notion that "blood is thicker than water." Derrick mentions two heterosexual couples at their local church whom he considers family. In response to a question as to why he considers them such, he reflects: "Why yes, without a doubt, they care about us. They are like our godparents. They adopted us. We are real close with them. They are our family." His partner, Andrew, comments on the same heterosexual couples: "They took us under their wing when we first got here. I think of them as our family, I don't know what else you would call them." These competing views of the importance of ethnic/racial distinctions upon family that exist among African-, Asian-, and Latino-American lesbigay families point to the influence of factors related to but different from ethnicity that play a role in conceptions and constructions of family life. In the case of Andrew and Derrick, they migrated to the Bay Area and established connections to a church community. Their biolegal relatives remain in the East and far away from their day-to-day lives. Andrew reports that he last spoke with a biolegal relative more than a year ago. What really seems to divide those African-, Asian-, and Latino-American lesbigay families who redefine family in non-biolegal terms from those who do is social class. All of those families who blur the distinctions between biolegal and chosen families possess bachelor's degrees, work in professional careers, and earn higher incomes. Ceasar and Derrick both work as social workers, Andrew works as a secondary education teacher, and Andy works in higher education administration.

Kin Work and the Creation of Family

In its extensiveness, its focused character, and its reflection of genuine bonds of love and affection, kin work contributes much to the creation and sustenance of lesbigay life. The family that results from this kin work is not, as many opponents of lesbigay people would have one believe, a rough approximation of the real thing or a sad substitute for genuine biolegal relations. Nor is it just a group of friends. Far from it. The bonds created within and among these families are far more extensive than what most middle-class Americans would conventionally view as friendship bonds (Rapp 1992). Middle-class Americans infrequently take in their friends and provide them housing, food, and medical care while they are dying. Moreover, any number of the lesbigay families in this study would not dream of sacrificing the lesbigay kin ties they have created in favor of some biolegally defined entity. Not to mention that many lesbigay families don't have to make that choice because their biolegal kin have not excluded them, and therein they have been able to integrate biolegal and lesbigay kin into a greater whole. Surely, many lesbigay families are struggling to create and sustain kin ties against socioeconomic conditions that deter them, but the effort is paradoxical and often threatening to the broader culture. These families are struggling to create and sustain kin relations with the qualities associated with family ideals in American culture, but not necessarily with the forms most citizens associate with family.

REFERENCES

Badgett, L., and M. King. 1997. Lesbian and gay occupational strategies. In A. Gluckman and B. Reed, eds., *Homo Economics: Capitalism, Community and Lesbian and Gay Life.* New York: Routledge.

Berk, S. Fenstermacher. 1985. *The Gender Factory: The Apportionment of Work in American Households.* New York: Plenum Press.

Blumstein, P., and P. Schwarz. 1983. *American Couples.* New York: Morrow.

Coontz, S. 1992. *The Way We Never Were: American Families and the Nostalgia Trap.* New York: Basic Books.

Curtis, R., and E. Jackson. 1977. *Inequality in American Communities.* New York: Academic Press.

D'Emilio, J. 1983. Capitalism and gay identity. In Ann Snitow, ed., *Powers of Desire: The Politics of Sexuality.* New York: Monthly Press Review.

Di Leonardo, M. 1987. The female world of cards and holidays: Women, families, and the work of kinship. *Signs* 12 (Summer): 440–52.

Dizard, J., and H. Gadlin. 1990. *The Minimal Family.* Amherst: University of Massachusetts Press.

Gerstel, N., and S. Gallagher. 1993. Kinkeeping and distress: Gender, recipients of care, and work-family conflict. *Journal of Marriage and Family* 55 (Aug.): 598–607.

———. 1994. Caring for kith and kin: Gender, employment, and privatization of care. *Social Problems* 41 (4): 519–39.

Harry, J. 1984. *Gay couples.* New York: Praeger.

Hodges, H. 1964. *Social Stratification: Class in America.* Cambridge, Mass.: Schenkman.

Lewin, E. 1993. *Lesbian Mothers: Accounts of Gender in American Culture.* Ithaca, N.Y.: Cornell University Press.

———. 1998. *Recognizing Ourselves: Ceremonies of Lesbian and Gay Commitment.* New York: Columbia University Press.

Matthews, G. 1987. *Just a Housewife: The Rise and Fall of Domesticity in America.* New York: Oxford.

Mohr, R. 1994. *A More Perfect Union: Why Straight America Must Stand Up for Gay Rights.* Boston: Beacon.

Nardi, P. 1992. That's what friends are for: Friends as family in the gay and lesbian community. In K. Plummer, ed., *Modern Homosexualities.* London: Routledge.

Nardi, P., and D. Sherrod. 1994. Friendship in the lives of gay men and lesbians. *Journal of Social and Personal Relationships* 11:185–99.

Newton, E. 1993. *Cherry Grove, Fire Island: Sixty Years in America's First Gay and Lesbian Town.* Boston: Beacon.

Rosenthal, C. 1985. Kinkeeping in the family division of labor. *Journal of Marriage and the Family* 47 (4): 965–74.

Schneider, D. 1984. *A Critique of the Study of Kinship.* Ann Arbor: University of Michigan Press.

Schneider, D., and R. Smith. 1973. *Class Differences and Sex Roles in American Kinship and Family Structure.* Englewood Cliffs, N.J.: Prentice Hall.

Skolnick, A. 1991. *Embattled Paradise: The American Family in an Age of Uncertainty.* New York: Basic Books.

Stacey, J. 1990. *Brave New Families: Stories of Upheaval in the Late Twentieth Century.* New York: Basic Books.

———. 1996. *In the Name of the Family: Rethinking Family Values in the PostModern Age.* Boston: Beacon.

Stack, C. 1974. *All Our Kin: Strategies for Survival in a Black Community.* New York: Harper and Row.

Steinberg, Stephen. 1989. *The Ethnic Myth: Race, Ethnicity, and Class in America.* Boston: Beacon.

U.S. Bureau of the Census. 1991. *Money Income of Households, Families, and Persons in the United States: 1990.* Series P-60, no. 174. Washington, D.C.

Voydanoff, P. 1992. Economic distress and family relations: A review of the eighties. *Journal of Marriage and the Family* 52:1099–1115.

West, C., and D. Zimmerman. 1987. Doing gender. *Gender and Society* I (2): 125–51.

Westkott, M. 1986. *The Feminist Legacy of Karen Horney.* New Haven, Conn.: Yale University Press.

Weston, K. 1990. *Families We Choose: Lesbians, Gays, Kinship.* New York: Columbia University Press.

THINKING ABOUT THE READING

What is "kin work"? Do you agree that kin work is what creates and sustains families? Should two people who consistently love and care for each other and who engage in the day-to-day tasks necessary to maintain a household be considered a family and be eligible for all the benefits that legal families are entitled to? If, as Carrington argues, the family-defining activities that gay and lesbian couples engage in are no different from those that heterosexual couples engage in, why is there such strong public opposition to the legal recognition of gay couples as families? Carrington implies that individuals should have the freedom to define their own living arrangements as a family. Do you agree? Does society have an interest in controlling who can and can't be considered a family?

Jesus Christ's Half-Brother Is Alive and Well on the Spokane Indian Reservation

Sherman Alexie

1966

Rosemary MorningDove gave birth to a boy today and seeing as how it was nearly Christmas and she kept telling everyone she was still a virgin even though Frank Many Horses said it was his we all just figured it was an accident. Anyhow she gave birth to him but he came out all blue and they couldn't get him to breathe for a long time but he finally did and Rosemary MorningDove named him ———, which is unpronounceable in Indian and English but it means: *He Who Crawls Silently Through the Grass with a Small Bow and One Bad Arrow Hunting for Enough Deer to Feed the Whole Tribe.*

We just call him James.

1967

Frank Many Horses and Lester FallsApart and I were drinking beers in the Breakaway Bar playing pool and talking stories when we heard the sirens. Indians get all excited when we hear sirens because it means fires and it means they need firefighters to put out the fires and it means we get to be firefighters and it means we get paid to be firefighters. Hell somebody always starts a fire down at the Indian burial grounds and it was about time for the Thirteenth Annual All-Indian Burial Grounds Fire so Frank and Lester and I ran down to the fire station expecting to get hired but we see smoke coming from Commodity Village where all the really poor Indians live so we run down there instead and it was Rosemary MorningDove's house that was on fire. Indians got buckets of water but this fire was way too big and we could hear a baby crying and Frank Many Horses gets all excited even though

it's Lillian Many's baby right next to us. But Frank knows James is in the house so he goes running in before any of us can stop him and pretty soon I see Frank leaning out the upstairs window holding James and they're both a little on fire and Frank throws James out the window and I'm running my ass over to catch him before he hits the ground making like a high school football hero again but I miss him just barely slipping through my fingers and James hits the ground hard and I pick him up right away and slap the flames out with my hands all the while expecting James to be dead but he's just looking at me almost normal except the top of his head looks all dented in like a beer can.

He wasn't crying.

1967

I went down to the reservation hospital to see how James and Frank and Rosemary were doing and I got drunk just before I went so I wouldn't be scared of all the white walls and the sound of arms and legs getting sawed off down in the basement. But I heard the screams anyway and they were Indian screams and those can travel forever like all around the world and sometimes from a hundred years ago so I close my ears and hide my eyes and just look down at the clean clean floors. Oh Jesus I'm so drunk I want to pray but I don't and before I can change my mind about coming here Moses MorningDove pulls me aside to tell me Frank and Rosemary have died and since I saved James's life I should be the one who raises him. Moses says it's Indian tradition but somehow since Moses is going on about two hundred years old and still drinking and screwing like he was twenty I figure he's just trying to get out of his grandfatherly duties. I don't really want any of it and I'm sick and the hospital is making me sicker and my heart is shaking and confused like when the nurse wakes you up in the middle of the night to give you a sleeping pill but I know James will end up some Indian kid at a welfare house making baskets and wearing itchy clothes and I'm only twenty myself but I take one look at James all lumpy and potato looking and I look in the mirror and see myself holding him and I take him home.

Tonight the mirror will forgive my face.

1967

All dark tonight and James couldn't sleep and just kept looking at the ceiling so I walk on down to the football field carrying James so we can both watch the stars looking down at the reservation. I put James down on the fifty-yard line and I run and run across the frozen grass wishing there was snow enough to make a trail and let the world know I was there in the morning. Thinking I could spell out my name or James's name or every name I could think of until I stepped on every piece of snow on the field like it was every piece of the world or at least every piece of this reservation that has so many pieces it might just be the world. I want to walk circles around James getting closer and closer to him in a new dance and a better kind of healing which could make James talk and walk before he learns to cry. But he's not crying and he's not walking and he's not talking and I see him sometimes like an old man passed out in the back of a reservation van with shit in his pants and a battered watch in his pocket that always shows the same damn time. So I pick James up from the cold and the grass that waits for spring and the sun to change its world but I can only walk home through the cold with another future on my back and James's future tucked in my pocket like an empty wallet or a newspaper that feeds the fire and never gets read.

Sometimes all of this is home.

1968

The world changing the world changing the world. I don't watch the TV anymore since it exploded and left a hole in the wall. The woodpile don't dream of me no more. It sits there by the ax and they talk about the cold that waits in corners and surprises you on a warm almost spring day. Today I stood at the window for hours and then I took the basketball from inside the wood stove and shot baskets at the hoop nailed to a pine tree in the yard. I shot and shot until the cold meant I was protected because my skin was too warm to feel any of it. I shot and shot until my fingertips bled and my feet ached and my hair stuck to the skin of my bare back. James waited by the porch with his hands in the dirt and his feet stuck into leather shoes I found in the dump under a washing machine. I can't believe the details I am forced to remember with each day that James comes closer to talking. I change his clothes and his dirty pants and I wash his face and the crevices of his little body until he shines like a new check.

This is my religion.

1968

Seems like the cold would never go away and winter would be like the bottom of my feet but then it is gone in one night and in its place comes the sun so large and laughable. James sitting up in his chair so young and he won't talk and the doctors at the Indian clinic say it's way too early for him to be talking anyhow but I see in his eyes something and I see in his eyes a voice and I see in his eyes a whole new set of words. It ain't Indian or English and it ain't cash register and it ain't traffic light or speed bump and it ain't window or door. Late one day James and I watch the sun fly across the sky like a basketball on fire until it falls down completely and lands in Benjamin Lake with a splash and shakes the ground and even wakes up Lester FallsApart who thought it was his father come back to slap his face again.

Summer coming like a car from down the highway.

1968

James must know how to cry because he hasn't cried yet and I know he's waiting for that one moment to cry like it was five hundred years of tears. He ain't walked anywhere and there are no blisters on his soles but there are dreams worn clean into his rib cage and it shakes and shakes with each breath and I see he's trying to talk when he grabs at the air behind his head or stares up at the sky so hard. All of this temperature rising hot and I set James down in the shade by the basketball court and I play and I play until the sweat of my body makes it rain everywhere on the reservation. I play and I play until the music of my shoes against pavement sounds like every drum. Then I'm home alone and I watch the cockroaches live their complicated lives.

I hold James with one arm and my basketball with the other arm and I hold everything else inside my whole body.

1969

I take James to the Indian clinic because he ain't crying yet and because all he does sometimes is stare and stare and sometimes he'll wrap his arms around the stray dogs and let them carry him around the yard. He's strong enough to hold his body off the ground but he ain't strong enough to lift his tongue from the bottom of his mouth to use the words for love or anger or hunger or good morning. Maybe he's only a few years old but he's got eyes that are ancient and old and dark like a castle or a lake where the turtles go to die and sometimes even to live. Maybe he's going to howl out the words when I least expect it or want it and he'll yell out a cuss word in church or a prayer in the middle of a grocery store. Today I moved through town and walked and walked past the people who hadn't seen me in so long maybe for months and they asked questions about me and James and no one bothered to knock on the door and look for the answers. It's just me and James walking and walking except he's on my back and his eyes are looking past the people who are looking past us

for the coyote of our soul and the wolverine of our heart and the crazy crazy man that touches every Indian who spends too much time alone. I stand in the Trading Post touching the canned goods and hoping for a vision of all the miles until Seymour comes in with a twenty-dollar bill and buys a couple cases of beer and we drink and drink all night long. James gets handed from woman to woman and from man to man and a few children hold this child of mine who doesn't cry or recognize the human being in his own body. All the drunks happy to see me drunk again and back from the wagon and I fell off that wagon and broke my ass and dreams and I wake up the next morning in a field watching a cow watch me. With piss in my pants I make the long walk home past the HUD houses and abandoned cars and past the powwow grounds and the Assembly of God where the sinless sing like they could forgive us all. I get home and James is there with Suzy Song feeding him and rocking him like a boat or a three-legged chair.

I say no and I take James away and put him in his crib and I move into Suzy's arms and let her rock and rock me away from my stomach and thin skin. . . .

1969

We played our first basketball game of the season tonight in the community center and I had Suzy Song watch James while I played and all of us warriors roaring against the air and the nets and the clock that didn't work and our memories and our dreams and the twentieth-century horses we called our legs. We played some Nez Percé team and they ran like they were still running from the cavalry and they were kicking the shit out of us again when I suddenly steal the ball from their half-white point guard and drive all the way to the bucket. I jump in the air planning to dunk it when the half-white point guard runs under me knocking my ass to the floor and when I land I hear a crunch and my leg bends in half the wrong way. They take me to the reservation hospital and later they tell me my leg has exploded and I can't play ball for a long time or maybe forever and when Suzy comes by with James and they ask me if this is my wife and son and I tell them yes and James still doesn't make a noise and so they ask me how old he is. I tell them he's almost four years old and they say his physical development is slow but that's normal for an Indian child. Anyhow I have to have an operation and all but since I don't have the money or the strength or the memory and it's not covered by Indian Health I just get up and walk home almost crying because my leg and life hurt so bad. Suzy stays with me that night and in the dark she touches my knee and asks me how much it hurts and I tell her it hurts more than I can talk about so she kisses all my scars and she huddles up close to me and she's warm and she talks into my ear close. She isn't always asking questions and sometimes she has the answers. In the morning I wake up before her and I hobble into the kitchen and make some coffee and fix a couple of bowls of cornflakes and we sit in bed eating together while James lies still in his crib watching the ceiling so Suzy and I watch the ceiling too.

The ordinary can be like medicine. . . .

1970

I took James down to the reservation hospital again because he was almost five years old and still hadn't bothered to talk yet or crawl or cry or even move when I put him on the floor and once I even dropped him and his head was bleeding and he didn't make a sound. They looked him over and said there was nothing wrong with him and that he's just a little slow developing and that's what the doctors always say and they've been saying that about Indians for five hundred years. Jesus I say don't you know that James wants to dance and to sing and to pound a drum so hard it hurts your ears and he ain't ever going to drop an eagle feather and he's always going to be respectful to elders at least the Indian elders and he's going to change the world. He's going to dynamite Mount Rushmore or hijack a plane and make it land on the reservation highway. He's going to be a father and a mother and a son

and a daughter and a dog that will pull you from a raging river.

He'll make gold out of commodity cheese.

1970

Happy birthday James and I'm in the Breakaway Bar drinking too many beers when the Vietnam war comes on television. The white people always want to fight someone and they always get the dark-skinned people to do the fighting. All I know about this war is what Seymour told me when he came back from his tour of duty over there and he said all the gooks he killed looked like us and Seymour said every single gook he killed looked exactly like someone he knew on the reservation. Anyhow I go to a Christmas party over at Jana Wind's house and leave James with my auntie so I could get really drunk and not have to worry about coming home for a few days or maybe for the rest of my life. We all get really drunk and Jana's old man Ray challenges me to a game of one-on-one since he says I'm for shit now and was never any good anyway but I tell him I can't since my knee is screwed up and besides there's two feet of snow on the ground and where are we going to play anyhow? Ray says I'm chickenshit so I tell him come on and we drive over to the high school to the outside court and there's two feet of snow on the court and we can't play but Ray smiles and pulls out a bottle of kerosene and pours it all over the court and lights it up and pretty soon the snow is all melted down along with most of Lester FallsApart's pants since he was standing too close to the court when Ray lit the fire. Anyhow the court is clear and Ray and I go at it and my knee only hurts a little and everyone was cheering us on and I can't remember who won since I was too drunk and so was everyone else. Later I hear how Ray and Joseph got arrested for beating some white guy half to death and I say that Ray and Joseph are just kids but Suzy says nobody on the reservation is ever a kid and that we're all born grown up anyway. I look at James and I think maybe Suzy is wrong about Indian kids being born adults and that maybe James was born this way and wants to stay this way like a baby because he doesn't want to grow up and see and do everything we all do?

There are all kinds of wars.

1971

So much time alone with a bottle of one kind or another and James and I remember nothing except the last drink and a drunk Indian is like the thinker statue except nobody puts a drunk Indian in a special place in front of a library. For most Indians the only special place in front of a library might be a heating grate or a piece of sun-warmed cement but that's an old joke and I used to sleep with my books in piles all over my bed and sometimes they were the only thing keeping me warm and always the only thing keeping me alive.

Books and beer are the best and worst defense. . . .

1971

Been in A.A. for a month because that was the only way to keep James with me and my auntie and Suzy Song both moved into the house with me to make sure I don't drink and to help take care of James. They show the same old movies in A.A. and it's always the same white guy who almost destroys his life and his wife and his children and his job but finally realizes the alcohol is killing him and he quits overnight and spends the rest of the movie and the rest of his whole life at a picnic with his family and friends and boss all laughing and saying we didn't even recognize you back then Bob and we're glad to have you back Daddy and we'll hire you back at twice the salary you old dog you. Yesterday I get this postcard from Pine Ridge and my cousin says all the Indians there are gone and do I know where they went? I write back and tell him to look in the A.A. meeting and then I ask him if there are more birds with eyes that look like his and I ask him if the sky is more blue and the sun more yellow because those are the colors we all become when we die. I tell him to search his dreams for a

man dressed in red with a red tie and red shoes and a hawk head. I tell him that man is fear and will eat you like a sandwich and will eat you like an ice cream cone and will never be full and he'll come for you in your dreams like he was a bad movie. I tell him to turn his television toward the wall and to study the walls for imperfections and those could be his mother and father and the stain on the ceiling could be his sisters and maybe the warped floorboard squeaking and squeaking is his grandfather talking stories.

Maybe they're all hiding on a ship in a bottle.

1972

Been sober so long it's like a dream but I feel better somehow and Auntie was so proud of me she took James and me into the city for James's checkup and James still wasn't talking but Auntie and James and I ate a great lunch at Woolworth's before we headed back to the reservation. I got to drive and Auntie's uranium money Cadillac is a hell of a car and it was raining a little and hot so there were rainbows and the pine trees looked like wise men with wet beards or at least I thought they did. That's how I do life sometimes by making the ordinary just like magic and just like a card trick and just like a mirror and just like the disappearing. Every Indian learns how to be a magician and learns how to misdirect attention and the dark hand is always quicker than the white eye and no matter how close you get to my heart you will never find out my secrets and I'll never tell you and I'll never show you the same trick twice.

I'm traveling heavy with illusions.

1972

Every day I'm trying not to drink and I pray but I don't know who I'm praying to and if it's the basketball gathering ash on the shelf or the blank walls crushing me into the house or the television that only picks up public channels. I've seen only painters and fishermen and I think they're both the same kind of men who made a different choice one time in their lives. The fisherman held a rod in his hand and said yes and the painter held a brush in his hand and said yes and sometimes I hold a beer in my hand and say yes. At those moments I want to drink so bad that it aches and I cry which is a strange noise in our house because James refuses tears and he refuses words but sometimes he holds a hand up above his head like he's reaching for something. Yesterday I nearly trip over Lester FallsApart lying drunk as a skunk in front of the Trading Post and I pick him up and he staggers and trembles and falls back down. Lester I say you got to stand up on your own and I pick him up and he falls down again.

Only a saint would have tried to pick him up the third time.

1972

The streetlight outside my house shines on tonight and I'm watching it like it could give me vision. James ain't talked ever and he looks at that streetlight like it was a word and maybe like it was a verb. James wanted to streetlight me and make me bright and beautiful so all the moths and bats would circle me like I was the center of the world and held secrets. Like Joy said that everything but humans keeps secrets. Today I get my mail and there's a light bill and a postcard from an old love from Seattle who asks me if I still love her like I used to and would I come to visit?

I send her my light bill and tell her I don't ever want to see her again.

1973

James talked today but I had my back turned and I couldn't be sure it was real. He said potato like any good Indian would because that's all we eat. But maybe he said I love you because that's what I wanted him to say or maybe he said geology or mathematics or college basketball. I pick him up and ask him again and again what did you say? He just smiles and I take him to the clinic and the doctors say it's about time but are you sure you didn't imagine his voice? I said James's voice

sounded like a beautiful glass falling off the shelf and landing safely on a thick shag carpet.

The doctor said I had a very good imagination.

1973

I'm shooting hoops again with the younger Indian boys and even some Indian girls who never miss a shot. They call me old man and elder and give me a little bit of respect like not running too fast or hard and even letting me shoot a few more than I should. It's been a long time since I played but the old feelings and old moves are there in my heart and in my fingers. I see these Indian kids and I know that basketball was invented by an Indian long before the Naismith guy ever thought about it. When I play I don't feel like drinking so I wish I could play twenty-four hours a day seven days a week and then I wouldn't wake up shaking and quaking and needing just one more beer before I stop for good. James knows it too and he sits on the sideline clapping when my team scores and clapping when the other team scores too. He's got a good heart. He always talks whenever I'm not in the room or I'm not looking at him but never when anybody else might hear so they all think I'm crazy. I am crazy. He says things like I can't believe. He says $E = MC^2$ and that's why all my cousins drink themselves to death. He says the earth is an oval marble that nobody can win. He says the sky is not blue and the grass is not green.

He says everything is a matter of perception.

1973

Christmas and James gets his presents and he gives me the best present of all when he talks right at me. He says so many things and the only thing that matters is that he says he and I don't have the right to die for each other and that we should be living for each other instead. He says the world hurts. He says the first thing he wanted after he was born was a shot of whiskey. He says all that and more. He tells me to get a job and to grow my braids. He says I better learn how to shoot left-handed if I'm going to keep playing basketball. He says to open a fireworks stand.

Every day now there are little explosions all over the reservation.

1974

Today is the World's Fair in Spokane and James and I drive to Spokane with a few cousins of mine. All the countries have exhibitions like art from Japan and pottery from Mexico and mean-looking people talking about Germany. In one little corner there's a statue of an Indian who's supposed to be some chief or another. I press a little button and the statue talks and moves its arms over and over in the same motion. The statue tells the crowd we have to take care of the earth because it is our mother. I know that and

James says he knows more. He says the earth is our grandmother and that technology has become our mother and that they both hate each other. James tells the crowd that the river just a few yards from where we stand is all we ever need to believe in. One white woman asks me how old James is and I tell her he's seven and she tells me that he's so smart for an Indian boy. James hears this and tells the white woman that she's pretty smart for an old white woman. I know this is how it will all begin and how the rest of my life will be. I know when I am old and sick and ready to die that James will wash my body and take care of my wastes. He'll carry me from HUD house to sweathouse and he will clean my wounds. And he will talk and teach me something new every day.

But all that is so far ahead.

THINKING ABOUT THE READING

Would you consider the narrator of the story to be James's father? Would you consider the two of them a family? How is the narrator's daily caring for James similar to or different from what you'd expect in a "typical" family? In the last paragraph the narrator expresses a sense of hope for his future with James. Do you think this hope is realistic? He's also telling us that, despite all the hardships, James will be in his life forever. Is this kind of commitment enough to sustain a family? Do you think James would have been better off if he'd been sent to a foster home or an institution off of the reservation? What do you suppose would have happened to him if he was an orphaned, handicapped child who came from more affluent surroundings? In what ways does James's presence change the narrator's life?

The Time Bind

When Work Becomes Home and Home Becomes Work

Arlie Russell Hochschild

. . . I had come to Spotted Deer [Day Care Center] to explore a question I'd been left with after finishing my last book, *The Second Shift: Working Parents and the Revolution at Home.* In that work I had examined the tensions that arise at home in two-job marriages when working women also do the lion's share of the childcare and housework. Such marriages were far less strained, I found, when men committed themselves to sharing what I came to call "the second shift," the care of children and home. But even with the work shared out, there seemed to be less and less time for the second shift, not to mention relaxed family life. Something was amiss, and whatever it was, I sensed that I would not find out simply by looking at home life by itself.

Everything I already knew or would soon learn pointed to the workplace as the arena that needed to be explored. As a start, I was well aware that, while in 1950 12.6 percent of married mothers with children under age seventeen worked for pay, by 1994, 69 percent did so; and 58.8 percent of wives with children age one or younger were in the workforce. Many of these wives also had a hand in caring for elderly relatives. In addition, the hours both men and women put in at work had increased—either for college-educated workers or, depending on which scholars you read, for all workers. In her book *The Overworked American,* the economist Juliet Schor has claimed that over the last two decades the average worker has added an extra 164 hours—a month of work—to his or her work year. Workers now take fewer unpaid leaves, and even fewer paid ones. In the 1980s alone, vacations shortened by 14 percent. According to the economist Victor Fuchs, between 1960 and 1986 parental time available to children per week fell ten hours in white households and twelve hours in black households. It was also evident, however you cut the figures, that life was coming to center more on work. More women were on board the work train, and the train was moving faster. It wasn't just that ever larger numbers of mothers of young children were taking paying jobs, but that fewer of those jobs were part time; and fewer of those mothers were taking time off even in the summer, as they might once have done, to care for school-aged children on vacation. Women moving into the workforce—whether or not they were mothers—were less inclined than ever to move out of it. It was apparent, in fact, that working mothers were increasingly fitting the profile of working fathers. But those fathers, far from cutting back to help out at home, studies told us, were now working even longer hours. In fact, their hours were as long as those of childless men.

All this could be read in the numbers—as well as in the tensions in many of the households I had visited. I was left with a nagging question: given longer workdays—and more of them—how could parents balance jobs with family life? Or, to put the matter another way, was life at work winning out over life at home? If so, was there not some way to organize work to avoid penalizing employees, male and female, for having lives outside of work and to ease the burden on their children?

I was thinking about these questions when a surprising event occurred. I was asked to give a talk at Amerco, a company about which I knew little except that it had been identified as one of the ten most "family-friendly" companies in

America by the Families and Work Institute, by *Working Mother* magazine, and by the authors of *Companies That Care.* At a dinner given after my talk, a company spokesman seated next to me asked if I had ever thought of studying family-friendly policies in the workplace itself. To tell the truth, I could not believe my luck. If there was ever a chance for families to balance home and work, I thought to myself, it would be at a place like this. Amerco's management clearly hoped my findings would help them answer a few questions of their own. In the late 1980s, the company had been distressed to discover a startling fact: they were losing professional women far faster than they were losing professional men. Each time such a worker was lost, it cost the company a great deal of money to recruit and train a replacement. The company had tried to eliminate this waste of money and talent by addressing one probable reason women were leaving: the absence of what was called "work-family balance." Amerco now offered a range of remedial programs including options for part-time work, job sharing, and flextime. Did these policies really help Amerco? Given current trends, it seemed crucial to top management to know the answer. Six months later I found myself lodged at a cozy bed-and-breakfast on a tree-lined street in Spotted Deer, ready to begin finding out. . . .

I interviewed top and middle managers, clerks and factory workers—a hundred and thirty people in all. Most were part of two-job couples, some were single parents, and a few were single without children. Sometimes we met in their offices or in a plant breakroom, sometimes in their homes, often in both places. Early mornings and evenings, weekends and holidays, I sat on the lawn by the edge of a series of parking lots that circled company headquarters, watching people walk to and from their vans, cars, or pick-up trucks to see when they came to work and when they left.

I talked with psychologists in and outside the company, childcare workers hired by Amerco, homemakers married to Amerco employees, and company consultants. Along with the Spotted

Deer Childcare Center, I visited local YWCA after-school programs as well as a Parent Resource Center funded by the company. I attended company sessions of the Women's Quality Improvement Team and the Work Family Progress Committee, a Valuing Diversity workshop, and two High Performance Team meetings. A team in Amerco's Sales Division allowed me to sit in on its meetings. To their surprise—and mine—I also became the fifth wheel on a golfing expedition designed to build team spirit. During several night shifts at an Amerco factory, tired workers patiently talked with me over coffee in the breakroom. One even took me to a local bar to meet her friends and relatives.

The company gave me access to a series of its internal "climate surveys" of employee attitudes, and I combed through research reports on other companies, national opinion polls, and a burgeoning literature on work and family life. I also attended work-family conferences held in New York, San Francisco, Los Angeles, and Boston by The Conference Board, a respected organization that gathers and disseminates information of interest to the benefit of the business management community.

[In addition,] six families—four two-parent families and two single-mother families—allowed me to follow them on typical workdays from dawn until dusk and beyond. . . .

An Angel of an Idea

Almost from the beginning of my stay in Spotted Deer, I could tell that the family-friendly reforms introduced with so much fanfare in 1985 were finding a curious reception. Three things seemed true. First, Amerco's workers declared on survey after survey that they were strained to the limit. Second, the company offered them policies that would allow them to cut back. Third, almost no one cut back. . . . Programs that allowed parents to work undistracted by family concerns were endlessly in demand, while policies offering shorter hours that allowed workers more free or family time languished.

To try to make sense of this paradox I began, first of all, to scrutinize the text of the policy and the results of employee surveys. Amerco defines a part-time job as one that requires thirty-five hours or less, with full or prorated benefits.[1] A job share is a full-time position shared by two people with benefits and salary prorated. As with all attempts to change work schedules, I learned, the worker has to get the permission of a supervisor, a division head, or both. In addition, workers under union contract—a full half of Amerco's workforce including factory hands and maintenance crews—were not eligible for policies offering shorter or more flexible hours.

But I discovered that among eligible employees with children thirteen and under, only 3 percent worked part time. In fact, in 1990, only 53 out of Amerco's 21,070 employees in the United States, less than one-quarter of 1 percent of its workforce, were part-timers, and less than 1 percent of Amerco's employees shared a job.

Amerco also offered its employees a program called "flexplace," which allowed workers to do their work from home or some other place. One percent of employees used it. Likewise, under certain circumstances, an employee could take a temporary leave from full-time work. The standard paid parental leave for a new mother was six weeks (to be divided with the father as the couple wished). If permission was granted, a parent could then return to work part time with full benefits, to be arranged at his or her supervisor's discretion. Most new mothers took the paid weeks off, and sometimes several months more of unpaid leave, but then returned to their full-time schedules. Almost no Amerco fathers took advantage of parental leave, and no Amerco father has ever responded to the arrival of a new baby in the family by taking up a part-time work schedule.

By contrast, "flextime," a policy allowing workers to come and go early or late, or to be in other ways flexible about when they do their work, was quite popular. By 1993, a quarter of all workers—and a third of working parents—used it. In other words, of Amerco's family-friendly policies only flextime, which rearranged but did

not cut back on hours of work, had any significant impact on the workplace. According to one survey, 99 percent of Amerco employees worked full time, and full-time employees averaged forty-seven hours a week. As I looked more closely at the figures I discovered some surprising things. Workers with young children actually put in more hours at work as those without children. Although a third of all parents had flexible schedules, 56 percent of employees with children regularly worked on weekends. Seventy-two percent of parents regularly worked overtime; unionized hourly workers were paid for this time (though much of their overtime was required), while salaried workers weren't. In fact, during the years I was studying Amerco, parents and nonparents alike began to work *longer* hours. By 1993, virtually everyone I spoke with told me they were working longer hours than they had only a few years earlier, and most agreed that Amerco was "a pretty workaholic place."

Amerco is not alone. A 1990 study of 188 Fortune 500 manufacturing firms found that while 88 percent of them informally offered part-time work, only 3 to 5 percent of their employees made use of it. Six percent of the companies surveyed formally offered job sharing, but only 1 percent or less of their employees took advantage of that. Forty-five percent of these companies officially offered flextime, but only 10 percent of their employees used it. Three percent of the companies offered flexplace—work at home—and less than 3 percent of their employees took advantage of it.[2*]

As Amerco's experience would suggest, American working parents seem to be putting in longer and longer hours. Of workers with children aged twelve and under, only 4 percent of men, and 13 percent of women, worked less than forty hours a week.[3] According to a study

---

*The 1993 Family and Medical Leave Act requires all companies employing fifty or more workers to offer three months of unpaid time off for medical or family emergencies. Although it is not yet clear what effect this law will have, research suggests few workers are likely to take advantage of it. Studies of earlier state family and medical leave laws show that less than 5 percent of employees actually use the leave.

by Arthur Emlen of Portland State University, whether or not a worker has a child makes remarkably little difference to his or her attendance record at work. Excluding vacation and holidays, the average employee misses nine days of work a year. The average parent of a child who is left home alone on weekdays misses fourteen and a half days a year: only five and a half days more. Fathers with young children only miss half a day more a year than fathers without children.[4]

The idea of more time for family life seems to have died, gone to heaven, and become an angel of an idea. But why? Why don't working parents, and others too, take the opportunity available to them to reduce their hours at work?

The most widely accepted explanation is that working parents simply can't *afford* to work shorter hours. With the median income of U.S. households in 1996 at $32,264, it is true that many workers could not pay their rent and food bills on three-quarters or half of their salaries. But notwithstanding the financial and time pressures most parents face, why do the majority not even take all of the paid vacation days due to them? Even more puzzling, why are the best-paid employees—upper-level managers and professionals—among the least interested in part-time work or job sharing? In one Amerco survey, only one-third of top-level female employees (who belong to what is called the "A-payroll") thought part time was of "great value." The percentage of women favoring part time rose as pay levels went down: 45 percent of "B-payroll" (lower-level managers and professionals) and "administrative" women (who provide clerical support) thought part time was of "great value." Thus, those who earned more money were less interested in part-time work than those who earned less. Few men at any level expressed interest in part-time work.

Again, if income alone determined how often or how long mothers stayed home after the birth of their babies, we would expect poorer mothers to go back to work more quickly, and richer mothers to spend more time at home. But that's not what we find. Nationwide, well-to-do new mothers are not significantly more likely to stay

home with a new baby than low-income new mothers. A quarter of poor new mothers in one study returned to work after three months, but so did a third of well-to-do new mothers. Twenty-three percent of new mothers with household incomes of $15,000 or under took long leaves (fifty-three weeks or more), and so did 22 percent of new mothers with household incomes of $50,000 or more.[5]

In a 1995 national study, 48 percent of American working women and 61 percent of men claimed they would still want to work even if they had enough money to live as "comfortably as you would like."[6] When asked what was "very important" to their decision to take their current job, only 35 percent of respondents in one national study said "salary/wage," whereas 55 percent mentioned "gaining new skills" as very important, and 60 percent mentioned "effect on personal/family life."[7] Money matters, of course, but other things do too.

According to a second commonly believed explanation, workers extend their hours, not because they need the money, but because they are afraid of being laid off. They're working scared. By fostering a climate of fear, the argument goes, many companies take away with one hand the helpful policies they lightly offer with the other.

Downsizing is a serious problem in American companies in the 1990s but there's scant evidence that employees at Amerco were working scared. During the late 1980s and early 1990s, there was very little talk of layoffs. When I asked employees whether they worked long hours because they were afraid of getting on a layoff list, virtually everyone said no. (Although there were, in fact, small-scale layoffs in certain divisions of the company, the process was handled delicately through "internal rehiring" and "encouraged" early retirement.) And when I compared hours of work in the few downsized Amerco divisions with those in non-downsized divisions, they were basically the same. Supervisors in the two kinds of divisions received just about the same number of requests for shorter hours. . . .

One possible explanation is that workers interested in and eligible for flexible or shorter hours don't know they can get them. After all, even at a place like Amerco, such policies are fairly new. Yet on closer inspection, this proved not to be the case. According to a 1990 survey, most Amerco workers were aware of company policies on flextime and leaves. Women were better informed than men, and higher-level workers more so than lower-level workers. The vast majority of people I talked with knew that the company offered "good" policies and were proud to be working for such a generous company. Employees who weren't clear about the details knew they could always ask someone who was. As one secretary remarked, "I don't know exactly how long the parental leave is, but I know how to find out." So why didn't they? . . .

Family Values and Reversed Worlds

If working parents are "deciding" to work full time and longer, what experiences at home and work might be influencing them to do so? When I first began [my] research, . . . I assumed that home was "home" and work was "work"—that each was a stationary rock beneath the moving feet of working parents. I assumed as well that each stood in distinct opposition to the other. In a family, love and commitment loom large as ends in themselves and are not means to any further end. As an Amerco parent put it, "I work to live; I don't live to work." However difficult family life may be at times, we usually feel family ties offer an irreplaceable connection to generations past and future. Family is our personal embrace with history.

Jobs, on the other hand, earn money that, to most of us, serves as the means to other ends. To be sure, jobs can also allow us to develop skills or friendships, and to be part of a larger work community. But we seldom envision the workplace as somewhere workers would freely choose to spend their time. If in the American imagination the family has a touch of the sacred, the realm of work seems profane.

In addition, I assumed, as many of us do, that compared to the workplace, home is a more pleasant place to be. This is after all one reason why employers pay workers to work and don't pay them to stay home. The very word "work" suggests to most of us something unpleasant, involuntary, even coerced.

If the purpose and nature of family and work differ so drastically in our minds, it seemed reasonable to assume that people's emotional experiences of the two spheres would differ profoundly, too. In *Haven in a Heartless World,* the social historian Christopher Lasch drew a picture of family as a "haven" where workers sought refuge from the cruel world of work.[8] Painting in broad strokes, we might imagine a picture like this: At the end of a long day, a weary worker opens his front door and calls out, "Hi, Honey! I'm home!" He takes off his uniform, puts on a bathrobe, opens a beer, picks up the paper, and exhales. Whatever its strains, home is where he's relaxed, most himself. At home, he feels that people know him, understand him, appreciate him for who he really is. At home, he is safe.

At work, our worker is "on call," ready to report at a moment's notice, working flat out to get back to the customer right away. He feels "like a number." If he doesn't watch out, he can take the fall for somebody else's mistakes. This, then, is Lasch's "heartless world." . . .

It was just such images of home and work that were challenged in one of my first interviews at Amerco. Linda Avery, a friendly thirty-eight-year-old mother of two daughters, is a shift supervisor at the Demco Plant, ten miles down the valley from Amerco headquarters. Her husband, Bill, is a technician in the same plant. Linda and Bill share the care of her sixteen-year-old daughter from a previous marriage and their two-year-old by working opposite shifts, as a full fifth of American working parents do. "Bill works the 7 A.M. to 3 P.M. shift while I watch the baby," Linda explained. "Then I work the 3 P.M. to 11 P.M. shift and he watches the baby. My older daughter works at Walgreens after school."

When we first met in the factory's breakroom over a couple of Cokes, Linda was in blue jeans and a pink jersey, her hair pulled back in a long blond ponytail. She wore no makeup, and her manner was purposeful and direct. She was working overtime, and so I began by asking whether Amerco required the overtime, or whether she volunteered for it. "Oh, I put in for it," she replied with a low chuckle. But, I wondered aloud, wouldn't she and her husband like to have more time at home together, finances and company policy permitting. Linda took off her safety glasses, rubbed her whole face, folded her arms, resting her elbows on the table, and approached the question by describing her life at home:

> I walk in the door and the minute I turn the key in the lock my older daughter is there. Granted, she needs somebody to talk to about her day. . . . The baby is still up. She should have been in bed two hours ago and that upsets me. The dishes are piled in the sink. My daughter comes right up to the door and complains about anything her stepfather said or did, and she wants to talk about her job. My husband is in the other room hollering to my daughter, "Tracy, I don't *ever* get any time to talk to your mother, because you're always monopolizing her time before I even get a chance!" They all come at me at once.

To Linda, her home was not a place to relax. It was another workplace. Her description of the urgency of demands and the unarbitrated quarrels that awaited her homecoming contrasted with her account of arriving at her job as a shift supervisor:

> I usually come to work early just to get away from the house. I get there at 2:30 P.M., and people are there waiting. We sit. We talk. We joke. I let them know what's going on, who has to be where, what changes I've made for the shift that day. We sit there and chit-chat for five or ten minutes. There's laughing, joking, fun. My coworkers aren't putting me down for any reason. Everything is done with humor and fun from beginning to end, though it can get stressful when a machine malfunctions.

For Linda, home had become work and work had become home. Somehow, the two worlds had been reversed. Indeed, Linda felt she could only get relief from the "work" of being at home by going to the "home" of work. As she explained,

> My husband's a great help watching our baby. But as far as doing housework or even taking the baby when I'm at home, no. He figures he works five days a week; *he's* not going to come home and clean. But he doesn't stop to think that I work *seven* days a week. Why should I have to come home and do the housework without help from anybody else? My husband and I have been through this over and over again. Even if he would just pick up from the kitchen table and stack the dishes for me, that would make a big difference. He does nothing. On his weekends off, I have to provide a sitter for the baby so he can go fishing. When I have a day off, I have the baby all day long without a break. He'll help out if I'm not here, but the minute I am, all the work at home is mine.

With a light laugh, she continued, "So I take a lot of overtime. The more I get out of the house, the better I am. It's a terrible thing to say, but that's the way I feel." Linda said this not in the manner of a new discovery, a reluctant confession, or collusion between two working mothers—"Don't you just want to get away sometimes?"—but in a matter-of-fact way. This was the way life was.

Bill, who was fifty-six when I first met him, had three grown children from a contentious first marriage. He told me he felt he had already "put in his time" to raise them and now was at a stage of life in which he wanted to enjoy himself Yet when he came home afternoons he had to "babysit for Linda."

In a previous era, men regularly escaped the house for the bar, the fishing hole, the golf course, the pool hall, or, often enough, the sweet joy of work. Today, as one of the women who make up 45 percent of the American workforce, Linda Avery, overloaded and feeling unfairly treated at home, was escaping to work, too. Nowadays, men and women both may leave unwashed dishes, unresolved quarrels, crying tots, testy teenagers, and unresponsive mates behind to arrive at work early and call out, "Hi, fellas, I'm here!"

Linda would have loved a warm welcome from her family when she returned from work, a reward for her day of labors at the plant. At a minimum, she would have liked to relax, at least for a little while. But that was hard to do because Bill, on *his* second shift at home, would nap and watch television instead of engaging the children. The more Bill slacked off on his shift at home, the more Linda felt robbed of rest when she was there. The more anxious the children were, or the messier the house was when she walked in the door, the more Linda felt she was simply returning to the task of making up for being gone.

For his part, Bill recalled that Linda had wanted a new baby more than he had. So now that they were the parents of a small child, Bill reasoned, looking after the baby should also be more Linda's responsibility. Caring for a two-year-old after working a regular job was hard enough. Incredibly, Linda wanted him to do more. That was her problem though, not his. He had "earned his stripes" with his first set of children. . . .

Both Linda and Bill felt the need for time off, to relax, to have fun, to feel free, but they had not agreed that it was Bill who needed a break more than Linda. Bill simply . . . took his free time. This irritated Linda because she felt he *took* it at her expense. Largely in response to her resentment, Linda grabbed what she also called "free time"—at work.

Neither Linda nor Bill Avery wanted more time at home, not as things were arranged. Whatever images they may have carried in their heads about what family and work should be like, the Averys did not feel their actual home was a haven or that work was a heartless world.

Where did Linda feel most relaxed? She laughed more, joked more, listened to more interesting stories while on break at the factory than at home. Working the 3 P.M. to 11 P.M. shift, her hours off didn't coincide with those of her mother or older sister who worked in town, nor with those of her close friends and neighbors. But even if they had, she would have felt that the true center of her social world was her plant, not her neighborhood. The social life that once

might have surrounded her at home she now found at work. The sense of being part of a lively, larger, ongoing community—that, too, was at work. In an emergency, Linda told me, she would sacrifice everything for her family. But in the meantime, the everyday "emergencies" she most wanted to attend to, that challenged rather than exhausted her, were those she encountered at the factory. Frankly, life there was more fun.

How do Linda and Bill Avery fit into the broader picture of American family and work life? Psychologist Reed Larson and his colleagues studied the daily emotional experiences of mothers and fathers in fifty-five two-parent Chicago families with children in the fifth to eighth grades. Some of the mothers cared for children at home, some worked part time, others full time, while all the fathers in the study worked full time. Each participant wore a pager for a week, and whenever they were beeped by the research team, each wrote down how he or she felt: "happy, unhappy, cheerful-irritable, friendly-angry." The researchers found that men and women reported a similar range of emotional states across the week. But fathers reported more "positive emotional states" at home; mothers, more positive emotional states at work. This held true for every social class. Fathers like Bill Avery relaxed more at home; while mothers like Linda Avery did more housework there. Larson suggests that "because women are constantly on call to the needs of other family members, they are less able to relax at home in the way men do."[9] Wives were typically in better moods than their husbands at home only when they were eating or engaging in "family transport." They were in worse moods when they were doing "child-related activities" or "socializing" there.[10] Men and women each felt most at ease when involved in tasks they felt less obliged to do, Larson reports. For women, this meant first shift work; for men, second.

A recent study of working mothers made another significant discovery. Problems at home tend to upset women more deeply than problems at work. The study found that women were most deeply affected by family stress—and were more likely to be made depressed or physically ill by it—even when stress at the workplace was greater. For women, current research on stress does not support the common view of home as a sanctuary and work as a "jungle." However hectic their lives, women who do paid work, researchers have consistently found, feel less depressed, think better of themselves, and are more satisfied with life than women who don't do paid work.[11] One study reported that, paradoxically, women who work feel more valued at home than women who stay home.[12]

In sum, then, women who work outside the home have better physical and mental health than those who do not, and not simply because healthier women go to work. Paid work, the psychologist Grace Baruch argues, "offers such benefits as challenge, control, structure, positive feedback, self-esteem . . . and social ties."[13] Reed Larson's study found, for example, that women were no more likely than men to see coworkers as friendly, but when women made friendly contact it was far more likely to lift their spirits.[14]

As a woman quoted by Baruch put it, "A job is to a woman as a wife is to a man."[15]

For Linda Avery self-satisfaction, well-being, high spirits, and work were inextricably linked. It was mainly at work, she commented, that she felt really good about herself As a supervisor, she saw her job as helping people, and those she helped appreciated her. . . .

Often relations at work seemed more manageable. The "children" Linda Avery helped at work were older and better able to articulate their problems than her own children. The plant where she worked was clean and pleasant. She knew everyone on the line she supervised. Indeed, all the workers knew each other, and some were even related by blood, marriage, or, odd as it may sound, by divorce. One coworker complained bitterly that a friend of her husband's ex-wife was keeping track of how much overtime she worked in order to help this ex-wife make a case for increasing the amount of his child support. Workers sometimes carried such hostilities generated at home into the workplace. Yet despite the common assumption that relations

at work are emotionally limited, meaningful friendships often blossom. When Linda Avery joined coworkers for a mug of beer at a nearby bar after work to gossip about the "spy" who was tracking the deadbeat dad's new wife's overtime, she was among real friends. Research shows that work friends can be as important as family members in helping both men and women cope with the blows of life. The gerontologist Andrew Sharlach studied how middle-aged people in Los Angeles dealt with the death of a parent. He found that 73 percent of the women in the sample, and 64 percent of the men, responded that work was a "helpful resource" in coping with a mother's death.[16]

Amerco regularly reinforced the family-like ties of coworkers by holding recognition ceremonies honoring particular workers or entire self-managed production teams. The company would decorate a section of the factory and serve food and drink. The production teams, too, had regular get-togethers. The halls of Amerco were hung with plaques praising workers for recent accomplishments. Such recognition luncheons, department gatherings, and, particularly in the ranks of clerical and factory workers, exchange of birthday gifts were fairly common workday events.

At its white-collar offices, Amerco was even more involved in shaping the emotional culture of the workplace and fostering an environment of trust and cooperation in order to bring out everyone's best. At the middle and top levels of the company, employees were invited to periodic "career development seminars" on personal relations at work. The centerpiece of Amerco's personal-relations culture was a "vision" speech that the CEO had given called "Valuing the Individual," a message repeated in speeches, memorialized in company brochures, and discussed with great seriousness throughout the upper reaches of the company. In essence, the message was a parental reminder to respect others. Similarly, in a new-age recasting of an old business slogan ("The customer is always right"), Amerco proposed that its workers "Value the internal customer." This meant: Be as polite and considerate to your coworkers as you would be to Amerco customers. "Value the internal customer" extended to coworkers the slogan "Delight the customer." Don't just work with your coworkers, delight them.

"Employee empowerment," "valuing diversity," and "work-family balance"—these catch-phrases, too, spoke to a moral aspect of work life. Though ultimately tied to financial gain, such exhortations—and the policies that followed from them—made workers feel the company was concerned with people, not just money. In many ways, the workplace appeared to be a site of benign social engineering where workers came to feel appreciated, honored, and liked. On the other hand, how many recognition ceremonies for competent performance were going on at home? Who was valuing the internal customer there?

After thirty years with Amerco, Bill Avery felt, if anything, overqualified for his job, and he had a recognition plaque from the company to prove it. But when his toddler got into his fishing gear and he blew up at her and she started yelling, he felt impotent in the face of her rageful screams— and nobody was there to back him up. When his teenage stepdaughter reminded him that she saw him, not as an honorable patriarch, but as an infantile competitor for her mother's attention, he felt humiliated. At such moments, he says, he had to resist the impulse to reach for the whiskey he had given up five years earlier.

Other fathers with whom I talked were less open and self-critical about such feelings, but in one way or another many said that they felt more confident they could "get the job done" at work than at home. As one human resource specialist at Amerco reflected,

> We used to joke about the old "Mother of the Year Award." That doesn't exist anymore. Now, we don't know a meaningful way to reward a parent. At work, we get paid and promoted for doing well. At home, when you're doing the right thing, chances are your kids are giving you hell for it.

If a family gives its members anything, we assume it is surely a sense of belonging to an ongoing community. In its engineered corporate cultures, capitalism has rediscovered communal ties and is using them to build its new version of capitalism. Many Amerco employees spoke warmly, happily, and seriously of "belonging to the Amerco family," and everywhere there were visible symbols of this belonging. While some married people have dispensed with their wedding rings, people proudly wore their "Total Quality" pins or "High Performance Team" tee-shirts, symbols of their loyalty to the company and of its loyalty to them. In my interviews, I heard little about festive reunions of extended families, while throughout the year, employees flocked to the many company-sponsored ritual gatherings. . . .

We may be seeing here a trend in modern life destined to affect us all. To be sure, few people feel totally secure either at work or at home. In the last fifteen years, massive waves of downsizing have reduced the security workers feel even in the most apparently stable workplaces. At the same time, a rising divorce rate has reduced the security they feel at home. Although both Linda and Bill felt their marriage was strong, over the course of their lives, each had changed relationships more often than they had changed jobs. Bill had worked steadily for Amerco for thirty years, but he had been married twice; and in the years between marriages, he had lived with two women and dated several more. Nationwide, half the people who marry eventually divorce, most within the first seven years of marriage. Three-quarters of divorced men and two-thirds of divorced women remarry, but remarried couples are more likely than those in first marriages to divorce. Couples who only live together are even more likely to break up than couples who marry. Increasing numbers of people are getting their "pink slips" at home. Work may become their rock. . . .

The social world that draws a person's allegiance also imparts a pattern to time. The more attached we are to the world of work, the more its deadlines, its cycles, its pauses and interruptions shape our lives and the more family time is forced to accommodate to the pressures of work.

In recent years at Amerco it has been possible to detect a change in the ways its workers view the proper use of their time: Family time, for them, has taken on an "industrial" tone.

As the social worlds of work and home reverse, working parents' experience of time in each sphere changes as well. Just how, and how much, depends on the nature of a person's job, company, and life at home. But at least for people . . . at Amerco, it's clear that family time is succumbing to a cult of efficiency previously associated with the workplace. Meanwhile, work time, with its ever longer hours, becomes newly hospitable to sociability—periods of talking with friends on e-mail, patching up quarrels, gossiping. . . .

The Third Shift

. . .

. . . Why *weren't* Amerco working parents putting up a bigger fight for family time, given the fact that most said they needed more? Many of them may have been responding to a powerful process that is devaluing what was once the essence of family life. The more women and men do what they do in exchange for money and the more their work in the public realm is valued or honored, the more, almost by definition, private life is devalued and its boundaries shrink. For women as well as men, work in the marketplace is less often a simple economic fact than a complex cultural value. If in the early part of the century it was considered unfortunate that a woman had to work, it is now thought surprising when she doesn't.

People generally have the urge to spend more time on what they value most and on what they are most valued for. . . . The valued realm of work is registering its gains in part by incorporating the best aspects of home. The devalued realm, the home, is meanwhile taking on what were once considered the most alienating attributes of work. However one explains the failure of Amerco to create a good program of work-family balance, though, the fact is that in a cultural contest between work and home, work-

ing parents are voting with their feet, and the workplace is winning.

In this respect, we may ask, are working parents at Amerco an anomaly or are they typical of working parents nationwide? In search of an answer, I contacted a company called Bright Horizons, which runs 125 company-based childcare centers associated with corporations, hospitals, real estate developers, and federal agencies in nineteen states.[17] Bright Horizons allowed me to add a series of new questions to a questionnaire the company was sending out to seven thousand parents whose children were attending Bright Horizons Children's Centers. A third of the parents who received questionnaires filled them out. The resulting 1,446 responses came from mainly middle- or upper-middle-class parents in their early thirties.[18] Since many of them worked for Fortune 500 companies—including IBM, American Express, Sears, Roebuck, Eastman Kodak, Xerox, Bausch and Lomb, and Dunkin' Donuts—this study offers us a highly suggestive picture of what is happening among managers and professional working parents at Amerco's counterparts nationwide.

These parents reported time pressures similar to those Amerco parents complained about. As at Amerco, the longest hours at work were logged by the most highly educated professionals and managers, among whom six out of ten regularly averaged over forty hours a week. A third of the parents in this sample had their children in childcare forty hours a week or more.[19] As at Amerco, the higher the income of their parents, the longer the children's shifts in childcare.

When asked, "Do you ever consider yourself a workaholic?" a third of fathers and a fifth of mothers answered yes. One out of three said their *partner* was workaholic. In response to the question "Do you experience a problem of 'time famine'?" 89 percent responded yes. Half reported that they typically brought work home from the office.[20] Of those who complained of a time famine, half agreed with the statement "I feel guilty that I don't spend enough time with my child." Forty-three percent agreed that they "very often" felt "too much of the time I'm tired when I'm with my child." When asked, "Overall, how well do you feel you can balance the demands of your work and family?" only 9 percent said "very well."

If many of these Bright Horizons working parents were experiencing a time bind of the sort I heard about from Amerco employees, were they living with it because they felt work was more rewarding than family life? To find out, I asked, "Does it sometimes feel to you like home is a 'workplace'?" Eighty-five percent said yes (57 percent "very often"; 28 percent "fairly often"). Women were far more likely to agree than men. I asked this question the other way around as well: "Is it sometimes true that work feels like home should feel?" Twenty-five percent answered "very often" or "quite often," and 33 percent answered "occasionally." Only 37 percent answered "very rarely."

One reason some workers may feel more "at home" at work is that they feel more appreciated and more competent there. Certainly, this was true for many Amerco workers I interviewed, and little wonder, for Amerco put great effort into making its workers feel appreciated. In a large-scale nationwide study, sociologists Diane Burden and Bradley Googins found that 59 percent of employees rated their family performances "good or unusually good," while 86 percent gave that rating to their performances on the job—that is, workers appreciated *themselves* more at work than at home.[21] In the Bright Horizons national survey, only 29 percent felt appreciated "mainly at home," and 52 percent "equally" at home and work. Surprisingly, women were not more likely than men to say they felt more appreciated at home.

Often, working parents feel more at home at work because they come to expect that emotional support will be more readily available there. As at Amerco, work can be where their closest friends are, a pattern the Bright Horizons survey reflected. When asked, "Where do you have the most friends?" 47 percent answered "at work"; 16 percent, "in the neighborhood"; and 6 percent, "at my church or temple." Women were

far more likely than men to have the most friends at work.[22]

Some workers at Amerco felt more at home at work because work was where they felt most relaxed. To the question "Where do you feel the most relaxed?" only a slight majority in the Bright Horizons survey, 51 percent, said "home." To the question "Do you feel as if your life circumstances or relationships are more secure at work or at home?" a similarly slim majority answered "home." I also asked, "How many times have you changed jobs since you started working?" The average was between one and two times. Though I didn't ask how many times a person had changed primary loved ones, the national picture suggests that by the early thirties, one or two such changes is not unusual. Work may not "always be there" for the employee, but then home may not either. . . .

For this sample, then, we find some evidence that a cultural reversal of workplace and home is present at least as a theme. Unsurprisingly, more people in the survey agreed that home felt like work than that work felt like home. Still, only to half of them was home a main source of relaxation or security. For many, work seemed to function as a backup system to a destabilizing family. For women, in particular, to take a job is often today to take out an emotional insurance policy on the uncertainties of home life. . . .

The Hydro-Compressed Sterilized Mouth Wiper

Working parents often face difficult problems at home without much outside support or help in resolving them. In itself time is, of course, no cure-all. But having time together is an important precondition for building family relations. What, then, is happening to family time?

Working parents exhibit an understandable desire to build sanctuaries of family time, free from pressure, in which they can devote themselves to only one activity or one relationship. So, for instance, the time between 8 and 8:45 P.M. may be cordoned off as "quality time" for parents and child, and that between 9:15 and 10 P.M. as quality time for a couple (once the children are in bed). Such time boundaries must then be guarded against other time demands—calls from the office, from a neighbor to arrange tomorrow's car pool, from a child's friend about homework. Yet these brief respites of "relaxed time" themselves come to look more and more like little segments of job time, with parents punching in and out as if on a time clock. . . .

Paradoxically, what may seem to harried working parents like a solution to their time bind—efficiency and time segmentation—can later feel like a problem in itself. To be efficient with whatever time they do have at home, many working parents try to go faster if for no other reason than to clear off some space in which to go slowly. They do two or three things at once. They plan ahead. They delegate. They separate home events into categories and try to outsource some of them. In their efficiency, they may inadvertently trample on the emotion-laden symbols associated with particular times of day or particular days of the week. They pack one activity closer to the next and disregard the "framing" around each of them, those moments of looking forward to or looking back on an experience, which heighten its emotional impact. They ignore the contribution that a leisurely pace can make to fulfillment, so that a rapid dinner, followed by a speedy bath and bedtime story for a child—if part of "quality time"—is counted as "worth the same" as a slower version of the same events. As time becomes something to "save" at home as much as or even more than at work, domestic life becomes quite literally a second shift; a cult of efficiency, once centered in the workplace, is allowed to set up shop and make itself comfortable at home. Efficiency has become both a means to an end—more home time—and a way of life, an end in itself. . . .

. . . *Working Mother* magazine, for example, carries ads that invite the working mother to cook "two-minute rice," a "five-minute chicken casserole," a "seven-minute Chinese feast." One ad features a portable phone to show that the working mother can make business calls while baking cookies with her daughter.

Another typical ad promotes cinnamon oatmeal cereal for breakfast by showing a smiling mother ready for the office in her square-shouldered suit, hugging her happy son. A caption reads, "In the morning, we are in such a rush, and my son eats so slowly. But with cinnamon oatmeal cereal, I don't even have to coax him to hurry up!" . . .

A Third Shift: Time Work

As the first shift (at the workplace) takes more time, the second shift (at home) becomes more hurried and rationalized. The longer the workday at the office or plant, the more we feel pressed at home to hurry, to delegate, to delay, to forgo, to segment, to hyperorganize the precious remains of family time. Both their time deficit and what seem like solutions to it (hurrying, segmenting, and organizing) force parents . . . to engage in a third shift—noticing, understanding, and coping with the emotional consequences of the compressed second shift.

Children respond to the domestic work-bred cult of efficiency in their own ways. Many, as they get older, learn to protest it. Parents at Amerco and elsewhere then have to deal with their children, as they act out their feelings about the sheer scarcity of family time. For example, Dennis Long, an engineer at Amerco, told me about what happened with his son from a previous marriage when he faced a project deadline at work. Whenever Dennis got home later than usual, four-year-old Joshua greeted him with a tantrum. As Dennis ruefully explained,

> Josh gets really upset when I'm not home. He's got it in his head that the first and third weeks of every month, he's with me, not with his mom. He hasn't seen me for a while, and I'm supposed to be there. When a project deadline like this one comes up and I come home late, he gets to the end of his rope. He gives me hell. I understand it. He's frustrated. He doesn't know what he can rely on.

This father did his "third shift" by patiently sitting down on the floor to "receive" Josh's tantrum, hearing him out, soothing him, and giving him some time. For a period of six months, Joshua became upset at almost any unexpected delay or rapid shift in the pace at which events were, as he saw it, supposed to happen. Figuring out what such delays or shifts in pace meant to Joshua became another part of Dennis Long's third shift.

Such episodes raise various questions: If Josh's dad keeps putting off their dates to play together, does it mean he doesn't care about Josh? Does Josh translate the language of time the same way his father does? What if time symbolizes quite different things to the two of them? Whose understanding counts the most? Sorting out such emotional tangles is also part of the third shift.

Ironically, many Amerco parents were challenged to do third-shift work by their children's reactions to "quality time." As one mother explained,

> Quality time is seven-thirty to eight-thirty at night, and then it's time for bed. I'm ready at seven-thirty, but Melinda has other ideas. As soon as quality time comes she wants to have her bath or watch TV; *no way* is she going to play with Mommy. Later, when I'm ready to drop, *then* she's ready for quality time.

. . .

In such situations, pressed parents often don't have time to sort through their children's responses. They have no space to wonder what their gift of time means. Or whether a parent's visit to daycare might seem to a child like a painfully prolonged departure. Is a gift of time what a parent wants to give, or what a child wants to receive? Such questions are often left unresolved.

Time-deficit "paybacks" lead to another kind of difficult emotional work. For example, like many salespeople at Amerco, Phyllis Ramey spent about a fifth of her work time traveling. She always kept in touch by phone with her husband and their two children—Ben, three, and Pete, five—and at each sales stop, she bought the boys gifts. Ben enjoyed them but thought little about them; Pete, on the other hand, fixated anxiously on "what mommy's bringing me"—a

Tonka truck, a Batman cape, a bubble-making set. . . . Phyllis believed that Pete "really needed more time" with her, and she sensed that she was buying him things out of guilt. Indeed, she talked and joked about guilt-shopping with co-workers. But in Pete's presence she had a hard time separating his anxiety about gifts from his relationship with her.

Amerco parents like Phyllis are not alone, of course. Spending on toys has soared from $6.7 billion in 1980 to $17.5 billion in 1995. According to psychologist Marilyn Bradford, preschoolers looking forward to Christmas ask for an average of 3.4 toys but receive on average 11.6.[23] As employers buy growing amounts of time from employees, parents half-consciously "buy" this time from their children. But children rarely enter into these "trades" voluntarily, and parents are tempted to avoid the "time work" it takes to cope with their children's frustration. . . .

Most Amerco working parents held on to some fantasy of a more leisurely and gratifying family life. Their wishes seemed so modest—to have time to throw a ball with their children, or to read to them, or simply to witness the small dramas of their development, not to speak of having a little fun and romance themselves. Yet often even those modest wishes seemed strangely out of reach. So many of these parents had come to live in a small town and work for a family-friendly company precisely because they thought it would be a good place to raise children. They had wanted some kind of balance. . . .

Still, family-friendly Amerco put steady pressure on its employees to lead a more work-centered life, and while some working parents resisted, most did not. As a result, they were giving their children, their marriages, their communities, and themselves far less time than they imagined giving. They were, in a sense, leading one life and imagining another. . . .

But how are working parents at Amerco—or any of us—to face the time bind? And once we face it, what are we to do about it—not just in our imaginations but in real life? One course of action is to deal with the time bind as a purely personal problem, and to develop personal strategies for coping with it in one's own life. At Amerco the most common response by far was to try to limit the pull of home by needs reduction, outsourcing, and dreams of a potential time-rich self, but these strategies merely avoided, and even exacerbated, the time bind. . . .

A more daunting yet ultimately more promising approach to unknotting the time bind requires collective—rather than individual—action: workers must directly challenge the organization, and the organizers, of the American workplace. For this to occur, Amerco employees and their counterparts across the country would have to become new kinds of political activists who would—to borrow a slogan from the environmental movement—"think globally and act locally." Together, they might create a time movement. For the truth of the matter is that many working parents lack time because the workplace has a prior claim on it. It solves very little to either adapt to that claim or retreat from the workplace. The moment has come to address that claim, to adjust the old workplace to the new workforce. . . .

. . . A movement to reform work time should not limit itself to encouraging companies to offer policies allowing shorter or more flexible hours. . . . Such policies may serve as little more than fig leaves concealing long-hour work cultures. A time movement would also need to challenge the premises of that work culture. It would ask, Are workers judged mainly on the excellence of their performance, or mainly on the amount of time they are present in the workplace? Is there a "culture of trust" that allows workers to pinch-hit for one another as needs arise? Is there job security? The answers to these questions are crucial, for there can be little appeal to shorter hours when employees fear that the long hours they now work may disappear entirely. . . .

A time movement cannot stop at the company level, however. In the long run, no work–family balance will ever fully take hold if the social conditions that might make it possible—men who are willing to share parenting and housework, communities that value work in the home as highly as work on the job, and policymakers and

elected officials who are prepared to demand family-friendly reforms—remain out of reach. And it is by helping foster these broader conditions that a social movement could have its greatest effect.

Any push for more flexible work time must confront a complex reality: many working families are both prisoners and architects of the time bind in which they find themselves. A time movement would have to explore the question of why working parents have yet to protest collectively the cramped quarters of the temporal "housing" in which they live. It would have to force a public reckoning about the private ways out of the time bind—emotional asceticism, the love affair with capitalism, the repeatedly postponed plans of the potential self—that only seem to worsen the situation.

Then, too, a time movement must not shy away from opening a national dialogue on the most difficult and frightening aspect of our time bind: the need for "emotional investment" in family life in an era of familial divestiture and deregulation. How much time and energy ought we to devote to the home? How much time and energy do we dare subtract from work? Current arguments about what should and should not count as "a family" do little to help the families that already exist. What is needed instead is a public debate about how we can properly value relationships with loved ones and ties to communities that defy commodification.

NOTES

1. These part-time jobs are not to be confused with jobs without benefits or job security, jobs in the so-called contingency labor force. The growth of "bad" part-time jobs may, indeed, be chilling the quest for "good" ones. See Vicki Smith, "Flexibility in Work and Employment: Impact on Women," *Research in the Sociology of Organizations* 11 (1993): 195–216.

2. . . . See also Galinsky et al., *The Corporate Reference Guide* (1991), pp. 85–87. Nationwide, a far higher proportion of firms claim to offer flexible schedules than report workers using them. In one study of flexible staffing and scheduling, of the twenty-nine firms

offering the family-friendly benefit flexplace, for example, eighteen of the companies had five or fewer employees working from home (Kathleen Christensen, *Flexible Staffing and Scheduling in U.S. Corporations* [New York: The Conference Board, 1989], p. 18).

What people *do* with the time freed up by flexible schedules is another story. One study of the use of flex benefits by workers in two federal agencies found no increase in working parents' time spent with children—although they did find an increase in women's time doing housework (Halcyone Bohen and Anamaria Viveros-Long, *Balancing Jobs and Family Life: Do Flexible Schedules Help?* [Philadelphia: Temple University Press, 1981]).

A 1992 study conducted by Johnson & Johnson Company found that only 6 percent of employees used their "family-care leave" (unpaid leave for up to a year), and 18 percent used the "family-care absence" (time off with pay for short-term emergency care) (Families and Work Institute, "An Evaluation of Johnson and Johnson's Work-Family Initiative," April 1993, p. 20). Despite the fact that in 1983, 37 percent of American companies made parental leave available to new fathers, one study of 384 companies found that only nine reported even one father taking a formal leave (Dana Friedman, *Linking Work–Family Issues to the Bottom Line* [New York: The Conference Board, 1991], p. 50).

3. Galinsky et al., *The Corporate Reference Guide* (1991), p. 123.

4. Arthur Emlen, "Employee Profiles: 1987 Dependent Care Survey, Selected Companies" (Portland: Oregon Regional Research Institute for Human Services, Portland State University, 1987), reported in Friedman, *Linking Work–Family Issues to the Bottom Line* (1991), p. 13.

5. Hofferth et al., *National Child Care Survey 1990* (1991), p. 374. See also Bond and Galinksy, *Beyond the Parental Leave Debate* (1991), p. 74.

6. Families and Work Institute, *Women: The New Providers*, Whirlpool Foundation Study, Part 1, survey conducted by Louis Harris and Associates, Inc., May 1995, p. 12.

7. See Galinsky et al., *The Changing Workforce* (1993), p. 17.

8. Christopher Lasch, *Haven in a Heartless World* (New York: Basic Books, 1977). To Lasch what matters about the family is its privacy, its capacity to protect the individual from the "cruel world of politics and work"; this privacy has been invaded, he argues, by the cruel world it was set up to guard against.

9. Reed Larson, Maryse Richards, and Maureen Perry-Jenkins, "Divergent Worlds: The Daily Emotional Experience of Mothers and Fathers in the Domestic and Public Spheres," *Journal of Personality and Social Psychology* 67 (1994):1035.

10. Larson et al., "Divergent Worlds" (1994), pp. 1039, 1040.

11. Grace Baruch, Lois Biener, and Rosalind Barnett, "Women and Gender in Research on Work and Family Stress," *American Psychologist* 42 (1987):130–136; Glenna Spitze, "Women's Employment and Family Relations: A Review," *Journal of Marriage and the Family* 50 (1988):595–618. Even when researchers take into account the fact that the depressed or less mentally fit would be less likely to find or keep a job in the first place, working women come out slightly ahead in mental health (see Rena Repetti, Karen Matthews, and Ingrid Waldron, "Employment and Women's Health: Effects of Paid Employment on Women's Mental and Physical Health," *American Psychologist* 44 [1989]:1394–1401).

12. Families and Work Institute, *Women: The New Providers* (1995), p. 10.

13. Baruch et al., "Women and Gender in Research" (1987), p. 132.

14. Larson et al., "Divergent Worlds" (1994), p. 1041. See also Shelley MacDermid, Margaret Williams, Stephen Marks, and Gabriela Heilbrun, "Is Small Beautiful? Influence of Workplace Size on Work-Family Tension," *Family Relations* 43 (1994):159–167.

15. For supporting research about the importance of work to women, see Baruch et al., "Women and Gender in Research" (1987), esp. p. 132. Also see Diane Burden and Bradley Googins, "Boston University Balancing Job and Homelife Study: Managing Work and Family Stress in Corporations" (Boston: Boston University School of Social Work, 1987). Researchers also find that simply being a mother doesn't raise satisfaction with life (E. Spreitzer, E. Snyder, and D. Larson, "Multiple Roles and Psychological Well-Being," *Sociological Focus* 12 [1979]: 141–148; and Ethel Roskies and Sylvie Carrier, "Marriage and Children for Professional Women: Asset or Liability?" paper presented at the APA convention "Stress in the 90s," Washington, D.C., 1992).

See also L. Verbrugge, "Role Burdens and Physical Health of Women and Men," in Faye Crosby, ed., *Spouse, Parent, Worker: On Gender and Multiple Roles* (New Haven, CT: Yale University Press, 1987). However, many factors come into play when we talk about working mothers' emotional well-being and mental health. For example, Kessler and McCrae found that a job improved mental health for women only if their husbands shared the load at home (R. Kessler and J. McCrae, "The Effect of Wives' Employment on the Mental Health of Men and Women," *American Sociological Review* 47 [1982]:216–227).

16. Andrew Scharlach and Esme Fuller-Thomson, "Coping Strategies Following the Death of an Elderly Parent," *Journal of Gerentological Social Work* 21 (1994): 90. In response to a mother's death, work was a more "helpful resource" than spouse or religion for women. For men, work was more helpful than family, friends, and religion.

17. Founded in 1986, Bright Horizons was named the nation's leading work-site childcare organization in 1991 by the Child Care Information Exchange. The company offers a range of services: drop-in care, weekend programs, and programs for infants, toddlers, preschoolers, and school-age children. Bright Horizons pays its teachers 10 percent more than whatever the going rate may be at nearby childcare centers and has a rate of teacher turnover that averages only half of the industry-wide 40 to 50 percent a year.

18. Thirty-five percent of parents responded (9 percent were male and 90 percent female; 92 percent were married and 7 percent single). Percentages may not add up to 100 for some questions either because some respondents didn't answer that question or because the percentages that are reported were rounded to the nearest whole number.

19. Twenty percent of parents reported that their children were in childcare 41–45 hours a week; 13 percent, 46–50 hours; 2 percent, 51–60 hours. In the lowest income group in the study ($45,000 or less), 25 percent of parents had children in childcare 41 hours a week or longer. In the highest income group ($140,000 or higher), 39 percent did.

20. Parents were asked how many hours they spent doing work they brought home from the office "on a typical weekday." Eighteen percent didn't answer. Of those remaining, half said they did bring work home. The largest proportion—19 percent—brought home "between six and ten hours of work [per week]." They estimated even longer hours for their partners.

21. Burden and Googins, "Boston University Balancing Job and Homelife Study" (1987), p. 30.

22. Yet friends may not be a working parent's main source of social support. When asked which were the "three most important sources of support in your life," nine out of ten men and women mentioned their spouses or partners. Second came their mothers, and third "other relatives." So people turned for support to kin first. Among *friendships*, however, those at work proved more significant than those around home. As sources of emotional support, 10 percent of the respondents also mentioned "books and magazines," the same percentage as mentioned "church or temple"; only 5 percent mentioned neighbors. Thirteen percent turned for support first to friends at work—as many as turned to their own fathers.

23. Gary Cross, "If Not the Gift of Time, At Least Toys," *New York Times*, 3 December 1995.

THINKING ABOUT THE READING

What does Hochschild mean when she says that "work has become home and home has become work"? Why does she think home life has become so stressful and harried in recent years? Think of the enduring effects of the shift that Hochschild describes. How will these changes influence people's expectations about their family lives? What impact will they have on marriage? On the bearing and rearing of children? If people aren't taking advantage of available family leave policies as Hochschild claims, how might the workplace change in the coming years? Hochschild implies that, in the past, people's work and family lives were very different than they are today. Was the workplace of the past as awful and dehumanizing as she implies? Was home life as warm and glorious?

PART III

Social Structure, Institutions, and Everyday Life

The Structure of Society:
Organizations and Social Institutions

One of the great sociological paradoxes of our existence is that in a society that so fiercely extols the virtues of rugged individualism and personal accomplishment, we spend most of our lives responding to the influence of larger organizations and social institutions. From the nurturing environments of our churches and schools to the cold depersonalizations of massive bureaucracies, organizations and institutions are a fundamental part of our everyday lives.

The organization that is perhaps most relevant to your life right now is your college or university. In "When Hope and Fear Collide: A Portrait of Today's College Student," Arthur Levine and Jeanette Cureton compare the lives of today's college students to past generations of students. They point out that the dominant cultural messages in a society tend to be cyclical. Sometimes the cultural emphasis is on individual self-interest; other times it is on collective responsibility and the well-being of the community. These different emphases are reflected in the attitudes of alternating generations of college students. The profound economic, demographic, global, and technological changes of the late 20th century created a period of dizzying transition for college students. The authors argue that contemporary social institutions have not adapted well to these changes and have failed today's college students. They conclude that universities must drastically revise their curricula to reinstill in students feelings of hope and responsibility.

Another important organization in which you will eventually spend a great deal of your life (if you don't already) is your place of employment. Many people define themselves by their work. But just how much of our time and energy we should devote to our jobs is a matter of some debate and concern. In "The Overworked American," economist Juliet Schor demonstrates that Americans work more and have less leisure time than people in other developed countries. She feels that this phenomenon is not a result of Americans being hard workers but instead is a consequence of what she calls "the work-spend cycle." Americans have become accustomed to working longer hours so they can earn more money to spend on more things. She contrasts this situation with other countries in which the culture promotes a concept of working less and taking more leisure time.

No matter how powerful and influential they are, organizations are more than structures, rules, policies, goals, job descriptions, and standard operating procedures. Each organization, and each division within an organization, develops its own norms, values, and language. Furthermore, no matter how strict and unyielding a particular organization may appear to be, individuals within them are usually able to exert some control over their lives. Rarely is an organization what it appears to be on the surface.

In larger organizations, distinct cultures develop where similar meanings and perspectives are cultivated. As in society as a whole, however, distinct subcultures can develop. In "The Smile Factory," John Van Maanen examines the organizational culture of one of American society's most enduring icons: Disney theme parks. Disneyland and Disneyworld have a highly codified and strict set of conduct standards. Variations from tightly defined employee norms are not tolerated. You'd expect in such a place that employees would be a rather homogeneous group. However, Van Maanen discovers that beneath the surface of this self-proclaimed "Happiest Place on Earth" lies a mosaic of distinct groups that have created their own status system and that work hard to maintain the status boundaries between one another.

When Hope and Fear Collide
A Portrait of Today's College Student

Arthur Levine and Jeanette S. Cureton

In 1980, Arthur Levine wrote a book titled *When Dreams and Heroes Died.* It was a portrait of the college students of the late 1970s, based on national surveys and interviews of undergraduates and college administrators conducted by the Carnegie Council on Policy Studies in Higher Education.

The picture that emerged was of a generation optimistic about their personal futures but pessimistic about the future of the country. Students had adopted what might be described as a "*Titanic* ethic," a belief that they were being forced to ride on a doomed ship called the United States (or the world). But so long as the ship was afloat, they were determined to make the voyage as luxurious as possible and go first class.

With this outlook, students turned inward, focusing increasingly on "me." They became more vocationally oriented, with an emphasis on careers in the platinum professions: business, law, and medicine. Material goods assumed a greater importance in their lives. Two out of three students said it was essential or very important for them to be very well off financially.

Students reported the key social and political events that shaped their generation were Vietnam and Watergate. For three out of four undergraduates, the effect of these events was profoundly negative; they caused students to reject politics, political involvement, and government. When asked who their heroes were, "no one" topped the undergraduates' lists, followed distantly by God, entertainers, and athletes.

Student political attitudes grew more conservative than those of their predecessors, with increasing proportions favoring the death penalty, less coddling of criminals, and cessation of school busing. Nonetheless, student activism persisted on campus. One in five undergraduates reported having participated in a demonstration. But the issues shifted from prior years; instead of civil rights and Vietnam, students now protested over college costs and financial aid, faculty and staff hiring and firing, institutional facilities, and administrative policy. The agenda shifted from national to local issues and from social policy questions to consumer concerns.

Academically, students were entering higher education less well prepared in basic skills. Even so, they were getting higher grades in college than their predecessors. In growing proportion, undergraduates were selecting majors in the professions rather than the liberal arts. And they were taking more of their courses in their majors than in the past.

Socially, the feeling of community declined on college campuses, while individualism became more dominant. Self-interest clubs and groups proliferated, with a focus on gender, race, religious, and ethnic differences. Team sports diminished in popularity; individual sports grew. Students became more liberal about social issues, particularly those emphasizing individual rights and freedoms; they were more supportive than students in past years of premarital sex, legalization of marijuana, and liberalization of divorce laws. . . .

. . . Levine decided to continue the student interviews. Each year, he would visit more than a dozen campuses around the country. During the 1980s, he asked undergraduates on those campuses the same set of questions he had for the Carnegie Council studies. They kept giving him the same set of answers, with the notable exception that the proportion saying it was essential or very important to be very well off financially kept rising.

That is, until 1990. Then the answers started changing dramatically in such basic areas as optimism about the future, social involvement, and life goals. It was like flipping a light switch, so sudden was the change. At first, Levine dismissed the differences, chalking them up to having selected unrepresentative institutions, having arrived at a college at a strange moment, or having talked with an atypical group of students. But the differences persisted. Levine found them at colleges and universities across the country. Undergraduate attitudes, values, and beliefs appeared to be changing, and he wanted to find out how and why.

With this goal in mind, Levine repeated the Carnegie Council research of a decade and a half earlier. Jeanette Cureton joined him in planning and carrying out the research. In summer and fall 1992, they surveyed a nationally representative sample of 270 chief student affairs officers. In 1993, with support from the Lilly Endowment, a similarly representative sample of ninety-one hundred undergraduates was surveyed. These students were of both traditional and nontraditional age, as were the undergraduates of the earlier Carnegie studies. In addition to the 1993 survey, interviews were conducted from 1993 to 1995 with student body presidents, student newspaper editors, more chief student affairs officers, and small focus groups of students (averaging eight to ten in number and diverse in age, gender, and ethnicity) on twenty-eight campuses across the nation, selected to reflect the variety of American higher education. In 1995, the student newspaper editors and student body presidents were interviewed once again. In 1997, a chief student affairs officer survey was conducted one last time. . . .

A Transitional Generation: Historical Cycles Revisited

. . . In this century, the most profound change in the character of the nation's undergraduates has been their multiplying numbers. Between 1900,

when 4 percent of all eighteen-year-olds attended college, and 1997, when 65 percent of all high school graduates went on to some form of postsecondary education, the nation moved from what has been characterized as elite to mass to universal higher education. As a result, college students have come to look more and more like the rest of the country. As the nation changes in character, college students change in character.

The changes in both occur cyclically. Societies are a lot like people. They go through periods of wakeful, strenuous, and even frenetic activity, and then they must rest. A period of waking, a period of rest, a period of waking, a period of rest . . . the cycle goes on and on. In this century, war has been the dividing line, marking the end of wakefulness—a final outpouring of frenzied activity—and the beginning of rest—the onset of exhausted slumber.

Periods of waking are change oriented and reform minded. They are times when the dominant focus of the country is on community. Indeed, they could be called *periods of community ascendancy*. These periods emphasize duty to others, responsibility, the need to give, and the commonalties all Americans share. They are at once future oriented and ascetic. In this century, there have been three periods of community ascendancy: the Progressive Era, from the turn of the century through World War I; the Roosevelt to Great Depression era, from 1932 through World War II; and the 1960s, actually from the late 1950s through the Vietnam War. These periods have seen the election of progressive presidents: Theodore Roosevelt, Harry Truman, John Kennedy, and Lyndon Johnson. Their administrations were activist socially, called for national improvement, and demanded citizen involvement. Capturing the spirit of such eras is John Kennedy's famed inaugural injunction, "Ask not what your country can do for you—ask what you can do for your country."

In contrast, periods of rest occurred after World War I, World War II, and Vietnam. These are times in which people are tired, having been asked in previous years to give and give more, and, finally, if necessary, to give lives—their own, those of family members, or their friends'—to fight a war. People are weary and want a break. Thoughts and actions that were directed outward turn inward to concerns that have been neglected: to getting one's life and the lives of one's family in order. The focus shifts from the community to the individual. These times can be called *periods of individual ascendancy.* They tend to be present oriented rather than future oriented. They are more hedonistic than ascetic, more concerned with individual rights than community responsibility, more rooted in getting than in giving, and more focused on self than on others. In such times, the nation has elected presidents (such as Warren Harding, Calvin Coolidge, Herbert Hoover, Dwight Eisenhower, Richard Nixon, Ronald Reagan, and George [H. W.] Bush) who champion the individual and oppose big government that places large burdens on its citizens. President Reagan caught the mood of those times when he said, "We are going to put an end to the notion that the American taxpayer exists to fund the American government. The federal government exists to serve the American people. . . . Work and family are at the center of our lives" (Reagan, 1985a, p. 268). Reagan called for an end of government that "sees people only as members of groups" in favor of government that "sees all the people of America as individuals" (Reagan, 1985b, p. 310). With the exception of the Harding administration, which promised "a return to normalcy," periods of individual ascendancy have been associated with a president's name, not a motto or a call to action, suggesting a social crusade. Their theme has been less government, less social control, and more individual freedom. . . .

As Ernest Boyer and Arthur Levine have written, this movement back and forth between periods of individual and community ascendancy is a reflection of what John Locke called the social contract. All the members of a society are bound together by a tacit agreement, a compact among the individuals, in which they cede a portion of their autonomy for what is defined as the greater good. In exchange, they receive common services, protections, and agreed-upon freedoms.

The history of all societies is a continuing effort to find the perfect balance between the community and the individual. Societies move first in one direction, then the other, in the search for that balance. They overcompensate in both directions, and correct the balance by moving in the opposite direction. When too great an emphasis is placed on the community, individuals feel herded, smothered, and restrained. They lament the lack of privacy and the intrusion of social obligations. They then demand the opportunity to express their individuality and uniqueness. In contrast, when the pendulum swings too far toward individualism and independence, people are apt to feel alone and isolated in an apathetic and uncaring world. In response, they move in the opposite direction, seeking to renew ties with their fellow human beings (Boyer and Levine, 1981).

This perennial tension between the individual and the community is mirrored in changes in the character of college students. Indeed, colleges, like all other social institutions, and undergraduates, like the rest of the population, follow the cycles of community and individual ascendancy.

During periods of individual ascendancy, students are less activist than in periods of community ascendancy. . . . During periods of individual ascendancy, student politics is more centrist and conservative. Ideological and political interest is relatively low. The proportion of undergraduates who are politically far right, far left, or adherents of ideologies of any type decreases. Isolationism grows and international concern declines during such times.

During periods of individual ascendancy, students are more socially rather than intellectually active. Membership in fraternities and sororities rises. Sports and intercollegiate athletics grow in popularity. Drinking increases. Fads are more likely to occur: flagpole sitting, mah-jongg, and marathon dance contests in the 1920s; panty raids, piano wrecking, and telephone booth stuffing during the 1950s; and streaking, skateboarding, hacking, "Dallas," and toga parties in the 1970s and 1980s.

During periods of individual ascendancy, student social attitudes tend to be more liberal, allowing for increased personal freedom. The 1920s were the age of women smoking and voting for the first time, increased sexual freedom, and Freud. The 1940s and 1950s—aside from inaugurating the pill and panty raids—were a time when students, particularly returning veterans, fought strenuously against hazing and rules based on the *in loco parentis* doctrine. The 1970s and 1980s were a period in which concern with personal freedom was perhaps the hallmark of the era.

During periods of individual ascendancy, students are more likely to be involved in religious activities, and campuses are more prone to experience religious revivals and to serve as launching pads for new religious movements.

During periods of individual ascendancy, students tend to be less academically oriented and less concerned with "relevance" in education; that is, they are less desirous of instruction that treats the burning social concerns of the day, in contrast to periods of community ascendancy.

During periods of individual ascendancy, students are more committed to the material aspects of the American dream and believe more strongly in their likelihood of attaining them.

During periods of community ascendancy, trends move in exactly the opposite directions. In this context, current undergraduates do not fit into traditional cycles as well as their predecessors did. Indeed, the students of the Progressive Era, the 1930s, and the 1960s exhibited in general the characteristics of periods of community ascendancy. The undergraduates of the 1920s, 1940s, 1950s, and the seventies and eighties showed the characteristics associated with periods of individual ascendancy.

A Time of Discontinuity

The 1992 presidential election should have marked a transition from a period of individual to community ascendancy. The Reagan and Bush years drew to a close and a progressive Democrat entered the White House. But this is not what happened.

The reason is that, in the words of Rip Van Winkle, "everything's changed." The periodic os-cillations from individualism to community are a phenomenon only of mature or very stable societies. They are a mechanism for maintaining the health of society by continually finding the appropriate balance between common goals and personal needs. In this manner, the competing demands of the individual and the community can both be met. This juggling act is what keeps society from flying apart and allows it to carry out business as usual under ordinary circumstances.

However, there are rare times in the history of a society in which rapid and profound change occurs. The change is so broad and so deep that the routine and ordinary cycles of readjustment cease. There is a sharp break between the old and the new. It is a time of discontinuity. In the history of this country, there have been two such break points.

The first was the Industrial Revolution, which began in earnest in the first decades of the nineteenth century. It brought about a transformation in the United States from an agricultural to an industrial society. For those who lived through it, everything appeared to be in flux. The nation's economy was turbulent and uncertain, with wide swings both up and down. New technologies with the capacity to remake the nation's daily life, ranging from steamboats and canals to railroads and mechanized factories, were burgeoning. Old industries were dying, and new industries were being born. Demographics were shifting dramatically as the population moved west and south, from rural to urban areas. Large numbers of immigrants, with relatively little formal education, were coming to America. All of the country's major social institutions—church, family, government, work, and media—were being transformed. Reflecting on the vastness of the changes, Henry Adams concluded that "the old universe was thrown into the ash heap and a new one created" (Adams, [1918] 1931, p. 5).

Adams's assessment was very close to the mark. The effects of industrialization have been well documented. Among the consequences are family disorganization, attenuation of kinship ties, and a splintering of connections between generations. Mate selection and marital patterns are retarded. Gender roles change. Homogeneity gives way to heterogeneity. Apathy and alienation grow. New and higher literacy levels are required to function in society, causing sharp differentiation in the wealth and status of the populace. Mass communication expands, and isolation within society declines. Interest groups and associations multiply (Moore, 1963).

As the reader will have guessed, the second break point or time of discontinuity is occurring now. . . . The United States is currently undergoing profound demographic, economic, global, and technological change. Demographically, the U. S. population is aging, changing color, coming from other countries, and redistributing itself across the country at astounding rates.

Economically, change is occurring at what appears an even quicker pace. In one generation, the United States has moved from being the largest creditor to the largest debtor nation in the world. In one generation, the country has gone from having a resource-rich government to a resource-poor one. In six generations, the nation has shifted from a rural and agrarian society to an urban and industrial nation and then to a suburban and information-based global economy. The signs of the change are all around us: the ailing farms in the heartland, a rust belt dotting the Midwest and East, roller-coastering high-technology centers, and troubled inner cities.

Globally, the United States has become a part of an interconnected world. Four of the last five presidential elections were determined by events in the Middle East. Creation of jobs in Japan and Korea exacts a price in terms of jobs in New York, Pennsylvania, and California. When countries in central Europe come apart and others in western Europe join together, the stock market plunges and surges. This interdependence is a new experience for the United States.

Technologically, our daily lives are filled with devices and realities that were the stuff of science fiction a few decades ago. The authors' grandparents were born before the airplane was invented, and our children were born after men landed on the moon. This is a dizzying rate of change.

The nature and degree of change today is very much like that of the Industrial Revolution. Henry Adams's description of his own times seems an apt characterization of ours as well. However, several important elements might be added to what Adams said. First, the razing of the old order and the building of the new may go on simultaneously, but they are not experienced that way by most people. The emerging order is unknowable and unrecognizable; it is the future. The old order appears to be falling apart; nothing works as well as it used to. The dominant emotion is necessarily one of loss. We can see that today. All of our major social institutions, which were created for an industrial society, now appear to be broken; government, education, manufacturing, health care, the family. The reaction of the nation is not one of potential and promise, but rather of loss and frustration.

Second, we name periods of profound change only in retrospect. During the antebellum period of the nineteenth century, people did not wake up in the morning and say, "No wonder the old rules seem to have been thrown out and nothing works as well as it used to; it is the Industrial Revolution!" Instead, they were confused, frustrated, angry, lost, flailing, and often failing. It was not until the 1890s that the name *Industrial Revolution* came to stick. Prior to that time, there was a plethora of possibilities to describe the massive change the nation had been through. Only when the period assumed a single agreed-upon name could the pattern of change be comprehended. This recurring process is not wholly different from our penchant for naming generations of young people.

Third, it is impossible to say with any sense of accuracy where we are or where we are going in terms of the current wave of change. To describe our society in the decades ahead is a guessing game; it is fantasy. Which of the ongoing changes is most important? Which will dominate? Will the era we are living through be called the Demographic Revolution? Perhaps the Economic Revolution? Maybe the Technological Revolution? How about the Global Revolution? No one knows, nor will anyone know for years to come. Business writer Jane Bryant Quinn put it best when she said in a 1992 conversation, "If you are not confused by what is going on today, you don't understand it."

For today's college students, this world of change dominates their lives. The cycles of community and individualism have given way to a world of unceasing, unknowable change.

This reality is compounded by the enormous size of the population attending college today. As a consequence, the benefit of a college education has diminished. When only a small proportion of an age group graduates from college, they are virtually guaranteed the best jobs a society offers. When the majority attend college, this is no longer possible. The guarantee of the best jobs expires along with the guarantee of *any* job. In short, the students who attended college at the turn of the century were shopping at the educational equivalent of Tiffany's. Today's undergraduates are at something much more akin to Kmart. The multiplication in size of the college student population means they are subject to exactly the same social forces as the rest of the nation's population. A smaller, more elite group might have been protected from the waves of change crashing upon the rest of the country. The college cohort is simply too large today to be sheltered in any fashion.

Moreover, higher education has become a mature industry. Throughout this century, higher education was a growth industry, increasing in size annually, except for wars and two years of the Depression. During that time, the sole demand of government and the public made on colleges and universities was to increase capacity—make it possible for more and more students to enroll. Today, there are few in government who want further growth. In the state houses of America, there is no clamor to increase the proportion of college attendance to 70 or 80 percent of the age group. Even President Clinton [focused] on reducing the cost of college through tax incentives rather than increasing the pool of students attending college. As a result, government [asked] hard questions it never asked before about the appropriate size of higher education and the effectiveness and efficiency of its work.

With growth industries, the focus is on providing resources for expansion and eliminating the impediments that retard it. With mature industries, the aim is just the opposite; the goal is to control growth, reduce cost, measure achievement, and require accountability. The result is that current undergraduates are coming to college at a time in which there are fewer public financial incentives for them to attend, and there is less public support for the institutions in which they are enrolled, causing colleges to scale back their programs and staffing levels. This means that colleges are also less able to shelter or protect their students from social conditions than they were once able to.

This is a generation that is feeling the full brunt of massive social change, more so than their predecessors ever did. For instance, even at the height of the Great Depression of the 1930s, the federal government provided financial aid to colleges in order to get more students to attend. The rationale was *not* to protect students; it was to keep them out of the labor market. Nonetheless, the infusion of dollars did have a simultaneous sheltering effect on Depression-era undergraduates.

The consequence of rapid social change and shifting conditions in higher education today is a generation straddling two worlds, one dying and another being born. Each makes competing and conflicting demands on today's college generation; they are torn between both. A dying world makes them want security, and a world being born makes urgent their call for change. In the same fashion, pragmatism wrestles with idealism, doing well with doing good, and fear with hope. They are, above all else, a transitional generation, not unlike the young people of Henry Adams's day, and they are experiencing the same symptoms as did those who lived through the Industrial Revolution.

Education for a Transitional Generation

As a group, current undergraduates might be described as having the following characteristics. They are

- Frightened
- Demanding of change
- Desirous of security
- Disenchanted with politics and the nation's social institutions
- Bifurcated in political attitudes between left and right; the middle is shrinking
- Liberal in social attitudes
- Socially conscious and active
- Consumer oriented
- Locally rather than globally focused
- Sexually active, but socially isolated
- Heavy users of alcohol
- Hardworking
- Tired
- Diverse and divided
- Weak in basic skills and able to learn best in ways different from how their professors teach
- Pragmatic, career oriented, and committed to doing well
- Idealistic, altruistic, and committed to doing good
- Optimistic about their personal futures
- Optimistic about our collective future
- Desperately committed to preserving the American dream

This generation is no better and no worse than any other generation, but, like every other generation before, it is unique. As a result, this generation requires a unique brand of education that will enable it to attain its personal dreams and to serve the society it must lead. The education we offered to previous generations, whether successful or not, will not work for these students. They are different, and their times are different. Above all, current undergraduates are in need of an education that provides them with four things.

Hope

The first is hope. When we speak about hope, we do not mean the flabby or groundless, rosy-eyed, Pollyannaish brand. Rather, we mean the kind of conviction that allows a person to rise each morning and face the new day. It is the stuff

Shakespeare talked of when he wrote, "True hope is swift and flies with swallow's wings; / Kings it makes gods, and meaner creatures kings" (*Richard III* 5.2.23). Current students profess to being optimistic about the future; but . . . that optimism is frail.

By way of example, in the course of our research we talked with a student who told us she was majoring in business. We asked how she liked it. She said she hated it. We asked what she would rather be majoring in. She said dance. We asked, Why not major in dance? She looked at us the way one would look at a dumb younger sibling and said, "Rich is nice. Poor is not nice. I want nice," and she walked off. We had no answer that day, but over time we have thought about that student a lot. She gave up all of her dreams to study a subject she hated. If she follows a career that flows from her major, she will probably dislike that too. The saddest, saddest part of the story is that she did not have to make the choice she did. This student may not have become a professional dancer, but she could manage a dance company, or be a dance teacher, or a critic, or perhaps operate a store selling dance equipment. The tragedy of the story is not that she made a bad selection. It is that the young woman gave up her hope. It was so tenuous that she dared not hold onto it. In one form or another, this was true of many of the students we interviewed.

Responsibility

The second attribute is responsibility. Despite all we said about the adversities this generation is facing, current college students are still among the most fortunate people in the world. They owe something to others. Indeed, they are more involved in service activities than their predecessors, but at the same time they are not convinced that they can both do good and do well. Many feel that when it comes to security and responsibility, a choice must be made.

At a New England liberal arts college, all first-year students were required to participate in an exercise called "Freshman Inquiry." Students were required to prepare an essay talking about what they had learned and not learned in college so far, their hopes and aspirations for the future, and how they planned to use the remainder of their college education. After the essay was written, each student met with a panel composed of a faculty member, an administrator, and a fellow student to discuss it. One student submitted an essay to a panel, saying when she grew up she wanted to be CEO of a multinational corporation, become a U.S. senator, head a foundation that provided scholarships for college students, and work for nuclear disarmament. The student was asked what she needed out of college to accomplish all this. After a little thought, she answered, "A killer instinct." Her listeners sought clarification. She said this meant the ability to step on people or walk over them when necessary to get what she wanted. She was asked about altruism. This time she asked for clarification, and the word was defined for her. She said that was not part of her game plan. The panel reminded her of her desire to work for nuclear arms control. Surely that was altruistic. She told the panel they did not get it: "If there were a nuclear war, I would not get to be CEO of a multinational corporation." Three years later, the student graduated, plans and opinions intact. Her grades were high, and several years later she was attending one of the nation's better business schools. All of her dreams may come true, but one is forced to conclude that her college experience was inadequate. It never taught her about responsibility, what she had an obligation to do for others.

Appreciation of Differences

The third attribute is understanding and appreciation of differences. Today's undergraduates are living in a world in which differences are multiplying and change is the norm, but they attend colleges that are often segregated on the basis of differences and where relationships between diverse populations are strained. They were unable to talk about those differences in our focus group interviews. When they did talk awkwardly about them, diverse students could not even face one another. . . . It is imperative that college students learn to recognize, respect, and accept their difference.

Efficacy

The final attribute is efficacy, that is, a sense that one can make a difference. Here again, current undergraduates affirmed this belief at the highest rates recorded in a quarter century, but in focus group interviews they expressed serious doubts. It brings to mind a group we met at a well-known liberal arts college. The college had created a special program for its most outstanding seniors to prepare them for the nation's most prestigious graduate fellowships. Levine was asked to talk to the students about leadership. After a few minutes of watching the students squirming in their seats, looking out the windows, and staring at their watches, he concluded the talk was not going well.

He told the group what he suspected; they agreed. They traded hypotheses back and forth about what had gone wrong. Finally, one student said, "Life is short. This leadership stuff is bullshit. We could not make a difference even if we wanted to." Levine took a quick poll of the group to see how many agreed with the student. Twenty-two out of twenty-five hands went up.

Today's students need to believe that they can make a difference. Not every one of them will become president of the United States, but each of them will touch scores of lives far more directly and tangibly—family, friends, neighbors, and coworkers. For ill or for good, in each of those lives students will make a difference. They need to be convinced that making a difference is their birthright. They should not give it away. No one can take it away.

Preparation of a Transitional Generation

These four attributes—hope, responsibility, appreciation of differences, and efficacy—are things that people learn or fail to learn growing up. They are taught by the entire community around them: a family, a neighborhood, youth groups, schools, churches, media, and government. Collectively and individually, these institutions have failed the current generation of college students. Each has declined in influence and power, decreased in trust and public confidence, diminished in its capacity or willingness to care for children, and eroded in stature as a role model and teacher for young people. They have been unable to develop the four attributes in our college students because they themselves are lacking in the very same attributes.

A Curriculum

This failure in preparing a generation of students forces colleges into the position of having to provide "remedial" education, not in the usual sense of needing to offer courses in reading, writing, and arithmetic (though they do this too). Rather, the education is remedial in the sense of having to compensate for what the other social institutions have failed to give young people over eighteen or more years.

Today's undergraduates need an education that includes five specific elements. These ideas are not new or shocking, but the content must be different from how these areas have been generically described for the past millennium. They must be fitted to today's undergraduates and their specific needs.

Communication

The first of these elements is communication and thinking skills. At the most basic level, current students need to be fluent in two languages: words and numbers. All learning is premised on mastery of these skills. For a generation that is weak in both languages, it is essential that each be included in the college curriculum.

The enormous change in the world in which current students will live their lives also necessitates that they master what might be called transition skills. These skills could be named the three C's. *Critical thinking* is imperative in an age in which information is multiplying geometrically,

ideologies masquerade as facts, and hard policy choices need to be faced. *Continuous learning*, the ability to learn independently throughout one's life, is also mandatory in an era in which the half-life of knowledge is declining precipitously and new learning technologies are burgeoning. *Creativity* is essential as well for a period in which the tried and true understandings of the past are quickly becoming aged and less useful.

As a corollary to mastering these transition skills, however, students must also understand how to access knowledge and use it effectively. Modern technology has revolutionized the process of recording, storing, and retrieving information. Learning how to access a vast body of knowledge that is constantly expanding and being revised is a critical first step in its acquisition. But the process of learning does not end there. The ability to make connections between, build on, and synthesize knowledge is crucial if purposeful learning and understanding are to take place.

For this generation of students, finding context for pieces of information is more complex than it used to be. At a time when books and libraries once provided discrete context for the information they contained, the process of acquiring and using knowledge was much simpler. Today, the contexts have changed or don't exist. For students of the 1990s, the process of acquiring pieces of information is like trying to fill a teacup with a fire hose. Using that information and knowledge effectively is the true challenge. Those who learn to think critically, learn continuously, and act creatively—those who have mastered the three C's and are able to put them to good use—have acquired techniques to enable them to convert the knowledge they acquire into value.

Human Heritage

The second element is the study of human heritage. True hope demands an understanding of the past as well as of the present. Society, in the words of Edmund Burke, is a contract, "a partnership not only between those who are living, but between those who are dead, and those who are to be born" ([1790] 1967, p. 318). The goal for this study is not for students to memorize a list of great names and key dates, but rather to understand how societies and people have responded to an ever-changing economic, political, social, and technological world. Only if we can teach students about the successes and failures, the evolutions and transitions, and the rises and declines of humanity and society can their hopes and fears be realistically grounded.

In the past, this was accomplished by teaching undergraduates about the United States and the Western world. This is no longer sufficient. Today they live in an interconnected global society in which the Koran has more influence on their daily lives than the Gettysburg Address does. It is a time in which our college students draw greater inspiration from Boris Yeltsin and Nelson Mandela than from their own political leaders. It is imperative that we educate current undergraduates about humankind in the fullest sense of the term.

The Environment

The third element is education regarding the environment in which students will live their lives. This is a "green" generation, one that deeply fears the desecration of the environment. They have no confidence in the groups now controlling the environment—government, business, and the press, among others. Many have turned away from the environment writ large. Their focus is chiefly local; their vision needs to be enlarged. Even if students ultimately choose to act locally, they must think globally. This means they need to understand both the natural environment and the humanmade environment in which we live, and take responsibility for caring for each.

With regard to the natural environment, students need to become literate scientifically; they need to know the basic facts and ways of thinking that constitute science. They must come to understand the inhabitants, planet, and universe in which we live. They must be educated to serve as effective citizens for the environment, that is,

learn about the public policy choices they will need to make and the criteria for making those choices.

With regard to the humanmade environment, the agenda is larger and even more difficult. Ralph Waldo Emerson wrote, "We do not make a world of our own, but fall into institutions already made and have to accommodate ourselves to them. . . ." (Emerson, 1909, p. 448). Current undergraduates are more negative about those institutions and more distrusting of their leaders than any group we have surveyed. They are rejecting both. It is essential that before turning their backs, they learn about what the range of social institutions—political, cultural, aesthetic, economic, and spiritual—is intended to accomplish. Students should learn how these institutions come into being, how they change over time, how they function and malfunction, and how they impose obligations and can be held accountable.

Individual Roles

The individual but multifaceted role that each of us plays is the fourth element in the curriculum. This is essential if students are to develop a sense of efficacy. Doing so is critical for a generation that believes that an individual can make a difference, while government is failing. It is invaluable for undergraduates who want families but have never witnessed happy marriages. It is a must for students who can't figure out whether to do well or do good. Shakespeare eloquently described this facet of our being, saying "All the world is a stage / And all the men and women merely players. / They have their entrances and their exits. / And one man in his time plays many parts" (*As You Like It* 2.7.139). Students need to know about each of those parts, all of the roles they will have to play: individual, friend, lover, family member, worker, citizen, leader, and follower. They must understand the nature of relationships, the choices they can make, the expectations associated with each role, the ways in which balance can be achieved among the various roles, and the part each role plays in creating a full and complete life. The curriculum must give them the skills, knowledge, and experience to perform each role. This is the career planning and preparation that today's students so desperately need, in its broadest and most basic form.

Values

The fifth and final element in the curriculum is values. This is critically important if students are to gain an appreciation of differences, or respect one another, or understand why cheating is wrong. But it also underlies each of the other attributes. Bertrand Russell explained the need for this fifth study when he wrote, "Without civic morality, communities perish; without personal morality, their survival has no value" (Russell, 1949, p. 70). Students must learn the meaning of values, be able to distinguish between values and facts, understand the difference between relative and absolute values, and differentiate between good, better, and best values. They also need to develop mechanisms for weighing and choosing among values. Finally, they need to comprehend how values function in our society and in their lives: the changing nature of values over time, how values fit into cultures, the place of values in an individual's life, and what happens to minority values in a society.

A Curriculum for Living

These five elements spell out a formal curriculum that colleges and universities can adopt. It differs from the traditional curriculum in that it is not rooted in the familiar disciplines and subject areas that higher education usually employs. Instead, it is grounded in the life needs of students. It is a curriculum designed specifically to prepare current undergraduates for the life they will lead and the world in which they will live. It seeks to marry intellectual vitality, which is intrinsic to academe, with the practical education students so urgently require today.

At bottom, what is being proposed is a contemporary vision of liberal education. Under-

graduate education has changed dramatically over its more than three-and-a-half-century history in this country, to meet the twin needs of remaining intellectually vital and providing useful or practical education. Whenever societies change quickly, there is a tendency for the curriculum to lose these anchor points. In a short period of time, a course of study becomes anachronistic. It no longer prepares students for the world in which they will live, and it imparts an intellectual tradition that has become outdated.

In the early decades of the nineteenth century, as America underwent the Industrial Revolution, the classic collegiate curriculum faced . . . such a challenge. The study of the trivium and quadrivium, which had been excellent preparation intellectually and practically for a theocratic, agrarian community, no longer fit an industrializing republic. The result, after decades of innovation and experiment, was creation of a new undergraduate curriculum that would prepare its students for an industrial democracy. It is the curriculum that continues to the present, rooted in a structure of courses, disciplines, specialization, and breadth.

Today, as our society once again is being transformed, it is necessary to develop a new curriculum, and educational program that will prepare our students to live simultaneously in two societies, one dying and the other being born. Our current students are a transitional generation, and they need a curriculum that prepares them to assume the enormous responsibilities of building a new world while living in an old and rapidly changing society. The proposed curriculum is offered with the hope that it might achieve this purpose.

What is being suggested is not simply a formal set of courses. Indeed, each of the five curricular elements could be translated into a set of discrete courses. However, the five elements are interdependent and overlapping. For instance, the transitional skills could be translated into three different courses, one for each of the C's. That would be a mistake. It would be preferable to teach transitional skills as part of each of the other four elements. Similarly, values could be made into a freshman seminar or the senior capstone course of the nineteenth century college, but it would be more desirable to teach values across the entire curriculum. In a like manner, learning about individual roles could be an isolated set of subjects, but in reality these roles cannot be understood without the context that studying our shared environment provides.

Moreover, the proposed curriculum is not only about subject matter and contents, it is also about pedagogy. As noted earlier, there is a growing gap between how professors prefer to teach and how students best learn. This curriculum benefits from joining the two approaches, that is, marrying concrete and abstract knowledge acquired both through active and passive methods of learning. The classics need to be augmented with case studies, and the classroom needs to be supplemented with field experiences for this curriculum to work. One of the most potent approaches is to combine the very popular community service activities in which students are now involved with in-class instruction; that is, make service an integral part of the formal curriculum rather than just another extracurricular opportunity.

Furthermore, the education being proposed needs to go beyond the formal curriculum. The five elements can better be attained by infusing them throughout collegiate life. They should be underlined in the awards an institution gives, in the speakers who are invited to campus, in widely attended events such as orientation and graduation, in the publications an institution distributes, in the services students are provided, and in the activities in which students are involved. The cocurriculum is as powerful a vehicle for teaching these elements as the curriculum.

Colleges and universities cannot be expected to embrace this agenda alone. Government, churches, social organizations, and business can make an important contribution. They can do this by supporting community service programs for their constituents, members, and employees. Community service is one of the most effective methods we know for teaching hope, responsibility, appreciation of differences, and efficacy. The overwhelming majority of college students are already participating in service programs; they need to find ways to sustain their involvement beyond the college years. They also need to find ways to sustain or, better yet, enhance their sense of hope, responsibility, appreciation of differences, and efficacy after college. Without nourishment, these attributes dry up and die. With continual reinforcement, they just might empower a transitional generation and be passed on from that generation to their children.

REFERENCES

Adams, H. *The Education of Henry Adams.* (T.J. Adams, intro.). New York: Modern Library, 1931 (Originally published in 1918).

Altbach, P.G. *Student Politics in America: A Historical Analysis.* New York: McGraw-Hill, 1974.

Boyer, E.L. and Levine, A. *A Quest for Common Learning: The Aims of General Education.* Washington, D.C.: Carnegie Foundation for the Advancement of Teaching, 1981.

Burke, E. "Reflections on the Revolution in France." In R.J.S. Hoffman and P. Levack (eds.), *Burke's Politics: Selected Writings.* New York: Knopf, 1967 (Originally published in 1790).

Emerson, R.W. *Journals of Ralph Waldo Emerson* (E.W. Emerson and W.E. Forbes, eds.) Vol. 2. Boston: Houghton Mifflin, 1909.

Levine, A. *When Dreams and Heroes Died: A Portrait of Today's College Student.* San Francisco: Jossey-Bass, 1980.

Quinn, J.B. Conversation with Arthur Levine. Middlebury, Vt.: Middlebury College, 1992.

Russell, B. *Authority and the Individual.* New York: Simon & Schuster, 1949.

THINKING ABOUT THE READING

What is the significance of the title of this article, "When Hope and Fear Collide"? What do Levine and Cureton mean when they call today's college students a "transitional generation"? Examine the list of characteristics on page 258. Do you think these traits accurately characterize today's undergraduates? Do you feel, as the authors argue, that important institutions such as families, schools, churches, the media, and the government have failed you (the current generation of college students)? The authors identify five elements they think all universities should include in their curricula. Does your university provide any training in these areas? Although the authors, for the most part, paint a pessimistic picture of contemporary university life, they conclude that community service can be the key to renewing hope among college students. Do you agree? Does your university require or encourage community service? What role should such programs play in the overall curriculum?

The Overworked American

Juliet B. Schor

In the last twenty years the amount of time Americans have spent at their jobs has risen steadily. Each year the change is small, amounting to about nine hours, or slightly more than one additional day of work. In any given year, such a small increment has probably been imperceptible. But the accumulated increase over two decades is substantial. When surveyed, Americans report that they have only sixteen and a half hours of leisure a week, after the obligations of job and household are taken care of. Working hours are already longer than they were forty years ago. If present trends continue, . . . Americans will [soon] be spending as much time at their jobs as they did back in the nineteen twenties.

The rise of worktime was unexpected. For nearly a hundred years, hours had been declining. When this decline abruptly ended in the late 1940s, it marked the beginning of a new era in worktime. But the change was barely noticed. Equally surprising, but also hardly recognized, has been the deviation from Western Europe. After progressing in tandem for nearly a century, the United States veered off into a trajectory of declining leisure, while in Europe work has been disappearing. Forty years later, the differences are large. U.S. manufacturing employees currently work 320 more hours—the equivalent of over two months—than their counterparts in . . . Germany or France.

The decline in American's leisure time is in sharp contrast to the potential provided by the growth of productivity. Productivity measures the goods and services that result from each hour worked. When productivity rises, a worker can either produce the current output in less time, or remain at work the same number of hours and produce more. Every time productivity increases, we are presented with the possibility of either more free time or more money. That's the productivity dividend.

Since 1948, productivity has failed to rise in only five years. The level of productivity of the U.S. worker has more than doubled. In other words, we could now produce our 1948 standard of living (measured in terms of marketed goods and services) in less than half the time it took in that year. We actually could have chosen the four-hour day. Or a working year of six months. Or, *every worker in the United States could now be taking every other year off from work—with pay.* Incredible as it may sound, this is just the simple arithmetic of productivity growth in operation.

But between 1948 and the present we did not use any of the productivity dividend to reduce hours. . . . [By] 1990, the average American owned and consumed more than twice as much as he or she did in 1948, but also had less free time.[1]

How did this happen? Why has leisure been such a conspicuous casualty of prosperity? In part, the answer lies in the difference between the markets for consumer products and free time. Consider the former, the legendary American market. It is a veritable consumer's paradise, offering a dazzling array of products varying in style, design, quality, price, and country of origin. The consumer is treated to GM versus Toyota. Kenmore versus GE, Sony, or Magnavox, the Apple versus the IBM. We've got Calvin Klein, Anne Klein, Liz Claiborne, and Levi-Strauss; McDonald's, Burger King, and Colonel Sanders. Marketing experts and advertisers spend vast sums of money to make these choices appealing—even irresistible. And they have been successful. In cross-country comparisons, Americans have been found to spend more time shopping than anyone else. They also spend a higher fraction of the money they earn. And with the explosion of consumer debt, many are now spending what they haven't earned.

After four decades of this shopping spree, the American standard of living embodies a level of material comfort unprecedented in human history. The American home is more spacious and luxurious than the dwellings of any other nation. Food is cheap and abundant. The typical family owns a fantastic array of household and consumer appliances: we have machines to wash our clothes and dishes, mow our lawns, and blow away our snow. . . .

On the other hand, the "market" for free time hardly even exists in America. With few exceptions, employers (the sellers) don't offer the chance to trade off income gains for a shorter work day or the occasional sabbatical. They just pass on income, in the form of annual pay raises or bonuses, or, if granting increased vacation or personal days, usually do so unilaterally. Employees rarely have the chance to exercise an actual choice about how they will spend their productivity dividend. The closest substitute for a "market in leisure" is the travel and other leisure industries that advertise products to occupy our free time. But this indirect effect has been weak, as consumers crowd increasingly expensive leisure spending into smaller periods of time. . . .

Sleep has become another casualty of modern life. According to sleep researchers, studies point to a "sleep deficit" among Americans, a majority of whom are currently getting between 60 and 90 minutes less a night than they should for optimum health and performance. The number of people showing up at sleep disorder clinics with serious problems has skyrocketed in the last decade. Shiftwork, long working hours, the growth of a global economy (with its attendant continent-hopping and twenty-four-hour business culture), and the accelerating pace of life have all contributed to sleep deprivation. If you need an alarm clock, the experts warn, you're probably sleeping too little.

The juggling act between job and family is another problem area. Half the population now says they have too little time for their families. The problem is particularly acute for women: in one study, half of all employed mothers reported it caused either "a lot" or an "extreme" level of stress. The same proportion feel that "when I'm at home I try to make up to my family for being away at work and as a result I rarely have any time for myself." This stress has placed tremendous burdens on marriages. Two-earner couples have less time together, which researchers have found reduces the happiness and satisfaction of a marriage. These couples often just don't have enough time to talk to each other. And growing numbers of husbands and wives are like ships passing in the night, working sequential schedules to manage their child care. Among young parents, the prevalence of at least one partner working outside regular daytime hours is now close to one half. But this "solution" is hardly a happy one. According to one parent: "I work 11–7 to accommodate my family—to eliminate the need for babysitters. However, the stress on myself is tremendous."[2] . . .

Time Squeeze: The Extra Month of Work

Time squeeze has become big news. . . .The première episode of Jane Pauley's television show, "Real Life," highlighted a single father whose computer job was so demanding that he found himself at 2:00 A.M. dragging his child into the office. A Boston-area documentary featured the fourteen- to sixteen-hour workdays of a growing army of moonlighters. CBS's "Forty-Eight Hours" warned of the accelerating pace of life for everyone from high-tech business executives (for whom there are only two types of people—"the quick and the dead") to assembly workers at Japanese-owned automobile factories (where a car comes by every sixty seconds). Employees at fast-food restaurants, who serve in twelve seconds, report that the horns start honking if the food hasn't arrived in fifteen. Nineteen-year-olds work seventy-hour weeks, children are "penciled" into their parents' schedules, and second-graders are given "half an hour a day to unwind" from the pressure to get good grades so they can get into a good college. By the beginning of the 1990s, the time squeeze had become a national focus of attention, appearing in almost all the nation's major media outlets. . . .

At cutting-edge corporations, which emphasize commitment, initiative, and flexibility, the time demands are often the greatest. "People who work for me should have phones in their bathrooms," says the CEO from one aggressive American company. Recent research on managerial habits reveals that work has become positively absorbing. When a deadline approached in one corporation, "people who had been working twelve-hour days and Saturdays started to come in on Sunday, and instead of leaving at midnight, they would stay a few more hours. Some did not go home at all, and others had to look at their watches to remember what day it was." The recent growth in small businesses has also contributed to overwork. When Dolores Kordek started a dental insurance company, her strategy for survival was to work harder than the competition. So the office was open from 7 A.M. to 10 P.M. three hundred and sixty-five days a year. And she was virtually always in it.

This combination of retrenchment, economic competition, and innovative business management has raised hours substantially. One poll of senior executives found that weekly hours rose during the 1980s, and vacation time fell. Other surveys have yielded similar results. By the end of the decade, overwork at the upper echelons of the labor market had become endemic—and its scale was virtually unprecedented in living memory.

If the shortage of time had been confined to Wall Street or America's corporate boardrooms, it might have remained just a media curiosity. The number of people who work eighty hours a week and bring home—if they ever get there—a six-figure income is very small. But while the incomes of these rarefied individuals were out of

reach, their schedules turned out to be down right common. As Wall Street waxed industrious, the longer schedules penetrated far down the corporate ladder, through middle management, into the secretarial pool, and even onto the factory floor itself.[3] Millions of ordinary Americans fell victim to the shortage of time. . . .

A twenty-eight-year-old Massachusetts factory worker explains the bind many fathers are in: "Either I can spend time with my family, or support them—not both." Overtime or a second job is financially compelling: "I can work 8–12 hours overtime a week at time and a half, and that's when the real money just starts to kick in. . . . If I don't work the OT my wife would have to work much longer hours to make up the difference, and our day care bill would double. . . . The trouble is, the little time I'm home I'm too tired to have any fun with them or be any real help around the house." Among white-collar employees the problem isn't paid overtime, but the regular hours. To get ahead, or even just to hold on to a position, long days may be virtually mandatory.

Overwork is also rampant among the nation's poorly paid workers. At $5, $6, or even $7 an hour, annual earnings before taxes and deductions range from $10,000 to $14,000. Soaring rents alone have been enough to put many of these low earners in financial jeopardy. For the more than one-third of all workers now earning hourly wages of $7 and below, the pressure to lengthen hours has been inexorable. Valerie Connor, a nursing-home worker in Hartford, explains that "you just can't make it on one job." She and many of her co-workers have been led to work two eight-hour shifts a day. According to an official of the Service Employees International Union in New England, nearly one-third of their nursing-home employees now hold two full-time jobs. Changes in the low end of the labor market have also played a role. There is less full-time, stable employment. "Twenty hours here, thirty hours there, and twenty hours here. That's what it takes to get a real paycheck," says Domenic Bozzotto, president of Boston's hotel and restaurant workers union, whose members are drowning in a sea of work. Two-job families? Those were the good old days, he says. "We've got four-job families." . . .

More People Working

The mythical American family of the 1950s and 1960s was comprised of five people, only one of whom "worked"—or at least did what society called work. Dad went off to his job every morning, while Mom and the three kids stayed at home. Of course, the 1950s-style family was never as common as popular memory has made it out to be. Even in the 1950s and 1960s, about one-fourth of wives with children held paying jobs. The nostalgia surrounding the family is especially inaccurate for African-American women, whose rates of job holding have historically been higher than whites'. Even so, in recent years, the steady growth of married women's participation in the labor force has made the "working woman" the rule rather than the exception. By 1990, two-thirds of married American women were participating in the paid labor market. . . .

Female employment has justifiably received widespread attention: it is certainly the most significant development afoot. But the expansion of work effort in the American family is not occurring just among women. American youth are also working harder in a reversal of a long decline of teenage job holding, the result of increased schooling and economic prosperity. The likelihood that a teenager would hold a job began to rise in the mid-1960s, just as adult hours began their upward climb. By 1990, the labor force participation rate of teens had reached 53.7 percent, nearly 10 points higher than it had been twenty-five years earlier. . . .

Not only are more of the nation's young people working, but they are working longer hours. A 1989 nationwide sweep by government inspectors uncovered widescale abuses of child labor laws—violations of allowable hours, permissible activities, and ages of employment. Low-wage service sector establishments have been voracious in their appetite for teen labor,

especially in regions with shortages of adult workers. In middle-class homes, much of this work is motivated by consumerism: teenagers buy clothes, music, even cars. Some observers are worried that the desire to make money has become a compulsion, with many young Americans now working full-time, in addition to full-time school. A New Hampshire study found that 85 percent of the state's tenth- to twelfth-graders hold jobs, and 45 percent of them work more than twenty hours a week. At 10 P.M. on a school night, Carolyn Collignon is just beginning hour eight on her shift at Friendly's restaurant. Teachers report that students are falling asleep in class, getting lower grades, and cannot pursue after-school activities. Robert Pimentel works five days a week at Wendy's to pay off loans on his car and a $5,600 motorcycle, the purchase of which he now describes as a "bad move." Pimentel averages "maybe six hours of sleep a night. If you consider school a job, which it pretty much is, I put in a long day." He wants to go to college, but his grades have suffered.

This is the picture in suburban America. In large urban centers, such as New York and Los Angeles, the problem is more serious. Inspectors have found nineteenth-century-style sweatshops where poor immigrants—young girls of twelve years and above—hold daytime jobs, missing out on school altogether. And a million to a million and a half migrant farmworker children—some as young as three and four years—are at work in the nation's fields. These families cannot survive without the effort of all their members. . . .

So what's pushing up hours? One factor is moonlighting—the practice of holding more than one job at a time. Moonlighting is now more prevalent than at any time during the three decades for which we have statistics. As of May 1989, more than seven million Americans, or slightly over 6 percent of those employed, officially reported having two or more jobs, with extremely high increases occurring among women. The real numbers are higher, perhaps twice as high—as tax evasion, illegal activities, and employer disapproval of second jobs make people reluctant to speak honestly. The main impetus behind this extra work is financial. Close to one-half of those polled say they hold two jobs in order to meet regular household expenses or pay off debts. . . .

A second factor, operating largely on weekly hours, is that Americans are working more overtime. After the recession of the early 1980s, many companies avoided costly rehiring of workers and, instead, scheduled extra overtime. Among manufacturing employees, paid overtime hours rose substantially after the recession and, by the end of 1987, accounted for the equivalent of an additional five weeks of work per year. One automobile worker noted, "You have to work the hours, because a few months later they'll lay you off for a model changeover and you'll need the extra money when you're out of work. It never rains but it pours—either there's more than you can stand, or there isn't enough." While many welcome the chance to earn premium wages, the added effort can be onerous. Older workers are often compelled to stretch themselves, because many companies calculate pension benefits only on recent earnings. A fifty-nine-year-old male worker explains:

> Just at the point in my life where I was hoping I could ease up a little bit on the job and with the overtime, I find that I have to work harder than ever. If I'm going to have enough money when I retire, I have to put in five good years now with a lot of overtime because that is what they will base my pension on. With all the overtime I have to work to build my pension, I hope I live long enough to collect it.

[Apparently he didn't—he was diagnosed with incurable cancer not long after this interview.]

The Shrinking Vacation

One of the most notable developments of the 1980s [and 1990s] is that paid time off is actually shrinking. European workers have been gaining vacation time—minimum allotments are now in the range of four to five weeks in many coun-

tries—but Americans are losing it. In the last decade, U.S. workers have gotten *less* paid time off—on the order of three and a half fewer days each year of vacation time, holidays, sick pay, and other paid absences. . . .

Part of the shrinkage has been caused by the economic squeeze many companies faced in the 1980s [and 1990s]. Cost-cutting measures often included reductions in vacations and holidays. DuPont reduced its top vacation allotment from seven to four weeks and eliminated three holidays a year. Personnel departments also tightened up on benefits such as sick leave and bereavement time. As employees became more fearful about job loss, they spent less time away from the workplace. Days lost to illness fell dramatically. So did unpaid absences—which declined for the first time since 1973.

The other factor reducing vacations has been the restructuring of the labor market. Companies have turned to more "casual" workforces—firing long-term employees and signing on consultants, part-timers, or temporaries. Early retirements among senior workers also reduced vacation time. Because the length of vacations in this country is based on duration of employment, these changes have all contributed to lowering the amount of time off people actually receive. The growth of service sector occupations, where the duration of employment tends to be shortest, has also been a factor. . . .

Involuntary Leisure:
Underemployment and Unemployment

There is at least one group of Americans for whom time squeeze is not a problem. These are the millions who cannot get enough work or who cannot get any at all. They have plenty of "leisure" but can hardly enjoy it. One of the great ironies of our present situation is that overwork for the majority has been accompanied by the growth of enforced idleness for the minority. The proportion of the labor force who cannot work as many hours as they would like has more than doubled in the last twenty years. Just as surely as our economic system is "underproducing" leisure for some, it is "overproducing" it for others.

Declining industries provide poignant illustrations of the coexistence of long hours and unemployment. The manufacturing sector lost over a million jobs in the 1980s. At the same time (from 1980 to 1987), overtime hours rose by fifty per year. Many of those on permanent layoff watch their former co-workers put in steady overtime, week after week, year after year. Outside manufacturing, unemployment also rose steadily. At the height of each business expansion (1969, 1973, 1979, and 1987), the proportion of the labor force without a job was higher—rising from only 3.4 percent in 1969 to almost twice that—6.1 percent—in 1987.

Enforced idleness is not just confined to those who have been laid off. Underemployment is also growing. The fraction of the labor force working part-time but desiring full-time work increased more than seven times . . . [to] almost 17 percent. . . .

The trend toward underemployment and unemployment signals a disturbing failure of the labor market: the U.S. economy is increasingly unable to provide work for its population. It is all the more noticeable that growing idleness is occurring at a time when those who are fully employed are at their workplaces for ever longer hours. Like long hours, the growth of unemployment stems from the basic structure of the economy. Capitalist systems such as our own do not operate in order to provide employment. Their guiding principle is the pursuit of profitability. If profitability results in high employment, that is a happy coincidence for those who want jobs. If it does not, bottom-line oriented companies will not take it upon themselves to hire those their plans have left behind. . . . Full employment typically occurs only when government commits itself to the task. . . .

. . . Employers have strong incentives to keep hours long. And these incentives have been instrumental in raising hours and keeping them high. In retrospect, the reformers underestimated the obstacles within capitalism itself to solving both the nation's shortage of jobs and its shortage of time.

The Insidious Cycle of Work-and-Spend

Shop 'Til You Drop

We live in what may be the most consumer-oriented society in history. Americans spend three to four times as many hours a year shopping as their counterparts in Western European countries. Once a purely utilitarian chore, shopping has been elevated to the status of a national passion.

Shopping has become a leisure activity in its own right. Going to the mall is a common Friday or Saturday night's entertainment, not only for the teens who seem to live in them, but also for adults. Shopping is also the most popular weekday evening "out-of-home entertainment." And malls are everywhere. Four billion square feet of our total land area has been converted into shopping centers, or about 16 square feet for every American man, woman, and child. Actually, shopping is no longer confined to stores or malls but is permeating the entire geography. Any phone line is a conduit to thousands of products. Most homes are virtual retail outlets, with cable shopping channels, mail-order catalogues, toll-free numbers, and computer hookups. We can shop during lunch hour, from the office. We can shop while traveling, from the car. We can even shop in the airport, where video monitors have been installed for immediate on-screen purchasing.

Some of the country's most popular leisure activities have been turned into extended shopping expeditions. National parks, music concerts, and art museums are now acquisition opportunities. When the South Street Seaport Museum in New York City opened in the early 1980s as a combination museum-shopping center, its director explained the commercialization as a bow to reality: "The fact is that shopping is the chief cultural activity in the United States." Americans used to visit Europe to see the sights or meet the people. Now "Born to Shop" guides are replacing Fodor and Baedeker, complete with walking tours from Ferragamo to Fendi. Even island paradises, where we go "to get away from it all," are not immune: witness titles such as *Shopping in Exciting Australia and Papua New Guinea.*

Debt has been an important part of the shopping frenzy. Buying is easier when there's no requirement to pay immediately, and credit cards have seduced many people beyond their means: "I wanted to be able to pick up the tab for ten people, or take a cab when I wanted. I thought that part of being an adult was being able to go to a restaurant, look at the menu, and go in if you like the food, not because you're looking at the prices." This young man quickly found himself with $18,000 of credit card debt, and realized that he and his wife "could have gone to Europe last year on [the] interest alone." For some people, shopping has become an addiction, like alcohol or drugs. "Enabled" by plastic, compulsive shoppers spend money they don't have on items they absolutely "can't" do without and never use. The lucky ones find their way to self-help groups like Debtors Anonymous and Shopaholics Limited. And for every serious compulsive shopper, there are many more with mild habits. Linda Weltner was lucky enough to keep her addiction within manageable financial bounds, but still her "mindless shopping" grew into a "troubling preoccupation . . . which was impoverishing [her] life." . . .

The Pitfalls of Consumerism

The consumerism that took root in the 1920s was premised on the idea of *dis*satisfaction. As much as one has, it is never enough. The implicit mentality is that the next purchase will yield happiness, and then the next. In the words of the baby-boom writer, Katy Butler, it was the new couch, the quieter street, and the vacation cottage. Yet happiness turned out to be elusive. Today's luxuries became tomorrow's necessities, no longer appreciated. When the Joneses also got

a new couch or a second home, these acquisitions were no longer quite as satisfying. Consumerism turned out to be full of pitfalls—a vicious pattern of wanting and spending which failed to deliver on its promises.

The inability of the consumerist life style to create durable satisfaction can be seen in the syndrome of "keeping up with the Joneses." This competition is based on the fact that it is not the absolute level of consumption that matters, but how much one consumes relative to one's peers. The great English economist John Maynard Keynes made this distinction over fifty years ago: "[Needs] fall into two classes—those which are absolute in the sense that we feel them whatever the situation of our fellow human beings may be, and those which are relative only in that their satisfaction lifts us above, makes us feel superior to, our fellows." Since then, economists have invented a variety of terms for "keeping up with the Joneses": "relative income or consumption," "positional goods," or "local status." A brand-new Toyota Corolla may be a luxury and status symbol in a lower-middle-class town, but it appears paltry next to the BMWs and Mercedes that fill the driveways of the fancy suburb. A 10-percent raise sounds great until you find that your co-workers all got 12 percent. The cellular phone, fur coat, or _____ (fill in the blank) gives a lot of satisfaction only before everyone else has one. In the words of one . . . investment banker: "You tend to live up to your income level. You see it in relation to the people of your category. They're living in a certain way and you want to live in that way. You keep up with other people of your situation who have also leveraged themselves."

Over time, keeping up with the Joneses becomes a real trap—because the Joneses also keep up with you. If everyone's income goes up by 10 percent, then relative positions don't change at all. No satisfaction is gained. The more of our happiness we derive from comparisons with others, the less additional welfare we get from general increases in income—which is probably why happiness has failed to keep pace with economic growth. This dynamic may be only partly conscious. We may not even be aware that we are competing with the Joneses, or experience it as a competition. It may be as simple as the fact that exposure to their latest "life-style upgrade" plants the seed in our own mind that we must have it, too—whether it be a European vacation, this year's fashion statement, or piano lessons for the children.

In the choice between income and leisure, the quest for relative standing has biased us toward income. That's because status comparisons have been mostly around commodities—cars, clothing, houses, even second houses. If Mrs. Jones works long hours, she will be able to buy the second home, the designer dresses, or the fancier car. If her neighbor Mrs. Smith opts for more free time instead, her two-car garage and walk-in closet will be half empty. As long as the competition is more oriented to visible commodities, the tendency will be for both women to prefer income to time off. But once they both spend the income, they're back to where they started. Neither is *relatively* better off. If free time is less of a "relative" good than other commodities, then true welfare could be gained by having more of it, and worrying less about what the Joneses are buying.

It's not easy to get off the income treadmill and into a new, more leisured life style. Mrs. Smith won't do it on her own, because it'll set her back in comparison to Mrs. Jones. And Mrs. Jones is just like Mrs. Smith. . . . We also know their employers won't initiate a shift to more leisure, because they prefer employees to work long hours.

A second vicious cycle arises from the fact that the satisfactions gained from consumption are often short-lived. For many, consumption can be habit forming. Like drug addicts who develop a tolerance, consumers need additional hits to maintain any given level of satisfaction. The switch from black and white to color television was a real improvement when it occurred. But soon viewers became habituated to color. Going back to black and white would have reduced well-being, but having color may not have yielded a permanently higher level of satisfac-

tion. Telephones are another example. Rotary dialing was a major improvement. Then came touch-tone, which made us impatient with rotaries. Now numbers are preprogrammed and some people begin to find any dialing a chore.

Our lives are filled with goods to which we have become so habituated that we take them for granted. Indoor plumbing was once a great luxury—and still is in much of the world. Now it is so ingrained in our life style that we don't give it a second thought. The same holds true for all but the newest household appliances—stoves, refrigerators, and vacuum cleaners are just part of the landscape. We may pay great attention to the kind of automobile we drive, but the fact of having a car is something adults grew accustomed to long ago. . . .

. . . The consumption traps I have described are just the flip side of the bias toward long hours embedded in the production system. We are not merely caught in a pattern of spend-and-spend—the problem identified by many critics of consumer culture. The whole story is that we work, and spend, and work and spend some more.

Causes of the Work-and-Spend Cycle

The irony in all the consuming Americans do is that, when asked, they reject materialist values. The Gallup Poll recently asked respondents to choose what was most important to them—family life, betterment of society, physical health, a strict moral code, and so on. Among a list of nine, the materialist option—"having a nice home, car and other belongings"—ranked *last*. In a second survey, respondents ranked "having nice things" twenty-sixth in a list of twenty-eight. . . . Over two-thirds of the population says it would "welcome less emphasis money." Yet behavior is often contrary to these stated values. Millions of working parents see their children or spouses far less than they should or would like to. "Working" mothers complain they have no time for themselves. Volunteer work is on the decline, presumably because people have little time for it. Employed Americans spend long hours at jobs that are adversely affecting their health—through injury, occupationally induced diseases, and stress. My explanation for this paradoxical behavior is that people are operating under a powerful set of constraints: they are trapped by the cycle of work-and-spend.

Work-and-spend is driven by productivity growth. Whether the annual increment is 3 percent, as it was for much of the postwar period, or less, as it has been in recent years, growth in productivity provides the chance either to raise income or to reduce working hours. This is where the cycle begins, with the employer's reaction to the choice between "time and money." Usually a company does not offer this choice to its employees but unilaterally decides to maintain existing hours and give a pay increase instead. As we have seen, for forty years, only a negligible portion of productivity increase has been channeled into free time. Using productivity to raise incomes has become the firmly entrenched "default option." . . .

Once a pay increase is granted, it sets off the consumption cycles I have described. The additional income will be spent. . . . The employee will become habituated to this spending and incorporate it into his or her usual standard of living. Gaining free time by *reducing* income becomes undesirable, both because of relative comparisons (Joneses versus Smiths) and habit formation. The next year, when another increase in productivity occurs, the process starts again. The company offers income, which the employee spends and becomes accustomed to. This interpretation is consistent with the history of the last half-century. Annual productivity growth has made possible higher incomes or more free time. Repeatedly, the bulk of the productivity increase has been channeled into the former. Consumption has kept pace. . . .

The Social Nature of Work-and-Spend

Part of the power of the work-and-spend cycle is its social pervasiveness. Although individuals are the proximate decision makers, their actions are influenced and constrained by social norms and conventions. The social character of the cycle of work-and-spend means that individuals have a hard time breaking out of it on their own. This is part of why, despite evidence of growing desires for less demanding jobs and disillusionment with "work-and-spend," hours are still rising.

To see the difficulties individuals have in deviating from the status quo, consider what would happen to an ordinary couple who have grown tired of the rat race. John and Jane Doe, like nearly half of all Americans, want more time to spend with their children and each other. What will happen if they both decide to reduce their hours by half and are willing to live on half their usual earnings?

The transition will be most abrupt for John. Few men work part-time, with the exception of teens, students, and some seniors. Among males aged twenty-five to forty-four, virtually none . . . voluntarily choose part-time schedules. Most report that they are not able to reduce their hours of work at all. And of those who do have the freedom to work fewer hours, it is likely that only a small percentage can reduce hours by as much as half. Unless John has truly unusual talents, his employer will probably refuse to sanction a change to part-time work. Chances are he'll have to find a new job.

Given the paucity of part-time jobs for men, John's choices will be limited. It will be almost impossible to secure a position in a managerial, professional, or administrative capacity. Most part-time jobs are in the service sector. When he does land a job, his pay will fall far short of what he earned in full-time work. The median hourly wage rate among male workers is about $10.50, with weekly earnings of $450. As a part-time worker paid by the hour, his median wage will be about $4, or $80 a week. He will also lose many of the benefits that went with his full-time job. Only 15 percent of part-time workers are given health insurance.[4] The total income loss John will suffer is likely to exceed 80 percent. Under these conditions, part-time work hardly seems feasible.

The social nature of John's choice is revealed by the drama of his attempt to go against the grain. Since few adult men choose part-time work, there is almost none to be had. The social convention of full-time work gives the individual little choice about it. Those who contemplate a shift to part-time will be deterred by the economic penalty. There may even be many who would prefer shorter hours, but they will exert very little influence on the actual choices available, because their desires are latent. Exit from existing jobs—one channel for influencing the market—is not available, because they cannot find part-time jobs to exit to. Unless people begin to speak up and collectively demand that employers provide alternatives, they will probably remain trapped in full-time work.

Jane's switch to part-time will be less traumatic. She will find more job possibilities, because more women work part-time. Her earnings loss will be less, because women are already discriminated against in full-time work. . . . If Jane can get health insurance through John's employment, part-time work may be feasible. But a great deal depends on his earnings and benefits. Even under the best of assumptions, Jane will have to forgo a wide variety of occupations, including most of those with the best pay and working conditions. She will most likely be relegated to the bottom part of the female labor market—the service, sales, and clerical jobs where the majority of women part-timers reside. Social convention and the economic incentives it creates will reproduce inequalities of gender. Despite their original intentions, Jane, rather than John, will end up in part-time employment.

These are the obstacles on the labor market side—low wages, few benefits, and severe limitations on choice of occupations. The dominance of full-time jobs also has effects on the consumption side. Imagine that Jane and John still want to cut back their hours, even under the adverse circumstances I have described. Their income will now be very low, and they will be forced to economize greatly on their purchases. This will affect their ability to fit in socially. As half-time workers, they will find many social occasions too expensive (lunches and dinners out, movies). At first, friends will be understanding,

but eventually the clash in life styles will create a social gap. Their children will have social difficulties if they don't have access to common after-school activities or the latest toys and clothes. They'll drop off the birthday party circuit because they can't afford to bring gifts. We can even see these pressures with full-time workers, as parents take on extra employment to live up to neighborhood standards. After her divorce Celeste Henderson worked two jobs to give her children the things their schoolmates had. Ms. Henderson's daughter says her mother "saved her the embarrassment of looking poor to the other children."[5] For a family with only part-time workers, the inability to consume in the manner of their peers is likely to lead to some social alienation. Unless they have a community of others in similar circumstances, dropping down will include an element of dropping out. Many Americans, especially those with children, are not willing to risk such a fate.

Even with careful budgeting, a couple like the Does may have trouble procuring the basics (housing, food, and clothing), because the U.S. standard of living is geared to at least one full-time income and, increasingly, to two. Rents will be high relative to the Does' income. In part, this is because of price increases in the last decade. But there is also a more fundamental impediment. As I have argued, contemporary houses and apartments are large and luxurious. They have indoor plumbing, central heating, stoves, and refrigerators. They have expensive features such as closets, garages, and individual bedrooms. In our society, housing must conform to legal and social conventions that define the acceptable standard of housing. The difficulty is that the social norm prevailing in the housing market is matched to a full-time income (or incomes). It is not only that the cost of living is high these days. It is also that bare-bones housing, affordable on only half a salary, is rare. Even if the Does were willing to go without closets, garages, and central heating in order to save money, they would be hard-pressed to find such a dwelling.

This problem is common to many goods and services. In an economy where nearly everyone works full-time, manufacturers cater to the purchasing power of the full-time income. There is a limited market for products that are desired only by those with half an income. A whole range of cheap products are not even available. Only the better-quality goods will be demanded, and hence only they will be produced. We can see this phenomenon in the continual upscaling of products. We've gone from blender to Cuisinart, from polyester to cotton, from one-speed Schwinn to fancy trail bike. Remember the things that were available forty years ago but have disappeared? The semiautomatic washing machine. The hand-driven coffee grinder. The rotary dial telephone. For those who are skeptical about this point, consider the markets of poor countries. In India, one can find very cheap, low-quality clothing—at a fraction of the price of the least expensive items in the United States. Semiautomatic washers and stripped-down cars are the norm. On a world scale, the American consumer market is very upscale, which means that Americans need an upscale income to participate in it.

The strength of social norms does not mean that the nature of work cannot be changed. Part-time employment *could* become a viable option for larger numbers of people. But the existence of social norms suggests that change will not come about . . . [without] intervention on a social level—from government, unions, professional associations, and other collective organizations. . . .

[Although] most Americans may find it hard to understand that such changes are in their interest, many who have made them are confident that getting off the consumer treadmill yields a deeper and truer sense of well-being. When Linda Weltner, a former shopping addict, stopped buying, she didn't "suffer pangs of self-denial" but felt "filled to the brim." Her life has become far richer. And not only will we help ourselves. Forswearing a bankrupting consumerist path, the new consumer of the twenty-first century will be in a far better position to address issues of global inequality and move us off our current collision course with nature. But to do these things, we must be open to major changes in how we run our businesses, households, and the connections between them. And we must organize ourselves to make those changes happen—in spite of all-too-certain opposition from those who benefit from the status quo. . . .

NOTES

1. These are from my calculations of total working hours per capita and per labor force from the National Income and Product Accounts. Between 1948 and 1969, per-capita hours rose from 1,069 to 1,124, or 55 hours. Annual hours per labor force participant fell slightly—from 1,968 to 1,944 hours. . . .

On a per-person basis, gross national product went from $9,060 in 1948 to $19,900 at the end of 1988 (measured in constant 1988 dollars). See *ERP*, 1989 ed., 308, table B–1 and 344, table B–32.

2. MassMutual Family Values Study. (Washington, D.C.: Mellman & Lazarus, 1989), 3, on families and time.

Diane S. Burden and Bradley Googins, *Boston University Balancing Job and Homelife Study* (Boston University: mimeo, 1987), 26, on women and stress.

"When I'm at home," from Harris, *Inside America*, 95.

Paul Williams Kingston and Steven L. Nock, "Time Together Among Dual-Earner Couples," *American Sociological Review,* 52 (June 1987): 391–400. See also Arlie Hochschild, *The Second Shift: Working Parents and the Revolution at Home* (New York: Viking Penguin, 1989).

Harriet Presser, "Shift Work and Child Care Among Young Dual-Earner American Parents," *Journal of Marriage and the Family* 50, 1 (February 1988): 133–48. This figure is for couples in which the wife works full time. Among part-timers, the proportion is over one-half.

Quote from Parents United for Child Care (PUCC) survey comments, mimeo, Boston, Massachusetts, 1989.

3. See Amanda Bennett, *The Death of the Organization Man* (New York: William Morrow, 1990), and Rosabeth Moss Kanter's *When Giants Learn to Dance* (New York: Simon & Schuster, 1989), chap. 10, p. 275, for evidence from case-study research on individual companies.

4. Median wage rate from Mishel and Frankel, *Working America,* 79, table 3.6.

Eighty percent of part-timers are paid by the hour. Earl F. Mellor and Steven E. Haugen, "Hourly Paid Workers: Who They Are and What They Earn," *Monthly Labor Review* (February 1986): 21–22, tables 1 and 2.

Health insurance data pertain to those who work 19 or fewer hours a week. Diane S. Rothberg and Barbara Ensor Cook, *Employee Benefits for Part-Timers,* 2nd ed. (McLean, Va.: Association of Part-Time Professionals, 1987), 6, table 4. Among workers at 20 to 29 hours, 49 percent have medical benefits.

5. Quoted in Peter T. Kilborn, "For Many Women, One Job Just Isn't Enough," *New York Times,* 15 February 1990.

REFERENCES

Bennett, Amanda. *The Death of the Organization Man.* New York: William Morrow, 1990.

Burden, Diane S., and Googins, Bradley. *Boston University Balancing Job and Homelife Study.* Boston University, 1987, Mimeographed.

Economic Report of the President. Washington, D.C.: Government Printing Office, 1989 and 1991.

Harris, Louis. *Inside America.* New York: Vintage, 1987.

Hochschild, Arlie. *The Second Shift: Working Parents and the Revolution at Home.* New York: Viking Penguin, 1989.

Kanter, Rosabeth Moss. *When Giants Learn to Dance: Mastering the Challenge of Strategy, Management and Careers in the 1990s.* New York: Simon & Schuster, 1989.

Kilborn, Peter T. "For Many Women, One Job Isn't Enough." *New York Times,* 15 February 1990.

Kingston, Paul Williams, and Nock, Steven L. "Time Together Among Dual-Earner Couples." *American Sociological Review* 52 (June 1987): 391–400.

MassMutual Family Values Study. Washington, D.C.: Mellman & Lazarus, 1989.

Mellor, Earl F., and Haugen, Steven E. "Hourly Paid Workers: Who They Are and What They Earn." *Monthly Labor Review* 109 (February 1986): 20–26.

Mishel, Lawrence, and Frankel, David M. *The State of Working America.* Armonk, N.Y.: M. E. Sharpe, 1990–91 Edition.

Parents United for Child Care (PUCC). Survey comments, Boston, Massachusetts, 1989. Mimeographed.

Presser, Harriet. "Shift Work and Child Care Among Young Dual-Earner American Parents." *Journal of Marriage and the Family* 50 (February 1988): 133–48.

Rothberg, Dianne S., and Cook, Barbara Ensor. *Employee Benefits for Part-Timers.* McLean, Va.: Association of Part-Time Professionals, 1987.

THINKING ABOUT THE READING

Schor argues that American workers are working longer hours because they want more money to buy things. Arlie Hochschild in Chapter 8 argued that people work more because the workplace has become a more nurturing and enjoyable place to be than the home. Who do you think is right? Can they both be? Why is the trend toward working longer hours among U.S. workers so different from the trend among western European workers of wanting more leisure time? What role do other social institutions play in perpetuating this trend? Schor originally wrote this piece almost 10 years ago. Do you think the situation she describes (increasing work hours coupled with decreasing leisure time) has gotten better, worse, or stayed the same in the past decade? (You may use your own work experiences to help answer this question.) Is this condition something that individuals can remedy on their own or is it something that requires societal-level changes carried out by corporations or by the government?

The Smile Factory
Work at Disneyland

John Van Maanen

Part of Walt Disney Enterprises includes the theme park Disneyland. In its pioneering form in Anaheim, California, this amusement center has been a consistent money maker since the gates were first opened in 1955. Apart from its sociological charm, it has, of late, become something of an exemplar for culture vultures and has been held up for public acclaim in several best-selling publications as one of America's top companies. . . . To outsiders, the cheerful demeanor of its employees, the seemingly inexhaustible repeat business it generates from its customers, the immaculate condition of park grounds, and, more generally, the intricate physical and social order of the business itself appear wondrous.

Disneyland as the self-proclaimed "Happiest Place on Earth" certainly occupies an enviable position in the amusement and entertainment worlds as well as the commercial world in general. Its product, it seems, is emotion—"laughter and well-being." Insiders are not bashful about promoting the product. Bill Ross, a Disneyland executive, summarizes the corporate position nicely by noting that "although we focus our attention on profit and loss, day-in and day-out we cannot lose sight of the fact that this is a feeling business and we make our profits from that."

The "feeling business" does not operate, however, by management decree alone. Whatever services Disneyland executives believe they are providing to the 60 to 70 thousand visitors per day that flow through the park during its peak summer season, employees at the bottom of the organization are the ones who most provide them. The work-a-day practices that employees adopt to amplify or dampen customer spirits are therefore a core concern of this feeling business. The happiness trade is an interactional one. It rests partly on the symbolic resources put into place by history and park design but it also rests on an animated workforce that is more or less eager to greet the guests, pack the trams, push the buttons, deliver the food, dump the garbage, clean the streets, and, in general, marshal the will to meet and perhaps exceed customer expectations. False moves, rude words, careless disregard, detected insincerity, or a sleepy and bored presence can all undermine the enterprise and ruin a sale. The smile factory has its rules.

It's a Small World

. . . This rendition is of course abbreviated and selective. I focus primarily on such matters as the stock appearance (vanilla), status order (rigid), and social life (full), and swiftly learned codes of conduct (formal and informal) that are associated with Disneyland ride operators. These employees comprise the largest category of hourly workers on the payroll. During the summer months, they number close to four thousand and run the 60-odd rides and attractions in the park.

Author's Note: This paper has been cobbled together using three-penny nails of other writings. Parts come from a paper presented to the American Anthropological Association Annual Meetings in Washington D.C. on November 16, 1989 called "Whistle While You Work." Other parts come from J. Van Maanen and G. Kunda, 1989. "Real feelings: Emotional expressions and organization culture." In B. Staw & L. L. Cummings (Eds.), *Research in Organization Behavior* (Vol. 11, pp. 43–103). Greenwich, CT: JAI Press. In coming to this version, I've had a good deal of help from my friends Steve Barley, Nicloe Biggart, Michael Owen Jones, Rosanna Hertz, Gideon Kunda, Joanne Martin, Maria Lydia Spinelli, Bob Sutton, and Bob Thomas.

They are also a well-screened bunch. There is—among insiders and outsiders alike—a rather fixed view about the social attributes carried by the standard-make Disneyland ride operator. Single, white males and females in their early twenties, without facial blemish, of above average height and below average weight, with straight teeth, conservative grooming standards, and a chin-up, shoulder-back posture radiating the sort of good health suggestive of a recent history in sports are typical of these social identifiers. There are representative minorities on the payroll but because ethnic displays are sternly discouraged by management, minority employees are rather close copies of the standard model Disneylander, albeit in different colors.

This Disneyland look is often a source of some amusement to employees who delight in pointing out that even the patron saint, Walt himself, could not be hired today without shaving off his trademark pencil-thin mustache. But, to get a job in Disneyland and keep it means conforming to a rather exacting set of appearance rules. These rules are put forth in a handbook on the Disney image in which readers learn, for example, that facial hair or long hair is banned for men as are aviator glasses and earrings and that women must not tease their hair, wear fancy jewelry, or apply more than a modest dab of makeup. Both men and women are to look neat and prim, keep their uniforms fresh, polish their shoes, and maintain an upbeat countenance and light dignity to complement their appearance—no low spirits or cornball raffishness at Disneyland.

The legendary "people skills" of park employees, so often mentioned in Disneyland publicity and training materials, do not amount to very much according to ride operators. Most tasks require little interaction with customers and are physically designed to practically insure that is the case. The contact that does occur typically is fleeting and swift, a matter usually of only a few seconds. In the rare event sustained interaction with customers might be required, employees are taught to deflect potential exchanges to area supervisors or security. A Training Manual offers the proper procedure: "On misunderstandings, guests should be told to call City Hall. . . . In everything from damaged cameras to physical injuries, don't discuss anything with guests . . . there will always be one of us nearby." Employees learn quickly that security is hidden but everywhere. On Main Street security cops are Keystone Kops; in Frontierland, they are Town Marshalls; on Tom Sawyer's Island, they are Cavalry Officers, and so on.

Occasionally, what employees call "line talk" or "crowd control" is required of them to explain delays, answer direct questions, or provide directions that go beyond the endless stream of recorded messages coming from virtually every nook and cranny of the park. Because such tasks are so simple, consisting of little more than keeping the crowd informed and moving, it is perhaps obvious why management considers the sharp appearance and wide smile of employees so vital to park operations. There is little more they could ask of ride operators whose main interactive tasks with visitors consist of being, in their own terms, "information booths," "line signs," "pretty props," "shepherds," and "talking statues."

A few employees do go out of their way to initiate contact with Disneyland customers but, as a rule, most do not and consider those who do to be a bit odd. In general, one need do little more than exercise common courtesy while looking reasonably alert and pleasant. Interactive skills that are advanced by the job have less to do with making customers feel warm and welcome than they do with keeping each other amused and happy. This is, of course, a more complex matter.

Employees bring to the job personal badges of status that are of more than passing interest to peers. In rough order, these include: good looks, college affiliation, career aspirations, past achievements, age (directly related to status up to about age 23 or 24 and inversely related thereafter), and assorted other idiosyncratic matters. Nested closely alongside these imported status badges are organizational ones that are also of concern and value to employees.

Where one works in the park carries much social weight. Postings are consequential because the ride and area a person is assigned provide rewards and benefits beyond those of wages. In-the-park stature for ride operators turns partly on whether or not unique skills are required. Disneyland neatly complements labor market theorizing on this dimension because employees with the most differentiated skills find themselves at the top of the internal status ladder, thus making their loyalties to the organization more predictable.

Ride operators, as a large but distinctly middle-class group of hourly employees on the floor of the organization, compete for status not only with each other but also with other employee groupings whose members are hired for the season from the same applicant pool. A loose approximation of the rank ordering among these groups can be constructed as follows:

1. The upper-class prestigious Disneyland Ambassadors and Tour Guides (bilingual young women in charge of ushering—some say rushing—little bands of tourists through the park);
2. Ride operators performing coveted "skilled work" such as live narrations or tricky transportation tasks like those who symbolically control customer access to the park and drive the costly entry vehicles (such as the antique trains, horse-drawn carriages, and Monorail);
3. All other ride operators;
4. The proletarian Sweepers (keepers of the concrete grounds);
5. The sub-prole or peasant status Food and Concession workers (whose park sobriquets reflect their lowly social worth—"pancake ladies," "peanut pushers," "coke blokes," "suds divers," and the seemingly irreplaceable "soda jerks").

Pay differentials are slight among these employee groups. The collective status adheres, as it does internally for ride operators, to assignment or functional distinctions. As the rank order suggests, most employee status goes to those who work jobs that require higher degrees of special skill, relative freedom from constant and direct supervision, and provide the opportunity to organize and direct customer desires and behavior rather than to merely respond to them as spontaneously expressed.

The basis for sorting individuals into these various broad bands of job categories is often unknown to employees—a sort of deep, dark secret of the casting directors in personnel. When prospective employees are interviewed, they interview for "a job at Disneyland," not a specific one. Personnel decides what particular job they will eventually occupy. Personal contacts are considered by employees as crucial in this job-assignment process as they are in the hiring decision. Some employees, especially those who wind up in the lower ranking jobs, are quite disappointed with their assignments as is the case when, for example, a would-be Adventureland guide is posted to a New Orleans Square restaurant as a pot scrubber. Although many of the outside acquaintances of our pot scrubber may know only that he works at Disneyland, rest assured, insiders will know immediately where he works and judge him accordingly.

Uniforms are crucial in this regard for they provide instant communication about the social merits or demerits of the wearer within the little world of Disneyland workers. Uniforms also correspond to a wider status ranking that casts a significant shadow on employees of all types. Male ride operators on the Autopia wear, for example, untailored jump-suits similar to pit mechanics and consequently generate about as much respect from peers as the grease-stained outfits worn by pump jockeys generate from real motorists in gas stations. The ill-fitting and homogeneous "whites" worn by Sweepers signify lowly institutional work tinged, perhaps, with a reminder of hospital orderlies rather than street cleanup crews. On the other hand, for males, the crisp, officer-like Monorail operator stands alongside the swashbuckling Pirate of the Caribbean, the casual cowpoke of Big Thunder Mountain, or the smartly vested Riverboat pilot as carriers of valued symbols in and outside the park. Employees lust for these higher status positions and the rights to small advantages such uniforms provide. A lively internal labor market exists wherein there is much scheming for the more prestigious assignments.

For women, a similar market exists although the perceived "sexiness" of uniforms, rather than social rank, seems to play a larger role. To wit, the rather heated antagonisms that developed years ago when the ride "It's a Small World" first opened and began outfitting the ride operators with what were felt to be the shortest skirts and most revealing blouses in the park. Tour Guides, who traditionally headed the fashion vanguard at Disneyland in their above-the-knee kilts, knee socks, tailored vests, black English hats, and smart riding crops were apparently appalled at being upstaged by their social inferiors and lobbied actively (and, judging by the results, successfully) to lower the skirts, raise the necklines, and generally remake their Small World rivals.

Important, also, to ride operators are the break schedules followed on the various rides. The more the better. Work teams develop inventive ways to increase the number of "time-outs" they take during the work day. Most rides are organized on a rotational basis (e.g., the operator moving from a break, to queue monitor, to turnstile overseer, to unit loader, to traffic controller, to driver, and, again, to a break). The number of break men or women on a rotation (or ride) varies by the number of employees on duty and by the number of units on line. Supervisors, foremen, and operators also vary as to what they regard as appropriate break standards (and, more importantly, as to the value of the many situational factors that can enter the calculation of break rituals—crowd size, condition of ride, accidents, breakdowns, heat, operator absences, special occasions, and so forth). Self-monitoring teams with sleepy supervisors and lax (or savvy) foremen can sometimes manage a shift comprised of 15 minutes on and 45 minutes off each hour. They are envied by others, and rides that have such a potential are eyed hungrily by others who feel trapped by their more rigid (and observed) circumstances.

Movement across jobs is not encouraged by park management, but some does occur (mostly within an area and job category). Employees claim that a sort of "once a sweeper, always a sweeper" rule obtains but all know of at least a few exceptions to prove the rule. The exceptions offer some (not much) hope for those working at the social margins of the park and perhaps keep them on the job longer than might otherwise be expected. Dishwashers can dream of becoming Pirates, and with persistence and a little help from their friends, such dreams just might come true next season (or the next).

These examples are precious, perhaps, but they are also important. There is an intricate pecking order among very similar categories of employees. Attributes of reward and status tend to cluster, and there is intense concern about the cluster to which one belongs (or would like to belong). To a degree, form follows function in Disneyland because the jobs requiring the most abilities and offering the most interest also offer the most status and social reward. Interaction patterns reflect and sustain this order. Few Ambassadors or Tour Guides, for instance, will stoop to speak at length with Sweepers who speak mostly among themselves or to Food workers. Ride operators, between the poles, line up in ways referred to above with only ride proximity (i.e., sharing a break area) representing a potentially significant intervening variable in the interaction calculation. . . .

Paid employment at Disneyland begins with the much renowned University of Disneyland whose faculty runs a day-long orientation program (Traditions I) as part of a 40-hour apprenticeship program, most of which takes place on the rides. In the classroom, however, newly hired ride operators are given a very thorough introduction to matters of managerial concern and are tested on their absorption of famous Disneyland fact, lore, and procedure. Employee demeanor is governed, for example, by three rules:

First, we practice the friendly smile.

Second, we use only friendly and courteous phrases.

Third, we are not stuffy—the only Misters in Disneyland are Mr. Toad and Mr. Smee.

Employees learn too that the Disneyland culture is officially defined. The employee handbook put it in this format:

Dis-ney Cor-po-rate Cul-ture (diz'ne kor'pr'it kul'cher) *n* 1. Of or pertaining to the Disney organization, as a: the philosophy underlying all business decisions; b: the commitment of top leadership and management to that philosophy; c: the actions taken by individual cast members that reinforce the image.

Language is also a central feature of university life, and new employees are schooled in its proper use. Customers at Disneyland are, for instance, never referred to as such, they are "guests." There are no rides at Disneyland, only "attractions." Disneyland itself is a "Park," not an amusement center, and it is divided into "backstage," "on-stage," and "staging" regions. Law enforcement personnel hired by the park are not policemen, but "security hosts." Employees do not wear uniforms but check out fresh "costumes" each working day from "wardrobe." And, of course, there are no accidents at Disneyland, only "incidents." . . .

The university curriculum also anticipates probable questions ride operators may someday face from customers, and they are taught the approved public response. A sample:

Question (posed by trainer): What do you tell a guest who requests a rain check?
Answer (in three parts): We don't offer rain checks at Disneyland because (1) the main attractions are all indoors; (2) we would go broke if we offered passes; and (3) sunny days would be too crowded if we gave passes.

Shrewd trainees readily note that such an answer blissfully disregards the fact that waiting areas of Disneyland are mostly outdoors and that there are no subways in the park to carry guests from land to land. Nor do they miss the economic assumption concerning the apparent frequency of Southern California rains. They discuss such matters together, of course, but rarely raise them in the training classroom. In most re-

spects, these are recruits who easily take the role of good student.

Classes are organized and designed by professional Disneyland trainers who also instruct a well-screened group of representative hourly employees straight from park operations on the approved newcomer training methods and materials. New-hires seldom see professional trainers in class but are brought on board by enthusiastic peers who concentrate on those aspects of park procedure thought highly general matters to be learned by all employees. Particular skill training (and "reality shock") is reserved for the second wave of socialization occurring on the rides themselves as operators are taught, for example, how and when to send a mock bobsled caroming down the track or, more delicately, the proper ways to stuff an obese adult customer into the midst of children riding the Monkey car on the Casey Jones Circus Train or, most problematically, what exactly to tell an irate customer standing in the rain who, in no uncertain terms, wants his or her money back and wants it back now.

During orientation, considerable concern is placed on particular values the Disney organization considers central to its operations. These values range from the "customer is king" verities to the more or less unique kind, of which "everyone is a child at heart when at Disneyland" is a decent example. This latter piety is one few employees fail to recognize as also attaching to everyone's mind as well after a few months of work experience. Elaborate checklists of appearance standards are learned and gone over in the classroom and great efforts are spent trying to bring employee emotional responses in line with such standards. Employees are told repeatedly that if they are happy and cheerful at work, so, too, will the guests at play. Inspirational films, hearty pep talks, family imagery, and exemplars of corporate performance are all representative of the strong symbolic stuff of these training rites. . . .

Yet, like employees everywhere, there is a limit to which such overt company propaganda can be effective. Students and trainers both seem to agree on where the line is drawn, for there is much satirical banter, mischievous winking, and playful exaggeration in the classroom. As young seasonal employees note, it is difficult to take seriously an organization that provides its retirees "Golden Ears" instead of gold watches after 20 or more years of service. All newcomers are aware that the label "Disneyland" has both an unserious and artificial connotation and that a full embrace of the Disneyland role would be as deviant as its full rejection. It does seem, however, because of the corporate imagery, the recruiting and selection devices, the goodwill trainees hold toward the organization at entry, the peer-based employment context, and the smooth fit with real student calendars, the job is considered by most ride operators to be a good one. The University of Disneyland, it appears, graduates students with a modest amount of pride and a considerable amount of fact and faith firmly ingrained as important things to know (if not always accept).

Matters become more interesting as new hires move into the various realms of Disneyland enterprise. There are real customers "out there" and employees soon learn that these good folks do not always measure up to the typically well mannered and grateful guest of the training classroom. Moreover, ride operators may find it difficult to utter the prescribed "Welcome Voyager" (or its equivalent) when it is to be given to the 20-thousandth human being passing through the Space Mountain turnstile on a crowded day in July. Other difficulties present themselves as well, but operators learn that there are others onstage to assist or thwart them.

Employees learn quickly that supervisors and, to a lesser degree, foremen are not only on the premises to help them, but also to catch them when they slip over or brazenly violate set procedures or park policies. Because most rides are tightly designed to eliminate human judgment and minimize operational disasters, much of the supervisory monitoring is directed at activities ride operators consider trivial: taking too long a break; not wearing parts of one's official uniform such as a hat, standard-issue belt, or correct shoes; rushing the ride (although more frequent violations seem to be detected for the provision of longer-than-usual rides for lucky customers); fraternizing with guests beyond the call of duty; talking back to quarrelsome or sometimes merely querisome customers; and so forth. All are matters covered quite explicitly in the codebooks ride operators are to be familiar with, and violations of such codes are often subject to instant and harsh discipline. The firing of what to supervisors are "malcontents," "trouble-makers," "bumblers," "attitude problems," or simply "jerks" is a frequent occasion at Disneyland, and among part-timers, who are most subject to degradation and being fired, the threat is omnipresent. There are few workers who have not witnessed firsthand the rapid disappearance of a co-worker for offenses they would regard as "Mickey Mouse." Moreover, there are few employees who themselves have not violated a good number of operational and demeanor standards and anticipate, with just cause, the violation of more in the future.

In part, because of the punitive and what are widely held to be capricious supervisory practices in the park, foremen and ride operators are usually drawn close and shield one another from suspicious area supervisors. Throughout the year, each land is assigned a number of area supervisors who, dressed alike in short-sleeved white shirts and ties with walkie-talkies hitched to their belts, wander about their territories on the lookout for deviations from park procedures (and other signs of disorder). Occasionally, higher level supervisors pose in "plainclothes" and ghost-ride the various attractions just to be sure everything is up to snuff. Some area supervisors are well-known among park employees for the variety of surreptitious techniques they employ when going about their monitoring duties. Blind observation posts are legendary, almost sacred, sites within the park ("This is where Old Man Weston hangs out. He can see Dumbo, Storybook, the Carousel, and the Tea Cups from here"). Supervisors in Tomorrowland are, for example, famous for their penchant of hiding in the bushes above the submarine caves, timing the arrivals and departures of the supposedly fully loaded boats making the $8\frac{1}{2}$ minute cruise under the polar icecaps. That they might also catch a submarine captain furtively enjoying a cigarette (or worse) while inside the conning tower (his upper body out of view of the crowd on the vessel) might just make a supervisor's day—and unmake the employee's. In short, supervisors, if not foremen, are regarded by ride operators as sneaks and tricksters out to get them and representative of the dark side of park life. Their presence is, of course, an orchestrated one and does more than merely watch over the ride operators. It also draws operators together as cohesive little units who must look out for one another while they work (and shirk). . . .

Employees are also subject to what might be regarded as remote controls. These stem not from supervisors or peers but from thousands of paying guests who parade daily through the park. The public, for the most part, wants Disneyland employees to play only the roles for which they are hired and costumed. If, for instance, Judy of the Jets is feeling tired, grouchy, or bored, few customers want to know about it. Disneyland employees are expected to be sunny and helpful; and the job, with its limited opportunities for sustained interaction, is designed to support such a stance. Thus, if a ride operator's behavior drifts noticeably away from the norm, customers are sure to point it out—"Why aren't you smiling?" "What's wrong with you?" "Having a bad day?" "Did Goofy step on your foot?" Ride operators learn swiftly from the constant hints, glances, glares, and tactful (and tactless) cues sent by their audience what their role in the park is to be, and as long as they keep to it, there will be no objections from those passing by.

> I can remember being out on the river looking at the people on the Mark Twain looking down on the people in the Keel Boats who are looking up at them. I'd come by on my raft and the y'd all turn and stare at me. If I gave them a little wave and a grin, they'd all wave back and smile; all ten thousand of them. I always wondered what would happen if I gave them the finger? (Ex-ride operator, 1988)

Ride operators also learn how different categories of customers respond to them and the parts they are playing on-stage. For example, infants and small children are generally timid, if not frightened, in their presence. School-age children are somewhat curious, aware that the operator is at work playing a role but sometimes in awe of the role itself. Nonetheless, these children can be quite critical of any flaw in the operator's performance. Teenagers, especially males in groups, present problems because they sometimes go to great lengths to embarrass, challenge, ridicule, or outwit an operator. Adults are generally appreciative and approving of an operator's conduct provided it meets their rather minimal standards, but they sometimes overreact to the part an operator is playing (positively) if accompanied by small children. . . .

The point here is that ride operators learn what the public (or, at least, their idealized version of the public) expects of their role and find it easier to conform to such expectations than not. Moreover, they discover that when they are bright and lively others respond to them in like ways. This . . . balancing of the emotional exchange is such that ride operators come to expect good treatment. They assume, with good cause, that most people will react to their little waves and smiles with some affection and perhaps joy. When they do not, it can ruin a ride operator's day.

With this interaction formula in mind, it is perhaps less difficult to see why ride operators detest and scorn the ill-mannered or unruly guest. At times, these grumpy, careless, or otherwise unresponsive characters insult the very role the operators play and have come to appreciate—"You can't treat the Captain of the USS Nautilus like that!" Such out-of-line visitors offer breaks from routine, some amusement, consternation, or the occasional job challenge that occurs when remedies are deemed necessary to restore employee and role dignity.

By and large, however, the people-processing tasks of ride operators pass good naturedly and smoothly, with operators hardly noticing much more than the bodies passing in front of view (special bodies, however, merit special attention as when crew members on the subs gather to assist a young lady in a revealing outfit on board and then linger over the hatch to admire the view as she descends the steep steps to take her seat on the boat). Yet, sometimes, more than a body becomes visible, as happens when customers overstep their roles and challenge employee authority, insult an operator, or otherwise disrupt the routines of the job. In the process, guests become "dufusses," "ducks," and "assholes" (just three of many derisive terms used by ride operators to label those customers they believe to have gone beyond the pale). Normally, these characters are brought to the attention of park security officers, ride foremen, or area supervisors who, in turn, decide how they are to be disciplined (usually expulsion from the park).

Occasionally, however, the alleged slight is too personal or simply too extraordinary for a ride operator to let it pass unnoticed or merely inform others and allow them to decide what, if anything, is to be done. Restoration of one's respect is called for, and routine practices have been developed for these circumstances. For example, common remedies include: the "seatbelt squeeze," a small token of appreciation given to a deviant customer consisting of the rapid cinching-up of a required seatbelt such that the passenger is doubled-over at the point of departure and left gasping for the duration of the trip; the "break-toss," an acrobatic gesture of the Autopia trade whereby operators jump on the outside of a norm violator's car, stealthily unhitching the safety belt, then slamming on the brakes, bringing the car to an almost instant stop while the driver flies on the hood of the car (or beyond); the "seatbelt slap," an equally distinguished (if primitive) gesture by which an offending customer receives a sharp, quick snap of a hard plastic belt across the face (or other parts of the body) when entering or exiting a seatbelted ride; the "break-up-the-party" gambit, a queuing device put to use in officious fashion whereby bothersome pairs are separated at the last minute into different units, thus forcing on them the pain of strange companions for the duration of a ride through the Haunted Mansion or a ramble on Mr. Toad's Wild Ride; the

"hatch-cover ploy," a much beloved practice of Submarine pilots who, in collusion with mates on the loading dock, are able to drench offensive guests with water as their units pass under a waterfall; and, lastly, the rather ignoble variants of the "Sorry-I-didn't-see-your-hand" tactic, a savage move designed to crunch a particularly irksome customer's hand (foot, finger, arm, leg, etc.) by bringing a piece of Disneyland property to bear on the appendage, such as the door of a Thunder Mountain railroad car or the starboard side of a Jungle Cruise boat. This latter remedy is, most often, a "near miss" designed to startle the little criminals of Disneyland.

All of these unofficial procedures (and many more) are learned on the job. Although they are used sparingly, they are used. Occasions of use provide a continual stream of sweet revenge talk to enliven and enrich colleague conversation at break time or after work. Too much, of course, can be made of these subversive practices and the rhetoric that surrounds their use. Ride operators are quite aware that there are limits beyond which they dare not pass. If they are caught, they know that restoration of corporate pride will be swift and clean.

In general, Disneyland employees are remarkable for their forbearance and polite good manners even under trying conditions. They are taught, and some come to believe, for a while at least, that they are really "on-stage" at work. And, as noted, surveillance by supervisory personnel certainly fades in light of the unceasing glances an employee receives from the paying guests who tromp daily through the park in the summer. Disneyland employees know well that they are part of the product being sold and learn to check their more discriminating manners in favor of the generalized countenance of a cheerful lad or lassie whose enthusiasm and dedication is obvious to all.

At times, the emotional resources of employees appear awesome. When the going gets tough and the park is jammed, the nerves of all employees are frayed and sorely tested by the crowd, din, sweltering sun, and eyeburning smog. Customers wait in what employees call "bullpens" (and park officials call "reception areas") for up to several hours for a $3\frac{1}{2}$ minute ride that operators are sometimes hell-bent on cutting to $2\frac{1}{2}$ minutes. Surely a monument to the human ability to suppress feelings has been created when both users and providers alike can maintain their composure and seeming regard for one another when in such a fix.

It is in this domain where corporate culture and the order it helps to sustain must be given its due. Perhaps the depth of a culture is visible only when its members are under the gun. The orderliness—a good part of the Disney formula for financial success—is an accomplishment based not only on physical design and elaborate procedures, but also on the low-level, part-time employees who, in the final analysis, must be willing, even eager, to keep the show afloat. The ease with which employees glide into their kindly and smiling roles is, in large measure, a feat of social engineering. Disneyland does not pay well; its supervision is arbitrary and skin-close; its working conditions are chaotic; its jobs require minimal amounts of intelligence or judgment; and asks a kind of sacrifice and loyalty of its employees that is almost fanatical. Yet, it attracts a particularly able workforce whose personal backgrounds suggest abilities far exceeding those required of a Disneyland traffic cop, people stuffer, queue or line manager, and button pusher. As I have suggested, not all of Disneyland is covered by the culture put forth by management. There are numerous pockets of resistance and various degrees of autonomy maintained by employees. Nonetheless, adherence and support for the organization are remarkable. And, like swallows returning to Capistrano, many part-timers look forward to their migration back to the park for several seasons.

The Disney Way

Four features alluded to in this unofficial guide to Disneyland seem to account for a good deal of the social order that obtains within the park. First, socialization, although costly, is of a most selective, collective, intensive, serial, sequential, and closed sort. These tactics are notable for their penetration into the private spheres of individual thought and feeling. . . . Incoming identities are not so much dismantled as they are set aside as employees are schooled in the use of new identities of the situational sort. Many of these are symbolically powerful and, for some, laden with social approval. It is hardly surprising that some of the more problematic positions in terms of turnover during the summer occur in the food and concession domains where employees apparently find little to identify with on the job. Cowpokes on Big Thunder Mountain, Jet Pilots, Storybook Princesses, Tour Guides, Space Cadets, Jungle Boat Skippers, or Southern Belles of New Orleans Square have less difficulty on this score. Disneyland, by design, bestows identity through a process carefully set up to strip away the job relevance of other sources of identity and learned response and replace them with others of organizational relevance. It works.

Second, this is a work culture whose designers have left little room for individual experimentation. Supervisors, as apparent in their focused wandering and attentive looks, keep very close tabs on what is going on at any moment in all the lands. Every bush, rock, and tree in Disneyland is numbered and checked continually as to the part it is playing in the park. So too are employees. Discretion of a personal sort is quite limited while employees are "on-stage." Even "back-stage" and certain "off-stage" domains have their corporate monitors. Employees are indeed aware that their "off-stage" life beyond the picnics, parties, and softball games is subject to some scrutiny, for police checks are made on potential and current employees. Nor do all employees discount the rumors that park officials make periodic inquiries on their own as to a person's habits concerning sex and drugs. Moreover, the sheer number of rules and regulations is striking, thus making the grounds for dismissal a matter of multiple choice for supervisors who discover a target for the use of such grounds. The feeling of being watched is, unsurprisingly, a rather prevalent complaint among Disneyland people, and it is one that employees must live with if they are to remain at Disneyland.

Third, emotional management occurs in the park in a number of quite distinct ways. From the instructors at the university who beseech recruits to "wish every guest a pleasant good day," to the foremen who plead with their charges to, "say thank you when you herd them through the gate," to the impish customer who seductively licks her lips and asks, "what does Tom Sawyer want for Christmas?" appearance, demeanor, and etiquette have special meanings at Disneyland. Because these are prized personal attributes over which we normally feel in control, making them commodities can be unnerving. Much self-monitoring is involved, of course, but even here self-management has an organizational side. Consider ride operators who may complain of being "too tired to smile" but, at the same time, feel a little guilty for uttering such a confession. Ride operators who have worked an early morning shift on the Matterhorn (or other popular rides) tell of a queasy feeling they get when the park is opened for business and they suddenly feel the ground begin to shake under their feet and hear the low thunder of the hordes of customers coming at them, oblivious of civil restraint and the small children who might be among them. Consider, too, the discomforting pressures of being "on-stage" all day and the cumulative annoyance of having adults ask permission to leave a line to go to the bathroom, whether the water in the lagoon is real, where the well-marked entrances might be, where Walt Disney's cryogenic tomb is to be found, or—the real clincher—whether or not one is "really real."

The mere fact that so much operator discourse concerns the handling of bothersome guests suggests that these little emotional disturbances have costs. There are, for instance, times in all employee careers when they put themselves on "automatic pilot," "go robot," "can't feel a thing," "lapse into a dream," "go into a trance," or otherwise "check out" while still on duty. Despite a crafty supervisor's (or curious visitor's) attempt to measure the glimmer in an employee's eye, this sort of willed emotional numbness is common to many of the "on-stage" Disneyland personnel. Much of this numbness is, of course, beyond the knowledge of supervisors and guests because most employees have little trouble appearing as if they are present even when they are not. It is, in a sense, a passive form of resistance that suggests there still is a sacred preserve of individuality left among employees in the park.

Finally, taking these three points together, it seems that even when people are trained, paid, and told to be nice, it is hard for them to do so all of the time. But, when efforts to be nice have succeeded to the degree that is true of Disneyland, it appears as a rather towering (if not always admirable) achievement. It works at the collective level by virtue of elaborate direction. Employees—at all ranks—are stage-managed by higher ranking employees who, having come through themselves, hire, train, and closely supervise those who have replaced them below. Expression rules are laid out in corporate manuals. Employee time-outs intensify work experience. Social exchanges are forced into narrow bands of interacting groups. Training and retraining programs are continual. Hiding places are few. Although little sore spots and irritations remain for each individual, it is difficult to imagine work roles being more defined (and accepted) than those at Disneyland. Here, it seems, is a work culture worthy of the name.

THINKING ABOUT THE READING

What is the significance of the title, "The Smile Factory"? What, exactly, is the factory-made product that Disney sells in its theme parks? How does the Disney organizational culture shape the lives of employees? Disney is frequently criticized for its strict—some would say oppressive—employee rules and regulations. But would it be possible to run a "smile factory" with a more relaxed code of conduct where employees could regularly make their own decisions and act as they pleased? Explain. Disney theme parks abroad (in Japan and France, for instance) have not been nearly as successful as Disneyland and Disneyworld. Why has it been so difficult to export the "feeling business" to other countries? Consider also how Van Maanen describes the ways in which employees define the social rank of different positions within Disneyland. Describe an organizational situation you've been in where such a ranking of members occurred. What were the criteria upon which such rankings were made?

The Architecture of Stratification: Social Class and Inequality

Inequality is woven into the fabric of all societies through a structured system of *social stratification*. Social stratification is a ranking of entire groups of people that perpetuates unequal rewards and life chances in society. The structural-functionalist explanation of stratification is that the stability of society depends on all social positions being filled—that is, there are people around to do all the jobs that need to be done. Higher rewards, such as prestige and large salaries, are afforded to the most important positions, thereby ensuring that the most qualified individuals will occupy the highest positions. In contrast, conflict theory argues that stratification reflects an unequal distribution of power in society and is a primary source of conflict and tension.

Social class is the primary means of stratification in American society. Contemporary sociologists are likely to define one's class standing as a combination of income, wealth, occupational prestige, and educational attainment. It is tempting to see class differences as simply the result of an economic stratification system that exists at a level above the individual. Although inequality is created and maintained by larger social institutions, however, it is often felt most forcefully and is reinforced most effectively in the chain of interactions that take place in our day-to-day lives.

In "Software Entrepreneurship Among the Urban Poor," Alice Amsden and Jon Collins Clark examine the subtle but powerful ways stratification conveys advantages on some at the expense of others. They pose the deceptively simple question: If Bill Gates was poor and black would he be as successful as he is? In the process of answering their own question, they identify what they consider to be the factors necessary to become a successful entrepreneur: "gumption," connections, financial backing, and so on. Notice that none of these factors have anything to do with actual skill.

It is impossible to fully examine the American stratification system without addressing the plight of those at the bottom. Despite the much publicized economic recovery of the late 1990s, poverty continues to be a large and, in many cases, deadly social problem. The face of American poverty has changed somewhat over the past several decades. The economic status of single mothers and their children has deteriorated while that of people over age 65 has improved somewhat.

What hasn't changed is the ever widening gap between the rich and the poor. Poverty persists because in a free-market and competitive society it serves economic and social functions. In addition, poverty receives institutional "support" in the form of segmented labor markets and inadequate educational systems. The ideology of competitive individualism—that to succeed in life all one has to do is work hard and win in competition with others—creates a belief that poor people are to blame for their own suffering. So although the problem of poverty remains serious, worse, public attitudes toward poverty and poor people are frequently indifferent or even hostile. Furthermore, important social institutions can perpetuate the problem.

In "Savage Inequalities in America's Schools," Jonathan Kozol provides a troubling portrait of inequality in the American educational system by comparing the school experiences of children in two very different cities. Although the children of destitute East St. Louis, Illinois, and affluent Rye, New York, are citizens of the same country, they live in two very different worlds. Kozol draws compelling contrasts between the broken-down classrooms, outdated textbooks, and faulty plumbing in East St. Louis and the sparkling new auditoriums and up-to-date computers in Rye. These vastly different educational experiences make it difficult to sustain the myth that all children, no matter where they live, are competing in a fair race for society's resources.

Sociologist Elijah Anderson digs deeper into the consequences of stratification in his article, "The Code of the Streets." Anderson shows us that for many African Americans growing up in poor, depressed neighborhoods, violence and despair are consistent parts of everyday life. The highly publicized economic boom of the late 1990s barely touched these areas. Access to jobs that pay a living wage—and therefore a traditional means of gaining respect—is almost nonexistent. The result is that many poor inner-city African-American youth develop a profound sense of alienation from mainstream society and its institutions. Anderson shows us that in such an environment a "code of the streets" emerges with a set of informal rules governing all aspects of public interaction, including violence. This code is so powerful that it even holds the most well-intentioned, "decent" families in its grip.

It is important to remember that inequality and stratification extend beyond national borders. Third-world laborers have become a crucial part of the global economic marketplace and an important foreign resource for multinational corporations. Low-skilled jobs are frequently exported to developing countries that have cheaper labor costs. On the surface, it would appear that such an arrangement benefits all involved: The multinational corporations benefit from higher profits, the developing countries benefit from higher rates of employment, the workers themselves benefit from earning a wage that would have otherwise been unavailable to them, and consumers in wealthy countries benefit from less expensive products.

But most of us are unaware of and unconcerned with the harsh conditions under which our most coveted products are made. William Greider, in "These Dark Satanic Mills," discusses the exploitative potential of relying on third-world factories. He uses a particular tragedy, the 1993 industrial fire at the Kader Industrial Toy Company in Thailand, to illustrate how global economics create and sustain international inequality. Greider shows us the complex paradox of the global marketplace: While foreign manufacturing facilities free factory workers from certain poverty, they also ensnare the workers in new and sometimes lethal forms of domination.

Software Entrepreneurship Among the Urban Poor

Could Bill Gates Have Succeeded If He Were Black? . . . Or Impoverished?

Alice H. Amsden and Jon Collins Clark

Introduction: The Gumption Factor

The computer software industry is a bastion of entrepreneurship in the late twentieth century. Drug dealing aside, it is one of the few industries associated with the "third industrial revolution" in which the individual entrepreneur can become a multimillionaire overnight.[1] The best example is Bill Gates, whose entrepreneurship and ten-digit financial fortune have been the subject of admiration and awe in at least three popular books in print in the 1990s.

The software industry has been identified as a fertile field for aspiring modern-day Horatio Algers because of its perceived low start-up requirements and barriers to entry. Take, for instance, the following citation from a contemporary conference on the subject of entrepreneurship: "The microcomputer software industry is both a throwback to the classic cottage industry of entrepreneurship and at the same time a leading edge of the new wave of technological entrepreneurship. Like the cottage industry of old, the barriers to entry are modest in the extreme. An investment of a few hundred dollars in hardware; a corner in a room; combined with commitment and hard work can, in most cases, produce a product, and in a few cases, a business" (Teach, Tarpley and Schwartz 1985, p. 546).

This supposed ease of entry for entrepreneurs into software production presumes that even society's most disadvantaged can reap potential gains in this industry. Because barriers to entry are supposedly so low, individuals from the ranks of the urban poor can make it as computer software entrepreneurs alongside individuals from the ranks of the wealthy and privileged. All that is needed is imagination, perseverance, and painstaking effort—"gumption" for short.

290

We have sought to examine the validity of this proposition. It is intriguing because entrepreneurship is an enchanted and extraordinary talent that seems to emerge from unexpected soils—impoverished youth, as in the case of Andrew Carnegie and Henry Ford, and especially the cultures of persecuted minority groups, as in the Jews, French Huguenots, Indians in East Africa, Chinese in Southeast Asia, and so forth. If entrepreneurship can blossom in these inhospitable climes, then why not in the software industry among the urban poor in American cities, which are typically rife with persecuted minorities?

By entrepreneurship we mean a process whereby an individual or group of individuals perceive a new profit-making opportunity, coordinate and mobilize the resources necessary to implement the original idea, and then monitor the implementation procedures necessary to ensure the efficient execution of plans. . . .

Certainly entrepreneurship is rare and inspired, and more of an art than a science. Nevertheless, from data on who has innovated in the American software industry, it appears that entrepreneurship is not nearly as quirky as once believed. As we hope to show:

1. American software entrepreneurs tend to have standard characteristics: a very large portion of them are white, male, and extremely well educated. They may all have gumption, but the gumption factor *alone* works in only a very small number of cases (the details of which are in any event unclear).

2. Entry barriers into the software industry may be low in terms of physical capital but are high in terms of human capital, which is gen-

erally a key difference between the second and third industrial revolutions. "Human capital" refers to education and work experience. Also important for success is "social capital," or the contacts and networks that facilitate business interactions (Putnam 1993).

3. The category of "entrepreneur" in the United States—which we proxy statistically with certain subcategories of "self-employed"—includes a large number of African Americans. Being black and being an entrepreneur (even in software) are not mutually exclusive, although blacks tend to have a lower incidence of entrepreneurship than whites for reasons that are discussed later in this [article].

4. We infer from this that what restrains entrepreneurship in industries like software in American inner cities is not race but rather *poverty,* with characteristics of low education and an absence of influential business contacts that are antagonistic to those required for entry into the new high-tech information sectors.

5. Quick fixes—like the dumping of computers into inner-city schools—may encourage the necessary tinkering with hardware that seems to flow in the veins of software engineers. But such gestures are far from sufficient to ensure even a small steady stream of inner-city entrepreneurial talent. Even before that flow can start to trickle, imbalances must first be addressed in the state of education in general, computer education in particular, job training and job availability, and other factors that currently serve to make real levels of human capital so disparate among different economic classes in the United States.

Entrepreneurship and the Software Industry

Who Are Entrepreneurs?

To understand software entrepreneurship, it is instructive to have some background information on the demographics of entrepreneurs in general. Most research concentrates on the cat-

egory of the "self-employed" rather than of the "entrepreneur" because no data are available directly on the latter. These two populations overlap considerably, but they are by no means identical (see Reynolds 1995 and Becker 1984). Some self-employed are not entrepreneurs and some entrepreneurs are not self-employed.[2]

The ranks of the self-employed contain many independent professionals who by most definitions including ours, would not be considered entrepreneurs. "More than half of all dentists, veterinarians, optometrists, podiatrists, and other health diagnosing technicians, authors, painters, and sculptors, auctioneers, street and door-to-door sales workers, barbers, child-care workers, and farm operators and managers were self employed in 1983" (Becker 1984, p. 17). Given the heterogeneity of this classification, inferences about entrepreneurs drawn from this population must be taken gingerly.

Research shows that the self-employed are disproportionately represented by native-born white males. Put another way, the self-employment rates among both women and minorities are significantly lower than those among white men. Among minorities, rates of self-employment are lowest among African Americans, somewhat higher among Hispanics, and in the case of Asian Americans, almost equal to that of native-born whites (Aronson 1991; Reynolds 1995; Butler 1991). Just why this has been the case has been the cause for much debate and will be discussed in further detail later in this [article].

The self-employed are generally older and have some work experience. "The probability of being self-employed increases with labor market experience" (Evans and Leighton 1989, p. 532). In other words, most self-employed are not high school dropouts, college dropouts, or even recent high school or college graduates; they are former employees with real job experience. . . . On average, the self-employed are better educated than the population at large. This holds true even when controlling for the "professional" contingent among the self-employed—that is, independent lawyers, doctors, and so on (see Evans and

Leighton 1989 and Light 1995). This suggests a quality about entrepreneurs that tends to make them better educated, all else being equal. . . .

Software Entrepreneurship

Fortunately, some specific research has been conducted on the demographic profile of software entrepreneurs themselves (Teach, Tarpley and Schwartz 1986). Perhaps the most important insight gained is that most software entrepreneurs *are extremely well educated.* A whopping 86 percent of the software entrepreneurs analyzed in one sample (approximately two hundred software firms) had at least a college degree, and 47 percent held advanced degrees (Teach, Tarpley and Schwartz 1985). Another study in 1987 found similar results among a sample of over two hundred high-tech firms (Goslin 1987). This entry qualification of high educational credentials appears to have accelerated over time. A follow-up study to the 1987 study provided evidence of ". . . the virtual disappearance of the 'computer jock' without a college degree" (Teach et al. 1987, p. 465).

Software entrepreneurs also usually have some work experience prior to opening their own businesses. The Haug 1991 study of the software industry in Washington state found that only 3 percent of software company founders launched their companies directly out of high school or college. Approximately 86 percent had previously held some position in industry working for another firm, and a majority (approximately 57 percent) had been employed by a software company. In the Teach, Tarpley and Schwartz 1985 study, less than 2 percent reported that their current position was their first position. Over 40 percent had worked as employees in the software industry.

Research confirms the notion that *physical* capital requirements for software entrepreneurs are relatively low. Initial capitalization levels of the firms in the Teach, Tarpley and Schwartz 1985 study were relatively small. Roughly 50 percent reported initial capitalization levels of $10,000 or less. A follow-up investigation in 1986 found that over 75 percent of firms were initially capitalized exclusively with the personal funds of the principals (Teach, Tarpley and Schwartz 1986).

The Haug 1991 study found that approximately 83 percent of software companies were initially capitalized through the personal funds of the principals and/or their families and friends. In the Goslin 1987 study, 71 percent of firms were capitalized exclusively with the personal funds of the principals. These findings are consistent with those of Light (1995) and others who have found that physical capital requirements for *all* entrepreneurs, regardless of industry, tend to be relatively lower than one might expect. . . .

Finally, software entrepreneurs appear to be predominantly male. Only 15 percent of those in the Teach, Tarpley and Schwartz 1985 sample were women. This proportion is significantly lower than the number of women found among the self-employed as a whole, most estimates of which range between 30 and 40 percent (Becker 1984 and Reynolds 1995).

The Urban Poor: Software Entrepreneurs-in-Waiting?

Urban Poor

The urban poor have become of greater interest to policymakers and social scientists alike because they represent an increasing proportion of the total poor in the United States (Sandefur 1988). The steady increase in the "spatial concentration" of poverty in American inner cities has led us to consider ways of addressing poverty particularly in these geographical centers. . . .

Poverty in U.S. urban centers often has a dual nature. Two kinds of poor are present in the inner city at any given time: first there are the transient poor (poor at a given moment but not likely to be so in the near future), and second are the "persistent poor" (those who have been and are likely to remain in a state of poverty) (Adams et al. 1988). We are mostly concerned with the persistent poor—not with those who are transiently poor on the basis of their reported income in a given year.[3]

Table 1   *Composition of the urban poor*

	Persistently poor (8 or more years, 1974–1983)	Poor in 1979	Total U.S. urban population
Ethnicity			
Black	66%	51%	21%
White	34%	49%	79%
Education Among Heads of Household			
K–8 grades	49%	29%	12%
9–11 grades	29%	27%	17%
12 grades	18%	32%	33%
13 or more	4%	11%	38%

Source: Survey Research Center, 1984, *User Guide to the Panel Study of Income Dynamics,* University of Michigan, Ann Arbor, as adapted from Adams et al. 1988.

As can be seen in table 1, the urban poor are mostly black. Notice that 66 percent of the *persistent* poor were black, whereas the corresponding number of blacks in the urban population as a whole was only 21 percent. Perhaps most significantly for the purposes of this study, the urban poor as described in table 1 are poorly educated. Among the persistently poor, 78 percent of the heads of the household did not graduate from high school. Only 4 percent had even one year of schooling beyond high school.

As a final note, it is important to recognize that the urban poor are often unemployed or out of the labor force altogether. The correlation between poverty and unemployment is widely acknowledged and is possibly becoming stronger (Wilson 1996). . . . For our purposes, it is important to be aware that those living in poverty, because they are often unemployed, are likely to have no recent job experience in any industry whatsoever. . . .

Urban Poor and Software Entrepreneurs: How Do They Match Up?

Now that we have two basic demographic portraits, of software entrepreneurs and of the urban poor, the question is how they match up. We know that software entrepreneurs are, on average, white, male, college-educated professionals with some job experience, often in the field of computers. Among the urban poor, we know that they are, on average, black, have not graduated from high school, and are often currently unemployed or out of the workforce altogether. Many are also female heads of households.[4] Clearly, these two groups do not seem to overlap very much.

Nevertheless, the set of general demographic characteristics among the urban poor that we have provided here does not altogether preclude the existence of entrepreneurship in urban areas. There are, in fact, urban entrepreneurs. Rates of entrepreneurship in the inner city, however, fall significantly below those in the country as a whole. . . .

Race and Entrepreneurship

Thus far the evidence does not suggest that skin color is a prerequisite for success in entrepreneurial endeavors, whatever their nature. It is true that rates of self-employment among blacks and Hispanics have lagged behind those of nonminorities . . . and there has been considerable debate as to the cause of this disparity.

Table 2   *Mean traits of above average versus below average earners of self-employment income*

	Low earners		High earners	
	Minorities	Nonminorities	Minorities	Nonminorities
Age	43.5	44.5	43.1	44.7
Education	10.9	12.3	12.1	13.4
Proportion female	0.322	0.337	0.133	0.091
1979 self-employment income	$4,446	$4,447	$22,689	$27,199
1979 income from all sources	$7,028	$8,878	$25,792	$31,676
1979 household income	$17,710	$20,211	$34,297	$38,263
No. of observations	13,845	3414	7119	1805

High earners are those earning self-employment income above the sample mean of $10,640. Low earners fall below the mean. Data exclude doctors and lawyers; nonfarm agricultural industries are included. Self-employment earnings include nonfarm earnings only.

Source: 1980 Census of Population Public Use Samples as cited in Bates 1987.

Much of the variation in rates of self-employment is *not* explained by independent variables such as education, age, and income (Butler 1991 and Light 1995).

Instead, some have argued that cultural differences among ethnic groups have been the greatest source of differing rates of self-employment (Light 1995). But other factors must also be considered. For instance, it may be that racial discrimination on the demand side may influence the decision of minorities to become self-employed. The more (perceived) discrimination, the greater the risk of failure and, therefore, the higher the opportunity costs of investing in entrepreneurship. . . . Others have suggested that a lack of past experience in business and a consequent underdevelopment of social and business networks for some ethnic groups is a crucial contributing factor (Fratoe 1988).

But despite variations in the proportions of those who are self-employed among different ethnic groups, there is still a substantial number of self-employed who are from minority groups. Moreover, concrete evidence suggests that their characteristics and experiences are remarkably similar to those of the nonminority self-employed. . . . Bate's 1987 study of the self-employed found that among those whose self-employment income was *below* average, the characteristics and earnings in minorities and nonminorities were almost identical. The results of this study are provided in table 2.

As can be seen in the table, the same commonalties cannot be said to be true among those with *above* average earnings. In the high-earner category, nonminorities appear to have earned approximately 20 percent more than their minority counterparts. Most of this disparity in earnings, however, can be accounted for by differences in three independent variables: age, education, and sex (Bates 1987). . . .

Research . . . shows that the qualities that make high-earning entrepreneurs among minorities are the same qualities that make high-earning entrepreneurs among nonminorities; namely, among both demographic groups, those with higher levels of education and with some working experience earn more than those with less education and experience (all else being equal) (Bates 1987; Fratoe 1988; Hisrich and Brush 1986).

Thus, as a step toward answering the question we posed in the title of this chapter—Could Bill Gates have succeeded were he black (or a member of another minority)?—our answer is yes, he could have succeeded, *all else being equal*. Nevertheless, all else is typically not equal. The incidence of poverty is significantly higher among most minorities than in the population at large. As we show in the following section, it is the pathology of poverty, including low levels of human and social capital, that is most inimical to entrepreneurship.

What Does It Take?

Human and Social Capital

Even though race may not be a determining factor in the success of prospective entrepreneurs, evidence strongly suggests that both human and social capital are critical ingredients of success. As mentioned in the previous section, successful minority entrepreneurs have the same characteristics as nonminority entrepreneurs: they are well educated and usually have relevant job experience. In other words, they have higher levels of human capital. They also have higher levels of social capital, in part as a result of their better education and richer job experience.

Research concerning the importance of formal education in the success of entrepreneurs has been extensive and conclusive. Study after study indicates that successful entrepreneurs have above-average levels of education. . . . We have every reason to believe, then, that formal schooling is becoming increasingly important as a determinant of high self-employed earnings, just as it is in the labor force at large. . . .

More specifically, advanced business degrees and entrepreneurial-specific training seem to serve as important assets to entrepreneurs in general, including those in software. One study of software venture teams found that those that contained at least one member with an advanced business degree were more successful than those that did not (Teach, Tarpley and Schwartz 1985). Specific courses that targeted potential entrepreneurs and taught them the practical know-how needed to start their own businesses have also been shown to be effective (Balkin 1989; Price 1991; Rush et al. 1987).

Not only an advanced degree but a college degree in any discipline seems to contribute to entrepreneurial success. The nature of that degree, if not in business, would most likely depend on the nature of the entrepreneur's intended industry. For instance, the Teach, Tarpley and Schwartz 1985 study of software entrepreneurs found that a majority of the respondents had undergraduate degrees in a technical field (engineering, math, science, or computer science). Another quarter of respondents, however, had degrees in liberal arts or humanities. This suggests that beyond the specific nature of the degree, there are other benefits that a college degree can provide to the potential entrepreneur.

One such potential benefit is the opportunity it can provide for the degree holder to gain relevant job experience and make social contacts. This is especially true when one considers what we already know about the importance to entrepreneurs of having previous job experience.

Another potential benefit of a college degree is the membership it can provide graduates in instrumental peer networks. A great deal of research has been done on the importance of social connections for entrepreneurial success. Researchers have found that higher levels of social capital contribute to an increased probability of entrepreneurial success (Fratoe 1988); for instance, peer networks have been shown to contribute to the development of marketing and subcontracting among new firms (Holt 1987 and Rush et al. 1987). It is this development of social capital no less than human capital that has contributed to entrepreneurial success among those with undergraduate and graduate degrees.

Computer Education and Software Entrepreneurship

Given the abundant evidence that successful entrepreneurship, whether in software or other endeavors, is strongly associated with high levels of education, the hypothesis of low entry barriers into the software industry requires serious revision. Barriers in the form of physical capital may be relatively low, but those in the form of human and social capital appear substantial. Thus, even though the eccentric individual with megadoses of gumption may succeed as an entrepreneur whatever his or her background, population groups with low levels of human and social capital are unlikely *on average* to pioneer new, legitimate business ventures, small or large.

Nevertheless, the cherished American ideal that anyone with gumption can make it as an entrepreneur lives on with respect to information technology. Consequently, there has been a vigorous attempt on the part of government and business to blanket the inner cities with computers and computer-related crash courses, the hardware and software supposedly needed for anyone with a dream to become a software entrepreneur. The increased proliferation of computers throughout American public schools has thus rekindled the old American dream of equal opportunity. Nevertheless, a closer look at the nature of computer education in poor urban schools shows why this dream is seriously out of focus.

It is true that in recent years much has been done to increase the number of computers in poor urban schools. Initiatives have been launched by large private corporations such as AT&T, Microsoft, and Xerox to place computers and develop computer networks in public schools (U.S. Department of Education 1996). Local private companies have complemented these initiatives by donating their outdated computers. Meanwhile, the federal government has begun to pay more attention to the importance of computer education, a visible example being [former] President Clinton's . . . campaign promise to "put a computer in every classroom" and to link these computers on the Internet. Nevertheless, the impact these developments have had on the overall quality of computer education among the poor remains suspect for the following reasons.

First, although the absolute number of computers in poorer schools has increased, it still appears to fall short of the number in more wealthy classrooms. Picciano's 1991 study comparing computer education in schools in Westchester County, New York, with those in New York City found that the ratio of computers to students was more than twice as high in Westchester. Another study found similar degrees of imbalance

in the computer-to-student ratio between suburban and urban districts (Quality Education Data 1991). Thus, although it may be true that some effort has been made to address the discrepancy in access to computers in poor and rich schools, serious imbalances persist.

Perhaps even more important, researchers have found that there are significant differences in how computers are used in school districts with different income levels. According to Owens (1995, p. 84), "urban schools with predominantly minority students have been found typically to use computers for tutorial and rote drill-and-practice programs, while suburban schools with students from higher-income families have generally been found to use computers for problem solving and programming." In eighth-grade mathematics classes, "urban teachers reported that they were more likely than suburban and rural teachers to use computers for remedial purposes" (Owens 1995, p. 90). Thus, there is reason to believe that the overall quality of computer education in inner-city schools suffers compared with that of suburban schools; the nature of "literacy" is different.

Alongside the inequities in computer education that exist in the nation's schools, one must further consider the inequities that characterize young people's access to computers at home. . . . Access to computers at home as well as at school is an important condition for the nurturing of software entrepreneurship. A 1994 national survey found that the degree of technology used in the home was largely dependent on income: "college graduates and families with high incomes were more likely to own several types of electronic technology" (Black Child Advocate 1995, p. 3).

Young people who have exposure to creative uses for computers, and continued access to and experience with computers in their own homes, are far more likely to tinker in creating software than those who do not. These and other inequities in asset endowments put the poor at a distinct disadvantage in fulfilling any entrepreneurial dreams with respect to information technology.

Conclusion

The urban poor are not likely on average to become software entrepreneurs for many of the same reasons they are not likely to become brain surgeons, investment bankers, or CEOs of Fortune 500 companies—they simply do not have the requisite educational and social capital. . . . Although [these are] not the only factor[s] inhibiting the development of high-earning entrepreneurs in the inner city, to our minds . . . [they are] primary . . . in light of the technological requirements of the third industrial revolution through which the U.S. and other advanced economies are now passing. Were education, training, and job experience brought up to par, then policymakers could begin to address other entry barriers to small-firm entrepreneurship, such as access to finance capital.[5] But these other barriers will remain moot as long as the urban poor remain insufficiently skilled to take the first step on the long road to successful entrepreneurship—the mere conception of a novel product or process that sufficient numbers of people with high enough levels of income are willing and able to buy.

Thus, even though Bill Gates may be the *un*characteristic software entrepreneur in having dropped out of college (Harvard no less), he is typical insofar as he enjoyed membership in a privileged American economic and social elite. The odds that he would have succeeded had his social world been that of the urban ghetto may be predicted to be infinitesimally small.

All this puts an enormous burden on education to bootstrap the poor. We would suggest, however, that although better education in poor neighborhoods may increase the number of successful entrepreneurs, it is insufficient for a technomodernization of the American inner city itself. This may be illustrated briefly by drawing an analogy between poor people in rich countries and poor countries in the world economy. After World War II a large number of extremely poor underdeveloped countries attempted to industrialize. Most failed because they started from a capital base (physical, human, and social) that

was too low to allow them to compete in world markets. But a few enjoyed spectacular success, in particular South Korea and Taiwan, which were very poor initially but which had exceptionally equal income distributions (a result of land reform) and unusually high levels of education (in part as a consequence of the geopolitics underlying American foreign aid allocation). What is noteworthy about South Korea and Taiwan, however, is that initially their high investments in education resulted not in rapid domestic economic growth but in a "brain drain"—the educated migrated abroad to high-wage countries and only returned home once endogenous growth had begun—by a variety of complex and controversial means, although none of these means involved the exploitation of high technology. The industries in which South Korea and Taiwan (and Japan before it) prospered involved first low- and then mid-technology, such as steel, industrial chemicals, and later automobiles (Hikino and Amsden 1994).

So, too, we would suggest, better education of the poor will initially result in their migration out of the inner city, and not necessarily in an immediate improvement in living standards of the inner city proper. What remains unclear—and controversial—is how the inner city itself is to be modernized, and what role high technology, specifically information technology, will play in that process.

NOTES

1. The "third industrial revolution" is associated with innovations in electronics, communications, chemicals, and pharmaceuticals, including biotechnology, which is also friendly toward the small entrepreneur (Chandler Jr. and Hikino 1997).

2. "Downsizing" in large American corporations appears to have swelled the ranks of the "self-employed" in the form of a burgeoning number of underemployed "consultants."

3. We are concerned with the persistent poor in order to understand the entrepreneurship among the most disadvantaged. . . .

4. Roughly 70 percent of a sample of poor urban households were found to be headed by females (Adams et al. 1988).

5. Teach, Tarpley and Schwartz (1985) found that a large percentage of software entrepreneurs borrowed large sums of money from friends and family. How many among the urban poor could do so?

REFERENCES

Adams, T., G. Duncan, and W. Rogers. 1988. "The Persistence of Urban Poverty." In *Quiet Riots,* edited by F. Harris and R. Wilkins pp. 78–99. New York: Pantheon Books.

Aronson, R. L. 1991. *Self-Employment: A Labor Market Perspective.* Ithaca: NY: ILR Press.

Balkin, S. 1989. *Self Employment for Low-Income People.* New York: Praeger.

Bates, T. 1987. "Self-Employed Minorities: Traits and Trends." *Social Science Quarterly* 68: 539–551.

Becker, E. 1984. "Self-Employed Workers: An Update to 1983." *Monthly Labor Review* 107(7): 14–18.

Butler, J. S. C. H. 1991. "Ethnicity and Entrepreneurship in America: Toward an Explanation of Racial and Ethnic Group Variations in Self-Employment." *Sociological Perspectives* 34(1): 79–94.

Chandler Jr., A. D., and T. Hikino. 1997. The Large Industrial Enterprise and the Dynamics of Modern Economic Growth. In *Big Business and the Wealth of Nations,* edited by A. D. Chandler Jr., F. Amatori, and T. Hikino. Cambridge: Cambridge University Press.

Danziger, S. P. G. 1987. "Continuing Black Poverty: Earnings Inequality, the Spatial Concentration of Poverty, and the Underclass." *American Economic Review* 77(2): 211–215.

Evans, D., and B. Jovanovic. 1989. "An Estimated Model of Entrepreneurial Choice Under Liquidity Constraints." *Journal of Political Economy* 97(4): 808–827.

Evans, D., and L. Leighton. 1989. "Some Empirical Aspects of Entrepreneurship." *American Economic Review* 79(3): 519–535.

Field, A., and C. Harris. 1986. "Software: The Growing Gets Rough." *Business Week:* (March 24): 128–134.

Fratoe, F. 1988. "Social Capital in Black Business Owners." *Development of Black Political Economy* 16(4): 33–50.

Glade, W. P. 1967. "Approaches to a Theory of Entrepreneurship Formation." *Explorations in Entrepreneurial History* 5(3).

Goslin, L. N. 1987. "Characteristics of Successful High-Tech Start-Up Firms." In *Frontiers of Entrepreneurship Research,* edited by N. Churchill, B. Kirchoff, W. Krasner, and K. Vesper. Wellesley, MA: Babson College.

Harbison, F. H. 1956. "Entrepreneurial Organization as a Factor in Economic Development." *Quarterly Journal of Economics* 70(3).

Haug, P. 1991. "Regional Formation of High-Technology Service Industries: The Software Industry in Washington State." *Environment and Planning A* 23: 869–884.

Hikino, T., and A. H. Amsden 1994. "Staying Behind, Stumbling Back, Sneaking Up, Soaring Ahead: Late Industrialization in Historical Perspective." In *Convergence of Productivity: Cross-National Studies and Historical Evidence,* edited by W. J. Baumol, R. R. Nelson and E. N. Wolff, pp. 285–315. New York: Oxford University Press.

Hisrich, R., and C. Brush. 1986. "Characteristics of the Minority Entrepreneur." *Journal of Small Business Management* 24(4): 1–8.

Holt, D. 1987. "Network, Support Systems: How Communities Can Encourage Entrepreneurship." In *Frontiers of Entrepreneurship Research,* edited by N. Churchill, R. Kirchoff, W. Krasner, and K. Vespero. Wellesley, MA: Babson College.

Juliussen, K., and E. Juliussen. 1993. *The 1993 Computer Industry Almanac.* Austin: The Reference Press Inc.

Lichter, D. 1988. "Racial Differences in Underemployment in American Cities." *American Journal of Sociology* 93(4): 771–792.

Light, I. C. R. 1995. *Race, Ethnicity, and Entrepreneurship in Urban America.* New York: Aldine De Gruyter.

Marris, P. 1968. "The Social Barriers to African Entrepreneurship." *Journal of Development Studies* 5(1).

Merges, R. P. 1996. "A Comparative Look at Intellectual Property Rights and the Software Industry." In *The International Computer Software Industry,* edited by D. Mowery, pp. 272–303. New York: Oxford University Press.

Owens, E. H. W. 1995. "Differences Among Urban, Suburban, and Rural Schools on Technology Access and Use in Eighth-Grade Mathematics Classrooms." *Journal of Educational Technology Systems* 24(1): 83–92.

"Parents Must Ensure That Children Have Access to Information Technologies." 1995. *Black Child Advocate* (Summer): 3–7.

Picciano, A. 1991. "Computers, City and Suburb: A Study of New York City and Westchester County Public Schools." *The Urban Review* 23(3): 191–203.

Price, C. D. F., 1991. "Four Year Study of Colorado Entrepreneurship with Minority and Women Business Owners." In *Frontiers of Entrepreneurship Research,* edited by W. Bygrave. Wellesley, MA: Babson College.

Putnam, R. D. 1993. *Making Democracy Work: Civic Traditions in Modern Italy.* Princeton, NJ: Princeton University Press.

Quality Education Data. 1991. Microcomputer Uses in Schools: A 1990 –91 Q.E.D. Update. Denver.

Reynolds, P. 1995. "Who Starts New Firms? Linear Additive Versus Interaction Based Models." In *Frontiers of Entrepreneurship Research.* W. Bygrave. Wellesley, MA: Babson College.

Rush, B. et al. 1987. "The Use of Peer Networks in the Start-Up Process." *Frontiers of Entrepreneurship Research.* N. Churchill, B. Kirchoff, W. Krasner, and K. Vespero. Wellesley, MA: Babson College.

Sandefur, G. D. M. T., ed. 1988. *Divided Opportunities: Minorities, Poverty, and Social Policy.* New York: Plenum Press.

Teach, R., F. Tarpley, and R. Schwartz. 1985. "Who Are the Microcomputer Software Entrepreneurs?" In *Frontiers of Entrepreneurship Research.* B. Kirchoff. Wellesley, MA: Babson College.

Teach, R., F. Tarpley, R. Schwartz, and D. Brawley. 1987. "Maturation in the Microcomputers Software Industry: Venture Teams and Their Firms." In *Frontiers of Entrepreneurship Research,* 1987. N. Churchill, B. Kirchoff, W. Krasner, and K. Vesper. Wellesley, MA: Babson College.

U.S. Department of Education. 1996. "Private Companies Already Offering Computer Aid to Schools." *Department of Education Reports* 17(9): 5–8.

Wilson, W. J. 1987. *The Truly Disadvantaged.* Chicago: University of Chicago Press.

Wilson, W. J. 1996. *When Work Disappears: The World of the New Urban Poor.* New York: Random House.

THINKING ABOUT THE READING

What do the authors mean when they say that entry barriers into the software industry are low in physical capital but high in human and social capital? If a person doesn't have access to higher education and social networks, but has a lot of drive and "gumption," what sorts of other money-making activities might he or she be inclined to get into? Amsden and Clark point out that high levels of education are strongly associated with successful entrepreneurship. But there is a perception today that many young people are foregoing higher education and moving instead into high-paying jobs in the dot com industries. Given the data Amsden and Clark present, what sorts of jobs are these young people likely to have? Why do the authors feel that providing poor, inner-city people with computers and computer instruction is not sufficient to correct imbalances in software entrepreneurship? If they're correct, how would you go about increasing entrepreneurship among the urban poor? Use this article to discuss how stratification provides those at the top with important, nonmonetary social advantages.

Savage Inequalities in America's Schools
Life on the Mississippi: East St. Louis, Illinois

Jonathan Kozol

"East of anywhere," writes a reporter for the *St. Louis Post-Dispatch*, "often evokes the other side of the tracks. But, for a first-time visitor suddenly deposited on its eerily empty streets, East St. Louis might suggest another world." The city, which is 98 percent black, has no obstetric services, no regular trash collection, and few jobs. Nearly a third of its families live on less than $7,500 a year; 75 percent of its population lives on welfare of some form. The U.S. Department of Housing and Urban Development describes it as "the most distressed small city in America."

Only three of the 13 buildings on Missouri Avenue, one of the city's major thoroughfares, are occupied. A 13-story office building, tallest in the city, has been boarded up. Outside, on the sidewalk, a pile of garbage fills a ten-foot crater.

The city, which by night and day is clouded by the fumes that pour from vents and smokestacks at the Pfizer and Monsanto chemical plants, has one of the highest rates of child asthma in America.

It is, according to a teacher at the University of Southern Illinois, "a repository for a nonwhite population that is now regarded as expendable." The *Post-Dispatch* describes it as "America's Soweto."

Fiscal shortages have forced the layoff of 1,170 of the city's 1,400 employees in the past 12 years. The city, which is often unable to buy heating fuel or toilet paper for the city hall, recently announced that it might have to cashier all but 10 percent of the remaining work force of 230. In 1989 the mayor announced that he might need to sell the city hall and all six fire stations to raise needed cash. Last year the plan had to be scrapped after the city lost its city hall in a court

judgment to a creditor. East St. Louis is mortgaged into the next century but has the highest property-tax rate in the state.

Since October 1987, when the city's garbage pickups ceased, the backyards of residents have been employed as dump sites. In the spring of 1988 a policeman tells a visitor that 40 plastic bags of trash are waiting for removal from the backyard of his mother's house. Public health officials are concerned the garbage will attract a plague of flies and rodents in the summer. The policeman speaks of "rats as big as puppies" in his mother's yard. They are known to the residents, he says, as "bull rats." Many people have no cars or funds to cart the trash and simply burn it in their yards. The odor of smoke from burning garbage, says the *Post-Dispatch*, "has become one of the scents of spring" in East St. Louis.

Railroad tracks still used to transport hazardous chemicals run through the city. "Always present," says the *Post-Dispatch*, "is the threat of chemical spills. . . . The wail of sirens warning residents to evacuate after a spill is common." The most recent spill, the paper says, "was at the Monsanto Company plant. . . . Nearly 300 gallons of phosphorous trichloride spilled when a railroad tank was overfilled. About 450 residents were taken to St. Mary's Hospital. . . . The frequency of the emergencies has caused Monsanto to have a 'standing account' at St. Mary's." . . .

The dangers of exposure to raw sewage, which backs up repeatedly into the homes of residents in East St. Louis, were first noticed, in the spring of 1989, at a public housing project, Villa Griffin. Raw sewage, says the *Post-Dispatch*, overflowed into a playground just behind the housing project, which is home to 187 children, "forming an oozing lake of . . . tainted water." Two schoolgirls, we are told, "experienced hair loss since raw sewage flowed into their homes."

While local physicians are not certain whether loss of hair is caused by the raw sewage, they have issued warnings that exposure to raw sewage can provoke a cholera or hepatitis outbreak. A St. Louis health official voices her dismay that children live with waste in their backyards. "The development of working sewage systems made cities livable a hundred years ago," she notes. "Sewage systems separate us from the Third World."

The sewage, which is flowing from collapsed pipes and dysfunctional pumping stations, has also flooded basements all over the city. The city's vacuum truck, which uses water and suction to unclog the city's sewers, cannot be used because it needs $5,000 in repairs. Even when it works, it sometimes can't be used because there isn't money to hire drivers. A single engineer now does the work that 14 others did before they were laid off. By April the pool of overflow behind the Villa Griffin project has expanded into a lagoon of sewage. Two million gallons of raw sewage lie outside the children's homes. . . .

The Daughters of Charity, whose works of mercy are well known in the Third World, operate a mission at the Villa Griffin homes. On an afternoon in early spring of 1990, Sister Julia Huiskamp meets me on King Boulevard and drives me to the Griffin homes.

As we ride past blocks and blocks of skeletal structures, some of which are still inhabited, she slows the car repeatedly at railroad crossings. A seemingly endless railroad train rolls past us to the right. On the left: a blackened lot where garbage has been burning. Next to the burning garbage is a row of 12 white cabins, charred by fire. Next: a lot that holds a heap of auto tires and a mountain of tin cans. More burnt houses. More trash fires. The train moves almost imperceptibly across the flatness of the land.

Fifty years old, and wearing a blue suit, white blouse, and blue head-cover, Sister Julia points to the nicest house in sight. The sign on the front reads MOTEL. "It's a whorehouse," Sister Julia says.

When she slows the car beside a group of teen-age boys, one of them steps out toward the car, then backs away as she is recognized.

The 99 units of the Villa Griffin homes—two-story structures, brick on the first floor, yellow wood above—form one border of a recessed park and playground that were filled with fecal matter last year when the sewage mains exploded. The sewage is gone now and the grass is very green and looks inviting. When nine-year-old Serena and her seven-year-old brother take me for a walk, however, I discover that our shoes sink into what is still a sewage marsh. An inch-deep residue of fouled water still remains.

Serena's brother is a handsome, joyous little boy, but troublingly thin. Three other children join us as we walk along the marsh: Smokey, who is nine years old but cannot yet tell time; Mickey, who is seven; and a tiny child with a ponytail and big brown eyes who talks a constant stream of words that I can't always understand.

"Hush, Little Sister," says Serena. I ask for her name, but "Little Sister" is the only name the children seem to know.

"There go my cousins," Smokey says, pointing to two teen-age girls above us on the hill.

The day is warm, although we're only in the second week of March; several dogs and cats are playing by the edges of the marsh. "It's a lot of squirrels here," says Smokey. "There go one!"

"This here squirrel is a friend of mine," says Little Sister.

None of the children can tell me the approximate time that school begins. One says five o'clock. One says six. Another says that school begins at noon.

When I ask what song they sing after the flag pledge, one says "Jingle Bells."

Smokey cannot decide if he is in the second or third grade.

Seven-year-old Mickey sucks his thumb during the walk.

The children regale me with a chilling story as we stand beside the marsh. Smokey says his sister was raped and murdered and then dumped behind his school. Other children add more details: Smokey's sister was 11 years old. She was beaten with a brick until she died. The murder was committed by a man who knew her mother.

The narrative begins when, without warning, Smokey says, "My sister has got killed."

"She was my best friend," Serena says.

"They had beat her in the head and raped her," Smokey says.

"She was hollering out loud," says Little Sister.

I ask them when it happened. Smokey says, "Last year." Serena then corrects him and she says, "Last week."

"It scared me because I had to cry," says Little Sister.

"The police arrested one man but they didn't catch the other," Smokey says.

Serena says, "He was some kin to her."

But Smokey objects, "He weren't no kin to me. He was my momma's friend."

"Her face was busted," Little Sister says.

Serena describes this sequence of events: "They told her go behind the school. They'll give her a quarter if she do. Then they knock her down and told her not to tell what they had did."

I ask, "Why did they kill her?"

"They was scared that she would tell," Serena says.

"One is in jail," says Smokey. "They can't find the other."

"Instead of raping little bitty children, they should find themselves a wife," says Little Sister.

"I hope," Serena says, "her spirit will come back and get that man."

"And *kill* that man," says Little Sister.

"Give her another chance to live," Serena says.

"My teacher came to the funeral," says Smokey.

"When a little child dies, my momma say a star go straight to Heaven," says Serena.

"My grandma was murdered," Mickey says out of the blue. "Somebody shot two bullets in her head."

I ask him, "Is she really dead?"

"She dead all right," says Mickey. "She was layin' there, just dead."

"I love my friends," Serena says. "I don't care if they no kin to me. I care for them. I hope his mother have another baby. Name her for my friend that's dead."

"I have a cat with three legs," Smokey says.

"Snakes hate rabbits," Mickey says, again for no apparent reason.

"Cats hate fishes," Little Sister says.

"It's a lot of hate," says Smokey.

Later, at the mission, Sister Julia tells me this: "The Jefferson School, which they attend, is a decrepit hulk. Next to it is a modern school, erected two years ago, which was to have replaced the one that they attend. But the construction was not done correctly. The roof is too heavy for the walls, and the entire structure has begun to sink. It can't be occupied. Smokey's sister was raped and murdered and dumped between the old school and the new one."

As the children drift back to their homes for supper, Sister Julia stands outside with me and talks about the health concerns that trouble people in the neighborhood. In the setting sun, the voices of the children fill the evening air. Nourished by the sewage marsh, a field of wild daffodils is blooming. Standing here, you wouldn't think that anything was wrong. The street is calm. The poison in the soil can't be seen. The sewage is invisible and only makes the grass a little greener. Bikes thrown down by children lie outside their kitchen doors. It could be an ordinary twilight in a small suburban town.

Night comes on and Sister Julia goes inside to telephone a cab. In another hour, the St. Louis taxis will not come into the neighborhood. . . .

East St. Louis—which the local press refers to as "an inner city without an outer city"—has some of the sickest children in America. Of 66 cities in Illinois, East St. Louis ranks first in fetal death, first in premature birth, and third in infant death. Among the negative factors listed by the city's health director are the sewage running in the streets, air that has been fouled by the local plants, the high lead levels noted in the soil, poverty, lack of education, crime, dilapidated housing, insufficient health care, unemployment. Hospital care is deficient too. There is no place to have a baby in East St. Louis. The maternity ward at the city's Catholic hospital, a 100-year-old structure, was shut down some years ago. The only other hospital in town was forced by lack of funds to close in 1990. The closest obstetrics service open to the women here is seven miles away. The infant death rate is still rising.

As in New York City's poorest neighborhoods, dental problems also plague the children here. Although dental problems don't command the instant fears associated with low birth weight, fetal death or cholera, they do have the consequence of wearing down the stamina of children and defeating their ambitions. Bleeding gums, impacted teeth and rotting teeth are routine matters for the children I have interviewed in the South Bronx. Children get used to feeling constant pain. They go to sleep with it. They go to school with it. Sometimes their teachers are alarmed and try to get them to a clinic. But it's all so slow and heavily encumbered with red tape and waiting lists and missing, lost or canceled welfare cards, that dental care is often delayed. Children live for months with pain that grown-ups would find unendurable. The gradual attrition of accepted pain erodes their energy and aspiration. I have seen children in New York with teeth that look like brownish, broken sticks. I have also seen teenagers who were missing half their teeth. But, to me, most shocking is to see a child with an abscess that has been inflamed for weeks and that he has simply lived with and accepts as part of the routine of life. Many teachers in the urban schools have seen this. It is almost commonplace.

Compounding these problems is the poor nutrition of the children here—average daily food expenditure in East St. Louis is $2.40 for one child—and the underimmunization of young children. Of every 100 children recently surveyed in East St. Louis, 55 were incompletely immunized for polio, diphtheria, measles and whooping cough. In this context, health officials look with all the more uneasiness at those lagoons of sewage outside public housing.

On top of all else is the very high risk of death by homicide in East St. Louis. In a recent year in

which three cities in the state of roughly the same size as East St. Louis had an average of four homicides apiece, there were 54 homicides in East St. Louis. But it is the heat of summer that officials here particularly dread. The heat that breeds the insects bearing polio or hepatitis in raw sewage also heightens asthma and frustration and reduces patience. "The heat," says a man in public housing, "can bring out the beast. . . ."

The fear of violence is very real in East St. Louis. The CEO of one of the large companies out on the edge of town has developed an "evacuation plan" for his employees. State troopers are routinely sent to East St. Louis to put down disturbances that the police cannot control. If the misery of this community explodes someday in a real riot (it has happened in the past), residents believe that state and federal law-enforcement agencies will have no hesitation in applying massive force to keep the violence contained. . . .

The problems of the streets in urban areas, as teachers often note, frequently spill over into public schools. In the public schools of East St. Louis this is literally the case.

"Martin Luther King Junior High School," notes the *Post-Dispatch* in a story published in the early spring of 1989, "was evacuated Friday afternoon after sewage flowed into the kitchen. . . . The kitchen was closed and students were sent home." On Monday, the paper continues, "East St. Louis Senior High School was awash in sewage for the second time this year." The school had to be shut because of "fumes and backed-up toilets." Sewage flowed into the basement, through the floor, then up into the kitchen and the students' bathrooms. The backup, we read, "occurred in the food preparation areas."

School is resumed the following morning at the high school, but a few days later the overflow recurs. This time the entire system is affected, since the meals distributed to every student in the city are prepared in the two schools that have been flooded. School is called off for all 16,500 students in the district. The sewage backup, caused by the failure of two pumping stations, forces officials at the high school to shut down the furnaces.

At Martin Luther King, the parking lot and gym are also flooded. "It's a disaster," says a legislator. "The streets are underwater; gaseous fumes are being emitted from the pipes under the schools," she says, "making people ill."

In the same week, the schools announce the layoff of 280 teachers, 166 cooks and cafeteria workers, 25 teacher aides, 16 custodians and 18 painters, electricians, engineers and plumbers. The president of the teachers' union says the cuts, which will bring the size of kindergarten and primary classes up to 30 students, and the size of fourth to twelfth grade classes up to 35, will have "an unimaginable impact" on the students. "If you have a high school teacher with five classes each day and between 150 and 175 students . . . , it's going to have a devastating effect." The school system, it is also noted, has been using more than 70 "permanent substitute teachers," who are paid only $10,000 yearly, as a way of saving money.

Governor Thompson, however, tells the press that he will not pour money into East St. Louis to solve long-term problems. East St. Louis residents, he says, must help themselves. "There is money in the community," the governor insists. "It's just not being spent for what it should be spent for."

The governor, while acknowledging that East St. Louis faces economic problems, nonetheless refers dismissively to those who live in East St. Louis. "What in the community," he asks, "is being done right?" He takes the opportunity of a visit to the area to announce a fiscal grant for sewer improvement to a relatively wealthy town nearby.

In East St. Louis, meanwhile, teachers are running out of chalk and paper, and their paychecks are arriving two weeks late. The city warns its teachers to expect a cut of half their pay until the fiscal crisis has been eased.

The threatened teacher layoffs are mandated by the Illinois Board of Education, which, because of the city's fiscal crisis, has been given supervisory control of the school budget. Two weeks later the state superintendent partially relents. In a tone very different from that of the governor, he notes that East St. Louis does not have the means to solve its education problems on its own. "There is no natural way," he says, that "East St. Louis can bring itself out of this situation." Several cuts will be required in any case—one quarter of the system's teachers, 75 teacher aides, and several dozen others will be given notice—but, the state board notes, sports and music programs will not be affected.

East St. Louis, says the chairman of the state board, "is simply the worst possible place I can imagine to have a child brought up. . . . The community is in desperate circumstances." Sports and music, he observes, are, for many children here, "the only avenues of success." Sadly enough, no matter how it ratifies the stereotype, this is the truth; and there is a poignant aspect to the fact that, even with class size soaring and one quarter of the system's teachers being given their dismissal, the state board of education demonstrates its genuine but skewed compassion by attempting to leave sports and music untouched by the overall austerity.

Even sports facilities, however, are degrading by comparison with those found and expected at most high schools in America. The football field at East St. Louis High is missing almost everything—including goalposts. There are a couple of metal pipes—no crossbar, just the pipes. Bob Shannon, the football coach, who has to use his personal funds to purchase footballs and has had to cut and rake the football field himself, has dreams of having goalposts someday. He'd also like to let his students have new uniforms. The ones they wear are nine years old and held together somehow by a patchwork of repairs. Keeping them clean is a problem, too. The school cannot afford a washing machine. The uniforms are carted to a corner laundromat with fifteen dollars' worth of quarters. . . .

In the wing of the school that holds vocational classes, a damp, unpleasant odor fills the halls. The school has a machine shop, which cannot be used for lack of staff, and a woodworking shop. The only shop that's occupied this morning is the auto-body class. A man with long blond hair and wearing a white sweat suit swings a paddle to get children in their chairs. "What we need the most is new equipment," he reports. "I have equipment for alignment, for example, but we don't have money to install it. We also need a better form of egress. We bring the cars in through two other classes." Computerized equipment used in most repair shops, he reports, is far beyond the high school's budget. It looks like a very old gas station in an isolated rural town.

The science labs at East St. Louis High are 30 to 50 years outdated. John McMillan, a soft-spoken man, teaches physics at the school. He shows me his lab. The six lab stations in the room have empty holes where pipes were once attached. "It would be great if we had water," says McMillan. . . .

Leaving the chemistry labs, I pass a double-sized classroom in which roughly 60 kids are sitting fairly still but doing nothing. "This is supervised study hall," a teacher tells me in the corridor. But when we step inside, he finds there is no teacher. "The teacher must be out today," he says.

Irl Solomon's history classes, which I visit next, have been described by journalists who cover East St. Louis as the highlight of the school. Solomon, a man of 54 whose reddish hair is turning white, has taught in urban schools for almost 30 years. A graduate of Brandeis University in 1961, he entered law school but was drawn away by a concern with civil rights. "After one semester, I decided that the law was not for me. I said, 'Go and find the toughest place there is to teach. See if you like it.' I'm still here. . . ."

Teachers like Mr. Solomon, working in low-income districts such as East St. Louis, often tell me that they feel cut off from educational developments in modern public schools. "Well, it's amazing," Solomon says. "I have done without so much so long that, if I were assigned to a suburban school, I'm not sure I'd recognize what they are doing. We are utterly cut off."

"Very little education in the school would be considered academic in the suburbs. Maybe 10 to 15 percent of students are in truly academic programs. Of the 55 percent who graduate, 20 percent may go to four-year colleges: something like 10 percent of any entering class. Another 10 to 20 percent may get some other kind of higher education. An equal number join the military. . . .

"Sometimes I get worried that I'm starting to burn out. Still, I hate to miss a day. The department frequently can't find a substitute to come here, and my kids don't like me to be absent."

Solomon's advanced class, which soon comes into the room, includes some lively students with strong views.

"I don't go to physics class, because my lab has no equipment," says one student. "The typewriters in my typing class don't work. The women's toilets. . . ." She makes a sour face. "I'll be honest," she says. "I just don't use the toilets. If I do, I come back into class and I feel dirty."

"I wanted to study Latin," says another student. "But we don't have Latin in this school."

"We lost our only Latin teacher," Solomon says.

A girl in a white jersey with the message DO THE RIGHT THING on the front raises her hand. "You visit other schools," she says. "Do you think the children in this school are getting what we'd get in a nice section of St. Louis?"

I note that we are in a different state and city.

"Are we citizens of East St. Louis or America?" she asks. . . .

Clark Junior High School is regarded as the top school in the city. I visit, in part, at the request of school officials, who would like me to see education in the city at its very best. Even here, however, there is a disturbing sense that one has entered a backwater of America.

"We spend the entire eighth grade year preparing for the state exams," a teacher tells me in a top-ranked English class. The teacher seems devoted to the children, but three students sitting near me sleep through the entire period. The teacher rouses one of them, a girl in the seat next to me, but the student promptly lays her head back on her crossed arms and is soon asleep again. Four of the 14 ceiling lights are broken. The corridor outside the room is filled with voices. Outside the window, where I see no schoolyard, is an empty lot.

In a mathematics class of 30 children packed into a space that might be adequate for 15 kids, there is one white student. The first white student I have seen in East St. Louis, she is polishing her nails with bright red polish. A tiny black girl next to her is writing with a one-inch pencil stub.

In a seventh grade social studies class, the only book that bears some relevance to black concerns—its title is *The American Negro*—bears a publication date of 1967. The teacher invites me to ask the class some questions. Uncertain where to start, I ask the students what they've learned about the civil rights campaigns of recent decades.

A 14-year-old girl with short black curly hair says this: "Every year in February we are told to read the same old speech of Martin Luther King. We read it every year. 'I have a dream. . . .' It does begin to seem—what is the word?" She hesitates and then she finds the word: "perfunctory."

I ask her what she means.

"We have a school in East St. Louis named for Dr. King," she says. "The school is full of sewer water and the doors are locked with chains. Every student in that school is black. It's like a terrible joke on history."

It startles me to hear her words, but I am startled even more to think how seldom any press reporter has observed the irony of naming segregated schools for Martin Luther King. Children reach the heart of these hypocrisies much quicker than the grown-ups and the experts do.

Public Education in New York

The train ride from Grand Central Station to suburban Rye, New York, takes 35 to 40 minutes. The high school is a short ride from the station. Built of handsome gray stone and set in a landscaped campus, it resembles a New England prep school. On a day in early June of 1990, I enter the school and am directed by a student to the office.

The principal, a relaxed, unhurried man who, unlike many urban principals, seems gratified to have me visit in his school, takes me in to see the auditorium, which, he says, was recently restored with private charitable funds ($400,000) raised by parents. The crenellated ceiling, which is white and spotless, and the polished dark-wood paneling contrast with the collapsing structure of the auditorium at Morris High. The principal strikes his fist against the balcony: "They made this place extremely solid." Through a window, one can see the spreading branches of a beech tree in the central courtyard of the school.

In a student lounge, a dozen seniors are relaxing on a carpeted floor that is constructed with a number of tiers so that, as the principal explains, "they can stretch out and be comfortable while reading."

The library is wood-paneled, like the auditorium. Students, all of whom are white, are seated at private carrels, of which there are approximately 40. Some are doing homework; others are looking through the *New York Times*. Every student that I see during my visit to the school is white or Asian, though I later learn there are a number of Hispanic students and that 1 or 2 percent of students in the school are black.

According to the principal, the school has 96 computers for 546 children. The typical student, he says, studies a foreign language for four or five years, beginning in the junior high school, and a second foreign language (Latin is available) for two years. Of 140 seniors, 92 are now enrolled in AP classes. Maximum teacher salary will soon reach $70,000. Per-pupil funding is above $12,000 at the time I visit.

The students I meet include eleventh and twelfth graders. The teacher tells me that the class is reading Robert Coles, Studs Terkel, Alice Walker. He tells me I will find them more than willing to engage me in debate, and this turns out to be correct. Primed for my visit, it appears, they arrow in directly on the dual questions of equality and race.

Three general positions soon emerge and seem to be accepted widely. The first is that the fiscal inequalities "do matter very much" in shaping what a school can offer ("That is obvious," one student says) and that any loss of funds in Rye, as a potential consequence of future equalizing, would be damaging to many things the town regards as quite essential.

The second position is that racial integration—for example, by the busing of black children from the city or a nonwhite suburb to this school—would meet with strong resistance, and the reason would not simply be the fear that certain standards might decline. The reason, several students say straightforwardly, is "racial" or, as others say it, "out-and-out racism" on the part of adults.

The third position voiced by many students, but not all, is that equity is basically a goal to be desired and should be pursued for moral reasons, but "will probably make no major difference" since poor children "still would lack the motivation" and "would probably fail in any case because of other problems."

At this point, I ask if they can truly say "it wouldn't make a difference" since it's never been attempted. Several students then seem to rethink their views and say that "it might work, but it would have to start with preschool and the elementary grades" and "it might be 20 years before we'd see a difference."

At this stage in the discussion, several students speak with some real feeling of the present inequalities, which, they say, are "obviously unfair," and one student goes a little further and proposes that "we need to change a lot more than the schools." Another says she'd favor racial integration "by whatever means—including busing —even if my parents disapprove." But a contradictory opinion also is expressed with a good deal of fervor and is stated by one student in a rather biting voice: "I don't see why we should do it. How could it be of benefit to us?"

Throughout the discussion, whatever the views the children voice, there is a degree of unreality about the whole exchange. The children are lucid and their language is well chosen and their arguments well made, but there is a sense that they are dealing with an issue that does not feel very vivid, and that nothing that we say about it to each other really matters since it's "just a theoretical discussion." To a certain degree, the skillfulness and cleverness that they display seem to derive precisely from this sense of unreality. Questions of unfairness feel more like a geometric problem than a matter of humanity or conscience. A few of the students do break

through the note of unreality, but, when they do, they cease to be so agile in their use of words and speak more awkwardly. Ethical challenges seem to threaten their effectiveness. There is the sense that they were skating over ice and that the issues we addressed were safely frozen underneath. When they stop to look beneath the ice they start to stumble. The verbal competence they have acquired here may have been gained by building walls around some regions of the heart.

"I don't think that busing students from their ghetto to a different school would do much good," one student says. "You can take them out of the environment, but you can't take the environment out of *them*. If someone grows up in the South Bronx, he's not going to be prone to learn." His name is Max and he has short black hair and speaks with confidence. "Busing didn't work when it was tried," he says. I ask him how he knows this and he says he saw a television movie about Boston.

"I agree that it's unfair the way it is," another student says. "We have AP courses and they don't. Our classes are much smaller." But, she says, "putting them in schools like ours is not the answer. Why not put some AP classes into *their* school? Fix the roof and paint the halls so it will not be so depressing."

The students know the term "separate but equal," but seem unaware of its historical associations. "Keep them where they are but make it equal," says a girl in the front row.

A student named Jennifer, whose manner of speech is somewhat less refined and polished than that of the others, tells me that her parents came here from New York. "My family is originally from the Bronx. Schools are hell there. That's one reason that we moved. I don't think it's our responsibility to pay our taxes to provide for *them*. I mean, my parents used to live there and they wanted to get out. There's no point in coming to a place like this, where schools are good, and then your taxes go back to the place where you began."

I bait her a bit: "Do you mean that, now that you are not in hell, you have no feeling for the people that you left behind?"

"It has to be the people in the area who want an education. If your parents just don't care, it won't do any good to spend a lot of money. Someone else can't want a good life for you. You have got to want it for yourself." Then she adds, however, "I agree that everyone should have a chance at taking the same courses. . . ."

I ask her if she'd think it fair to pay more taxes so that this was possible.

"I don't see how that benefits me," she says.

It occurs to me how hard it would have been for anyone to make that kind of statement, even in the wealthiest suburban school, in 1968. Her classmates would have been unsettled by the voicing of such undisguised self-interest. Here in Rye, in 1990, she can say this with impunity. She's an interesting girl and I reluctantly admire her for being so straightforward.

Max raises a different point. "I'm not convinced," he says, "that AP courses would be valued in the Bronx. Not everyone is going to go to college."

Jennifer picks up on this and carries it a little further. "The point," she says, "is that you cannot give an equal chance to every single person. If you did it, you'd be changing the whole economic system. Let's be honest. If you equalize the money, someone's got to be shortchanged. I don't doubt that children in the Bronx are getting a bad deal. But do we want *everyone* to get a mediocre education?"

"The other point," says Max, "is that you need to match the money that you spend to whether children in the school can profit from it. We get twice as much as kids in the South Bronx, but our school is *more* than twice as good and that's because of who is here. Money isn't the whole story. . . ."

"In New York," says Jennifer, "rich people put their kids in private school. If we equalize between New York and Rye, you would see the same thing happen here. People would pull out their kids. Some people do it now. So it would happen a lot more."

An eleventh grader shakes her head at this. "Poor children need more money. It's as simple

as that," she says. "Money comes from taxes. If we have it, we should pay it."

It is at this point that a boy named David picks up on a statement made before. "Someone said just now that this is not our obligation, our responsibility. I don't think that that's the question. I don't think you'd do it, pay more taxes or whatever, out of obligation. You would do it just because . . . it is unfair the way it is." He falters on these words and looks a bit embarrassed. Unlike many of the other students who have spoken, he is somewhat hesitant and seems to choke up on his words. "Well, it's easy for me to be sitting here and say I'd spend my parents' money. I'm not working. I don't earn the money. I don't need to be conservative until I do. I can be as open-minded and unrealistic as I want to be. You can be a liberal until you have a mortgage."

I ask him what he'd likely say if he were ten years older. "Hopefully," he says, "my values would remain the same. But I know that having money does affect you. This, at least, is what they tell me."

Spurred perhaps by David's words, another student says, "The biggest tax that people pay is to the federal government. Why not take some money from the budget that we spend on armaments and use it for the children in these urban schools?"

A well-dressed student with a healthy tan, however, says that using federal taxes for the poor "would be like giving charity," and "charitable things have never worked. . . . Charity will not instill the poor with self-respect."

Max returns to something that he said before: "The environment is everything. It's going to take something more than money." He goes on to speak of inefficiency and of alleged corruption in the New York City schools. "Some years ago the chancellor was caught in borrowing $100,000 from the schools. I am told that he did not intend to pay it back. These things happen too much in New York. Why should we pour money in, when they are wasting what they have?"

I ask him, "Have we *any* obligations to poor people?"

"I don't think the burden is on us," says Jennifer again. "Taxing the rich to help the poor—we'd be getting nothing out of it. I don't understand how it would make a better educational experience for me."

"A child's in school only six hours in a day," says Max. "You've got to deal with what is happening at home. If his father's in the streets, his mother's using crack . . . how is money going to make a difference?"

David dismisses this and tells me, "Here's what we should do. Put more money into preschool, kindergarten, elementary years. Pay college kids to tutor inner-city children. Get rid of the property tax, which is too uneven, and use income taxes to support these schools. Pay teachers more to work in places like the Bronx. It has to come from taxes. Pay them extra to go into the worst schools. You could forgive their college loans to make it worth their while."

"Give the children Head Start classes," says another student. "If they need more buildings, give them extra money so they wouldn't need to be so crowded."

"It has got to come from taxes," David says again.

"I'm against busing," Max repeats, although this subject hasn't been brought up by anybody else in a long while.

"When people talk this way," says David, "they are saying, actually—" He stops and starts again: "They're saying that black kids will never learn. Even if you spend more in New York. Even if you bring them here to Rye. So what it means is—you are writing people off. You're just dismissing them. . . ."

"I'd like it if we had black students in this school," the girl beside him says.

"It seems rather odd," says David when the hour is up, "that we were sitting in an AP class discussing whether poor kids in the Bronx deserve to get an AP class. We are in a powerful position."

THINKING ABOUT THE READING

What do you suppose would happen if a student from a place like East St. Louis were to attend a school in a place like Rye? Or vice versa? At one point in the reading, one of the students from Rye says, "You can take them [that is, poor, underprivileged students] out of the environment, but you can't take the environment out of them." Do you agree or disagree with that assessment of the problem of unequal education? Do you think this is a common attitude in American society? Does it enhance or impede progress regarding inequality in this country?

The Code of the Streets

Elijah Anderson

Of all the problems besetting the poor inner-city black community, none is more pressing than that of interpersonal violence and aggression. It wreaks havoc daily with the lives of community residents and increasingly spills over into downtown and residential middle-class areas. Muggings, burglaries, carjackings, and drug-related shootings, all of which may leave their victims or innocent bystanders dead, are now common enough to concern all urban and many suburban residents. The inclination to violence springs from the circumstances of life among the ghetto poor—the lack of jobs that pay a living wage, the stigma of race, the fallout from rampant drug use and drug trafficking, and the resulting alienation and lack of hope for the future.

Simply living in such an environment places young people at special risk of falling victim to aggressive behavior. Although there are often forces in the community which can counteract the negative influences, by far the most powerful being a strong, loving, "decent" (as inner-city residents put it) family committed to middle-class values, the despair is pervasive enough to have spawned an oppositional culture, that of "the streets," whose norms are often consciously opposed to those of mainstream society. These two orientations—decent and street—socially organize the community, and their coexistence has important consequences of residents, particularly children growing up in the inner city. Above all, this environment means that even

Elijah Anderson is the Charles and William Day Distinguished Professor of the Social Sciences and Professor of Sociology at the University of Pennsylvania.

youngsters whose home lives reflect mainstream values—and the majority of homes in the community do—must be able to handle themselves in a street-oriented environment.

This is because the street culture has evolved what may be called a code of the streets, which amounts to a set of informal rules governing interpersonal public behavior, including violence. The rules prescribe both a proper comportment and a proper way to respond if challenged. They regulate the use of violence and so allow those who are inclined to aggression to precipitate violent encounters in an approved way. The rules have been established and are enforced mainly by the street-oriented, but on the streets the distinction between street and decent is often irrelevant; everybody knows that if the rules are violated, there are penalties. Knowledge of the code is thus largely defensive; it is literally necessary for operating in public. Therefore, even though families with a decency orientation are usually opposed to the values of the code, they often reluctantly encourage their children's familiarity with it to enable them to negotiate the inner-city environment.

At the heart of the code is the issue of respect—loosely defined as being treated "right," or granted the deference one deserves. However, in the troublesome public environment of the inner city, as people increasingly feel buffeted by forces beyond their control, what one deserves in the way of respect becomes more and more problematic and uncertain. This in turn further opens the issue of respect to sometimes intense interpersonal negotiation. In the street culture, especially among young people, respect is viewed as almost and external entity that is hard-won but easily lost, and so must constantly be guarded. The rules of the code in fact provide a framework for negotiating respect. The person whose very appearance—including his clothing, demeanor, and way of moving—deters transgressions feels that he possesses, and may be considered by others to possess, a measure of respect. With the right amount of respect, for instance, he can avoid "being bothered" in public. If he is bothered, not only may he be in physical danger but he has been disgraced or "dissed" (disrespected). Many of the forms that dissing can take might seem petty to middle-class people (maintaining eye contact for too long, for example), but to those invested in the street code, these actions become serious indications of the other person's intentions. Consequently, such people become very sensitive to advances and slights, which could well serve as warnings of imminent physical confrontation.

This hard reality can be traced to the profound sense of alienation from mainstream society and its institutions felt by many poor inner-city black people, particularly the young. The code of the streets is actually a cultural adaptation to a profound lack of faith in the police and the judicial system. The police are most often seen as representing the dominant white society and not caring to protect inner-city residents. When called, they may not respond, which is one reason many residents feel they must be prepared to take extraordinary measures to defend themselves and their loved ones against those who are inclined to aggression. Lack of police accountability has in fact been incorporated into the status system: the person who is believed capable of "taking care of himself" is accorded a certain deference, which translates into a sense of physical and psychological control. Thus the street code emerges where the influence of the police ends and personal responsibility for one's safety is felt to begin. Exacerbated by the proliferation of drugs and easy access to guns, this volatile situation results in the ability of the street-oriented minority (or those who effectively "go for bad") to dominate the public spaces.

Decent and Street Families

Although almost everyone in poor inner-city neighborhoods is struggling financially and therefore feels a certain distance from the rest of America, the decent and the street family in a real sense represent two poles of value orientation, two contrasting conceptual categories. The labels "decent" and "street," which the residents themselves use, amount to evaluative judgments that confer status on local residents. The labeling is often the result of a social contest among individuals and families of the neighborhood. Individuals of the two orientations often coexist in the same extended family. Decent residents judge themselves to be so while judging others to be of the street, and street individuals often present themselves as decent, drawing distinctions between themselves and other people. In addition, there is quite a bit of circumstantial behavior—that is, one person may at different times exhibit both decent and street orientations, depending on the circumstances. Although these designations result from so much social jockeying, there do exist concrete features that define each conceptual category.

Generally, so-called decent families tend to accept mainstream values more fully and attempt to instill them in their children. Whether married couples with children or single-parent (usually female) households, they are generally "working poor" and so tend to be better off financially than their street-oriented neighbors. They value hard work and self-reliance and are willing to sacrifice for their children. Because they have a certain amount of faith in mainstream society, they harbor hopes for a better future for their children, if not for themselves. Many of them go to church and take a strong interest in their children's schooling. Rather than dwelling on the real hardships and inequities facing them, many such decent people, particularly the increasing number of grandmothers raising grandchildren, see their difficult situation as a test from God and derive great support from their faith and from the church community.

Extremely aware of the problematic and often dangerous environment in which they reside, decent parents tend to be strict in their child-rearing practices, encouraging children to respect authority and walk a straight moral line. They have an almost obsessive concern about trouble of any kind and remind their children to be on the lookout for people and situations that might lead to it. At the same time, they are themselves polite and considerate of others, and teach their children to be the same way. At home, at work, and in church, they strive hard to maintain a positive mental attitude and a spirit of cooperation.

So-called street parents, in contrast, often show a lack of consideration for other people and have a rather superficial sense of family and community. Though they may love their children, many of them are unable to cope with the physical and emotional demands of parenthood, and find it difficult to reconcile their needs with those of their children. These families, who are more fully invested in the code of the streets than the decent people are, may aggressively socialize their children into it in a normative way. They believe in the code and judge themselves and others according to its values.

In fact the overwhelming majority of families in the inner-city community try to approximate the decent-family model, but there are many others who clearly represent the worst fears of the decent family. Not only are their financial resources extremely limited, but what little they have may easily be misused. The lives of the street-oriented are often marked by disorganization. In the most desperate circumstances people frequently have a limited understanding of priorities and consequences, and so frustrations mount over bills, food, and, at times, drink, cigarettes, and drugs. Some tend toward self-destructive behavior; many street-oriented women are crack-addicted ("on the pipe"), alcoholic, or involved in complicated relationships with men who abuse them. In addition, the seeming intractability of their situation, caused in large part by the luck of well-paying jobs and

the persistence of racial discrimination, has engendered deep-seated bitterness and anger in many of the most desperate and poorest blacks, especially young people. The need both to exercise a measure of control and to lash out at somebody is often reflected in the adults' relations with their children. At the least, the frustrations of persistent poverty shorten the fuse in such people—contributing to a lack of patience with anyone, child or adult, who irritates them.

In these circumstances a woman—or a man, although men are less consistently present in children's lives—can be quite aggressive with children, yelling at and striking them for the least little infraction of the rules she has set down. Often little if any serious explanation follows the verbal and physical punishment. This response teaches children a particular lesson. They learn that to solve any kind of interpersonal problem one must quickly resort to hitting or other violent behavior. Actual peace and quiet, and also the appearance of calm, respectful children conveyed to her neighbors and friends, are often what the young mother most desires, but at times she will be very aggressive in trying to get them. Thus she may be quick to beat her children, especially if they defy her law, not because she hates them but because this is the way she knows to control them. In fact, many street-oriented women love their children dearly. Many mothers in the community subscribe to the notion that there is a "devil in the boy" that must be beaten out of him or that socially "fast girls need to be whupped." Thus much of what borders on child abuse in the view of social authorities is acceptable parental punishment in the view of these mothers.

Many street-oriented women are sporadic mothers whose children learn to fend for themselves when necessary, foraging for food and money any way they can get it. The children are sometimes employed by drug dealers of become addicted themselves. These children of the street, growing up with little supervision, are said to "come up hard." They often learn to fight at an early age, sometimes using short-tempered adults around them as role models. The street-oriented home may be fraught with anger, verbal disputes, physical aggression, and even mayhem. The children observe these goings-on, learning the lesson that might makes right. They quickly learn to hit those who cross them, and the dog-eat-dog mentality prevails. In order to survive, to protect oneself, it is necessary to marshal inner resources and be ready to deal with adversity in a hands-on way. In these circumstances physical prowess takes on great significance.

In some of the most desperate cases, a street-oriented mother may simply leave her young children alone and unattended while she goes out. The most irresponsible women can be found at local bars and crack houses, getting high and socializing with other adults. Sometimes a troubled woman will leave very young children alone for days at a time. Reports of crack addicts abandoning their children have become common in drug-infested inner-city communities. Neighbors or relatives discover the abandoned children, often hungry and distraught over the absence of their mother. After repeated absences, a friend or relative, particularly a grandmother, will often step in to care for the young children, sometimes petitioning the authorities to send her, as guardian of the children, the mother's welfare check, if the mother gets one. By this time, however, the children may well have learned the first lesson of the streets: survival itself, let alone respect, cannot be taken for granted; you have to fight for your place in the world.

Campaigning for Respect

These realities of inner-city life are largely absorbed on the streets. At an early age, often even before they start school, children from street-oriented homes gravitate to the streets, where they "hang"—socialize with their peers. Children from these generally permissive homes have a great deal of latitude and are allowed to "rip and run" up and down the street. They often come home from school, put their books down, and go right back out the door. On school nights eight- and nine-year-olds remain out until nine or ten o'clock (and teenagers typically come in whenever they want to). On the streets they play in groups that often become the source of their primary social bonds. Children from decent homes tend to be more carefully supervised and are thus likely to have curfews and to be taught how to stay out of trouble.

When decent and street kids come together, a kind of social shuffle occurs in which children have a chance to go either way. Tension builds as a child comes to realize that he must choose an orientation. The kind of home he comes from influences but does not determine the way he will ultimately turn out—although it is unlikely that a child from a thoroughly street-oriented family will easily absorb decent values on the streets. Youths who emerge from street-oriented families but develop a decency orientation almost always learn those values in another setting—in school, in a youth group, in church. Often it is the result of their involvement with a caring "old head" (adult role model).

In the street, through their play, children pour their individual life experiences into a common knowledge pool, affirming, confirming, and elaborating on what they have observed in the home and matching their skills against those of others. And they learn to fight. Even small children test one another, pushing and shoving, and are ready to hit other children over circumstances not to their liking. In turn, they are readily hit by other children, and the child who is toughest prevails. Thus the violent resolution of disputes, the hitting and cursing, gains social reinforcement. The child in effect is initiated into a system that is really a way of campaigning for respect.

In addition, younger children witness the disputes of older children, which are often resolved through cursing and abusive talk, if not aggression or outright violence. They see that one child succumbs to the greater physical and mental abilities of the other. They are also alert and attentive witnesses to the verbal and physical fights of adults, after which they compare notes and share their interpretations of the event. In almost every case the victor is the person who physically won the altercation, and this person often enjoys the esteem and respect of onlookers. These experiences reinforce the lessons the children have learned at home: might makes right, and toughness is a virtue, while humility is not. In effect they learn the social meaning of fighting. When it is left virtually unchallenged, this understanding becomes an ever more important part of the child's working conception of the world. Over time the code of the streets becomes refined.

Those street-oriented adults with whom children come in contact—including mothers, fathers, brothers, sisters, boyfriends, cousins, neighbors, and friends—help them along in forming this understanding by verbalizing the messages they are getting through experience: "Watch your back." "Protect yourself." "Don't punk out." "If somebody messes with you, you got to pay them back." "If someone disses you, you got to straighten them out." Many parents actually impose sanctions if a child is not sufficiently aggressive. For example, if a child loses a fight and comes home upset, the parent might respond, "Don't you come in here crying that somebody beat you up; you better get back out there and whup his ass. I didn't raise no punks! Get back out there and whup his ass. If you don't whup his ass, I'll whup your ass when you come home." Thus the child obtains reinforcement for being tough and showing nerve.

While fighting, some children cry as though they are doing something they are ambivalent about. The fight may be against their wishes, yet they may feel constrained to fight or face the consequences—not just from peers but also from caretakers or parents, who may administer another beating if they back down. Some adults recall receiving such lessons from their own parents and justify repeating them to their children as a way to toughen them up. Looking capable of taking care of oneself as a form of self-defense is a dominant theme among both street-oriented and decent adults who worry about the safety of

their children. There is thus at times a convergence in their child-rearing practices, although the rationales behind them may differ.

Self-Image Based on "Juice"

By the time they are teenagers, most youths have either internalized the code of the streets or at least learned the need to comport themselves in accordance with its rules, which chiefly have to do with interpersonal communication. The code revolves around the presentation of self. Its basic requirement is the display of a certain predisposition to violence. Accordingly, one's bearing must send the unmistakable if sometimes subtle message to "the next person" in public that one is capable of violence and mayhem when the situation requires it, that one can take care of oneself. The nature of this communication is largely determined by the demands of the circumstances but can include facial expressions, gait, and verbal expressions—all of which are geared mainly to deterring aggression. Physical appearance, including clothes, jewelry, and grooming, also plays an important part in how a person is viewed; to be respected, it is important to have the right look.

Even so, there are no guarantees against challenges, because there are always people around looking for a fight to increase their share of respect—or "juice," as it is sometimes called on the street. Moreover, if a person is assaulted, it is important, not only in the eyes of his opponent but also in the eyes of his "running buddies," for him to avenge himself. Otherwise he risks being "tried" (challenged) or "moved on" by any number of others. To maintain his honor he must show he is not someone to be "messed with" or "dissed." In general, the person must "keep himself straight" by managing his position of respect among others; this involves in part his self-image, which is shaped by what he thinks others are thinking of him in relation to his peers.

Objects play an important and complicated role in establishing self-image. Jackets, sneakers, gold jewelry, reflect not just a person's taste, which tends to be tightly regulated among adolescents of all social classes, but also a willingness to possess things that may require defending. A boy wearing a fashionable, expensive jacket, for example, is vulnerable to attack by another who covets the jacket and either cannot afford to buy one or wants the added satisfaction of depriving someone else of his. However, if they boy forgoes the desirable jacket and wears one that isn't "hip," he runs the risk of being teased and possibly even assaulted as an unworthy person. To be allowed to hang with certain prestigious crowds, a boy must wear a different set of expensive clothes—sneakers and athletic suit—every day. Not to be able to do so might make him appear socially deficient. The youth comes to covet such items—especially when he sees easy prey wearing them.

In acquiring valued things, therefore, a person shores up his identity—but since it is an identity based on having things, it is highly precarious. This very precariousness gives a heightened sense of urgency to staying even with peers, with whom the person is actually competing. Young men and women who are able to command respect through their presentation of self—by allowing their possessions and their body language to speak for them—may not have to campaign for regard but may, rather, gain it by the force of their manner. Those who are unable to command respect in this way must actively campaign for it—and are thus particularly alive to slights.

One way of campaigning for status is by taking the possessions of others. In this context, seemingly ordinary objects can become trophies imbued with symbolic value that far exceeds their monetary worth. Possession of the trophy can symbolize the ability to violate somebody—to "get in his face," to take something of value from him, to "dis" him, and thus to enhance one's own worth by stealing someone else's. The trophy does not have to be something material. It can be another person's sense of honor, snatched away with a derogatory remark. It can be the outcome of a fight. It can be the imposition of a certain standard, such as a girl's getting herself recognized as the most beautiful. Material things, however, fit easily into the pattern. Sneakers, a pistol, even somebody else's girlfriend, can become a trophy. When a person can take something from another and then flaunt it, he gains a certain regard by being the owner, or the controller, of that thing. But this display of ownership can then provoke other people to challenge him. This game of who controls what is thus constantly being played out on inner-city streets, and the trophy—extrinsic or intrinsic, tangible or intangible—identifies the current winner.

An important aspect of this often violent give-and-take is its zero-sum quality. That is, the extent to which one person can raise himself up depends on his ability to put another person down. This underscores the alienation that permeates the inner-city ghetto community. There is a generalized sense that very little respect is to be had, and therefore everyone competes to get what affirmation he can of the little that is available. The craving for respect that results gives people thin skins. Shows of deference by others can be highly soothing, contributing to a sense of security, comfort, self-confidence, and self-respect. Transgressions by others which go unanswered diminish these feelings and are believed to encourage further transgressions. Hence one must be ever vigilant against the transgressions of others or even *appearing* as if transgressions will be tolerated. Among young people, whose sense of self-esteem is particularly vulnerable, there is an especially heightened concern with being disrespected. Many inner-city young men in particular crave respect to such a degree that they will risk their lives to attain and maintain it.

The issue of respect is thus closely tied to whether a person has an inclination to be violent, even as a victim. In the wider society people may not feel required to retaliate physically after an attack, even though they are aware that they have been degraded or taken advantage of. They may feel a great need to defend themselves *during* an attack, or to behave in such a way as to deter aggression (middle-class people certainly can and do become victims of street-oriented youths), but they are much more likely than street-oriented people to feel that they can walk away from a possible altercation with their self-esteem intact. Some people may even have the strength of character to flee, without any thought that their self-respect or esteem will be diminished.

In impoverished inner-city black communities, however, particularly among young males and perhaps increasingly among females, such flight would be extremely difficult. To run away would likely leave one's self-esteem in tatters. Hence people often feel constrained not only to stand up and at least attempt to resist during an assault but also to "pay back"—to seek revenge—after a successful assault on their person. This may include going to get a weapon or even getting relatives involved. Their very identity and self-respect, their honor, is often intricately tied up with the way they perform on the streets during and after such encounters. This outlook reflects the circumscribed opportunities of the inner-city poor. Generally people outside the ghetto have other ways of gaining status and regard, and thus do not feel so dependent on such physical displays.

By Trial of Manhood

On the street, among males these concerns about things and identity have come to be expressed in the concept of "manhood." Manhood in the inner city means taking the prerogatives of men with respect to strangers, other men, and women—being distinguished as a man. It implies physicality and a certain ruthlessness. Regard and respect are associated with this concept in large part because of its practical application: if others have little or no regard for a person's manhood, his very life and those of this loved ones could be in jeopardy. But there is a chicken-and-egg aspect to this situation: one's physical safety is more likely to be jeopardized in public *because* manhood is associated with respect. In other words, an existential link has been created between the idea of manhood and one's self-esteem, so that it has become hard to say which is

primary. For many inner-city youths, manhood and respect are flip sides of the same coin; physical and psychological well-being are inseparable, and both require a sense of control, of being in charge.

The operating assumption is that a man, especially a real man, knows what other men know—the code of the streets. And if one is not a real man, one is somehow diminished as a person, and there are certain valued things one simply does not deserve. There is thus believed to be a certain justice to the code, since it is considered that everyone has the opportunity to know it. Implicit in this is that everybody is held responsible for being familiar with the code. If the victim of a mugging, for example, does not know the code and so responds "wrong," the perpetrator may feel justified even in killing him and may feel no remorse. He may think, "Too bad, but it's his fault. He should have known better."

So when a person ventures outside, he must adopt the code—a kind of shield, really—to prevent others from "messing with" him. In these circumstances it is easy for people to think they are being tried or tested by others even when this is not the case. For it is sensed that something extremely valuable is at stake in every interaction, and people are encouraged to rise to the occasion, particularly with strangers. For people who are unfamiliar with the code—generally people who live outside the inner city—the concern with respect in the most ordinary interactions can be frightening and incomprehensible. But for those who are invested in the code, the clear object of their demeanor is to discourage strangers from even thinking about testing their manhood. And the sense of power that attends the ability to deter others can be alluring even to those who know the code without being heavily invested in it—the decent inner-city youths. Thus a boy who has been leading a basically decent life can, in trying circumstances, suddenly resort to deadly force.

Central to the issue of manhood is the widespread belief that one of the most effective ways of gaining respect is to manifest "nerve." Nerve is shown when one takes another person's posses-sions (the more valuable the better), "messes with" someone's woman, throws the first punch, "gets in someone's face," or pulls a trigger. Its proper display helps on the spot to check others who would violate one's person and also helps to build a reputation that works to prevent future challenges. But since such a show of nerve is a forceful expression of disrespect toward the per-son on the receiving end, the victim may be greatly offended and seek to retaliate with equal or greater force. A display of nerve, therefore, can easily provoke a life-threatening response, and the background knowledge of that possibility has of-ten been incorporated into the concept of nerve.

True nerve exposes a lack of fear of dying. Many feel that it is acceptable to risk dying over the principle of respect. In fact, among the hard-core street-oriented, the clear risk of violent death may be preferable to being "dissed" by an-other. The youths who have internalized this atti-tude and convincingly display it in their public bearing are among the most threatening people of all, for it is commonly assumed that they fear no man. As the people of the community say, "They are the baddest dudes on the street." They often lead an existential life that may acquire meaning only when they are faced with the pos-sibility of imminent death. Not to be afraid to die is by implication to have few compunctions about taking another's life. Not to be afraid to die is the quid pro quo of being able to take somebody else's life—for the right reasons, if the situation demands it. When others believe this is one's position, it gives one a real sense of power on the streets. Such credibility is what many inner-city youths strive to achieve, whether they are decent or street-oriented, both because of its practical defensive value and because of the posi-tive way it makes them feel about themselves. The difference between the decent and the street-oriented youth is often that the decent youth makes a conscious decision to appear tough and manly; in another setting—with teachers, say, or at his part-time job—he can be polite and defer-ential. The street-oriented youth, on the other

hand, has made the concept of manhood a part of his very identity; he has difficulty manipulat-ing it—it often controls him.

Girls and Boys

Increasingly, teenage girls are mimicking the boys and trying to have their own version of "manhood." Their goal is the same—to get re-spect, to be recognized as capable of setting or maintaining a certain standard. They try to achieve this end in the ways that have been es-tablished by the boys, including posturing, abu-sive language, and the use of violence to resolve disputes, but the issues for the girls are different. Although conflicts over turf and status exist among the girls, the majority of disputes seem rooted in assessments of beauty (which girl in a group is "the cutest"), competition over boy-friends, and attempts to regulate other people's knowledge of and opinions about a girl's behav-ior or that of someone close to her, especially her mother.

A major cause of conflicts among girls is "he say, she say." This practice begins in the early school years and continues through high school. It occurs when "people," particularly girls, talk about others, thus putting their "business in the streets." Usually one girl will say something nega-tive about another in the group, most often be-hind the person's back. The remark will then get back to the person talked about. She may retali-ate or her friends may feel required to "take up for" her. In essence this is a form of group gos-siping in which individuals are negatively as-sessed and evaluated. As with much gossip, the things said may or may not be true, but the point is that such imputations can cast aspersions on a person's good name. The accused is required to defend herself against the slander, which can re-sult in arguments and fights, often over little of real substance. Here again is the problem of low self-esteem, which encourages youngsters to be highly sensitive to slights and to be vulnerable to feeling easily "dissed." To avenge the dissing, a fight is usually necessary.

Because boys are believed to control violence, girls tend to defer to them in situations of conflict. Often if a girl is attacked or feels slighted, she will get a brother, uncle, or cousin to do her fighting for her. Increasingly, however, girls are doing their own fighting and are even asking their male relatives to teach them how to fight. Some girls form groups that attack other girls or take things from them. A hard-core segment of inner-city girls inclined toward violence seems to be developing. As one thirteen-year-old girl in a detention center for youths who have committed violent acts told me, "To get people to leave you alone, you gotta fight. Talking don't always get you out of stuff." One major difference between girls and boys: girls rarely use guns. Their fights are therefore not life-or-death struggles. Girls are not often willing to put their lives on the line for "manhood." The ultimate form of respect on the male-dominated inner-city street is thus reserved for men.

"Going for Bad"

In the most fearsome youths such a cavalier attitude toward death grows out of a very limited view of life. Many are uncertain about how long they are going to live and believe they could die violently at any time. They accept this fate; they live on the edge. Their manner conveys the message that nothing intimidates them; whatever turn the encounter takes, they maintain their attack—rather like a pit bull, whose spirit many such boys admire. The demonstration of such tenacity "shows heart" and earns their respect.

This fearlessness has implications for law enforcement. Many street-oriented boys are much more concerned about the threat of "justice" at the hands of a peer than at the hands of the police. Moreover, many feel not only that they have little to lose by going to prison but that they have something to gain. The toughening-up one experiences in prison can actually enhance one's reputation on the streets. Hence the system loses influence over the hard core who are without jobs, with little perceptible stake in the system. If mainstream society has done nothing *for* them,

they counter by making sure it can do nothing *to* them.

At the same time, however, a competing view maintains that true nerve consists in backing down, walking away from a fight, and going on with one's business. One fights only in self-defense. This view emerges from the decent philosophy that life is precious, and it is an important part of the socialization process common in decent homes. It discourages violence as the primary means of resolving disputes and encourages youngsters to accept nonviolence and talk as confrontational strategies. But "if the deal goes down," self-defense is greatly encouraged. When there is enough positive support for this orientation, either in the home or among one's peers, then nonviolence has a chance to prevail. But it prevails at the cost of relinquishing a claim to being bad and tough, and therefore sets a young person up as at the very least alienated from street-oriented peers and quite possibly a target of derision or even violence.

Although the nonviolent orientation rarely overcomes the impulse to strike back in an encounter, it does introduce a certain confusion and so can prompt a measure of soul-searching, or even profound ambivalence. Did the person back down with his respect intact or did he back down only to be judged a "punk"—a person lacking manhood? Should he or she have acted? Should he or she have hit the other person in the mouth? These questions beset many young men and women during public confrontations. What is the "right" thing to do? In the quest for honor, respect, and local status—which few young people are uninterested in—common sense most often prevails, which leads many to opt for the tough approach, enacting their own particular versions of the display of nerve. The presentation of oneself as rough and tough is very often quite acceptable until one is tested. And then that presentation may help the person pass the test, because it will cause fewer questions to be asked about what he did and why. It is hard for a person to explain why he lost the fight or why he backed down. Hence many will strive to appear to "go for bad," while hoping they will never be tested. But when they are tested, the outcome of the situation may quickly be out of their hands, as they become wrapped up in the circumstances of the moment.

An Oppositional Culture

The attitudes of the wider society are deeply implicated in the code of the streets. Most people in inner-city communities are not totally invested in the code, but the significant minority of hard-core street youths who are have to maintain the code in order to establish reputations, because they have—or feel they have—few other ways to assert themselves. For these young people the standards of the street code are the only game in town. The extent to which some children—particularly those who through upbringing have become most alienated and those lacking in strong and conventional social support—experience, feel, and internalize racist rejection and contempt from mainstream society may strongly encourage them to express contempt for the more conventional society in turn. In dealing with this contempt and rejection, some youngsters will consciously invest themselves and their considerable mental resources in what amounts to an oppositional culture to preserve themselves and their self-respect. Once they do, any respect they might be able to garner in the wider system pales in comparison with the respect available in the local system; thus they often lose interest in even attempting to negotiate the mainstream system.

At the same time, many less alienated young black have assumed a street-oriented demeanor as a way of expressing their blackness while really embracing a much more moderate way of life; they, too, want a nonviolent setting in which to live and raise a family. These decent people are trying hard to be part of the mainstream culture, but the racism, real and perceived, that they encounter helps to legitimate the oppositional culture. And so on occasion they adopt street behavior. In fact, depending on the demands of the situation, many people in the community slip back and forth between decent and street behavior.

A vicious cycle has thus been formed. The hopelessness and alienation many young inner-city black men and women feel, largely as a result of endemic joblessness and persistent racism, fuels the violence they engage in. This violence serves to confirm the negative feelings many whites and some middle-class blacks harbor toward the ghetto poor, further legitimating the oppositional culture and the code of the streets in the eyes of many poor young blacks. Unless this cycle is broken, attitudes on both sides will become increasingly entrenched, and the violence, which claims victims, black and white, poor and affluent, will only escalate.

THINKING ABOUT THE READING

What is Anderson referring to when he speaks of a "code of the streets"? What role do poverty and racism play in the development of such a code? He makes a distinction between "street families" and "decent families." How useful is such a distinction? How do these different types of families adapt to the code of the streets? Anderson implies that *all* young people in the inner city, no matter how mainstream their values, must know, and at times live by, the code of the streets. Do you agree? If it's true that young people feel that in order to gain respect they must show a willingness to be aggressive when publicly confronted, how can the vicious cycle of violence in the inner city ever be broken?

These Dark Satanic Mills

William Greider

... If the question were put now to everyone, everywhere—do you wish to become a citizen of the world?—it is safe to assume that most people in most places would answer, no, they wish to remain who they are. With very few exceptions, people think of themselves as belonging to a place, a citizen of France or Malaysia, of Boston or Tokyo or Warsaw, loyally bound to native culture, sovereign nation. The Chinese who aspire to get gloriously rich, as Deng instructed, do not intend to become Japanese or Americans. Americans may like to think of themselves as the world's leader, but not as citizens of "one world."

The deepest social meaning of the global industrial revolution is that people no longer have free choice in this matter of identity. Ready or not, they are already of the world. As producers or consumers, as workers or merchants or investors, they are now bound to distant others through the complex strands of commerce and finance reorganizing the globe as a unified marketplace. The prosperity of South Carolina or Scotland is deeply linked to Stuttgart's or Kuala Lumpur's. The true social values of Californians or Swedes will be determined by what is tolerated in the factories of Thailand or Bangladesh. The energies and brutalities of China will influence community anxieties in Seattle or Toulouse or Nagoya.

. . . Unless one intends to withdraw from modern industrial life, there is no place to hide from the others. Major portions of the earth, to be sure, remain on the periphery of the system, impoverished bystanders still waiting to be included in the action. But the patterns of global interconnectedness are already the dominant reality. Commerce has leapt beyond social con-

sciousness and, in doing so, opened up challenging new vistas for the human potential. Most people, it seems fair to say, are not yet prepared to face the implications. . . .

The process of industrialization has never been pretty in its primitive stages. Americans or Europeans who draw back in horror at the present brutalities in Asia or Latin America should understand that they are glimpsing repetitions of what happened in their own national histories, practices that were forbidden as inhumane in their own countries only after long political struggle. To make that historical point complicates the moral responses, but does not extinguish the social question.

The other realm, of course, is the wealthy nation where the established social structure is under assault, both from market forces depressing wages and employment and from the political initiatives to dismantle the welfare state. The governments' obligations to social equity were erected during the upheavals of the last century to ameliorate the harsher edges of unfettered capitalism; now they are in question again. The economic pressures to shrink or withdraw public benefits are relentless, yet no one has explained how wealthy industrial nations will maintain the social peace by deepening their inequalities.

A standard response to all these social concerns is the reassuring argument that market forces will eventually correct them—if no one interferes. The new wealth of industrialization, it is said, will lead naturally to middle-class democracy in the poorer countries and the barbarisms will eventually be eradicated. In the older societies, it is assumed that technology will create new realms of work that in time replace the lost employment, restore living wages and spread the prosperity widely again. People need only be patient with the future and not interrupt the revolution.

The global system has more or less been proceeding on these assumptions for at least a generation and one may observe that the unfolding reality has so far gravely disappointed these expectations. Nor does the free-market argument conform with the actual history of how democratic development or social equity was advanced over the last two centuries, neither of which emerged anywhere without titanic political struggles. A more pointed contradiction is the hypocrisy of those who make these arguments. If multinational enterprises truly expect greater human freedom and social equity to emerge from the marketplace, then why do they expend so much political energy to prevent these conditions from developing?

In any case, the theoretical arguments about the future do not satisfy the moral question that exists concretely at present. If one benefits tangibly from the exploitation of others who are weak, is one morally implicated in their predicament? Or are basic rights of human existence confined to those civilized societies wealthy enough to afford them? Everyone's values are defined by what they will tolerate when it is done to others. Everyone's sense of virtue is degraded by the present reality. . . .

Two centuries ago, when the English industrial revolution dawned with its fantastic invention and productive energies, the prophetic poet William Blake drew back in moral revulsion. Amid the explosion of new wealth, human destruction was spread over England—peasant families displaced from their lands, paupers and poorhouses crowded into London slums, children sent to labor at the belching ironworks or textile looms. Blake delivered a thunderous rebuke to the pious Christians of the English aristocracy with these immortal lines:

And was Jerusalem builded here
Among these dark Satanic mills?

Blake's "dark Satanic mills" have returned now and are flourishing again, accompanied by the same question.[1]

On May 10, 1993, the worst industrial fire in the history of capitalism occurred at a toy factory on the outskirts of Bangkok and was reported on page 25 of the *Washington Post*. The *Financial Times* of London, which styles itself as the daily newspaper of the global economy, ran a brief item on page 6. The *Wall Street Journal* followed a day late with an account on page 11. The *New York Times* also put the story inside, but printed a dramatic photo on its front page: rows of small shrouded bodies on bamboo pallets—dozens of them—lined along the damp pavement, while dazed rescue workers stood awkwardly among the corpses. In the background, one could see the collapsed, smoldering structure of a mammoth factory where the Kader Industrial Toy Company of Thailand had employed three thousand workers manufacturing stuffed toys and plastic dolls, playthings destined for American children.[2]

The official count was 188 dead, 469 injured, but the actual toll was undoubtedly higher since the four-story buildings had collapsed swiftly in the intense heat and many bodies were incinerated. Some of the missing were never found; others fled home to their villages. All but fourteen of the dead were women, most of them young, some as young as thirteen years old. Hundreds of the workers had been trapped on upper floors of the burning building, forced to jump from third- or fourth-floor windows, since the main exit doors were kept locked by the managers, and the narrow stairways became clotted with trampled bodies or collapsed.

When I visited Bangkok about nine months later, physical evidence of the disaster was gone—the site scraped clean by bulldozers—and Kader was already resuming production at a new toy factory, built far from the city in a rural province of northeastern Thailand. When I talked with Thai labor leaders and civic activists, people who had rallied to the cause of the fire victims, some of them were under the impression that a worldwide boycott of Kader products was under way, organized by conscience-stricken Americans and Europeans. I had to inform them that the civilized world had barely noticed their tragedy.

As news accounts pointed out, the Kader fire surpassed what was previously the worst industrial fire in history—the Triangle Shirtwaist Company fire of 1911—when 146 young immigrant women died in similar circumstances at a garment factory on the Lower East Side of Manhattan. The Triangle Shirtwaist fire became a pivotal event in American politics, a public scandal that provoked citizen reform movements and energized the labor organizing that built the International Ladies Garment Workers Union and other unions. The fire in Thailand did not produce meaningful political responses or even shame among consumers. The indifference of the leading newspapers merely reflected the tastes of their readers, who might be moved by human suffering in their own communities but were inured to news of recurring calamities in distant places. A fire in Bangkok was like a typhoon in Bangladesh, an earthquake in Turkey.

The Kader fire might have been more meaningful for Americans if they could have seen the thousands of soot-stained dolls that spilled from the wreckage, macabre litter scattered among the dead. Bugs Bunny, Bart Simpson and the Muppets. Big Bird and other *Sesame Street* dolls. Playskool "Water Pets." Santa Claus. What the initial news accounts did not mention was that Kader's Thai factory produced most of its toys for American companies—Toys "R" Us, Fisher-Price, Hasbro, Tyco, Arco, Kenner, Gund and J. C. Penney—as well as stuffed dolls, slippers and souvenirs for Europe.[3]

Globalized civilization has uncovered an odd parochialism in the American character: Americans worried obsessively over the everyday safety of their children, and the U.S. government's regulators diligently policed the design of toys to avoid injury to young innocents. Yet neither citizens nor government took any interest in the brutal and dangerous conditions imposed on the people who manufactured those same toys, many of whom were mere adolescent children themselves. Indeed, the government position, both in Washington and Bangkok, assumed that there was no social obligation connecting consumers with workers, at least none that governments could enforce without disrupting free trade or invading the sovereignty of other nations.

The toy industry, not surprisingly, felt the same. Hasbro Industries, maker of Playskool, subsequently told the *Boston Globe* that it would no longer do business with Kader, but, in general, the U.S. companies shrugged off responsibility. Kader, a major toy manufacturer based in Hong Kong, "is extremely reputable, not sleaze bags," David Miller, president of the Toy Manufacturers of America, assured *USA Today*. "The responsibility for those factories," Miller told ABC News, "is in the hands of those who are there and managing the factory."[4]

The grisly details of what occurred revealed the casual irresponsibility of both companies and governments. The Kader factory compound consisted of four interconnected, four-story industrial barns on a three-acre lot on Buddhamondhol VI Road in the Sampran district west of Bangkok. It was one among Thailand's thriving new industrial zones for garments, textiles, electronics and toys. More than 50,000 people, most of them migrants from the Thai countryside, worked in the district at 7,500 large and small firms. Thailand's economic boom was based on places such as this, and Bangkok was almost choking on its own fantastic growth, dizzily erecting luxury hotels and office towers.

The fire started late on a Monday afternoon on the ground floor in the first building and spread rapidly upward, jumping to two adjoining buildings, all three of which swiftly collapsed. Investigators noted afterwards that the structures had been cheaply built, without concrete reinforcement, so steel girders and stairways crumpled easily in the heat. Thai law required that in such a large factory, fire-escape stairways must be sixteen to thirty-three feet wide, but Kader's were a mere four and a half feet. Main doors were locked and many windows barred to prevent pilfering by the employees. Flammable raw materials—fabric, stuffing, animal fibers—

were stacked everywhere, on walkways and next to electrical boxes. Neither safety drills nor fire alarms and sprinkler systems had been provided.

Let some of the survivors describe what happened.

A young woman named Lampan Taptim: "There was the sound of yelling about a fire. I tried to leave the section but my supervisor told me to get back to work. My sister who worked on the fourth floor with me pulled me away and insisted we try to get out. We tried to go down the stairs and got to the second floor; we found that the stairs had already caved in. There was a lot of yelling and confusion. . . . In desperation, I went back up to the windows and went back and forth, looking down below. The smoke was thick and I picked the best place to jump in a pile of boxes. My sister jumped, too. She died."

A young woman named Cheng: "There is no way out [people were shouting], the security guard has locked the main door out! It was horrifying. I thought I would die. I took off my gold ring and kept it in my pocket and put on my name tag so that my body could be identifiable. I had to decide to die in the fire or from jumping down from a three stories' height." As the walls collapsed around her, Cheng clung to a pipe and fell downward with it, landing on a pile of dead bodies, injured but alive.

An older woman named La-iad Nada-nguen: "Four or five pregnant women jumped before me. They died before my eyes." Her own daughter jumped from the top floor and broke both hips.

Chauweewan Mekpan, who was five months pregnant: "I thought that if I jumped, at least my parents would see my remains, but if I stayed, nothing would be left of me." Though her back was severely injured, she and her unborn child miraculously survived.

An older textile worker named Vilaiwa Satieti, who sewed shirts and pants at a neighboring factory, described to me the carnage she encountered: "I got off work about five and passed by Kader and saw many dead bodies lying around, uncovered. Some of them I knew. I tried to help the workers who had jumped from the factory. They had broken legs and broken arms and bro-

ken heads. We tried to keep them alive until they got to the hospital, that's all you could do. Oh, they were teenagers, fifteen to twenty years, no more than that, and so many of them, so many."

This was not the first serious fire at Kader's factory, but the third or fourth. "I heard somebody yelling 'fire, fire,'" Tumthong Podhirun testified, ". . . but I did not take it seriously because it has happened before. Soon I smelled smoke and very quickly it billowed inside the place. I headed for the back door but it was locked. . . . Finally, I had no choice but to join the others and jumped out of the window. I saw many of my friends lying dead on the ground beside me."[5]

In the aftermath of the tragedy, some Bangkok activists circulated an old snapshot of two smiling peasant girls standing arm in arm beside a thicket of palm trees. One of them, Praphai Prayonghorm, died in the 1993 fire at Kader. Her friend, Kammoin Konmanee, had died in the 1989 fire. Some of the Kader workers insisted afterwards that their factory had been haunted by ghosts, that it was built on the site of an old graveyard, disturbing the dead. The folklore expressed raw poetic truth: the fire in Bangkok eerily resembled the now-forgotten details of the Triangle Shirtwaist disaster eighty years before. Perhaps the "ghosts" that some workers felt present were young women from New York who had died in 1911.

Similar tragedies, large and small, were now commonplace across developing Asia and elsewhere. Two months after Kader, another fire at a Bangkok shirt factory killed ten women. Three months after Kader, a six-story hotel collapsed and killed 133 people, injuring 351. The embarrassed minister of industry ordered special inspections of 244 large factories in the Bangkok region and found that 60 percent of them had basic violations similar to Kader's. Thai industry was growing explosively—12 to 15 percent a year—but workplace injuries and illnesses were growing even faster, from 37,000 victims in 1987 to more than 150,000 by 1992 and an estimated 200,000 by 1994.

In China, six months after Kader, eighty-four women died and dozens of others were severely burned at another toy factory fire in the burgeoning industrial zone at Shenzhen. At Dongguan, a Hong Kong–owned raincoat factory burned in 1991, killing more than eighty people (Kader Industries also had a factory at Dongguan where two fires have been reported since 1990). In late 1993, some sixty women died at the Taiwanese-owned Gaofu textile plant in Fuzhou Province, many of them smothered in their dormitory beds by toxic fumes from burning textiles. In 1994, a shoe factory fire killed ten persons at Jiangmen; a textile factory fire killed thirty-eight and injured 160 at the Qianshan industrial zone.[6]

"Why must these tragedies repeat themselves again and again?" the *People's Daily* in Beijing asked. The official *Economic Daily* complained: "The way some of these foreign investors ignore international practice, ignore our own national rules, act completely lawlessly and immorally and lust after wealth is enough to make one's hair stand on end."[7]

America was itself no longer insulated from such brutalities. When a chicken-processing factory at Hamlet, North Carolina, caught fire in 1991, the exit doors there were also locked and twenty-five people died. A garment factory discovered by labor investigators in El Monte, California, held seventy-two Thai immigrants in virtual peonage, working eighteen hours a day in "sub-human conditions." One could not lament the deaths, harsh working conditions, child labor and subminimum wages in Thailand or across Asia and Central America without also recognizing that similar conditions have reappeared in the United States for roughly the same reasons.

Sweatshops, mainly in the garment industry, scandalized Los Angeles, New York and Dallas. The grim, foul assembly lines of the poultry-processing industry were spread across the rural South; the *Wall Street Journal's* Tony Horwitz won a Pulitzer Prize for his harrowing description of this low-wage work. "In general," the U.S. Government Accounting Office reported in 1994, "the description of today's sweatshops differs little from that at the turn of the century."[8]

That was the real mystery: Why did global commerce, with all of its supposed modernity and wondrous technologies, restore the old barbarisms that had long ago been forbidden by law? If the information age has enabled multinational corporations to manage production and marketing spread across continents, why were their managers unable—or unwilling—to organize such mundane matters as fire prevention?

The short answer, of course, was profits, but the deeper answer was about power: Firms behaved this way because they could, because nobody would stop them. When law and social values retreated before the power of markets, then capitalism's natural drive to maximize returns had no internal governor to check its social behavior. When one enterprise took the low road to gain advantage, others would follow.

The toy fire in Bangkok provided a dramatic illustration for the much broader, less visible forms of human exploitation that were flourishing in the global system, including the widespread use of children in manufacturing, even forced labor camps in China or Burma. These matters were not a buried secret. Indeed, American television has aggressively exposed the "dark Satanic mills" with dramatic reports. ABCs *20/20* broadcast correspondent Lynn Sherr's devastating account of the Kader fire; CNN ran disturbing footage. Mike Wallace of CBS's *60 Minutes* exposed the prison labor exploited in China. NBC's *Dateline* did a piece on Wal-Mart's grim production in Bangladesh. CBS's *Street Stories* toured the shoe factories of Indonesia.

The baffling quality about modern communications was that its images could take us to people in remote corners of the world vividly and instantly, but these images have not as yet created genuine community with them. In terms of human consciousness, the "global village" was still only a picture on the TV screen.

Public opinion, moreover, absorbed contradictory messages about the global reality that were difficult to sort out. The opening stages of industrialization presented, as always, a great paradox: the process was profoundly liberating for millions, freeing them from material scarcity and limited life choices, while it also ensnared other millions in brutal new forms of domination. Both aspects were true, but there was no scale on which these opposing consequences could be easily balanced, since the good and ill effects were not usually apportioned among the same people. Some human beings were set free, while other lives were turned into cheap and expendable commodities.

Workers at Kader, for instance, earned about 100 baht a day for sewing and assembling dolls, the official minimum wage of $4, but the constant stream of new entrants meant that many at the factory actually worked for much less—only $2 or $3 a day—during a required "probationary" period of three to six months that was often extended much longer by the managers. Only one hundred of the three thousand workers at Kader were legally designated employees; the rest were "contract workers" without permanent rights and benefits, the same employment system now popularized in the United States.

"Lint, fabric, dust and animal hair filled the air on the production floor," the International Confederation of Free Trade Unions based in Brussels observed in its investigative report. "Noise, heat, congestion and fumes from various sources were reported by many. Dust control was nonexistent; protective equipment inadequate. Inhaling the dust created respiratory problems and contact with it caused skin diseases." A factory clinic dispensed antihistamines or other drugs and referred the more serious symptoms to outside hospitals. Workers paid for the medication themselves and were reimbursed, up to $6, only if they had contributed 10 baht a month to the company's health fund.

A common response to such facts, even from many sensitive people, was: yes, that was terrible, but wouldn't those workers be even worse off if civil standards were imposed on their employers since they might lose their jobs as a result? This was the same economic rationale offered by American manufacturers a century before to explain why American children must work in the

coal mines and textile mills. U.S. industry had survived somehow (and, in fact, flourished) when child labor and the other malpractices were eventually prohibited by social reforms. Furthermore, it was not coincidence that industry always assigned the harshest conditions and lowest pay to the weakest members of a society—women, children, uprooted migrants. Whether the factory was in Thailand or the United States or Mexico's *maquiladora* zone, people who were already quite powerless were less likely to resist, less able to demand decency from their employers.

Nor did these enterprises necessarily consist of small, struggling firms that could not afford to treat their workers better. Small sweatshops, it was true, were numerous in Thailand, and I saw some myself in a working-class neighborhood of Bangkok. Behind iron grillwork, children who looked to be ten to twelve years old squatted on the cement floors of the open-air shops, assembling suitcases, sewing raincoats, packing T-shirts. Across the street, a swarm of adolescents in blue smocks ate dinner at long tables outside a two-story building, then trooped back upstairs to the sewing machines.

Kader Holding Company, Ltd., however, was neither small nor struggling. It was a powerhouse of the global toy industry—headquartered in Hong Kong, incorporated in Bermuda, owned by a wealthy Hong Kong Chinese family named Ting that got its start after World War II making plastic goods and flashlights under procurement contracts from the U.S. military. Now Kader controlled a global maze of factories and interlocking subsidiaries in eight countries, from China and Thailand to Britain and the United States, where it owned Bachmann toys.[9]

After the fire Thai union members, intellectuals and middle-class activists from social rights organizations (the groups known in developing countries as nongovernmental organizations, or NGOs) formed the Committee to Support Kader Workers and began demanding justice from the employer. They sent a delegation to Hong Kong to confront Kader officials and investigate the complex corporate linkages of the enterprise.

What they discovered was that Kader's partner in the Bangkok toy factory was actually a fabulously wealthy Thai family, the Chearavanonts, ethnic Chinese merchants who own the Charoen Pokphand Group, Thailand's own leading multi-national corporation.

The CP Group owns farms, feed mills, real estate, air-conditioning and motorcycle factories, food-franchise chains—two hundred companies worldwide, several of them listed on the New York Stock Exchange. The patriarch and chairman, Dhanin Chearavanont, was said by *Fortune* magazine to be the seventy-fifth richest man in the world, with personal assets of $2.6 billion (or 65 billion baht, as the *Bangkok Post* put it). Like the other emerging "Chinese multinationals," the Pokphand Group operates through the informal networks of kinfolk and ethnic contacts spread around the world by the Chinese diaspora, while it also participates in the more rigorous accounting systems of Western economies.

In the mother country, China, the conglomerate nurtured political-business alliances and has become the largest outside investor in new factories and joint ventures. In the United States, it maintained superb political connections. The Chearavanonts co-sponsored a much-heralded visit to Bangkok by ex-president George Bush, who delivered a speech before Thai business leaders in early 1994, eight months after the Kader fire. The price tag for Bush's appearance, according to the Bangkok press, was $400,000 (equivalent to one month's payroll for all three thousand workers at Kader). The day after Bush's appearance, the Chearavanonts hosted a banquet for a leading entrepreneur from China—Deng Xiaoping's daughter.[10]

The Pokphand Group at first denied any connection to the Kader fire, but reformers and local reporters dug out the facts of the family's involvement. Dhanin Chearavanont himself owned 11 percent of Honbo Investment Company and with relatives and corporate directors held majority control. Honbo, in turn, owned half of KCP Toys (KCP stood for Kader Charoen Pokphand), which, in turn, owned 80 percent of Kader Industrial (Thailand) Company. Armed with these facts, three hundred workers from the destroyed factory marched on the Pokphand Group's corporate tower on Silom Road, where they staged a gentle sit-down demonstration in the lobby, demanding just compensation for the victims.[11]

In the context of Thai society and politics, the workers' demonstration against Pokphand was itself extraordinary, like peasants confronting the nobility. Under continuing pressures from the support group, the company agreed to pay much larger compensation for victims and their families—$12,000 for each death, a trivial amount in American terms but more than double the Thai standard. "When we worked on Kader," said Professor Voravidh Charoenloet, an economist at Chulalongkorn University, "the government and local entrepreneurs and factory owners didn't want us to challenge these people; even the police tried to obstruct us from making an issue. We were accused of trying to destroy the country's reputation."

The settlement, in fact, required the Thai activists to halt their agitation and fall silent. "Once the extra compensation was paid," Voravidh explained, "we were forced to stop. One of the demands by the government was that everything should stop. Our organization had to accept it. We wanted to link with the international organizations and have a great boycott, but we had to cease."

The global boycott, he assumed, was going forward anyway because he knew that international labor groups like the ICFTU and the AFL-CIO had investigated the Kader fire and issued stinging denunciations. I told him that aside from organized labor, the rest of the world remained indifferent. There was no boycott of Kader toys in America. The professor slumped in his chair and was silent, a twisted expression on his face.

"I feel very bad," Voravidh said at last. "Maybe we should not have accepted it. But when we came away, we felt that was what we could accomplish. The people wanted more. There must be something more."

In the larger context, this tragedy was not explained by the arrogant power of one wealthy family or the elusive complexities of interlocking corporations. The Kader fire was ordained and organized by the free market itself. The toy industry—much like textiles and garments, shoes, electronics assembly and other low-wage sectors—existed (and thrived) by exploiting a crude ladder of desperate competition among the poorest nations. Its factories regularly hopped to new locations where wages were even lower, where the governments would be even more tolerant of abusive practices. The contract work assigned to foreign firms, including thousands of small sweatshops, fitted neatly into the systems of far-flung production of major brand names and distanced the capital owners from personal responsibility. The "virtual corporation" celebrated by some business futurists already existed in these sectors and, indeed, was now being emulated in some ways by advanced manufacturing—cars, aircraft, computers.

Over the last generation, toy manufacturers and others have moved around the Asian rim in search of the bottom-rung conditions: from Hong Kong, Korea and Taiwan to Thailand and Indonesia, from there to China, Vietnam and Bangladesh, perhaps on next to Burma, Nepal or Cambodia. Since the world had a nearly inexhaustible supply of poor people and suppliant governments, the market would keep driving in search of lower rungs; no one could say where the bottom was located. Industrial conditions were not getting better, as conventional theory assured the innocent consumers, but in many sectors were getting much worse. In America, the U.S. diplomatic opening to Vietnam was celebrated as progressive politics. In Southeast Asia, it merely opened another trapdoor beneath wages and working conditions.

A country like Thailand was caught in the middle: if it conscientiously tried to improve, it would pay a huge price. When Thai unions lobbied to win improvements in minimum-wage standards, textile plants began leaving for Vietnam and elsewhere or even importing cheaper "guest workers" from Burma. When China opened its fast-growing industrial zones in Shenzhen, Dongguan and other locations, the new competition had direct consequences on the factory floors of Bangkok.

Kader, according to the ICFTU, opened two new factories in Shekou and Dongguan where young people were working fourteen-hour days, seven days a week, to fill the U.S. Christmas orders for Mickey Mouse and other American dolls. Why should a company worry about sprinkler systems or fire escapes for a dusty factory in Bangkok when it could hire brand-new workers in China for only $20 a month, one fifth of the labor cost in Thailand?

The ICFTU report described the market forces: "The lower cost of production of toys in China changes the investment climate for countries like Thailand. Thailand competes with China to attract investment capital for local toy production. With this development, Thailand has become sadly lax in enforcing its own legislation. It turns a blind eye to health violations, thus allowing factory owners to ignore safety standards. Since China entered the picture, accidents in Thailand have nearly tripled."

The Thai minister of industry, Sanan Kachornprasart, described the market reality more succinctly: "If we punish them, who will want to invest here?" Thai authorities subsequently filed charges against three Kader factory managers, but none against the company itself nor, of course, the Chearavanont family.[12]

In the aftermath, a deputy managing director of Kader Industrial, Pichet Laokasem, entered a Buddhist monastery "to make merit for the fire victims," *The Nation* of Bangkok reported. Pichet told reporters he would serve as a monk until he felt better emotionally. "Most of the families affected by the fire lost only a loved one," he explained. "I lost nearly two hundred of my workers all at once."

The fire in Bangkok reflected the amorality of the marketplace when it has been freed of social obligations. But the tragedy also mocked the moral claims of three great religions, whose adherents were all implicated. Thais built splendid golden temples exalting Buddha, who taught them to put spiritual being before material wealth. Chinese claimed to have acquired superior social values, reverence for family and community, derived from the teachings of Confucius. Americans bought the toys from Asia to celebrate the birth of Jesus Christ. Their shared complicity was another of the strange convergences made possible by global commerce. . . .

In the modern industrial world, only the ignorant can pretend to self-righteousness since only the primitive are truly innocent. No advanced society has reached that lofty stage without enduring barbaric consequences and despoliation along the way; no one who enjoys the uses of electricity or the internal combustion engine may claim to oppose industrialization for others without indulging in imperious hypocrisy.

Americans, one may recall, built their early national infrastructure and organized large-scale agriculture with slave labor. The developing American nation swept native populations from their ancient lands and drained the swampy prairies to grow grain. It burned forests to make farmland, decimated wildlife, dammed the wild rivers and displaced people who were in the way. It assigned the dirtiest, most dangerous work to immigrants and children. It eventually granted political rights to all, but grudgingly and only after great conflicts, including a terrible civil war.

The actual history of nations is useful to remember when trying to form judgments about the new world. Asian leaders regularly remind Americans and Europeans of exactly how the richest nation-states became wealthy and observe further that, despite their great wealth, those countries have not perfected social relations among rich and poor, weak and powerful. The maldistribution of incomes is worsening in America, too, not yet as extreme as Thailand's, but worse than many less fortunate nations.

Hypocrisies run the other way, too, however. The fashionable pose among some leaders in developing Asia is to lecture the West on its decadent ways and hold up "Asian values" as morally superior, as well as more productive. If their cultural claims sound plausible at a distance, they seem less noble, even duplicitous up close. The Asian societies' supposed reverence for family, for instance, is expressed in the "dark Satanic mills" where the women and children are sent to work.

"Family" and "social order" are often mere euphemisms for hierarchy and domination. A system that depends upon rigid control from above or the rank exploitation of weaker groups is not about values, but about power. Nothing distinctive about that. Human societies have struggled to overcome those conditions for centuries.

My point is that any prospect of developing a common global social consciousness will inevitably force people to reexamine themselves first and come to terms with the contradictions and hypocrisies in their own national histories. Americans, in particular, are not especially equipped for that exercise. A distinguished historian, Lawrence Goodwyn of Duke University, once said to me in frustration: You cannot teach American history to American students. You can teach the iconic version, he said, that portrays America as beautiful and unblemished or you can teach a radical version that demonizes the country. But American culture does not equip young people to deal with the "irreconcilable conflicts" embedded in their own history, the past that does not yield to patriotic moralisms. "Race is the most obvious example of what I mean," he said.

Coming to terms with one's own history ought not only to induce a degree of humility toward others and their struggles, but also to clarify what one really believes about human society. No one can undo the past, but that does not relieve people of the burden of making judgments about the living present or facing up to its moral implications. If the global system has truly created a unified marketplace, then every worker, every consumer, every society is already connected to the other. The responsibility exists and invoking history is not an excuse to hide from the new social questions.

Just as Americans cannot claim a higher morality while benefiting from inhumane exploitation, neither can developing countries pretend to become modern "one world" producers and expect exemption from the world's social values. Neither can the global enterprises. The future asks: Can capitalism itself be altered and reformed? Or is the world doomed to keep renewing these inhumanities in the name of economic progress?

The proposition that human dignity is indivisible does not suppose that everyone will become equal or alike or perfectly content in his or her circumstances. It does insist that certain well-understood social principles exist internationally which are enforceable and ought to be the price of admission in the global system. The idea is very simple: every person—man, woman and child—regardless of where he or she exists in time and place or on the chain of economic development, is entitled to respect as an individual being.

For many in the world, life itself is all that they possess; an economic program that deprives them of life's precious possibilities is not only unjust, but also utterly unnecessary. Peasants may not become kings, but they are entitled to be treated with decent regard for their sentient and moral beings, not as cheap commodities. Newly industrialized nations cannot change social patterns overnight, any more than the advanced economies did before them, but they can demonstrate that they are changing.

This proposition is invasive, no question, and will disturb the economic and political arrangements within many societies. But every nation has a sovereign choice in this matter, the sort of choice made in the marketplace every day. If Thailand or China resents the intrusion of global social standards, it does not have to sell its toys to America. And Americans do not have to buy them. If Singapore rejects the idea of basic rights for women, then women in America or Europe may reject Singapore—and multinational firms that profit from the subordination of women. If people do not assert these values in global trade, then their own convictions will be steadily coarsened.

In Bangkok, when I asked Professor Voravidh to step back from Thailand's problems and suggest a broader remedy, he thought for a long time and then said: "We need cooperation among nations because the multinational corporations can shift from one country to another. If they don't like Thailand, they move to Vietnam or China. Right now, we are all competing and the world is getting worse. We need a GATT on labor conditions and on the minimum wage, we need a standard on the minimum conditions for work and a higher standard for children."

The most direct approach, as Voravidh suggested, is an international agreement to incorporate such standards in the terms of trade, with penalties and incentives, even temporary embargoes, that will impose social obligations on the global system, the firms and countries. Most of the leading governments, including the United States, have long claimed to support this idea—a so-called social clause for GATT—but the practical reality is that they do not. Aside from rhetoric, when their negotiators are at the table, they always yield readily to objections from the multinational corporations and developing nations. Both the firms and the governing elites of poor countries have a strong incentive to block the proposition since both profit from a free-running system that exploits the weak. A countering force has to come from concerned citizens. Governments refuse to act, but voters and consumers are not impotent, and, in the meantime, they can begin the political campaign by purposefully targeting the producers—boycotting especially the well-known brand names that depend upon lovable images for their sales. Americans will not stop buying toys at Christmas, but they might single out one or two American toy companies for Yuletide boycotts, based on their scandalous relations with Kader and other manufacturers. Boycotts are difficult to organize and sustain, but every one of the consumer-goods companies is exquisitely vulnerable.

In India, the South Asian Coalition on Child Servitude, led by Kailash Satyarthi, has created a promising model for how to connect the social obligations of consumers and workers. Indian carpet makers are notorious for using small children at their looms—bonded children like Thailand's bonded prostitutes—and have always claimed economic necessity. India is a poor nation and the work gives wage income to extremely poor families, they insist. But these children will never escape poverty if they are deprived of schooling, the compulsory education promised by law.

The reformers created a "no child labor" label that certifies the rugs were made under honorable conditions and they persuaded major importers in Germany to insist upon the label. The exporters in India, in turn, have to allow regular citizen inspections of their workplaces to win the label for their rugs. Since this consumer-led certification system began, the carpet industry's use of children has fallen dramatically. A Textile Ministry official in New Delhi said: "The government is now contemplating the total eradication of child labor in the next few years."[13]

Toys, shoes, electronics, garments—many consumer sectors are vulnerable to similar approaches, though obviously the scope of manufacturing is too diverse and complex for consumers to police it. Governments have to act collectively. If a worldwide agreement is impossible to achieve, then groups of governments can form their own preferential trading systems, introducing social standards that reverse the incentives for developing countries and for capital choosing new locations for production.

The crucial point illustrated by Thailand's predicament is that global social standards will help the poorer countries escape their economic trap. Until a floor is built beneath the market's social behavior, there is no way that a small developing country like Thailand can hope to overcome the downward pull of competition from other, poorer nations. It must debase its citizens to hold on to what it has achieved. The path to improvement is blocked by the economics of an irresponsible marketplace.

Setting standards will undoubtedly slow down the easy movement of capital—and close down the most scandalous operations—but that is not a harmful consequence for people in struggling nations that aspire to industrial prosperity or for a global economy burdened with surpluses and inadequate consumption. When global capital makes a commitment to a developing economy, it ought not to acquire the power to blackmail that nation in perpetuity. Supported by global rules, those nations can begin to improve conditions and stabilize their own social development. At least they would have a chance to avoid the great class conflicts that others have experienced.

In the meantime, the very least that citizens can demand of their own government is that it

no longer use public money to finance the brutal upheavals or environmental despoliation that have flowed from large-scale projects of the World Bank and other lending agencies. The social distress in the cities begins in the countryside, and the wealthy nations have often financed it in the name of aiding development. The World Bank repeatedly proclaims its new commitment to strategies that address the development ideas of indigenous peoples and halt the destruction of natural systems. But social critics and the people I encountered in Thailand and elsewhere have not seen much evidence of real change.

The terms of trade are usually thought of as commercial agreements, but they are also an implicit statement of moral values. In its present terms, the global system values property over human life. When a nation like China steals the property of capital, pirating copyrights, films or technology, other governments will take action to stop it and be willing to impose sanctions and penalty tariffs on the offending nation's trade. When human lives are stolen in the "dark Satanic mills," nothing happens to the offenders since, according to the free market's sense of conscience, there is no crime.

NOTES

1. William Blake's immortal lines are from "Milton," one of his "prophetic books" written between 1804 and 1808. *The Portable Blake*, Alfred Kazin, editor (New York: Penguin Books, 1976).

2. *Washington Post, Financial Times* and *New York Times,* May 12, 1993, and *Wall Street Journal,* May 13, 1993.

3. The U.S. contract clients for Kader's Bangkok factory were cited by the International Confederation of Free Trade Unions headquartered in Brussels in its investigatory report, "From the Ashes: A Toy Factory Fire in Thailand," December 1994. In the aftermath, the ICFTU and some nongovernmental organizations attempted to mount an "international toy campaign" and a few sporadic demonstrations occurred in Hong Kong and London, but there never was a general boycott of the industry or any of its individual companies. The labor federation met with associations of British and American toy manufacturers and urged them to adopt a "code of conduct" that might discour-

age the abuses. The proposed codes were inadequate, the ICFTU acknowledged, but it was optimistic about their general adoption by the international industry.

4. Mitchell Zuckoff of the *Boston Globe* produced a powerful series of stories on labor conditions in developing Asia and reported Hasbro's reaction to the Kader fire, July 10, 1994. David Miller was quoted in *USA Today*, May 13, 1993, and on ABC News *20/20*, July 30, 1993.

5. The first-person descriptions of the Kader fire are but a small sampling from survivors' horrifying accounts, collected by investigators and reporters at the scene. My account of the disaster is especially indebted to the investigative report by the International Confederation of Free Trade Unions; Bangkok's English-language newspapers, the *Post* and *The Nation;* the Asia Monitor Resource Center of Hong Kong; and Lynn Sherr's devastating report on ABCs *20/20*, July 30, 1993. Lampan Taptim and Tumthong Podhirun, "From the Ashes," ICFTU, December 1994; Cheng: *Asian Labour Update*, Asia Monitor Resource Center, Hong Kong, July 1993; La-iad Nads-nguen: *The Nation*, Bangkok, May 12, 1993; and Chaweewan Mekpan: *20/20.*

6. Details on Thailand's worker injuries and the litany of fires in China are from the ICFTU report and other labor bulletins, as well as interviews in Bangkok.

7. The *People's Daily* and *Economic Daily* were quoted by Andrew Quinn of Reuters in *The Daily Citizen* of Washington, DC, January 18, 1994.

8. Tony Horwitz described chicken-processing employment as the second fastest growing manufacturing job in America: *Wall Street Journal,* December 1, 1994. U.S. sweatshops were reviewed in "Garment Industry: Efforts to Address the Prevalence and Conditions of Sweatshops," U.S. Government Accounting Office, November 1994.

9. Corporate details on Kader are from the ICFTU and the Asia Monitor Resource Center's *Asian Labour Update*, July 1993.

10. Dhanin Chearavanont's wealth: *Bangkok Post,* June 15, 1993; Pokphand Group ventures in China and elsewhere: *Far Eastern Economic Review,* October 21, 1993; George Bush's appearance in Bangkok: *Bangkok Post,* January 22, 1994. The dinner for Deng's daughter, Deng Nan, was reported in *The Nation,* Bangkok, January 28, 1994.

11. The complex structure of ownership was used to deflect corporate responsibility. Kader's Kenneth Ting protested after the fire that his family's firm owned only a 40 percent stake in the Thai factory, but people blamed them "because we have our name on it. That's the whole problem." The lesson, he said, was to "never lend your name or logo to any company if you don't have managing control in the company." That lesson, of course, contradicted the basic structure of how the global toy industry was organized: *Bangkok Post,* May 17, 1993. The chain of ownership was reported in several places, including *The Nation* of Bangkok, May 28, 1993. Details of the Kader workers' sit-in: *Bangkok Post,* July 13, 1993.

12. Sanan was quoted in the *Bangkok Post,* May 29, 1993.

13. The New Delhi–based campaign against child labor in the carpet industry is admittedly limited to a narrow market and expensive product, but its essential value is demonstrating how retailers and their customers can be connected to a distant factory floor. See, for instance, Hugh Williamson, "Stamp of Approval," *Far Eastern Economic Review,* February 2, 1995, and N. Vasuk Rao in the *Journal of Commerce,* March 1, 1995.

THINKING ABOUT THE READING

Greider argues that the tragedy of the Kader industrial fire cannot be explained simply by focusing on greedy families and multinational corporations. Instead, he blames global economics and the organization of the international toy industry. He writes, "The Kader fire was ordained and organized by the free market itself." What do you suppose he means by this? Given the enormous economic pressures that this and other multinational industries operate under, are such tragedies inevitable? Why have attempts to improve the working conditions in Third World factories been so ineffective?

The Architecture of Inequality: Race and Ethnicity

The history of race in American society is an ambivalent one. Our famous sayings about equality conflict with the experiences of most racial and ethnic minorities: oppression, violence, and exploitation. Opportunities for life, liberty, and the pursuit of happiness have always been distributed along racial and ethnic lines. U.S. society is built on the assumption that different immigrant groups will ultimately assimilate, changing their way of life to conform to that of the dominant culture. But the increasing diversity of the population has shaped people's ideas about what it means to be an American and has influenced our relationships with one another and with our social institutions.

Racial inequality is both a personal and structural phenomenon. On the one hand, it is lodged in individual prejudice and discrimination. On the other hand, it resides in our language, collective beliefs, and important social institutions. This latter manifestation of racism is more difficult to detect than personal racism, hence it is more difficult to stop. Because such racism exists at a level above personal attitudes, it will not disappear simply by reducing people's prejudices.

"Stephen Cruz" is taken from a book of interviews by Studs Terkel called *American Dreams: Lost and Found*. In this piece, Stephen Cruz talks about the contradictions and frustrations he feels as a Chicano who has worked hard to achieve the American Dream. As he assesses the way others perceive him, he becomes less and less certain of exactly why he has become so successful. Is it because of his skills or because of his ethnicity? In pondering this question, he experiences a growing rift between the predominantly white, middle class world he has entered and the world of his fellow Chicanos.

It has been said that white people in the United States have the luxury of "having no color." When someone is described with no mention of race, the default assumption is that he or she is white. In other words, "White" is used far less often as a modifying adjective than "Black," "Asian," or "Latino." As a result, "whiteness" is rarely questioned or examined as a racial category. Only recently have scholars begun to explore the origins and characteristics of whiteness. In "Whiteness as an 'Unmarked' Cultural Category," Ruth Frankenberg describes how white people perceive their race. She conducted extensive interviews with white women and found that many of them had difficulty describing what whiteness was or if there was such a thing as a white culture. The irony, of course, is that although "whiteness" is a formless entity, white culture has enormous power.

While Frankenberg describes the nature of whiteness, Maxine Thompson and Verna Keith explore the complex nuances of "blackness" in "The Blacker the Berry." They examine the highly emotional issue of skin color prejudice *within* the African-American community and the different effects such prejudice has for men and women. They analyzed the responses of a sample of over 2,000 African Americans to questions on the National Survey of Black Americans to draw conclusions about how gender and skin tone combine to influence evaluations of self-worth and self-competence among African Americans.

Cultural attitudes toward race can sometimes be internalized to the point of individuals trying to surgically alter their appearance to conform to Anglo standards. In her article, "'Opening' Faces," Eugenia Kaw describes how some Asian-American women have come to judge their own bodies through the eyes of White America. Although many of these women claim that by undergoing cosmetic surgery they are simply exercising their right to become more desirable and don't see any racism in their decisions, their attitudes reflect a deeper belief in the social inferiority of Asian features.

Stephen Cruz

Studs Terkel

. . . The speaker here, Stephen Cruz, is a man who at first glance seems to be living the American dream of success and upward mobility; he is never content, however, and he comes to question his own values and his place in the predominantly Anglo society where he is "successful."

He is thirty-nine.

"The family came in stages from Mexico. Your grandparents usually came first, did a little work, found little roots, put together a few bucks, and brought the family in, one at a time. Those were the days when controls at the border didn't exist as they do now."

You just tried very hard to be whatever it is the system wanted of you. I was a good student and, as small as I was, a pretty good athlete. I was well liked, I thought. We were fairly affluent, but we lived down where all the trashy whites were. It was the only housing we could get. As kids, we never understood why. We did everything right. We didn't have those Mexican accents, we were never on welfare. Dad wouldn't be on welfare to save his soul. He woulda died first. He worked during the depression. He carries that pride with him, even today.

Of the five children, I'm the only one who really got into the business world. We learned quickly that you have to look for opportunities and add things up very quickly. I was in liberal arts, but as soon as *Sputnik*[1] went up, well, golly, hell, we knew where the bucks were. I went right over to the registrar's office and signed up for engineering. I got my degree in '62. If you had a master's in business as well, they were just paying all kinds of bucks. So that's what I did. Sure enough, the market was super. I had fourteen job offers. I could have had a hundred if I wanted to look around.

I never once associated these offers with my being a minority. I was aware of the Civil Rights Act of 1964, but I was still self-confident enough to feel they wanted me because of my abilities. Looking back, the reason I got more offers than the other guys was because of the government edict. And I thought it was because I was so goddamned brilliant. (Laughs.) In 1962, I didn't get as many offers as those who were less qualified. You have a tendency to blame the job market. You just don't want to face the issue of discrimination.

I went to work with Procter & Gamble. After about two years, they told me I was one of the best supervisors they ever had and they were gonna promote me. Okay, I went into personnel. Again, I thought it was because I was such a brilliant guy. Now I started getting wise to the ways of the American Dream. My office was glass-enclosed, while all the other offices were enclosed so you couldn't see into them. I was the visible man.

They made sure I interviewed most of the people that came in. I just didn't really think there was anything wrong until we got a new plant manager, a southerner. I received instructions from him on how I should interview blacks. Just check and see if they smell, okay? That was the beginning of my training program. I started asking: Why weren't we hiring more minorities? I realized I was the only one in a management position.

I guess as a Mexican I was more acceptable because I wasn't really black. I was a good compromise. I was visibly good. I hired a black secretary, which was *verboten*. When I came back from my vacation, she was gone. My boss fired her while I was away. I asked why and never got a good reason.

Until then, I never questioned the American Dream. I was convinced if you worked hard, you could make it. I never considered myself different. That was the trouble. We had been discriminated against a lot, but I never associated it with society. I considered it an individual matter. Bad people, my mother used to say. In '68 I began to question.

I was doing fine. My very first year out of college, I was making twelve thousand dollars. I left Procter & Gamble because I really saw no opportunity. They were content to leave me visible, but my thoughts were not really solicited. I may have overreacted a bit, with the plant manager's attitude, but I felt there's no way a Mexican could get ahead here.

I went to work for Blue Cross. It's 1969. The Great Society[2] is in full swing. Those who never thought of being minorities before are being turned on. Consciousness raising is going on. Black programs are popping up in universities. Cultural identity and all that. But what about the one issue in this country: economics? There were very few management jobs for minorities, especially blacks.

The stereotypes popped up again. If you're Oriental, you're real good in mathematics. If you're Mexican, you're a happy guy to have around, pleasant but emotional. Mexicans are either sleeping or laughing all the time. Life is just one big happy kind of event. *Mañana.* Good to have as part of the management team, as long as you weren't allowed to make decisions.

I was thinking there were two possibilities why minorities were not making it in business. One was deep, ingrained racism. But there was still the possibility that they were simply a bunch of bad managers who just couldn't cut it. You see, until now I believed everything I was taught about the dream: the American businessman is omnipotent and fair. If we could show these turkeys there's money to be made in hiring

minorities, these businessmen—good managers, good decision makers—would respond. I naïvely thought American businessmen gave a damn about society, that given a choice they would do the right thing. I had that faith.

I was hungry for learning about decision-making criteria. I was still too far away from top management to see exactly how they were working. I needed to learn more. Hey, just learn more and you'll make it. That part of the dream hadn't left me yet. I was still clinging to the notion of work your ass off, learn more than anybody else, and you'll get in that sphere.

During my fifth year at Blue Cross, I discovered another flaw in the American Dream. Minorities are as bad to other minorities as whites are to minorities. The strongest weapon the white manager had is the old divide and conquer routine. My mistake was thinking we were all at the same level of consciousness.

I had attempted to bring together some blacks with the other minorities. There weren't too many of them anyway. The Orientals never really got involved. The blacks misunderstood what I was presenting, perhaps I said it badly. They were on the cultural kick: a manager should be crucified for saying "Negro" instead of "black." I said as long as the Negro or the black gets the job, it doesn't mean a damn what he's called. We got into a huge hassle. Management, of course, merely smiled. The whole struggle fell flat on its face. It crumpled from divisiveness. So I learned another lesson. People have their own agenda. It doesn't matter what group you're with, there is a tendency to put the other guy down regardless.

The American Dream began to look so damn complicated, I began to think: Hell, if I wanted, I could just back away and reap the harvest myself. By this time, I'm up to twenty-five thousand dollars a year. It's beginning to look good, and a lot of people are beginning to look good. And they're saying: "Hey, the American Dream, you got it. Why don't you lay off?" I wasn't falling in line.

My bosses were telling me I had all the "ingredients" for top management. All that was required was to "get to know our business." This term comes up all the time. If I could just warn all minorities and women whenever you hear "get to know our business," they're really saying "fall in line." Stay within that fence, and glory can be yours. I left Blue Cross disillusioned. They offered me a director's job at thirty thousand dollars before I quit.

All I had to do was behave myself. I had the "ingredients" of being a good Chicano, the equivalent of the good nigger. I was smart. I could articulate well. People didn't know by my speech patterns that I was of Mexican heritage. Some tell me I don't look Mexican, that I have a certain amount of Italian, Lebanese, or who knows. (Laughs.)

One could easily say: "Hey, what's your bitch? The American Dream has treated you beautifully. So just knock it off and quit this crap you're spreading around." It was a real problem. Every time I turned around, America seemed to be treating me very well.

Hell, I even thought of dropping out, the hell with it. Maybe get a job in a factory. But what happened? Offers kept coming in. I just said to myself: God, isn't this silly? You might as well take the bucks and continue looking for the answer. So I did that. But each time I took the money, the conflict in me got more intense, not less.

Wow, I'm up to thirty-five thousand a year. This is a savings and loan business. I have faith in the executive director. He was the kind of guy I was looking for in top management: understanding, humane, also looking for the formula. Until he was up for consideration as executive v.p. of the entire organization. All of a sudden everything changed. It wasn't until I saw this guy flip-flop that I realized how powerful vested interests are. Suddenly he's saying: "Don't rock the boat. Keep a low profile. Get in line." Another disappointment.

Subsequently, I went to work for a consulting firm. I said to myself: Okay, I've got to get close to the executive mind. I need to know how they work. Wow, a consulting firm.

Consulting firms are saving a lot of American businessmen. They're doing it in ways that defy the whole notion of capitalism. They're not al-

lowing these businesses to fail. Lockheed was successful in getting U.S. funding guarantees because of the efforts of consulting firms working on their behalf, helping them look better. In this kind of work, you don't find minorities. You've got to be a proven success in business before you get there.

The American Dream, I see now, is governed not by education, opportunity, and hard work, but by power and fear. The higher up in the organization you go, the more you have to lose. The dream is *not losing*. This is the notion pervading America today: Don't lose.

When I left the consulting business, I was making fifty thousand dollars a year. My last performance appraisal was: You can go a long way in this business, you can be a partner, but you gotta know our business. It came up again. At this point, I was incapable of being disillusioned any more. How easy it is to be swallowed up by the same set of values that governs the top guy. I was becoming that way. I was becoming concerned about losing that fifty grand or so a year. So I asked other minorities who had it made. I'd go up and ask 'em: "Look, do you owe anything to others?" The answer was: "We owe nothing to anybody." They drew from the civil rights movement but felt no debt. They've quickly forgotten how it happened. It's like I was when I first got out of college. Hey, it's really me, I'm great. I'm great. I'm as angry with these guys as I am with the top guys.

Right now, it's confused. I've had fifteen years in the business world as "a success." Many Anglos would be envious of my progress. Fifty thousand dollars a year puts you in the one or two top percent of all Americans. Plus my wife making another thirty thousand. We had lots of money. When I gave it up, my cohorts looked at me not just as strange, but as something of a traitor. "You're screwing it up for all of us. You're part of our union, we're the elite, we should govern. What the hell are you doing?" So now I'm looked at suspiciously by my peer group as well.

I'm teaching at the University of Wisconsin at Platteville. It's nice. My colleagues tell me what's on their minds. I got a farm next-door to

Platteville. With farm prices being what they are (laughs), it's a losing proposition. But with university work and what money we've saved, we're gonna be all right.

The American Dream is getting more elusive. The dream is being governed by a few people's notion of what the dream is. Sometimes I feel it's a small group of financiers that gets together once a year and decides all the world's issues.

It's getting so big. The small-business venture is not there any more. Business has become too big to influence. It can't be changed internally. A counterpower is needed.

NOTES

1. *Sputnik:* satellite launched by the Soviet Union in 1957; this launch signaled the beginning of the "space race" between the United States and the USSR.

2. *The Great Society:* President Lyndon B. Johnson's term for the American society he hoped to establish through social reforms, including an antipoverty program.

THINKING ABOUT THE READING

By most people's standards—including his own—Stephen Cruz has achieved the American Dream. Yet he seems to have some doubts about just how he reached it. Why is it so hard for him to be certain that his accomplishments have to do with his abilities rather than other factors? Does he think he has been successful *because of* his minority status or *in spite of* it? What does he think is wrong with the American Dream? What does he mean when he says that this dream is governed not by education, opportunity, and hard work, but by power and fear? How common do you suppose this sort of uncertainty is for members of racial or ethnic minorities who have achieved economic success?

Whiteness as an "Unmarked" Cultural Category

Ruth Frankenberg

America's supposed to be the melting pot. I know that I've got a huge number of nationalities in my blood, but how do I—what do I call myself? And hating this country as I do, I don't like to say I'm an American. Even though it is what I am. I hate identifying myself as only an American, because I have so many objections to Americans' place in the world. I don't know how I felt about that when I was growing up, but I never—I didn't like to pledge allegiance to the flag. . . . Still, at this point in my life, I wonder what it is that somebody with all this melting pot blood can call their own. . . .

Especially growing up in the sixties, when people *did* say "I'm proud to be Black," "I'm proud to be Hispanic," you know, and it became very popular to be proud of your ethnicity. And even feminists, you know, you could say, "I'm a woman" and be proud of it. But there's still a majority of the country that can't say they are proud of anything!

Suzie Roberts's words powerfully illustrate the key themes . . . that stirred the women I interviewed as they examined their own identities: what had formed them, what they counted as (their own or others') cultural practice(s), and what constituted identities of which they could be proud.* This [discussion] explores perceptions of whiteness as a location of culture and identity, focusing mainly on white feminist women's views and contrasting their voices with those of more politically conservative women. . . .

*Between 1984 and 1986 I interviewed 30 white women, diverse in age, class, region of origin, sexuality, family situation and political orientation, all living in California at the time of the interviews.

[M]any of the women I interviewed, including even some of the conservative ones, appeared to be self-conscious about white power and racial inequality. In part because of their sense of the links and parallels between white racial dominance in the United States and U.S. domination on a global scale, there was a complex interweaving of questions about race and nation—whiteness and Americanness—in these women's thoughts about white culture. Similarly, conceptions of racial, national, and cultural belonging frequently leaked into one another.

On the one hand, then, these women's views of white culture seemed to be distinctively modern. But at the same time, their words drew on much earlier historical moments and participated in long-established modes of cultural description. In the broadest sense, Western colonial discourses on the while self, the nonwhite Other, and the white Other too, were very much in evidence. These discourses produced dualistic conceptualizations of whiteness versus other cultural forms. The women thus often spoke about culture in ways that reworked, and yet remained tied to, "older" forms of racism.

For a significant number of young white women, being white felt like being cultureless. Cathy Thomas, in the following description of whiteness, raised many of the themes alluded to by other feminist and race-cognizant women. She described what she saw as a lack of form and substance:

. . . the formlessness of being white. Now if I was a middle western girl, or a New Yorker, if I had a fixed regional identity that was something palpable, then I'd be a white New Yorker, no doubt, but I'd still be a New Yorker. . . . Being a Californian, I'm sure it has its hallmarks, but to me they were invisible. . . . If I had an ethnic base to identify from, if I was even Irish American, that would have been something formed, if I was a working-class woman, that would have been something formed. But to be a Heinz 57 American, a white, class-confused American, land of the Kleenex type American, is so formless in and of itself. It only takes shape in relation to other people.

Whiteness as a cultural space is represented here as amorphous and indescribable, in contrast with a range of other identities marked by race, ethnicity, region, and class. Further, white culture is viewed here as "bad" culture. In fact, the extent to which identities can be named seems to show an inverse relationship to power in the U.S. social structure. The elisions, parallels, and differences between characterizations of white people, Americans, people of color, and so-called white ethnic groups will be explored [here].

Cathy's own cultural positioning seemed to her impossible to grasp, shapeless and unnameable. It was easier to know others and to know, with certainty, what one was *not*. Providing a clue to one of the mechanisms operating here is the fact that, while Cathy viewed New Yorkers and midwesterners as having a cultural shape or identity, women from the East Coast and the Midwest also described or mourned their own seeming lack of culture. The self, where it is part of a dominant cultural group, does not have to name itself. In this regard, Chris Patterson hit the nail on the head, linking the power of white culture with the privilege not to be named:

I'm probably at the stage where I'm beginning to see that you can come up with a definition of white. Before, I didn't know that you could turn it around and say, "Well what *does* white mean?" One thing is it's taken for granted. . . . [To be white means to] have some sort of advantage or privilege, even if it's something as simple as not having a definition.

The notion of "turning it around" indicates Chris's realization that, most often, whites are the nondefined definers of other people. Or, to put it another way, whiteness comes to be an unmarked or neutral category, whereas other cultures are specifically marked "cultural."

Many of the women shared the habit of turning to elements of white culture as the unspoken norm. This assumption of a white norm was so prevalent that even Sandy Alverez and Louise Glebocki, who were acutely aware of racial inequality as well as being members of racially mixed families, referred to "Mexican" music versus "regular" music, and regular meant "white."

Similarly, discussions of race difference and cultural diversity at times revealed a view in which people of color actually embodied difference and whites stood for sameness. Hence, Margaret Phillips said of her Jamaican daughter-in-law that: "She *really* comes with diversity." In spite of its brevity, and because of its curious structure, this short statement says a great deal. It implicitly designates whiteness as norm, and Jamaicans as having or bearing with them "differentness." At the risk of being crass, one might say that in this view, diversity is to the daughter-in-law as "the works" is to a hamburger—added on, adding color and flavor, but not exactly essential. Whiteness, seen by many of these women as boring, but nonetheless definitive, could also follow this analogy. This mode of thinking about "difference" expresses clearly the double-edged sword of a color- and power-evasive repertoire, apparently valorizing cultural difference but doing to in a way that leaves racial and cultural hierarchies intact.

For a seemingly formless entity, then, white culture had a great deal of power, difficult to dislodge from its place in white consciousness as a point of reference for the measuring of others. Whiteness served simultaneously to eclipse and marginalize others (two modes of making the other inessential). Helen Standish's description of her growing-up years in a small New England town captured these processes well. Since the community was all white, the differences at issue were differences between whites. (This also enables an assessment of the links between white and nonwhite "marked" cultures.) Asked about her own cultural identity, Helen explained that "it didn't seem like a culture because everyone else was the same." She had, however, previously mentioned Italian Americans in the town, so I asked about their status. She responded as follows, adopting at first the voice of childhood:

> They are different, but I'm the same as everybody else. They speak Italian, but everybody else in the U.S. speaks English. They eat strange, different food, but I eat the same kind of food as everybody else in the U.S. . . . The way I was brought up was to think that everybody who was the same as me were "Americans," and the other people were of "such and such descent."

Viewing the Italian Americans as different and oneself as "same" serves, first, to marginalize, to push from the center, the former group. At the same time, claiming to be the same as *everyone* else makes other cultural groups invisible or eclipses them. Finally, there is a marginalizing of all those who are not like Helen's own family, leaving a residual core or normative group who are the true Americans. The category of "American" represents simultaneously the normative and the residual, the dominant culture and a nonculture.

Although Helen talked here about whites, it is safe to guess that people of color would not have counted among the "same" group but among the communities of "such and such descent" (Mexican American, for example). Whites, within this discursive repertoire, became conceptually the real Americans, and only certain kinds of whites actually qualified. Whiteness and Americanness both stood as normative and exclusive categories in relation to which other cultures were identified and marginalized. And this clarifies that there are two kinds of whites, just as there are two kinds of Americans: those who are truly or only white, and those who are white but also something more—or is it something less?

In sum, whiteness often stood as an unmarked marker of others' differentness—whiteness not

so much void or formlessness as norm. I associate this construction with colonialism and with the more recent asymmetrical dualisms of liberal humanist views of culture, race, and identity. For the most part, this construction views nonwhite cultures as lesser, deviant, or pathological. However, another trajectory has been the inverse: conceptualizations of the cultures of peoples of color as somehow better than the dominant culture, perhaps more natural or more spiritual. These are positive evaluations of sort, but they are equally dualistic. Many of the women I interviewed saw white culture as less appealing and found the cultures of the "different" people more interesting. As Helen Standish put it:

> [We had] Wonder bread, white bread. I'm more interested in, you know, "What's a bagel?" in other people's cultures rather than my own.

The claim that whiteness lacks form and content says more about the definitions of culture being used than it does about the content of whiteness. However, I would suggest that in describing themselves as cultureless these women are in fact identifying specific kinds of unwanted absences or presences in their own culture(s) as a generalized lack or nonexistence. It thus becomes important to look at what they *did* say about the cultural content of whiteness.

Descriptions of the content of white culture were thin, to say the least. But despite the paucity of signifiers, there was a great deal of consistency across the narratives. First, there was naming based on color, the linking of white culture with white objects—the clichéd white bread and mayonnaise, for example. Freida Kazen's identification of whiteness as "bland," together with Helen Standish's "blah," also signified paleness or neutrality. The images connote several things—color itself (although exaggerated, and besides, bagels are usually white inside, too), lack of vitality (Wonder bread is highly processed), and homogeneity. However, these images are perched on a slippery slope, at once suggesting "white" identified as a color (though an unappealing one) and as an absence of color, that is, white as the unmarked marker.

Whiteness was often signified in these narratives by commodities and brands: Wonder bread, Kleenex, Heinz 57. In this identification whiteness came to be seen as spoiled by capitalism, and as being linked with capitalism in a way that other cultures supposedly are not. Another set of signifiers that constructed whiteness as uniquely tainted by capitalism had to do with the "modern condition": Dot Humphrey described white neighborhoods as "more privatized," and Cathy Thomas used "alienated" to describe her cultural condition. Clare Traverso added to this theme, mourning her own feeling of lack of identity, in contrast with images of her husband's Italian American background (and here, Clare is again talking about perceived differences between whites):

> Food, old country, mama. Stories about a grandmother who can't speak English. . . . Candles, adobe houses, arts, music. [It] has emotion, feeling, belongingness that to me is unique.

In linking whiteness to capitalism and viewing nonwhite cultures as untainted by it, these women were again drawing on a colonial discourse in which progress and industrialization were seen as synonymous with Westernization, while the rest of the world is seen as caught up in tradition and "culture." In addition, one can identify, in white women's mourning over whiteness, elements of what Raymond Williams has called "pastoralism," or nostalgia for a golden era now gone by (but in fact, says Williams, one that never existed).[1]

The image of whiteness as corrupted and impoverished by capitalism is but one of a series of ways in which white culture was seen as impure or tainted. White culture was also seen as tainted by its relationship to power. For example, Clare Traverso clearly counterposed white culture and white power, finding it difficult to value the former because of the overwhelming weight of the latter:

> The good things about whites are to do with folk arts, music. Because other things have power associated with them.

For many race-cognizant white women, white culture was also made impure by its very efforts to maintain race purity. Dot Humphrey, for example, characterized white neighborhoods as places in which people were segregated by choice. For her, this was a good reason to avoid living in them.

The link between whiteness and domination, however, was frequently made in ways that both artificially isolated culture from other factors and obscured economics. For at times, the traits the women envied in Other cultures were in fact at least in part the product of poverty or other dimensions of oppression. Lack of money, for example, often means lack of privacy or space, and it can be valorized as "more street life, less alienation." Cathy Thomas's notion of Chicanas' relationship to the kitchen ("the hearth of the home") as a cultural "good" might be an idealized one that disregards the reality of intensive labor.

Another link between class and culture emerged in Louise Glebocki's reference to the working-class Chicanos she met as a child as less pretentious, "closer to the truth," more "down to earth." And Marjorie Hoffman spoke of the "earthy humor" of Black people, which she interpreted as, in the words of Langston Hughes, a means of "laughing to keep from crying." On the one hand, as has been pointed out especially by black scholars and activists, the positions of people of color at the bottom of a social and economic hierarchy create the potential for a critique of the system as a whole and consciousness of the need to resist.[2] From the standpoint of race privilege, the system of racism is thus made structurally invisible. On the other hand, descriptions of this kind leave in place a troubling dichotomy that can be appropriated as easily by the right as by the left. For example, there is an inadvertent affinity between the image of Black people as "earthy" and the conservative racist view that African American culture leaves African American people ill equipped for advancement in the modern age. Here, echoing essentialist racism, both Chicanos and African Americans are placed on the borders of "nature" and "culture."

By the same token, often what was criticized as "white" was as much the product of middle-class status as of whiteness as such. Louise Glebocki's image of her fate had she married a white man was an image of a white-collar, nuclear family:

Him saying, "I'm home, dear," and me with an apron on—ugh!

The intersections of class, race, and culture were obscured in other ways. Patricia Bowen was angry with some of her white feminist friends who, she felt, embraced as "cultural" certain aspects of African American, Chicano, and Native American cultures (including, for example, artwork or dance performances) but would reject as "tacky" (her term) those aspects of daily life that communities of color shared with working-class whites, such as the stores and supermarkets of poor neighborhoods. This, she felt, was tantamount to a selective expansion of middle-class aesthetic horizons, but not to true antiracism or to comprehension of the cultures of people of color. Having herself grown up in a white working-class family, Pat also felt that middle-class white feminists were able to use selective engagement to avoid addressing their class privilege.

I have already indicated some of the problems inherent in this kind of conceptualization, suggesting that it tends to keep in place dichotomous constructions of "white" versus Other cultures, to separate "culture" from other dimensions of daily life, and to reify or strip of history *all* cultural forms. There are, then, a range of issues that need to be disentangled if we are to understand the location of "whiteness" in the terrain of culture. It is, I believe, useful to approach this question by means of a reconceptualization of the concept of culture itself. A culture, in the sense of the set of rules and practices by means of which a group organizes itself and its values, manners, and worldview—in other words, culture as "a field articulating the lifeworld of subjects . . . and the structures created by human activity"[3]—is an indispensable precondition to any individual's existence in the world. It is nonsensical in terms of this kind of definition to suggest that anyone could actually have "no culture." But this is not, as I have suggested, the mode of thinking about culture that these women are employing.

Whiteness emerges here as inextricably tied to domination partly as an effect of a discursive "draining process" applied to both whiteness and Americanness. In this process, any cultural practice engaged in by a white person that is not identical to the dominant culture is automatically counted as either "not really white"—and, for that matter, not really American, either—(but rather of such and such descent), or as "not really cultural" (but rather "economic"). There is a slipperiness to whiteness here: it shifts from "no culture" to "normal culture" to "bad culture" and back again. Simultaneously, a range of marginal or, in Trinh T. Minh-ha's terminology, "bounded" cultures are generated. These are viewed as enviable spaces, separate and untainted by relations of dominance or by linkage to other structures or systems. By contrast, whiteness is conceived as axiomatically tied to dominance, to economics, to political structures. In this process, both whiteness and nonwhiteness are reified, made into objects rather than processes, and robbed of historical context and human agency. As long as the discussion remains couched in these terms, a critique of whiteness remains a double-edged sword: for one thing, whiteness remains normative because there is no way to name the cultural practices associated with it *as* cultural. Moreover, as I have suggested, whether whiteness is viewed as artificial and dominating (and therefore "bad") or civilized (and therefore "good"), whiteness and all varieties of nonwhiteness continue to be viewed as ontologically different from one another.

A genuine sadness and frustration about the meaning of whiteness at this moment in history motivated these women to decry white culture. It becomes important, then, to recognize the grains of truth in their views of white culture. It is important to acknowledge their anger and frustration about the meaning of whiteness as we reach toward a politicized analysis of culture that is freer of colonial and pastoral legacies.

The terms "white" and "American" as these women used them signified domination in international and domestic terms. This link is both accurate and inaccurate. While it is true that, by and large, those in power in the United States are white, it is also true that not all those who are white are in power. Nor is the axiomatic linkage between Americanness and power accurate, because not all Americans have the same access to power. At the same time, the link between whiteness, Americanness, and power *are* accurate because, as we have seen, the terms "white" and "American" both function discursively to exclude people from normativity—including white people "of such and such descent." But here we need to distinguish between the fates of people of color and those of white people. Notwithstanding a complicated history, the boundaries of Americanness and whiteness have been much more fluid for "white ethnic" groups than for people of color.

There have been border skirmishes over the meaning of whiteness and Americanness since the inception of those terms. For white people, however, those skirmishes have been resolved through processes of assimilation, not exclusion. The late nineteenth and early twentieth centuries in the United States saw a systematic push toward the cultural homogenization of whites carried out through social reform movements and the schools. This push took place alongside the expansion of industrial capitalism, giving rise to the sense that whiteness signifies the production and consumption of commodities under capitalism.[4] But recognition of this history should not be translated into an assertion that whites were stripped of culture (for to do that would be to continue to adhere to a colonial view of "culture"). Instead one must argue that certain cultural practices replaced others. Were one to undertake a history of this "generic" white culture, it would fragment into a thousand tributary elements, culturally specific religious observances, and class survival mechanisms as

well as mass-produced commodities and mass media.

There are a number of dangers inherent in continuing to view white culture as no culture. Whiteness appeared in the narratives to function as both norm or core, that against which everything else is measured, and as residue, that which is left after everything else has been named. A far-reaching danger of whiteness coded as "no culture" is that it leaves in place whiteness as defining a set of normative cultural practices against which all are measured and into which all are expected to fit. This normativity has underwritten oppression from the beginning of colonial expansion and has had impact in multiple ways: from the American pioneers' assumption of a norm of private property used to justify appropriation of land that within their worldview did not have an owner, and the ideological construction of nations like Britain as white,[5] to Western feminism's Eurocentric shaping of its movements and institutions. It is important for white feminists not to continue to participate in these processes.

And if whiteness has a history so do the cultures of people of color, which are worked on, crafted, and created, rather than just "there." For peoples of color in the United States, this work has gone on as much in the context of relationships to imperialism and capitalism as has the production of whiteness, though it has been premised on exclusion and resistance to exclusion more than on assimilation. Although not always or only forged in resistance, the visibility and recognition of the cultures of U.S. peoples of color in recent times *is* the product of individual and collective struggle. Only a short time has elapsed since those struggles made possible the introduction into public discourse of celebration and valorization of their cultural forms. In short, it is important not to reify any culture by failing to acknowledge its createdness, and not to view it as always having been there in unchanging form.

Rather than feeling "cultureless," white women need to become conscious of the histories and specificities of our cultural positions, and of the political, economic, and creative fusions that form all cultures. The purpose of such an exercise is not, of course, to reinvent the dualisms and valorize whiteness so much as to develop a clearer sense of where and who we are.

NOTES

1. Raymond Williams, *The Country and the City* (New York: Oxford University Press, 1978).

2. The classic statement of this position is W. E. B. Du Bois's concept of the "double consciousness" of Americans of African descent. Two recent feminist statements of similar positions are Patricia Hill Collins, *Black Feminist Thought: Knowledge, Consciousness, and the Politics of Empowerment* (Boston: Unwin Hyman, 1990); and Aida Hurtado, "Relating to Privilege: Seduction and Rejection in the Subordination of White Women and Women of Color," *Signs* 14, no. 4:833–55.

3. Paul Gilroy, *There Ain't No Black in the Union Jack.* London: Hutchinson, 1987.

4. See, for example, Winthrop Talbot, ed., *Americanization* (New York: H. W. Wilson, 1917), esp. Sophonisba P. Brechinridge, "The Immigrant Family," 251–52; Olivia Howard Dunbar, "Teaching the Immigrant Woman," 252–56, and North American Civic League for Immigrants," 256–58; and Kathie Friedman Kasaba. "'To Become a Person': The Experience of Gender, Ethnicity and Work in the Lives of Immigrant Women, New York City, 1870–1940," doctoral dissertation. Department of Sociology, State University of New York, Binghamton, 1991. I am indebted to Kathie Friedman Kasaba for these references and for her discussion with me about working-class European immigrants to the United States at the turn of this century.

5. Gilroy. *There Ain't No Black in the Union Jack.*

THINKING ABOUT THE READING

In what ways does the invisibility of "whiteness" confer privileges on white people? Make a list of what you consider to be the typical characteristics of a white person. How easy/difficult is it to compile such a list? Does it contain primarily positive or negative attributes? When the women in Frankenberg's study did manage to describe whiteness, they tended to talk about blandness, paleness, and a lack of vitality. Such unappealing characterizations are actually quite common, but they don't seem to serve as a catalyst for discrimination the way the negative characterizations of other groups do. Why not? Why is it that we can laugh at or trivialize the stereotypes of whites but find the stereotypes of other racial groups demeaning and dangerous? Is there a link between these women's perceptions of their own whiteness and their social class standing? In what ways have you used the color of your skin to your advantage?

The Blacker the Berry

Gender, Skin Tone, Self-Esteem, and Self-Efficacy

Maxine S. Thompson and Verna M. Keith

She should have been a boy, then color of skin wouldn't have mattered so much, for wasn't her mother always saying that a Black boy could get along, but that a Black girl would never know anything but sorrow and disappointment? But she wasn't a boy; she was a girl, and color did matter, mattered so much that she would rather have missed receiving her high school diploma than have to sit as she now sat, the only odd and conspicuous figure on the auditorium platform of the Boise high school . . .

Get a diploma?—What did it mean to her? College?—Perhaps. A job?—Perhaps again. She was going to have a high school diploma, but it would mean nothing to her whatsoever. (Thurman 1929, 4–5).

Wallace Thurman (1929) speaking through the voice of the main character, Emma Lou Morgan, in his novel, "The Blacker the Berry," about skin color bias within the African American community, asserts that the disadvantages and emotional pain of being "dark skinned" are greater for women than men and that skin color, not achievement, determines identity and attitudes about the self. Thurman's work describes social relationships among African Americans that were shaped by their experiences in the white community during slavery and its aftermath. In the African American community, skin color, an ascribed status attribute, played an integral role in determining class distinctions. Mulattoes, African Americans with white progenitors, led a more privileged existence when compared with their Black counterparts, and in areas of the Deep South (i.e., most notably Louisiana and South Carolina), mulattoes served as a buffer class be-

tween whites and Blacks (Russell, Wilson, and Hall 1992). In the *Black Bourgeoisie,* Frazier (1957) describes affluent organized clubs within the Black community called "blue vein" societies. To be accepted into these clubs, skin tone was required to be lighter than a "paper bag" or light enough for visibility of "blue veins" (Okazawa Rey, Robinson, and Ward 1987). Preferential treatment given by both Black and white cultures to African Americans with light skin have conveyed to many Blacks that if they conformed to the white, majority standard of beauty, their lives would be more rewarding (Bond and Cash 1992; Gatewood 1988).

Although Thurman's novel was written in 1929, the issue of *colorism* (Okazawa Rey, Robinson, and Ward 1987), intraracial discrimination based on skin color, continues to divide and shape life experiences within the African American community. The status advantages afforded to persons of light complexion continue despite the political preference for dark skin tones in the Black awareness movement during the 1960s. No longer an unspoken taboo, color prejudice within the African American community has been a "hot" topic of talk shows, novels, and movies and an issue in a court case on discrimination in the workplace (Russell, Wilson, and Hall 1992). In addition to discussions within lay communities, research scholars have had considerable interest in the importance of skin color. At the structural levels, studies have noted that skin color is an important determinant of educational and occupational attainment: Lighter skinned Blacks complete more years of schooling, have more prestigious jobs, and earn more than darker skinned Blacks (Hughes and

Hertel 1990; Keith and Herring 1991). In fact, one study notes that the effect of skin color on earnings of "lighter" and "darker" Blacks is as great as the effect of race on the earnings of whites and all Blacks (Hughes and Hertel 1990). The most impressive research on skin tone effects is studies on skin tone and blood pressure. Using a reflectometer to measure skin color, research has shown that dark skin tone is associated with high blood pressure in African Americans with low socioeconomic status (Klag et al. 1991; Tryoler and James 1978). And at the social-psychological level, studies find that skin color is related to feelings of self-worth and attractiveness, self-control, satisfaction, and quality of life (Bond and Cash 1992; Boyd Franklin 1991; Cash and Duncan 1984; Chambers et al. 1994; Neal and Wilson 1989; Okazawa Rey, Robinson, and Ward 1987).

It is important to note that skin color is highly correlated with other phenotypic features—eye color, hair texture, broadness of nose, and fullness of lips. Along with light skin, blue and green eyes, European-shaped noses, and straight as opposed to "kinky" hair are all accorded higher status both within and beyond the African American community. Colorism embodies preference and desire for both light skin as well as these other attendant features. Hair, eye color, and facial features function along with color in complex ways to shape opportunities, norms regarding attractiveness, self-concept, and overall body image. Yet, it is color that has received the most attention in research on African Americans.[1] The reasons for this emphasis are not clear, although one can speculate that it is due to the fact that color is the most visible physical feature and is also the feature that is most enduring and difficult to change. As Russell, Wilson, and Hall (1992) pointed out, hair can be straightened with chemicals, eye color can be changed with contact lenses, and a broad nose can be altered with cosmetic surgery. Bleaching skin to a lighter tone, however, seldom meets with success (Okazawa Rey, Robinson, and Ward 1987). Ethnographic research also suggests that the research focus on skin color is somewhat justified.

For example, it played the central role in determining membership in the affluent African American clubs.

Although colorism affects attitudes about the self for both men and women, it appears that these effects are stronger for women than men. In early studies, dark-skinned women were seen as occupying the bottom rungs of the social ladder, least marriageable, having the fewest options for higher education and career advancement, and as more color conscious than their male counterparts (Parrish 1944; Warner, Junker, and Adams 1941). There is very little empirical research on the relationship between gender, skin color, and self-concept development. In this article, we evaluate the relative importance of skin color to feelings about the self for men and women within the African American community. . . .

. . . Using an adult sample of respondents who are representative of the national population, we examine[d] the relationship of skin tone to self-concept development. . . . More important, we examine[d] the way in which gender socially constructs the impact of skin tone on self-concept development. . . .

The Sample

Data for this study come from the National Survey of Black Americans (NSBA) (Jackson and Gurin 1987). . . . Only self-identified Black American citizens were eligible for the study. Face-to-face interviews were carried out by trained Black interviewers, yielding a sample of 2,107 respondents. The response rate was approximately 69 percent. For the most part, the NSBA is representative of the national Black population enumerated in the 1980 census, with the exception of a slight overrepresentation of women and older Blacks and a small underrepresentation of southerners (Jackson, Tucker, and Gurin 1987). . . . [Using these data we were able to study the relationship between skin tone, gender, and self-evaluation. (For a description of the methods and results see the complete article.)]

Skin Tone and Gender

Issues of skin color and physical attractiveness are closely linked and because expectations of physical attractiveness are applied more heavily to women across all cultures, stereotypes of attractiveness and color preference are more profound for Black women (Warner, Junker, and Adams 1941). In the clinical literature (Boyd Franklin 1991; Grier and Cobbs 1968; Neal and Wilson 1989; Okazawa Rey, Robinson, and Ward 1987), issues of racial identity, skin color, and attractiveness were central concerns of women. The "what is beautiful is good" stereotype creates a "halo" effect for light-skinned persons. The positive glow generated by physical attractiveness includes a host of desirable personality traits. Included in these positive judgments are beliefs that attractive people would be significantly more intelligent, kind, confident, interesting, sexy, assertive, poised, modest, and successful, and they appear to have higher self-esteem and self-worth (Dion, Berscheid, and Walster 1972). When complexion is the indicator of attractiveness, similar stereotypic attributes are found. There is evidence that gender difference in response to the importance of skin color to attractiveness appears during childhood. Girls as young as six are twice as likely as boys to be sensitive to the social importance of skin color (Porter 1971; Russell, Wilson, and Hall 1992, 68). In a study of facial features, skin color, and attractiveness, Neal (cited in Neal and Wilson 1989, 328) found that

> unattractive women were perceived as having darker skin tones than attractive women and that women with more Caucasoid features were perceived as more attractive to the opposite sex, more successful in their love lives and their careers than women with Negroid features.

Frequent exposure to negative evaluations can undermine a woman's sense of self. "A dark skinned Black woman who feels herself unattractive, however, may think that she has nothing to offer society no matter how intelligent or inventive she is" (Russell, Wilson, and Hall 1992, 42).

Several explanations are proffered for gender differences in self-esteem among Blacks. One is that women are socialized to attend to evaluations of others and are vulnerable to negative appraisals. Women seek to validate their selves through appraisal from others more than men do. And the media has encouraged greater negative self-appraisals for dark-skinned women. A second explanation is that colorism and its associated stressors are not the same for dark-skinned men and women. For men, stereotypes associated with perceived dangerousness, criminality, and competence are associated with dark skin tone, while for women the issue is attractiveness (Russell, Wilson, and Hall 1992, 38). Educational attainment is a vehicle by which men might overcome skin color bias, but changes in physical features are difficult to accomplish. Third, women may react more strongly to skin color bias because they feel less control of their lives. Research studies show that women and persons of low status tend to feel fatalistic (Pearlin and Schooler 1978; Turner and Noh 1983) and to react more intensely than comparable others to stressors (Kessler and McLeod 1984; Pearlin and Johnson 1977; Thoits 1982, 1984; Turner and Noh 1983). This suggests a triple jeopardy situation: black women face problems of racism and sexism, and when these two negative status positions—being Black and being female—combine with colorism, a triple threat lowers self-esteem and feelings of competence among dark Black women.

Skin Tone and Self-Evaluation

William James (1890) conceived of the self as an integrating social product consisting of various constituent parts (i.e., the physical, social, and spiritual selves). Body image, the aspect of the self that we recognize first, is one of the major components of the self and remains important throughout life. One can assume that if one's bodily attributes are judged positively, the impact on one's self is positive. Likewise, if society devalues certain physical attributes, negative feelings about the self are likely to ensue. Body image is influenced by a number of factors including skin color, size, and shape. In our society, dark-skinned men and women are raised to believe that "light" skin is preferred. They see very light-skinned Blacks having successful experiences in advertisements, in magazines, in professional positions, and so forth. They are led to believe that "light" skin is the key to popularity, professional status, and a desirable marriage. Russell, Wilson, and Hall (1992) argue that the African American gay and lesbian community is also affected by colorism because a light-skinned or even white mate confers status. Whether heterosexual, gay, or lesbian, colorism may lead to negative self-evaluations among African Americans with dark skin.

Self-evaluations are seen as having two dimensions, one reflecting the person's moral worth and the other reflecting the individual's competency or agency (Gecas 1989). The former refers to self-esteem and indicates how we feel about ourselves. The latter refers to self-efficacy and indicates our belief in the ability to control our own fate. These are two different dimensions in that people can feel that they are good and useful but also feel that what happens to them is due to luck or forces outside themselves.

Self-esteem and skin tone. Self-esteem consists of feeling good, liking yourself, and being liked and treated well. Self-esteem is influenced both by the social comparisons we make of ourselves with others and by the reactions that other people have toward us (i.e., reflected appraisals). The self-concept depends also on the attributes of others who are available for comparison. Self-evaluation theory emphasizes the importance of consonant environmental context for personal comparisons; that is, Blacks will compare themselves with other Blacks in their community. Consonant environmental context assumes that significant others will provide affirmation of one's identity and that similarity between oneself and others shapes the self. Thus, a sense of personal connectedness to other African Americans is most important for fostering and reinforcing positive self-evaluations. This explains why the personal self-esteem of Blacks, despite their lower status position, was as high as that of whites (Por-

ter and Washington 1989, 345; Rosenberg and Simmons 1971).[2] It does not explain the possible influence of colorism on self-esteem within the African American community. Evidence suggests that conflictual and dissonant racial environments have negative effects on self-esteem, especially within the working class (Porter and Washington 1989, 346; Verna and Runion 1985). The heterogeneity of skin tone hues and colorism create a dissonant racial environment and become a source of negative self-evaluation.

Self-efficacy and skin tone. Self-efficacy, as defined by Bandura (1977, 1982), is the belief that one can master situations and control events. Performance influences self-efficacy such that when faced with a failure, individuals with high self-efficacy generally believe that extra effort or persistence will lead to success (Bandura 1982). However, if failure is related to some stable personal characteristic such as "dark skin color" or social constraints such as blocked opportunities resulting from mainstreaming practices in the workplace, then one is likely to be discouraged by failure and to feel less efficacious than his or her lighter counterparts. In fact, Pearlin and colleagues (1981) argue that stressors that seem to be associated with inadequacy of one's efforts or lack of success are implicated in a diminished sense of self. Problems or hardships "to which people can see no end, those that seem to become fixtures of their existence" pose the most sustained affront to a sense of mastery and self-worth (Pearlin et al. 1981, 345). For Bandura, however, individual agency plays a role in sustaining the self. Individuals actively engage in activities that are congenial with a positive sense of self. Self-efficacy results not primarily from beliefs or attitudes about performance but from undertaking challenges and succeeding. Thus, darker skinned Blacks who experience success in their everyday world (e.g., work, education, etc.) will feel more confident and empowered.

Following the literature, we predict a strong relationship between skin tone and self-esteem and self-efficacy, but the mechanisms are different for the two dimensions. The effect of skin tone on self-efficacy will be partially mediated by occupation and income. The effect will be direct for self-esteem. That is, the direct effect will be stronger for self-esteem than for self-efficacy. Furthermore, we expect a stronger relationship between skin tone and self-esteem for women than men because women's self-esteem is conditioned by the appraisals of others, and the media has encouraged negative appraisals for dark-skinned women.

Discussion [of the Study]

The data in this study indicate that gender—mediated by socioeconomic status variables such as education, occupation, and income—socially constructs the importance of skin color evaluations of self-esteem and self-efficacy. Self-efficacy results not primarily from beliefs or attitudes about performance but rather reflects an individual's competency or agency from undertaking challenges and succeeding at overcoming them. Self-esteem consists of feeling good about oneself and being liked and treated favorably by others. However, the effect of skin color on these two domains of self is different for women and men. Skin color is an important predictor of perceived efficacy for Black men but not Black women. And skin color predicts self-esteem for Black women but not Black men. This pattern conforms to traditional gendered expectations (Hill Collins 1990, 79–80). The traditional definitions of masculinity demand men specialize in achievement outside the home, dominate in interpersonal relationships, and remain rational and self-contained. Women, in contrast, are expected to seek affirmation from others, to be warm and nurturing. Thus, consistent with gendered characteristics of men and women, skin color is important in self-domains that are central to masculinity (i.e., competence) and femininity (i.e., affirmation of the self).[3]

Turning our attention to the association between skin color and self-concept for Black men, the association between skin color and self-efficacy increases significantly as skin color lightens. And this is independent of the strong positive contribution of education—and ultimately socioeconomic status—to feelings of competence

of men. We think that the effect of skin tone on self-efficacy is the result of widespread negative stereotyping and fear associated with dark-skinned men that pervade the larger society and operates independent of social class. Correspondingly, employers view darker African American men as violent, uncooperative, dishonest, and unstable (Kirschenman and Neckerman, 1998). As a consequence, employers exclude "darker" African American men from employment and thus block their access to rewards and resources.

Evidence from research on the relationship between skin tone and achievement supports our interpretation. The literature on achievement and skin tone shows that lighter skinned Blacks are economically better off than darker skinned persons (Hughes and Hertel 1990; Keith and Herring 1991). Hughes and Hertal (1990), using the NSBA data, present findings that show that for every dollar a light-skinned African American earns, the darker skinned person earns 72 cents. Thus, it seems colorism is operative within the workplace. Lighter skinned persons are probably better able to predict what will happen to them and what doors will open and remain open, thus leading to a higher sense of control over their environment. Our data support this finding and add additional information on how that process might work, at least in the lives of Black men. Perhaps employers are looking to hire African American men who will assimilate into the work environment, who do not alienate their clients (Kirschenman and Neckerman 1998), and who are nonthreatening. One consequence of mainstreaming the workplace is that darker skinned Black men have fewer opportunities to demonstrate competence in the breadwinner role. It is no accident that our inner cities where unemployment is highest are filled with darker skinned persons, especially men (Russell, Wilson, and Hall 1992, 38). During adolescence, lighter skinned boys discover that they have better job prospects, appear less threatening to whites, and have a clearer sense of who they are and their competency (Russell, Wilson, and Hall 1992, 67). In contrast, darker skinned African American men may feel powerless and less able to affect change through the "normal" channels available to light skinned African American men (who are able to achieve a more prestigious socioeconomic status).

While skin color is an important predictor of self-efficacy for African American men, it is more important as a predictor of self-esteem for African American women. These data confirm much of the anecdotal information from clinical studies of clients in psychotherapy that found that dark-skinned Black women have problems with self-worth and confidence. Our findings suggest that this pattern is not limited to experiences of women who are in therapy but that colorism is part of the everyday reality of black women. Black women expect to be judged by their skin tone. No doubt messages from peers, the media, and family show a preference for lighter skin tones. Several studies cited in the literature review point out that Black women of all ages tend to prefer lighter skin tones and believe that lighter hues are perceived as most attractive by their Black male counterparts (Bond and Cash 1992; Chambers et al. 1994; Porter 1971; T. L. Robinson and Ward 1995).

Evidence from personal accounts reported by St. John and Feagin (1998, 75) in research on the impact of racism in the everyday lives of Black women supports this interpretation. One young woman describes her father's efforts to shape her expectations about the meaning of beauty in our society and where Black women entered this equation.

> Beauty, beauty standards in this country, a big thing with me. It's a big gripe, because I went through a lot of personal anguish over that, being Black and being female, it's a real big thing with me, because it took a lot for me to find a sense of self . . . in this white-male-dominated society. And just how beauty standards are so warped because like my daddy always tell me, "white is right." The whiter you are, somehow the better you are, and if you look white, well hell, you've got your ticket, and anything you want, too.

Nevertheless, the relationship between skin color and self-esteem among African American women is moderated by socioeconomic status. For example, there is no correlation between skin color and self-esteem among women who have a more privileged socioeconomic status. Consequently, women who are darker and "successful" evaluate themselves just as positively as women of a lighter color. On the other hand, the relationship between skin color and self-esteem is stronger for African American women from the less privileged socioeconomic sectors. In other words, darker skinned women with the lowest incomes display the lowest levels of self-esteem, but self-esteem increases as their skin color lightens. Why does skin color have such importance for self-regard in the context of low income or poverty? Low income shapes self-esteem because it provides fewer opportunities for rewarding experiences or affirming relationships. In addition, there are more negative attributes associated with behaviors of individuals from less privileged socioeconomic status than with those of a more prestigious one. For example, the derisive comment "ghetto chick" is often used to describe the behaviors, dress, communication and interaction styles of women from low-income groups. Combine stereotypes of classism and colorism, and you have a mixture that fosters an undesirable if not malignant context for self-esteem development. An important finding of this research is that skin color and income determine self-worth for Black women and especially that these factors can work together. Dark skin and low income produce Black women with very low self-esteem. Accordingly, [our study] help[s] refine [the] understanding of gendered racism and of "triple oppression" involving race, gender, and class that places women of color in a subordinate social and economic position relative to men of color and the larger white population as well (Segura 1986). More important, the data suggest that darker skinned African American women actually experience a "quadruple" oppression originating in the convergence of social inequalities based on gender, class, race, and color. . . . We noted the absence of an interaction effect between skin tone and education, and we can only speculate on the explanation for this nonfinding. Perhaps education does not have the same implications for self-esteem as income because it is a less visible symbol of success. Financial success affords one the ability to purchase consumer items that tell others, even at a distance, that an individual is successful. These visible symbols include the place where we live, the kind of car we drive, and the kind of clothing that we wear. Educational attainment is not as easily grasped, especially in distant social interactions—passing on the street, walking in the park, or attending a concert event. In other words, for a dark-skinned African American woman, her M.A. or Ph.D. may be largely unknown outside her immediate friends, family, and coworkers. Her Lexus or Mercedes, however, is visible to the world and is generally accorded a great deal of prestige.

Finally, the data indicate that self-esteem increases as skin color becomes lighter among African American women who are judged as having "low and average levels of attractiveness." There is no relationship between skin color and self-esteem for women who are judged "highly attractive," just as there is no correlation between skin color and self-esteem for women of higher socioeconomic status. That physical attractiveness influenced feelings of self-worth for Black women is not surprising. Women have traditionally been concerned with appearance, regardless of ethnicity. Indeed, the pursuit and preoccupation with beauty are central features of female sex-role socialization. Our findings suggest that women who are judged "unattractive" are more vulnerable to color bias than those judged attractive.

NOTES

1. Skin color bias has also been investigated among Latino groups, although more emphasis has been placed on the combination of both color and European phenotype facial characteristics. Studies of Mexican Americans have documented that those with lighter skin and European features attain more schooling (Telles and Murguia 1990) and generally have higher socioeconomic status (Acre, Murguia, and Frisbie 1987) than those of darker complexion with more Indian features. Similar findings have been reported for Puerto Ricans (Rodriguez 1989), a population with African admixture.

2. Self-concept theory argued that the experience of social inequality would foster lower self-concept of persons in lower status positions compared with their higher status counterparts. However, when comparing the self-concept of African American schoolboys and schoolgirls, Rosenberg and Simmons (1971) found that their self-feelings were as high and in some instances higher than those of white schoolchildren. This "unexpected" finding was explained by strong ties and bonds within the African American community as opposed to identifying with the larger community.

3. These findings also reflect the dual nature of colorism as it pertains to Black women. Colorism is an aspect of racism that results in anti-Black discrimination in the wider society and, owing to historical patterns, also occurs within the Black community. The finding that the effects of skin tone on self-efficacy become nonsignificant when socioeconomic status variables are added suggests that the interracial discrimination aspect of colorism is more operational for Black women's self-efficacy via access to jobs and income. The finding that the effect of skin tone is more central to Black women's self-esteem indicates that colorism within the Black community is the more central mechanism. Self-esteem is derived from family, friends, and close associates.

REFERENCES

Acre, Carlos, Edward Murguia, and W. P. Frisbie, 1987. Phenotype and life chances among Chicanos. *Hispanic Journal of Behavioral Sciences* 9(1): 19–32.

Aiken, Leona S., and Stephen G. West. 1991. *Multiple regression: Testing and interpreting interactions.* Newbury Park, CA: Sage.

Bachman, J. G., and Johnson. 1978. *The monitoring the future project: Design and procedures.* Ann Arbor: University of Michigan, Institute for Social Research.

Bandura, A. 1977. Self efficacy: Towards a unifying theory of behavioral change. *Psychological Review* 84: 191–215.

———. 1982. Self efficacy mechanism in human agency. *American Psychologist* 37: 122–47.

Bond, S., and T. F. Cash. 1992. Black beauty: Skin color and body images among African-American college women. *Journal of Applied Social Psychology* 22 (11): 874–88.

Boyd Franklin, N. 1991. Recurrent themes in the

treatment of African-American women in group psychotherapy. *Women and Therapy.* 11 (2): 25–40.

Cash, T. S., and N. C. Duncan. 1984. Physical attractiveness stereotyping among Black American college students. *Journal of Social Psychology* 1:71–77.

Chambers, J. W., T. Clark, L. Dantzler, and J. A. Baldwin. 1994. Perceived attractiveness, facial features, and African self-consciousness. *Journal of Black Psychology* 20 (3): 305–24.

Dion, K., E. Berscheid, and E. Walster. 1972. What is beautiful is good. *Journal of Personality and Social Psychology* 24:285–90.

Frazier, E. Franklin. 1957. *Black bourgeoise: The rise of the new middle class.* New York: Free Press.

Freeman, H. E., J. M. Ross, S. Armor, and R. F. Pettigrew. 1966. Color gradation and attitudes among middle class income Negroes. *American Sociological Review* 31: 365–74.

Gatewood, W. B. 1988. Aristocrat of color: South and North and the Black elite, 1880–1920. *Journal of Southern History* 54: 3–19.

Gecas, Viktor. 1989. The social psychology of self-efficacy. *Annual Review of Sociology* 15: 291–316.

Grier, W., and P. Cobbs. 1968. *Black rage.* New York: Basic Books.

Hill Collins, Patricia. 1990. *Black feminist thought: Knowledge, consciousness, and the politics of empowerment.* Boston: Unwin Hyman.

Hughes, M., and B. R. Hertel. 1990 The significance of color remains: A study of life chances, mate selection, and ethnic consciousness among Black Americans. *Social Forces* 68(4): 1105-20.

Hughes, Michael, and David H. Demo. 1989. Self perceptions of Black Americans: Self-esteem and personal efficacy. *American Journal of Sociology* 95: 132–59.

Jackson, J., and G. Gurin. 1987. *National survey of Black Americans, 1979–1980* (machine-readable codebook). Ann Arbor: University of Michigan, Inter-University Consortium for Political and Social Research

Jackson, J. S., B. Tucker, and G. Gurin. 1987. *National survey of Black Americans 1979–1980* (MRDF). Ann Arbor, MI: Institute for Social Research.

James, W. 1890. *The principles of psychology.* New York: Smith.

Keith, V. M., and C. Herring. 1991. Skin tone and stratification in the Black community. *American Journal of Sociology* 97 (3): 760–78.

Kessler, R. C., and J. D. McLeod. 1984. Sex differences in vulnerability to undesirable life events. *American Sociological Review* 49: 620–31.

Kirschenman, J., and K. M. Neckerman. 1998. We'd love to hire them, but . . . In *The meaning of race for employers in working American: Continuity, conflict, and change,* edited by Amy S. Wharton. Mountain View, CA: Mayfield.

Klag, Michael, Paul Whelton, Josef Coresh, Clarence Grim, and Lewis Kuller. 1991. The association of skin color with blood pressure in US Blacks with low socioeconomic status. *Journal of the American Medical Association* 65(5): 599–602.

Miller, Herman P. 1964. *Rich man, poor man.* New York: Corwell.

Neal, A., and M. Wilson. 1989. The role of skin color and features in the Black community: Implications for Black women in therapy. *Clinical Psychology Review* 9 (3): 323–33.

Okazawa Rey, Margo, Tracy Robinson, and Janie V. Ward. 1987. *Black women and the politics of skin color and hair.* New York: Haworth.

Parrish, Charles. 1944. The significance of skin color in the Negro community. Ph.D. diss., University of Chicago.

Pearlin, L. I., and J. S. Johnson. 1977. Marital status, life strains, and depression. *American Sociological Review* 42: 704–15.

Pearlin, L. I., M. A. Liberman, E. G. Meneghan, and J. T. Mullan. 1981. The stress process. *Journal of Health and Social Behavior* 22 (December): 337–56.

Pearlin, L. I., and C., Schooler. 1978. The structure of coping. *Journal of Health and Social Behavior* 19: 2–21.

Porter, J. 1971. *Black child, white child: The development of racial attitudes.* Cambridge, MA: Harvard University Press.

Porter, J. R., and R. E. Washington. 1989. Developments in research on black identity and self esteem: 1979–88. *Review of International Psychology and Sociology* 2:341–53.

Ransford, E. H. 1970. Skin color, life chances and anti-white attitudes. *Social Problems* 18:164–78.

Robinson, J. P., and P. R. Shaver. 1969. *Measures of social psychological attitudes.* Ann Arbor: University of Michigan, Institute of Social Research.

Robinson, T. L., and J. V. Ward. 1995. African American adolescents and skin color. *Journal of Black Psychology* 21 (3): 256–74.

Rodriguez, Clara. 1989. *Puerto Ricans: Born in the USA.* Boston: Unwin Hyman.

Rosenberg, M. 1979. *Conceiving the self.* New York: Basic Books.

Rosenberg, M., and R. Simmons. 1971. *Black and white self-esteem: The urban school child.* Washington, DC: American Sociological Association.

Russell, Kathy, Midge Wilson, and Ronald Hall. 1992. *The color complex: The politics of skin color among African Americans.* New York: Harcourt Brace Jovanovich.

Segura, Denise. 1986. Chicanas and triple oppression in the labor force. In *Chicana voices: Intersections of class, race, and gender,* edited by Teresa Cordova and the National Association of Chicana Studies Editorial Committee. Austin, TX: Center for Mexican American Studies.

St. John, Y., and J. R. Reagin. 1998. *Double burden: Black women and everyday racism.* New York: M. E. Sharpe.

Telles, Edward E., and Edward Murguia. 1990. Phenotypic discrimination and income differences among Mexican Americans. *Social Science Quarterly* 71 (4): 682–95.

Thoits, Peggy A. 1982. Life stress, social support, and psychological vulnerability: Epidemiological considerations. *Journal of Community Psychology* 10: 341–62.

———. 1984. Explaining distributions of psychological vulnerability: Lack of social support in the face of life stress. *Social Forces* 63: 452–81.

Thurman, Wallace. 1929. *The blacker the berry: A novel of Negro life.* New York: Macmillan.

Tryoler, H. A., and S. A. James. 1978. Blood pressure and skin color. *American Journal of Public Health* 58: 1170–72.

Turner, R. J., and S. Noh. 1983. Class and psychological vulnerability among women: The significance of social support and personal control. *Journal of Health and Social Behavior* 24: 2–15.

Udry, J. R., K. E. Baumann, and C. Chase. 1969. Skin color, status, and mate selection. *American Journal of Sociology* 76: 722–33.

Verna. G., and K. Runion. 1985. The effects of contextual dissonance on the self concept of youth from high vs. low socially valued group. *Journal of Social Psychology* 125: 449–58.

Warner, W. L., B. H. Junker, and W. A. Adams. 1941. *Color and human nature.* Washington, DC: American Council on Education.

Wright, B. 1976. *The dissent of the governed: Alienation and democracy in America.* New York: Academic Press.

THINKING ABOUT THE READING

Describe the different effects skin tone has on black men and women. How can you explain the gender differences in the relationship between skin tone and self-esteem and between skin tone and self-efficacy? What role does socioeconomic status play in mediating these relationships? What are the long-term economic and political consequences of skin color bias? Thompson and Keith state that *colorism*—intraracial discrimination based on skin color—still divides and shapes the lives of African Americans. How does this skin color bias within the African-American community compare to the prejudice and discrimination blacks are subjected to by non-blacks? Is there comparable *within-group* prejudice among other races? If so, how does it compare to what Thompson and Keith describe? If not, why is such prejudice unique to the African-American community?

"Opening" Faces

The Politics of Cosmetic Surgery and Asian American Women

Eugenia Kaw

Ellen, a Chinese American in her forties, informed me she had had her upper eyelids surgically cut and sewed by a plastic surgeon twenty years ago in order to get rid of "the sleepy look," which her naturally "puffy" eyes gave her. She pointed out that the sutures, when they healed, became a crease above the eye which gave the eyes a more "open appearance." She was quick to tell me that her decision to undergo "double-eyelid" surgery was not so much because she was vain or had low self-esteem, but rather because the "undesirability" of her looks before the surgery was an undeniable fact.

During my second interview with Ellen, she showed me photos of herself from before and after her surgery in order to prove her point. When Stacy, her twelve-year-old daughter, arrived home from school, Ellen told me she wanted Stacy to undergo similar surgery in the near future because Stacy has only single eyelids and would look prettier and be more successful in life if she had a fold above each eye. Ellen brought the young girl to where I was sitting and said, "You see, if you look at her you will know what I mean when I say that I had to have surgery done on my eyelids. Look at her eyes. She looks just like me before the surgery." Stacy seemed very shy to show me her face. But I told the girl truthfully that she looked fine and beautiful the way she was. Immediately she grinned at her mother in a mocking, defiant manner, as if I had given her courage, and put her arm up in the manner that bodybuilders do when they display their bulging biceps.

As empowered as Stacy seemed to feel at the moment, I could not help but wonder how many times Ellen had shown her "before" and "after"

photos to her young daughter with the remark that "Mommy looks better after the surgery." I also wondered how many times Stacy had been asked by Ellen to consider surgically "opening" her eyes like "Mommy did." And I wondered about the images we see on television and in magazines and their often negative, stereotypical portrayal of "squinty-eyed" Asians (when Asians are featured at all). I could not help but wonder how normal it is to feel that an eye without a crease is undesirable and how much of that feeling is imposed. And I shuddered to think how soon it might be before twelve-year-old Stacy's defenses gave away and she allowed her eyes to be cut.

The permanent alteration of bodies through surgery for aesthetic purposes is not a new phenomenon in the United States. As early as World War I, when reconstructive surgery was performed on disfigured soldiers, plastic surgery methods began to be refined for purely cosmetic purposes (that is, not so much for repairing and restoring but for transforming natural features a person is unhappy with). Within the last decade, however, an increasing number of people have opted for a wide array of cosmetic surgery procedures, from tummy tucks, facelifts, and liposuction to enlargement of chests and calves. By 1988, two million Americans had undergone cosmetic surgery (Wolf 1991:218), and a 69 percent increase had occurred in the number of cosmetic surgery procedures between 1981 and 1990, according to the ASPRS, or American Society of Plastic and Reconstructive Surgeons (n.d.).

Included in these numbers are an increasing number of cosmetic surgeries undergone by people like Stacy who are persons of color

(American Academy of Cosmetic Surgery press release, 1991). In fact, Asian Americans are more likely than any other ethnic group (white or nonwhite) to pursue cosmetic surgery. ASPRS reports that over thirty-nine thousand of the aesthetic procedures performed by its members in 1990 (or more than 6 percent of all procedures performed that year) were performed on Asian Americans, who make up 3 percent of the U.S. population (Chen 1993:15). Because Asian Americans seek cosmetic surgery from doctors in Asia and from doctors who specialize in fields other than surgery (e.g., ear, nose, and throat specialists and opthamologists), the total number of Asian American patients is undoubtedly higher (Chen 1993:16).

The specific procedures requested by different ethnic groups in the United States are missing from the national data, but newspaper reports and medical texts indicate that Caucasians and nonwhites, on the average, seek significantly different types of operations (Chen 1993; Harahap 1982; Kaw 1993; LeFlore 1982; McCurdy 1980; Nakao 1993; Rosenthal 1991). While Caucasians primarily seek to augment breasts and to remove wrinkles and fat through such procedures as facelifts, liposuction, and collagen injection, African Americans more often opt for lip and nasal reduction operations; Asian Americans more often choose to insert an implant on their nasal dorsum for a more prominent nose or undergo double-eyelid surgery whereby parts of their upper eyelids are excised to create a fold above each eye, which makes the eye appear wider.[1]

Though the American media, the medical establishment, and the general public have debated whether such cosmetic changes by nonwhite persons reflect a racist milieu in which racial minorities must deny their racial identity and attempt to look more Caucasian, a resounding no appears to be the overwhelming opinion of people in the United States.[2] Many plastic surgeons have voiced the opinion that racial minorities are becoming more assertive about their right to choose and that they are choosing not to look Caucasian. Doctors say that nonwhite per-

sons' desire for thinner lips, wider eyes, and pointier noses is no more than a wish to enhance their features in order to attain "balance" with all their other features (Kaw 1993; Merrell 1994; Rosenthal 1991).

Much of the media and public opinion also suggests that there is no political significance inherent in the cosmetic changes made by people of color which alter certain conventionally known, phenotypic markers of racial identity. On a recent Phil Donahue show where the racially derogatory nature of blue contact lenses for African American women was contested, both white and nonwhite audience members were almost unanimous that African American women's use of these lenses merely reflected their freedom to choose in the same way that Bo Derek chose to wear corn rows and white people decided to get tans (Bordo 1990). Focusing more specifically on cosmetic surgery, a *People Weekly* magazine article entitled "On the Cutting Edge" (January 27, 1992, p. 3) treats Michael Jackson (whose nose has become narrower and perkier and whose skin has become lighter through the years) as simply one among many Hollywood stars whose extravagant and competitive lifestyle has motivated and allowed them to pursue cosmetic self-enhancement. Clearly, Michael Jackson's physical transformation within the last decade has been more drastic than Barbara Hershey's temporary plumping of her lips to look younger in *Beaches* or Joan Rivers's facelift, yet his reasons for undergoing surgery are not differentiated from those of Caucasian celebrities; the possibility that he may want to cross racial divides through surgery is not an issue in the article.

When critics speculate on the possibility that a person of color is attempting to look white, they often focus their attack on the person and his or her apparent lack of ethnic pride and self-esteem. For instance, a *Newsweek* article, referring to Michael Jackson's recent television interview with Oprah Winfrey, questioned Jackson's emphatic claim that he is proud to be a black American: "Jackson's dermatologist confirmed that the star has vitiligo, a condition that blocks the skin's ability to produce pigment . . . [however,] most vitiligo sufferers darken their light patches with makeup to even the tone. Jackson's makeup solution takes the other tack: less ebony, more ivory" (Fleming and Talbot 1993:57). Such criticisms, sadly, center around Michael Jackson the person instead of delving into his possible feelings of oppression or examining society as a potential source of his motivation to alter his natural features so radically.

. . . Based on structured, open-ended interviews with Asian American women like Ellen who have or are thinking about undergoing cosmetic surgery for wider eyes and more heightened noses, I attempt to convey more emphatically the lived social experiences of people of color who seek what appears to be conventionally recognized Caucasian features. Rather than mock their decision to alter their features or treat it lightly as an expression of their freedom to choose an idiosyncratic look, I examine everyday cultural images and social relationships which influence Asian American women to seek cosmetic surgery in the first place. Instead of focusing, as some doctors do (Kaw 1993), on the size and width of the eyelid folds the women request as indicators of the women's desire to look Caucasian, I examine the cultural, social, and historical sources that allow the women in my study to view their eyes in a negative fashion—as "small" and "slanted" eyes reflecting a "dull," "passive" personality, a "closed" mind, and a "lack of spirit" in the person. I explore the reasons these women reject the natural shape of their eyes so radically that they willingly expose themselves to a surgery that is at least an hour long, costs one thousand to three thousand dollars, entails administering local anesthesia and sedation, and carries the following risks: "bleeding and hematoma," "hemorrhage," formation of a "gaping wound," "discoloration," scarring, and "asymmetric lid folds" (Sayoc 1974:162–166).

In our feminist analyses of femininity and beauty we may sometimes find it difficult to account for cosmetic surgery without undermining the thoughts and decisions of women who opt for it (Davis 1991). However, I attempt to show that the decision of the women in my study to undergo cosmetic surgery is often carefully thought out. Such a decision is usually made only after a long period of weighing the psychological pain of feeling inadequate prior to surgery against the possible social advantages a new set of features may bring. Several of the women were aware of complex power structures that construct their bodies as inferior and in need of change, even while they simultaneously reproduced these structures by deciding to undergo surgery (Davis 1991:33).

I argue that as women and as racial minorities, the psychological burden of having to measure up to ideals of beauty in American society falls especially heavy on these Asian-American women. As women, they are constantly bombarded with the notion that beauty should be their primary goal (Lakoff and Scherr 1984, Wolf 1991). As racial minorities, they are made to feel inadequate by an Anglo American–dominated cultural milieu that has historically both excluded them and distorted images of them in such a way that they themselves have come to associate those features stereotypically identified with their race (i.e., small, slanty eyes, and a flat nose) with negative personality and mental characteristics.

In a consumption-oriented society such as the United States, it is often tempting to believe that human beings have an infinite variety of needs which technology can endlessly fulfill, and that these needs, emerging spontaneously in time and space, lack any coherent patterns, cultural meanings, or political significance (Bordo 1991; Goldstein 1993; O'Neill 1985:98). However, one cannot regard needs as spontaneous, infinite, harmless, and amorphous without first considering what certain groups feel they lack and without first critically examining the lens with which the larger society has historically viewed this lack. Frances C. MacGregor, who between 1946 and 1959 researched the social and cultural motivations of such white ethnic minorities as Jewish and Italian Americans to seek rhinoplasty, wrote, "The statements of the patients . . . have a certain face validity and explicitness that reflect both the values of our society and the degree to which these are perceived as creating problems for the deviant individual" (MacGregor 1967:129).

Social scientific analyses of ethnic relations should include a study of the body. As evident in my research, racial minorities may internalize a body image produced by the dominant culture's racial ideology and, because of it, began to loathe, mutilate, and revise parts of their bodies. Bodily adornment and mutilation (the cutting up and altering of essential parts of the body; see Kaw 1993) are symbolic mediums most directly and concretely concerned with the construction of the individual as social actor or cultural subject (Turner 1980). Yet social scientists have only recently focused on the body as a central component of social self-identity (Blacking 1977; Brain 1979; Daly 1978; Lock and Scheper-Hughes 1990; ONeill 1985; Turner 1980; Sheets-Johnstone 1992). Moreover, social scientists, and sociocultural anthropologists in particular, have not yet explored the ways in which the body is central to the everyday experience of racial identity.

Method and Description of Subjects

In this article, I present the findings of an ethnographic research project completed in the San Francisco Bay Area. I draw on data from structured interviews with doctors and patients, basic medical statistics, and relevant newspaper and magazine articles. The sampling of informants for this research was not random in the strictly statistical sense since informants were difficult to find. Both medical practitioners and patients treat cases of cosmetic surgery as highly confidential, as I later discuss in more detail. To find a larger, more random sampling of Asian American informants, I posted fliers and placed advertisements in various local newspapers. Ultimately, I was able to conduct structured, open-ended interviews with eleven Asian American women, four of whom were referred to me by the doctors in my study and six by mutual acquaintances; I found one through an advertisement. Nine had had cosmetic surgery of the eye or the nose; one recently considered a double-eyelid operation; one is con-

sidering undergoing double-eyelid operation in the next few years. The women in my study live in the San Francisco Bay Area, except for two who reside in the Los Angeles area. Five were operated on by doctors who I also interviewed for my study, while four had their operations in Asia—two in Seoul, Korea, one in Beijing, China, and one in Taipei, Taiwan. Of the eleven women in my study, only two (who received their operations in China and in Taiwan) had not lived in the United States prior to their operations.[3] The ages of the Asian American women in my study range from eighteen to seventy-one; one woman was only fifteen at the time of her operation. Their class backgrounds are similar in that they were all engaged in middle-class, white-collar occupations: there were three university students, one art student, one legal assistant, one clerk, one nutritionist, one teacher, one law student, and two doctors' assistants.

Although I have not interviewed Asian American men who have or are thinking of undergoing cosmetic surgery, I realize that they too undergo double-eyelid and nose bridge operations. Their motivations are, to a large extent, similar to those of the women in my study (Iwata 1991). Often their decision to undergo surgery also follows a long and painful process of feeling marginal in society (Iwata 1991). I did not purposely exclude Asian American male patients from my study; rather, none responded to my requests for interviews.

To understand how plastic surgeons view the cosmetic procedures performed on Asian Americans, five structured, open-ended interviews were conducted with five plastic surgeons, all of whom practice in the Bay Area. I also examined several medical books and plastic surgery journals which date from the 1950s to 1990. And I referenced several news releases and informational packets distributed by such national organizations as the American Society of Plastic and Reconstructive Surgeons, an organization which represents 97 percent of all physicians certified by the American Board of Plastic Surgery.

To examine popular notions of cosmetic surgery, in particular how the phenomenon of

Asian American women receiving double-eyelid and nose bridge operations is viewed by the public and the media, I have referenced relevant newspaper and magazine articles.

I obtained national data on cosmetic surgery from various societies for cosmetic surgeons, including the American Society of Plastic and Reconstructive Surgeons. Data on the specific types of surgery sought by different ethnic groups in the United States, including Asian Americans, were missing from the national statistics. At least one public relations coordinator told me that such data are unimportant to plastic surgeons. To compensate for this lack of data, I asked the doctors in my study to provide me with figures from their respective clinics. Most told me they had little data on their cosmetic patients readily available.

Colonization of Asian American Women's Souls: Internalization of Gender and Racial Stereotypes

Upon first talking with my Asian American women informants, one might conclude that the women were merely seeking to enhance their features for aesthetic reasons and that there is no cultural meaning or political significance in their decision to surgically enlarge their eyes and heighten their noses. As Elena, a twenty-one-year-old Chinese American who underwent double-eyelid surgery three years ago from a doctor in my study, stated: "I underwent my surgery for personal reasons. It's not different from wanting to put makeup on . . . I don't intend to look Anglo-Saxon. I told my doctor, 'I would like my eyes done with definite creases on my eyes, but I don't want a drastic change.' "Almost all the other women similarly stated that their unhappiness with their eyes and nose was individually motivated and that they really did not desire Caucasian features. In fact, one Korean American woman, Nina, age thirty-four, stated she was not satisfied with the results of her surgery from three years ago because her doctor made her eyes "too round" like that of Caucasians. One might deduce from such statements that the women's

decision to undergo cosmetic surgery of the eye and nose is harmless and may be even empowering to them, for their surgery provides them with a more permanent solution than makeup for "personal" dissatisfactions they have about their features.

However, an examination of their descriptions of the natural shape of their eyes and nose suggests that their "personal" feelings about their features reflect the larger society's negative valuation and stereotyping of Asian features in general. They all said that "small, slanty" eyes and a "flat" nose suggest, in the Asian person, a personality that is "dull," "unenergetic," "passive," and "unsociable" and a mind that is narrow and "closed." For instance, Elena said, "When I look at other Asians who have no folds and their eyes are slanted and closed, I think of how they would look better more awake." Nellee, a twenty-one-year-old Chinese American, said that she seriously considered surgery for double eyelids in high school so that she could "avoid the stereotype of the 'oriental bookworm' " who is "dull and doesn't know how to have fun." Carol, a thirty-seven-year-old Chinese American who received double eyelids seven years ago, said: "The eyes are the window of your soul . . . [yet] lots of oriental people have the outer corners of their eyes a little down, making them look tired. [The double eyelids] don't make a big difference in the size of our eyes but they give your eyes more spirit." Pam, a Chinese American, age forty-four, who received double-eyelid surgery from another doctor in my study, stated, "Yes. Of course. Bigger eyes look prettier. . . . Lots of Asians' eyes are so small they become little lines when the person laughs, making the person look sleepy." Likewise, Annie, an eighteen-year-old Korean American woman who had an implant placed on her nasal dorsum to build up her nose bridge at age fifteen, said: "I guess I always wanted that sharp look—a look like you are smart. If you have a roundish kind of nose it's like you don't know what's going on. If you have that sharp look, you know, with black eyebrows, a pointy nose, you look more alert. I always thought that was cool." The women were influenced by the larger society's negative valuation of stereotyped Asian features in such a way that they evaluated themselves and Asian women in general with a critical eye. Their judgments were based on a set of standards, stemming from the eighteenth- and nineteenth-century European aesthetic ideal of the proportions in Greek sculpture, which are presumed by a large amount of Americans to be within the grasp of every woman (Goldstein 1993:150, 160).

Unlike many white women who may also seek cosmetic surgery to reduce or make easier the daily task of applying makeup, the Asian American women in my study hoped more specifically to ease the task of creating with makeup the illusion of features they do not have as women who are Asian. Nellee, who has not yet undergone double-eyelid surgery, said that at present she has to apply makeup everyday "to give my eyes an illusion of a crease. When I don't wear makeup I feel my eyes are small." Likewise, Elena said that before her double-eyelid surgery she checked almost every morning in the mirror when she woke up to see if a fold had formed above her right eye to match the more prominent fold above her left eye: "[on certain mornings] it was like any other day when you wake up and don't feel so hot, you know. My eye had no definite folds, because when Asians sleep their folds change in and out—it's not definite." Also, Jo, a twenty-eight-year-old Japanese American who already has natural folds above each eye but wishes to enlarge them through double-eyelid surgery, explained:

> I guess I just want to make a bigger eyelid [fold] so that they look bigger and not slanted. I think in Asian eyes it's the inside corner of the fold [she was drawing on my notebook] that goes down too much. . . . Right now I am still self-conscious about leaving the house without any makeup on, because I feel just really ugly without it. I try to curl my eyelashes and put on mascara. I think it makes my eyes look more open. But surgery can permanently change the shape of my eyes. I don't think that a bigger eyelid fold will actually change the slant but I

think it will give the perception of having less of it, less of an Asian eye.

For the women in my study, their oppression is a double encounter: one under patriarchal definitions of femininity (i.e., that a woman should care about the superficial details of her look), and the other under Caucasian standards of beauty. The constant self-monitoring of their anatomy and their continuous focus on detail exemplify the extent to which they feel they must measure up to society's ideals.

In the United States, where a capitalist work ethic values "freshness," "a quick wit," and assertiveness, many Asian American women are already disadvantaged at birth by virtue of their inherited physical features which society associates with dullness and passivity. In this way, their desire to look more spirited and energetic through the surgical creation of folds above each eye is of a different quality from the motivation of many Anglo Americans seeking facelifts and liposuction for a fresher, more youthful appearance. Signs of aging are not the main reason Asian American cosmetic patients ultimately seek surgery of the eyes and the nose; often they are younger (usually between eighteen and thirty years of age) than the average Caucasian patient (Kaw 1993). Several of the Asian American women in my study who were over thirty years of age at the time of their eyelid operation sought surgery to get rid of extra folds of skin that had developed over their eyes due to age; however, even these women decided to receive double eyelids in the process. When Caucasian patients undergo eyelid surgery, on the other hand, the procedure is almost never to create a double eyelid (for they already possess one); in most cases, it is to remove sagging skin that results from aging. Clearly, Asian American women's negative image of their eyes and nose is not so much a result of their falling short of the youthful, energetic beauty ideal that influences every American as it is a direct product of society's racial stereotyping.

The women in my study described their own features with metaphors of dullness and passivity in keeping with many Western stereotypes of

Asians. Stereotypes, by definition, are expedient caricatures of the "other," which serve to set them apart from the "we"; they serve to exclude instead of include, to judge instead of accept (Gilman 1985:15). Asians are rarely portrayed in the American print and electronic media. For instance, Asians (who constitute 3 percent of the U.S. population) account for less than 1 percent of the faces represented in magazine ads, according to a 1991 study titled "Invisible People" conducted by New York City's Department of Consumer Affairs (cited in Chen 1993:26). When portrayed, they are seen in one of two forms, which are not representative of Asians in general: as Eurasian-looking fashion models and movie stars (e.g., Nancy Kwan who played Suzy Wong) who already have double eyelids and pointy noses; and as stereotypically Asian characters such as Charlie Chan, depicted with personalities that are dull, passive, and nonsociable (Dower 1986; Kim 1986; Ramsdell 1983; Tajima 1989). The first group often serves as an ideal toward which Asian American women strive, even when they say they do not want to look Caucasian. The second serves as an image from which they try to escape.

Asian stereotypes, like all kinds of stereotypes, are multiple and have changed throughout the years; nevertheless they have maintained some distinct characteristics. Asians have been portrayed as exotic and erotic (as epitomized by Suzie Wong, or the Japanese temptress in the film *The Berlin Affair*), and especially during the U.S. war in the Pacific during World War II, they were seen as dangerous spies and mad geniuses who were treacherous and stealthy (Dower 1986; Huhr and Kim 1989). However, what remains consistent in the American popular image of Asians is their childishness, narrow-mindedness, and lack of leadership skills. Moreover, these qualities have long been associated with the relatively roundish form of Asian faces, and in particular with the "puffy" smallness of their eyes. Prior to the Japanese attack on Pearl Harbor, for instance, the Japanese were considered incapable of planning successful dive bombing attacks due to their "myopic," "squinty" eyes. During the war

in the Pacific, their soldiers were caricatured as having thick horn-rimmed glasses through which they must squint to see their targets (Dower 1986). Today, the myopic squinty-eyed image of the narrow-minded Asian persists in the most recent stereotype of Asians as "model minorities" (as eptimoized in the Asian exchange student character in the film *Sixteen Candles*). The term *model minority* was first coined in the 1960s when a more open-door U.S. immigration policy began allowing an unprecedented number of Asian immigrants into the United States, many of whom were the most elite and educated of their own countries (Takaki 1989). Despite its seemingly complimentary nature, *model minority* refers to a person who is hardworking and technically skilled but desperately lacking in creativity, worldliness, and the ability to assimilate into mainstream culture (Huhr and Kim 1989; Takaki 1989). Representations in the media, no matter how subtle, of various social situations can distort and reinforce one's impressions of one's own nature (Goffman 1979).

Witnessing society's association of Asian features with negative personality traits and mental characteristics, many Asian Americans become attracted to the image of Caucasian, or at least Eurasian, features. Several of the women in my study stated that they are influenced by images of fashion models with Western facial types. As Nellee explained: "I used to read a lot of fashion magazines which showed occidental persons how to put makeup on. So I used to think a crease made one's eyes prettier. It exposes your eyelashes more. Right now they all go under the hood of my eyes." Likewise, Jo said she thought half of her discontent regarding her eyes is a self-esteem problem, but she blames the other half on society: "When you look at all the stuff that they portray on TV and in the movies and in Miss America Pageants, the epitome of who is beautiful is that all-American look. It can even include African Americans now but not Asians." According to Jo, she is influenced not only by representations of Asians as passive, dull, and narrow-minded, but also by a lack of representation of Asians in general because society considers them un-American, unassimilable, foreign, and to be excluded.

Similar images of Asians also exist in East and Southeast Asia, and since many Asian Americans are immigrants from Asia, they are likely influenced by these images as well. Multinational corporations in Southeast Asia, for example, consider the female work force biologically suited for the most monotonous industrial labor because they claim the "Oriental girl" is "diligent" and has "nimble fingers" and a "slow-wit" (Ong 1987:151). In addition, American magazines and films have become increasingly available in many parts of Asia since World War II, and Asian popular magazines and electronic media depict models with Western facial types, especially when advertizing Western products. In fact, many of my Asian American women informants possessed copies of such magazines, available in various Asian stores and in Chinatown. Some informants, like Jane, a twenty-year-old Korean American who underwent double-eyelid surgery at age sixteen and nasal bridge surgery at age eighteen, thumbed through Korean fashion magazines which she stored in her living room to show me photos of the Western and Korean models who she thought looked Caucasian, Eurasian, or had had double-eyelid and nasal bridge surgeries. She said these women had eyes that were too wide and noses that were too tall and straight to be on Asians. Though she was born and raised in the United States, she visits her relatives in Korea often. She explained that the influences the media had on her life in Korea and in the United States were, in some sense, similar: "When you turn on the TV [in Korea] you see people like Madonna and you see MTV and American movies and magazines. In any fashion magazine you don't really see a Korean-type woman; you see Cindy Crawford. My mother was telling me that when she was a kid, the ideal beauty was someone with a totally round, flat face. Kind of small and five feet tall. I guess things began to change in the 1950s when Koreans started to have a lot of contact with the West." The environment within which Asian women develop a perspective on the value and

meaning of their facial features is most likely not identical in Asia and the United States, where Asian women are a minority, but in Asia one can still be influenced by Western perceptions of Asians.

Some of the women in my study maintained that although racial inequality may exist in many forms, their decision to widen their eyes had little to do with racial inequality; they were attempting to look like other Asians with double eyelids, not like Caucasians. Nina, for example, described a beautiful woman as such: "Her face should not have very slender eyes like Chinese, Korean, or Japanese but not as round as Europeans. Maybe Filipino, Thai, or other Southeast Asian faces are ideal. Basically I like an Asian's looks. . . . I think Asian eyes [not really slender ones] are sexy and have character." The rest of her description, however, makes it more difficult for one to believe that the Asian eyes she is describing actually belong on an Asian body: "The skin should not be too dark . . . and the frame should be a bit bigger than that of Asians." Southeast Asians, too, seek cosmetic surgery for double eyelids and nose bridges. One doctor showed me "before" and "after" photos of many Thai, Indonesian, and Vietnamese American women, who, he said, came to him for wider, more definite creases so that their eyes, which already have a double-eyelid, would look deeper-set.

In the present global economy, where the movement of people and cultural products is increasingly rapid and frequent and the knowledge of faraway places and trends is expanding, it is possible to imagine that cultural exchange happens in a multiplicity of directions, that often people construct images and practices that appear unconnected to any particular locality or culture (Appadurai 1990). One might perceive Asian American women in my study as constructing aesthetic images of themselves based on neither a Caucasian ideal nor a stereotypical Asian face. The difficulty with such constructions, however, is that they do not help Asian Americans to escape at least one stereotypical notion of Asians in the United States—that they are "foreign" and "exotic." Even when Asians are considered sexy, and attractive in the larger American society, they are usually seen as exotically sexy and attractive (Yang and Ragaz 1993:21). Since their beauty is almost always equated with the exotic and foreign, they are seen as members of an undifferentiated mass of people. Even though the women in my study are attempting to be seen as individuals, they are seen, in some sense, as less distinguishable from each other than white women are. As Lumi, a Japanese former model recently told *A. Magazine: The Asian American Quarterly,* "I've had bookers tell me I'm beautiful, but that they can't use me because I'm 'type.' All the agencies have their one Asian girl, and any more would be redundant" (Chen 1993:21).

The constraints many Asian Americans feel with regard to the shape of their eyes and nose are clearly of a different quality from almost every American's discontent with weight or signs of aging; it is also different from the dissatisfaction many women, white and nonwhite alike, feel about the smallness or largeness of their breasts. Because the features (eyes and nose) Asian Americans are most concerned about are conventional markers of their racial identity, a rejection of these markers entails, in some sense, a devaluation of not only oneself but also other Asian Americans. It requires having to imitate, if not admire, the characteristics of another group more culturally dominant than one's own (i.e., Anglo Americans) in order that one can at least try to distinguish oneself from one's own group. Jane, for instance, explains that looking like a Caucasian is almost essential for socioeconomic success: "Especially if you go into business, or whatever, you kind of have to have a Western facial type and you have to have like their features and stature—you know, be tall and stuff. So you can see that [the surgery] is an investment in your future."

Unlike those who may want to look younger or thinner in order to find a better job or a happier social life, the women in my study must take into consideration not only their own socioeconomic future, but also more immediately that of their offspring, who by virtue of heredity, inevi-

tably share their features. Ellen, for instance, said that "looks are not everything. I want my daughter, Stacy, to know that what's inside is important too. Sometimes you can look beautiful because your nice personality and wisdom inside radiate outward, such as in the way you talk and behave." Still, she has been encouraging twelve-year-old Stacy to have double-eyelid surgery because she thinks "having less sleepy looking eyes would make a better impression on people and help her in the future with getting jobs." Ellen had undergone cosmetic surgery at the age of twenty on the advice of her mother and older sister and feels she has benefited.[4] Indeed, all three women in the study under thirty who have actually undergone cosmetic surgery did so on the advice of their mother and in their mother's presence at the clinic. Elena, in fact, received her double-eyelid surgery as a high school graduation present from her mother, who was concerned for her socioeconomic future. The mothers, in turn, are influenced not so much by a personal flaw of their own which drives them to mold and perfect their daughters as by a society that values the superficial characteristics of one race over another.

A few of the women's dating and courtship patterns were also affected by their negative feelings toward stereotypically Asian features. Jo, for example, who is married to a Caucasian man, said she has rarely dated Asian men and is not usually attracted to them, partly because they look too much like her: "I really am sorry to say that I am not attracted to Asian men. And it's not to say that I don't find them attractive on the whole. But I did date a Japanese guy once and I felt like I was holding my brother's hand [she laughs nervously]."

A Mutilation of the Body

Although none of the women in my study denied the fact of racial inequality, almost all insisted that the surgical alteration of their eyes and nose was a celebration of their bodies, reflecting their right as women and as minorities to do what they wished with their bodies. Many, such as Jane, also said the surgery was a rite of passage or a routine ceremony, since family members and peers underwent the surgery upon reaching eighteen. Although it is at least possible to perceive cosmetic surgery of the eyes and nose for many Asian Americans as a celebration of the individual and social bodies, as in a rite of passage, this is clearly not so. My research has shown that double-eyelid and nasal bridge procedures performed on Asian Americans do not hold, for either the participants or the larger society, cultural meanings that are benign and spontaneous. Rather, these surgeries are a product of society's racial ideologies, and for many of the women in my study, the surgeries are a calculated means for socioeconomic success. In fact, most describe the surgery as something to "get out of the way" before carrying on with the rest of their lives.

Unlike participants in a rite of passage, these Asian American women share little *communitas* (an important element of rites of passage) with each other or with the larger society. Arnold Van Gennup defined rites of passage as "rites which accompany every change of place, state, social position, and age" (quoted in Turner 1969:94). These rites create an almost egalitarian type of solidarity (communitas) between participants and between the participants and a larger social group. A body modification procedure which is an example of such a rite is the series of public head-scarification rituals for pubescent boys among the Kabre of Togo, West Africa (Brain 1979:178). The final scars they acquire make them full adult members of their group. Their scarification differs considerably from the cosmetic surgery procedures of Asian American women in my study in at least two of its aspects: (1) an egalitarian bond is formed between the participants (between and among those who are doing the scarring and those who are receiving it); and (2) both the event and the resulting feature (i.e., scars) signify the boy's incorporation into a larger social group (i.e., adult men), and therefore, both are unrelentingly made public.

The Asian American women who undergo double-eyelid and nasal bridge surgeries do not usually create bonds with each other or with their plastic surgeons. Their surgery, unlike the

scarification rite of the Kabre, is a private event that usually occurs in the presence of the patient, the doctor, and the doctor's assistants only. Moreover, there is little personal connection between doctor and patient. Though a few of the Asian American women in my study were content with their surgery and with their doctors, most describe their experience on the operating table as one of fear and loneliness, and some described their doctors as impersonal, businesslike, and even tending toward profit-making. Annie, for instance, described the fear she felt being alone with the doctor and his assistants in the operating room, when her mother suddenly left the room because she could not bear to watch:

> They told me to put my thumbs under my hips so I didn't interfere with my hands. I received two anesthesia shots on my nose—this was the only part of the operation that hurt, but it hurt! I closed my eyes. I didn't want to look. I didn't want to see like the knives or anything. I could feel like the snapping of scissors and I was aware when they were putting that thing up my nose. My mom didn't really care. They told her to look at my nose. They were wondering if I wanted it sharper and stuff. She said, "Oh no. I don't want to look" and just ran away. She was sitting outside. I was really pissed.

Elena described her experience of surgery in a similar manner: "I had no time to be nervous. They drugged me with valium, I think. I was awake but drugged, conscious but numb. I remember being on the table. They [doctor and nurses] continued to keep up a conversation. I would wince sometimes because I could feel little pinches. He [the doctor] would say, 'Okay. Pumpkin, Sweetheart, it will be over soon.' . . . I didn't like it, being called Pumpkin and being touched by a stranger. . . . I wanted to say Shut up! to all three people." Clearly, the event of surgery did not provide an opportunity or the atmosphere for the women in my study to forge meaningful relationships with their doctors.

Asian American women who undergo cosmetic surgery also have a very limited chance of bonding with each other by sharing experiences of the surgery, because unlike participants in a Kabre puberty rite, these women do not usually publicize either their operation or their new features. All informed me that apart from me and their doctors, few people knew about their surgery since at the most they had told three close friends and/or family members about it. As Annie stated, "I don't mind if people found out [that I had a nose operation], but I won't go around telling them." Jane explained: "It's nothing to be ashamed of, not at all, but it's not something you brag about either. . . . To this day my boyfriend doesn't notice I had anything done. That makes me feel pretty good. It's just that you want to look good, but you don't want them [other people] to know how much effort goes into it." In fact, all the women in my study said they wanted a "better" look, but one that was not so drastically different from the original that it looked "unnatural." Even those who underwent revision surgeries to improve on their first operation said they were more at ease and felt more effective in social situations (with boyfriends, classmates, and employers) after their primary operation, mainly because they looked subtly "better," not because they looked too noticeably different from the way they used to look. Thus, it is not public awareness of these women's cosmetic surgery or the resulting features which win them social acceptance. Rather, the successful personal concealment of the operation and of any glaring traces of the operation (e.g., scars or an "unnatural" look) is paramount for acceptance. Clearly, the alteration of their features is not a rite of passage celebrating the incorporation of individual bodies into a larger social body; rather, it is a personal quest by marginal people seeking acceptance in a society where the dominant culture's ideals loom large and are constraining. The extent to which the Asian American women have internalized society's negative valuation of their natural features is best exemplified by the fact that these women feel more self-confident in social interactions as a result of this slight alteration of their eyelids—that is, with one minor alteration in their whole anatomy—which others may not even notice.

Medicine and the "Disembodiment" of the Asian American Female Consumer

Some sectors of the medical profession fail to recognize that Asian American women's decision to undergo cosmetic surgery of the eyelid and the nose is not so much triggered by a simple materialistic urge to feel better with one more status item that money can buy as much as it is an attempt to heal a specific doubt about oneself which society has unnecessarily brought on. For instance, one doctor in my study stated the following about double-eyelid surgery on Asian American women: "It's like when you wear certain shoes, certain clothes, or put certain makeup on, well—why do you wear those? Why this brand of clothes and not another? . . . You can label these things different ways, but I think that it [the double-eyelid surgery of Asian Americans] is just a desire to look better. You know, it's like driving a brand-new car down the street or having something bought from Nordstrom." By viewing cosmetic surgery and items bought from a department store as equally arbitrary, plastic surgeons, like economists, sometimes assume that the consumer (in this case, the cosmetic surgery client) is disembodied (O'Neill 1985:103). They view her as an abstract, nonhuman subject whose choice of items is not mediated by any historical circumstances, symbolic meaning, or political significance.

With "advances" in science and technology and the proliferation of media images, the number of different selves one can become appears arbitrary and infinite to many Americans, including the women in my study. Thus, many of them argue, as do some plastic surgeons (see Kaw 1993), that the variation in the width of the crease requested by Asian Americans (from six to ten millimeters) is indicative of a whole range of personal and idiosyncratic styles in double-eyelid operations. The idea is that the women are not conforming to any standard, that they are molding their own standards of beauty. However, they ignore that a primary goal in all double-eyelid operations, regardless of how high or how far across the eyelid the crease is cut, is to have a more open appearance of the eye, and the trend in all cases is to create a fold where there was none. These operations are an instance of the paradoxical "production of variety within standardization" in American consumer culture (Goldstein 1993:152). Thus, there is a double bind in undergoing a double-eyelid operation. On the one hand, the women are rebelling against the notion that one must be content with the physical features one is born with, that one cannot be creative in molding one's own idea of what is beautiful. On the other hand, they are conforming to Caucasian standards of beauty.

The women in the study seem to have an almost unconditional faith that science and technology will help them feel satisfied with their sense of self. And the plastic surgery industry, with its scientific advances and seemingly objective stance, makes double-eyelid surgery appear routine, necessary, and for the most part, harmless (Kaw 1993). The women in my study had read advertisements of cosmetic surgery clinics, many of them catering to their specific "needs." In my interviews with Nellee, who had once thought about having double-eyelid surgery, and Jo, who is thinking about it for the near future, I did not have to tell them that the operation entailed creating a crease on the upper eyelid through incision and sutures. They told me. Jo, for instance, said, "I know the technology and it's quite easy, so I am not really afraid of it messing up."

Conclusion: Problem of Resistance in a Culture Based on Endless Self-Fashioning

My research has shown that Asian American women's decision to undergo cosmetic surgery for wider eyes and more prominent noses is very much influenced by society's racial stereotyping of Asian features. Many of the women in my study are aware of the racial stereotypes from which they suffer. However, all have internalized these negative images of themselves and of other Asians, and they judge the Asian body, including their own, with the critical eye of the oppressor. Moreover, almost all share the attitude of certain sectors of the media and medicine in regard to

whether undergoing a surgical operation is, in the end, harmful or helpful to themselves and other Asian Americans; they say it is yet another exercise of their freedom of choice.

The American value of individualism has influenced many of the women to believe that the specific width and shape they choose for their eyelid folds and nose bridges indicate that they are molding their own standards of beauty. Many said they wanted a "natural" look that would be uniquely "in balance" with the rest of their features. However, even those such as Jane, who openly expressed the idea that she is conforming to a Western standard of beauty, emphasized that she is not oppressed but rather empowered by her surgical transformation: "Everything is conforming as I see it. It's just a matter of recognizing it. . . . Other people—well, they are also conforming to something else. Nothing anybody has ever done is original. And it's very unlikely that people would go out and be dressed in any way if they hadn't seen it somewhere. So I don't think it's valid to put a value judgment on [the type of surgery I did]. I'm definitely for self-improvement. So if you don't like a certain part of your body, there's no reason not to change it."

The constraints Asian American women in my study feel every day with regard to their natural features are a direct result of unequal race relationships in the United States. These women's apparent lack of concern for their racial oppression is symptomatic of a certain postmodern culture arising in the United States which has the effect of hiding structural inequalities from public view (Bordo 1990). In its attempt to celebrate differences and to shun overgeneralizations and totalizing discourses that apparently efface diversity among people in modern life, this postmodern culture actually obscures differences; that is, by viewing differences as all equally arbitrary, it effaces from public consciousness historically determined differences in power between groups of people. Thus, blue contact lenses for African American women, and double eyelids and nose bridges for Asian women are both seen as forms of empowerment and indistinguishable in form and function from perms for white women, corn rows on Bo Derek, and tans on Caucasians. All cosmetic changes are seen in the same way—as having no cultural meaning and no political significance. In this process, what is trivialized and obscured is the difficult, and often frustrated struggle with which subordinate groups must assert their difference as something to be proud of in the face of dominant ideologies (Bordo 1990:666).

With the proliferation of scientific and technological industries, the many selves one can become appear infinite and random. Like the many transformations of the persona of Madonna throughout her career or the metamorphosis of Michael Jackson's face during his "Black and White" video, the alteration of bodies through plastic surgery has become for the American public simply another means of self-expression and self-determination. As Ellen said, "You can be born Chinese. But if you want to look like a more desirable one, and if surgery is available like it is now, then why not do it?" She said that instead of having to undergo the arduous task of placing thin strips of transparent plastic tape over the eyelids to create a temporary crease (a procedure which, she said, many Asians unhappy with single eyelids used to do), Asians now have the option to permanently transform the shape of their eyes.

Thus, instead of becoming a battleground for social and cultural resistance, the body has become a playground (Bordo 1990:667). Like Michael Jackson's lyrics in the song "Man in the Mirror" ("If you want to make the world a better place, then take a look at yourself and make a change"; Jackson 1987), it is ambiguous whether political change and social improvement are best orchestrated through changing society or through an "act of creative interpretation" (Bordo 1990) of the superficial details of one's appearance. The problem and dilemma of resistance in U.S. society are best epitomized in this excerpt of my interview with Jo, the twenty-eight-year-old law student who is thinking of having double-eyelid surgery:

JO: In my undergraduate college, every Pearl Harbor Day I got these phone calls and people would say, "Happy Pearl Harbor Day," and they made noises like bombs and I'd find little toy soldiers at my dorm door. Back then, I kind of took it as a joke. But now, I think it was more malicious. . . . [So] I think the surgery is a lot more superficial. Affecting how society feels about a certain race is a lot more beneficial. And it goes a lot deeper and lasts a lot longer.

INTERVIEWER: Looking into the future, do you think you will do both?

JO: Yeah [nervous laughter]. I do. I do.

Jo recognizes that undergoing double-eyelid surgery, that is, confirming the undesirability of Asian eyes, is in contradiction to the work she would like to do as a teacher and legal practitioner. However, she said she cannot easily destroy the negative feelings she already possesses about the natural shape of her eyes.

Implications: Asian Americans and the American Dream

The psychological burden of having constantly to measure up has been often overlooked in the image of Asian Americans as model minorities, as people who have achieved the American dream. The model minority myth assumes not only that all Asian Americans are financially well-to-do, but also that those Asian Americans who are from relatively well-to-do, non-working-class backgrounds (like many of the women in my study) are free from the everyday constraints of painful racial stereotypes (see Takaki 1989; Hurh and Kim 1989). As my research has shown, the cutting up of Asian Americans' faces through plastic surgery is a concrete example of how, in modern life, Asian Americans, like other people of color, can be influenced by the dominant culture to loathe themselves in such a manner as to begin mutilating and revising parts of their body.

Currently, the eyes and nose are those parts of the anatomy which Asian Americans most typically cut and alter since procedures for these are relatively simple with the available technology. However, a few of the women in my study said that if they could, they would also want to increase their stature, and in particular, to lengthen their legs; a few also suggested that when safer implants were found, they wanted to augment their breasts; still others wanted more prominent brow bridges and jawlines. On the one hand, it appears that through technology women can potentially carve an endless array of new body types, breaking the bounds of racial categories. On the other hand, these desired body types are constructed in the context of the dominant culture's beauty ideals. The search for the ideal body may have a tremendous impact, in terms of racial discrimination, on patterns of artificial genetic selection, such as occurs at sperm banks, egg donation centers, and in the everyday ritual of courtship.

ACKNOWLEDGMENTS

I first thank the many women who generously gave their time and shared their thoughts in interviews with me. Without their contributions, this research project would not have been possible.

I continue to thank Cecilia de Mello, without whose encouragement I never would have begun to formulate my research. I am also grateful to Nancy Scheper-Hughes, Aihwa Ong, Paul Rabinow, Lynn Kwiatkowski, and Steve McGraw, as well as the various anonymous reviewers, for their insightful comments on earlier versions of this [article].

This [article] appeared, in slightly different form, in *Medical Anthropology* 7,1 (March 1993). . . .

NOTES

1. I have not yet found descriptions, in medical texts and newspaper articles, of the types of cosmetic surgery specifically requested by Latinos. However, one newspaper article (Ellison 1990) reports that an increasing number of Mexicans are purchasing a device by which they can attain a more Nordic and Anglo-Saxon "upturned" nose. It requires inserting plastic hooks in the nostrils.

2. The shapes of the eye and nose of Asians are not meant in this [article] to be interpreted as categories which define a group of people called Asians. Categories of racial groups are arbitrarily defined by society. Likewise, the physical traits people in a racial group are recognized are arbitrary (see Molnar 1983).

Also, I use the term *Asian American* to name collectively the women in this study who have undergone or are thinking about undergoing cosmetic surgery. Although I recognize their ethnic, generational, and geographical diversity, people of Asian ancestry in the United States share similar experiences in that they are subject to many of the same racial stereotypes (see Hurh and Kim 1989; Takaki 1989).

3. Cosmetic surgeries for double eyelids, nasal tip refinement, and nose bridges are not limited to Asians in the United States. Asians in East and Southeast Asia have requested such surgeries since the early 1950s, when U.S. military forces began long-term occupations of such countries as Korea and the Philippines. Some American doctors (such as Millard) were asked by Asians in these countries to perform the surgeries. See Harahap 1982; Kristof 1991; Millard 1964; Sayoc 1954.

4. Ellen's mother, however, did not receive double-eyelid or nose bridge surgery. It appears that the trend of actually undergoing such surgeries began with Asian women who are now about forty to fifty years of age. Jane and Annie, sisters in their early twenties, said that though their mother who is about fifty had these surgeries, their grandmother did not. They also said that their grandmother encouraged them to have the operation, as did their mother.

None of the women in my study mentioned their father or other males in their household or social networks as verbally encouraging them to have the surgeries. However, many said they felt their resulting features would or did help them in their relationships with men, especially boyfriends (Asians and non-Asians alike). We did not discuss in detail their father's reaction to their surgery, but those who mentioned their father's reaction summed it up mainly as indifference.

REFERENCES

American Society of Plastic and Reconstructive Surgeons (ASPRS). N.d. "Estimated Number of Cosmetic Surgery Procedures Performed by ASPRS Members in 1990." Pamphlet.

Appadurai, Arjun. 1990. "Disjuncture and Difference in the Global Cultural Economy." *Public Culture* 2(2): 1–24.

Blacking, John. 1977. *The Anthropology of the Body.* London: Academic Press.

Bordo, Susan. 1990. "Material Girl: The Effacements of Postmodern Culture." *Michigan Quarterly Review* 29:635–676.

Brain, Robert. 1979. *The Decorated Body.* New York: Harper and Row.

Chen, Joanne. 1993. "Before and After: For Asian Americans, the Issues Underlying Cosmetic Surgery Are Not Just Skin Deep." *A. Magazine: The Asian American Quarterly* 2(1): 15–18, 26–27.

Daly, Mary. 1978. *Gyn/ecology: The Metaethics of Radical Feminism.* Boston: Beacon Press.

Davis, Kathy. 1991. "Remaking the She-Devil: A Critical Look at Feminist Approaches to Beauty." *Hypatia* 6(2): 21–43.

Dower, John. 1986. *War without Mercy: Race and Power in the Pacific War.* New York: Pantheon.

Ellison, Katherine. 1990. "Mexico Puts on a Foreign Face." *San Jose Mercury News,* December 16, p. 14a.

Fleming, Charles, and Mary Talbot. 1993. "The Two Faces of Michael Jackson." *Newsweek,* February 22, p. 57.

Gilman, Sander L. 1985. *Difference and Pathology: Stereotypes of Sexuality, Race and Madness.* Ithaca, NY: Cornell University Press.

Goffman, Erving. 1979. *Gender Advertisement.* Cambridge: Harvard University Press.

Goldstein, Judith. 1993. "The Female Aesthetic Community." *Poetics Today* 14(1): 143–163.

Harahap, Marwali. 1982. "Oriental Cosmetic Blepharoplasty." In *Cosmetic Surgery for Non-white Patients,* ed. Harold Pierce, pp. 79–97. New York: Grune & Stratton.

Hurh, Won Moo, and Kwang Chung Kim. 1989. "The 'Success' Image of Asian Americans: Validity, and Its Practical and Theoretical Implications." *Ethnic and Racial Studies* 12(4):512–537.

Iwata, Edward. 1991. "Race without Face." *San Francisco Image Magazine,* May, pp. 51–55.

Jackson, Michael. 1987. "Man in the Mirror." On *Bad.* Epic Records, New York.

Kaw. Eugenia. 1993. "Medicalization of Racial Features: Asian American Women and Cosmetic Surgery." *Medical Anthropology Quarterly* 7(1):74–89.

Kim, Elaine. 1986. "Asian-Americans and American Popular Culture." In *Dictionary of Asian-American History,* ed. Hyung-Chan Kim. New York: Greenwood Press.

Kristof, Nicholas. 1991. "More Chinese Look 'West.' " *San Francisco Examiner and Chronicle,* July 7.

Lakoff, Robin T., and Raquel L. Scherr. 1984. *Face Value: The Politics of Beauty.* Boston: Routledge & Kegan Paul.

LeFlore, Ivens C. 1982. "Face Lift, Chin Augmentation and Cosmetic Rhinoplasty in Blacks." In *Cosmetic Surgery in Non-White Patients,* ed. Harold Pierce. New York: Grune & Stratton.

Lock, Margaret, and Nancy Scheper-Hughes. 1990. "A Critical-Interpretive Approach in Medical Anthropology: Rituals and Routines of Discipline and Dissent." In *Medical Anthropology: Contemporary Theory and Method,* ed., Thomas Johnson and Carolyn Sargent, pp. 47–72. New York: Praeger.

McCurdy, John A. 1990. *Cosmetic Surgery of the Asian Face.* New York: Thieme Medical Publishers.

MacGregor, Frances C. 1967. "Social and Cultural Components in the Motivations of Persons Seeking Plastic Surgery of the Nose." *Journal of Health and Social Behavior* 8(2):125–135.

Merrell, Kathy H. 1994. "Saving Faces." *Allure,* January, pp. 66–68.

Millard, Ralph, Jr. 1964. "The Original Eyelid and Its Revision." *American Journal of Opthamology* 57:546–649.

Molnar, Stephen. 1983. *Human Variation: Races, Types, and Ethnic Groups.* Englewood Cliffs, NJ: Prentice Hall.

Nakao, Annie. 1993. "Faces of Beauty: Light Is Still Right." *San Francisco Examiner and Chronicle,* April 11, p. D4.

O'Neill, John. 1985. *Five Bodies.* Ithaca, NY: Cornell University Press.

Ong, Aihwa. 1987. *Spirits of Resistance and Capitalist Discipline: Factory Women in Malaysia.* Albany: State University of New York Press.

Ramsdell, Daniel. 1983. "Asia Askew: U.S. Best-sellers on Asia. 1931–1980." *Bulletin of Concerned Asian Scholars* 15(4):2–25.

Rosenthal, Elisabeth. 1991. "Ethnic Ideals: Rethinking Plastic Surgery." *New York Times,* September 25, p. B7.

Sayoc, B. T. 1954. "Plastic Construction of the Superior Palpebral Fold." *American Journal of Opthamology* 38:556–559.

———. 1974. "Surgery of the Oriental Eyelid." *Clinics in Plastic Surgery* 1(1): 157–171.

Sheets-Johnstone, Maxine, ed. 1992. *Giving the Body Its Due.* Albany: State University of New York Press.

Tajima, Renee E. 1989. "Lotus Blossoms Don't Bleed: Images of Asian Women." In *Making Waves: An Anthology of Writings by and about Asian American Women,* ed. Diane Yeh-Mei Wong, pp. 308–317. Boston: Beacon Press.

Takaki. Ronald. 1989. *Strangers from a Different Shore.* Boston: Little, Brown.

Turner, Terence. 1980. "The Social Skin." In *Not Work Alone,* ed. J. Cherfas and R. Lewin, pp. 112–114. London: Temple Smith.

Turner, Victor. 1969. *The Ritual Process: Structure and Anti-Structure.* Chicago: Aldine.

Wolf, Naomi. 1991. *The Beauty Myth: How Images of Beauty Are Used Against Women.* New York: Morrow.

Yang, Jeff, and Angelo Ragaz. 1993. "The Beauty Machine." *A. Magazine: The Asian American Quarterly* 2(1):20–21.

THINKING ABOUT THE READING

What is meant by the term "the politics of cosmetic surgery"? How can the private act of undergoing plastic surgery be linked to broader political or, for that matter, economic or cultural issues? Is there anything wrong with Asian-American women trying to look more Caucasian? When considering an alteration to their physical appearance, should people feel obligated to maintain their "ethnically unique" features? In other words, at what point does loyalty to one's ethnic group identity override a personal desire to enhance one's attractiveness? Is there any difference between altering one's body to fit prevailing White standards and, say, changing one's name or one's wardrobe to accomplish the same goal?

12 The Architecture of Inequality: Sex and Gender

Along with racial and class inequality, sexual inequality—and the struggle against it—has been a fundamental part of the historical development of our national identity. Along the way it has influenced the lives and dreams of individual people, shaped popular culture, and created or maintained social institutions. Gender is a major criterion for the distribution of important economic, political, and educational resources in most societies. Sexual inequality is perpetuated by a dominant cultural ideology that devalues women on the basis of presumed biological differences between men and women. This ideology overlooks the equally important role of social forces in determining male and female behavior.

In "The Mismeasure of Woman," Carol Tavris takes a close look at the biological ideology that underlies beliefs about the different behavioral tendencies and social positions of men and women. She argues that our cultural preoccupation with discovering biochemical, hormonal, or neurological differences between men and women has created a pervasive tendency to see male characteristics as the norm against which female characteristics (perceived as "flaws," "curiosities," or "deficiencies") are measured and judged. She traces the development of "premenstrual syndrome" to show how male standards of health are used to turn natural biological processes into problems in need of urgent attention.

Like the article, "The Blacker the Berry . . ." in the previous chapter, Bart Landry explores the intersections of race and gender in "Black Women and a New Definition of Womanhood." Landry examines the difficulties black women have faced throughout history in being seen by others as virtuous and moral. This article provides a fascinating picture of women's struggle for equality from the perspective of black women, a group that is often ignored and marginalized in discussions of the "Women's Movement." Although much of the article focuses on black women's activism in the 19th century, it provides important insight into the intersection of race and gender today.

Institutional sexism exists in the law, in the family (in terms of such things as the domestic division of labor), and in economics. Not only are social institutions sexist, in that women are systematically segregated, exploited, and excluded, they are also gendered. Institutions themselves are structured along gender lines so that traits associated with success are usually stereotypically male characteristics: tough-mindedness, rationality, assertiveness, competitiveness, and so forth.

Women have made significant advances politically, economically, educationally, and socially over the past decades. The traditional obstacles to advancement continue to fall. Women have entered the labor force in unprecedented numbers. Yet despite their growing presence in the labor force and their entry into historically male occupations, rarely do women work alongside men or perform the same tasks and functions.

Jobs within an occupation still tend to be divided into "men's work" and "women's work." Such sex segregation has serious consequences for women in the form of blocked advancement and lower salaries. But looking at sex segregation on the job as something that happens only to women gives us an incomplete picture of the situation. It is just as important to examine what keeps men out of "female" jobs as it is to examine what keeps women out of "male" jobs. The proportion of women in male jobs has increased over the past several decades, but the proportion of men in female jobs has remained virtually unchanged. In "Still a Man's World," Christine Williams looks at the experiences of male nurses, social workers, elementary school teachers, and librarians. She finds that although these men do feel somewhat stigmatized by their nontraditional career choices, they still enjoy significant gender advantages.

The Mismeasure of Woman

Carol Tavris

The Universal Male

Man is the measure of all things.
—Protagoras (c. 485–410 B.C.)

Join me, if you will, in a brief flight of fancy. George Jones, age thirty-four, visits the "psychology and health" section of his local bookstore. There he finds an assortment of books designed to solve his problems with love, sex, work, stress, and children:

- *Women Who Hate Men and the Men Who Love Them* explains why he remains in a self-defeating relationship with Jane.
- *The X Spot and other new findings about male sexuality* tells him exactly how to have the right kind of multiple orgasm that women have.
- *The Male Manager* shows why his typically male habits of competitiveness and individualism prevent him from advancing in the female-dominated, cooperative corporate world.
- *Cooperation Training* offers practical instructions for overcoming his early competitive socialization as a man, showing him how to get along more smoothly with others.
- *The Superman Syndrome* explains that because men are physically less hardy than women throughout their lives, men find it difficult to combine work and family. They would live as long as women do if they would scale down their efforts to seek power and success.
- *The Father Knot* and *The Reproduction of Fathering* explore the reasons that George feels

so guilty about the way he is raising his children. Women feel comfortable with motherhood, these books argue, because they bear and nurse their offspring. But men for basic anatomical reasons are doomed to feel insecure and guilty in their role as fathers because unconsciously they never quite believe the child is theirs.

- *Erratic Testosterone Syndrome (ETS)—What it is and how to live with it* provides medical and psychological information to help George cope with his hormonal ups and downs. Because men do not have a visible monthly reminder of hormonal changes, they fail to realize that their moodiness and aggressive outbursts are hormonally based. A special concluding chapter helps the wives of men with ETS learn to live with their husband's unpredictable mood swings.

Lucky George. He will never feel obliged to read books like these, were anyone ever to write them; but of course women feel obliged to read the comparable volumes directed at them. It's a puzzle that they do, actually, because most of these books imply that women aren't doing anything right. Women are irrational and moody because of their hormones. They cry too much. They love too much. They talk too much. They think differently. They are too dependent on unworthy men, but if they leave the men to fend for themselves, they are too independent, and if they stay with the men they are codependent. They are too emotional, except when the emotion in question is anger, in which case they aren't emotional enough. They don't have correct orgasms, the correct way, with the correct frequency. They pay too much attention to their children, or not enough, or the wrong kind. They are forever subject to syndromes: the Superwoman Syndrome causes the Stress Syndrome, which is exacerbated by Premenstrual Syndrome, which is followed by a Menopausal Deficiency Syndrome.

Why do women buy so many self-help books every year to improve their sex lives, moods, relationships, and mental health? Simone de Beauvoir gave us one answer in 1949: because women are the second sex, the other sex, the sex to be explained. Men and women are not simply considered different from one another, as we speak of people differing in eye color, movie tastes, or preferences for ice cream. In almost every domain of life, men are considered the normal human being, and women are "ab-normal," deficient because they are different from men. Therefore, women constantly worry about measuring up, doing the right thing, being the right way. It is normal for women to worry about being abnormal, because male behavior, male heroes, male psychology, and even male physiology continue to be the standard for normalcy against which women are measured and found wanting.

Despite women's gains in many fields in the last twenty years, the fundamental belief in the normalcy of men, and the corresponding abnormality of women, has remained virtually untouched. Now even this entrenched way of thinking is being scrutinized and the reverberations are echoing across the land. Everywhere we look, it seems, teachers, courses, theories, and books are being challenged to examine their implicit assumption that man is the measure of all things. . . .

Not long ago the firm of Price Waterhouse was charged with discrimination in not granting partnership status to a woman named Ann Hopkins. Everyone agreed that Hopkins did her job well. She brought in over $40 million in new business to the firm, far more than any of the eighty-seven other nominees, all of whom were male, and forty-seven of whom were invited to become partners. Most of the opposition to

Hopkins came from brief comments from the partners who had had limited contact with her and were unaware of her track record. They described her as "macho," harsh, and aggressive, and one speculated that she "may have overcompensated for being a woman." One man, trying to be helpful, advised her to "walk more femininely, talk more femininely, dress more femininely, wear make-up, have her hair styled and wear jewelry."

Hopkins's supporters described her behavior as outspoken, independent, self-confident, assertive, and courageous. Her detractors interpreted the same behavior as overbearing, arrogant, self-centered, and abrasive. "Why is it," asked Lynn Hecht Schafran, an attorney on Hopkins's case, "that men can be bastards and women must wear pearls and smile?"[1]

At the same time that the Hopkins case was wending its way to the Supreme Court (where she eventually won), an attorney named Brenda Taylor lost her job because she was *too* feminine: she favored short skirts, designer blouses, ornate jewelry, and spike heels. Her boss told her that she looked like a "bimbo," and she was fired after she complained about his remarks to the Equal Employment Opportunity Commission.

Ann Hopkins and Brenda Taylor illustrate the pressures on modern women to be feminine *and* masculine, to be different from men but also the same. How is a woman supposed to behave: like an ideal male, in which case her male colleagues will accuse her of not being feminine enough, or like an ideal female, in which case her male colleagues will accuse her of not being masculine enough?

We will never know the truth about Ann Hopkins—whether she is outspoken or overbearing, confident or arrogant—because both sets of perceptions are true, from the beholder's standpoint. But by framing the problem as one of her personality, her colleagues deflected attention from the systematic practices of their company and from their own behavior. Suppose, instead, we ask: *Under what conditions* is the negative stereotype of women like Hopkins more likely to occur? The answer, according to research summarized in a brief prepared by the American Psychological Association on behalf of Hopkins, is that men are likely to behave like the Price Waterhouse partners under three conditions: when the woman (or other minority) is a token member of the organization; when the criteria used to evaluate the woman are ambiguous; and when observers lack necessary information to evaluate the woman's work.[2] All three conditions were met in Hopkins's situation. She could have read 435 books on how to behave, and they would have failed her. She could have gone to work dressed in a muu-muu or Saran Wrap, and she still would have lost that promotion. In this case, her personality had nothing to do with it.

Ann Hopkins's dilemma—whether a woman is supposed to behave like a man or a woman—is played out a thousand times a day, in the varied domains of women's lives. A woman who leaves her child in day care worries that she is failing as a mother; but if she leaves her job temporarily to stay home with her child, she worries that she will fail in her career. A woman who cries at work worries whether crying is good, since she is a woman, or wrong, since she is a professional. A woman who spends endless hours taking care of her husband and ailing parents feels that she is doing the right thing as a woman, but the wrong thing as an independent person. A woman who cannot penetrate her husband's emotional coolness alternates between trying to turn him into one of her expressive girlfriends and trying to cure her "dependency" on him.

Of the countless self-help books on the market that address these dilemmas, most direct the reader's attention to women's alleged inner flaws and psychological deficiencies. Women's unhappiness, in many of these accounts, is a result of their fear of independence, fear of codependence, fear of success, fear of failure, or fear of fear. Women are told to be more masculine in some ways and more feminine in others. Each of these explanations has a brief moment in the sun. And each eventually fades from sight, to be replaced by similar explanations that flourish briefly and die, because they do not touch the

basic reasons for women's dilemma: Inequities and ambiguities about "women's place" are built into the structure of our lives and society. These dilemmas are normal for women. They will persist as long as women look exclusively inward to their psyches and biology instead of outward to their circumstances, and as long as women blame themselves for not measuring up.

It may seem, after [three] decades of the modern women's movement, that issues of difference and equality have been talked into the ground, that equality has been won. Unquestionably, women have made great progress. But our society continues to fight a war over the proper place of women, and the battleground is the female body. Once again we are in the midst of a pronatalist revival that praises motherhood as women's basic need and talent, and that persists in trying to limit and control women's reproductive choices. Once again we are hearing arguments about women's nature, their unreliable physiology, their unmasculine hormones and brains. And once again we are hearing about the problems that face women who wish to combine careers and families, as experts warn of the dangers of day care, the stresses of being superwomen, the empty satisfactions of being corporate executives.

Researchers in the fields of science, medicine, and psychology all celebrate a renewed emphasis on biological explanations of women's behavior and a medical approach to women's problems and their cures. They enthusiastically seek physiological differences in brain structure and function, biochemical reasons that more women than men suffer from depression, and hormonal changes that supposedly account for women's (but not men's) moods and abilities. Their assertions are more likely to make the news than is the evidence that contradicts them. Similarly, women hear much less these days about the psychological benefits of having many roles and sources of esteem, let alone the benefits of having a personal income.

In *The Mismeasure of Man*, the scientist Stephen Jay Gould showed how science has been used and abused in the study of intelligence to serve a larger social and political agenda: to confirm the prejudice that some groups are assigned to their subordinate roles "by the harsh dictates of nature."[3] The mismeasure of women persists because it, too, reflects and serves society's prejudices. Views of woman's "natural" differences from man justify a status quo that divides work, psychological qualities, and family responsibilities into "his" and "hers." Those who are dominant have an interest in maintaining their difference from others, attributing those differences to "the harsh dictates of nature," and obscuring the unequal arrangements that benefit them. . . .

Brain: Dissecting the Differences

It must be stated boldly that conceptual thought is exclusive to the masculine intellect . . . [but] it is no deprecation of a woman to state that she is more sensitive in her emotions and less ruled by her intellect. We are merely stating a difference, a difference which equips her for the special part for which she was cast. . . . Her skull is also smaller than man's; and so, of course, is her brain.[4]
—T. Lang, *The Difference Between a Man and a Woman*

In recent years the sexiest body part, far and away, has become the brain. Magazines with cover stories on the brain fly off the newsstands, and countless seminars, tapes, books, and classes teach people how to use "all" of their brains. New technologies, such as PET scans, produce gorgeous photographs of the brain at work and play. Weekly we hear new discoveries about this miraculous organ, and it seems that scientists will soon be able to pinpoint the very neuron, and very neurotransmitter, responsible for joy, sadness, rage, and suffering. At last we will know the reasons for all the differences between women and men that fascinate and infuriate, such as why men won't stop to ask directions and why women won't stop asking men what they are feeling.

In all this excitement, it seems curmudgeonly to sound words of caution, but the history of brain research does not exactly reveal a noble

and impartial quest for truth, particularly on sensitive matters such as sex and race differences. Typically, when scientists haven't found the differences they were seeking, they haven't abandoned the goal or their belief that such differences exist; they just moved to another part of the anatomy or a different corner of the brain.

A century ago, for example, scientists tried to prove that women had smaller brains than men did, which accounted for women's alleged intellectual failings and emotional weaknesses. Dozens of studies purported to show that men had larger brains, making them smarter than women. When scientists realized that men's greater height and weight offset their brain-size advantage, however, they dropped this line of research like a shot. The scientists next tried to argue that women had smaller frontal lobes and larger parietal lobes than men did, another brain pattern thought to account for women's intellectual inferiority. Then it was reported that the parietal lobes might be associated with intellect. Panic in the labs—until anatomists suddenly found that women's parietal lobes were *smaller* than they had originally believed. Wherever they looked, scientists conveniently found evidence of female inferiority, as Gustave Le Bon, a Parisian, wrote in 1879:

In the most intelligent races, as among the Parisians, there are a large number of women whose brains are closer in size to those of gorillas than to the most developed male brains. This inferiority is so obvious that no one can contest it for a moment; only its degree is worth discussion.[5]

We look back with amusement at the obvious biases of research a century ago, research designed to prove the obvious inferiority of women and minorities (and non-Parisians). Today, many researchers are splitting brains instead of weighing them, but they are no less determined to find sex differences. Nevertheless, skeptical neuroscientists are showing that biases and values are just as embedded in current research—old prejudices in new technologies.

The brain, like a walnut, consists of two hemispheres of equal size, connected by a bundle of fibers called the corpus callosum. The left hemisphere has been associated with verbal and reasoning ability, whereas the right hemisphere is associated with spatial reasoning and artistic ability. Yet by the time these findings reached the public, they had been vastly oversimplified and diluted. Even the great neuroscientist Roger Sperry, the grandfather of hemispheric research, felt obliged to warn that the "left-right dichotomy . . . is an idea with which it is very easy to run wild."[6] And many people have run wild with it: Stores are filled with manuals, cassettes, and handbooks that promise to help people become fluent in "whole-brain thinking," to beef up the unused part of their right brain, and to learn to use the intuitive right brain for business, painting, and inventing.

The fact that the brain consists of two hemispheres, each characterized by different specialties, provides a neat analogy to the fact that human beings consist of two genders, each characterized by different specialties. The analogy is so tempting that scientists keep trying to show that it is grounded in physical reality. Modern theories of gender and the brain are based on the idea that the left and right hemispheres develop differently in boys and girls, as does the corpus callosum that links the halves of the brain.

According to one major theory, the male brain is more "lateralized," that is, its hemispheres are specialized in their abilities, whereas females use both hemispheres more symmetrically because their corpus callosum is allegedly larger and contains more fibers. Two eminent scientists, Norman Geschwind and Peter Behan, maintained that this sex difference begins in the womb, when the male fetus begins to secrete testosterone—the hormone that will further its physical development as a male. Geschwind and Behan argued that testosterone in male fetuses washes over the brain, selectively attacking parts of the left hemisphere, briefly slowing its development, and producing right-hemisphere dominance in men. Geschwind speculated that the effects of testosterone on the prenatal brain produce "superior right hemisphere talents, such as artistic, musical, or mathematical talent."[7]

Right-hemisphere dominance is also thought to explain men's excellence in some tests of "visual-spatial ability"—the ability to imagine objects in three-dimensional space (the skill you need for mastering geometry, concocting football formations, and reading maps). This is apparently the reason that some men won't stop and ask directions when they are lost; they prefer to rely on their right brains, whereas women prefer to rely on a local informant. It is also supposed to be the reason that men can't talk about their feelings and would rather watch television or wax the car. Women have interconnected hemispheres, which explains why they excel in talk, feelings, intuition, and quick judgments. Geschwind and Behan's theory had tremendous scientific appeal, and it is cited frequently in research papers and textbooks. *Science* hailed it with the headline "Math Genius May Have Hormonal Basis."[8] . . .

Now it may be true that men and women, on the average, differ in the physiology of their brains. . . . But given the disgraceful history of bias and sloppy research designed more to confirm prejudices than to enlighten humanity, I think we would all do well to be suspicious and to evaluate the evidence for these assertions closely.

This is difficult for those of us who are not expert in physiology, neuroanatomy, or medicine. We are easily dazzled by words like "lateralization" and "corpus callosum." Besides, physiology seems so *solid;* if one study finds a difference between three male brains and three female brains, that must apply to all men and women. How do I know what my corpus callosum looks like? Is it bigger than a man's? Should I care?

For some answers, I turned to researchers in biology and neuroscience who have critically examined the research and the assumptions underlying theories of sex differences in the brain.[9] The first discovery of note was that, just like the nineteenth-century researchers who kept changing their minds about which *lobe* of the brain accounted for male superiority, twentieth-century researchers keep changing their minds about which *hemisphere* of the brain accounts for male superiority. Originally, the left hemisphere was considered the repository of intellect and reason.

The right hemisphere was the sick, bad, crazy side, the side of passion, instincts, criminality, and irrationality. Guess which sex was thought to have left-brain intellectual superiority? (Answer: males.) In the 1960s and 1970s, however, the right brain was resuscitated and brought into the limelight. Scientists began to suspect that it was the source of genius and inspiration, creativity and imagination, mysticism and mathematical brilliance. Guess which sex was now thought to have right-brain specialization? (Answer: males.)

It's all very confusing. Today we hear arguments that men have greater left-brain specialization (which explains their intellectual advantage) *and* that they have greater right-brain specialization (which explains their mathematical and artistic advantage). *Newsweek* recently asserted as fact, for instance, that "Women's language and other skills are more evenly divided between left and right hemisphere; in men, such functions are concentrated in the left brain."[10]

But fundamentalists Smalley and Trent asserted that:

> most women spend the majority of their days and nights camped out on the right side of the brain [which] harbors the center for feelings, as well as the primary relational, language, and communication skills . . . and makes an afternoon devoted to art and fine music actually enjoyable.[11]

You can hear the chuckling from men who regard art museums and concert halls as something akin to medieval torture chambers, but I'm sure that the many men who enjoy art and fine music, indeed who create art and fine music, would not find that last remark so funny. Geschwind and Behan, of course, had argued that male specialization of the right hemisphere explained why men *excel* in art and fine music. But since Smalley and Trent apparently do not share these prissy female interests, they relegate them to women—to women's brains.

The two hemispheres of the brain do have different specialties, but it is far too simple-minded (so to speak) to assume that human abilities clump up in opposing bunches. Most brain re-

searchers today believe that the two hemispheres complement one another, to the extent that one side can sometimes take over the functions of a side that has been damaged. Moreover, specific skills often involve components from both hemispheres: one side has the ability to tell a joke, and the other has the ability to laugh at one. Math abilities include both visual-spatial skills and reasoning skills. The right hemisphere is involved in creating art, but the left hemisphere is involved in appreciating and analyzing art. As neuropsychologist Jerre Levy once said, "Could the eons of human evolution have left half of the brain witless? Could a bird whose existence is dependent on flying have evolved only a single wing?"[12]

These qualifications about the interdependence of brain hemispheres have not, however, deterred those who believe that there are basic psychological differences between the sexes that can be accounted for in the brain. So let's consider their argument more closely.

The neuroscientist Ruth Bleier, who at her untimely death was Professor of Neurophysiology at the University of Wisconsin, carefully examined Geschwind and Behan's data, going back to many of their original references.[13] In one such study of 507 fetal brains of 10 to 44 weeks gestation, the researchers had actually stated that they found *no significant sex differences* in these brains. If testosterone had an effect on the developing brain, it would surely have been apparent in this large sample. Yet Geschwind and Behan cited this study for other purposes and utterly ignored its findings of no sex differences.

Instead, Geschwind and Behan cited as evidence for their hypothesis a study of *rats'* brains. The authors of the rat study reported that in male rats, two areas of the cortex that are believed to be involved in processing visual information were 3 percent thicker on the right side than on the left. In one of the better examples of academic gobbledygook yet to reach the printed page, the researchers interpreted their findings to mean that "in the male rat it is necessary to have greater spatial orientation to interact with a female rat during estrus and to integrate that input into a meaningful output." Translation: When having sex with a female, the male needs to be able to look around in case a dangerous predator, such as her husband, walks in on them.

Bleier found more holes in this argument than in a screen door. No one knows, she said, what the slightly greater thickness in the male rat's cortex means for the rat, let alone what it means for human beings. There is at present no evidence that spatial orientation is related to asymmetry of the cortex, or that female rats have a lesser or deficient ability in this regard. . . .

Bleier wrote to *Science,* offering a scholarly paper detailing these criticisms. *Science* did not publish it, on the grounds, as one reviewer put it, that Bleier "tends to err in the opposite direction from the researchers whose results and conclusions she criticizes" and because "she argues very strongly for the predominant role of environmental influences."[14] Apparently, said Bleier, one is allowed to err in only direction if one wants to be published in *Science.* The journal did not even publish her critical Letter to the Editor.

At about the same time, however, *Science* saw fit to publish a study by two researchers who claimed to have found solid evidence of gender differences in the splenium (posterior end) of the corpus callosum.[15] In particular, they said, the splenium was larger and more bulbous in the five female brains than in the nine male brains they examined, which had been obtained at autopsy. The researchers speculated that "the female brain is less well lateralized—that is, manifests less hemispheric specialization—than the male brain for visuospatial functions." Notice the language: The female brain is *less specialized* than, and by implication inferior to, the male brain. They did not say, as they might have, that the female brain was *more integrated* than the male's. The male brain is the norm, and specialization, in the brain as in academia, is considered a good thing. . . .

Ultimately, the most damning blow to all of these brain-hemisphere theories is that the formerly significant sex differences that brain theories are attempting to account for—in verbal, spatial, and math abilities—are fading rapidly. Let's start with the famed female superiority in verbal ability. Janet Hyde, a professor of psychology at the University of Wisconsin, and her colleague Marcia Linn reviewed 165 studies of verbal ability (including skills in vocabulary, writing, anagrams, and reading comprehension), which represented tests of 1,418,899 people. Hyde and Linn reported that at present in America, there simply are no gender differences in these verbal skills. They noted: "Thus our research pulls out one of the two wobbly legs on which the brain lateralization theories have rested."[16]

Hyde recently went on to kick the other leg, the assumption of overall male superiority in mathematics and spatial ability. No one disputes that males do surpass females at the highly gifted end of the math spectrum. But when Hyde and her colleagues analyzed 100 studies of mathematics performance, representing the testing of 3,985,682 students, they found that gender differences were smallest and favored *females* in samples of the general population, and grew larger, favoring males, only in selected samples of precocious individuals.[17]

What about spatial abilities, another area thought to reveal a continuing male superiority? When psychologists put the dozens of existing studies on spatial ability into a giant hopper and looked at the overall results, this was what they reported: Many studies show no sex differences. Of the studies that do report sex differences, the magnitude of the difference is often small. And finally, there is greater variation *within* each sex than *between* them. As one psychologist who reviewed these studies summarized: "The observed differences are very small, the overlap [between men and women] large, and abundant biological theories are supported with very slender or no evidence."[18] . . .

Now, it is possible that reliable sex differences in the brain will eventually be discovered. . . . Should we then all make sure we have a male brain and a female brain in every household? Should we then worry about the abnormality of households like mine, in which the male is better at intuitive judgments and the female has the adding-machine mentality?

The answers are no, for three reasons. First, theories of sex differences in the brain cannot account for the complexities of people's everyday behavior. They cannot explain, for instance, why, if women are better than men in verbal ability, so few women are auctioneers or diplomats, or why, if women have the advantage in making rapid judgments, so few women are air-traffic controllers or umpires. Nor can brain theories explain why abilities and ambitions change when people are given opportunities previously denied to them. Two decades ago, theorists postulated biological limitations that were keeping women out of men's work like medicine and bartending. When the external barriers to these professions fell, the speed with which women entered them was dizzying. Did everybody's brain change? Today we would be amused to think that women have a brain-lateralization deficiency that is keeping them out of law school. But we continue to hear about the biological reasons that keep women out of science, math, and politics. For sex differences in cognitive abilities to wax and wane so rapidly, they must be largely a result of education, motivation, and opportunity, not of innate differences between male and female brains.

Second, the meanings of terms like "verbal ability" and "spatial reasoning" keep changing too, depending on who is using them and for what purpose. For example, when conservatives like Dobson speak of women's verbal abilities, they usually mean women's interest in and willingness to talk about relationships and feelings. But in studies of total talking time in the workplace, men far exceed women in the talk department. In everyday life, men interrupt women more than vice versa, dominate the conversation, and are more successful at introducing new topics and having their comments remembered in group discussions.[19] What does this mean for judgments of which sex has the better "verbal ability"?

Third, the major key problem with biological theories of sex differences is that they deflect attention from the far more substantial evidence for sex similarity. The finding that men and women are more alike in their abilities and brains than different almost never makes the news. Researchers and the public commit the error of focusing on the small differences—usually of the magnitude of a few percentage points—rather than on the fact that the majority of women and men overlap. For example, this is what the author of a scientific paper that has been widely quoted as *supporting* sex differences in brain hemispheres actually concluded:

> Thus, one must not overlook perhaps the most obvious conclusion, which is that basic patterns of male and female brain asymmetry seem to be more similar than they are different. [20]

Everyone, nevertheless, promptly overlooked it.

The habit of seeing women and men as two opposite categories also leads us to avoid the practical question: How much ability does it take to do well in a particular career? When people hear that men are better than women in spatial ability, many are quick to conclude that perhaps women, with their deficient brains, should not try to become architects or engineers. This reaction is not merely unfortunate; it is cruel to the women who *do* excel in architectural or engineering ability. The fields of math and science are losing countless capable women because girls keep hearing that women aren't as good as men in these fields.

None of this means that biology is irrelevant to human behavior. But whenever the news trumpets some version of "biology affects behavior," it obscures the fact that biology and behavior form a two-way street. Hormones affect sexual drive, for instance, but sexual activity affects hormone levels. An active brain seeks a stimulating environment, but living in a stimulating environment literally changes and enriches the brain. Fatigue and boredom cause poor performance on the job, but stultifying job conditions produce fatigue and boredom. Scientists and writers who reduce our personalities, problems, and abilities to biology thereby tell only half the story, and miss half the miracle of how human biology works. . . .

Misdiagnosing the Body

Premenstrual Syndrome, Postmenstrual Syndrome, and Other Normal "Diseases"

. . . Hormone studies are part of an ongoing tidal wave of biological research in general, and much of this research has benefited women. Women should know that the physiological changes of the menstrual cycle vary enormously, that *normal* women range from having no pain or discomfort to having considerable though temporary pain. It is important for women to know that morning sickness during pregnancy is entirely a hormonal matter, and not, as a male physician once said to a friend of mine, "a woman's way of saying she doesn't want to be pregnant." It is important for women to know that hot flashes and vaginal dryness during menopause are likewise due to temporary hormonal changes, not to a neurotic loss of femininity or sexual inhibitions.

In short, it is beneficial and empowering for women to understand the normal changes of their bodies, and not to have their feelings dismissed as psychosomatic whining....

But ... there are many dangers to the over-psychologizing of normal biological processes [and] there are also dangers of reducing all of our feelings, problems, and conflicts to them. Everywhere we look today, we find that the normal changes of menstruation and menopause are increasingly being regarded as diseases, problems, and causes of women's emotional woes and practical difficulties. In particular, biomedical researchers have taken a set of bodily changes that are normal to women over the menstrual cycle, packaged them into a "Premenstrual Syndrome," and sold them back to women as a disorder, a problem that needs treatment and attention. Of course, the only thing worse for women than menstruating is not menstruating. When women cease having the monthly "disease" of PMS, they suffer the "disease" of Menopausal Estrogen Deficiency.

The biological mismeasurement of women's bodies poses many emotional and intellectual conflicts for women, who are caught between defending their reproductive differences from men and asserting their intellectual equality and competence. The story of "premenstrual syndrome" highlights this conflict perfectly. Research on the menstrual cycle was long overdue, as it were, and feminist scholars had to press for research funds and scientific attention to be given to a bodily process that only women experience. Many

women themselves have responded positively to the language of PMS, feeling validated at last by the attention being paid to menstrual changes. But the enthusiastic support for PMS masks the more important fact that the menstrual cycle does not affect a healthy woman's ability to do what she needs to do. It also diverts public attention from other matters, such as the effects of hormones on men and the fact that men's and women's moods and physical symptoms are more alike than different....

The Manufacture of "PMS"

Let's start by trying to identify the problem. A small percentage of women report having particularly difficult emotional symptoms associated with the premenstrual phase. Some describe severe Jekyll-and-Hyde-like personality changes that recur cyclically and predictably. In my lifetime of knowing hundreds of women, I have never met such a Jekyll-and-Hyde-like female, but there is something compelling about the testimony of women themselves and of researchers who have observed their behavior clinically. A woman in one study described herself this way:

> Something seems to snap in my head. I go from a normal state of mind to anger, when I'm really nasty. Usually I'm very even tempered, but in these times it is as if someone else, not me, is doing all this, and it is very frightening. [21]

A larger percentage of women describe premenstrual mood changes, notably depression and irritability, that they swear occur as predictably as ragweed in spring. "Unbeknownst to me, my husband kept track of my irritability days in his office diary," one friend reports, "and he could predict like clockwork when I was within a week of my period."

Which group has the premenstrual syndrome? The Jekyll-and-Hyde phenomenon reflects an abnormality in degree, kind, and severity of symptoms. But many researchers, the media, and women themselves now confuse mood changes that are abnormal and occur in *few* women with mood changes that are normal for *all* women—and, as it turns out, for all men, too.

This confusion is apparent in virtually all contemporary discussions of PMS in the media. Most of the media today regard PMS as if it were a clearly defined disorder that most, if not all, women "suffer." For example, *Science News* called it "the monthly menace," and the *Orange County Register* called it "an internal earthquake." An article in *Psychology Today* began: "Premenstrual Syndrome (PMS) remains as baffling to researchers as it is troublesome to women." *Troublesome?* To *all* women, as implied? The article turns out to be about a study of 188 nursing students and tea factory workers in China. In the tea factory, "almost 80% suffered from PMS." *Suffered?* "Overall, nearly 74% rated their symptoms as mild, 24% as moderate and 3% said they were severe." In other words, for 97 percent of the women the symptoms of this "syndrome" were no big deal.

Likewise, an article in the *Baltimore Sun,* headlined "Why PMS Triggers Hunger," begins by asking "Why is it so hard to diet when you're suffering from premenstrual syndrome?" (There we are "suffering" again.) The answer turns out to have nothing at all to do with PMS, or, for that matter, with suffering. According to the research, women feel hungrier in the few days before menstruation because their metabolism has increased. This is normal, the article states: "Your body is working as it should, building up the uterine lining . . ." Working as it should? Then why am I suffering from a syndrome?

It's easy to understand the media's confusion, because the list of symptoms thought to characterize "PMS" doesn't leave much out. One popular paperback book offers a "complete checklist" of physical, behavioral, and emotional changes, including weight gain, eye diseases, asthma, nausea, blurred vision, skin disorders and lesions, joint pains, headaches, backaches, general pains, epilepsy, cold sweats and hot flashes, sleeplessness, forgetfulness, confusion, impaired judgment, accidents, difficulty concentrating, lowered school or work performance, lethargy, decreased efficiency, drinking or eating too

much, mood swings, crying and depression, anxiety, restlessness, tension, irritability, and loss of sex drive. [22] That's just for starters. Other alleged symptoms include allergies, alcoholism, anemia, low self-esteem, problems with identity, and cravings for chocolate. Some physicians have specified as many as *150* different symptoms.

Mercy! With so many symptoms, accounting for most of the possible range of human experience, who wouldn't have "PMS"? Obviously, the more symptoms that are listed, the more likely that someone will have them, at least sometimes. This likelihood is increased in checklists that include mutually contradictory symptoms (such as "was less interested in sex" *and* "was more sexually active," or "had less energy" *and* "couldn't sit still") and the entire range of negative emotions ("irritable or angry," "sad or lonely," "anxious or nervous"). [23] On these lists, there is no way you can't have some symptoms. . . .

Many institutions and individuals now benefit from the concept of PMS. Biomedical researchers, medical schools, and drug companies profit financially. Gynecologists, many of whom have closed their obstetrical services because of malpractice insurance costs, have lost a traditional source of income and are turning to new patient groups and new diagnoses for replenishment. Many psychiatrists have shifted from conducting long-term psychotherapy to prescribing short-term (repeatable) drug treatments. Indeed, obstetricians and psychiatrists are already engaged in turf wars over who is best suited to diagnose and treat all those women with premenstrual symptoms.

But the success of PMS is not entirely a conspiracy of big institutions, although, as [psychologist Mary Brown] Parlee says, if PMS didn't exist as a "psychologically disturbing, socially disruptive, biologically caused disease" they would have needed to invent it. (They did.) We must also ask why so many women have responded so favorably to the term and use it so freely. Parlee suggests that "the language of 'PMS' is a means by which many women can have their experiences of psychological distress, or actions they do not understand, validated as 'real' and taken seriously."[24] In that sense the language of PMS is empowering for women, she believes, because it gives a medical and social reality to experiences that were previously ignored, trivialized, or misunderstood.

Like all psychological diagnoses, then, PMS cuts two ways: It validates women, but it also stigmatizes them. Psychiatrist Leslie Hartley Gise directs a PMS program at Mt. Sinai Hospital in New York, yet she too is worried about the stigmatizing effects of making PMS a psychiatric diagnosis. . . . Gise told an interviewer, "think of what a PMS diagnosis would mean for a woman seeking public office."[25] . . .

Of Menstruation and Men: The Story Behind the Headlines

The research on the physiology and psychology of the menstrual cycle paints a very different picture from the popular impression that PMS is a proven, biomedical syndrome. It is clear that some physical changes normally occur: breast tenderness, water retention, and increased metabolism being the most common. The key word here is *normally.* It is normal for premenstrual women to have some aches and pains, to gain a few pounds (because of temporary water retention), or to crave food (because of increased metabolism). Leslie Gise puts it this way: "Although PMS is used for convenience, *premenstrual changes* is a more accurate term."[26]

You might think, with all the studies trying to document the existence of a "widespread" biological disorder that so many women are "suffering" from, that researchers would have some idea of what causes it. Yet in spite of more than a decade of biomedical research, no biological marker has been found that distinguishes women who have severe premenstrual symptoms from those who do not. There is no support for theories suggesting that premenstrual symptoms are caused by abnormally high (or low) hormones, low magnesium, high sodium, abnormal thyroids, a deficiency of hormonelike substances called prostaglandins, steroid fluctuations, or the like.

Moreover, thus far, no drug or vitamin has been found to be effective. There is no evidence that vitamins help, and megadoses of B-6 supplements, which are commonly recommended, carry significant risks, such as causing nerve damage, for some individuals. In most of the double-blind treatment studies, in which neither the women nor her physician knows whether she is being given an active drug or a placebo, the placebo effect is as strong as the drug. Upward of 60 to 70 percent of the women who are given a placebo report improvement in their symptoms.[27]

For many years, the treatment of choice for PMS was progesterone suppositories, in spite of a lack of clinical evidence demonstrating their effectiveness. Recently, however, Ellen Freeman and her colleagues, who conducted the largest and best-controlled study to date of the effects of progesterone, found that "progesterone suppositories have no clinically significant therapeutic effect greater than that of placebo for premenstrual symptoms."[28] Progesterone did not improve individual symptoms or severity of symptoms in any way. If anything, symptoms remained *higher* in the women given progesterone than in those on the placebo!

So what is going on here? Up to the mid-1970s, researchers kept finding what they called the "classic" menstrual mood pattern: greater happiness and self-esteem during ovulation (mid-cycle), followed by depression, irritability, and low self-esteem premenstrually. But as Mary Brown Parlee noticed back in 1973, the professional journals were not publishing negative results—that is, studies that were finding *no* premenstrual differences or mood variations over the menstrual cycle. In the last fifteen years, more of these disconfirming studies have been published, and many errors have been discovered in the earlier research. The new evidence finds that most of the so-called emotional and behavioral symptoms of Premenstrual Syndrome may not have much to do with menstruation, and in any case are not limited to women.

The problem of memory. One major problem with much of the research that supposedly documented Premenstrual Syndrome is that many women recall having had premenstrual mood changes when, in fact, they did not. When you ask women retrospectively to describe their symptoms over the month, many of them will cheerfully tell you that they become depressed, weepy, irritable, and moody just before menstruation. Yet when most of these same women keep a daily diary of their moods, their *actual* moods are often unrelated to what they *recall* their moods as having been. Many women "remember" symptoms that didn't occur, and forget changes that did occur.[29]

Moreover, menstruation itself provides women with the cue they need to decide when they have been "premenstrual." Psychologist Randi Koeske finds that many women *retrospectively* make sense of troublesome moods and actions ("Aha, so that's why I was so grumpy Tuesday; I was about to get my period").[30] Yet a large percentage of women claiming to experience PMS fail to demonstrate a cyclic pattern of negative moods when they actually keep daily records. Nevertheless, many physicians and medical researchers, to this day, diagnose PMS by relying on a woman's memory, asking her to fill out a checklist of what she believes her symptoms have been for the last month or two. Survey questionnaires in popular magazines make the same mistake.

The "premenstrual elation" syndrome and the "no symptoms at all" syndrome. The way to correct the error of retrospective memory, it would appear, is to ask women to keep daily mood and symptom diaries for a couple of months. When they do, it turns out that women, like men, vary widely over a thirty-five-day span. Some women . . . do tend to become irritable and grouchy premenstrually. But others have no premenstrual symptoms at all—not a twitch or jiggle. Others are grumpiest during the luteal phase (midcycle). Many women report feeling *better* before menstruation; they describe having a "burst of creativity" and energy. Few studies and checklists ever included this possibility; one questionnaire measure of "Menstrual Distress" contains forty-two negative mood adjectives and only five positive ones. The popular

books, likewise, list all manner of negative emotions but no positive ones. Their checklists contain anger, hostility, irritability, depression, nervousness, worry, anxiety, sadness, and loneliness, but not enthusiasm, cheerfulness, happiness, satisfaction, optimism, and increased energy.

Mary Brown Parlee asked seven women to fill out mood and activity questionnaires every day for ninety days, but these women did not know that they were in a study of menstruation. The results showed patterns that were exactly the opposite of what those PMS checklists would predict: Depression, fatigue, sleepiness, and hostility were *lower* premenstrually and menstrually than during ovulation! Parlee concluded, wryly, that she had found evidence for a "premenstrual elation syndrome." Yet when she interviewed the women at the end of the study and told them its purpose, they all believed that they had been more anxious, irritable and depressed premenstrually, although their own diaries failed to bear them out.[31]

The power of expectations and circumstances. The belief in PMS has, itself, a powerful influence on a woman's likelihood of noticing some symptoms and ignoring others at different times of the month. This is why even the day-by-day method of tracking symptoms has a problem: For some women, the strong belief that their moods change predictably over the menstrual cycle affects their actual experience of symptoms.

In one fascinating study, for example, two groups of women and a comparable group of men filled out daily inventories of their moods and physical symptoms. Half of the women were aware that menstrual-cycle changes were a focus of the study, and half were unaware. During the premenstrual phase of their cycles, the "aware" women reported a significantly higher level of negative moods and uncomfortable physical changes (such as headaches and muscle tension), and fewer positive feelings, than did either the "unaware" women or the men.[32] The belief in PMS and the expectation of negative symptoms, apparently, influence a woman's likelihood of noticing some symptoms and ignoring others at different times. And it's a big likelihood. In this study, the "aware" women, premenstrually, reported a 76 percent increase in negative emotions (anxiety, depression, anger) and a whopping 193 percent increase in physical complaints. The "unaware" women did not.

Being aware of bodily changes or expecting them to occur can make us more sensitive to them; conversely, distracting influences can override them. This fact may explain why moods have less to do with a woman's time of the month than with her time of the week. Women's positive moods (and men's) peak on the weekends![33] If you want to predict when a woman will feel happiest, according to several studies, you do better to know when it's a Saturday or Sunday than when she is ovulating.

As this research suggests, the mood effects of the menstrual cycle often depend on whether a woman is paying more attention to her bodily changes or to her immediate situation. A friend of mine put it this way:

> If, one day, I'm aware of feeling too easily annoyed by telephone interruptions, or if my threshold for bureaucratic stupidity plummets, I may suddenly realize that I'm "premenstrual." This mood can be easily overturned, though, if I do something I enjoy, like taking a hike or going to the movies. It just depends on whether I want to indulge my moods or break them.

The male comparison. One of the most misleading consequences of the popular focus on Premenstrual Syndrome is that it omits men as a comparison group. Yet if you give men those same checklists of symptoms (reduced or increased energy, irritability and other negative moods, back pain, sleeplessness, headaches, confusion, etc.), men report having as many "premenstrual symptoms" as women do—when the symptoms aren't called PMS. (You do have to omit the female-specific symptoms, such as breast tenderness.) If the identical checklist is titled "Menstrual Distress Questionnaire," however, men miraculously lose their headaches, food cravings, and insomnia.[34]

When men are included as a comparison group in menstrual-cycle research, it turns out that their moods also change over the course of a month, just as much as women's moods do. Among men, as among women, individuals vary enormously in their moodiness, frequency of mood swings, and general levels of grumpiness. It's just that men can't blame their mood changes on a menstrual cycle, and their mood changes are more unpredictable and idiosyncratic.

Psychologist Jessica McFarlane and her associates, who conducted the "weekend happiness" study, observed mood fluctuations in women and men over a span of seventy days. Their findings reinforce all of the points I have been making here:

> . . . the women in this study did not actually experience the classic menstrual mood pattern but when they were asked to recall their moods, they reported that pattern. . . . [They] were relatively unaffected emotionally by menstrual hormonal fluctuations.
>
> . . . young women's moods fluctuated more over days of the week than across the menstrual cycle, and young men also experienced emotional fluctuations over days of the week. The women were not "moodier" than the men; their moods were not less stable within a day or from day-to-day. Evidence of weekday mood cycles in both sexes suggest that *treating emotional fluctuations as unhealthy symptoms, and assuming that only women usually manifest them, is misleading.*[35] [My emphasis.]

Yet very little research has been done specifically on men's hormones and moods; testosterone, in most men, is as much as 25 percent higher in the mornings than in the afternoons, but no one regards these normal fluctuations as symptoms of anything. If you look up research on testosterone and mood, you will find more studies on women than on men. (Both sexes have both sex hormones, although in different proportion.)

But in one nice study, psychologist Betsy Bosak Houser worked with five young men three times a week for ten weeks. She took blood samples to determine levels of serum testosterone and other hormones; she gave the men mood inventories, behavioral tests (e.g., of reaction time and arm-hand steadiness), and the Menstrual Distress Questionnaire, omitting only its title and one item—"painful breasts." Houser found significant links between hormone levels and moods; for instance, as plasma testosterone increased, the men's hand steadiness and good humor decreased. (Alarm! What does this finding mean for millions of men doing brain surgery or assembly-line detail work?) However, she also found—as is the case for women—huge individual variations in the specific links between hormones and mood.[36]

The ultimate question: What do hormones have to do with abilities and behavior? . . . The behavior question is important. We should be worried if the premenstrual workers in America are costing the economy millions. We should be worried if premenstrual college students are flubbing their exams in great numbers. And we should be worried if growing numbers of premenstrual (or postpartum) females are crashing their cars or murdering their lovers.

Fortunately, we can all relax. Unsung by the media, study after study has confirmed that women manage to manage their households, thoughts, exams, families, and jobs at any phase of the cycle. Hormonal changes in women have never been reliably linked to problems in behavior or intellectual performance. (Few experts have suggested that women's hormones might *improve* their performance in any sphere, except, perhaps, child care.[37])

For example, psychologist Sharon Golub reviewed all the studies that have tried to find effects of menstruation on women's ability to work. The studies measured everything from the ability to perform simple motor tasks to complex problem-solving. The results, she reports, "confirmed the findings of almost 50 years of research in this area. *The menstrual cycle has no consistent demonstrable effect on cognitive tasks, work, or academic performance* despite beliefs to the contrary that persist"[38] (my emphasis). . . .

In contrast, male hormones *are* related to behavior. In a major study of 4,462 male veterans, psychologists James Dabbs, Jr., and Robin Morris, of Georgia State University, found that unusually high testosterone was associated with delinquency, drug use, having many sex partners, conduct disorders, abusiveness, and violence. Of course, these are correlational data and it is also true that some behaviors raise testosterone levels. But Dabbs and Morris noted that testosterone is directly associated only with negative actions: "While high testosterone theoretically might lead to prosocial behavior, the present data provide no indication of such redeeming social value."[39] Testosterone can be restrained, it appears, by money and success. Men of higher socio-economic status had lower testosterone levels and were less likely to commit antisocial acts.

When *The New York Times* eventually published a report on these findings (not, by the way, on the front page, but in the science section), the bad news of the link between testosterone and antisocial behavior was buried late in the story. The headline was "Aggression in Men: Hormone Levels Are a Key," with the subtitle "Testosterone is linked to dominance and competitiveness."[40] Aggression, competitiveness, and dominance are considered desirable for men, of course; the implication of the title was that these qualities are hormonally determined. It is only halfway through the article that the writer cites Dabbs's study and quotes him as saying: "The overall picture among the high-testosterone men is one of delinquency, substance abuse and a tendency toward excess." This point, which is the real news, is not featured in the headline.

I do not wish to replace the biological reductionism of women's behavior with a biological reductionism of men's behavior, but rather to highlight the different diagnoses that society favors and to raise some questions. Of course women are influenced by their bodies—by aches, pains, puffiness, water retention, and headaches—but so are men. Why, then, are women's mood changes a "syndrome," but men's mood changes just "normal ups and downs"? Why are women, but not men, considered "moody," and why are mood changes, which are normal, considered undesirable? Why are variations in testosterone not considered a medieval and social problem, whereas variations in female hormones are a focus of national concern? . . .

Reading the Body: The Psychology of Symptoms

Many women are highly resistant to the evidence that their beliefs and expectations about PMS might be influencing their symptoms, or that their memories of symptoms might not be entirely accurate. It sounds as if psychologists are refusing to believe them, singing the old refrain that was so patronizing for so long: "It's all in your head." When I've talked to women about this research, many say, "Well, the research is plain wrong; I *know* my body changes and I *know* I become irritable," or "That research may apply to other women, but not to me."

Something is going on, therefore, between the evidence of the research and the private experience of the body. How might women (and men) begin to regard the normal symptoms of the menstrual cycle, without transmogrifying them into a problem or syndrome, yet recognizing their influences in daily life and emotional well-being?

Recall these puzzles of PMS. There is no special biological marker or abnormality that characterizes women who report having PMS from those who do not. The symptoms include contradictory conditions, such as irritability and euphoria, lack of energy and increased energy, and every sort of emotion. Some women feel "impelled" to yell at their husbands when they are premenstrual, but others feel equally impelled to bake bread. Both women and men have hormonal fluctuations and mood changes in the course of a month, but only women's moods are attributed to their hormones. And although women everywhere in the world experience similar physical symptoms along with menstruation (cramps, tender breasts, aches and pains), a World Health Organization survey of hundreds of women in each of ten nations found that "PMS" and its associated mood shifts are a Western phenomenon.[41]

This collection of anomalous facts suggests that the changes associated with the menstrual cycle are "real," are felt physically, and that they provide a fuel for moods and feelings. But the *content* of those moods and wishes often depends on a woman's attitudes, expectations, situation, personal history, and immediate problems and concerns. To try another metaphor, hormone changes provide the clay; the mind and experience shape and mold it into a form. It's real clay, but it's only clay.

Symptoms are therefore not "all in the mind," but they aren't exactly "all in the body," either. No hormone could, by itself, account for yelling *and* bread-baking. But hormonal changes can make a woman feel edgy, bloated, and "not herself." They can create a feeling of fatigue and enervation. A woman then interprets these bodily changes in a particular way: as symptoms to be ignored, as signs of temporary insanity, as a sickness to be medicated, as an opportunity to tell her husband what she is afraid to say otherwise, as a liberating opportunity to write poetry. This is why the same physiological process expresses itself in so many different psychological forms.

In a series of studies. Randi Koeske has found that positive *and* negative emotions are often enhanced premenstrually and that it is the situation a woman is in, more than her hormones, that determines which emotions (if any) she feels. Her reactions also depend on how she explains her feelings. A woman who says to herself "water retention makes my tear ducts feel full" is going to feel different from one who regards the same physical sensation as evidence that "I am about to cry and must be depressed."[42]

Sometimes women are aware of how their attitudes and expectations affect their experience of the menstrual cycle, as in the case of my friend who decides whether she wants to overrule her premenstrual symptoms or indulge them. But usually women are unaware of the combined and invisible impact of their unique package of physical histories, family attitudes, culture's views of menstruation, and individual experiences. They are usually unaware, for example, of the fact that they selectively notice certain physical signs or emotional states and ignore others. (So do men.) As one woman I spoke with said:

> If I feel irritable and then get my period a day or two later, I'll say, "Oh, it was just my period speaking, thank goodness. What a relief; it wasn't important." But if I feel irritable at other times, I don't usually put it down as just being in a bad mood; I try to figure out why.

PMS is one illustration of the mind-body link in the experience of any noticeable physiological change, such as pain. Of course pain isn't "all in the mind," but psychologists have demonstrated that the mind affects how severely the pain is felt and what pain sufferers do about it.[43] Many if not most human beings live with some recurring or chronic discomfort, such as lower back pain, migraines, stomach problems, or arthritis. All of us draw a personal line that determines when we acknowledge, worry about, and seek treatment for our pains, and when we will say, "Oh, the hell with it" and carry on as if it weren't there.

In general, men are expected to fall on the "carry on" side of pain management, whereas women are expected to fall on the "worry about it" side. Each strategy has its strengths. The ability to talk about the experiences of the body often evokes useful support, sympathy, and advice from others; the "carry on" approach has the virtue of distracting the pain sufferer, which itself is often a successful technique of pain control. But each strategy, pursued to extremes, has its pitfalls: on the one hand, ignoring symptoms that are signs of a serious problem; on the other, overemphasizing or overmedicating symptoms that are not serious problems. . . .

Doctoring the Failed Female

Ultimately, the belief that menstruation and menopause are problems for women is part of a larger assumption that female physiology itself is abnormal, deficient, and diseased. Because this view is so pervasive, it is easy to forget that it is not the only one possible.

In fact, the idea that menstruation is a problem for women (and their families) is new to this century. For most of human history, from the ancient Greeks until the late eighteenth century, medical writers assumed that male and female bodies were structurally similar, and that there was nothing inherently pathological or debilitating about menstruation. (They held many misconceptions about the magical powers of menstrual blood, but that's another story.) For example, in seventeenth- and eighteenth-century America, when women were believed to be biologically similar to men, menstruation was considered a natural, unproblematic process.[44]

In the nineteenth century, . . . a major transformation took place in the scientific and popular views of the female body. It was no longer seen as analogous to the male body, but as distinctly opposite, different. Menstruation became a symbol of that difference. Walter Heape, a zoologist at Cambridge University, wrote in his 1913 book *Sex Antagonism* that "the reproductive system is not only structurally but functionally fundamentally different in the Male and the Female; and since all other organs and systems of organs are affected by this system, it is certain that the Male and Female are essentially different throughout."[45] Heape's description of menstruation, a "severe, devastating, periodic action," was, dare I say, hysterical. The menstrual flow, he wrote, leaves behind "a ragged wreck of tissue, torn glands, ruptured vessels, jagged edges of stroma, and masses of blood corpuscles, which it would seem hardly possible to heal satisfactorily without the aid of surgical treatment."[46]

Today, Heape's descriptions seem as outdated as the old brain studies do, and it would surely surprise no one to learn that Heape was a militant antisuffragist. Yet the legacy of this attitude survives. It is much toned down, to be sure, but no less influential, and just as much a part of the political and social culture in which it occurs.

The view of menstruation as a monthly wound from which women must recover, along with the view of its sister sickness, menopause, are subtly enshrined in our language as processes that involve weaknesses, losses, and debilities. In a dazzling analysis of the language that describes menstruation and menopause in medical textbooks, Emily Martin showed how physicians, anatomists, and the public have come to regard these processes. Menstruation is *failed* conception; menopause is *failed* reproductive functions.

Thus, textbooks describe the process of menstruation in terms of deprivation, deficiency, loss, shedding, and sloughing. The fall in hormones "deprives" the uterine wall of its "hormonal support," "constriction" of blood vessels leads to a "diminished" supply of oxygen and nutrients, and finally "disintegration starts, the entire lining begins to slough, and the menstrual flow begins." The imagery of menstruation that Martin found in textbook after textbook is one of "catastrophic disintegration: 'ceasing,' 'dying,' 'losing,' 'denuding,' and 'expelling.' "[47]

I certainly learned about menstruation in those terms, and my first reaction to Martin's criticism of physiology textbooks was to say, "Well, how else would you describe it?" The answer is immediately apparent, she shows, in the way textbooks describe other bodily processes that are analogous to menstruation. For example, the lining of the stomach is shed and replaced regularly, in order to protect itself from self-destruction by the hydrochloric acid produced for digestion. Textbooks do not describe this process as one of degenerating, weakening, or sloughing of the stomach lining. They emphasize the "secretion" and "production" of mucus, Martin reports, and "—in a phrase that gives the story away—the periodic *renewal* of the lining of the stomach" (emphasis in original).[48] Here is Martin's summary:

> One can choose to look at what happens to the lining of stomachs and uteruses negatively as breakdown and decay needing repair or positively as continual production and replenishment. Of these two sides of the same coin, stomachs, which women *and* men have, fall on the positive side; uteruses, which only women have, fall on the negative.[49]

. . . Menopause fares no better in textbooks, Martin shows. If menstruation is a monthly deterioration and failure, menopause represents a permanent deterioration and failure: "ovaries cease to respond and fail to produce. Everywhere else there is regression, decline, atrophy, shrinkage, and disturbance."[50] This condition is apparently so dire and potentially dangerous to women that in 1981 the World Health Organization actually defined menopause as an estrogen-deficiency disease.

Now this is curious. Why should a process that is normal for all women be construed as a disease? Why, instead, aren't we asking whether there might be advantages to women of ceasing reproduction? After all, women don't faint or die at the end of menopause; most live another twenty-five or thirty active years. So how deadly could this disease be? Of course menopause does involve losses, such as a reduced production of estrogen by the ovaries and the inability to conceive (if one wanted to at that age). It is true that the risks of osteoporosis and heart disease rise significantly after menopause. Nevertheless, *most* women do *not* die from these conditions. The uniformly negative description of menopause is by no means the only one possible. Martin found one current textbook that describes the changes of menopause positively, if tentatively so:

> . . . although menopausal women do have an estrogen milieu which is lower than that necessary for *reproductive* function, it is not negligible or absent but is perhaps satisfactory for *maintenance* of *support tissues.* The menopause could then be regarded as a physiologic phenomenon which is protective in nature— protective from undesirable reproduction and the associated growth stimuli.[51] [Emphasis in original.]

The negative view of menstruation and menopause is part of a larger perspective that regards female anatomy as designed entirely for reproduction. When it starts to "fail" and "run down," therefore, it can only be seen as a "problem," a "crisis"; the relevant body parts become "superfluous" or in need of a little medical bolstering. . . .

If the female reproductive process were regarded as the norm (or at least as being normal) in this society, our ways of thinking about and treating the female body would be entirely different. Consider just a few changes that would occur:

Women and men would regard changes in moods, efficiency, and good humor as expected and normal variations, not as abnormal deviations from the (impossible) male ideal of steadiness and implacability. Why must women defend themselves from the charge of having mood changes, anyway? Mood changes are perfectly normal. Everyone has them. Even men.

We would, by understanding the interplay of mind and body, be better able to distinguish emotions that signify something important (such as a family conflict that should be dealt with) from those that are momentary blips on the screen of life. . . .

We would regard the changes of menstruation and menopause as normal, not as failures, losses, deficiencies, and weaknesses. Some bodily states or transitions (for both sexes) may not be comfortable one hundred percent of the time, but, under normal circumstances, the best remedies are patience, a moderate diet, exercise, and good humor. Morning sickness, menstrual cramps, and hot flashes are hormonal; they will pass.

We would not confuse normal physical changes with symptoms of a disorder or a disease. We can protest the mindless application of the term "PMS" and speak instead of the variety of premenstrual changes in women *and* of hormonal changes in men. The same applies to menopause; we can try to nip in the bud the forthcoming onslaught of diagnoses that will try to turn this healthy, beneficial, and to most women liberating change into an estrogen-deficiency disease. We can also learn how to live with the normal hormonal effects of menopause without regarding them as major psychological disorders. . . .

We would regard surgical procedures and drugs as treatments of last resort, when medically necessary to save a woman's life or when, on balance, they will significantly improve the quality of a woman's life. We would not resort to them casually, to "cure" normal female processes. Instead, we would regard menstruation and menopause as processes of renewal and change, processes that do not need to be conquered, cured, or altered.

Most of all, we would recognize that if hormones affect one sex, they also affect the other. The current embrace of hormonal diagnoses of women's behavior feeds the belief that women aren't really responsible for their actions—not in the way men are, anyway. Hormones affect behavior, but we must think carefully and critically about whose hormones, and which behaviors, are legitimate legal defenses, let alone personal excuses to use around the house.

I believe that women long to achieve legitimacy for the unique experiences of the normal female body, and that they embrace the biomedical language of PMS and Estrogen Deficiency Disease as a way of getting there. But trusting to a language that proclaims these experiences deficient and diseased is not the solution. The price, for women's psychological well-being and for their status in society, is too great.

NOTES

1. Joan S. Girgus, Susan Nolen-Hoeksema, and Martin E. P. Seligman, "Why Do Sex Differences in Depression Emerge During Adolescence?" Paper presented at the annual meeting of the American Psychological Association, New Orleans, 1989; Attie and Brooks-Gunn, 1987.

2. Quoted in Carol Tavris, "Is Thin Still In?" *Woman's Day,* March 3, 1987, p. 35.

3. Susan Wooley and O. Wayne Wooley, "Thinness Mania," *American Health,* October 1986, pp. 68–74. Quote, p. 72.

4. T. Lang, *The Difference Between a Man and a Woman* (New York: The John Day Co., 1971), pp. 203–204.

5. Le Bon quoted in *The Mismeasure of Man,* Gould, Stephen J. (New York: W. W. Norton & Co., 1981).

6. Roger W. Sperry, "Some Effects of Disconnecting the Cerebral Hemisphere," *Science,* 212, 1223–1226.

7. Quoted in Gina Kolata, "Math Genius May Have Hormonal Basis," *Science,* 222 (December 23, 1983), p. 1312.

8. Ibid., p. 1312.

9. See Ruth Bleier, "Sex Differences Research: Science or Belief?" In R. Bleier (Ed.) *Feminist Approaches to Science* (New York: Pergamon, 1988); Anne Fausto-Sterling, *Myths of Gender: Biological Theories about Women and Men* (New York: Basic Books, 1985); Anne Harrington, *Medicine, Mind, and the Double Brain: A Study in 19th-Century Thought* (Princeton, NJ: Princeton University Press, 1987); Ruth Hubbard, *The Politics of Women's Biology* (New Brunswick, NJ: Rutgers University Press, 1990). For an excellent history of psychological revisionism in the study of the brain, see Stephanie A Shields, "Functionalism, Darwinism, and the Psychology of Women: A Study in Social Myth," *American Psychologist* 30, 1975, pp. 998–1002.

10. *Newsweek,* "Guns and Dolls," May 28, 1990, p. 59.

11. Gary Smalley and John Trent, *The Language of Love* (Pomona, CA: Focus on the Family Publishing, 1988), p. 36.

12. Jerre Levy, "Language, Cognition, and the Right Hemisphere: A Response to Gazzaniga," *American Psychologist* 38, 1983, pp. 538–541.

13. The discussion and critique of Geschwind and Behan, 1982, is from Bleier, 1988.

14. Ruth Bleier, "Sex Differences Research in the Neurosciences." Paper presented at the annual meeting of the American Association for the Advancement of Science, Chicago, 1987.

15. The study of the corpus callosum is from Christine de Lacoste-Utamsing and Ralph L. Holloway," Sexual Dimorphism in the Human Corpus Callosum," *Science* 216, 1982, pp. 1431–1432.

16. Janet S. Hyde and Marcia C. Linn (Eds.) *The Psychology of Gender: Advances through Meta-analysis* (Baltimore: Johns Hopkins University Press, 1986) and "Gender Differences in Verbal Ability: A Meta-analysis," *Psychological Bulletin* 104, 1988, pp. 53–69. Males are more likely to have speech problems, such as stuttering, and to be referred for treatment for dyslexia—though not more likely to actually be dyslexic (see Shaywitz et al., 1990). See also Alan Feingold, "Cognitive Gender Differences Are Disappearing," *American Psychologist* 43, 1988, pp. 95–103, who found that gender differences in SAT scores have "declined precipitously" in the last forty years. In 1950, school-age boys and girls differed markedly in verbal ability (girls excelled), abstract reasoning (boys excelled), and "clerical ability" (girls excelled). By 1980, boys had completely caught up with girls in verbal ability. Girls had completely caught up in verbal and abstract reasoning and numerical ability, and halved the difference in mechanical reasoning and space relations. The only exception to the rule of "vanishing gender differences," Feingold found, was the gender gap at the highest levels of math performance.

17. Janet S. Hyde, Elizabeth Fennema, and Susan J. Lamon, "Gender Differences in Mathematics Performance: A Meta-analysis," *Psychological Bulletin* 107, 1990, pp. 139–155.

18. Paula J. Caplan, Gael M. MacPherson, and Patricia Tobin, "Do Sex-Related Differences in Spatial Abilities Exist?," *American Psychologist* 40, 1985, pp. 786–799. Researcher quoted on p. 786.

19. Pamela M. Fishman, "Interaction: The Work Women Do," In B. Thorne, C. Kramarae, and N. Hurley (Eds.), *Language, Gender and Society* (Rowley, MA: Newbury House, 1983); Robin T. Lakoff, *Talking Power: The Politics of Language* (New York: Basic Books, 1990); Sally McConnell-Ginet, "Intonation in a Man's World," in B. Thorne, C. Kramarae, and N. Hinley (Eds.), *Language, Gender, and Society* (Rowley, MA: Newbury House, 1983) and "The Orgins of Sexist Language in Discourse," In S. J. White and V. Teller (Eds.) *Discourses in Reading and Linguistics (Annals of the New York Academy of Sciences, Vol. 433)* (New York: New York Academy of Sciences, 1984); Deborah Tannen, *You Just Don't Understand* (New York: William Morrow, 1990).

20. Jeannette McGlore, "Sex Differences in Human Brain Asymmetry: A Critical Survey," *The Behavioral and Brain Sciences* 3, 1980, pp. 215–263.

21. Woman interviewed by Emily Martin, *The Woman in the Body: A Cultural Analysis of Reproduction* (Boston: Beacon, 1987), p. 132.

22. Judy Lever and Michael G. Brush, *Premenstrual Tension* (New York: Bantam, 1981).

23. For example, see "A Nightly Checklist of PMS," *American Health,* December 1989, p. 58.

24. Mary Brown Parlee, "The Science and Politics of PMS Research." Invited address presented at the annual meeting of the Association for Women in Psychology, Newport, R.I., 1989.

25. Quoted in Lynn Payer, "Hell Week," *Ms.,* March 1989, pp. 28–31. Quoted on p. 28.

26. Leslie H. Gise (Ed.) The Premenstrual Syndromes (New York: Churchill Livingstone, 1988).

27. Parlee, 1989. See also Freeman et al., "Ineffectiveness of Progesterone Suppository Treatment for Premenstrual Syndrome," *Journal of the American Medical Association* 264, July 18, 1990, pp. 349–353.

28. Freeman et al., 1990, p. 349. Katharina Dalton, however, who at age seventy-five still operates a private practice in London as of this writing (1991), continues to prescribe progesterone; Suzie Mackenzie, "A Woman's Problems," *The Guardian,* May 8, 1991.

29. U. Halbreich and J. Endicott, "Retrospective Report of Premenstual Changes: Factors Affecting Confirmation of Daily Ratings," *Psychopharmacology Bulletin* 18, 1983, pp. 109–112; Sheryle J. Gallant and Jean Hamilton, "On a Premenstrual Psychiatric Diagnosis: What's in a Name?" *Professional Psychology: Research and Practice* 79, 1988, pp. 271–278; Hamilton et al., "Premenstrual Mood Changes: A Guide to Evaluation and Treatment," *Psychiatric Annals* 14, 1984, pp. 426–435; Randi D. Koeske, "Premenstrual Emotionality: Is Biology Destiny?" In M. R. Walsh (Ed.) *The Psychology of Women: Ongoing Debates* (New Haven, CT: Yale University Press, 1987).

30. Koeske, 1987, p. 141.

31. Parlee, 1982.

32. P. G. AuBuchon and F. S. Calhoun, "Menstrual Cycle Symptomatology: The Role of Social Expectancy and Experimental Demand Characteristics," *Psychosomatic Medicine* 47, 1985, pp. 35–45.

33. Jessica McFarlane, Carol L. Martin, and Tannis M. Williams, "Mood Fluctuations: Women versus Men and Menstrual versus Other Cycles," *Psychology of Women Quarterly* 12, 1988, pp. 201–223.

34. AuBuchon and Calhoun, 1985; Gallant and Hamilton, 1988.

35. McFarlane, Martin, and Williams, 1988, pp. 216, 217.

36. Betsy B. Houser, "An Investigation between Hormonal Levels in Males and Mood, Behavior , and Physical Discomfort," *Hormones and Behavior* 12, 1979, pp. 185–197.

37. See Lynda Birke and Sandy Best, "The Tyrannical Womb: Menstruation and Menopause," In The Brighton Women and Science Group (Eds.) *Alice through the Microscope: The Power of Science over Women's Lives* (London: Virago, 1980).

38. Sharon Golub, "A Developmental Perspective," In L. H. Gise (Ed.), *The Premenstrual Syndromes* (New York: Churchill Livingstone, 1988), p. 17.

39. James M. Dabbs, Jr. and Robin Morris, "Testosterone, Social Class, and Antisocial Behavior in a Sample of 4,462 Men," *Psychological Science* 1, 1990, pp. 209–211.

40. Daniel Goleman, "Aggression in Men: Hormone Levels Are a Key," *The New York Times,* July 17, 1990, pp. B1, B8.

41. The WHO study consisted of 500 women from each of ten different nations. See Karen P. Ericksen, "Menstrual Symptoms and Menstrual Beliefs: National and Cross-National Patterns," In B. E. Ginsburg and B. F. Carter (Eds.), *Premenstrual Syndrome* (New York: Plenum, 1987).

42. Koeske, 1987.

43. On the psychological interpretation of physical symptoms of all kinds, see James W. Pennebaker, *The Psychology of Physical Symptoms* (New York: Springer-Verlag, 1982).

44. See Emily Martin, *The Woman in the Body: A Cultural Analysis of Reproduction* (Boston: Beacon, 1987); Thomas Laqueur, "Orgasm, Generation, and the Politics of Reproductive Biology," In C. Gallagher and T. Laqueur (Eds.), *The Making of the Modern Body* (Berkeley, CA: University of California Press, 1987).

45. Quoted in Laqueur, 1987, p. 31.

46. Ibid., p. 32.

47. Martin, 1987, general description of menstruation, p. 45; "catastrophic disintegration," p. 48.

48. Ibid., p. 50.

49. Ibid.

50. Ibid., p. 43.

51. Quoted in Martin, 1987, p. 52.

REFERENCES

AuBuchon, P. G., Calhoun, K. S. (1985). Menstrual cycle symptomatology: The role of social expectancy and experimental demand characteristics. *Psychosomatic Medicine, 47,* 35–45.

Birke, Lynda, & Best, Sandy (1980). The tyrannical womb: Menstruation and menopause. In The Brighton Women and Science Group (Eds.), *Alice through the microscope: The power of science over women's lives.* London: Virago.

Bleier, Ruth (1988). Sex differences research: Science or belief? In R. Bleier (Ed.), *Feminist approaches to science.* New York: Pergamon.

Caplan, Paula J.; MacPherson, Gael M.; & Tobin, Patricia (1985). Do sex-related differences in spatial abilities exist? *American Psychologist, 40,* 786–799.

Dabbs, James M., Jr., & Morris, Robin (1990). Testosterone, social class, and antisocial behavior in a sample of 4,462 men. *Psychological Science, 1,* 209–211.

de Lacoste-Utamsing, Christine, & Holloway, Ralph L. (1982). Sexual dimorphism in the human corpus callosum. *Science, 216,* 1431–1432.

Ericksen, Karen P. (1987). Menstrual symptoms and menstrual beliefs: National and cross-national patterns. In B. E. Ginsburg & B. F. Carter (Eds.), *Premenstrual syndrome.* New York: Plenum.

Fausto-Sterling, Anne (1985). *Myths of gender: Biological theories about women and men.* New York: Basic Books.

Feingold, Alan (1988). Cognitive gender differences are disappearing. *American Psychologist, 43,* 95–103.

Fishman, Pamela M. (1983). Interaction: The work women do. In B. Thorne, C. Kramarae, & N. Henley (Eds.), *Language, gender and society.* Rowley, MA: Newbury House.

Freeman, Ellen; Rickels, Karl; Sondheimer, S. J.; & Polansky, M. (1990, July 18). Ineffectiveness of progesterone suppository treatment for premenstrual syndrome. *Journal of the American Medical Association, 264,* 349–353.

Gallant, Sheryle J., & Hamilton, Jean (1988). On a premenstrual psychiatric diagnosis: What's in a name? *Professional Psychology: Research and Practice, 19,* 271–278.

Geschwind, Norman, & Behan, Peter (1982). Left-handedness: Association with immune disease, migraine, and developmental learning disorder. *Proceedings of the National Academy of Sciences, 79,* 5097–5100.

Gise, Leslie H. (Ed.) (1988). *The premenstrual syndromes.* New York: Churchill Livingstone.

Golub, Sharon (1988). A developmental perspective. In L. H. Gise (Ed.), *The premenstrual syndromes.* New York: Churchill Livingstone.

Gould, Stephen J. (1981). *The mismeasure of man.* New York: W. W. Norton & Co.

Halbreich, U., & Endicott, J. (1983). Retrospective report of premenstrual changes: Factors affecting confirmation of daily ratings. *Psychopharmacology Bulletin, 18,* 109–112.

Hamilton, Jean A.; Parry, Barbara L.; Blumenthal, S.; Algana, S.; & Herz, E. (1984). Premenstrual mood changes: A guide to evaluation and treatment. *Psychiatric Annals, 14,* 426–435.

Harrington, Anne (1987). *Medicine, mind, and the double brain: A study in 19th-century thought.* Princeton, NJ: Princeton University Press.

Houser, Betsy B. (1979). An investigation of the correlation between hormonal levels in males and mood, behavior, and physical discomfort. *Hormones and Behavior, 12,* 185–197.

Hubbard, Ruth (1990). *The politics of women's biology.* New Brunswick, NJ: Rutgers University Press.

Hyde, Janet S.; Fennema, Elizabeth; & Lamon, Susan J. (1990). Gender differences in mathematics performance: A meta-analysis. *Psychological Bulletin, 107,* 139–155.

Hyde, Janet S., & Linn, Marcia C. (Eds.) (1986). *The psychology of gender: Advances through meta-analysis.* Baltimore, MD: Johns Hopkins University Press.

——— (1988). Gender differences in verbal ability: A meta-analysis. *Psychological Bulletin, 104,* 53–69.

Koeske, Randi D. (1987). Premenstrual emotionality: Is biology destiny? In M. R. Walsh (Ed.), *The psychology of women: Ongoing debates.* New Haven, CT: Yale University Press.

Lakoff, Robin T. (1990). *Talking power: The politics of language.* New York: Basic Books.

Laqueur, Thomas (1987). Orgasm, generation, and the politics of reproductive biology. In C. Gallagher & T. Laqueur (Eds.), *The making of the modern body.* Berkeley, CA: University of California Press.

Levy, Jerre (1983). Language, cognition, and the right hemisphere: A response to Gazzaniga. *American Psychologist, 38,* 538–541.

Martin, Emily (1987). *The woman in the body: A cultural analysis of reproduction.* Boston: Beacon.

McConnell-Ginet, Sally (1983). Intonation in a man's world. In B. Thorne, C. Kramarae, & N. Henley (Eds.), *Language, gender and society.* Rowley, MA: Newbury House.

——— (1984). The origins of sexist language in discourse. In S. J. White & V. Teller (Eds.), *Discourses in reading and linguistics (Annals of the New York Academy of Sciences, vol. 433).* New York: New York Academy of Sciences.

McFarlane, Jessica; Martin, Carol L.; & Williams, Tannis M. (1988). Mood fluctuation: Women versus men and menstrual versus other cycles. *Psychology of Women Quarterly, 12,* 201–223.

McGlone, Jeannette (1980). Sex differences in human brain asymmetry: A critical survey. *The Behavioral and Brain Sciences, 3,* 215–263.

Parlee, Mary B. (1973). The premenstrual syndrome. *Psychological Bulletin, 80,* 454–465.

———— (1982). Changes in moods and activation levels during the menstrual cycle in experimentally naïve subjects. *Psychology of Women Quarterly, 7,* 119–131.

———— (1987). Media treatment of premenstrual syndrome. In B. E. Ginsburg & B. F. Carter (Eds.), *Premenstrual syndrome.* New York: Plenum.

Pennebaker, James W. (1982). *The psychology of physical symptoms.* New York: Springer-Verlag.

Sperry, Roger W. (1982). Some effects of disconnecting the cerebral hemispheres. *Science, 217,* 1223–1226.

Tannen, Deborah (1990). *You just don't understand.* New York: William Morrow.

THINKING ABOUT THE READING

What does Tavris mean by the term "Universal Male"? How do you respond to her contention that maleness is synonymous with normality and femaleness is synonymous with abnormality? How does pre-menstrual syndrome simultaneously validate and stigmatize women? How is the focus on biological differences between men and women related to economic discrimination? Tavris focuses on how women are hurt by a reliance on biological explanations for gender differences in behavior. The implication is that men benefit from such explanations. What are some of these benefits? Try to think of some ways in which men suffer from a reliance on biological explanations for gender differences in social behavior.

Black Women and a New Definition of Womanhood

Bart Landry

A popular novel of 1852 chirped that the white heroine, Eoline, "with her fair hair, and celestial blue eyes bending over the harp . . . really seemed 'little lower than the angels,' and an aureola of purity and piety appeared to beam around her brow."[1] By contrast, in another popular antebellum novel, *Maum Guinea and Her Plantation Children* (1861), black women are excluded from the category of true womanhood without debate: "The idea of modesty and virtue in a Louisiana colored-girl might well be ridiculed; as a general thing, she has neither."[2] Decades later, in 1902, a commentator for the popular magazine *The Independent* noted, "I sometimes hear of a virtuous Negro woman, but the idea is absolutely inconceivable to me. . . . I cannot imagine such a creature as a virtuous Negro woman."[3] Another writer, reflecting early-twentieth-century white male stereotypes of black and white women, remarked that, like white women, "Black women had the brains of a child, [and] the passions of a woman" but, unlike white women, were "steeped in centuries of ignorance and savagery, and wrapped about with immoral vices."[4]

Faced with the prevailing views of white society that placed them outside the boundaries of true womanhood, black women had no choice but to defend their virtue. Middle-class black women led this defense, communicating their response in words and in the actions of their daily lives. In doing so they went well beyond defending their own virtue to espouse a broader conception of womanhood that anticipated modern views by more than half a century. Their vision of womanhood combined the public and the private spheres and eventually took for granted a role for women as paid workers outside the home. More than merely an abstract vision, it was a philosophy of womanhood embodied in the lives of countless middle-class black women in both the late nineteenth and the early twentieth centuries.

Virtue Defended

Although black women were seen as devoid of all four of the cardinal virtues of true womanhood—piety, purity, submissiveness, and domesticity—white attention centered on purity. As Hazel Carby suggests, this stemmed in part from the role assigned to black women in the plantation economy. She argues that "two very different but interdependent codes of sexuality operated in the antebellum South, producing opposite definitions of motherhood and womanhood for white and black women which coalesce in the figures of the slave and the mistress."[5] In this scheme, white mistresses gave birth to heirs, slave women to property. A slave woman who attempted to preserve her virtue or sexual autonomy was a threat to the plantation economy. In the words of Harriet Jacobs's slave narrative, *Incidents in the Life of a Slave Girl* (1861), it was "deemed a crime in her [the slave woman] to wish to be virtuous."[6]

Linda Brent, the pseudonym Jacobs used to portray her own life, was an ex-slave struggling to survive economically and protect herself and her daughter from sexual exploitation. In telling her story, she recounts the difficulty all black women faced in practicing the virtues of true womanhood. The contrasting contexts of black and white women's lives called for different, even opposite, responses. While submissiveness and passivity brought protection to the white mistress, these characteristics merely exposed black women to sexual and economic exploitation. Black women, therefore, had to develop strength rather than glory in fragility, and had to be active and assertive rather than passive and submissive.

Though "conventional principles of morality were rendered impossible by the conditions of the slave," as Jacobs argued,[7] Linda Brent embodied the virtues required by black women to survive with dignity in a hostile environment. It was a world in which "Freedom replaced and transcended purity."[8] In the conventional sentimental novels of the period, white heroines who lost their purity chose death or went mad. Black women saw death as an alternative to slavery. "As I passed the wreck of the old meeting house," Linda Brent mused, "where, before Nat Turner's time, the slaves had been allowed to meet for worship, I seemed to hear my father's voice come from it, bidding me not to tarry till I reached freedom or the grave."[9] Painfully aware of her inability to meet the standards of conventional white womanhood ("I do not sit with my children in a home of my own. I still long for a hearthstone of my own, however humble."[10]), Linda Brent nevertheless represented a fundamental challenge to this ideology and the beginnings of an alternative, broader definition of womanhood, one that incorporated resourcefulness and independence.

Three decades later, in the 1890s, black women found reasons to defend their moral integrity with new urgency against attacks from all sides. Views such as those in *The Independent* noted earlier were given respectability by a report of the Slater Fund, a foundation that supported welfare projects for blacks in this period. The foundation asserted without argument, "The negro women of the South are subject to temptations . . . which come to them from the days of their race enslavement. . . . To meet such temptations the negro woman can only offer the resistance of a low moral standard, an inheritance from the system of slavery, made still lower from a lifelong residence in a one-room cabin."[11]

At the 1893 World Columbian Exposition in Chicago, where black women were effectively barred from the exhibits on the achievements of American women, the few black women allowed to address a women's convention there felt compelled to publicly challenge these views. One speaker, Fannie Barrier Williams, shocked her audience by her forthrightness. "I regret the necessity of speaking of the moral question of our women," but "the morality of our home life has been commented on so disparagingly and meanly that we are placed in the unfortunate position of being defenders of our name."[12] She went on to emphasize that black women continued to be the victims of sexual harassment by white men and chided her white female audience for failing to protect their black sisters. In the same vein, black activist and educator Anna Julia Cooper told the audience that it was not a question of "temptations" as much as it was "the painful, patient, and silent toil of mothers to gain title to the bodies of their daughters."[13] Williams was later to write on the same theme. "It is a significant and shameful fact that I am constantly in receipt of letters from the still unprotected women in the South, begging me to find employment for their daughters . . . to save them from going into the homes of the South as servants as there is nothing to save them from dishonor and degradation."[14] Another black male writer was moved to reveal in *The Independent:* "I know of more than one colored woman who was openly importuned by White women to become the mistress of their husbands, on the ground that they, the white wives, were afraid that, if their husbands did not associate with colored women they would certainly do so with outside white women. . . . And the white wives, for reasons which ought to be perfectly obvious, preferred to have all their husbands do wrong with colored women in order to keep their husbands *straight!*"[15] The attacks on black women's virtue came to a head with a letter written by James Jacks, president of the Missouri Press Association, in which he alleged, "The Negroes in this country were wholly devoid of morality, the women were prostitutes and all were natural thieves and liars."[16] These remarks, coming from such a prominent individual, drew an immediate reaction from black women throughout the country. The most visible was Josephine St. Pierre Ruffin's invitation to black club women to a national convention in Boston in 1895; one hundred women from ten states came to Boston in response. In a memorable address to representatives of some twenty clubs, Ruffin directly attacked the scurrilous accusations:

> Now for the sake of the thousands of self-sacrificing young women teaching and preaching in lonely southern backwoods, for the noble army of mothers who gave birth to these girls, mothers whose intelligence is only limited by their opportunity to get at books, for the cultured women who have carried off the honors at school here and often abroad, for the sake of our own dignity, the dignity of our race and the future good name of our children, it is "meet, right and our bounden duty" to stand forth and declare ourselves and our principles, to teach an ignorant and suspicious world that our aims and interests are identical with those of all good, aspiring women. Too long have we been silent under unjust and unholy charges. . . . It is to break this silence, not by noisy protestations of what we are not, but by a dignified showing of what we are and hope to become, that we are impelled to take this step, to make of this gathering an object lesson to the world.[17]

At the end of three days of meetings, the National Federation of Afro-American Women was founded, uniting thirty-six black women's clubs in twelve states.[18] The following year, the National Federation merged with the National League of Colored Women to form the National Association of Colored Women (NACW).

Racial Uplift: In Defense of the Black Community

While the catalyst for these national organizations was in part the felt need of black women to defend themselves against moral attacks by whites, they soon went beyond this narrow goal.

Twenty years after its founding, the NACW had grown to fifty thousand members in twenty-eight federations and more than one thousand clubs.[19] The founding of these organizations represented a steady movement by middle-class black women to assume more active roles in the community. Historian Deborah Gray White argues that black club women "insisted that only black women could save the black race," a position that inspired them to pursue an almost feverish pace of activities.[20]

These clubs, however, were not the first attempts by black women to participate actively in their communities. Since the late 1700s black women had been active in mutual-aid societies in the North, and in the 1830s northern black women organized anti-slavery societies. In 1880 Mary Ann Shadd Cary and six other women founded the Colored Women's Progressive Franchise Association in Washington, D.C. Among its stated goals were equal rights for women, including the vote, and the even broader feminist objective of taking "an aggressive stand against the assumption that men only begin and conduct industrial and other things."[21] Giving expression to this goal were a growing number of black women professionals, including the first female physicians to practice in the South.[22] By the turn of the twentieth century, the National Business League, founded by Booker T. Washington, could report that there were "160 Black female physicians, seven dentists, ten lawyers, 164 ministers, assorted journalists, writers, artists, 1,185 musicians and teachers of music, and 13,525 school instructors."[23]

Black women's activism was spurred by the urgency of the struggle for equality, which had led to a greater acceptance of black female involvement in the abolitionist movement. At a time when patriarchal notions of women's domestic role dominated, historian Paula Giddings asserts, "There is no question that there was greater acceptance among Black men of women in activist roles than there was in the broader society."[24] This is not to say that all black men accepted women as equals or the activist roles that many were taking. But when faced with resistance, black women often *demanded* acceptance of their involvement. In 1849, for example, at a black convention in Ohio, "Black women, led by Jane P. Merritt, threatened to boycott the meetings if they were not given a more substantial voice in the proceedings."[25]

In the postbellum period black women continued their struggle for an equal voice in activities for racial uplift in both secular and religious organizations. Historian Evelyn Brooks Higginbotham has offered a detailed account of the successful struggle of black women in the Baptist Church during the late nineteenth century to win acceptance of independent organizations led by themselves.[26] These women's organizations then played a significant role not only in missionary activities, but also in general racial uplift activities in both rural and urban areas.[27] . . .

Black Women and the Suffrage Movement

In their struggle for their own rights, black women moved into the political fray and eagerly joined the movement for passage of a constitutional amendment giving women the right to vote. Unlike white women suffragists, who focused exclusively on the benefits of the vote for their sex, black women saw the franchise as a means of improving the condition of the black community generally. For them, race and gender issues were inseparable. As historian Rosalyn Terborg-Penn emphasizes, black feminists believed that by "increasing the black electorate" they "would not only uplift the women of the race, but help the children and the men as well."[28]

Prominent black women leaders as well as national and regional organizations threw their support behind the suffrage movement. At least twenty black suffrage organizations were founded, and black women participated in rallies and demonstrations and gave public speeches.[29] Ironically, they often found themselves battling white women suffragists as well as men. Southern white women opposed including black women under a federal suffrage as a matter of principle. Northern white women suffragists, eager to retain the support of southern white women, leaned to-

ward accepting a wording of the amendment that would have allowed the southern states to determine their own position on giving black women the vote, a move that would have certainly led to their exclusion.[30]

After the Nineteenth Amendment was ratified in 1920 in its original form, black women braved formidable obstacles in registering to vote. All across the South white registrars used "subterfuge and trickery" to hinder them from registering, including a "grandmother clause" in North Carolina, literacy tests in Virginia, and a $300 poll tax in Columbia, South Carolina. In Columbia, black women "waited up to twelve hours to register" while white women were registered first.[31] In their struggle to register, black women appealed to the NAACP, signed affidavits against registrars who disqualified them, and finally asked for assistance from national white women suffrage leaders. They were especially disappointed in this last attempt. After fighting side by side with white women suffragists for passage of the Nineteenth Amendment, they were rebuffed by the National Woman's Party leadership with the argument that theirs was a race rather than a women's rights issue.[32] Thus, white women continued to separate issues of race and sex that black women saw as inseparable.

Challenging the Primacy of Domesticity

A conflicting conception of the relationship between gender and race issues was not the only major difference in the approaches of black and white women to their roles in the family and society. For most white women, their domestic roles as wives and mothers remained primary. In the late nineteenth century, as they began increasingly to argue for acceptance of their involvement on behalf of child-labor reform and growing urban problems, white women often defended these activities as extensions of their housekeeping role. Historian Barbara Harris comments, "The [white women] pioneers in women's education, who probably did more than anyone else in this period to effect change in the female sphere, advocated education for women and their entrance into the teaching profession on the basis of the values proclaimed by the cult of true womanhood. In a similar way, females defended their careers as authors and their involvement in charitable, religious, temperance, and moral reform societies."[33] Paula Giddings notes that in this way white women were able "to become more active outside the home while still preserving the probity of 'true womanhood.' "[34] From the birth of white feminism at the Seneca Falls Convention in 1848, white feminists had a difficult time advancing their goals. Their numbers were few and their members often divided over the propriety of challenging the cult of domesticity. . . .

In the late nineteenth century the cult of domesticity remained primary even for white women graduates of progressive women's colleges such as Vassar, Smith, and Wellesley. For them, no less than for those with only a high-school education, "A Woman's Kingdom" was "a well-ordered home."[35] In a student essay, one Vassar student answered her rhetorical question, "Has the educated woman a duty towards the kitchen?" by emphasizing that the kitchen was "exactly where the college woman belonged" for "the orderly, disciplined, independent graduate is the woman best prepared to manage the home, in which lies the salvation of the world."[36] This essay reflects the dilemma faced by these young white women graduates. They found little support in white society to combine marriage and career. In *Beyond Her Sphere* historian Barbara Harris comments, "To a degree that is hard for us to appreciate, a [white] woman had to make a choice: she either married and had children, or she remained single and had a career. . . . Yet, after their exhilarating years at college, many women were far too committed to the pursuit of knowledge or the practical application of their education to retreat willingly to the narrow confines of Victorian domesticity. And so, in surprising numbers, they chose the other alternative and rejected marriage."[37] Historian Carl Degler estimates that in 1900 25 percent of white women college graduates and 50 percent of those receiving Ph.D.s remained single. Graduates of elite women's colleges in the East were even less likely to marry: 45 and 57 percent, respectively, of Bryn Mawr and Wellesley graduates between 1889 and 1909. While the increasing numbers of white women receiving college degrees did contribute to the ranks of activists, this did not result in a frontal attack on the cult of domesticity. In fact, a number of prominent feminists such as Angelina Grimké and Antoinette Brown Blackwell "disappeared from the ranks of feminist leaders after their marriage," and Alice Freeman Palmer, the president of Wellesley College, resigned after her marriage in 1887 to Herbert Palmer, a philosophy professor at Harvard.[38] Society sanctioned only three courses for the middle-class white woman in the Progressive period: "marriage, charity work or teaching."[39] Marriage and motherhood stood as the highest calling. If there were no economic need for them to work, single women were encouraged to do volunteer charity work. For those who needed an independent income, teaching was the only acceptable occupation.

Historian John Rousmaniere suggests that the white college-educated women involved in the early settlement house movement saw themselves as fulfilling the "service norm" so prominent among middle-class women of the day. At the same time, he argues, it was their sense of uniqueness as college-educated women and their felt isolation upon returning home that led them to this form of service. The settlement houses, located as they were in white immigrant, working-class slums, catered to these women's sense of noblesse oblige; they derived a sense of accomplishment from providing an example of genteel middle-class virtues to the poor. Yet the settlement houses also played into a sense of adventure, leading one resident to write, "We feel that we know life for the first time."[40] For all their felt uniqueness, however, with some notable exceptions these women's lives usually offered no fundamental challenge to the basic assumptions of true womanhood. Residency in settlement houses was for the most part of short duration, and most volunteers eventually embraced their true roles of wife and mother without significant outside involvement. The exceptions were women like Jane Addams, Florence Kelley, Julia Lathrop, and Grace Abbott, who became major figures in the public sphere. Although their lives disputed the doctrine of white women's confinement to the private sphere, the challenge was limited in that most of them did not themselves combine the two spheres of marriage and a public life. Although Florence Kelley was a divorced mother, she nevertheless upheld "the American tradition that men support their families, their wives throughout life," and bemoaned the "retrograde movement" against man as the breadwinner.[41]

Most college-educated black middle-class women also felt a unique sense of mission. They accepted Lucy Laney's 1899 challenge to lift up their race and saw themselves walking in the footsteps of black women activists and feminists of previous generations. But their efforts were not simply "charity work"; their focus was on "racial uplift" on behalf of themselves as well as of the economically less fortunate members of their race.[42] The black women's club movement, in contrast to the white women's, tended to concern themselves from the beginning with the "social and legal problems that confronted both black women and men."[43] While there was certainly some elitism in the NACW's motto, "Lifting as We Climb," these activists were always conscious that they shared a common experience of exploitation and discrimination with the masses and could not completely retreat to the safe haven of their middle-class homes.[44] On the way to meetings they shared the black experience of riding in segregated cars or of being ejected if they tried to do otherwise, as Ida B. Wells did in 1884.[45] Unlike white women for whom, as black feminist Frances Ellen Watkins Harper had emphasized in 1869, "the priorities in the struggle for human rights were sex, not race,"[46] black women could not separate these twin sources of their oppression. They understood that, together with their working-class sisters, they were assumed by whites to have "low animalistic urges." Their exclusion from the category of true womanhood was no less complete than for their less educated black sisters.

It is not surprising, therefore, that the most independent and radical of black female activists led the way in challenging the icons of true womanhood, including on occasion motherhood and marriage. Not only did they chafe under their exclusion from true womanhood, they viewed its tenets as strictures to their efforts on behalf of racial uplift and their own freedom and integrity as women. In 1894 *The Woman's Era* (a black women's magazine) set forth the heretical opinion that "not all women are intended for mothers. Some of us have not the temperament for family life. . . . Clubs will make women think seriously of their future lives, and not make girls think their only alternative is to marry."[47] Anna Julia Cooper, one of the most dynamic women of the period, who had been married and widowed, added that a woman was not "compelled to look to sexual love as the one sensation capable of giving tone and relish, movement and vim to the life she leads. Her horizon is extended."[48] Elsewhere Cooper advised black women that if they married they should seek egalitarian relationships. "The question is not now with the woman 'How shall I so cramp, stunt, and simplify and nullify myself as to make me eligible to the honor of being swallowed up into some little man?' but the problem . . . rests with the man as to how he can so develop . . . to reach the ideal of a generation of women who demand the noblest, grandest and best achievements of which he is capable."[49]

. . . Black activists were far more likely to combine marriage and activism than white activists. . . . Historian Linda Gordon found this to be the case in her study of sixty-nine black and seventy-six white activists in national welfare reform between 1890 and 1945. Only 34 percent of the white activists had ever been married, compared to 85 percent of the black activists. Most of these women (83 percent of blacks and 86 percent of whites) were college educated.[50] She also found that "The white women [reformers], with few exceptions, tended to view married women's economic dependence on men as desirable, and their employment as a misfortune. . . ."[51] On the other hand, although there were exceptions, Gordon writes, ". . . most black women activists projected a favorable view of working women and women's professional aspirations."[52] Nor could it be claimed that these black activists worked out of necessity, since the majority were married to prominent men "who could support them."[53]

Witness Ida B. Wells-Barnett (married to the publisher of Chicago's leading black newspaper) in 1896, her six-month-old son in tow, stumping from city to city making political speeches on behalf of the Illinois Women's State Central Committee. And Mary Church Terrell dismissing the opinion of those who suggested that studying higher mathematics would make her unappealing as a marriage partner with a curt, "I'd take a chance and run the risk."[54] She did eventually marry and raised a daughter and an adopted child. Her husband, Robert Terrell, a Harvard graduate, was a school principal, a lawyer, and eventually a municipal court judge in Washington, D.C. A biographer later wrote of Mary Terrell's life, "But absorbing as motherhood was, it never became a full-time occupation."[55] While this could also be said of Stanton, perhaps what most distinguished black from white feminists and activists was the larger number of the former who unequivocally challenged domesticity and the greater receptivity they found for their views in the black community. As a result, while the cult of domesticity remained dominant in the white community at the turn of the twentieth century, it did not hold sway within the black community.

Rejection of the Public/Private Dichotomy

Black women of the nineteenth and early twentieth centuries saw their efforts on behalf of the black community as necessary for their own survival, rather than as noblesse oblige. "Self preservation," wrote Mary Church Terrell in 1902, "demands that [black women] go among the lowly, illiterate and even the vicious, to whom they are bound by ties of race and sex . . . to reclaim them."[56] These women rejected the confinement to the private sphere mandated by the cult of domesticity. They felt women could enter the public sphere without detriment to the home. As historian Elsa Barkley Brown has emphasized, black women believed that "Only a strong and unified community made up of both women and men could wield the power necessary to allow black people to shape their own lives. Therefore, only when women were able to exercise their full strength would the community be at its full strength. . . ."[57]

In her study of black communities in Illinois during the late Victorian era (1880–1910), historian Shirley Carlson contrasts the black and white communities' expectations of the "ideal woman" at that time:

> The black community's appreciation for and development of the feminine intellect contrasted sharply with the views of the larger society. In the latter, intelligence was regarded as a masculine quality that would "defeminize" women. The ideal white woman, being married, confined herself almost exclusively to the private domain of the household. She was demure, perhaps even self-effacing. She often deferred to her husband's presumably superior judgment, rather than formulating her own views and vocally expressing them, as black women often did. A woman in the larger society might skillfully manipulate her husband for her own purposes, but she was not supposed to confront or challenge him directly. Black women were often direct, and frequently won community approval for this quality, especially when such a characteristic was directed toward achieving racial uplift. Further, even after her marriage, a black woman might remain in the public domain, possibly in paid employment. The ideal black woman's domain, then, was both the private and public spheres. She was wife and mother, but she could also assume other roles such as schoolteacher, social activist, or businesswoman, among others. And she was intelligent.[58]

In their struggle for an expansion of roles beyond the domestic sphere, black women sometimes had to contend with opposition from within the black community, especially from men, as well as with the larger society's definition of women's proper role. When Ida Wells-Barnett was elected financial secretary of the Afro-American Council, the *Colored American* newspaper suggested that a man should hold the position. While recognizing that "She is a woman of unusual mental powers," the newspaper argued that "the proprieties would have been observed by giving her an assignment more in keeping with the popular idea of women's work and which would not interfere so disastrously with her domestic duties."[59]

Feminist Maggie Lena Walker, the first woman in the nation (and the first African American, male or female) to establish and head a bank and founder of the Richmond Council of Colored Women in Virginia, also met with male opposition in her efforts for racial uplift and expanded women's roles. She too opposed these limitations to the domestic sphere, contending, "Men should not be so pessimistic and down on women's clubs. They don't seek to destroy the home or disgrace the race."[60] The Woman's Union, a Richmond female insurance company founded in 1898, took as its motto, "The Hand That Rocks the Cradle Rules the World." As Brown has clarified, however, "unlike nineteenth-century white women's rendering of that expression to signify the limitation of woman's influence to that which she had by virtue of rearing her sons, the idea as these women conceived it transcended the separation of private and public spheres and spoke to the idea that women, while not abandoning their roles as wives and mothers, could also move into economic and political activities in ways that would support rather than conflict with family and community."[61]

Although many black males, like most white males, opposed the expansion of black women's roles, many other black males supported women's activism and even criticized their brethren for their opposition. Echoing Maggie Walker's sentiments, T. Thomas Fortune wrote, "The race could not succeed nor build strong citizens, until we have a race of women competent to do more than hear a brood of negative men."[62] Support for women's suffrage was espe-

cially strong among black males. . . . Black men saw women's suffrage as advancing the political empowerment of the race. For black women, suffrage promised to be a potent weapon in their fight for their rights, for education and jobs.[63]

A Threefold Commitment

An expanded role for black women did not end at the ballot box or in activities promoting racial uplift. Black middle-class women demanded a place for themselves in the paid labor force. Theirs was a threefold commitment to family, career, and social movements. According to historian Rosalyn Terborg-Penn, "most black feminists and leaders had been wives and mothers who worked yet found time not only to struggle for the good of their sex, but for their race." Such a threefold commitment "was not common among white women."[64]

In her study of eighty African American women throughout the country who worked in "the feminized professions" (such as teaching) between the 1880s and the 1950s, historian Stephanie Shaw comments on the way they were socialized to lives dedicated to home, work, and community. When these women were children, she indicates, "the model of womanhood held before [them] was one of achievement in *both* public and private spheres. Parents cast domesticity as a complement rather than a contradiction to success in public arenas."[65] Later, in her discussion of one woman whose husband opposed her desire to work outside the home, Shaw observes, "It seems, then, that Henry Riddick subscribed to an old tradition (which was becoming less and less influential in general, and which *had never been a real tradition among most black families*) wherein the wife of a 'good' husband did not need to work for pay."[66]

An analysis of the lives of 108 of the first generation of black clubwomen bears this out. "The career-oriented clubwomen, comments Paula Giddings, "seemed to have no ambivalence concerning their right to work, whether necessity dictated it or not."[67] According to Giddings, three-quarters of these 108 early clubwomen were married, and almost three-quarters worked outside the home, while one-quarter had children.

A number of these clubwomen and other black women activists not only had careers but also spoke forcefully about the importance of work, demonstrating surprisingly progressive attitudes with a very modern ring. "The old doctrine that a man marries a woman to support her," quipped Walker, "is pretty nearly threadbare to-day."[68] "Every dollar a woman makes," she declared in a 1912 speech to the Federation of Colored Women's Clubs, "some man gets the direct benefit of same. Every woman was by Divine Providence created for some man; not for some man to marry, take home and support, but for the purpose of using her powers, ability, health and strength, to forward the financial . . . success of the partnership into which she may go, if she will. . . ."[69] Being married with three sons and an adopted daughter did not in any way dampen her commitment to gender equality and an expanded role for wives.

Such views were not new. In a pamphlet entitled *The Awakening of the Afro-American Woman,* written in 1897 to celebrate the earlier founding of the National Association of Colored Women, Victoria Earle Matthews referred to black women as "co-breadwinners in their families."[70] Almost twenty years earlier, in 1878, feminist writer and activist Frances Ellen Harper sounded a similar theme of equality when she insisted, "The women as a class are quite equal to the men in energy and executive ability." She went on to recount instances of black women managing small and large farms in the post-bellum period.[71]

It is clear that in the process of racial uplift work, black middle-class women also included membership in the labor force as part of their identity. They were well ahead of their time in realizing that their membership in the paid labor force was critical to achieving true equality with men. For this reason, the National Association of Wage Earners insisted that all black women should be able to support themselves.[72] . . .

. . . A number of women began their fight for careers when still very young and continued this battle throughout their lives. Braving the opposition of family and friends, Terrell dared to earn an A.B. degree in mathematics from Oberlin, even though "It was held by most people that women were unfitted to do their work in the home if they studied Latin, Greek and higher mathematics." Upon graduation, she defied her father's furious objection to her employment and took a teaching job at Wilberforce College. For her act of rebellion she was "disinherited" by her irate father, who "refused to write to me for a year."[73] But Terrell enjoyed the full support of her husband, Robert.

In 1963 in *The Feminine Mystique,* Betty Friedan wrote, "I never knew a woman, when I was growing up, who used her mind, played her own part in the world, and also loved, and had children."[74] Her experience, however, was only of white middle-class women. In fact, many black middle-class women did fit this description, and Friedan's lack of acquaintance with these women attests to the deep chasm that has historically separated the worlds of black and white women. As W. E. B. Du Bois commented as early as 1924, "Negro women more than the women of any other group in America are the protagonists in the fight for an economically independent womanhood in modern countries. . . . The matter of economic independence is, of course, the central fact in the struggle of women for equality."[75]

Defining Black Womanhood

In the late 1930s when Mary McLeod Bethune, the acknowledged leader of black women at the time and an adviser to President Franklin Roosevelt on matters affecting the black community, referred to herself as the representative of "Negro womanhood" and asserted that black women had "room in their lives to be wives and mothers as well as to have careers," she was not announcing a new idea.[76] As Terborg-Penn emphasizes:

> . . . most black feminists and leaders had been wives and mothers who worked yet found time not only to struggle for the good of their sex,

but for their race. Until the 1970s, however, this threefold commitment—to family and to career and to one or more social movements—was not common among white women. The key to the uniqueness among black feminists of this period appears to be their link with the past. The generation of the woman suffrage era had learned from their late nineteenth-century foremothers in the black women's club movement, just as the generation of the post World War I era had learned and accepted the experiences of the preceding generation. Theirs was a sense of continuity, a sense of group consciousness that transcended class.[77]

This "sense of continuity" with past generations of black women was clearly articulated in 1917 by Mary Talbert, president of the NACW. Launching an NACW campaign to save the home of the late Frederick Douglass, she said, "We realize today is the psychological moment for us women to show our true worth and prove the Negro women of today measure up to those sainted women of our race, who passed through the fire of slavery and its galling remembrances."[78] Talbert certainly lived up to her words, going on to direct the NAACP's anti-lynching campaign and becoming the first woman to receive the NAACP's Spingarn Medal for her achievements.

What then is the expanded definition of true womanhood found in these black middle-class women's words and embodied in their lives? First, they tended to define womanhood in an inclusive rather than exclusive sense. Within white society, true womanhood was defined so narrowly that it excluded all but a small minority of white upper- and upper-middle-class women with husbands who were able to support them economically. Immigrant women and poor women—of any color—did not fit this definition. Nor did black women as a whole, regardless of class, because they were all seen as lacking an essential characteristic of true womanhood— virtue. For black women, however, true womanhood transcended class and race boundaries. Anna Julia Cooper called for "reverence for

woman as woman regardless of rank, wealth, or culture."[79] Unlike white women, black women refused to isolate gender issues from other forms of oppression such as race and nationality, including the struggles of colonized nations of Africa and other parts of the world. Women's issues, they suggested, were tied to issues of oppression, whatever form that oppression might assume.

As discussed above, black women organized to defend their virtue against the vicious attacks of white society. They pointed out—Fannie Barrier Williams and Ida B. Wells-Barnett forcefully among them—that the real culprits were white males who continued to harass and prey upon them with the tacit support of white women. At times they also chastised black males for failing to protect them. Black women obviously saw themselves as virtuous, both individually and as a group. Yet, apart from defending themselves against these attacks, black women did not dwell upon virtue in defining womanhood. theirs was not the sexless purity forced on white women by white males who placed their women on pedestals while seeking out black women for their pleasure....

The traditional white ideology of true womanhood separated the active world of men from the passive world of women. As we have seen, women's activities were confined to the home, where their greatest achievement was maintaining their own virtue and decorum and rearing future generations of male leaders. Although elite black women did not reject their domestic roles as such, many expanded permissible public activities beyond charity work to encompass employment and participation in social progress. They founded such organizations as the Atlanta Congress of Colored Women, which historian Erlene Stetson claims was the first grassroots women's movement organized "for social and political good."[80]

The tendency of black women to define womanhood inclusively and to see their roles extending beyond the boundaries of the home led them naturally to include other characteristics in their vision. One of these was intellectual equality. While the "true" woman was portrayed as submissive ("conscious of inferiority, and therefore grateful for support"),[81] according to literary scholar Hazel Carby, black women such as Anna Julia Cooper argued for a "partnership with husbands on a plane of intellectual equality."[82] Such equality could not exist without the pursuit of education, particularly higher education, and participation in the labor force. Cooper, like many other black women, saw men's opposition to higher education for women as an attempt to make them conform to a narrow view of women as "sexual objects for exchange in the marriage market."[83] Education for women at all levels became a preoccupation for many black feminists and activists. Not a few—like Anna Cooper, Mary L. Europe, and Estelle Pinckney Webster—devoted their entire lives to promoting it, especially among young girls. Womanhood, as conceived by black women, was compatible with—indeed, required—intellectual equality. In this they were supported by the black community. While expansion of educational opportunities for women was a preoccupation of white feminists in the nineteenth century, as I noted above, a college education tended to create a dilemma in the lives of white women who found little community support for combining marriage and career. In contrast, as Shirley Carlson emphasizes, "The black community did not regard intelligence and femininity as conflicting values, as the larger society did. That society often expressed the fear that intelligent women would develop masculine characteristics—a thickening waist, a diminution of breasts and hips, and finally, even the growth of facial hair. Blacks seemed to have had no such trepidations, or at least they were willing to have their women take these risks."[84]

In addition, to women's rights to an education, Cooper Walker, Alexander, Terrell, the leaders of the National Association of Wage Earners, and countless other black feminists and activists insisted on their right to work outside the home. They dared to continue very active lives after marriage. Middle-class black women's insistence on the right to pursue careers paralleled their view that a true woman could move in both the private and the public spheres and that marriage did not require submissiveness or subordination. In fact, as Shirley Carlson has observed in her study of black women in Illinois in the late Victorian period, many activist black women "continued to be identified by their maiden names—usually as their middle names or as part of their hyphenated surnames—indicating that their own identities were not subsumed in their husbands."[85]

While the views of black women on womanhood were all unusual for their time, their insistence on the right of all women—including wives and mothers—to work outside the home was the most revolutionary. In their view the need for paid work was not merely a response to economic circumstances, but the fulfillment of women's right to self-actualization. Middle-class black women like Ida B. Wells-Barnett, Margaret Washington, and Mary Church Terrell, married to men who were well able to support them, continued to pursue careers throughout their lives, and some did so even as they reared children. These women were far ahead of their time, foreshadowing societal changes that would not occur within the white community for several generations. . . .

Rather than accepting white society's views of paid work outside the home as deviant, therefore, black women fashioned a competing ideology of womanhood—one that supported the needs of an oppressed black community and their own desire for gender equality. Middle-class black women, especially, often supported by the black community, developed a consciousness of themselves as persons who were competent and capable of being influential. They believed in higher education as a means of sharpening their talents, and in a sexist world that looked on men as superior, they dared to see themselves as equals both in and out of marriage.

This new ideology of womanhood came to have a profound impact on the conception of black families and gender roles. Black women's insistence on their role as co-breadwinners clearly foreshadows today's dual-career and dual-worker families. Since our conception of the family is inseparably tied to our views of women's and men's roles, the broader definition of womanhood advocated by black women was also an argument against the traditional family. The cult of domesticity was anchored in a patriarchal notion of women as subordinate to men in both the family and the larger society. The broader definition of womanhood championed by black middle-class women struck a blow for an expansion of women's rights in society and a more egalitarian position in the home, making for a far more progressive system among blacks at this time than among whites.

NOTES

1. Quoted in Hazel V. Carby, *Reconstructing Womanhood: The Emergence of the Afro-American Woman Novelist* (New York: Oxford University Press, 1987), p. 26.

2. Ibid.

3. Quoted in Paula Giddings, *When and Where I Enter: The Impact of Black Women and Race and Sex in America* (New York: Bantam Books, 1985), p. 82.

4. Ibid., p. 82.

5. Carby, *Reconstructing Womanhood,* p. 20.

6. Harriet Jacobs, *Incidents in the Life of a Slave Girl,* L. Baria Child, ed. (1861; paperback reprint, New York: Harcourt Brace Jovanovich, 1973), p. 29.

7. Carby, *Reconstructing Womanhood,* pp. 58–59.

8. Ibid., p. 60.

9. Jacobs, *Incidents in the Life of a Slave Girl,* p. 93.

10. Ibid., p. 207.

11. Quoted in Giddings, *When and Where I Enter,* p. 82.

12. Ibid., p. 86.

13. Ibid., p. 87.

14. Ibid., pp. 86–87.

15. Ibid., p. 87.

16. Quoted in Sharon Harley, "Black Women in a Southern City: Washington, D.C., 1890–78 in Joanne V. Hawks and Shiela L. Skemp, eds., *Sex, Race, and the Role of Women in the South* (Jackson, Miss.: University Press of Mississippi, 1983), p. 72.

17. Eleanor Flexner, *Century of Struggle: The Woman's Rights Movement in the United States* (Cambridge: Harvard University Press, 1959), p. 194.

18. Giddings, *When and Where I Enter,* p. 93.

19. Ibid., p. 95. For a discussion of elitism in the "uplift" movement and organizations, see Kevin K. Gains, *Uplifting the Race: Black Leadership, Politics, and Culture in the Twentieth Century* (Chapel Hill, N.C.: University of North Carolina Press, 1996). Black reformers, enlightened as they were, could not entirely escape being influenced by Social Darwinist currents of the times.

20. Deborah Gray White, *Too Heavy a Load: Black Women in Defense of Themselves, 1894–1994* (New York: W. W. Norton & Company, 1999), p. 36.

21. Quoted in Giddings, *When and Where I Enter,* p. 75.

22. Ibid.

23. Ibid.

24. Ibid., p. 59.

25. Ibid.

26. Evelyn Brooks Higginbotham, *Righteous Discontent: The Women's Movement in the Black Baptist Church, 1880–1920* (Cambridge: Harvard University Press, 1993).

27. Ibid., p. 20.

28. Rosalyn Terborg-Penn, "Discontented Black Feminists: Prelude and Postscript to the Passage of the Nineteenth Amendment," pp. 261–278 in Lois Scharf and Joan M. Jensen, eds., *Decades of Discontent: The Woman's Movement, 1920–1940* (Westport, Conn.: Greenwood Press, 1983), p. 264.

29. Ibid., p. 261.

30. Ibid., p. 264.

31. Ibid., p. 266.

32. Ibid., pp. 266–267.

33. Barbara J. Harris, *Beyond Her Sphere: Women and the Professions in American History* (Westport, Conn.: Greenwood Press, 1978), pp. 85–86.

34. Giddings, *When and Where I Enter,* p. 81.

35. John P. Rousmaniere, "Cultural Hybrid in the Slums: The College Woman and the Settlement House, 1889–1984," *American Quarterly* 22 (Spring 1970): p. 56.

36. Ibid., p. 55.

37. Barbara J. Harris, *Beyond Her Sphere,* pp. 101–102.

38. Ibid., pp. 101–102.

39. Rousmaniere, "Cultural Hybrid in the Slums," p. 56.

40. Ibid., p. 61.

41. Quoted in Linda Gordon, "Black and White Visions of Welfare: Women's Welfare Activism, 1890–

1945," *Journal of American History* 78 (September 1991): 583.

42. Giddings, *When and Where I Enter,* p. 97.

43. Estelle Freedman, "Separatism as Strategy: Female Institution Building and American Feminism, 1870–1930," pp. 445–462 in Nancy F. Cott, ed., *Women Together: Organizational Life* (New Providence, RI: K. G. Saur, 1994), p. 450; Nancy Forderhase, " 'Limited Only by Earth and Sky': The Louisville Woman's Club and Progressive Reform, 1900–1910," pp. 365–381 in Cott, ed. *Women Together: Organizational Life* (New Providence, RI: K. G. Saur, 1994); . . . Mary Dell Brady, "Kansas Federation of Colored Women's Clubs, 1900–1930," pp. 382–408 in Nancy F. Cott, *Women Together.*

44. Higginbotham, *Righteous Discontent,* pp. 206–207.

45. Giddings, *When and Where I Enter,* p. 22.

46. Terborg-Penn, "Discontented Black Feminists," p. 267.

47. Giddings, *When and Where I Enter,* p. 108.

48. Ibid., pp. 108–109.

49. Ibid., p. 113.

50. Linda Gordon, "Black and Whites Visions of Welfare," p. 583.

51. Ibid., p. 582.

52. Ibid., p. 585.

53. Ibid., pp. 568–69.

54. Ibid., p. 109.

55. Quoted in Giddings, ibid., p. 110.

56. Ibid., p. 97.

57. Elsa Barkley Brown, "Womanist Consciousness: Maggie Lena Walker and the Independent Order of Saint Luke," *Journal of Women in Culture and Society* 14, no. 3 (1989): 188.

58. Shirley J. Carlson, "Black Ideals of Womanhood in the Late Victorian Era," *Journal of Negro History* 77, no. 2 (Spring 1992): 62. Carlson notes that these black women of the late Victorian era also observed the proprieties of Victorian womanhood in their deportment and appearance but combined them with the expectations of the black community for intelligence, education, and active involvement in racial uplift.

59. Giddings, *When and Where I Enter,* pp. 110–111.

60. Brown, "Womanist Consciousness," p. 180.

61. Ibid., p. 178.

62. Quoted in Giddings, *When and Where I Enter,* p. 117.

63. See Rosalyn Terborg-Penn, *African American Women in the Struggle for the Vote, 1850–1920* (Bloomington, Ind.: Indiana University Press, 1998).

64. Rosalyn Terborg-Penn, "Discontented Black Feminists," p. 274.

65. Stephanie J. Shaw, *What a Woman Ought to Be and to Do: Black Professional Women Workers During the Jim Crow Era* (Chicago: University of Chicago Press, 1996), p. 29. Shaw details the efforts of family and community to socialize these women for both personal achievement and community service. The sacrifices some families made included sending them to private schools and sometimes relocating the entire family near a desired school.

66. Ibid., p. 126. Italics added.

67. Giddings, *When and Where I Enter,* p. 108.

68. Brown, "Womanist Consciousness," p. 622.

69. Ibid., p. 623.

70. Carby, *Reconstructing Womanhood,* p. 117.

71. Quoted in Giddings, *When and Where I Enter,* p. 72.

72. Brown, "Womanist Consciousness," p. 182.

73. Quoted in Giddings, *Where and When I Enter,* p. 109.

74. Betty Friedan, *The Feminine Mystique* (New York: Dell, 1963), p. 68.

75. Quoted in Giddings, *Where and When I Enter,* p. 197.

76. Quoted in Terborg-Penn, "Discontented Black Feminists," p. 274.

77. Ibid., p. 274.

78. Quoted in Giddings, *Where and When I Enter,* p. 138.

79. Quoted in Carby, *Reconstructing Womanhood,* p. 98.

80. Erlene Stetson, "Black Feminism in Indiana, 1893–1933," *Phylon* 44 (December 1983): 294.

81. Quoted in Barbara Welter, "The Cult of True Womanhood: 1820–1860," p. 318.

82. Carby, *Reconstructing Womanhood,* p. 100.

83. Ibid., p. 99.

84. Carlson, "Black Ideals of Womanhood in the Late Victorian Era," p. 69. This view is supported by historian Evelyn Brooks Higginbotham's analysis of schools for blacks established by northern Baptists in the postbellum period, schools that encouraged the attendance of both girls and boys. Although, as Higginbotham observes, northern Baptists founded these schools in part to spread white middle-class values among blacks, blacks nevertheless came to see higher education as an instrument of their own liberation (*Righteous Discontent,* p. 20).

85. Ibid., p. 67.

THINKING ABOUT THE READING

How were the needs of black women during the 19th century movement for gender equality different from those of white women? How did their lives differ with regard to the importance of marriage, motherhood, and employment? What does Landry mean when he says that for these women, "race and gender are inseparable"? What was the significance of the "clubs" for these black women? How does this article change what you previously thought about the contemporary Women's Movement?

Still a Man's World

Men Who Do "Women's Work"

Christine L. Williams

Gendered Jobs and Gendered Workers

A 1959 article in *Library Journal* entitled "The Male Librarian—An Anomaly?" begins this way:

> My friends keep trying to get me out of the library. . . . Library work is fine, they agree, but they smile and shake their heads benevolently and charitably, as if it were unnecessary to add that it is one of the dullest, most poorly paid, unrewarding, off-beat activities any man could be consigned to. If you have a heart condition, if you're physically handicapped in other ways, well, such a job is a blessing. And for women there's no question library work is fine; there are some wonderful women in libraries and we all ought to be thankful to them. But let's face it, no healthy man of normal intelligence should go into it.[1]

Male librarians still face this treatment today, as do other men who work in predominantly female occupations. In 1990, my local newspaper featured a story entitled "Men Still Avoiding Women's Work" that described my research on men in nursing, librarianship, teaching, and social work. Soon afterwards, a humor columnist for the same paper wrote a spoof on the story that he titled, "Most Men Avoid Women's Work Because It Is Usually So Boring."[2] The columnist poked fun at hairdressing, librarianship, nursing, and babysitting—in his view, all "lousy" jobs requiring low intelligence and a high tolerance for boredom. Evidently people still wonder why any "healthy man of normal intelligence" would willingly work in a "woman's occupation."

In fact, not very many men do work in these fields, although their numbers are growing. In 1990, over 500,000 men were employed in these four occupations, constituting approximately 6 percent of all registered nurses, 15 percent of all elementary school teachers, 17 percent of all librarians, and 32 percent of all social workers. These percentages have fluctuated in recent years: As Table 1 indicates, librarianship and social work have undergone slight declines in the proportions of men since 1975; teaching has remained somewhat stable; while nursing has experienced noticeable gains. The number of men in nursing actually doubled between 1980 and 1990; however, their overall proportional representation remains very low.

Very little is known about these men who "cross over" into these nontraditional occupations. While numerous books have been written about women entering male-dominated occupations, few have asked why men are underrepresented in traditionally female jobs.[3] The underlying assumption in most research on gender and work is that, given a free choice, both men and women would work in predominantly male occupations, as they are generally better paying and more prestigious than predominantly female occupations. The few men who willingly "cross over" must be, as the 1959 article suggests, "anomalies."

Popular culture reinforces the belief that these men are "anomalies." Men are rarely portrayed working in these occupations, and when they are, they are represented in extremely stereotypical ways. For example, in the 1990 movie *Kindergarten Cop*, muscle-man Arnold Schwarzenegger played a detective forced to work undercover as a

TABLE 1 *Men in the "Women's Professions":*
Number (in thousands) and Distribution of Men
Employed in the Occupations, Selected Years

Profession	1975	1980	1990
Registered Nurses			
Number of men	28	46	92
% men	3.0	3.5	5.5
Elementary Teachers[a]			
Number of men	194	225	223
% men	14.6	16.3	14.8
Librarians			
Number of men	34	27	32
% men	18.9	14.8	16.7
Social Workers			
Number of men	116	134	179
% men	39.2	35.0	21.8

Sources: U.S. Department of Labor, Bureau of Labor
Statistics, *Employment and Earnings* 38 no. 1 (January
1991), table 22 (employed civilians by detailed occupation),
p. 185; vol. 28, no. 1 (January 1981), table 23 (employed
persons by detailed occupation), p. 180; vol. 22, no. 7
(January 1976), table 2 (employed persons by detailed
occupation), p. 11.

[a]Excludes kindergarten teachers.

kindergarten teacher; the otherwise competent
Schwarzenegger was completely overwhelmed by
the five-year-old children in his class. . . .

[I] challenge these stereotypes about men who
do "women's work" through case studies of men
in four predominantly female occupations: nursing, elementary school teaching, librarianship,
and social work. I show that men maintain their
masculinity in these occupations, despite the
popular stereotypes. Moreover, male power and
privilege is preserved and reproduced in these occupations through a complex interplay between
gendered expectations embedded in organizations, and the gendered interests workers bring
with them to their jobs. Each of these occupations is "still a man's world" even though mostly
women work in them.

I selected these four professions as case studies
of men who do "women's work" for a variety of

reasons. First, because they are so strongly associated with women and femininity in our popular
culture, these professions highlight and perhaps
even exaggerate the barriers and advantages men
face when entering predominantly female environments. Second, they each require extended
periods of educational training and apprenticeship, requiring individuals in these occupations
to be at least somewhat committed to their work
(unlike those employed in, say, clerical or domestic work). Therefore I thought they would be re-
flective about their decisions to join these "nontraditional" occupations, making them "acute
observers" and, hence, ideal informants about the
sort of social and psychological processes I am
interested in describing.[4] Third, these occupations vary a great deal in the proportion of men
working in them. Although my aim was not to
engage in between-group comparisons, I believed
that the proportions of men in a work setting
would strongly influence the degree to which
they felt accepted and satisfied with their jobs.[5]

I traveled across the United States conducting
in-depth interviews with seventy-six men and
twenty-three women who work in nursing,
teaching, librarianship, and social work. Like the
people employed in these professions generally,
those in my sample were predominantly white
(90 percent). Their ages ranged from twenty to
sixty-six, and the average age was thirty-eight. I
interviewed women as well as men to gauge their
feelings and reactions to men's entry into "their"
professions. Respondents were intentionally selected to represent a wide range of specialties
and levels of education and experience. I interviewed students in professional schools, "front
line" practitioners, administrators, and retirees,
asking them about their motivations to enter
these professions, their on-the-job experiences,
and their opinions about men's status and prospects in these fields. . . .

Riding the Glass Escalator

Men earn more money than women in every occupation—even in predominantly female jobs

(with the possible exceptions of fashion modeling and prostitution).[6] Table 2 shows that men outearn women in teaching, librarianship, and social work; their salaries in nursing are virtually identical. The ratios between women's and men's earnings in these occupations are higher than those found in the "male" professions, where women earn 74 to 90 percent of men's salaries. That there is a wage gap at all in predominantly female professions, however, attests to asymmetries in the workplace experiences of male and female tokens. These salary figures indicate that the men who do "women's work" fare as well as, and often better than, the women who work in these fields. . . .

Hiring Decisions

Contrary to the experience of many women in the male-dominated professions, many of the men and women I spoke to indicated that there is a *preference* for hiring men in these four occupations. A Texas librarian at a junior high school said that his school district "would hire a male over a female":

[CW: Why do you think that is?]

Because there are so few, and the . . . ones that they do have, the library directors seem to really . . . think they're doing great jobs. I don't

know, maybe they just feel they're being progressive or something, [but] I have had a real sense that they really appreciate having a male, particularly at the junior high. . . . As I said, when seven of us lost our jobs from the high schools and were redistributed, there were only four positions at junior high, and I got one of them. Three of the librarians, some who had been here longer than I had with the school district, were put down in elementary school as librarians. And I definitely think that being male made a difference in my being moved to the junior high rather than an elementary school.

Many of the men perceived their token status as males in predominantly female occupations as an *advantage* in hiring and promotions. When I asked an Arizona teacher whether his specialty (elementary special education) was an unusual area for men compared to other areas within education, he said,

Much more so. I am extremely marketable in special education. That's not why I got into the field. But I am extremely marketable because I am a man.

. . . Sometimes the preference for men in these occupations is institutionalized. One man landed his first job in teaching before he earned the appropriate credential "because I was a wrestler

TABLE 2 *Median Weekly Earnings of Full-Time Professional Workers, by Sex, and Ratio of Female:Male Earnings, 1990*

Occupation	Both	Men	Women	Ratio
Registered Nurses	608	616	608	.99
Elementary Teachers	519	575	513	.89
Librarians	489	—*	479	—
Social Workers	445	483	427	.88
Engineers	814	822	736	.90
Physicians	892	978	802	.82
College Teachers	747	808	620	.77
Lawyers	1,045	1,178	875	.74

Source: U.S. Department of Labor, Bureau of Labor Statistics, *Employment and Earnings* 38, no. 1 (January 1991), table 56, p. 223.

*The Labor Department does not report income averages for base sample sizes consisting of fewer than 50,000 individuals.

and they wanted a wrestling coach." A female math teacher similarly told of her inability to find a full-time teaching position because the schools she applied to reserved the math jobs for people (presumably men) who could double as coaches. . . .

. . . Some men described being "tracked" into practice areas within their professions which were considered more legitimate for men. For example, one Texas man described how he was pushed into administration and planning in social work, even though "I'm not interested in writing policy; I'm much more interested in research and clinical stuff." A nurse who is interested in pursuing graduate study in family and child health in Boston said he was dissuaded from entering the program specialty in favor of a concentration in "adult nursing." And a kindergarten teacher described his difficulty finding a job in his specialty after graduation: "I was recruited immediately to start getting into a track to become an administrator. And it was men who recruited me. It was men that ran the system at that time, especially in Los Angeles."

This tracking may bar men from the most female-identified specialties within these professions. But men are effectively being "kicked upstairs" in the process. Those specialties considered more legitimate practice areas for men also tend to be the most prestigious, and better-paying specialties as well. For example, men in nursing are overrepresented in critical care and psychiatric specialties, which tend to be higher paying than the others.[7] The highest paying and most prestigious library types are the academic libraries (where men are 35 percent of librarians) and the special libraries which are typically associated with businesses or other private organizations (where men constitute 20 percent of librarians).[8]

A distinguished kindergarten teacher, who had been voted citywide "Teacher of the Year," described the informal pressures he faced to advance in his field. He told me that even though people were pleased to see him in the classroom, "there's been some encouragement to think about administration, and there's been some en-

couragement to think about teaching at the university level or something like that, or supervisory-type position."

The effect of this "tracking" is the opposite of that experienced by women in male-dominated occupations. Researchers have reported that many women encounter "glass ceilings" in their efforts to scale organizational and professional hierarchies. That is, they reach invisible barriers to promotion in their careers, caused mainly by the sexist attitudes of men in the highest positions.[9] In contrast to this "glass ceiling," many of the men I interviewed seem to encounter a "glass escalator." Often, despite their intentions, they face invisible pressures to move up in their professions. Like being on a moving escalator, they have to work to stay in place. . . .

Supervisors and Colleagues: The Working Environment

. . . Respondents in this study were asked about their relationships with supervisors and female colleagues to ascertain whether men also experienced "poisoned" work environments when entering nontraditional occupations.

A major difference in the experience of men and women in nontraditional occupations is that men are far more likely to be supervised by a member of their own sex. In each of the four professions I studied, men are overrepresented in administrative and managerial capacities, or, as in the case of nursing, the organizational hierarchy is governed by men. For example, 15 percent of all elementary school teachers are men, but men make up over 80 percent of all elementary school principals and 96 percent of all public school superintendents and assistant superintendents.[10] Likewise, over 40 percent of all male social workers hold administrative or managerial positions, compared to 30 percent of all female social workers.[11] And 50 percent of male librarians hold administrative positions, compared to 30 percent of female librarians, and the majority of deans and directors of major university and public libraries are men.[12] Thus, unlike women who enter "male fields," the men in these professions often work under the direct supervision of other men.

Many of the men interviewed reported that they had good rapport with their male supervisors. It was not uncommon in education, for example, for the male principal to informally socialize with the male staff, as a Texas special education teacher describes:

> Occasionally I've had a principal who would regard me as "the other man on the campus" and "it's us against them," you know? I mean, nothing really that extreme, except that some male principals feel like there's nobody there to talk to except the other man. So I've been in that position.

These personal ties can have important consequences for men's careers. For example, one California nurse, whose performance was judged marginal by his nursing superiors, was transferred to the emergency room staff (a prestigious promotion) due to his personal friendship with the physician in charge. And a Massachusetts teacher acknowledged that his principal's personal interest in him landed him his current job:

> [CW: You had mentioned that your principal had sort of spotted you at your previous job and had wanted to bring you here [to this school]. Do you think that has anything to do with the fact that you're a man, aside from your skills as a teacher?]
>
> Yes, I would say in that particular case, that was part of it. . . . We have certain things in common, certain interests that really lined up.
>
> [CW: Vis-à-vis teaching?]
>
> Well, more extraneous things—running specifically, and music. And we just seemed to get along real well right off the bat. It is just kind of a guy thing; we just liked each other. . . .

Interviewees did not report many instances of male supervisors discriminating against them, or refusing to accept them because they were male. Indeed, these men were much more likely to report that their male bosses discriminated against the *females* in their professions. . . .

Of course, not all the men who work in these occupations are supervised by men. Many of the men interviewed who had female bosses also reported high levels of acceptance—although the level of intimacy they achieved with women did not seem as great as with other men. But in some cases, men reported feeling shut-out from decision making when the higher administration was constituted entirely by women. I asked this Arizona librarian whether men in the library profession were discriminated against hiring because of their sex:

> Professionally speaking, people go to considerable lengths to keep that kind of thing out of their [hiring] deliberations. Personally, is another matter. It's pretty common around here to talk about the "old girl network." This is one of the few libraries that I've had any intimate knowledge of which is actually controlled by women. . . . Most of the department heads and upper level administrators are women. And there's an "old girl network" that works just like the "old boy network," except that the important conferences take place in the women's room rather than on the golf course. But the political mechanism is the same, the exclusion of the other sex from decision making is the same. The reasons are the same. It's somewhat discouraging. . . .

Although I did not interview many supervisors, I did include twenty-three women in my sample to ascertain their perspectives about the presence of men in their professions. All of the women I interviewed claimed to be supportive of their male colleagues, but some conveyed ambivalence. For example, a social work professor said she would like to see more men enter the social work profession, particularly in the clinical specialty (where they are underrepresented). She said she would favor affirmative action hiring guidelines for men in the profession, and yet, she resented the fact that her department hired "another white male" during a recent search. I confronted her about this apparent ambivalence:

> [CW: I find it very interesting that, on the one hand, you sort of perceive this preference and

perhaps even sexism with regard to how men are evaluated and how they achieve higher positions within the profession, yet, on the other hand, you would be encouraging of more men to enter the field. Is that contradictory to you, or . . . ?]

Yeah, it's contradictory. . . .

Men's reception by their female colleagues is thus somewhat mixed. It appears that women are generally eager to see men enter "their" occupations, and the women I interviewed claimed they were supportive of their male peers. Indeed, several men agreed with this social worker that their female colleagues had facilitated their careers in various ways (including college mentorship). At the same time, however, women often resent the apparent ease with which men seem to advance within these professions, sensing that men at the higher levels receive preferential treatment, and thus close off advancement opportunities for women.

But this ambivalence does not seem to translate into the "poisoned" work environment described by many women who work in male-dominated occupations. Among the male interviewees, there were no accounts of sexual harassment (indeed, one man claimed this was a disappointment to him!) However, women do treat their male colleagues differently on occasion. It is not uncommon in nursing, for example, for men to be called upon to help catheterize male patients, or to lift especially heavy patients. Some librarians also said that women asked them to lift and move heavy boxes of books because they were men. . . .

Another stereotype confronting men, in nursing and social work in particular, is the expectation that they are better able than women to handle aggressive individuals and diffuse violent situations. An Arizona social worker who was the first male caseworker in a rural district, described this preference for men:

They welcomed a man, particularly in child welfare. Sometimes you have to go into some tough parts of towns and cities, and they felt it was nice to have a man around to accompany them or be present when they were dealing with a difficult client. Or just doing things that males can do. I always felt very welcomed.

But this special treatment bothered some respondents: Getting assigned all the violent patients or discipline problems can make for difficult and unpleasant working conditions. Nurses, for example, described how they were called upon to subdue violent patients. A traveling psychiatric nurse I interviewed in Texas told how his female colleagues gave him "plenty of opportunities" to use his wrestling skills. . . .

But many men claimed that this differential treatment did not distress them. In fact, several said they liked being appreciated for the special traits and abilities (such as strength) they could contribute to their professions.

Furthermore, women's special treatment of men sometimes enhanced—rather than detracted from—the men's work environments. One Texas librarian said he felt "more comfortable working with women than men" because "I think it has something to do with control. Maybe it's that women will let me take control more than men will." Several men reported that their female colleagues often cast them into leadership roles. . . .

The interviews suggest that the working environment encountered by "nontraditional" male workers is quite unlike that faced by women who work in traditionally male fields. Because it is not uncommon for men in predominantly female professions to be supervised by other men, they tend to have closer rapport and more intimate social relationships with people in management. These ties can facilitate men's careers by smoothing the way for future promotions. Relationships with female supervisors were also described for the most part in positive terms, although in some cases, men perceived an "old girls'" network in place that excluded them from decision making. But in sharp contrast to the reports of women in nontraditional occupations, men in these fields did not complain of feeling discriminated against because they were men. If anything, they felt that being male was an asset that enhanced their career prospects.

Those men interviewed for this study also described congenial workplaces, and a very high level of acceptance from their female colleagues. The sentiment was echoed by women I spoke to who said that they were pleased to see more men enter "their" professions. Some women, however, did express resentment over the "fast-tracking" that their male colleagues seem to experience. But this ambivalence did not translate into a hostile work environment for men: Women generally included men in their informal social events and, in some ways, even facilitated men's careers. By casting men into leadership roles, presuming they were more knowledgeable and qualified, or relying on them to perform certain critical tasks, women unwittingly contributed to the "glass escalator effect" facing men who do "women's work."

Relationships with Clients

Workers in these service-oriented occupations come into frequent contact with the public during the course of their work day. Nurses treat patients; social workers usually have client case loads; librarians serve patrons; and teachers are in constant contact with children, and often with parents as well. Many of those interviewed claimed that the clients they served had different expectations of men and women in these occupations, and often treated them differently.

People react with surprise and often disbelief when they encounter a man in nursing, elementary school teaching, and, to a lesser extent, librarianship. (Usually people have no clear expectations about the sex of social workers.) The stereotypes men face are often negative. For example, according to this Massachusetts nurse, it is frequently assumed that male nurses are gay:

> Fortunately, I carry one thing with me that protects me from [the stereotype that male nurses are gay], and the one thing I carry with me is a wedding ring, and it makes a big difference. The perfect example was conversations before I was married. . . . [People would ask], "Oh, do you have a girlfriend?" Or you'd

hear patients asking questions along that idea, and they were simply implying, "Why is this guy in nursing? Is it because he's gay and he's a pervert?" And I'm not associating the two by any means, but this is the thought process.

. . . It is not uncommon for both gay and straight men in these occupations to encounter people who believe that they are "gay 'til proven otherwise," as one nurse put it. In fact, there are many gay men employed in these occupations. But gender stereotypes are at least as responsible for this general belief as any "empirical" assessment of men's sexual lifestyles. To the degree that men in these professions are perceived as not "measuring up" to the supposedly more challenging occupational roles and standards demanded of "real" men, they are immediately suspected of being effeminate—"like women"—and thus, homosexual.

An equally prevalent sexual stereotype about men in these occupations is that they are potentially dangerous and abusive. Several men described special rules they followed to guard against the widespread presumption of sexual abuse. For example, nurses were sometimes required to have a female "chaperone" present when performing certain procedures or working with specific populations. This psychiatric nurse described a former workplace:

> I worked on a floor for the criminally insane. Pretty threatening work. So you have to have a certain number of females on the floor just to balance out. Because there were female patients on the floor too. And you didn't want to be accused of rape or any sex crimes.

Teachers and librarians described the steps they took to protect themselves from suspicions of sexual impropriety. A kindergarten teacher said:

> I know that I'm careful about how I respond to students. I'm careful in a number of ways—in my physical interaction with students. It's mainly to reassure parents. . . . For example, a little girl was very affectionate, very anxious to give me a hug. She'll just throw herself at me. I need to tell her very carefully: "Sonia, you need

to tell me when you want to hug me." That way I can come down, crouch down. Because you don't want a child giving you a hug on your hip. You just don't want to do that. So I'm very careful about body position.

. . . Although negative stereotypes about men who do "women's work" can push men out of specific jobs, their effects can actually benefit men. Instead of being a source of negative discrimination, these prejudices can add to the "glass escalator effect" by pressuring men to move *out* of the most feminine-identified areas and *up* to those regarded as more legitimate for men. The public's reactions to men working in these occupations, however, are by no means always negative. Several men and women reported that people often assume that men in these occupations are more competent than women, or that they bring special skills and expertise to their professional practice. For example, a female academic librarian told me that patrons usually address their questions to the male reference librarian when there is a choice between asking a male or a female. A male clinical social worker in private practice claimed that both men and women generally preferred male psychotherapists. And several male nurses told me that people often assume that they are physicians and direct their medical inquiries to them instead of to the female nurses.[13]

The presumption that men are more competent than women is another difference in the experience of token men and women. Women who work in nontraditional occupations are often suspected of being incompetent, unable to survive the pressures of "men's work." As a consequence, these women often report feeling compelled to prove themselves and, as the saying goes, "work twice as hard as men to be considered half as good." To the degree that men are assumed to be competent and in control, they may have to be twice as incompetent to be considered half as bad. One man claimed that "if you're a mediocre male teacher, you're considered a better teacher than if you're a female and a mediocre teacher. I think there's that prejudice there." . . .

There are different standards and assumptions about men's competence that follow them into nontraditional occupations. In contrast, women in both traditional and nontraditional occupations must contend with the presumption that they are neither competent nor qualified. . . .

The reasons that clients give for preferring or rejecting men reflect the complexity of our society's stereotypes about masculinity and femininity. Masculinity is often associated with competence and mastery, in contrast to femininity, which is often associated with instrumental incompetence. Because of these stereotypes, men are perceived as being stricter disciplinarians and stronger than women, and thus better able to handle violent or potentially violent situations. . . .

Conclusion

Both men and women who work in nontraditional occupations encounter discrimination, but the forms and the consequences of this discrimination are very different for the two groups. Unlike "nontraditional" women workers, most of the discrimination and prejudice facing men in the "female" professions comes from clients. For the most part, the men and women I interviewed believed that men are given fair—if not preferential—treatment in hiring and promotion decisions, are accepted by their supervisors and colleagues, and are well-integrated into the workplace subculture. Indeed, there seem to be subtle mechanisms in place that enhance men's positions in these professions—a phenomenon I refer to as a "glass escalator effect."

Men encounter their most "mixed" reception in their dealings with clients, who often react negatively to male nurses, teachers, and to a lesser extent, librarians. Many people assume that the men are sexually suspect if they are employed in these "feminine" occupations either because they do or they do not conform to stereotypical masculine characteristics.

Dealing with the stress of these negative stereotypes can be overwhelming, and it probably pushes some men out of these occupations.[14] The challenge facing the men who stay in these fields is to accentuate their positive contribution to what our society defines as essentially "women's work." . . .

NOTES

1. Allan Angoff, "The Male Librarian—An Anomaly?" *Library Journal,* February 15, 1959, p. 553.

2. *Austin-American Statesman,* January 16, 1990; response by John Kelso, January 18, 1990.

3. Some of the most important studies of women in male-dominated occupations are: Rosabeth Moss Kanter, *Men and Women of the Corporation* (New York: Basic Books, 1977); Susan Martin, *Breaking and Entering: Policewomen on Patrol* (Berkeley: University of California Press, 1980); Cynthia Fuchs Epstein, *Women in Law* (New York: Basic Books, 1981); Kay Deaux and Joseph Ullman, *Women of Steel* (New York: Praeger, 1983); Judith Hicks Stiehm, *Arms and the Enlisted Woman* (Philadelphia: Temple University Press, 1989); Jerry Jacobs, *Revolving Doors: Sex Segregation and Women's Careers* (Stanford: Stanford University Press, 1989); Barbara Reskin and Patricia Roos, *Job Queues, Gender Queues: Explaining Women's Inroads into Male Occupations* (Philadelphia: Temple University Press, 1990).

Among the few books that do examine men's status in predominantly female occupations are Carol Tropp Schreiber, *Changing Places: Men and Women in Transitional Occupations* (Cambridge: MIT Press, 1979); Christine L. Williams, *Gender Differences at Work: Women and Men in Nontraditional Occupations* (Berkeley: University of California Press, 1989); and Christine L. Williams, ed., *Doing "Women's Work": Men in Nontraditional Occupations* (Newbury Park, CA: Sage Publications, 1993).

4. In an influential essay on methodological principles, Herbert Blumer counseled sociologists to "sedulously seek participants in the sphere of life who are acute observers and who are well informed. One such person is worth a hundred others who are merely unobservant participants." See "The Methodological Position of Symbolic Interactionism," in *Symbolic Interactionism: Perspective and Method* (Berkeley: University of California Press, 1969), p. 41.

5. The overall proportions in the population do not necessarily represent the experiences of individuals in my sample. Some nurses, for example, worked in groups that were composed almost entirely of men, while some social workers had the experience of being the only man in their group. The overall statistics provide a general guide, but relying on them exclusively can distort the actual experiences of individuals in the workplace. The statistics available for research on occupational sex segregation are not specific enough to measure internal divisions among workers. Research that uses firm-level data finds a far greater degree of segregation than research that uses national data. See William T. Bielby and James N. Baron, "A Woman's Place Is with Other Women: Sex Segregation within Organizations," in *Sex Segregation in the Workplace: Trends, Explanations, Remedies,* ed. Barbara Reskin (Washington, D.C.: National Academy Press, 1984), pp. 27–55.

6. Catharine MacKinnon, *Feminism Unmodified* (Cambridge: Harvard University Press, 1987), pp. 24–25.

7. Howard S. Rowland, *The Nurse's Almanac,* 2d ed. (Rockville, MD: Aspen Systems Corp., 1984), p. 153; Johw W. Wright, *The American Almanac of Jobs and Salaries,* 2d ed. (New York: Avon, 1984), p. 639.

8. King Research, Inc., *Library Human Resources: A Study of Supply and Demand* (Chicago: American Library Association, 1983), p. 41.

9. See, for example, Sue J. M. Freeman, *Managing Lives: Corporate Women and Social Change* (Amherst: University of Massachusetts Press, 1990).

10. Patricia A. Schmuck, "Women School Employees in the United States," in *Women Educators: Employees of Schools in Western Countries* (Albany: State University of New York Press, 1987), p. 85; James W. Grimm and Robert N. Stern, "Sex Roles and Internal Labor Market Structures: The Female Semi-Professions," *Social Problems* 21(1974): 690–705.

11. David A. Hardcastle and Arthur J. Katz, *Employment and Unemployment in Social Work: A Study of NASW Members* (Washington, D.C.: NASW, 1979), p. 41; Reginold O. York, H. Carl Henley and Dorothy N. Gamble, "Sexual Discrimination in Social Work: Is It Salary or Advancement?" *Social Work* 32 (1987): 336–340; Grimm and Stern, "Sex Roles and Internal Labor Market Structures."

12. Leigh Estabrook, "Women's Work in the Library/Information Sector," in *My Troubles Are Going to Have Trouble with Me,* ed. Karen Brodkin Sacks and Dorothy Remy (New Brunswick, NJ: Rutgers University Press, 1984), p. 165.

13. Liliane Floge and D. M. Merrill found a similar phenomenon in their study of male nurses. See "Tokenism Reconsidered: Male Nurses and Female Physicians in a Hospital Setting," Social Forces 64 (1986): 931–932.

14. Jim Allan makes this argument in "Male Elementary Teachers: Experiences and Perspectives," in Doing "Women's Work": Men in Nontraditional Occupations, ed. Christine L. Williams (Newbury Park, CA: Sage Publications, 1993), pp. 113–127.

THINKING ABOUT THE READING

Compare the discrimination men experience in traditionally female occupations to that experienced by women in traditionally male occupations. What is the "glass escalator effect"? In what ways can the glass escalator actually be harmful to men? What do you suppose might happen to the structure of the American labor force if men did in fact begin to enter predominantly female occupations in the same proportion as women entering predominantly male occupations?

13

The Global Dynamics of Population: Demographic Trends

In the past several chapters we have examined the various interrelated sources of social stratification. Race, class, and gender continue to determine access to cultural, economic, and political opportunities. Yet another source of inequality that we don't think much about but that has enormous local, national, and global significance is the changing size and shape of the human population. Globally, population imbalances between richer and poorer societies underlie most if not all of the other important forces for change that are taking place today. Poor, developing countries are expanding rapidly, while the populations in wealthy, developed countries have either stabilized or, in some cases, declined. When the population of a country grows rapidly, the age structure is increasingly dominated by young people. In slow-growth countries with low birthrates and high life expectancy, the population is much older.

Often overlooked in our quest to identify the structural factors that shape our everyday experiences are the effects of our *birth cohort*. Birth cohorts are more than just a collection of individuals born within a few years of each other; they are distinctive generations tied together by historical events, national and global population trends, and large-scale societal changes.

We hear a lot of criticism about the youthful generation of Americans in their teens and early twenties. The news media depict them as a directionless wasteland of academic underachievement, political apathy, disease-ridden sex, and reckless self-absorption. In their article, "Planet Pokémon," Neil Howe and William Strauss examine the lives and futures of the Millennial Generation, those individuals born after 1982. These young people take for granted the privileges and choices past generations struggled to obtain. As such, their world is a significantly more stable place than the world of young people as recently as 10 years ago. The authors predict that teenagers in North America will exert enormous—and for the most part, positive—global influence in the years to come. In describing the characteristics of this generation they provide a vivid illustration of the importance of birth cohorts on our everyday experiences.

As social and demographic conditions in poor, developing countries grow worse, pressures to migrate increase, creating a variety of cultural, political, and economic fears in countries experiencing high levels of immigration. Immigration—both legal and illegal—has become one of the most contentious political issues in the United States today. While politicians debate proposed immigration restrictions, people from all corners of the globe continue to come to this country looking for a better life. In

"Border Blues: Mexican Immigration and Mexican-American Identity," Farai Chideya describes life on the U.S.–Mexico border from the perspective of both border patrol agents and the immigrants themselves. Chideya points out that conflict over illegal immigration is not between the United States and Mexico, but between the various visions of what Mexican immigration means to the United States. Although some people decry the waves of illegal immigration as a burden and a scourge on society, others profit from the cheap labor that illegal immigrants provide.

Planet Pokémon

Neil Howe and William Strauss

Colors of the world
Spice up your life
—Spice Girls, "Spice Up Your Life"

Pokémon, you're my best friend
In the world we must defend
— *Pokémon* opening

On January 1, 2000, Nickelodeon broadcast clips of preteen kids from around the world, cheerily talking about the future. From all continents, kids of all cultures and races predicted how science and technology would solve problems large and small. Progress was a given. Scourges like war, poverty, and totalitarianism were seldom on their minds.

This program was distinctly Millennial. Back in the Boomer child years, satellites hadn't yet been launched to allow such conversations. In the Gen-X child years, the satellites were going up, but transoceanic discussions seldom included children, who had yet to become a global priority. The most interesting difference, though, lay in the new child sunniness. Turn-of-the-millennium triumphalism has touched not only American children, but those elsewhere as well.

Reflect on what earlier kids would have said (had such a global conversation been possible) during the Boomer, and Gen-X child eras. In 1960, kids knew that their parents had fought in terrible wars for or against terrible dictators, that science had invented H-bombs, and that computers might well empower Big Brother. In 1980, through a child's eye, the world was full of family and economic turmoil—overshadowed by a Cold War threat from two superpowers who had enough warheads to destroy the world in fifteen minutes. But today, the world's children pay little mind to those old anxieties. They're growing up in a different time.

Much as American millennials share a *national* location in history, kids around the world today share a *global* one, based on both cultural and family trends as well as changes in geopolitics and technology.

Are they a global generation? Indeed, is there ever such a thing as a global generation?

Since World War II, if not earlier, the answer to the second question is yes. Throughout the developed world, the Depression and total-war decades of the 1930s and (especially) 1940s left a life-cycle mark on everyone who participated, according to their age—on midlife parents, on young-adult soldiers, on growing children, and even on the babies born in the immediate aftermath. One could say that global generations began to take shape in the 1940s, even if no one yet spoke of humanity in those terms.

The first self-conscious announcement of a transatlantic youth kinship came with the "generation of 1968," when American and European collegians shared new bonds of music, drugs, blue jeans, and riots against whatever their parents expected them to do. In the years since, as global travel, culture, commerce, and telecommunications have grown, a larger share of the world's youths have come to share common life-cycle markers—the Berlin Wall's collapse, Tiananmen Square, Desert Storm, Princess Di's death, Michael Jordan, *Titanic*—prompting talk of a global Gen X. Every year, satellite news, pop culture, and the internet gain more cementing power over the world's young people.

Since World War II, much of the world has seen six generations, each with its own linkage with events, each with its own persona.

Global Generations

. . . The foot soldiers of World War I . . . became the generals and home-front managers of World War II—and, afterward, the initial shapers and leaders of a bipolar world. Through the Boomer childhood, they included Harry Truman, Dwight Eisenhower, Dean Acheson, and John Foster Dulles, the creators of survivalist Cold War defense posture that remained essentially intact through the 1980s. Overseas, this no-nonsense generation encompassed the likes of Konrad Adenauer, Charles de Gaulle, Nikita Khrushchev, and Mao Zedong (and the despised memories of Hitler, Tojo, and Mussolini). In the year 2000, their survivors are over age 100. Throughout the world, this is the group that, for ill or good, most deserves to be called the World War II Generation—but, instead, they're known in the United States as the Lost Generation, in Europe as the "generation of 1914" or (in France) *génération au feu.*

The next generation, now in their late seventies and beyond, is more familiar: Allied and Axis soldiers, revolution and resistance cadre, Rosie-the-Riveters and nuclear scientists. Their impact on world history peaked young, in the 1940s. Their global impact as national leaders peaked much later, around 1970, with several of their larger-than-life members staying at the helm well into the 1980s and '90s. In America, this G.I. Generation held the White House for thirty-two years, from John Kennedy through George [H. W.] Bush. Overseas, they have been known as the generation of the Long March (Chou En-lai, Deng Xiaoping), of the Blitz (Mrs. Miniver, Margaret Thatcher), of the Resistance (François Mitterand, Giulio Andreotti), and of the Great Patriotic War (Leonid Brezhnev, Yuri Andropov). From China to Russia to Europe to the United States, they are still associated with civic deeds and big institutions.

Next comes the grown-up children of World War II, now between their late fifties and early seventies, a generation that has produced the likes of Boris Yeltsin, Jiang Zemin, Helmut Kohl, Jacques Chirac, John Major, Kofi Annan, Romano Prodi, and Buru Utara Barat. Around the world, these war-era children grew up so seared by organized hatred that they have spent a lifetime trying to spare their own children from similar horrors. From one continent to another, they have become global technocrats who tout diplomacy, communication, and compromise—while old alliances meander and old empires splinter. In Europe, the peers of Anne Frank (in England, the "Air Raid" generation) grew up to be the '80s-era Eurocrats who staked their future on miltilaterlism, the Euro, and increased cross-border trade. In the Soviet Union, the "glasnost generation" presided over the dismantlement of their own empire over the objections of older war heroes. In Canada, today's sixtysomethings furnish the patient conciliators for endless separatist arguments. In America, the Silent Generation could become the first never to occupy the White House.

The familiar generation now rising to the top of the world's power pyramid consists of the middle-aged postwar children who lack personal memory of World War II; who came of age amid sixties youth riots, seventies anti-Americanism, and the Chinese Cultural Revolution; and who now mix varying degrees of moralism, nationalism, ironic detachment, and inward satisfaction. The name Boomers, now heard outside North America, is attachable to the likes of Tony Blair, Gerhard Schroeder, Javier Solana, Vladimir Putin, Joerg Haider, and Benyamin Netanyahu. While this generation has thus far made only a light impact on world affairs, its ethnic hatreds ravaged former Yugoslavia and its moralism transformed NATO into a more aggressive military body. A youth generation that announced itself with ideology and terror (Red Guard, Baader-Meinhof, the IRA, the Weathermen) has today matured into the global age bracket most inclined to use military force. Already its loud debates over values, standards, and "third way" realignments reflect the inner passions of Vladimir Putin–style nationalists and Falun Gong–style spiritualists, with more waiting in the wings.

Lately, the world generation receiving the most media attention has been the global "Gen X," a name used along with " '90s generation" and (in France) *génération bof,* as in "who cares?" Global Gen Xers are acquiring a reputation as fun-loving and rootless, pragmatic and market-oriented, environmentalist and entrepreneurial, technologically smarter but otherwise dumber than older people, and far less interested in politics than in business. From London to Singapore, young adults are the free-agent nomads at the cutting edge of the new global economy and its culture. The high-tech IPO is their pride, temp work their curse. In fledgling capitalist countries (China, Russia, Eastern Europe), young adults comprise the *byiznyizmyin* who are handling the transition to freer markets—and, typically, they're faring better than older pensioners. In more-settled societies (Japan, Western Europe), they're doing substantially worse. One-third of young-adult Italians not in school are jobless, with more living at home with parents than at any time since the Great Depression.

What about the world's teenagers? Only in the United States and Canada have educators, political leaders, and the media identified a post-X adolescent generation. Outside North America, the term "Generation X" is still used much more widely than any other term to refer to teenagers. The "global teen" focus is far less on politics or ideology than on technology, family success, moneymaking, fun, and other quality-of-life issues. They're rootless, with 38 percent not expecting to live in the country of their birth. They believe in their right to go wherever they want to work or play—or in having that work or play delivered to them in a nanosecond, on their doorstep or at their PC. In 1998, a British study of a so-called English "Millennial Generation" found youths between the ages of 16 and 21 to be cynical (44 percent thinking that "most people can't be believed"), risk takers, and strong Labour and

Blair supporters. Nearly half want to own their own business, and only 1 percent list a job in civil service as a career goal. Seven in ten see voting as pointless, and most oppose bans on smoking in public places.

Some of these traits clearly aren't in sync with the U.S. Millennial Generation. The reason? *Abroad, the leading edge of a new Millennial generation, in most countries, probably has not yet reached its teens.* This misalignment dates back to how different societies experienced World War II. "Most contemporary European and Asian generations are at least five years younger than their American counterparts," explains war historian Davis Kaiser, "because it took at least that long for their societies to become stabilized after the Second World War." Where Americans began to talk and feel "postwar" even before VJ Day, other nations—Japan, Germany, Italy, China, Russia, even (to a lesser degree) Britain—had to deal with far more residual wreckage and suffering. North America produced an earlier (and much larger) postwar "baby boom" than Europe or Asia. Among global Boomers, therefore, the "postwar" mind-set attached to different birth-year boundaries.

Similarly, the conditions that produced global Gen Xers came later to nations outside North America. Europe's youth tumult didn't begin until 1968, when America's was already well under way (explaining why even Parisians could learn from Berkeley "veterans" about what to do with a billowing tear gas cannister). Where America's youth unrest ebbed after 1971, China's persisted for another five years. Today's triumphal individualism reached America ahead of other societies. The Clinton era crescendoed a few years before Blair's "Cool Britannia," while global Boomers elsewhere are just now making their mark.

For Millennials, the difference came with America's prior (early '80s) shift in popular attitudes toward babies and small children—a trend that didn't reach the rest of the world until around 1989, the year the United Nations began taking children's issues seriously. While the first discovery of new-style teens occurred in the

United States and Canada in 1997, with the new teen pop music, this trend is just now reaching England and remains weaker elsewhere. And while youth violence is on the wane in the United States, it's still on the rise in Japan and much of Western Europe. Nowhere has there been nearly the same interest in post-X teens and children as in the primarily English-speaking countries.

America's Millennial-child fixation has had a global penumbra. Other nations see the same CNN camera shots Americans do, of global children in distress. Over the past two decades, the unrelenting pro-child crusading of the U.S. cultural elite has spread to the elites of other countries, helping to propel a new activism by multilateral agencies. European hysteria over child abuse (in Belgium) and school shootings (in Scotland) has furthered this momentum. In November 1989, just after the Berlin Wall fell, the United Nations hosted a Convention on the Rights of the Child (which, since then, has been ratified by every nation in the world except Somalia and the United States). In the ten years since, new multinational agreements have been reached on such agendas as discouraging the use of children as soldiers, regularizing cross-national adoptions, prohibiting the worst forms of child labor, and stepping up the prosecution of war crimes against children.

So even if the Millennial child era is arriving later in many countries, it has recently gained real force. In the 1990s, over fifty nations amended their constitutions or legal codes to improve the status of children. Japan, Thailand, and the Philippines, long the locus of "child sex holidays" and child pornography films, have imposed strict new laws against both. Sri Lanka raised the age of sexual consent from 12 to 16. In Indonesia, the World Bank is testing a new plan to pay school costs to keep small kids out of the work force. Sweden banned TV ads aimed at children, and Italy, Poland, Denmark, and Latvia may soon follow. Greece wants to ban ads targeting anybody under age 18. Brazil's national budget now shows how much money is spent on children. Through the spring of 2000, the fate of 6-year-old Elián

González dominated the news across the western hemisphere.

The only significant exception appears to be in the Islamic world, where World War II did not create similar generations, and whose cultural defenses are stronger. Islamic nations have joined neither the downward global fertility trend nor the trend toward market-oriented individualism.

In summary, global Millennials seem to be most concentrated in societies that share a fairly similar generational constellation: East Asia, China, all of Europe, Russia, and the more prosperous nations of Latin America. Their birth-year boundaries vary. American and Canadian teens are at the leading edge. In Britain and Australia, the Post-X generation seems to be two or three years younger, and in the non-English-speaking developed world, several years younger still. This means that Americans and Canadians born between 1982 and 1985 lie across a generational divide from like-aged teenagers in most other countries, who remain X-like. But today's global "tweeners" (born in the late '80s) and younger kids (born in the '90s) share tighter links—from their post–Cold War location in history to their more protective parental nurturing style to their elevated status in the national media.

To picture first-wave global Millennials, think of the age bracket corresponding to tens of millions of Pokémon fans, from 12-year-olds on master-trainer sites to 6-year-olds with their Pikachu figures. By the time these youth legions reach their teens and evolve to the next level, Millennials will begin to recognize themselves as a truly worldwide phenomenon.

Global Millennials

What distinguishes global Millennials from global Gen Xers? As in America, look at their location in history.

Look first at the worldwide fertility rate, whose change over the birth eras of the last three global generations reveals a sudden and stunning change. In the early 1950s (early global Boom births) the rate was 5.0 births per woman. In the late 1970s (early Gen-X births) it was nearly the

Total Fertility Rate for World and Selected Regions, 1950 to 2000

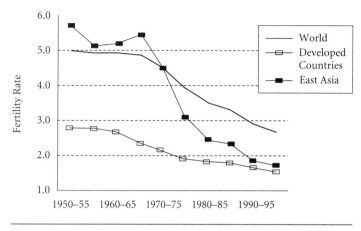

Rates are five-year averages; 1995–2000 is the official UN projection.
Source: United Nations (1999).

same, at 4.9 births per woman. But by the late 1980s (early global Millennial births), it had fallen to 3.3 births per woman—and by the year 2000, it has fallen even further to 2.7.

These declines were especially pronounced in Latin America (5.6 to 3.4) and in East Asia (5.5 to 2.4), led in the latter case by the antinatal policies of the Chinese government. In the developed countries, the average fertility rate by the late 1980s (1.8) had sunk well below the "replacement rate" necessary to keep the population from ultimately shrinking. The main global exceptions to rapidly falling fertility during the Gen-X birth era were the Islamic world and sub-Saharan Africa.

Where Boomers were the children of a fertility "boom" or plateau and Gen Xers the children of a fertility "bust," global Millennials are the children of a lower yet newly stable fertility pattern that reflects an emerging family ethnic favoring "quality over quantity." Throughout most of the developed (and developing) world—China, Japan, Russia, Mexico, Europe—smaller families are now the norm. Beijing's mandate limiting urban Han Chinese to one child per couple is producing what they call the "Peach" generation, only one seed per fruit. The Japanese

have their "Little Emperors," Latin societies their *hijos únicos.*

Look also at the signal event of the late twentieth century—the end of the Cold War—and how that separates today's two youngest generations. Where global Gen Xers grew up with the waning of the Cold War, global Millennials are the first true post–Cold War generation, with no personal recollection of what Ronald Reagan famously called "the Evil Empire." Global Gen Xers arrived in a dangerously armed yet more stable bipolar world, in which America led one of two competing world systems. Global Millenials entered a less immediately endangered yet more disordered unipolar world, in which America rides supreme. To most of the world's 1.5 billion preteens, no ideology competes with the American model—which to them means a world in which ordinary people can do basically what they want and prosper.

During the 1950s, when global Boomers were kids, adults feared that the natural outcome for low-civic-energy societies was totalitarian dictatorship. During the Gen-X child era, that perception gradually changed. Millennials are now arriving in a world replete with democratization and individualism, technology and commercialism—all triumphant, all still expanding, and all apparently requiring not one iota of civic effort to sweep everything else away. As many kids understand it, the tide is unstoppable and will soon wrap around the globe. According to Freedom House, 14 percent of the world's countries (with 31 percent of the world's population) were democracies in 1950, expanding to 62 percent of the countries (and 58 percent of the people) in the year 2000. Again, as with population, the Boomer child era was static, young Gen Xers witnessed the most change, and young Millennials are stepping into the new reality.

The Vietnam War seems odd, in the hindsight perspective of a middle schooler studying history for the first time: Why would the United States fight for years at such cost when it could have just quit and watched both North and South Vietnam become market-oriented societies within a year or two? Global Millennials have never known a world in which democracy had to pay an enormous price in lives and resources to defend itself against enemies. They only know a world in which high-tech wars can be waged and won with zero casualties to the richer side. They look upon the United States as a rich *and* easy society, running on its own momentum, presided over by leaders who symbolize good times, personal pleasures, and ever-expanding wallets.

For today's preteens, the freedom to move across borders is an established fact. Global Boomers assumed that you stayed put in the country in which you were born—unless (like some U.S. draft resisters) you had a political reason to leave. When global Gen Xers were children, that assumption gave way to a new, more economically driven mobility across borders. Yet even the youngest global Gen Xer can recall a time before the collapse of the Soviet "iron curtain." Today's global Millennials, by contrast, have trouble imagining a world in which any family cannot emigrate if it wants to or needs to badly enough.

The world's youth culture has shown a similar transition, dating back to the first postwar years. Global Boomers were children at a time when indigenous cultures reigned nearly everywhere and

"American culture"—then an oxymoron—was perceived as bland and corny by post-war youth nearly everywhere. This global perception changed during the 1960's and '70s. When Gen Xers were children, American TV, movies, and music began to innovate, experiment, and spread through much of the world. By the late '80s and '90s, while U.S. Millennials were children, the entertainment industry learned how to profit from the export of a culture consistently more profane and violent than the domestic culture. Today, to children around the world, "American culture" means the *opposite* of bland and corny. Anyone tired of feature-length cartoons, *Titanic,* and boy bands can easily turn the channel to unprintable song lyrics, sexually charged TV shows, and movies overflowing with casual violence.

Now add technology to this mix. The world's Boomers grew up with domestically produced movies and TV shows. Gen Xers grew up with VCRs and the rise of personal computers. The idea of worldwide high-tech linkages dawned while they were still children. Millennials are growing up *after* this has already happened. For most American children, satellites, cable TV, cell phones, and the internet are a given. For most children elsewhere, those devices remain dreams—but dreams they expect will soon become a shared reality. Even if the kids in some European town or remote Asian village don't yet have cable, the internet, and cell phones, they can assume they probably will by the time they reach adulthood. Where global Gen Xers feel they are pioneering a new high-tech frontier, Millennials are growing up as that frontier is being settled—and, in time, will adapt the new technologies to suit themselves.

Millennials Mobilize

While teens in the rest of the world still look very much like X, or (in Britain) its fading shadow, teens in the United States and Canada are taking the lead in showing the world what comes after X. Others, from Tokyo to Berlin, may contribute plenty of new fads in dress and language. And others may later catch up—as Europeans did with Boomers by the late '60s, and as Europeans, Asians, and Russians did with Gen Xers by the early '90s. But for now, U.S. and Canadian youths are the initiators, the pathbreakers, the exemplars of what's new.

Where North American teenagers stand in the year 2000 is similar to where the continent's Boomers stood around 1960 and Gen Xers around 1980—an as-yet-unheralded opening wedge of a global youth movement. To the extent U.S. and Canadian Millennials anticipate this global change—the more they correct for Boomers, turn away from the Gen-X style, and fill the roles vacated by G.I.s—the more leadership they can provide for today's global children when the latter pass through their teens. And to the extent North American teens can fuse bits and pieces of other cultures into a new generational amalgam, the more they can set the trends for the global approach of the Millennial teen.

To date, U.S. and Canadian teens have been doing this. From Boston to Vancouver, L.A. to Halifax, they have been tracking down offerings from all continents—toys and games from here, books and music from there. Whatever they decide they like, they make popular by chatting it up in various media (including the internet), after which younger kids around the world follow their lead.

No other North American child generation ever borrowed so much from so many cultures other than its own. The Boomer childhood was distinctly nativist—and when Boomers came of age, the geographic origin of their youth trends was always clear, whether music from England, clothing from Italy, philosophy from France, or religion from India. In the Gen-X child era, multiculturalism was spreading rapidly, and by the time they reached young adulthood, their global links were subsumed in a vast mishmash of trends. Among Millennial children, this mishmash is all they've ever known, and the multicultural linkages are so pervasive that the national identities of today's youth trends are often hard to pin down. A telling example is the Pokémon game and TV show, known to American kids by its Japanese name but still known to

Japanese kids by an earlier English name, Pocket Monsters.

True to the second-generation immigrant pattern, Millennials are today forging a mind-set borrowed from bits and pieces of their countries of origin. The amalgam is part Ricky Martin, part Harry Potter, part Lego, part Kwanzaa, and part Pokémon. Among those culture groups, kids find unprecedented diversity—and from each, they can extract elements that feel (to them) stylistically fresh and socially corrective. From Latino cultures they find family values, upbeat attitudes, bright colors, and wider gender roles (with men who actually dance with women). From Europeans, they find political history, rules and codes, puzzles and other geometric toys, challenging pedagogy, and structured knowledge. From Africans, they can obtain close community rituals and the courage to assist peers in need. From East Asia, they learn teamwork, honor, deference to tradition, and respect for elders. These cultures offer far broader values than just these, of course—but Millennials are selecting only the aspects of those cultures that comport with their global persona.

The cutting edge of this mind-set is less among today's teens than among "tweens" born in the late '80s and early '90s. By the time today's third through sixth graders fill U.S. high schools—and (unlike first-wave Millennials) feel a bona fide generational kinship with global peers—they could be even busier sifting and sorting from among the world's cultures, coming up with their own distinctly post-X blend and exporting it back to the world.

With the dawning of a new century, American Millennials are on the verge of broadcasting their viewpoint and style throughout the world. By the late '60s, American Boomers had launched their global peers on countless crusades of liberation (from technology, among other things). By the late '80s, Gen Xers were setting the global teen standard for a fully liberated consumerism, the commercialism to serve it, and new personal technologies. Millennials are well on the path to setting a global standard for a politics and economics that takes aggressive consumerism and unfettered commercialism as its starting point, and which seeks new community uses for technology.

U.S. and Canadian Millennial teens are already asserting a leadership role among their age mates around the world. One reason is that, in the manner of elder siblings, North Americans are reaching the new generational mind-set ahead of the others. That's what makes overseas kids *ready* to pay attention to them. Another reason is their extraordinary pan-global diversity, through which kids from nearly every corner of the world can find bits and pieces of themselves in what goes on here. That makes kids overseas *willing* to follow their lead. A third reason is the ability of kids from so many countries to communicate with one another—and develop a sense of shared community—through the internet. That's how kids elsewhere are *able* to keep up with American and Canadian Millennials.

Teens here are, along with Australians, the world's most aggressive and skillful navigators of the internet. For this, they owe a debt to older generations who provided the necessary tools and training. In 1999, 25 percent of U.S. households had web hookups, versus 13 percent in Japan, 9 percent in Great Britain, 7 percent in Germany, and 4 percent in Italy—and among all global teens on-line, North Americans are the ones most likely to use the web for news, entertainment, purchases, and political action.

Older North American generations are boosting their kids' leadership role by focusing so fervently on children's issues and by constantly repeating the mantra that children are the future. Their own kids naturally focus on these issues, accept this mantra, see their global dimensions, go on-line to learn more about them, link up with kids from other countries, and begin to take action.

Kids around the world are themselves noticing the high Clinton-era priority that Americans place on the welfare of children—not just in their own domestic policies but in their major actions abroad. What causes the United States to intervene in locales such as Somalia, Haiti, Bosnia, or Kosovo? U.S.-produced images of children, broadcast all over the world on satellite TV. Which nationality is most conspicuously willing to adopt orphaned children, no matter how sick? Whose army is most often used for humanitarian reasons? America's movie and CD exports may be violent and profane, its president may constantly preach morals to the world as the world snickers at his, its armies may be forward-positioned in more places than ever—all that may be true and more—but from the standpoint of today's global kids, no people stand readier than Americans to spend their treasure and risk their lives in order to help children anywhere who fall victim to wars, earthquakes, hurricanes, floods, famines, and disease.

These are positive things, duly noted around the planet, which have the effect of enhancing the American Millennials' budding leadership role among their global peers. In a letter to the *Junior Journal*, Taiwan teen Chen Jun-Lin quoted the Backstreet Boys to offer her view from across the Pacific: "I don't care who you are, where you're from, what you did, as long as you love me." Life remains wretched for millions of kids in a world where, each day, 32,000 children under the age of 5 die of preventable causes. Older people sympathize, but assume nothing much can be done. Today's kids are shedding that fatalism and are trying to find a new challenge by taking on soluble global ills every generation before them has come to tolerate.

"Through friendships and fibre-optic cables," says the web site of the global teen activist Nation 1, "youth are taking positive action to shape their planet. The Youth Movement consists of many remarkable projects all over the globe. However, for the true power of youth to be realised, it is imperative that we unite, by using what we know best: technology." Nation 1's organizing motto—"connecting and empowering youth"—speaks to this rising generation's *modus*. Its global-action web sites don't look anything like the noisy, dumbed-down sites older people often design to attract teen visitors. Instead, they are simple, uncluttered, and briskly informative, with trim fonts and clean designs, and proudly state their linkages with the adult institutional world without a trace of Boomer coyness or Gen-X cynicism. They bristle with action plans, lists of prior achievements, and no-nonsense requests for help,

Usually, Millennial internet activists target their own global peers—children on all continents who are abused, hungry, or otherwise hurting. The number-one geographic focus is Africa, whose kids inhabit a bottomless pit of suffering and need. In a vast arc reaching from Sudan across Rwanda and Congo to Angola, an estimated 60,000 children under 15 have been pressed into combat and fight in wars that rage on even after the next-older, soldier-age generation has been largely wasted. Tens of thousands of Sudanese children are enslaved, which has prompted a vast effort by a hundred American middle schools to demand, or buy, their freedom.

The cruelest childhood scourge is AIDS (in Africa, "slim disease"). It has killed so many parents that many villages now contain only the very old and very young. Through this year, nearly ten million African children under 15 have lost their mothers, or both parents, to AIDS. In 1997-98 alone, the number of new orphans was utterly staggering: over one million in Uganda alone, another million in Kenya, Zambia, and Zimbabwe, half a million in Tanzania—even 180,000 in the more prosperous South Africa. "Nobody has an excuse for apathy," writes *Newsweek*. Here lies a great Millennial challenge: Can they rescue their African peers? Can they apply science—or change human behavior—to prevent the next generation from being ravaged even worse? Surely, many will try.

When Millennials get busy, they get results. To date, no one has gotten more results than a 1982-born Canadian, Craig Kielburger. When he was 12, Craig read a *Toronto Star* article about a Pakistani boy his age who had been sold into bondage as a carpet weaver and who one day dared to speak out against child labor—and then was murdered.

Reading that story changed Craig's life. Within five years, Craig (now 17) and his friends had succeeded in establishing Free the Children, a power-packed global youth army with 100,000 volunteers in more than twenty countries. Using the internet and working closely with a variety of public and private organizations, Craig's group has helped build child-worker rehabilitation sites in Asia, set up job cooperatives for mothers of Latin American child workers (enabling the latter to go to school), create rescue homes for Middle Eastern camel jockeys, extract Filipino children from the sex trade, and organize a European boycott of carpets that lack a "rugmark" guaranteeing they are not made by small children. Their volunteers have aided hurricane relief in Nicaragua, sent health kits and baby items to Kosovo, campaigned to get the police to assist Mexico's child beggars, and sought to criminalize "child sex tourism." Free the Children's new goal is to mobilize global teens to get their governments to ban the worst forms of child labor and criminally punish those who are responsible.

When in history has any single group of kids launched so many activities, on so many continents, on behalf of so many less-fortunate members of their own generation? Kudos to Craig Kielburger—and to the internet, without which Free the Children might never have gained traction. Yet for this cause to have gone so far so fast, more was required than energetic kids with high-tech tools. Adults worldwide have been totally supportive in ways they would not have been in earlier eras. Teenage good-deed-doing on a global scale would have seemed incomprehensible in the 1940s, ridiculous in the 1960s, implausible in the 1980s. Today, it makes sense, and it happens.

More, much more, is still to come. As U.S. and Canadian Millennials get older, they will continue to mobilize their global generation. Perhaps, as young adults, they will not deem the plight of their African (and other Third World) peers so far beyond hope as today's older generations seem to think. Who knows what good they can someday do?

But the world cannot assume that Millennial deed-doing will always be so benign. What many of today's global Boomers now fear—a perpetuation of global Gen X, with all the splintery cynicism and hardscrabble nomadism that implies—will not be the coming youth problem. Instead, there will be other dangers, coming from unexpected directions. The budding power of this global generation could soon be a source of immense civic energy, for good *or* ill, throughout the world.

The children who have attracted such intense public concern throughout the developed world will reach their teens in the Oh-Ohs and come of age as adults in the Oh-Teens. As they do, their nations may be inclined to mobilize against any obstacle standing in their way. This could pit U.S. Millennials against Millennials abroad (the Chinese "Peach" generation?) or against young Islamics who will not share the same generational kinship. Let's hope that it will do neither—that it will instead pit Millennials *with* Millennials against some of the great unmet challenges facing all of humanity.

One prediction can safely be made. By the time today's "tweens" come fully of age as adults, the world will understand that it has not reached the end of history. And by the time today's newborns come fully of age about a quarter century from now, the world will understand that history has *restarted*, powerfully, with a new burst of youthful energy.

THINKING ABOUT THE READING

Even though the Millennial generation is more "global" than any previous generation, other countries don't seem to acknowledge it. Why not? Why is this generation such a powerful force in the United States and Canada but not elsewhere? How do Millennials differ from the cohort that immediately preceded them: Generation X? How are they alike? To what generation do you belong? Baby boom? Generation X? Millennial? How do you characterize those older and younger than you? In what ways do you think your generation (cohort) influences your everyday life?

Border Blues

Mexican Immigration and Mexican-American Identity

Farai Chideya

The land around El Paso, Texas, is an imposing desert scene painted in tones of ochre and red clay—stark mountains, vast sky, arid plains. It's so far west that it's the only major Texas city in the mountain, rather than the central, time zone. Atop a nearby mountain is the massive Christo Rey—an imposing figure of Jesus hewn out of tons of stone. It seems like a peaceful vista, but this land is the staging ground for a colossal clash of cultures—the meeting of Mexico and the United States at the border. The biggest clash is not between Mexico and the United States per se, but between many competing visions of what Mexican immigration means to the United States. Mexican immigration has been decried as an "illegal alien invasion," an erosion of American's job base, even the beginnings of a plot to return the Southwest to Mexican hands. And sometimes Mexican Americans themselves are perceived with suspicion, in the belief their allegiance is pledged to Mexico, not the United States.

What's the reality behind these perceptions? And what's life on the border like? . . . I've spent virtually my whole life living on the East Coast, where the Latino communities are dominated by Puerto Ricans, Dominicans, Cubans. I groove to Latin hip-hop and Afro-Cuban sounds, but I hadn't heard much Mexican-American music like ranchero and Tejano. I know a good plate of *pernil* when I eat one, but I couldn't tell you from *tortas*. And I've heard more opinions over whether Puerto Rico should become independent than I've heard firsthand accounts of life on the border. In other words, when I came to El Paso I was starting at ground zero. Why did I choose El Paso? Well, first, this border city has

been the site of a well-publicized crackdown on illegal immigration. Second, it's been deeply impacted by government policies like NAFTA. But third, and most important to me, El Paso is not majority Anglo but 70 percent Latino and Mexican American, a place where there are bound to be differences of opinion between members of the Latino community.

I head for El Paso in the summer of 1996, a time when the federal government is debating whether to bar the children of undocumented immigrants from going to schools and whether to tighten limits on even legal immigration. The measures are championed by Senator and presidential candidate Bob Dole. A bill that would have clamped down on legal immigration also withered on the vine. It is the continuation of a vigorous ongoing national debate over immigration. Three years before, the newly installed Clinton administration had pushed for and ultimately passed the hotly contested North American Free Trade Agreement. Proponents said NAFTA would stimulate U.S.-Mexican trade, putting dollars into America's economy. Opponents argued it would cost thousands of U.S. jobs when plants relocated to take advantage of Mexican workers who earn as little as five dollars per day. Then, in November of 1994, California voters passed Proposition 187, a referendum designed to deny all public services—health care, welfare, even elementary and secondary education—to illegal immigrants. Sixty-three percent of white Californians voted for Proposition 187, while 69 percent of Latinos voted against it. Before 187 could be implement, opponents challenged its constitutionality and sent the issue to the courts.

Like California, Texas is just under 30 percent Latino. But the state's governor and senators, all of them Republicans, didn't follow California's lead and try to impose new laws on illegal immigration. Instead, they voiced objections to anti-immigrant legislation. Public opinion, culture, and commerce all played a role. Polls show that most Texas residents still view immigration as a boon, not a burden, while the opposite is true in California. Texas draws identity from the Mexican border, whether it's the heritage of many of its citizens, historical events like the Alamo, or the hallmarks of everyday life, like food. (The term "Tex-Mex" says it all.) And an analysis by *The Economist* points to more tangible commodities. In 1995, Texas exported $24 billion in goods to Mexico, its leading trading partner. Mexico was only California's fourth trading partner, with $7 billion in goods.

But while trade with Mexico has been good for Texas in general, the NAFTA free trade treaty has hit El Paso's economy hard. The city already has an unemployment rate double the national average. Now plants that used to pay workers five dollars an hour in El Paso can pay them five dollars a day just across the border in Juarez—and not pay duty on the goods shipped back to the United States. Among the issues I want to explore here in El Paso are not just questions of Mexican-American identity—how they see themselves—but also how they see their (real or distant) cousins across the border. Do the residents of El Paso look upon the Mexicans as brothers, economic competitors—or a bit of both?

One of the first people I meet in El Paso gives me a hint of the differences in opinion about border issues. Nora is chic, almost out of place in the grungy alternative bar we're both sitting in, with high cheekbones, light skin, and curly black hair cut in a bob. "I hate to say it, but I agree with him," she says. "They need to learn English." The "him" Nora is talking about is a black city councilman who chewed out a citizen who addressed a town hall meeting in Spanish. The "they"—an implicit "they"—are recent Mexican immigrants. Nora, who used to model in New York and now works

in the local clothing industry, takes the councilman's side. But some local cartoonists lampooned the politician's outrage, and many residents wrote letters of protest to the newspaper.

Many El Paso residents are from first- or second-generation immigrant families, people who remember life in Mexico and have direct family ties across the border. But it's a mistake to think that they encompass all of El Paso's Latinos. A large proportion of El Paso families, like Nora's, are *Tejano,* a term which means that her forebears have lived in Texas for generations—i.e., even before it was part of the United States. (As many Tejanos like to say, "We didn't cross the border. The border crossed us.") The unique Tex-Mex culture of the Tejanos gave rise to one of the biggest Latina singing sensations, Selena, whose premature death in 1995 woke America up to the size of the Latino community. And one lesson America has yet to learn about the Latino community is how many different cultural and political perspectives there are—even within a single group, like Mexican Americans.

Those different perspectives come into direct conflict when it comes to an issue as controversial as the border. I focused on two groups of people familiar with El Paso: the enforcers who try to keep people out, and the border crossers desperate to stay in America.

The Enforcers

Melissa Lucio gets the radio call at noon on a scorching summer day. An electric sensor just inside the U.S. border's been tripped; agents are looking around but they haven't found anyone yet. She heads for the sensor's coordinates and pulls up alongside a couple of agents. They're beating the bushes around a splotch of water halfway between a pond and a puddle. After a minute, a guy about thirty-five years old steps out of a thicket with a resigned look on his face and a satchel slung over his shoulder. A Mexican worker who's crossed illegally into the States, he also happens to be wearing an OFFICIAL U.S. TAXPAYER baseball cap. When I laughingly point this out to Melissa, she goes me one better. "We had a guy who walked in with a Border Patrol hat the other day. We asked him where he got it and he said he found it on the bank of the river. The officer's name was still written on the inside—he'd lost it over a year ago."

Melissa's just one of the thousands of U.S. Border Patrol agents charged with the thankless (and some would say impossible) task of keeping illegal immigrants out of America and catching them once they come in. A Mexican-American El Paso native, she's also the wife of another Mexican-American Border Patrol agent. Just thirty years old, she's also the mother of five sons. With her thick black hair pulled back in a neat French braid, her brown uniform replete with two-way radio and gun, Melissa rides the Texas–Mexico–New Mexico border tracking and detaining border crossers. Sometimes she gets help from the electronic signals of hidden sensors, but much of the time she relies on her own eyes, scanning the horizon and bending toward the earth to interpret "signs"—the scant marks and footprints in the dry earth which she reads for vital clues of time and direction. The day is hot and clear. Recent rains have made it easier to track signs—and have also put desert flowers into bloom. Melissa's comments as she navigates the covered-cab truck around bumps and gullies are punctuated with interjections about the wildlife—"Beautiful bird!" "Really cool lizard!" "Check out that jackrabbit!" But her ear is always tuned to the radio, and she's tough when she has to be. If her truck gets stuck, she breaks off branches and digs it out; if a suspect in a vehicle takes off into a residential area, she pursues and radios the local police. As we traverse highways, dirt roads, and long stretches of pristine desert, we don't run into any other female agents out in the field.

The man Melissa has just picked up doesn't protest when she puts him in the covered back area of the truck. In fact, he reaches into his satchel, pulls out a newspaper, and starts to read. At my request, she asks him where he was going and what he was going to do.

"*¿Para dónde vas?*" she asks.

"*Para Coronodo,*" he answers.

Coronado is an affluent area, replete with a country club, where he was headed to cut yards. "He was actually closer to the east side of Juarez," Melissa translates, "and I asked him why he didn't cross over there. And he said there's a lot of *cholos* [bandits] stealing and robbing in that area. He says it's easier to cross over here. He says he doesn't come often, but every once in a while when he needs money."

One stereotype of illegal immigrants is that they're a bunch of welfare cheats. But this crosser, and most of the ones that Melissa picks up, are coming in strictly to work—sometimes to stay for the day and go back that night. The economics are clear cut. The starting wage in the *maquiladoras,* or twin plants—so named because they're owned by U.S. corporations who maintain both Mexican factories and their "twins" across the border—is about five dollars a day. The wages for yard work are far, far higher. "If they have their own tools, they could make sixty bucks a day," Melissa says. "If not, it could be thirty or forty." In other words, one day per week of work in the United States earns more than an entire week's labor in Mexico. Of course, there'd be no point crossing the border if U.S. employers weren't willing, even eager, to give undocumented workers jobs. If a border crosser makes it in every day, the payoff is good even relative to U.S. workers. "If you think about minimum wage, four sixty per hour with taxes taken out, [the border crossers] are going to make more," she says. "Even the Mexican police officers, some of them make four hundred dollars per month if they're lucky."

I ask Melissa if the people she picks up ever give her flack for being Mexican American and picking up Mexicans. "I've only had one person say, 'Don't you think you're being mean?'" she says. "And I say, if you had a job, you would do it to the best of your ability, right? They say 'Yeah.'"—she draws the word out to give it a dubious inflection. "And I say that's just what I'm doing. I've got five children. I want to maintain my household. And they understand."

"Like this education issue," she continues. "Let's say you educate them, and then what?

They're illegal in the United States so they can't obtain work. Or let's say they become legal, then they're going to be competing against my children or me for a job that could have very well been mine." She's no fan of NAFTA, which she believes has knocked the wind out of an already weakened local economy. "Not a month goes by that you don't hear about a local company that's up and relocating to Mexico," she says. "It may be a good law, but not for the people who live paycheck to paycheck."

We drop our passenger off at the Paso Del Norte processing station, a short-term holding area that seems appropriately located in the middle of nowhere. Inside the plain building is a bullpen of officers at their desks, surrounded by large cells where individuals are sorted by gender, age, and area of origin. Locals—people from Juarez and nearby border areas—are the easiest to process and return. People from the interior of Mexico, farther south, are interviewed by Mexican officials and given bus fare home. And last of all are detainees from Central America, some of whom have traveled hundreds upon hundreds of miles from Honduras and points south, only to be caught on the final leg of their journey. There are men and women, old and young—really young. One of the kids in the pen, who flashes me an impish grin when I check him out, looks about twelve.

"Oh, we get kids who are eight, nine, ten. I ask them, 'Your Mom, doesn't she worry about you?' And some of their parents do, but they really run wild. If they know a lady at a bakery [in the United States] will give them sweetbreads, stuff like that, they'll come. Some of them have friends they come to goof off with. This is what they do. This is recreation."

By the time they're sixteen—which is the age of the next border crosser we pick up—they're usually crossing to work. The teenager has tan skin and hair bleached nearly blond by the sun; he's carrying yard tools.

"*¿Con qué te posito entro los Estados Unidos?*" Melissa asks.

"*Trabajo.*"

"*¿Qué clase trabajo?*"

"*En yardas,*" he answers. He was headed to Coronado as well.

An Economic Judgment

Melissa Lucio is not only a Border Patrol agent, but a mother and a taxpayer as well. She believes the influx of illegal immigrants could curtail her children's chances at prosperity. "When people talk about immigration issues as being racial," she says, "you have Hispanics as well as Anglos as well as other ethnic groups that will say the same thing: 'We need to be strong on immigration issues.' Why should my tax dollars and my anything be funding someone else?"

Melissa's family immigrated from Mexico a couple of generations ago. "My grandma jokes that I'm going to send her back over the border," Melissa says. She had what she describes as a typical, happy coming of age in El Paso. She met her first love, Rick, who's also Mexican American, in high school, and married him right after she graduated. Like several members of both of their families, Rick went into law enforcement, joining the Border Patrol. Melissa dreamed about the same thing for ten years before she decided to take the plunge. "I had thought about going to college and to the FBI behavioral science department, to pursue some forensics. But the more and more children I started having, I just started to see that dream being pushed further and further away," she says.

Melissa found out the Border Patrol was hiring when Rick told her about a career day he was coordinating—but he tried to discourage her from trying out. It was an arduous process. First she had to take a written test to get admitted to the academy. Then she had to get in shape. After seven years of bearing and raising five sons (Daniel, David, Derek, Dario, and Andrew—"we ran out of Ds," she says), she was two hundred and twenty pounds. She quit her job and lost forty before going into the academy, and another ten once she was there. When it came time for the induction ceremony, she received her badge from an officer who'd specially requested the honor—her husband. "As he's pinning me he whispers in my ear, 'Oh Melissa, I never thought you would make it. You've never made me so proud.'" She beams. "It was absolutely great. It was amazing."

Now Melissa works just past the El Paso line in the Christo Rey area of New Mexico. Standing atop the hill that supports the huge statue of Christ, you can see Mexico, New Mexico, and Texas in panorama. You can also see the latest attempts to keep the border clamped down. Along the length of the border, construction crews are putting up an immense fence designed to eventually cover the entire U.S.-Mexico line. But Melissa for one is skeptical it will stop the crossings. "They'll just have to walk a little further," she says, to where mesas break the fence line.

Her division, which contains forty to sixty agents per day depending on scheduling, picks up about a hundred and fifty people per day, a thousand per week. It's labor-intensive work, particularly given the nature of the terrain. The El Paso Border Patrol region gained prominence in 1991 when Silvestre Reyes, the chief at the time, implemented a policy he called Operation Hold the Line. Instead of chasing border crossers after they walked over train tracks or through the Rio Grande (at the Juarez-El Paso border, the river is little more than a trickle in a concrete culvert), Reyes posted agents in vehicles along large stretches of the border. Their presence dropped the number of crossers at that juncture from eight thousand a day to virtually zero. But that meant more Mexicans who wanted to come to Texas chose to go through the New Mexico mountains. "You can't do that here. You'd have to have a ton of agents to watch every side of every hill. We have to be mobile," Melissa says.

It seems like an awful lot of work for each agent on an eight-hour shift to pick up the equivalent of three border jumpers a day. But the political stakes are far higher than those numbers would suggest. Tensions about immigration characterize the turn of this century as deeply as they marked the turn of the last one. But instead of Italians, Irish, and Jews who received a lukewarm welcome disembarking at Ellis Island in the late 1800s and early 1900s, Mexican Ameri-

cans crossing into the border for points as far flung as New York and the Midwest are the immigrants under scrutiny today. According to the Immigration and Naturalization Service, in 1995 eighty-six thousand Mexicans emigrated to the United States legally, to work, study, or join their families. They were the largest single group of U.S. immigrants, and joined approximately 6 million Mexican immigrants living legally in the United States. (All told, there are over 30 million Latinos living in the United States.) U.S. officials estimate there are more than 5 million illegal immigrants in the United States, 54 percent of them Mexicans, most of whom also came to work or go to school. While some agents are used as human scarecrows, keeping would-be border crossers out, Melissa's job is mainly to track and capture the people who do make it through.

The pickups don't always go smoothly. Some of the border crossers have passed out and nearly died from heat stroke or dehydration as they're being taken in; other times agents just find the bodies. (One agent tells me a gruesome, perhaps apocryphal tale of finding a body whose eyes had literally popped out of the scorched head.) Sometimes people resist or carry weapons. The agents also have to watch out for *cholos*—gang members who can come from either side of the border, and who often prey on those crossing the border to work. In a Wild West twist, some of the *cholos* rob trains passing through the region. "A bandit will board the trains out West and pilfer through first, and say, 'The Nike tennis shoes are here.' Then they have their buddies, twenty or thirty or forty guys, shunt the track so the little computer tells the train to stop. As soon as it stops, these guys start throwing the stuff down. They don't care if the nine hundred ninety-nine dollar television cracks open because the good ones will land somewhere and they will grab it and sell it. Or on the other hand, in the next two weeks you'll arrest a bunch of people that are all wearing brand new Nike tennis shoes."

Sometimes they prey on the individuals working along the border fence line. As our day together draws to a close, Melissa gets a radio call from one of the men erecting the new fence. He's worried because four men are approaching and he's alone. "Ten-four. Horse patrol and myself will thirteen over there and check it out." Melissa radios back. As we approach, two men on powerful horses gallop parallel, about twenty yards away. "I'm on the list for horseback," Melissa says. "I think it's so cool." She surveys the situation as we approach. "These guys are definitely up to no good." I ask how she can tell. "They don't have any bags, which means they're not crossing. They don't have any water and they're just hanging around with no attempt to go north." They might have wanted to get their hands on some of the construction supplies, she figures.

Every eight weeks Melissa and the other agents change shift—days, evenings, overnights (which start at midnight). Now she's working days and her husband is working evenings, making it easy for him to take the kids to and from school. They try to avoid both doing the evening shift, "because we've noticed that our kids' grades drop."

To help out, Rick and Melissa have hired a live-in housekeeper, which is a drama in and of itself. "I advertised for a housekeeper two years ago, [and] the first thing off the bat was, 'Are you a U.S. citizen or a legal resident? If not, I work for immigration and I can't hire you.' And half the people would hang up. A quarter of the people would say, 'I'm a border crosser,' but they were not permitted to work. The lady we hired, she's late forties, great with the kids, teaching the kids Spanish, and she's a legal resident, so it worked out really, really, well."

"So what's funny, a neighbor came up and said, 'Do you realize your house is under surveillance?' I was like 'Excuse me?'" One day, when both husband and wife were gone, an agent came to the home and asked their housekeeper for documents. Neighbors came out to watch, and she waved right back at them to say "I'm still here because I'm legal," Melissa says. The couple learned why the Immigration and Naturalization Service suspected them when they talked the

matter over with their chief. A neighbor had phoned in with an elaborate tale how the housekeeper, supposedly illegal, had begged up and down the street for work and found it with the Lucios. "It's just someone being vindictive. I thought, that is really terrible," Melissa says. "At the time we lived in the Coronado Country Club area. They were really unhappy about Hold the Line because their maids couldn't come in illegally." As we head back into the station, I think again about the economics of the illegal immigration debate. The reality is that for every undocumented immigrant who finds low-wage work in America, there is somebody willing to hire that person. And some of the same people benefiting from below-market labor loudly decry illegal immigration at the same time.

The Politics of the Border

America likes to think its immigration laws are tough. And while they're arguably harsh on people who cross the border, most penalties on the businesses that hire illegal immigrants are modest. And people like the border crossers Melissa Lucio picked up often don't work for "businesses" at all, but everyday U.S. citizens who usually suspect the person they've hired to cut their lawn or babysit their kids doesn't hold a green card. America decries the waves of illegal immigration. But some Americans on the border and throughout the United States profit from the cheap labor these immigrants provide.

The economics of the border are full of conflict and duplicity, people who profit, people who lose, and people who lie about which camp they're in. Most important, the economics are deeply intertwined. Downtown El Paso, an unremarkable collection of modest office buildings and low-priced shops, is tethered by a bridge to downtown Juarez, Mexico. The Mexicans who cross the bridge come to work, visit, and shop. The Anglos going the other way often buy cheap groceries and pharmaceuticals (you can purchase Valium and Prozac without a prescription there), and college students hit the bars, where the words "drinking age" are meaningless. What happens when the Border Patrol cracks down on illegal crossings? Many downtown El Paso businessmen say their shops suffer, deprived of the day workers that used to buy clothes and consumer goods.

Many Mexican residents of Juarez aren't happy about the increasingly fortified border, either. El Paso and Juarez are separated by an unimpressive trickle of water that, amazingly enough, is part of the mighty Rio Grande river. A cement aqueduct, fenced on both sides, contains the water and separates the people. Painted on the concrete are signs decrying the border fortifications:

One reads OJO MIGRA (eyes are painted into the *o*'s) ¡¡YA BASTA!!

Another says: POR CADA ILEGAL QUE NOS MALTRATEN EN LOS ESTADOS UNIDOS DE N.A. VAMOS A MALTRATAR UN VISITANTE GAVACHO. BIENVENIDOS LOS PAISANOS.

Their translations: "Look, Immigration—enough already!" and "For every illegal they mistreat in the United States, we are going to mistreat a visiting gringo. Welcome, countrymen."

It sounds like a bit of useless bravado, the "welcome, countrymen" sign. But the history of the Southwest is the history of what Mexico founded and America fought to win—not particularly fairly, either. Writes biographer Hugh Pearson:

> In 1845, hewing to the strictures of Manifest Destiny we annexed the Republic of Texas, which had been part of Mexico. Its American settlers decided to introduce slavery into the territory, which was illegal in Mexico. Then, as gratitude for the Mexican government's inviting them to settle the territory and because they wanted to keep their slaves, they fought for independence. As former President and Gen. Ulysses S. Grant wrote in his memoirs, "The occupation, separation and annexation were, from the inception of the movement to its final consummation, a conspiracy to acquire territory out of which slave states might be formed for the American union."

After accepting the Texas republic's petition to be annexed by the United States, a dispute between the United States and Mexico ensued, regarding where the exact boundary of Texas lay. Mexican and U.S. patrols clashed somewhere along the disputed territory and the United States declared war on Mexico. In the process of fighting the war, U.S. troops captured from Mexico what is now New Mexico and what the Mexicans called Upper California. As conditions for surrender, Mexico was forced to cede all of the captured territory north of the Rio Grande River, and an agreed upon jagged imaginary line that now separates California, Arizona and New Mexico from Mexico. So today, Mexicans crossing into U.S. California are treated as illegal aliens if they don't go through the proper channels for entering territory that was originally theirs.

I didn't learn any of this in high school, and I'd wager that many Americans don't know it today. What happened doesn't change the fact that America has the right to control its borders, but it does cast into sharper relief the interconnectedness of these two nations. Texas was birthed from Mexico. But—defying the stereotypes that pervade much of the news coverage about the border—many Mexican Americans are now the ones guarding the border.

Silvestre Reyes headed the Border Patrol for the entire El Paso region. After gaining recognition for starting Operation Hold the Line, Reyes resigned in November 1995 in order to run for a seat in the U.S. Congress, hoping the "sleeping giant" of Mexican-American political clout will work in his favor. (In November 1996, he won that seat.)

I meet the solid, handsome fifty-year-old in the offices where he's running his campaign with the help of his twenty-five-year-old daughter. Even in his civilian clothes, he's got the demeanor of a law enforcement officer. Reyes grew up in a small farming town where his high school graduating class was made up of just twenty-six students. When he was a child, he served as a lookout against *la migra*—the Border

Patrol—in the fields where Mexicans worked. He served in Vietnam, then worked as a Border Patrol agent for over twenty-five years. He believes that people's opinions about the border don't have anything to do with ethnic loyalty, but quality of life. "Hispanics, like every ethnic group in the country, have an expectation to be safe and secure in their neighborhoods," he says. "A Hispanic no more than anybody else appreciates undocumented people flowing through their backyards, creating a chaotic situation."

Still, Reyes says he'd like to find a way to benefit both Mexicans and Americans at the same time. "Mexican citizens don't want to come up here," he says. "They would rather stay home. But they stay home, they starve. We've got forces down in Mexico that want jobs, and people up here that want them to come up here. But the whole problem is, let's find a system that does it legally."

Despite its adverse effect on the El Paso economy, Reyes supports NAFTA as a way of increasing employment opportunities in Mexico. If things don't get better there, he reasons, illegal immigration will never stop. "Mexico has a surplus of manpower. I think 60 percent of Mexican citizens are under the age of twenty, if I remember my statistics right," he says. The problem with NAFTA in the short term is that it's relied on minimum-wage jobs, jobs that are the first to be transferred to the other side of the border. "In El Paso, we have a minimum-wage mentality. When they graduate, kids want to go someplace else. They don't want to stay here and work for four thirty-five or five fifteen or whatever the [minimum] wage finally ends up to be when they can go to Dallas, L.A., Denver, Chicago and participate in high-paying, high-tech kinds of jobs. Anybody with any kind of ambition knows that in order to make it, you've got to leave here."

One policy he doesn't support is California's Proposition 187, which voters passed in 1994 in an effort, among other things, to prevent illegal immigrants from receiving government medical care or public education. Reyes calls the measure "illegal and unconstitutional," and rejects the calls of national politicians like former Senator

Bob Dole to replicate it. "Should we amend the Constitution in order to deny children born in this country their citizenships? I think we're crazy," he says. "What's gonna keep someone from going back retroactively and saying, 'You know, your father was born to illegal parents back in 1924. Therefore he was illegal, therefore you're illegal.'" (Such logic recalls a joke by Mexican-American comedian Paul Rodriguez, who says he supports making deportations for illegal immigration retroactive and shipping the Anglos back home.) The idea of barring education to undocumented children is "insanity running amok. The way that people enslave whole segments of our society is by keeping them ignorant. . . . To me it doesn't matter whether it's black or Hispanics or Chinese or whites or who it is. I think it's just wrong for any country to guarantee a subculture of ignorance. And that's what you're doing when you don't educate the kids."

The wording of California's Proposition 187 was also openly militaristic, reading:

> WE CAN STOP ILLEGAL ALIENS. If the citizens and the taxpayers of our state wait for the politicians in Washington and Sacramento to stop the incredible flow of ILLEGAL ALIENS, California will be in economic and social bankruptcy. We have to act and ACT NOW! On our ballot, Proposition 187 will be the first giant stride in ultimately ending the ILLEGAL ALIEN invasion.

Some advocates say the border has already become militarized, infringing upon the rights of citizens and legal immigrants. El Paso's Border Rights Coalition says that in 1995, half of the individuals who complained to their group about mistreatment by the Border Patrol, Immigration and Naturalization Service, and U.S. Customs were U.S. citizens, not legal or illegal immigrants. The group helped students at El Paso's Bowie High School file a class action suit. They alleged that Border Patrol agents were routinely harassing individuals on and near campus—in one case, arresting a group of students, U.S. citizens, who were driving to school. Today, the Border Patrol is operating under a settlement that requires they meet higher standards before detaining individuals, and limits searches at schools and churches.

Of course, the ultimate military-style solution would be to create a physical wall between Mexico and the United States. Reyes strongly disagrees with such a plan. "That's impractical, you know. The Berlin wall didn't seal, and that was using mines and barbed wire and guards and concrete, and all of that, and still people got out of there," he says. Yet as Reyes and I talk, construction on just such a wall is happening along the border near El Paso. While I'm out with Melissa Lucio, she shows me the early stages of the construction site. It's impossible to cover the whole border, of course. But by 1998, several miles of what Reyes calls the "impractical" solution stand completed.

The Border Crossers

A Family Full of Contradictions

Gilberto, an eighteen-year-old undocumented immigrant from Chihuahua, has few marketable skills but one strong advantage on his side. He has family legally in the United States who are willing to help him. Gilberto is the brother-in-law of a naturalized U.S. citizen who emigrated from Hong Kong. Chiu, who went to college in the United States, met his wife Lorena, in a Juarez nightclub. Now they have two children, baby Jenny Anna and Andy, who turned three the day after I spoke with them. Both attend the University of Texas at El Paso, and they earn a living by running a home care facility for the elderly.

Gilberto helps out with the home care, meaning he's guaranteed a job as well as a place to stay far from the eyes of the Border Patrol. Like virtually all illegal immigrants, he's an unskilled laborer. Like many Mexicans, he finished the "secondario" level of schooling at fifteen and then started working. His first job was in a junkyard—hot, heavy work for very little money. Still, like a teenager, he used the remaining money he had to party rather than save. Asked if he's worried *la migra* will find him—something

they did once before, as he was out and about—he shakes his head confidently, "No."

Chiu and Lorena's generous brick house is nestled in a pristine, upper-middle-class enclave undergoing rapid development. Bold and self-assured, Chiu strongly opposes illegal immigration, a position it's hard not to think deeply about when you see Gilberto sitting sheepishly on the other side of the table. "My brother-in-law, he's an illegal alien. He come and go whenever he wants. When you're talking about Hold the Line, it's only to make the government look good," Chiu scolds. "Washington, D.C., will furnish a lot of money for this project because it's very successful—you catch ten billion illegal aliens. Oh great job!" he sneers. "Now they have this Hold the Line thing, OK, and then they say, 'Nobody coming across.' But in the reality it's not true. In Mexico, if the people over there are making three to five dollars a day and if they cannot support their kids, do you think they would just sit there and die?"

Gilberto isn't in the dire straits many border crossers are. In fact, he originally entered not to stay but to fulfill teenage longings. "All the boys, they have the same dream: you know, they wanted to come and get some money and buy a truck, a nice truck," his sister Lorena translates, "and then go back to Mexico and spend one or two months or whatever on the money they saved up. Then after that, they come back to the United States again and work and get some more money. That's the way they think." Now Gilberto's changed his mind. He wants to stay in the United States and become a nurse. "It's very important to learn to speak English, otherwise there's no way to find a job—well, maybe in El Paso a very low job. But I want to go further," he says. He's enrolled in a local high school, where his legal status proved no problem. "As a matter of fact, they are not allowed to ask you whether you have papers or not or whether you have a Social Security number of not, because if they do that they have violated federal law," Chiu says. "So they have to let him register although he's an illegal alien." In a clear example of how self-interest overrides politics, Chiu says that he's happy his brother-in-law can be enrolled, but that he is opposed to educating undocumented children. "When they do that they are inviting illegal immigrants to come to school here, you see. I would say no illegal immigrants to go to school in this country for free."

Neither Mexican nor American

A pensive seventeen-year-old named Diana finds herself in the opposite situation from Gilberto: with her near-perfect English and years of schooling in the United States, she seems culturally American, but this undocumented immigrant has no one to advocate for her or protect her. She's been caught between two worlds most of her life. Four years ago, Diana crossed into the United States at the Juarez–El Paso bridge that symbolizes the border so well. Now she's a senior at Fremont High School in Oakland, California. . . . Before crossing the Rio Grande, she spent her junior high school years near Durango, Mexico. And before that, from the ages of two until nine, she lived in the United States—attending American schools, playing with American toys, speaking both English and Spanish. Without a green card or citizenship, but with a keen understanding of American culture and her precarious position in it, she is neither fully American nor fully Mexican.

Diana remembers the day her family crossed over from Juarez to El Paso. "We used a raft to get across. It was really sunny that day. People were on the bridge watching us. They were like 'Oh look!'" she says. "I remember I saw this man with a little boy in his arms pointing at us." Once they got to El Paso, her family tried to blend in with the rest of the crowds in the downtown shopping area. "We crossed the street right in front of a Border Patrol car," Diana remembers. "The car stopped so we could cross the street! My Mom was praying and I was like, 'Mom, they're not going to do anything to us now.' They didn't."

While her experience in crossing the Rio Grande was a common one until recently, Diana's reasons for going back and forth between the United States and Mexico are personal and com-

plex. Like most families who cross over from Mexico, Diana's came to work and make a better life for their children. Her father has a green card, so he was able to live and work legally; but he brought Diana, her mother, and Diana's older brother into the country without papers. Diana's father began drinking too much, and after living in the United States for several years, he decided to move the family back to Mexico and pull himself together. But there's little work near Durango, so he ended up going back to the United States to earn a living (taking Diana's teenage brother along with him) and sending money to the family back home. It was only once her father had stopped drinking that he decided to reunite the family, arranging for a "coyote"—or someone who smuggles people across the border—to bring Diana and the rest of the family north through Mexico, on a raft over the Rio Grande, and by truck out of Texas.

Diana was too young to remember the first time she crossed the border. She was only two years old, and friends of the family who had papers for their own toddler smuggled her in as their child. "People told me I kept saying, 'I want my mother.' They needed me to be quiet," she says. From two on, Diana lived in Chico, California, as a normal Mexican-American kid—almost. When I ask her if she knew she was an "illegal immigrant," she says, "That question really bothered me and came into my head in, I think, the second grade. Most of my friends would go to Mexico on their summer vacations to see their grandparents, and I would ask, 'Why aren't we going to Mexico?' My mother would say, 'We can't.' Then," she continues, "one time in school I said, 'Um, I'm illegal.' And my teacher said, 'Honey, don't say that out loud. You could get your parents in a lot of trouble.' That's when I started feeling a little inferior to other kids."

Sometimes she still does. "Not because of who I am but because of what I can't do," she says, quietly breaking into tears. One thing she can't do is apply to college, even though she's a solid student. Without legal residence papers, she has little hope of attending school or getting anything but the most menial of jobs. Her older brother tried enrolling in college, but after they repeatedly asked him for a Social Security number, he simply left. Now he plays in a band. "I want to get a green card so I can work, so I can go to school, so I don't need to worry about getting deported and everything. But we have to pay a lawyer seven hundred dollars for each person applying for the green card," money her struggling family doesn't have. After she gets a green card, she wants to become a citizen "because I would like to be heard in this country. I would like to vote and be part of the process."

The most wrenching part of her experience is that Diana knows she could have been a legal resident by now. In 1987, she says, "we could have gotten our papers through the National Amnesty Program," a one-shot chance for illegal immigrants to declare themselves to officials in exchange for a green card. "My mother applied for us, but my Dad [who was drinking] felt that if we went back to Mexico, everything would be for the best." She remembers the day they left the United States. "I had to leave all my friends and the things I had. We left everything: the furniture, my toys, my Barbies. I had to practically leave my life there."

Yet Diana credits the time she spent in Mexico with helping her reconnect with her heritage. She became close with her grandmother, was in the Mexican equivalent of junior ROTC, and won dramatic speaking contests, reciting poetry. "In Mexico, I always wanted to be the one with the best grades—always wanted to be the center of attention," she says. "Maybe because I believed in myself and what I did," she says. That sense of confidence is lacking in Diana today. But if she had stayed in Mexico, it would have been difficult for her to continue her education considering how little money her family had. Most of the girls Diana knew stopped going to school at fourteen or fifteen, got married to a farmer or laborer, and started a family.

So, in one sense, Diana feels she was lucky to return to the United States. But when she first arrived, she had a difficult time readjusting. She returned in time for ninth grade, which in Oakland at the time was still a part of junior high school. Teachers put her in an English as a sec-

ond language program, probably because her shyness inhibited her from talking much. "It wasn't very helpful," she says. Luckily, as soon as one of her teachers found out how good Diana's English really was, Diana was moved into the regular track.

But Diana was dealing not only with educational displacement but ethnic culture shock. "In the ninth grade, there was only my Mexican friends . . . and we felt a little inferior to the rest." In her opinion, the Mexican kids broke down into two cliques: the "Mexican Mexicans," or hard-working immigrants, and the "little gangsters," or tough, Americanized teens. She hung out with the former—until tenth grade, when she went to Fremont and joined the Media Academy. There she make friends of several races. "When I got to Fremont there was African Americans, Asians, and Mexicans and everybody hangs out together and it was cool," she says.

What is heartbreaking to Diana today is that, though she loves school, she has little hope of continuing her education. She remembers a time that her teacher was leading them through an exercise in filling out college applications. "Everybody was like: 'Oh, I want to go to this place and I wanna go such and such and oh, my grades are good and everything.' My teacher was like, 'Aren't you going to fill out your applications?' And I was like, 'What for?'" Another girl in the class asked the question Diana was desperate to, but just couldn't. "What if you're not a legal resident?" Her teacher said to leave the Social Security number slot blank, but Diana says, dejected, "I didn't want to continue it."

The passage of Proposition 187 during Diana's junior year made the issues seem even more overwhelming. "I felt, Oh God, here goes another barrier. I'm trying to get over these little things and now here comes this big one." She's already experienced difficulty getting services. When she had a bad tooth, she went to the local clinic. They told her they could no longer help her if she didn't have a Social Security number. "My mom was like, 'We'll pay,' but no, she's like, 'We're sorry and everything is frozen until we get more orders.'"

As we drive through Oakland, she points out the tiny repair shop her father runs, nestled in an alley off of the East Fourteenth Street corridor. Her house, on a block of modest but well-kept homes with front and backyards, is filled with worn-out used furniture. Her mother, a warm, friendly woman who speaks little English, sits in the kitchen feeding an infant she babysits for extra cash. Her three younger siblings—adorable mischievous imps—run in and out of the house with their friends. Her youngest brother, who's five, doesn't have legal status, but her two middle siblings, both in elementary school, are U.S. citizens because they were born while her family was living in Chico. In California alone there are hundreds of thousands of families with mixed legal status (where some family members have green cards or citizenship and others have neither). Diana tries not to, but sometimes she resents the freedom that her two siblings have for being citizens. To her, their futures seem open, boundless; her own seems closed.

Still, "Regardless of all the barriers that are put between you and other people, America *is* the Land of Opportunity," says Diana. "No matter where you go, you will never find another place where even when you're not legal you can still get a job that pays you. There's no other place like it. In Mexico you can't even get a job. You depend on the crops on your land and live on what grows. There's nowhere for you to go, no McDonald's for you to hang out at. To me, it's better in America."

Mexicanizing America?

The unspoken fear that underlies much of our policy about the border is that an influx of immigrants will "Mexicanize" America. But my journey through El Paso illustrates the complex culture of Mexican Americans, and just how unfounded the fears about "Mexicanization" are. Those living on the U.S.-Mexican border face some difficult political and economic questions: whether Americans can compete with the low-wage workers in Mexico; whether Washington lawmakers can truly understand the issues facing Americans on the border; and, for Mexican Americans in particular, whether they should feel some connection to the problems facing Mexicans, or simply focus on their own issues. The influence of Mexican culture on America's should be seen as part of a continuum. Just as every immigration wave has shaped this country, so will the rise of the Latino population. In a best-case scenario, border towns like El Paso would help foster a rich appreciation for Mexican culture as *part* of American-style diversity. Silvestre Reyes describes his hopes for the next generation as quite literally out of this world. "You hope that someday you get to the point where *Star Trek* is today," he says. "That someday it doesn't matter who you are or what you look like or what your name is, but the important thing is that you're working in harmony."

THINKING ABOUT THE READING

Describe the various ways that illegal Mexican immigrants to the United States are victimized. Faced with the sorts of dangers mentioned in this article as well as the hostility of Border Patrol agents, why do you think people are still willing to take the risk and enter this country illegally? Do you consider illegal immigration to be a serious social problem? Do you think that tightening the border and increasing Border Patrol surveillance will ever reduce illegal immigration? If not, how would you go about reducing it? How do the Border Patrol agents' perceptions and attitudes affect your beliefs about illegal immigration? How would you now characterize the agents themselves? Why does Chideya think that the fear that illegal immigrants will "Mexicanize" the United States is unfounded?

14 Architects of Change: Reconstructing Society

Throughout this book you've seen examples of how society is socially constructed and how these social constructions, in turn, affect the lives of individuals. It's hard not to feel a little helpless when discussing the control that culture, massive bureaucratic organizations, social institutions, systems of social stratification and population trends have over our individual lives. However, social change is as much a part of society as social stability. Whether at the personal, cultural, or institutional level, change is the preeminent feature of modern societies.

Religious institutions are often intertwined with movements for widespread social change. Sometimes the religious ideology that underlies a particular movement is one that emphasizes peace and justice. The civil rights movement of the 1950s and the antiwar movement of the 1960s are two such examples. Other times, however, the supportive religious ideology of a movement can be used to deny civil rights and even incite violence. In his article, "Popular Christianity and Political Extremism in the United States," James Aho describes the relationship between Christianity and violent right-wing extremism. Every American generation, he argues, has experienced movements built on religiously inspired hatred. Today, however, these movements have been able to take advantage of sophisticated weapons and communications technology, making them especially lethal.

In the end, the nature of society, from its large institutions to its small, unspoken rules of everyday life, can be understood only by examining what people do and think. Individuals, acting collectively, can shape institutions, influence government policy, and alter the course of society. It's easy to forget that social movements consist of flesh-and-blood individuals acting together for a cause they believe in. In "Challenging Power," Celene Krauss examines the process by which white, working-class women with very traditional ideas about women's role in the family became community activists in toxic waste protests. She shows how these women became politicized not by the broader ideology of the environmentalist movement but by the direct health threats toxic waste posed to their children.

Popular Christianity and Political Extremism in the United States

James Aho

December 8, 1984. In a shootout on Puget Sound, Washington, involving several hundred federal and local law enforcement officials, the leader of a terrorist group compromised of self-proclaimed Christian soldiers is killed, ending a crime spree involving multi-state robberies, armored car heists, arson attacks, three murders, and a teenage suicide. (Flynn and Gerhardt 1989)

Christmas Eve, 1985. A "Christian patriot soldier" in Seattle trying to save America by eliminating the Jewish-Communist leader of the so-called one-world conspiracy, murders an innocent family of four, including two pre-teen children. (Aho 1994: 35–49)

August 1992. In northern Idaho, three persons are killed and two others critically injured in the course of a stand-off between federal marshals, ATF officers, the FBI, and a white separatist Christian family seeking refuge from the "Time of Tribulations" prophesied in the Book of Revelations. (Aho 1994: 50–65)

Three isolated incidents, twelve dead bodies, scores of young men imprisoned, shattered families, millions of dollars in litigation fees and investigation expenses. Why? What can sociology tell us about the causes of these events that they might be averted in the future? In particular, insofar as Christianity figures so prominently in these stories, what role has this religion played in them? Has Christianity been a cause of right-wing extremism in the United States? Or has it been an excuse for extremism occasioned by other factors? Or is the association between right-wing extremism and Christianity merely anecdotal and incidental? Our object is to address these questions.

Extremism Defined

The word "extremism" is used rhetorically in everyday political discourse to disparage and undermine one's opponents. In this sense, it refers essentially to anyone who disagrees with me politically. In this chapter, however, "extremism" will refer exclusively to particular kinds of behaviors, namely, to non-democratic actions, regardless of their ideology—that is, regardless of whether we agree with the ideas behind them or not (Lipset and Raab 1970: 4–17). Thus, extremism includes: (1) efforts to deny civil rights to certain people, including their right to express unpopular views, their right to due process at law, to own property, etc.; (2) thwarting attempts by others to organize in opposition to us, to run for office, or vote; (3) not playing according to legal constitutional rules of political fairness: using personal smears like "Communist Jew-fag" and "nigger lover" in place of rational discussion; and above all, settling differences by vandalizing or destroying the property or life of one's opponents. The test is not the end as such, but the means employed to achieve it.

Cycles of American Right-Wing Extremism

In this [article] we are concerned with the most rabid right-wing extremists, those who have threatened or succeeded in injuring and killing their opponents. We are interested, furthermore, only in such activities as are connected at least indirectly to Christianity. By no means is this limitation of focus intended to suggest that American Christians are characteristically more violent than their non-Christian neighbors. Nor are we arguing that American Christians engage only in right-wing activities. We are focusing on Christianity and on rightist extremism because in America today this connection has become newsworthy and because it is sociologically problematic.

American political history has long been acquainted with Christian-oriented rightist extremism. As early as the 1790s, for example, Federalist Party activists, inspired partly by Presbyterian and Congregationalist preachers, took-up arms against a mythical anti-Christian cabal known as the Illuminati—Illuminati = bringers of light = Lucifer, the devil.

The most notable result of anti-Illuminatism was what became popularly known as the "Reign of Terror": passage of the Alien and Sedition acts (1798). These required federal registration of recent immigrants to America from Ireland and France, reputed to be the homes of Illuminatism, lengthened the time of naturalization to become a citizen from five to fourteen years, restricted "subversive" speech and newspapers—that is, outlets advocating liberal Jeffersonian or what were known then as "republican" sentiments—and permitted the deportation of "alien enemies" without trial.

The alleged designs of the Illuminati were detailed in a three hundred-page book entitled *Proofs of a Conspiracy Against All the Religions and Governments of Europe Carried on in the Secret Meetings of . . . Illuminati* (Robison 1967 [1798]). Over two hundred years later *Proofs of a Conspiracy* continues to serve as a sourcebook for right-wing extremist commentary on American social issues. Its basic themes are: (1) *manichaenism:* that the world is divided into the warring principles of absolute good and evil; (2) *populism:* that the citizenry naturally would be inclined to ally with the powers of good, but have become indolent, immoral, and uninformed of the present danger to themselves; (3) *conspiracy:* that this is because the forces of evil have enacted a scheme using educators, newspapers, music,

and intoxicants to weaken the people's will and intelligence; (4) *anti-modernism:* that the results of the conspiracy are the very laws and institutions celebrated by the unthinking masses as "progressive": representative government, the separation of church and State, the extension of suffrage to the propertyless, free public education, public-health measures, etc.; and (5) *apocalypticism:* that the results of what liberals call social progress are increased crime rates, insubordination to "natural" authorities (such as royal families and property-owning Anglo-Saxon males), loss of faith, and the decline of common decency—in short, the end of the world.

Approximately every thirty years America has experienced decade-long popular resurrections of these five themes. While the titles of the alleged evil-doers in each era have been adjusted to meet changing circumstances, their program is said to have remained the same. They constitute a diabolic *Plot Against Christianity* (Dilling 1952). In the 1830s, the cabal was said to be comprised of the leaders of Masonic lodges: in the 1890s, they were accused of being Papists and Jesuits; in the 1920s, they were the Hidden Hand; in the 1950s, the Insiders or Force X; and today they are known as Rockefellerian "one-world" Trilateralists or Bilderbergers.

Several parallels are observable in these periods of American right-wing resurgence. First, while occasionally they have evolved into democratically-organized political parties holding conventions that nominate slates of candidates to run for office—the American Party, the Anti-Masonic Party, the People's Party, the Prohibition Party—more often, they have become secret societies in their own right, with arcane passwords, handshakes, and vestments, plotting campaigns of counter-resistance behind closed doors. That is, they come to mirror the fantasies against which they have taken up arms. Indeed, it is this ironic fact that typically occasions the public ridicule and undoing of these groups. The most notable examples are the Know Nothings, so-called because under interrogation they were directed to deny knowledge of the organization; the Ku Klux Klan, which during the 1920s had several million members; the Order of the Star Spangled Banner, which flourished during the 1890s; the Black Legion of Michigan, circa 1930; the Minutemen of the late 1960s; and most recently, the *Bruders Schweigen,* Secret Brotherhood, or as it is more widely known, The Order.

Secondly, the thirty-year cycle noted above evidently has no connection with economic booms and busts. While the hysteria of the 1890s took place during a nation-wide depression, McCarthyism exploded on the scene during the most prosperous era in American history. On close view, American right-wing extremism is more often associated with economic good times than with bad, the 1920s, the 1830s, and the 1980s being prime examples. On the contrary, the cycle seems to have more to do with the length of a modern generation than with any other factor.

Third, and most important for our purposes, Christian preachers have played pivotal roles in all American right-wing hysterias. The presence of Dan Gayman, James Ellison, and Bertrand Comparet spear-heading movements to preserve America from decline today continues a tradition going back to Jedidiah Morse nearly two centuries ago, continuing through Samuel D. Burchard, Billy Sunday, G. L. K. Smith, and Fred Schwarz's Christian Anti-Communist Crusade.

In the nineteenth century, the honorary title "Christian patriot" was restricted to white males with Protestant credentials. By the 1930s, however, Catholic ideologues, like the anti-Semitic radio priest Father Coughlin, had come to assume leadership positions in the movement. Today, somewhat uneasily, Mormons are included in the fold. The Ku Klux Klan, once rabidly anti-Catholic and misogynist, now encourages Catholic recruits and even allows females into its regular organization, instead of requiring them to form auxiliary groups.

Christianity: A Cause of Political Extremism?

The upper Rocky Mountain region is the heartland of American right-wing extremism in our time. Montana, Idaho, Oregon, and Washington have the highest per capita rates of extremist groups of any area in the entire country (Aho 1994: 152–153). Research on the members of these groups show that they are virtually identical to the surrounding population in all respects but one (Aho 1991: 135–163)—they are not less formally educated than the surrounding population. Furthermore, as indicated by their rates of geographic mobility, marital stability, occupational choice, and conventional political participation, they are no more estranged from their local communities than those with whom they live. And finally, their social status seems no more threatened than that of their more moderate neighbors. Indeed, there exists anecdotal evidence that American right-wing extremists today are drawn from the more favored, upwardly-mobile sectors of society. They are college-educated, professional suburbanites residing in the rapidly-growing, prosperous Western states (Simpson 1983).

In other words, the standard sociological theories of right-wing extremism—theories holding, respectively, that extremists are typically under-educated, if not stupid, transient and alienated from ordinary channels of belonging, and suffer inordinately from status insecurity—find little empirical support. Additionally, the popular psychological notion that right-wing extremists are more neurotic than the general population, perhaps paranoid to the point of psychosis, can not be confirmed. None of the right-wing political murderers whose psychiatric records this author has accessed have been medically certified as insane (Aho 1991: 68–82; Aho 1994: 46–49). If this is true for right-wing murderers, it probably also holds for extremists who have not taken the lives of others.

The single way in which right-wing extremists *do* differ from their immediate neighbors is seen in their religious biographies. Those with Christian backgrounds generally, and Presbyterians, Baptists and members of independent fundamentalist Protestant groups specifically, all are overrepresented among intermountain radical patriots (Aho 1991: 164–182). Although it concerns a somewhat different population, this finding is consistent with surveys of the religious affiliations of Americans with conservative voting and attitudinal patterns (Lipset and Raab 1970: 229–232, 359–361, 387–392, 433–437, 448–452; Shupe and Stacey 1983; Wilcox 1992).

Correlations do not prove causality. Merely because American extremists are members of certain denominations and sects does not permit the conclusion that these religious groups compel their members to extremism. In the first place, the vast majority of independent fundamentalists, Baptists, and Presbyterians are not political extremists, even if they are inclined generally to support conservative causes. Secondly, it is conceivable that violently-predisposed individuals are attracted to particular religions because of what they hear from the pulpit; and what they hear channels their *already* violent inclinations in political directions.

Today, a man named Gary Yarbrough, gaunt-faced and red-bearded, languishes in federal prison because of his participation in the *Bruders Schweigen*. Although he was recruited into terrorism from the Church of Jesus Christian—Aryan Nations—it was not the church itself that made him violent, at least not in a simplistic way. On the contrary, Yarbrough was the offspring of a notorious Pima, Arizona, family that one reporter (Ring 1985) describes as "very volatile—very anti-police, anti-social, anti-everybody." Charges against its various members have ranged from burglary and robbery to witness-intimidation.

Lloyd, Steve, and Gary Yarbrough are sons of a family of drifters. Red, the father, works as an itinerant builder and miner. Rusty, his wife, tends bar and waitresses. Child rearing, such as it was, is said to have been "severely heavy handed." Nor was much love lost between the parents. Fist fights were common and once Rusty stabbed Red so badly he was hospitalized. Not surprisingly, "the boys did not get very good schooling." Still, mother vehemently defends her boys. One night, she jumped over a bar to attack an overly inquisitive detective concerning their whereabouts.

After a spree of drugs, vandalism, and thievery, Gary, like his brothers, eventually found himself behind bars at the Arizona State Prison. It was there that he was contacted, first by letter and later personally, by the Aryan Nations prison ministry in Idaho. He was the kind of man the church was searching for: malleable, fearless, sentimental, tough. Immediately upon release, Yarbrough moved with his wife and daughter to Idaho to be close to church headquarters. He finally found his calling: working with like-minded souls in the name of Christ to protect God's chosen people, the white race, from mongrelization.

Yarbrough purchased the requisite dark blue twill trousers, postman's shirt, Nazi pins, Sam Browne holster-belt, and 9 mm. semi-automatic pistol. The pastor of the church assigned him to head the security detail. At annual church conventions, he helped conduct rifle training. But Yarbrough was a man of action; he soon became bored with the routine of guarding the compound against aliens who never arrived. He met others in the congregation who shared his impatience. Together in a farm building, deep in the woods, over the napping figure of one of the member's infant children, they founded the *Bruders Schweigen*, swearing together an oath to war against what they called ZOG—Zionist Occupation Government (Flynn and Gerhardt 1989).

The point is not that every extremist is a violent personality searching to legitimize criminality with religion. Instead, the example illustrates the subtle ways in which religious belief, practice, and organization all play upon individual psychology to produce persons prepared to violate others in the name of principle. Let us look at each of these factors separately, understanding that in reality they intermesh in complicated, sometimes contradictory ways that can only be touched upon here.

Belief

American right-wing politics has appropriated from popular Christianity several tenets: the concept of unredeemable human depravity, the idea of America as a specially chosen people, covenant theology and the right to revolt, the belief in a national mission, millennialism, and anti-Semitism. Each of these in its own way has inspired rightist extremism.

The New Israel

The notion of America as the new Israel, for example, is the primary axiom of a fast-growing religiously-based form of radical politics known as Identity Christianity. Idaho's Aryan Nations Church is simply the most well-known Identity congregation. The adjective "identity" refers to its insistence that Anglo-Saxons are in truth the Israelites. They are "Isaac's-sons"—the Saxons— and hence the Bible is *their* historical record, not that of the Jews (Barkun 1994). The idea is that after its exile to what today is northern Iran around seven hundred B.C., the Israelites migrated over the Caucasus mountains—hence their racial type, "caucasian"—and settled in various European countries. Several of these allegedly still contain mementos of their origins: the nation of Denmark is said to be comprised of descendants from the tribe of Dan; the German-speaking Jutland, from the tribe of Judah; Catalonia, Scotland, from the tribe of Gad.

Covenant Theology

Identity Christianity is not orthodox Christianity. Nevertheless, the notion of America as an especially favored people, or as Ronald Reagan once said, quoting Puritan founders, a "city on a hill," the New Jerusalem, is widely shared by Americans. Reagan and most conservatives, of course, consider the linkage between America and Israel largely symbolic. Many right-wing extremists, however, view the relationship literally as an historical fact and for them, just as the ancient Israelites entered into a covenant with the Lord, America has done the same. According to radical patriots America's covenant is what they call the "organic Constitution." This refers to the original articles of the Constitution plus the first ten amendments, the Bill of Rights. Other amendments, especially the 16th establishing a federal income tax, are considered to have ques-

tionable legal status because allegedly they were not passed according to constitutional strictures.

The most extreme patriots deny the constitutionality of the 13th, 14th, and 15th amendments—those outlawing slavery and guaranteeing free men civil and political rights as full American citizens. Their argument is that the organic Constitution was written by white men exclusively for themselves and their blood descendents (Preamble 1986). Non-caucasians residing in America are considered "guest peoples" with no constitutional rights. Their continued residency in this country is entirely contingent upon the pleasure of their hosts, the Anglo-Saxon citizenry. According to some, it is now time for the property of these guests to be confiscated and they themselves exiled to their places of origin (Pace 1985).

All right-wing extremists insist that if America adheres to the edicts of the organic Constitution, she, like Israel before her, shall be favored among the world's nations. Her harvests shall be bountiful, her communities secure, her children obedient to the voices of their parents, and her armies undefeated. But if she falters in her faith, behaving in ways that contravene the sacred compact, then calamities, both natural and human-made, shall follow. This is the explanation for the widespread conviction among extremists today for America's decline in the world. In short, the federal government has established agencies and laws contrary to America's divine compact: these include the Internal Revenue Service; the Federal Reserve System; the Bureau of Alcohol, Tobacco and Firearms; the Forest Service; the Bureau of Land Management; Social Security; Medicare and Medicaid; the Environmental Protection Agency; Housing and Urban Development; and the official apparatus enforcing civil rights for "so-called" minorities.

Essentially, American right-wing extremists view the entire executive branch of the United States government as little more than "jackbooted Nazi thugs," to borrow a phrase from the National Rifle Association fund-raising letter: a threat to freedom of religion, the right to carry weapons, freedom of speech, and the right to have one's property secure from illegal search and seizure.

Clumsy federal-agency assaults, first on the Weaver family in northern Idaho in 1992, then on the Branch Davidian sect in Waco, Texas, in 1993, followed by passage of the assault weapons ban in 1994, are viewed as indicators that the organic Constitution presently is imperiled. This has been the immediate impetus for the appearance throughout rural and Western America of armed militias since the summer of 1994. The terrorists who bombed a federal building in Oklahoma City in the spring of 1995, killing one hundred sixty-eight, were associated with militias headquartered in Michigan and Arizona. One month after the bombing, the national director of the United States Militia Association warned that after the current government falls, homosexuals, abortionists, rapists, "unfaithful politicians," and any criminal not rehabilitated in seven years will be executed. Tax evaders will no longer be treated as felons; instead they will lose their library privileges (Sherwood 1995).

Millennialism

Leading to both the Waco and Weaver incidents was a belief on the victims' parts that world apocalypse is imminent. The Branch Davidians split from the Seventh-Day Adventists in 1935 but share with the mother church its own millenarian convictions. The Weavers received their apocalypticism from *The Late Great Planet Earth* by fundamentalist lay preacher Hal Lindsey (1970), a book that has enjoyed a wide reading on the Christian right.

Both the Davidians and the Weavers were imbued with the idea that the thousand-year-reign of Christ would be preceded by a final battle between the forces of light and darkness. To this end both had deployed elaborate arsenals to protect themselves from the anticipated invasion of "Babylonish troops." These, they feared, would be comprised of agents from the various federal bureaucracies mentioned above, together with UN troops stationed on America's borders awaiting orders from Trilateralists. Ever alert to "signs"

of the impending invasion, both fired at federal officers who had come upon their property; and both ended up precipitating their own martyrdom. Far from quelling millenarian fervor, however, the two tragedies were immediately seized upon by extremists as further evidence of the approaching End Times.

Millenarianism is not unique to Christianity, nor to Western religions; furthermore, millenarianism culminating in violence is not new—in part because one psychological effect of end-time prophesying is a devaluation of worldly things, including property, honors, and human life. At the end of the first Christian millennium (A.D. 1000) as itinerant prophets were announcing the Second Coming, their followers were taking-up arms to prepare the way, and uncounted numbers died (Cohn 1967). It should not surprise observers if, as the second millennium draws to a close and promises of Christ's imminent return increase in frequency, more and more armed cults flee to the mountains, there to prepare for the final conflagration.

Anti-Semitism

Many post-Holocaust Christian and Jewish scholars alike recognize that a pervasive anti-Judaism can be read from the pages of the New Testament, especially in focusing on the role attributed to Jews in Jesus' crucifixion. Rosemary Ruether, for example, argues that anti-Judaism constitutes the "left-hand of Christianity," its archetypal negation (Ruether 1979). Although pre-Christian Greece and Rome were also critical of Jews for alleged disloyalty, anti-Semitism reached unparalleled heights in Christian theology, sometimes relegating Jews to the status of Satan's spawn, the human embodiments of Evil itself.

During the Roman Catholic era, this association became embellished with frightening myths and images. Jews—pictured as feces-eating swine and rats—were accused of murdering Christian children on high feast days, using their blood to make unleavened bread, and poisoning wells. Added to these legends were charges during the capitalist era that Jews control international banking and by means of usury have brought simple, kind-hearted Christians into financial ruin (Hay 1981 [1950]). All of this was incorporated into popular Protestant culture through, among other vehicles, Martin Luther's diatribe, *On the Jews and Their Lies,* a pamphlet that still experiences brisk sales from patriotic bookstores. This is one possible reason for a survey finding by Charles Glock and Rodney Stark that created a minor scandal in the late 1960s. Rigidly orthodox American Christians, they found, displayed far higher levels of Jew-hatred than other Christians, regardless of their education, occupation, race, or income (Glock and Stark 1966).

In the last thirty years there has been "a sharp decline" in anti-Semitic prejudice in America, according to Glock (1993: 68). Mainline churches have played some role in this decline by facilitating Christian-Jewish dialogue, de-emphasizing offensive scriptural passages, and ending missions directed at Jews. Nevertheless, ancient anti-Jewish calumnies continue to be raised by leaders of the groups that are the focus of interest in this [article]. Far from being a product of neurotic syndromes like the so-called Authoritarian (or fascist) Personality, the Jew-hatred of many right-wing extremists today is directly traceable to what they have absorbed from these preachments, sometimes as children.

Human Depravity

> There is none righteous, no not one; . . . there is none that doeth the good, no, no one. Their throat is an open sepulchre. With their tongues they have used deceit; the poison of asps in under their lips. In these words of the apostle Paul, John Calvin says God inveighs not against particular individuals, but against all mankind. "Let it be admitted, then, that men . . . are . . . corrupt . . . by a depravity of nature" (Calvin 1966: 34–36; see Romans 3:11–24).

One of the fundamentals of Calvinist theology, appropriated into popular American Christianity, is this: a transcendent and sovereign God resides in the heavens, relative to whom the earth and its human inhabitants are utterly, hopelessly fallen. True, Calvin only developed a line of thought already anticipated in Genesis and amplified repeatedly over the centuries. However, with a lawyer's penetrating logic, Calvin brought this tradition to its most stark, pessimistic articulation. It is this belief that accompanied the Pilgrims in their venture across the Atlantic, eventually rooting itself in the American psyche.

From its beginnings, a particular version of the doctrine of human depravity has figured prominently in American right-wing extremist discourse. It has served as the basis of its perennial misogyny, shared by both men and women. The female, being supposedly less rational and more passive, is said to be closer to earth's evil. Too, the theology of world devaluation is the likely inspiration for the right-wing's gossipy preoccupation with the body's appetites and the "perilous eroticism of emotion," for its prudish fulminations against music, dance, drink, and dress, and for its homophobia. Here, too, is found legitimation for the right-wing's vitriol against Satanist ouiji boards, "Dungeons and Dragons," and New Age witchcrafters with their horoscopes and aroma-therapies, and most recently, against "pagan-earth-worshippers" and "tree hugging idolaters" (environmentalists). In standing tall to "Satan's Kids" and their cravenness, certain neo-Calvinists in Baptist, Presbyterian, and fundamentalist clothing accomplish their own purity and sanctification.

Conspiratorialism

According to Calvin, earthquakes, pestilence, famine, and plague should pose no challenge to faith in God. We petty, self-absorbed creatures have no right to question sovereign reason. But even in Calvin's time, and more frequently later, many Christians have persisted in asking: if God is truly all-powerful, all-knowing, and all-good, then how is evil possible? Why do innocents suffer? One perennial, quasi-theological response is conspiratorialism. In short, there are AIDS epidemics, murderous holocausts, rampant poverty, and floods because counter-poised to God there exists a second hidden force of nearly equal power and omniscience: the Devil and His human consorters—Jews, Jesuits, Hidden Hands, Insiders, Masons, and Bilderbergers.

By conspiratorialism, we are not referring to documented cases of people secretly scheming to destroy co-workers, steal elections, or run competitors out of business. Conspiracies are a common feature of group life. Instead, we mean the attempt to explain the entirety of human history by means of a cosmic Conspiracy, such as that promulgated in the infamous *Protocols of the Learned Elders of Zion*. This purports to account for all modern institutions by attributing them to the designs of twelve or thirteen—one representing each of the tribes of Israel—Jewish elders (Aho 1994, 68–82). *The Protocols* enjoys immense and endless popularity on the right; and has generated numerous spin-offs: *The International Jew, None Dare Call It Conspiracy,* and the *Mystery of [Jewish] Iniquity,* to name three.

To posit the existence of an evil divinity is heresy in orthodox Christianity. But, theological objections aside, it is difficult indeed for some believers to resist the temptation of intellectual certitude conspiratorialism affords. This certainty derives from the fact that conspiratorialism in the cosmic sense can not be falsified. Every historical event can, and often is, taken as further verification of conspiracies. If newspapers report a case of government corruption, this is evidence of government conspiracy; if they do not, this is evidence of news media complicity in the conspiracy. If the media deny involvement in a cover-up, this is still further proof of their guilt; if they admit to having sat on the story, this is surely an admission of what is already known.

Practice

Christianity means more than adhering to a particular doctrine. To be Christian is to live righteously. God-fearing righteousness may either be understood as a *sign* of one's salvation, as in orthodox Christianity or, as in Mormonism, a way to *earn* eternal life in the celestial heavens.

Nor is it sufficient for the faithful merely to display righteousness in their personal lives and businesses, by being honest, hard-working, and reliable. Many Christians also are obligated to witness to, or labor toward, salvation in the political arena; to work with others to remake this charnel-house world after the will of God; to help establish God's kingdom on earth. Occasionally this means becoming involved in liberal causes—abolitionism, civil rights, the peace and ecological movements; often it has entailed supporting causes on the right. In either case it may require that one publicly stand up to evil. For, as Saint Paul said, to love God is to hate what is contrary to God.

Such a mentality may lead to "holy war," the organized effort to eliminate human fetishes of evil (Aho 1994: 23–34). For some, in cleansing the world of putrefaction their identity as Christian is recognized, it is re-known. This is not to argue that holy war is unique to Christianity, or that all Christians participate in holy wars. Most Christians are satisfied to renew their faith through the rites of Christmas, Easter, baptism, marriage, or mass. Furthermore, those who *do* speak of holy war often use it metaphorically to describe a private spiritual battle against temptation, as in "I am a soldier of Christ, therefore I am not permitted to fight" (Sandford 1966). Lastly, even holy war in the political sense does not necessarily imply the use of violence. Although they sometimes have danced tantalizingly close to extremism (in the sense defined earlier), neither Pat Robertson nor Jerry Falwell, for example, have advocated non-democratic means in their "wars" to avert America's decline.

Let us examine the notion of Christian holy war more closely. The sixteenth-century father of Protestant reform, Martin Luther, repudiated the concept of holy war, arguing that there exist two realms: holiness, which is the responsibility of the Church, and warfare, which falls under the State's authority (Luther 1974). Mixing these realms, he says, perverts the former while unnecessarily hamstringing the latter. This does not mean that Christians may forswear warfare, according to Luther. In his infinite wisdom, God has ordained princes to quell civil unrest and protect nations from invasion. Luther's exhortations to German officials that they spare no means in putting down peasant revolts are well known. Indeed, few theologians have "so highly praised the virtues of the State as Luther," says Ernst Troeltsch. Nevertheless, State violence is at best "sinful power to punish sin" for Luther. It is not a sacred instrument (Troeltsch 1960: 539–544, 656–677). To this day, Lutherans generally are less responsive to calls for holy wars than many other Christians.

John Calvin, on the other hand, rejected Luther's proposal to separate church from State. Instead, his goal was to establish a Christocracy in Geneva along Roman Catholic lines, and to attain this goal through force, if need be, as Catholicism had done. Calvin says that not only is violence to establish God's rule on earth permitted, it is commanded. "Good brother, we must bend unto all means that give furtherance to the holy cause" (Walzer 1965: 17, 38, 68–87, 90–91, 100–109; see Troeltsch 1960: 599–601, 651–652, 921–922 n. 399). This notion profoundly influenced Oliver Cromwell and his English revolutionary army known as the Ironsides, so named because of its righteously cold brutality (Solt 1971). And it was the Calvinist ethic, not that of Luther, that was imported to America by the Puritans, informing the politics of Presbyterians and Congregationalists—the immediate heirs of Calvinism—as well as some Methodists and many Baptists. Hence, it is not surprising that those raised in these denominations are often overrepresented in samples of "saints" on armed crusades to save the world for Christ.

Seminal to the so-called pedagogic or educational function of holy war are two requirements. First, the enemy against whom the saint fights must be portrayed in terms appropriate to his status as a fetish of evil. Second, the campaign against him must be equal to his diabolism. It must be terrifying, bloodthirsty, uncompromising.

"Prepare War!" was issued by the now defunct Covenant, Sword and the Arm of the Lord, a fundamentalist Christian paramilitary commune headquartered in Missouri. A raid on the compound in the late 1980s uncovered one of the largest private arms caches ever in American history. Evidently, this arsenal was to be used to combat what the pamphlet calls "Negro-beasts of the field . . . who eat the flesh of men. . . . This cannibalistic fervor shall cause them to eat the dead *and* the living during" the time of Tribulations, prophesied in The Book of Revelation (CSA n.d.: 19). The weapons were also to be directed against "Sodomite homosexuals waiting in their lusts to rape," "Seed-of-Satan Jews, who are today sacrificing people in darkness," and "do-gooders who've fought for the 'rights' of these groups" (CSA n.d.: 19). When the Lord God has delivered these enemies into our hands, warns the pamphlet quoting the Old Testament, "thou shalt save alive nothing that breatheth: but thou shalt utterly destroy them" (CSA n.d.: 20; see Deuteronomy 20: 10–18).

The 1990s saw a series of State-level initiatives seeking to deny homosexuals civil rights. Although most of these failed by narrow margins, one in Colorado was passed (later to be adjudged unconstitutional), due largely to the efforts of a consortium of fundamentalist Christian churches. One of the most influential of these was the Laporte, Colorado, Church of Christ, America's largest Identity congregation (more on Identity Christianity below). Acknowledging that the title of their pamphlet "Death Penalty for Homosexuals" would bring upon them the wrath of liberals, its authors insist that "such slanderous tactics" will not deter the anti-homosexual campaign. "For truth will ultimately prevail, no matter how many truth-bearers are stoned." And what precisely is this truth? It is that the Lord Himself has declared that "if a man also lie with mankind, as he lieth with a woman, both of them have committed an abomination: they shall surely be put to death; their blood shall be upon them" (Peters 1992: i; see Leviticus 20:13).

Like "Prepare War!," "Death Penalty for Homosexuals" is not satisfied merely to cite biblical references. To justify the extremity of its attack, it must paint the homosexual in luridly terrifying colors. Finding and citing a quote from the most extreme of radical gay activists, their pamphlet warns (CSA n.d.: 19):

> [They] shall sodomize [our] sons. . . . [They] shall seduce them in [our] schools, . . . in [our] locker rooms, . . . in [our] army bunkhouses . . . wherever men are with men together. [Our] sons shall become [their] minions and do [their] bidding. . . . All laws banning homosexual activity will be revoked. Instead, legislation shall be passed which engenders love between men. . . . [They] shall stage plays in which man openly caresses man. . . . The museums of the world will be filled only with paintings of . . . naked lads. . . . Love between men [will become] fashionable and de rigueur. [They] will eliminate heterosexual liaisons. . . . There will be no compromises. . . . Those who oppose [them] will be exiled. [They] shall raise vast private armies . . . to defeat [us]. . . . The family unit . . . will be abolished. . . . All churches who condemn [them] will be closed. . . . The society to emerge will be governed by . . . gay poets. . . . Any heterosexual man will be barred from . . . influence. All males who insist on remaining . . . heterosexual will be tried in homosexual courts of justice."

What should Christians do in the face of this looming specter, asks the pamphlet? "We, today, can and should have God's Law concerning Homosexuality and its judgment of the death penalty." For "they which commit such things," says the apostle Paul, "are worthy of death" (CSA n.d.: 15; see Romans 1:27–32). Extremism fans the flames of extremism.

Organization

Contrary to popular thinking, people rarely join right-wing groups because they have a prior belief in doctrines such as those enumerated above. Rather, they come to believe because they have first joined. That is, people first affiliate with right-wing activists and only then begin altering their intellectual outlooks to sustain and strengthen these ties. The original ties may develop from their jobs, among neighbors, among prison acquaintances, or through romantic relationships.

Take the case of Cindy Cutler, who was last seen teaching music at the Aryan Nations Church academy (Mauer, 1980). Reflecting on the previous decade she could well wonder at how far she had come in such a short time.

Cindy had been raised Baptist. "I was with the Jesus Christ thing, that Jesus was my savior and God was love. We'd go to the beach up to a perfect stranger and say, 'Are you saved?' " Such was the serene existence of an uncommonly pretty thrice born-again teenager then residing in San Diego—until she met Gary Cutler, a Navy man stationed nearby. Gary was fourteen years Cindy's senior and seemed the "good Christian man" she had been looking for when they met one Sunday at Baptist services.

Gary and Cindy were already dating when he discovered Identity Christianity. Brought up as a Mormon, he had left the church when it began granting priesthood powers to Black members during the 1970s. After several years searching for a new religious home, Gary claims to have first heard the Identity message one evening while randomly spinning the radio dial. An Identity preacher was extolling the white race as God's chosen people. Gary says the sermon gave him "new found pride."

In the meantime, Cindy's fondness for Gary was growing. The only problem was his espousal of Identity beliefs. As part of her faith, Cindy had learned that Jews, not Anglo-Saxons, were from Israel, and that Jesus was Jewish. Both of these notions were in conflict with what Gary was now saying. Perhaps, Cindy feared, she and Gary were incompatible after all. How could she ever find intellectual consensus with her fiance?

Gary and Cindy routinely spent time together in Bible study. One evening Cindy saw the light. She had already learned from church that Jews were supposedly "Christ killers." It was this information that enabled her to overcome what she calls her prideful resistance to Identity. The occasion of her conversion was this passage: "My sheep know me and hear my voice, and follow me" (John 10: 27). "That's how I got into Identity," she later said. "I questioned how they [the Jews] could be God's chosen people if they hate my Christ." Having discovered a shared theological ground upon which to stand, Gary and Cindy could now marry.

The point of this story is the sociological truth that the way in which some people become right-wing extremists is indistinguishable from the way others become vegetarians, peace activists, or members of mainline churches (Lofland and Stark 1965; Aho 1991: 185–211). *Their affiliations are mediated by significant others already in the movement.* It is from these others that they first learn of the cause; sometimes it is through the loaning of a pamphlet or videotape; occasionally it takes the form of an invitation to a meeting or workshop. As the relationship with the other tightens, the recruit's viewpoint begins to change. At this stage old friends, family members, and cohorts, observing the recruit spending inordinate time with "those new people," begin their interrogations: "What's up with you, man?" In answer, the new recruit typically voices shocking things: bizarre theologies, conspiracy theories, manichaeistic worldviews. Either because of conscious "disowning" or unconscious avoidance, the recruit finds the old ties loosening, and as they unbind, the "stupidity" and "backwardness" of prior acquaintances becomes increasingly evident.

Pushed away from old relationships and simultaneously pulled into the waiting arms of new friends, lovers, and comrades, the recruit is absorbed into the movement. Announcements of full conversion to extremism follow. To display commitment to the cause, further steps may be deemed necessary: pulling one's children out of public schools where "secular humanism" is taught; working for radical political candidates to stop America's "moral decline"; refusing to support ZOG with taxes; renouncing one's citizenship and throwing away social security card and driver's license; moving to a rugged wilderness to await the End Times. Occasionally it means donning camouflage, taking up high-powered weaponry, and confronting the "forces of satan" themselves.

There are two implications to this sociology of recruitment. First and most obviously, involvement in social networks is crucial to being mobilized into right-wing activism. Hence, contrary to the claims of the estrangement theory of extremism mentioned above, those who are truly isolated from their local communities are the last and least likely to become extremists themselves. My research (Aho 1991, 1994) suggests that among the most important of these community ties is membership in independent fundamentalist, Baptist, or Presbyterian congregations.

Secondly, being situated in particular networks is largely a matter of chance. None of us choose our parents. Few choose their co-workers, fellow congregants, or neighbors, and even friendships and marriages are restricted to those available to us by the happenstance of our geography and times. What this means is that almost any person could find themselves in a Christian patriot communications network that would position them for recruitment into right-wing extremism.

As we have already pointed out, American right-wing extremists are neither educationally nor psychologically different from the general population. Nor are they any more status insecure than other Americans. What makes them different is how they are socially positioned. This positioning includes their religious affiliation. Some people find themselves in churches that expose them to the right-wing world. This increases the likelihood of their becoming right-wingers.

Conclusion

Throughout American history, a particular style of Christianity has nurtured right-wing extremism. Espousing doctrines like human depravity, white America as God's elect people, conspiratorialism, Jews as Christ killers, covenant theology and the right to revolt, and millennialism, this brand of Christianity is party rooted in orthodox Calvinism and in the theologically questionable fantasies of popular imagination. Whatever its source, repeatedly during the last two centuries, its doctrines have served to prepare believers cognitively to assume hostile attitudes toward "un-Christian"—hence un-American—individuals, groups, and institutional practices.

This style of Christianity has also given impetus to hatred and violence through its advocacy of armed crusades against evil. Most of all, however, the cults, sects, and denominations wherein this style flourishes have served as mobilization centers for recruitment into right-wing causes. From the time of America's inception, right-wing political leaders in search of supporters have successfully enlisted clergymen who preach these principles to bring their congregations into the fold in "wars" to save America for Christ.

It is a mistake to think that modern Americans are more bigoted and racist than their ancestors were. Every American generation has experienced right-wing extremism, even that occasionally erupting into vigilante violence of the sort witnessed daily on the news today. What is different in our time is the sophistication and availability of communications and weapons technology. Today, mobilizations to right-wing causes has been infinitely enhanced by the availability of personal computer systems capable of storing and retrieving information on millions of potential recruits. Mobilization has also been facilitated by cheap shortwave radio and cable-television access, the telephone tree, desktop publishing, and readily available studio-quality recorders. Small coteries of extremists can now activate supporters across immense distances at the touch of a button. Add to this the modern instrumentality for maiming and killing available to the average American citizen: military-style assault weaponry easily convertible into fully automatic machine guns, powerful explosives manufacturable from substances like diesel oil and fertilizer, harmless in themselves, hence purchasable over-the-counter. Anti-tank and aircraft weapons, together with assault vehicles, have also been uncovered recently in private-arms caches in the Western states.

Because of these technological changes, religious and political leaders today have a greater responsibility to speak and write with care regarding those with whom they disagree. Specifi-

cally, they must control the temptation to demonize their opponents, lest, in their declarations of war they bring unforeseen destruction not only on their enemies, but on themselves.

REFERENCES

Aho, J. 1991. *The Politics of Righteousness: Idaho Christian Patriotism.* Seattle: University of Washington Press.

———. 1994. *This Thing of Darkness: A Sociology of the Enemy.* Seattle: University of Washington Press.

Barkun, M. 1994. *Religion and the Racist Right: The Origins of the Christian Identity Movement.* Chapel Hill: North Carolina University Press.

Calvin J. 1966. *On God and Man.* F. W. Strothmann (ed.). New York: Ungar.

Cohn, N. 1967. *The Pursuit of the Millennium.* New York: Oxford University Press.

CSA. n.d. "Prepare War!" Pontiac, Missouri: CSA Bookstore.

Dilling, E. 1952. *The Plot Against Christianity.* n.p.

Flynn, K. and G. Gerhardt. 1989. *The Silent Brotherhood: Inside America's Racist Underground.* New York: Free Press.

Glock, C. 1993. "The Churches and Social Change in Twentieth-Century America." *Annals of the American Academy of Political and Social Science.* 527: 67–83.

Glock, C. and R. Stark. 1966. *Christian Beliefs and Anti-Semitism.* New York: Harper & Row.

Hay, M. 1981 (1950). *The Roots of Christian Anti-Semitism.* New York: Anti-Defamation League of B'nai B'rith.

Lindsey, H. 1970. *The Late Great Planet Earth.* Grand Rapids: Zondervan.

Lipset, S. M. and E. Raab. 1970. *The Politics of Unreason: Right-Wing Extremism in America, 1790–1970.* New York: Harper & Row.

Lofland, J. and R. Stark. 1965. "Becoming a World-Saver: A Theory of Conversation to a Deviant Perspective." *American Sociological Review* 30: 862–875.

Luther, M. 1974. *Luther: Selected Political Writings,* J. M. Porter, ed. Philadelphia: Fortress Press.

Mannheim, K. 1952. "The Problem of Generations," in *Essays in the Sociology of Knowledge.* London: Routledge and Kegan Paul.

Mauer, D. 1980. "Couple Finds Answers in Butler's Teachings." *Idaho Statesman.* Sept. 14.

Nisbet, R. 1953. *The Quest for Community.* New York: Harper and Brothers.

Pace, J. O. 1985. *Amendment to the Constitution.* Los Angeles: Johnson, Pace, Simmons and Fennel.

Peters, P. 1992. *Death Penalty for Homosexuals.* LaPorte, Colorado: Scriptures for America. Preamble. 1986. "Preamble to the United States Constitution: Who Are the Posterity?" Oregon City, Oregon: Republic vs. Democracy Redress.

Ring, R. H. 1985. "The Yarbrough's." *The Denver Post.* Jan. 6.

Robison, J. 1967 (1798). *Proofs of a Conspiracy. . . .* Los Angeles: Western Islands.

Ruether, R. 1979. *Faith and Fratricide: The Theological Roots of Anti-Semitism.* New York: Seabury.

Sandford, F. W. 1966. *The Art of War for the Christian Soldier.* Amherst, New Hampshire: Kingdom Press.

Schlesinger, A. 1986. *The Cycles of American History.* Boston: Houghton Mifflin.

Sherwood, "Commander" S. 1995. Quoted in *Idaho State Journal.* May 21.

Shupe, A. and W. Stacey. 1983. "The Moral Majority Constituency" in *The New Christian Right,* R. Liebman and R. Wuthnow, eds. New York: Aldine.

Simpson, J. 1983. "Moral Issues and Status Politics" in *The New Christian Right,* R. Liebman and R. Wuthnow, eds. New York: Aldine.

Solt, L. 1971. *Saints in Arms: Puritanism and Democracy in Cromwell's Army.* New York: AMS Press.

Stark, R. and William Bainbridge. 1985. *The Future of Religion: Secularization, Revival and Cult Formation.* Berkeley: University of California Press.

Stouffer, S. A. 1966. *Communism, Conformity and Civil Liberties.* New York: John Wiley.

Troeltsch, E. 1960. *Social Teachings of the Christian Churches.* Trans. by O. Wyon. New York: Harper & Row.

Walzer, M. 1965. *The Revolution of the Saints.* Cambridge, MA: Harvard University Press.

Wilcox, C. 1992. *God's Warriors: The Christian Right in Twentieth Century America.* Baltimore, MD: Johns Hopkins University Press.

THINKING ABOUT THE READING

Describe the religious doctrines that typically characterize right-wing extremist groups in the United States. Compare the groups that Aho describes to the so-called Islamic extremist groups that became the focus of national attention after the attacks of September 11, 2001. How are they alike? How do they differ? After reading Aho's article, do you think that Christianity is a cause of right-wing extremism? If not, how can you account for the religiously inspired rhetoric of such movements? If so, what responsibility do "less extreme" churches have in suppressing extremist groups? In a more general sense, what role do you think religious institutions ought to play in movements for political and social change?

Challenging Power
Toxic Waste Protests and the Politicization of White, Working-Class Women

Celene Krauss

Over the past two decades, toxic waste disposal has been a central focus of women's grassroots environmental activism. Women of diverse racial, ethnic, and class backgrounds have assumed the leadership of community environmental struggles around toxic waste issues (Krauss 1993). Out of their experience of protest, these women have constructed ideologies of environmental justice that reveal broader issues of inequality underlying environmental hazards (Bullard 1990, 1994). Environmental justice does not exist as an abstract concept prior to these women's activism. It grows out of the concrete, immediate, everyday experience of struggles around issues of survival. As women become involved in toxic waste issues, they go through a politicizing process that is mediated by their experiences of class, race, and ethnicity (Krauss 1993).

Among the earliest community activists in toxic waste protests were white, working-class women. This [article] examines the process by which these women became politicized through grassroots protest activities in the 1980s, which led to their analyses of environmental justice, and in many instances to their leadership in regional and national toxic waste coalitions. These women would seem unlikely candidates for becoming involved in political protest. They came out of a culture that shares a strong belief in the existing political system, and in which traditional women's roles center around the private arena of family. Although financial necessity may have led them into the workplace, the primary roles from which they derived meaning, identity, and satisfaction are those of mothering and taking care of family. Yet, as we shall see, the threat that toxic wastes posed to family health and community survival disrupted the taken-for-granted fabric of their lives, politicizing women who had never viewed themselves as activists. . . .

This [article] shows how white, working-class women's involvement in toxic waste issues has wider implications for social change. . . . These women . . . fought to close down toxic waste dump sites, to prevent the siting of hazardous waste incinerators, to oppose companies' waste-disposal policies, to push for recycling projects, and so on. Their voices show us . . . that their single-issue community protests led them through a process of politicization and their broader analysis of inequities of class and gender in the public arena and in the family. Propelled into the public arena in defense of their children, they ultimately challenged government, corporations, experts, husbands, and their own insecurities as working-class women. Their analysis of environmental justice and inequality led them to form coalitions with labor and people of color around environmental issues. These women's traditional beliefs about motherhood, family, and democracy served a crucial function in this politicizing process. While they framed their analyses in terms of traditional constructions of gender and the state, they actively reinterpreted these constructions into an oppositional ideology, which became a resource of resistance and a source of power in the public arena.

Subjective Dimensions of Grassroots Activism

In most sociological analysis of social movements, the subjective dimension of protest has often been ignored or viewed as private and individualistic. . . . [Contemporary theories] show us how experience is not merely a personal, individualistic concept: it is social. People's experiences reflect where they fit into the social hierarchy. . . . Thus, white, working-class women interpret their experience of toxic waste problems within the context of their particular cultural history, arriving at a critique that reflects broader issues of class and gender. . . .

. . . This article focuses on the subjective process by which white, working-class women involved in toxic waste protests construct an oppositional consciousness out of their everyday lives, experiences, and identities. As these women became involved in the public arena, they confronted a world of power normally hidden from them. This forced them to re-examine their assumptions about private and public power and to develop a broad reconceptualization of gender, family, and government.

The experience of protest is central to this process and can reshape traditional beliefs and values (see Thompson 1963). My analysis reveals the contradictory ways in which traditional culture mediates white, working-class women's subjective experience and interpretation of structural inequality. Their protests are framed in terms of dominant ideologies of motherhood, family, and a deep faith in the democratic system. Their experience also reveals how dominant ideologies are appropriated and reconstructed as an instrument of their politicization and a legitimating ideology used to justify resistance. For example, as the political economy of growth displaces environmental problems into their communities, threatening the survival of children and family and creating everyday crises, government toxic waste policies are seen to violate their traditional belief that a democratic government will protect their families. Ideologies of motherhood and democracy become political resources which these women use to initiate and justify their resistance, their increasing politicization, and their fight for a genuine democracy.

Methodological Considerations

My analysis is based on the oral and written voices of white, working-class women involved in toxic waste protests. Sources include individual interviews, as well as conference presentations, pamphlets, books, and other written materials that have emerged from this movement. Interviews were conducted with a snowball sample of twenty white, working-class women who were leaders in grassroots protest activities against toxic waste landfills and incinerators during the 1980s. These women ranged in age from twenty-five to forty; all but one had young children at the time of their protest. They were drawn from a cross section of the country, representing urban, suburban, and rural areas. None of them had been politically active before the protest; many of them, however, have continued to be active in subsequent community movements, often becoming leaders in state-wide and national coalitions around environmental and social justice issues. I established contact with these women through networking at activist conferences. Open-ended interviews were conducted between May 1989, and December 1991, and lasted from two to four hours. The interview was designed to generate a history of these women's activist experiences, information about changes in political beliefs, and insights into their perceptions of their roles as women, mothers, and wives.

Interviews were also conducted with Lois Gibbs and four other organizers for the Citizens Clearinghouse for Hazardous Wastes (CCHW). CCHW is a nation-wide organization created by Gibbs, who is best known for her successful campaign to relocate families in Love Canal, New York. Over the past two decades, this organization has functioned as a key resource for community groups fighting around toxic waste issues in the United States. Its leadership and staff are composed primarily of women, and the organization played a key role in shaping the ideology of working-class women's environmental activism in the 1980s.

My scholarly interest in working-class women's community activism grew out of my own involvement as a community activist and organizer in the 1970s. This decade marked the period of my own politicization as a white, middle-class woman working with women from many different racial-ethnic backgrounds as they challenged corporate and governmental policies that were destroying urban, working-class neighborhoods. My subsequent academic research has focused on the community protests of working-class women, who are often forgotten in our understanding of movements for social change. My experiences within the environmental movement helped guide my research and deepen my analysis. Through the issue of toxic waste protests, I have examined different facets of working-class women's community activism, most recently the ways in which consciousness and agency are mediated by different experiences of race and ethnicity (Krauss 1993).

The Process of Politicization

Women identify the toxic waste movement as a women's movement, composed primarily of mothers. As one woman who fought against an incinerator in Arizona and subsequently worked on other anti-incinerator campaigns throughout the state stressed: "Women are the backbone of the grassroots groups, they are the ones who stick with it, the ones who won't back off." Because mothers are traditionally responsible for the health of their children, they are more likely than others within their communities to begin to make the link between toxic waste and their children's ill health. And in communities around the United States, it was women who began to uncover numerous toxin-related health problems: multiple miscarriages, birth defects, cancer, neurological symptoms, and so on. Given the placement of toxic waste facilities in working-class and low-income communities and communities of color, it is not surprising that women from these groups have played a particularly important role in fighting against environmental hazards.

White, working-class women's involvement in toxic waste issues is complicated by the political

reality that they, like most people, are excluded from the policy-making process. For the most part, corporate and governmental disposal policies with far-reaching social and political consequences are made without the knowledge of community residents. People may unknowingly live near (or even on top of) a toxic waste dump, or they may assume that the facility is well regulated by the government. Consequently, residents are often faced with a number of problems of seemingly indeterminate origin, and the information withheld from them may make them unwitting contributors to the ill health of their children.

The discovery of a toxic waste problem and the threat it poses to family sets in motion a process of critical questioning about the relationship between women's private work as mothers and the public arena of politics. The narratives of the women involved in toxic waste protests focus on political transformation, on the process of "becoming" an activist. Prior to their discovery of the link between their family's health and toxic waste, few of these women had been politically active. They saw their primary work in terms of the "private" sphere of motherhood and family. But the realization that toxic waste issues threatened their families thrust them into the public arena in defense of this private sphere. According to Penny Newman:

> We woke up one day to discover that our families were being damaged by toxic contamination, a situation in which we had little, if any, input. It wasn't a situation in which we chose to become involved, rather we did it because we had to . . . it was a matter of our survival. (Newman 1991, 8)

Lois Gibbs offered a similar account of her involvement in Love Canal:

> When my mother asked me what I wanted to do when I grew up, I said I wanted to have six children and be a homemaker. . . . I moved into Love Canal and I bought the American Dream: a house, two children, a husband, and HBO. And then something happened to me and that was Love Canal. I got involved because my son

Michael had epilepsy . . . and my daughter Melissa developed a rare blood disease and almost died because of something someone else did. . . . I never thought of myself as an activist or an organizer. I was a housewife, a mother, but all of a sudden it was my family, my children, and my neighbors. . . .

It was through their role as mothers that many of these women began to suspect a connection between the invisible hazard posed by toxic wastes and their children's ill health, and this was their first step toward political activism. At Love Canal, for example, Lois Gibbs's fight to expose toxic waste hazards was triggered by the link she made between her son's seizures and the toxic waste dump site. After reading about toxic hazards in a local newspaper, she thought about her son and then surveyed her neighbors to find that they had similar health problems. In Woburn, Massachusetts, Ann Anderson found that other neighborhood children were, like her son, being treated for leukemia, and she began to wonder if this was an unusually high incidence of the disease. In Denver, mothers comparing stories at Tupperware parties were led to question the unusually large number of sick and dying children in their community. These women's practical activity as mothers and their extended networks of family and community led them to make the connection between toxic waste and sick children—a discovery process rooted in what Sara Ruddick (1989) has called the everyday practice of mothering, in which, through their informal networks, mothers compare notes and experiences, developing a shared body of personal, empirical knowledge.

Upon making the link between their family's ill health and toxic wastes, the women's first response was to go to the government, a response that reflects a deeply held faith in democracy embedded in their working-class culture. They assumed that the government would protect the health and welfare of their children. Gibbs (1982, 12) reports:

I grew up in a blue-collar community, I was very patriotic, into democracy . . . I believed in

government. . . . I believed that if you had a complaint, you went to the right person in government. If there was a way to solve the problem, they would be glad to do it.

An Alabama activist who fought to prevent the siting of an incinerator describes a similar response:

We just started educating ourselves and gathering information about the problems of incineration. We didn't think our elected officials knew. Surely, if they knew that there was already a toxic waste dump in our county, they would stop it.

In case after case, however, these women described facing a government that was indifferent, if not antagonistic, to their concerns. At Love Canal, local officials claimed that the toxic waste pollution was insignificant, the equivalent of smoking just three cigarettes a day. In South Brunswick, New Jersey, governmental officials argued that living with pollution was the price of a better way of life. In Jacksonville, Arkansas, women were told that the dangers associated with dioxin emitted from a hazardous waste incinerator were exaggerated, no worse than "eating two or three tablespoons of peanut butter over a thirty-year period." Also in Arkansas, a woman who linked her ill health to a fire at a military site that produced agent orange was told by doctors that she was going through a "change of life." In Stringfellow, California, eight hundred thousand gallons of toxic chemical waste pumped into the community flowed directly behind the elementary school and into the playground. Children played in contaminated puddles yet officials withheld information from their parents because "they didn't want to panic the public."

Government's dismissal of their concerns about the health of their families and communities challenged these white, working-class women's democratic assumptions and opened a window on a world of power whose working they had not before questioned. Government explanations starkly contradicted the personal, empirical evidence which the women discovered as mothers, the everyday knowledge that their children and their neighbors' children were ill. Indeed, a recurring theme in the narratives of these women is the transformation of their beliefs about government. Their politicization is rooted in a deep sense of violation, hurt, and betrayal from finding out their government will not protect their families. Echoes of this disillusionment are heard from women throughout the country. In the CCHW publication *Empowering Women* (1989, 31) one activist noted:

> All our lives we are taught to believe certain things about ourselves as women, about democracy and justice, and about people in positions of authority. Once we become involved with toxic waste problems, we need to confront some our old beliefs and change the way we view things.

Lois Gibbs summed up this feeling when she stated:

> There is something about discovering that democracy isn't democracy as we know it. When you lose faith in your government, it's like finding out your mother was fooling around on your father. I was very upset. It almost broke my heart because I really believed in the system. I still believe in the system, only now I believe that democracy is of the people and by the people, that people have to move it, it ain't gonna move by itself.

These women's loss of faith in "democracy" as they had understood it led them to develop a more autonomous and critical stance. Their investigation shifted to a political critique of the undemocratic nature of government itself, making the link between government inaction and corporate power, and discovering that government places corporate interests and profit ahead of the health needs of families and communities. At Love Canal, residents found that local government's refusal to acknowledge the scope of the toxic waste danger was related to plans of Hooker Chemical, the polluting industry, for a multi-million dollar downtown development

project. In Woburn, Massachusetts, government officials feared that awareness of the health hazard posed by a dump would limit their plans for real-estate development. In communities throughout the United States, women came to see that government policies supported waste companies' preference of incineration over recycling because incineration was more profitable.

Ultimately, their involvement in toxic waste protests led these women to develop a perspective on environmental justice rooted in issues of class and a critique of the corporate state. They argued that government's claims—to be democratic, to act on behalf of the public interest, to hold the family sacrosanct—are false. One woman who fought an incinerator in Arizona recalled:

> I believed in government. When I heard EPA, I thought, "Ooh, that was so big." Now I wouldn't believe them if they said it was sunny outside. I have a list of the revolving door of the EPA. Most of them come from Browning Ferris or Waste Management, the companies that plan landfills and incinerators.

As one activist in Alabama related:

> I was politically naive. I was real surprised because I live in an area that's like the Bible belt of the South. Now I think the God of the United States is really economic development, and that has got to change.

Another activist emphasized:

> We take on government and polluters. . . . We are up against the largest corporations in the United States. They have lots of money to lobby, pay off, bribe, cajole, and influence. They threaten us. Yet we challenge them with the only things we have—people and the truth. We learn that our government is not out to protect our rights. To protect our families we are now forced to picket, protest and shout. (Zeff et al. 1989, 31)

In the process of protest, these women were also forced to examine their assumptions about the family as a private haven, separate from the public arena, which would however be protected by the policies and actions of government should the need arise. The issue of toxic waste shows the many ways in which government allows this haven to be invaded by polluted water, hazardous chemicals, and other conditions that threaten the everyday life of the family. Ultimately, these women arrived at a concept of environmental injustice rooted in the inequities of power that displace the costs of toxic waste unequally onto their communities. The result was a critical political stance that contributed to the militancy of their activism. Highly traditional values of democracy and motherhood remained central to their lives: they justified their resistance as mothers protecting their children and working to make the promise of democracy real. Women's politicization around toxic waste protests led them to transform their traditional beliefs into resources of opposition which enabled them to enter the public arena and challenge its legitimacy, breaking down the public/private distinction.

Appropriating Power in the Public Arena

Toxic waste issues and their threat to family and community prompted white, working-class women to redefine their roles as mothers. Their work of mothering came to extend beyond taking care of the children, husband, and housework; they saw the necessity of preserving the family by entering the public arena. In so doing, they discovered and overcame a more subtle process of intimidation, which limited their participation in the public sphere.

As these women became involved in toxic waste issues, they came into conflict with a public world where policy makers are traditionally white, male, and middle class. The Citizen's Clearinghouse for Hazardous Waste, in the summary of its 1989 conference on women and organizing, noted:

> Seventy to eighty percent of local leaders are women. They are women leaders in a community run by men. Because of this, many of the obstacles that these women face as leaders stem from the conflicts between their traditional

female role in the community and their new role as leader: conflicts with male officials and authorities who have not yet adjusted to these persistent, vocal, head-strong women challenging the system. . . . Women are frequently ignored by male politicians, male government officials and male corporate spokesmen.

Entering the public arena meant overcoming internal and external barriers to participation, shaped by gender and class. White, working-class women's reconstructed definition of motherhood became a resource for this process, and their narratives reveal several aspects of this transformation.

For these women, entering the public arena around toxic waste issues was often extremely stressful. Many of them were initially shy and intimidated, as simple actions such as speaking at a meeting opened up wider issues about authority, and experiences of gender and class combined to heighten their sense of inadequacy. Many of these women describe, for example, that their high-school education left them feeling ill-equipped to challenge "experts," whose legitimacy, in which they had traditionally believed, was based on advanced degrees and specialized knowledge.

One woman who fought to stop the siting of an incinerator in her community in Arizona recalled: "I used to cry if I had to speak at a PTA meeting. I was so frightened." An activist in Alabama described her experience in fighting the siting of an incinerator in her community:

> I was a woman . . . an assistant Sunday School teacher. . . . In the South, women are taught not to be aggressive, we're supposed to be hospitable and charitable and friendly. We don't protest, we don't challenge authority. So it was kind of difficult for me to get involved. I was afraid to speak. And all of a sudden everything became controversial. . . . I think a lot of it had to do with not knowing what I was. . . . The more I began to know, the better I was . . . the more empowered.

Male officials further exacerbated this intimidation by ignoring the women, by criticizing them for being overemotional, and by delegitimizing their authority by labeling them "hysterical housewives"—a label used widely, regardless of the professional status of the woman. In so doing, they revealed an antipathy to emotionality, a quality valued in the private sphere of family and motherhood but scorned in the public arena as irrational and inappropriate to "objective" discourse.

On several levels, the debate around toxic waste issues was framed by policy makers in such a way as to exclude women's participation, values, and expression. Women's concerns about their children were trivialized by being placed against a claim that the wider community benefits from growth and progress. Information was withheld from them. Discourse was framed as rational, technical, and scientific, using the testimony of "experts" to discredit the everyday empirical knowledge of the women. Even such details as seating arrangements reflected traditional power relations and reinforced the women's internalization of those relations.

These objective and subjective barriers to participation derived from a traditional definition of women's roles based on the separation of the public and private arenas. Yet it is out of these women's political redefinition of the traditional role of mother that they found the resources to overcome these constraints, ultimately becoming self-confident and assertive. They used the resources of their own experience to alter the power relations they had discovered in the public arena.

The traditional role of mother, of protector of the family and community, served to empower these activists on a number of levels. From the beginning, their view of this role provided the motivation for women to take risks in defense of their families and overcome their fears of participating in the public sphere. A woman who fought the siting of an incinerator in Arkansas described this power:

> I was afraid to hurt anyone's feelings or step on anyone's toes. But I'm protective and aggressive, especially where my children are concerned.

That's what brought it out of me. A mother protecting my kids. It appalled me that money could be more important than the health of my children.

A mother in New Jersey described overcoming her fear in dealing with male governmental officials at public hearings, "When I look at a male government official, I remember that he was once a little boy, born of a woman like me, and then I feel more powerful." In talking about Love Canal, Lois Gibbs showed the power of motherhood to carry women into activities alien to their experience:

> When it came to Love Canal, we never thought about ourselves as protestors. We carried signs, we barricaded, we blocked the gates, we were arrested. We thought of it as parents protecting our children. In retrospect, of course, we were protesting. I think if it had occurred to us we wouldn't have done it.

In these ways, they appropriated the power they felt in the private arena as a source of empowerment in the public sphere. "We're insecure challenging the authority of trained experts," notes Gibbs, "but we also have a title of authority, 'mother.'"

Working-class women's experiences as organizers of family life served as a further source of empowerment. Lois Gibbs noted that women organized at Love Canal by constantly analyzing how they would handle a situation in the family, and then translating that analysis into political action. For example, Gibbs explained:

> If our child wanted a pair of jeans, who would they go to? Well they would go to their father since their father had the money—that meant we should go to Governor Carey.

Gibbs drew on her own experience to develop organizing conferences that helped working-class women learn to translate their skills as family organizers into the political arena.

> I decided as a housewife and mother much of what I learned to keep the household running smoothly were skills that translated very well

into this new thing called organizing. I also decided that this training in running a home was one of the key reasons why so many of the best leaders in the toxic movement—in fact, the overwhelming majority—are women, and specifically women who are housewives and mothers. (Zeff 1989, 177)

Of her work with the CCHW, Gibbs stated:

In our own organization we're drawing out these experiences for women. So we say, what do you mean you're not an organizer? Are you a homemaker—then God damn it you can organize and you don't know it. So, for example, when we say you need to plan long-term and short-term goals, women may say, I don't know how to do that. . . . We say, what do you mean you don't know how to do that? Let's talk about something in the household—you plan meals for five, seven, fourteen days—you think about what you want for today and what you're going to eat on Sunday—that is short-term and long-term goals.

Movement language like "plug up the toilet," the expression for waste reduction, helped women to reinterpret toxic waste issues in the framework of their everyday experience. "If one does not produce the mess in the first place, one will not have to clean it up later," may sound like a maternal warning, but the expression's use in the toxic waste context implies a radical economic critique, calling for a change in the production processes of industry itself.

As women came to understand that government is not an objective, neutral mediator for the public good, they discovered that "logic" and "objectivity" are tools used by the government to obscure its bias in favor of industry, and motherhood became a strategy to counter public power by framing the terms of the debate. The labels of "hysterical housewives" or "emotional women," used by policy makers to delegitimize the women's authority, became a language of critique and empowerment, one which exposed the limits of the public arena's ability to address the importance of family, health, and community.

These labels were appropriated as the women saw that their emotionalism, a valued trait in the private sphere, could be transformed into a powerful weapon in the public arena.

What's really so bad about showing your feelings? Emotions and intellect are not conflicting traits. In fact, emotions may well be the quality that makes women so effective in the movement. . . . They help us speak the truth.

Finally, through toxic waste protests, women discovered the power they wield as mothers to bring moral issues to the public, exposing the contradictions of a society that purports to value motherhood and family, yet creates social policies that undermine these values:

We bring the authority of mother—who can condemn mothers? . . . It is a tool we have. Our crying brings the moral issues to the table. And when the public sees our children it brings a concrete, moral dimension to our experience. . . . They are not an abstract statistic.

White, working-class women's stories of their involvement in grassroots toxic waste protests reveal their transformations of initial shyness and intimidation into the self-confidence to challenge the existing system. In reconceptualizing their traditional roles as mothers, these women discovered a new strength. As one activist from Arizona says of herself, "Now I like myself better. I am more assertive and aggressive." These women's role in the private world of family ultimately became a source of personal strength, empirical knowledge, and political strategy in the public sphere. It was a resource of political critique and empowerment which the women appropriated and used as they struggled to protect their families.

Overcoming Obstacles to Participation: Gender Conflicts in the Family

In order to succeed in their fights against toxic wastes in their homes and communities, these women confronted and overcame obstacles not only in the public sphere, but also within the family itself, as their entry into the public arena disrupted both the power relationships and the highly traditional gender roles within the family. Divorce and separation were the manifestations of the crises these disruptions induced. All of the women I interviewed had been married when they first became active in the toxic waste movement. By the time of my interviews with them, more than half were divorced.

A central theme of these women's narratives is the tension created in their marriages by participation in toxic waste protests. This aspect of struggle, so particular to women's lives, is an especially hidden dimension of white, working-class women's activism. Noted one activist from New York:

> People are always talking to us about forming coalitions, but look at all we must deal with beyond the specific issue, the flack that comes with it, the insecurity of your husband that you have outgrown him. Or how do you deal with your children's anger, when they say you love the fight more than me. In a blue-collar community that is very important.

For the most part, white, working-class women's acceptance of a traditional gendered division of labor has also led them to take for granted the power relations within the family. Penny Newman, who was the West Coast Director of CCHW, reflected on the beginnings of her community involvement:

> I had been married just a couple of years. My husband is a fireman. They have very strict ideas of what family life is in which the woman does not work, you stay at home. . . . I was so insecure, so shy, that when I finally got to join an organization, a woman's club, . . . it would take me two weeks to build up the courage to ask my husband to watch the kids that night. I would really plan out my life a month ahead of time just to build in these little hints that there is a meeting coming up in two weeks, will you be available. Now, if he didn't want to do it, or had other plans, I didn't go to the meeting. (Zeff 1989, 183)

Involvement in toxic waste issues created a conflict between these traditional assumptions and women's concerns about protecting their children, and this conflict made visible the power relations within the family. The CCHW publication *Empowering Women* (1989, 33) noted that:

> Women's involvement in grassroots activism may change their views about the world and their relations with their husbands. Some husbands are actively supportive. Some take no stand: "Go ahead and do what you want. Just make sure you have dinner on the table and my shirts washed." Others forbid time away from the family.

Many of these women struggled to develop coping strategies to defuse conflict and accommodate traditional gender-based power relations in the family. The strategies included involving husbands in protest activities and minimizing their own leadership roles. As Lois Gibbs commented: "If you bring a spouse in, if you can make them part of your growth, then the marriage is more likely to survive, but that is real hard to do sometimes." Will Collette, a former director at CCHW, relates the ways in which he has observed women avoiding acknowledged leadership roles. He described this encounter with women involved in a toxic waste protest in New York:

> I was sitting around a kitchen table with several women who were leading a protest. And they were complaining about how Lou and Joe did not do their homework and weren't able to handle reports and so on. I asked them why they were officers and the women were doing all the work. They said, "That's what the guys like, it keeps them in and gives us a little peace at home."

In a similar vein, Collette recalled working with an activist from Texas to plan a large public hearing. Upon arriving at the meeting, he discovered that she was sitting in the back, while he was placed on the dais along with the male leadership, which had had no part in the planning process.

As the women became more active in the public arena, traditional assumptions about gender roles created further conflict in their marriages. Women who became visible community leaders experienced the greatest tension. In some cases, the husbands were held responsible for their wives' activities, since they were supposed to be able to "control" their wives. For example, a woman who fought against an incinerator in Arkansas related.

> When the mayor saw my husband, he wanted to know why he couldn't keep his pretty little wife's mouth shut. As I became more active and more outspoken, our marriage became rockier. My husband asked me to tone it down, which I didn't do.

In other cases, women's morals were often called into question by husbands or other community members. Collette relates the experience of an activist in North Dakota who was rumored to be having an affair. The basis for the rumor, as Collette describes, was that "an uppity woman has got to be promiscuous if she dares to organize. In this case, she was at a late-night meeting in another town, and she slept over, so of course she had to have had sex."

Toxic waste issues thus set the stage for tremendous conflict between these women and their husbands. Men saw their roles as providers threatened: the homes they had bought may have become valueless; their jobs may have been at risk; they were asked by their wives to take on housework and child care. Meanwhile, their wives' public activities increasingly challenged traditional views of gender roles. For the women, their husbands' negative response to their entry into the public sphere contradicted an assumption in the family that both husband and wife were equally concerned with the well-being of the children. In talking about Love Canal, Gibbs explained:

> The husband in a blue-collar community is saying, get your ass home and cook me dinner, it's either me or the issue, make your choice. The woman says: How can I make a choice,

> you're telling me choose between the health of my children and your fucking dinner, how do I deal with that?

When women were asked to choose between their children and their husbands' needs, they began to see the ways in which the children had to be their primary concern.

At times this conflict resulted in more equal power relations within the marriages, a direction that CCHW tried to encourage by organizing family stress workshops. By and large, however, the families of activist women did not tolerate this stress well. Furthermore, as the women began openly to contest traditional power relations in the family, many found that their marriages could not withstand the challenges. As one activist from Arkansas described:

> I thought [my husband] didn't care enough about our children to continue to expose them to this danger. I begged him to move. He wouldn't. So I moved my kids out of town to live with my mom.

All twenty women interviewed for this article were active leaders around toxic waste issues in their communities, but only two described the importance of their husband's continuing support. One white woman who formed an interracial coalition in Alabama credited her husband's support in sustaining her resolve:

> I've had death threats. I was scared my husband would lose his job, afraid that somebody's going to kill me. If it weren't for my husband's support, I don't think I could get through all this.

In contrast, most of these activists described the ongoing conflict within their marriages, which often resulted in their abandoning their traditional role in the family, a process filled with inner turmoil. One woman described that turmoil as follows:

> I had doubts about what I was doing, especially when my marriage was getting real rocky. I thought of getting out of [the protest]. I sat down and talked to God many, many times. I asked him to lead me in the right direction

because I knew my marriage was failing and I found it hard leaving my kids when I had to go to meetings. I had to struggle to feel that I was doing the right thing. I said a prayer and went on.

Reflecting on the strength she felt as a mother, which empowered her to challenge her government and leave her marriage, she continued:

It's an amazing ordeal. You always know you would protect your children. But it's amazing to find out how far you will go to protect your own kids.

The disruption of the traditional family often reflected positive changes in women's empowerment. Women grew through the protest; they became stronger and more self-confident. In some cases they found new marriages with men who respected them as strong individuals. Children also came to see their mothers as outspoken and confident.

Thus, for these women, the particularistic issue of toxic waste made visible oppression not only in the public sphere, but also in the family itself. As the traditional organization of family life was disrupted, inequities in underlying power relations were revealed. In order to succeed in fighting a toxic waste issue, these women had also to engage in another level of struggle as they reconceptualized their traditional role in family life in order to carry out their responsibilities as mothers.

Conclusion

The narratives of white, working-class women involved in toxic waste protests in the 1980s reveal the ways in which their subjective, particular experiences led them to analyses that extended beyond the particularistic issue to wider questions of power. Their broader environmental critique grew out of the concrete, immediate, everyday experience of struggling around survival issues. In the process of environmental protest, these women became engaged with specific governmental and corporate institutions and they were forced to reflect on the contradictions of

their family life. To win a policy issue, they had to go through a process of developing an oppositional or critical consciousness which informed the direction of their actions and challenged the power of traditional policy makers. The contradiction between a government that claimed to act on behalf of the family and the actual environmental policies and actions of that government were unmasked. The inequities of power between white, working-class women and middle-class, male public officials were made visible. The reproduction within the family of traditional power relationships was also revealed. In the process of protest these women uncovered and confronted a world of political power shaped by gender and class. This enabled them to act politically around environmental issues, and in some measure to challenge the social relationships of power, inside and outside the home.

Ideologies of motherhood played a central role in the politicizing of white, working-class women around toxic waste issues. Their resistance grew out of an acceptance of a sexual division of labor that assigns to women responsibility for "sustaining the lives of their children and, in a broader sense, their families, including husband, relatives, elders and community." . . .

The analysis of white, working-class women's politicization through toxic waste protests reveals the contradictory role played by dominant ideologies about mothering and democracy in the shaping of these women's oppositional consciousness. The analysis these women developed was not a rejection of these ideologies. Rather, it was a reinterpretation, which became a source of power in the public arena. Their beliefs provided the initial impetus for involvement in toxic waste protests, and became a rich source of empowerment as they appropriated and reshaped traditional ideologies and meanings into an ideology of resistance. . . .

REFERENCES

Bullard, Robert D. 1990. *Dumping in Dixie: Race, Class and Environmental Quality.* Boulder, CO: Westview Press.

Bullard, Robert D. 1994. *Communities of Color and Environmental Justice.* San Francisco: Sierra Club Books.

Citizen's Clearing House for Hazardous Wastes. 1989. *Empowering Women.* Washington, DC: Citizen's Clearinghouse for Hazardous Wastes.

Krauss, Celene. 1993. "Women and Toxic Waste Protests: Race, Class and Gender as Resources of Resistance." *Qualitative Sociology* 16(3):247–262.

Newman, Penny. 1991. "Women and the Environment in the United States of America." Paper presented at the Conference of Women and the Environment, Bangladore, India.

Ruddick, Sara. 1989. *Maternal Thinking: Towards a Politics of Peace.* New York: Ballantine Books.

Thompson, E. P. 1963. *The Making of the English Working Class.* New York: Pantheon Books.

Zeff, Robin Lee. 1989. "Not in My Backyard/Not in Anyone's Backyard: A Folklorist Examination of the American Grassroots Movement for Environmental Justice." Ph.D. dissertation, Indiana University.

THINKING ABOUT THE READING

Krauss describes how ordinary women became mobilized to construct a movement for social change when they felt their children's health was being threatened. Did their traditional beliefs about motherhood and family help or hinder their involvement in this protest movement? What effect did their participation have on their own families? Why do the women Krauss interviewed identify the toxic waste movement as a women's movement? Why don't men seem to be equally concerned about these health issues? How did the relative powerlessness of their working-class status shape the women's perspective on environmental justice?

Credits